THE NEW KEY TO COSTA RICA

"The Best."

—*Atlanta Journal-Constitution*

"Brings the traveler closer to the local culture."

—*San Antonio Express-News*

"Costa Rica's oldest guidebook remains the best! It's full of nuggets not found in the dozens of wannabes—information on ecotourism and local communities, cultural traditions, and out of the way adventures. Like no other writer, Beatrice Blake knows all of Costa Rica's nooks and crannies."

—Martha Honey, Ph.D., Executive Director of The International Ecotourism Society (TIES)

"Why is *The New Key to Costa Rica* one of Planeta.com's all-time favorite books? It places environmental conservation, biodiversity and responsible tourism in the spotlight with practical tips for the traveler. Highly recommended."

—Ron Mader, host of planeta.com

""The latest edition of *The New Key to Costa Rica* sets the standard for environmentally and socially responsible tourism guides. As well as a comprehensive wealth of great information on destinations, it also includes sections on community-based ecotourism."

—Andy Drumm, Director, Ecotourism Program, The Nature Conservancy

THE NEW KEY TO COSTA RICA

Seventeenth Edition

**BEATRICE BLAKE
ANNE BECHER**

DEIDRE HYDE
Illustrator

DAVID GILBERT
Photographer

Ulysses Press

Published by: Ulysses Press
P.O. Box 3440
Berkeley, CA 94703
www.ulyssespress.com

ISSN 1098-7398
ISBN 1-56975-430-6

Printed in Canada by Transcontinental Printing

20 19 18 17 16 15 14 13 12

Publishers: Ray Riegert, Leslie Henriques
Managing Editor: Claire Chun
Copy Editor: Lily Chou
Editorial Associates: Leona Benten, Laura Brancella, Jay Chung, Kaori Takee
Typesetting: James Meetze, Lisa Kester
Interior maps: XNR Productions except map on pages xviii–xix by Pease Press
Color map: Stellar Cartography
Indexer: Sayre Van Young
Front cover photography: Penélope Mendiguetti (Volcán Arenal)
Back cover photography: *top:* Beatrice Blake (Bridal Veil Falls in Karen Mogensen Reserve; *middle:* George Soriano (hanging bridge at Reserva Los Campesinos); *bottom:* Ken Weinberg (horseback riding in Yorkín)

Corcovado hiker and leaf-cutter ant photographs in color insert © Margaux Gibbons. Other photographs in insert © David Gilbert.

Illustrations on pages 104 and 105 by Anabel Maffioli

Part of Chapter Two was compiled by Sorrel Downer and J. Patrick O'Marr, and originally published by *Costa Rica Today*

Distributed in the United States by Publishers Group West and in Canada by Raincoast Books

For peace with justice in harmony with nature

Table of Contents

Maps

Acknowledgments

Thanks to Walter Odio of Selva Mar Travel Agency for sending me a copy of *Costa Rica Auténtica*, the colorful, bilingual guide to rural community tourism (available by e-mailing pequenas.donaciones.cr@undp.org). This led me to meet Gabriela Calderón, Arantxa Guereña, and Eduardo Mata of the UN Development Program and to visit the communities that have inspired this 17th edition of *The New Key*. Many thanks to my welcoming hosts: Hernán Ramírez and family of Nacientes Palmichal; Beto Chavez and family of El Copal; Miguel Mora, Misael Aguero, and Asdrubal Chacón of Reserva Los Campesinos; Luis Mena and Maria Teresa Cerdas of ASEPALECO; Diego Lynch and Benson Venegas of ANAI; Bernarda Morales of Yorkín; Luis Zuniga of Carbón Dos; Dolfi Goodman of Guías MANT; Juanita Sánchez and Gloria Mayorga of WaKaKoneke in the Kekoldi Indigenous Reserve; Xenia Jiménez of Tesoro Verde; Liliana and Isabel of Isla Chira; and Oscar Jiménez of Monte Alto. Sergio León and Yadira Mena of MINAE and Ana Báez of Turismo y Conservación helped me understand the evolution of community tourism and how it fits into Costa Rica's conservation system.

Many people updated me on the changes in their parts of the country and facilitated my research: Bob Bacher of Chen Taiji International in Pavones; Bobby Chappell of Coast2CostaRica and Philip Edwardes of Club del Mar in Jacó; Sarah Stuckey of Costa Rica Study Tours and Meg Laval and Susana Salas of Paseo de Stella in Monteverde; Pierre and Patricia of El Encanto in Cahuita; Sara and Berit of Casitas Laz Divaz in Sámara; Anja Seidel of Villas Macondo in Tamarindo; Miguel Pagán of Boritico Tours; Neta Talmor of La Finca Que Ama near Puriscal; Geinier

Guzmán of La Cusinga Lodge in Uvita de Osa; Lara of Luna Lodge; Joel Stewart and Belén Meoño of El Remanso; Lauren and Toby Cleaver of Iguana Lodge; Michael and Donna Butler of Playa Nicuesa Lodge in the Osa Peninsula; Gary and Edna Roberts of El Toucanet in Copey de Dota; Colocha and Mauricio Salazar of Chimuri Beach Cottages in Puerto Viejo; Aggie Wilhelm of Oasis del Pacifico in Playa Naranjo; Willis and Danny Rankin of All Rankins' Lodge in Tortuguero; Marisa and Guy Orfali of Hotel La Esperanza in Playa Carrillo; Ray Barry, Penelope Mendiguetti, and Rafa Hernandez of Silver King Lodge in Barra del Colorado; Jack and Diane Ewing and Georgie Wingfield of Hacienda Barú in Dominical; Bernie and Nhi of Hotel Pura Vida in Alajuela; Jim and Mary Jewett of Hotel La Rosa de America in Alajuela; Ginette Laurin of Casa Laurin in Escazú; Sabrina Vargas of Hotel 1492 in San José; Tom Douglas and his staff at Hotel Santo Tomás in San José; and Alex and Maria Mercedes Khajavi of Nature Air.

Many thanks to the hardy group of friends who joined me on the first CONSERVacations tour of community-based destinations: Kenny and Dan Weinberg, Allice Haidden, Pat Paine, Jan Carpenter, and Elizabeth Moran. Olger and Alex Porras and their friend Marlon were instrumental in helping us get around.

Cindy Taft, Luis Diego Vindas, Jennifer Reidy, and Carmen Maria Rojas all helped with vital research. Old friends Deirdre Hyde and Joan Martha provided much needed shelter, warmth, and laughter.

Thanks to my husband, Dennis Moran, for keeping the home fires burning, to our son Danny and our daughter Elizabeth, for being themselves, and to the joyful and generous spirit of my mother, Jean Wallace, who made Costa Rica her home back in 1970.

Even though Anne Becher was not involved in this edition, her words, spirit, and values still pervade the book, and we wish her well in her busy life as mother, professor, and freelance writer.

Thanks to the staff at Ulysses Press for supporting the changes necessary to make this edition focus on community tourism and for their ability to pound out yet another edition of manuscript into a user-friendly guide.

Beatrice Blake
November 2004

Campesinos, Conservation, and Your Vacation

When I first went to Costa Rica in 1971, it was easy to experience how the people lived. More recently, when prospective tourists asked me to recommend a place where they could see "how the people live," I was hard-pressed to think of a community that had not given itself over to tourism in a way that obliterated "how they live." Or else the emphasis was on ecology, and the Ticos were excellent guides, but usually not in their own territory.

But now there are whole rural communities that are proud of their commitment to conservation and willing to share their humble way of life with interested tourists. I am hoping the community control of these projects and their relative isolation will enable them to pick and choose what they want from tourism, while letting it supplement their farming incomes.

Family farms get very little support on this planet. In many of the projects highlighted in this edition, organic agriculture, appropriate energy technology, and preservation of forests and rivers are combined with tourism in a way that holds great promise for the future. By visiting these communities, you will not only meet some lovely people, but you will be inspired by their ability to put innovative principles into practice. You will also see the results of the intelligent, dedicated work of the United National Development Program, COOPRENA, ACTUAR, and other NGOs that, in a time of worldwide chaos, are faithfully sowing the seeds of peace.

THE EVOLUTION OF CONSERVATION AND ECOTOURISM IN COSTA RICA

Because it contains 4 percent of global biodiversity in its very small territory, Costa Rica has been a mecca for tropical biologists and ecologists for the last 50 years. These scientists worked with visionary Costa Ricans to establish the famous National Parks Service in the 1970s. As protected areas were established and research was carried out, biologists observed that most animals migrate from one altitude to another during the year. That led to the creation of more and more parks and protected areas during the 1980s.

The National Parks Service began a concerted effort to teach environmental education in the schools. Costa Rica also made a decision to rely on its biodiversity to attract tourism, instead of becoming yet another fun-and-sun tropical destination. Word spread, and soon Costa Ricans were seeing that their commitment to the protection of nature was providing jobs and opportunities for advancement.

At the same time, farmers who were struggling to make ends meet saw the tourism boom around them, and often decided to sell their farms in order to get funds to build tourist lodging, or to sell to foreigners who were paying exaggerated prices for land. Often foreigners knew how to establish and publicize nature tourism to people in North America and Europe, making for successful businesses. Setting up a B&B or an ecolodge became a dream for many foreigners who migrated here. Costa Rican families with large tracts of land also set up reserves to preserve wildlife habitats and gain government protection against squatters. Conservationists, farmers, and loggers often found themselves in a bitter race to gain control of the country's remaining unprotected forests.

In 1994, Costa Rica conducted a thorough survey of its richest ecosystems to determine how to conserve its remaining biodiversity. But the government, with 25 percent of national territory under some kind of protection, could not afford to buy and maintain more land. The government acknowledged that many privately owned reserves supported conservation by forming buffer zones and biological corridors around and between existing national parks. In 1995, the National System of Conservation Areas (SINAC) was formed. This divides the country into 11 conservation areas, ignoring provincial boundaries and concentrating on related ecosystems. In each area, private- and state-owned conservation activities are interrelated. SINAC's goals are to manage and promote the sustainable use of natural resources along with economic and social development.

Costa Rica's 1997 biodiversity law authorized a tax on gasoline in order to compensate the owners of forested land for the environmental services that their forests offer to society. These services are:

- reduction of greenhouse gases
- protection of drinking water
- protection of rivers that can be harnessed for hydroelectric power
- protection of biodiversity and its sustainable use for pharmaceuticals and science
- protection of ecosystems, life forms and scenic beauty.

Article 50 the Costa Rican Constitution states: "All people have the right to a healthy and ecologically balanced environment." Citizens have lived with environmental education, conservation, and ecotourism for a generation, and today it is rare to find Costa Ricans who are not wholeheartedly in favor of protecting nature. At the same time, poverty and lack of jobs still lead to illegal poaching. The struggle between exploiting nature and conserving forests and wildlife continues.

THE EVOLUTION OF THE MESOAMERICAN BIOLOGICAL CORRIDOR

Research biologists have discovered that many wild felines like panthers, jaguars, and pumas need hundreds of square miles of habitat in order to hunt and reproduce successfully. In fact, they have found that, in order for large cats to sustain their populations, each species requires a preserve big enough to support at least 500 to 5000 individuals of each species. If, through careless development, the original habitat is degraded into small, isolated pieces, the cats rapidly face extinction.

The end of the civil wars that plagued the rest of Central America in the 1970s and '80s has given these countries the opportunity to join Costa Rica in an organized effort to set aside land for conservation of native species of flora and fauna. In 1989, the countries of Central America formed a commission to promote and coordinate sound environmental policy throughout the isthmus.

In the early 1990s, area governments entertained the idea of the Paseo Pantera (Panther's Path): an unbroken strand of protected forest lands stretching along the Caribbean coast of Central America which would guarantee the range that wild animals need in order to survive. Although this project was funded by a consortium of conservation organizations, it floundered in the face of opposition from indigenous and campesino groups. Indigenous lands often have extensive forests, and governments have rarely been concerned with giving native people legal title to them. Poor farmers often lacked title as well. Both groups were aware of Central American history in which elites have taken the most desirable lands and pushed native people out. They feared a land grab that would banish them, once again, from their homes.

With time, even strict conservationists came to see that it was unnecessary to prohibit all human activity in order to preserve nature. They also began to understand that large tracts of land could never be assembled if the needs of local residents were not met. In 1998, a regional group of indigenous people and farmers asserted their role in the planning of a large, unbroken habitat for native animals and plants. And, by this time, southern Mexico, wanting to preserve the biological riches of the Yucatán peninsula, had joined the conservation activities of Central America. Through this coalition of governments, NGOs, and people, the Paseo Pantera expanded to become the Mesoamerican Biological Corridor.

Today, the aims of the Mesoamerican Biological Corridor are:

a) to protect key biodiversity sites

b) to connect these sites with corridors managed in such a way as to enable the movement and dispersal of animals and plants

c) to promote forms of social and economic development in and around these areas that conserve biodiversity while being socially equitable and culturally sensitive.

COSTA RICAN COMMUNITIES AND CONSERVATION

In order to make the Mesoamerican Biological Corridor work, local communities must be active and well organized. Costa Rica's vital grassroots democracy lends itself to the task. In contrast to most Latin American countries, Costa Rica celebrated its first democratic election in 1889. Elections have continued almost uninterrupted through the present day. But what is truly impressive is the level of community organization.

In the 1970s, President Daniel Oduber (1974–78) said, "Humans must not be the object, but the subject of their own development." He believed that the wellbeing of rural communities was intimately linked to the health of the nation. He formed the National Directorate for Community Development (DINADECO) to help communities organize themselves to address their needs for water, electricity, health care, and cultural activities. Advisors would travel by jeep, motorcycle, or horseback to make sure that communities had the tools they needed to form successful organizations. Today, DINADECO is no longer very active, but the culture of community involvement persists.

Building on its traditions of grassroots democracy, the Ministry of the Environment has encouraged citizens to form Natural Resource Vigilance Committees (COVIRENAS). These volunteer groups are active in almost every rural area of the country, educating their neighbors about illegal logging, poaching, fishing, trade in endangered species, water protection, and how each person's actions can make a difference. They work with art and theater to encourage children's awareness, carry out clean-up campaigns, and report environmental infractions to the authorities. They are given official ID cards as environmental inspectors ad honorem.

COMMUNITY-BASED ECOTOURISM

Through its Small Grants Program, the United Nations Development Program is now funding COVIRENAS groups, local conservation and development associations, and farmers' cooperatives so that rural communities with limited resources can have their own ecotourism businesses. This enables farmers to conserve their forests and rivers, keep their families on the land, and supplement their farming incomes. Many are turning to organic agriculture and are planting crops that provide habitat for a diversity of birds and wildlife.

In each chapter of this book, you will learn more about the biological corridors in each area, and you'll find highlighted reports on our adventures traveling to these communities.

Costa Rica still has the dreamy ecolodges that made it famous, where, after your massage and your yoga class, you can sit sipping rum-laced tropical smoothies and nibbling on delicate fish carpaccio while gazing out over the ocean. The extensive rainforest reserves owned by many of these lodges are also part of the conservation system. But make the effort to spend some time at the community-based places as well. Several travel agencies, like Cultourica, ACTUAR, Simbiosis Tours, and Horizontes organize tours to these destinations. You can find out more in these pages or by reading the colorful, bilingual guidebook to community-based tourism called *The Real Costa Rica (Costa Rica Autentica)* published by the Small Grants Program of the United Nations Development Program (296-1544 ext. 146; e-mail: pequenas.donaciones.cr@undp.org) and COOPRENA (248-2538; e-mail: cooprena@racsa.co.cr).

Text continued on page xx.

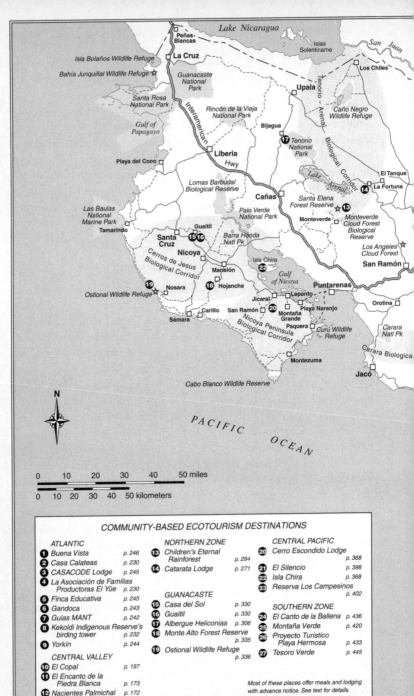

Lake Nicaragua

San Juan

Peñas-Blancas

Isla Bolaños Wildlife Refuge ☆
Bahía Junquillal Wildlife Refuge ☆

La Cruz

Islas Solentiname

Los Chiles

Guanacaste National Park

Santa Rosa National Park

Interamerican

Rincón de la Vieja National Park

Upala

Gulf of Papagayo

Bijagua

Caño Negro Wildlife Refuge

Liberia

17 Tenorio National Park

Tenorio - Arenal Biological Corridor

Playa del Coco

Hwy

El Tanque
14 La Fortuna

Lomas Barbudal Biological Reserve

Cañas

Lake Arenal

Santa Elena Forest Reserve ☆ 13

Las Baulas National Marine Park

Palo Verde National Park

Barra Honda Natl Pk

Monteverde

Monteverde Cloud Forest Biological Reserve

Tamarindo

Guaitil

15 16

Santa Cruz

Los Angeles Cloud Forest ☆

Nicoya

Isla Chira
22

San Ramón

Cerros de Jesus Biological Corridor

Mansión

Gulf of Nicoya

Puntarenas

19 Nosara

18 Hojancha

Jicaral

Lepanto

Orotina

Ostional Wildlife Refuge ☆

Carrillo

San Ramón
20 Montaña Grande

Playa Naranjo

Carara Natl Pk

Sámara

Nicoya Peninsula Biological Corridor

Paquera

Curú Wildlife Refuge

Carara Biológica

Montezuma

Jacó

Cabo Blanco Wildlife Reserve

N

PACIFIC OCEAN

| 0 | 10 | 20 | 30 | 40 | 50 miles |

| 0 | 10 | 20 | 30 | 40 | 50 kilometers |

COMMUNITY-BASED ECOTOURISM DESTINATIONS

Most of these places offer meals and lodging with advance notice. See text for details.

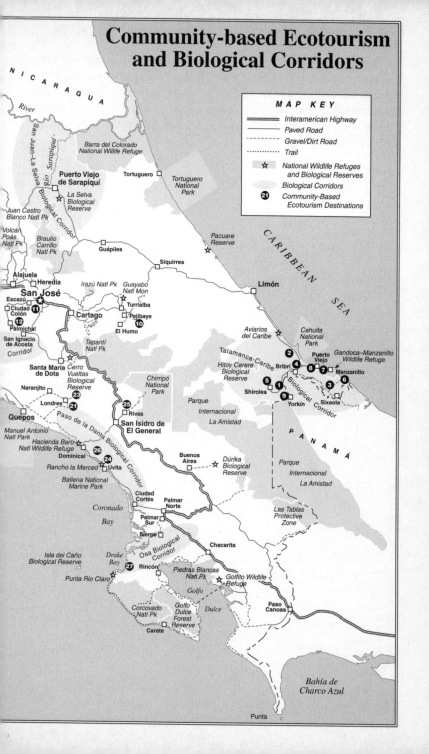

Community-based Ecotourism and Biological Corridors

MAP KEY

══════	Interamerican Highway
──────	Paved Road
- - - -	Gravel/Dirt Road
· · · · ·	Trail
☆	National Wildlife Refuges and Biological Reserves
▨	Biological Corridors
㉑	Community-Based Ecotourism Destinations

NICARAGUA

San Juan River

Sarapiquí River

San Juan–La Selva Biological Corridor

Barra del Colorado National Willife Refuge

Puerto Viejo de Sarapiquí

La Selva Biological Reserve

Tortuguero

Tortuguero National Park

Juan Castro Blanco Natl Pk

Volcán Poás Natl Pk

Braulio Carrillo Natl Pk

Guápiles

Pacuare Reserve

Siquirres

CARIBBEAN SEA

Alajuela

Heredia

Irazú Natl Pk

Guayabo Natl Mon

Limón

San José

Escazú

Ciudad Colón ⑪

⑫

Palmichal

Cartago

Turrialba

Pejibaye ⑩

El Humo

San Ignacio de Acosta Corridor

Tapantí Natl Pk

Santa María de Dota

Cerro Vueltas Biological Reserve

Chirripó National Park

Aviarios del Caribe

Cahuita National Park

Talamanca–Caribe

Bribri ④

Hitoy Cerere Biological Reserve

⑤ ①

Shiroles

⑨

Yorkín

Puerto Viejo ⑧ ⑦

Gandoca–Manzanillo Wildlife Refuge

Manzanillo

③ ⑥

Sixaola

Biological Corridor

Naranjito

Londres ㉑

Quepos

㉓

㉕

Rivas

San Isidro de El General

Parque Internacional La Amistad

PANAMÁ

Paso de la Danta Biological Corridor

Manuel Antonio Natl Park

Hacienda Barú Natl Wildlife Refuge

Dominical ㉖

Rancho la Merced ㉔ Uvita

Buenos Aires

Dúrika Biological Reserve

Parque Internacional La Amistad

Ballena National Marine Park

Ciudad Cortés

Palmar Norte

Las Tablas Protective Zone

Coronado Bay

Palmar Sur

Sierpe

Chacarita

Isla del Caño Biological Reserve

Drake Bay

Osa Biological Corridor

㉗ Rincón

Piedras Blancas Natl Pk

Golfito Wildlife Refuge

Punta Río Claro

Golfo

Paso Canoas

Corcovado Natl Pk

Golfo Dulce Forest Reserve

Dulce

Carate

Bahía de Charco Azul

Punta

We all know that clean air, water, soil, and trees are limited, and thus our most precious assets. Costa Rica is leading the way in valuing these resources and finding ways for humans to live in harmony with nature. Just by vacationing, adventuring, and learning at places that are involved in the Mesoamerican Biological Corridor in Costa Rica, you will be contributing to this world-changing work.

Sustainable Ecotourism Rating

A Sustainable Ecotourism Rating had been a feature of our book since the 1992 edition. In fact, *The New Key to Costa Rica* was the first guidebook to use a green-rating system. The focus of our rating system, however, has changed in this edition.

We are now relying on our personal observation of ecotourism businesses over the years. Very few people have the decades-long perspective that we do in Costa Rican ecotourism. All of the lodgings that we include in the book fit our criteria of being well-run, non-glitzy, environmentally aware, and pleasant places to spend one's vacation. We will maintain a list of our favorite hotels (all examples of best practices in ecotourism, with direct links to their websites) on the Green Rating page at www.keytocostarica.com.

We are also looking at ecotourism in a new way. Even though the lodges on our Sustainable Ecotourism list have been largely a positive force in Costa Rican society and culture, we can no longer ignore the fact that the majority of these ecolodges are owned by foreigners. There is hardly any beach property in Costa Rican hands, except for beaches protected by national parks. Prices of farmland are often out of the range of farmers, but easily accessible to foreigners. This neo-colonialism does not fit with Costa Rican history and values, and shows that it is very difficult for Costa Ricans to make a living from the land, as they have traditionally.

Over the last 30 years, we have observed how the conservation ethic has permeated the country. The most interesting thing Costa Rica has to share with tourists today is a network of rural communities that are devoted to sustainability: in agriculture, in the use of alternative energy, in learning how to work together, and in providing fascinating and beautiful experiences in nature.

In this edition, we give special recognition to these community-owned tourism enterprises. You will find them marked in the text with a ✿. Their locations are shown on the map on pages *xviii–xix*.

ONE

Costa Rica: A Brief History

To understand the unique character of the Costa Rican people today, it helps to know something of their history. Over the centuries, Costa Rica has taken some decidedly different turns from her Central American sister states.

PRE-COLUMBIAN COSTA RICA

The largest and most developed pre-Columbian population in Costa Rica was that of the Chorotegas, whose ancestors had migrated from Southern Mexico to the Nicoya Peninsula, probably in the 13th century. They were running away from enemies who wanted to enslave them—their name translates as "fleeing people."

Much of the information we have about the Chorotegas was collected by Gonzalo Fernández de Oviedo, a Spanish explorer who lived with them for a short period in 1529.

Outstanding farmers, the Chorotegas managed three harvests of corn per year. They also grew cotton, beans, fruits, and cacao, which they introduced to Costa Rica and whose seeds they used as currency. Land was communally owned and the harvest was divided according to need, so that old people and widows with children could be cared for.

The Chorotegas lived in cities of as many as 20,000 people, which had central plazas with a marketplace and a religious center. Only women could enter the market. Women wore skirts, the length of which depended upon their social level. Men could go naked, but often wore a large cloth or a woven and dyed sleeveless cotton shirt.

Women worked in ceramics, producing vessels painted in black and red, decorated with plumed serpents (the symbol for unity of matter and spirit),

1

jaguars, monkeys, and crocodiles. They carved stylized jade figures in human and animal shapes. The figures may have been used in fertility ceremonies or to bring good luck in the hunt. They wrote books on deerskin parchment and used a ritual calendar.

War was institutionalized. A permanent military organization fought to obtain land and slaves, who were used as human sacrifices. Eating someone who had been sacrificed to the gods was a purification rite. The Chorotegas also sacrificed virgins by throwing them into volcano craters.

The Chibcha people from Colombia migrated to the South Pacific region of Costa Rica, where they lived in permanent, well-fortified towns. Their concern with security could have arisen from their possession of gold—which they fashioned into human and animal figures (especially turtles, armadillos, and sharks). Both women and men fought for the best lands and for prisoners, who were used as slaves or as human sacrifices. They believed in life after death; vultures performed a vital role in transporting people to the other world by eating their corpses.

These people probably made the granite spheres that lie in linear formations in the valley of the Río Térraba and on the Isla del Caño off the coast of the Osa Peninsula. These spheres range in diameter from 7.5 centimeters (the size of an orange) to 2.5 meters. Their almost-perfect roundness and careful placement make them one of Costa Rica's pre-Columbian mysteries.

Peoples from the jungles of Brazil and Ecuador migrated to the lowland jungles of the Costa Rican Atlantic Coast. They lived semi-nomadically, hunting, fishing, and cultivating *yuca* (manioc), *pejibaye* (small cousin to the coconut), pumpkin, and squash. Their chief's nobility was hereditary, passed down through the female line of the family.

Social prestige was gained by good warriors. Apparently, decapitated heads of enemies were war trophies. Their stone figurines represent warriors with a knife in one hand and a head in the other.

They worshiped the sun, the moon, and the bones of their ancestors and believed that all things had souls. During religious festivals there was a ritual inebriation with a fermented *chicha* made from *yuca* or *pejibaye*. The burial mounds of these people have yielded the greatest number of pre-Columbian artifacts in the country.

COLONIAL COSTA RICA

On September 18, 1502, during his fourth and last voyage to the New World, Christopher Columbus anchored in the Bay of Cariari (now Limón) after a violent tempest wrecked his ships. During the 17 days that he and his crew were resting and making repairs, they visited a few coastal villages. The native people treated them well, and they left with the impression that Veragua (a name that Columbus used for the Caribbean Coast between Honduras and Panama) was a land rich in gold, whose gentle and friendly inhabitants could be easily conquered.

A few years later, in 1506, King Ferdinand of Spain sent a governor to colonize Veragua. Governor Diego de Nicuesa and his colonizers received a different welcome. First, their ship went aground on the coast of Panama, and they had to walk up the Atlantic shore. Food shortages and tropical diseases reduced the group by half. Then they met the native people, who burned their crops rather than feed the invaders. The Spanish realized that their task was not going to be easy. There was no centralized empire to conquer and sack, and the scattered tribes were at home in a climate and terrain that the explorers found devastating. This first attempt at colonization was a miserable failure.

After Vásco Núñez de Balboa discovered the Pacific Ocean in 1513, the Spaniards started exploring the west coast of Veragua. In 1522, an exploratory land expedition set out from northern Panama. Despite sickness, starvation, and tropical weather, the survivors of the long, hazardous trip called it a success: they had obtained gold and pearls, and their priest claimed he had converted more than 30,000 of the native people to Catholicism between Panama and Nicaragua.

More explorers and would-be colonizers arrived. There were attempted settlements on both coasts, but they ended in tragedy for the settlers, who died of hunger, were driven out by the native people, or fought among themselves and dissolved their communities.

Juan Vásquez de Coronado arrived as governor in 1562. He found a group of Spaniards and Spanish *mestizos* living inland from the Pacific Coast. Coronado explored Costa Rica, treating the Indians he met more humanely than had his predecessors. He decided that the highlands were more suitable for settlement, so he moved the settlers to the Cartago Valley, where the climate was pleasant and the soils were rich from the lava deposited by Volcán Irazú. In 1563, Cartago was established as the capital of Costa Rica.

In contrast to most other Spanish colonies, there was no large exploitable workforce in Costa Rica. The indigenous population had been

decimated early on by war and disease. Because it had no riches and was difficult to reach from Guatemala, the seat of Spain's Central American empire, Costa Rica was left free from foreign intrusion. Forgotten by its "mother country," Costa Rica was almost self-sufficient in its poverty. At one point, even the governor was forced to work his own small plot of land to survive.

While some Costa Ricans were slaveholders, they owned few compared to other countries. Most slaves tended cacao plantations in the Atlantic Coast town of Matina, or served in Central Valley homes. The Calvo Chinchilla household held 27 slaves, more than any other family in colonial Costa Rica. Their case illustrates a tendency that was common in colonial times. Son Miguel had five children with his parents' slave Ana Cardoso. He acknowledged them, and his parents eventually freed her and their grandchildren. The tendency of slaveowners to have children with their slaves—mostly by force, though not in this case—contributed to the "bleaching" of African roots in the Central Valley population. Historian and genealogist Mauricio Meléndez Obando identified several causes for African slaves not maintaining a strong identity: 1) forced and accelerated racial mixing; 2) a relatively small black population; 3) the heterogeneous nature of the slave population, since they were from various parts of Africa; and 4) their integration with other constituents of the population, including poor Spaniards, *mulattos*, *mestizos* (one parent Spanish and the other indigenous), and Zambos (one parent indigenous, the other black).

Costa Rica's Spanish population remained small and its lifestyle humble through the 17th century. In 1709, Spanish money became so scarce that settlers used cacao beans as currency, just like the Chorotegas. Women wore goat-hair skirts; soldiers had no uniforms. Volcán Irazú erupted in 1723, almost destroying Cartago. Nevertheless, the Spanish survived, and the area settled by Spaniards actually increased during the 1700s. Three new cities were founded in the Meseta Central (Central Valley): Cubujuquí (Heredia) in 1706, Villanueva de la Boca del Monte (San José) in 1737, and Villa Hermosa (Alajuela) in 1782.

INDEPENDENCE

In October 1821, word arrived from Guatemala that Spain had granted independence to its American colonies on September 15th. It had taken the news one month to travel through the mountains and valleys to Costa Rica. After a period of internal strife between conservative elements in Cartago who wanted to continue the monarchy and a more liberal faction in San José who wanted to join South America's liberation movement, Costa Rica declared itself a state in the short-lived Federal Republic of Central America, and the capital was moved from Cartago to San José.

The first president of free Costa Rica, Juan Mora Fernández, built roads and schools and gave land grants to anyone who would plant coffee, the most profitable export crop at the time. This epoch was one of the most influential in the evolution of Costa Rican democracy, because small farmers were encouraged to grow coffee and sell the beans to wealthier farmers, who would prepare the beans for export. Thus, rich and poor each had an important place in the coffee-growing process, and mutual respect was developed.

By the mid-1800s, coffee was Costa Rica's principal export, and coffee growers were a powerful and wealthy elite. They built a road to transport coffee from the Meseta Central to Costa Rica's port, Puntarenas. They exported first to Chile, then later to Germany and England. By mid-century, European money was entering the pockets of Costa Rican coffee growers, and Europeans were arriving en masse at this tropical frontier. Costa Rica was becoming cosmopolitan. A university was founded in 1844 to disseminate European thinking, and Costa Rican politicians sported European liberal ideologies.

By 1848, the coffee elite was influential enough to elect its own representative for president, Juan Rafael Mora. He was a self-made man who had become one of the most powerful coffee growers in the country. He was charismatic, astute, and respected by the coffee elite and the campesinos alike. He became a veritable national hero by leading an "army" of Costa Ricans to defend his country when it was invaded by one of the most detested figures in Central American history, the North American William Walker.

THE SAGA OF WILLIAM WALKER

A study of William Walker's early life gives one little indication of how he would later come to be the scourge of Central America. Walker graduated from the University of Nashville at the age of 14. By the time he was 19, he held both a law and a medical degree from the University of Pennsylvania. He followed this memorable academic record with two years of postgraduate study in Paris and Heidelberg.

His success stopped there. Returning from Europe, Walker quickly failed as a doctor, lawyer, and journalist. He had an ill-fated courtship with a beautiful deaf-mute New Orleans socialite, then in 1849 turned up as a gold miner in California. He didn't fare well in this occupation either, and soon started working as a hack writer in several California cities.

At this point, something happened in the mind of William Walker, and he launched himself on a career as a soldier of fortune. From then on, he succeeded in creating chaos wherever he took his five-foot, three-inch, one-hundred-pound frame.

In the early 1850s, Walker sailed with several hundred men on a "liberating expedition" to the Baja California Peninsula and Mexico. The expedition was financed by the Knights of the Golden Circle, a movement bent on promoting the "benefits" of slavery. Walker spent a year in Mexico, during which time he awarded himself the military title of colonel and proclaimed himself "President of Sonora and Baja California."

Back in the United States after several encounters with the Mexican Army, he was arrested for breaking the Neutrality Act of 1818. His acquittal of the charge gained him fame and followers. His next expedition was to Nicaragua.

Walker went with two main goals. One was to convert Central America into slave territory and annex it to the southern United States; the other was to conquer Nicaragua and ready it for the construction of a transisthmic canal. The new riches that were being discovered in California attracted many Easterners, but crossing the United States by land was slow and difficult. Walker had made contacts with a group of economically powerful North Americans who thought that a sea route could be more efficient and profitable. Southern Nicaragua would be a perfect site for the isthmus crossing; ships could sail up the San Juan River, which formed the Nicaragua–Costa Rica border, cross Lake Nicaragua, then pass through a to-be-built 18-mile canal from the lake to the Pacific Ocean.

Walker's contacts arranged for an invitation from the Liberal Party of Nicaragua, which at the time was embattled with the Conservatives. In June 1855, he landed in Nicaragua with 58 men. After losing his first encounter with the Conservatives, Walker managed to hold out until several hundred reinforcements arrived from California, bringing new model carbines and six-shooters. They soon overpowered the Conservatives, and, after an "open" election, Walker became "President of the Republic of Nicaragua."

Central Americans from throughout the isthmus rose to fight Walker and his band of *filibusteros*. In February 1856, President Juan Rafael Mora of Costa Rica declared war on Walker, but not on Nicaragua. Mora raised an Army of 9000 in less than a week. This "army," led by Mora and his brother-in-law José María Cañas, was composed of campesinos, merchants, and government bureaucrats ill-dressed for combat and armed only with farm tools, machetes, and old rifles. They marched for two weeks to Guanacaste, where they found 300 *filibusteros* resting at the Santa Rosa hacienda (now a national monument in Santa Rosa National Park). Having invaded Costa Rica, the *filibusteros* were preparing to conquer San José. The Costa Rican

Army, by then diminished to 2500 men, attacked the *filibusteros*, who fled back to Nicaragua after only 14 minutes of battle.

Two thousand Costa Ricans followed Walker up to Nicaragua and, in a generally masterful campaign, fought him to a standstill. The turning point came in Rivas, Nicaragua. Walker and his band were barricaded in a large wooden building from which they could not be dislodged. Juan Santamaría, a drummer boy, volunteered to set fire to the building and succeeded in forcing Walker's retreat. In his action, Santamaría lost his life, and became Costa Rica's national hero.

Walker's attempt to convert Nicaragua and the rest of Central America into slave territory was backed by U.S. President James Buchanan, and his failure angered the president. When Walker confiscated the transisthmic transportation concession that U.S. financier Cornelius Vanderbilt had already started installing, Vanderbilt began to finance some of Walker's enemies. This was the beginning of the end of Walker's career.

After another engagement in late 1856 on Lake Nicaragua, where the Costa Rican Army brilliantly cut Walker off from his support troops, the rag-tag *filibustero* forces were near defeat. On May 1, 1857, Walker surrendered to a U.S. warship.

The adventurer traveled to Nicaragua again in late 1857, but this time he was taken prisoner before he could wreak any havoc. When he was released in 1860, he sailed to Honduras, where, upon landing, he seized the custom house. This brought a British warship to the scene, upon which Walker, pursued by the Hondurans, eventually took refuge. Offered safe conduct into U.S. hands by the British commander, Walker insisted he was the rightful president of Honduras. The British therefore put Walker ashore again, where he was taken by the Hondurans and promptly shot.

La Casona,
scene of Walker's defeat

The net result of Walker's Central American marauding was the death of some 20,000 men. The inscription on William Walker's tombstone reads, "Glory to the patriots who freed Central America of such a bloody pirate! Curses to those who brought him and to those who helped him."

Juan Rafael Mora is now acclaimed for having saved Central America from Walker and the interests he represented, but he wasn't that popular when he returned from battle. People accused Mora of having been too ambitious and blamed him for an epidemic of cholera that infected Costa Rican soldiers in Nicaragua and spread to kill almost ten percent of the population.

Mora manipulated the 1859 election to win despite massive opposition. In August 1859, his enemies overthrew him. A year later, Mora led a coup d'etat against the new president, also a member of the coffee elite. His attempt failed, and he was shot by a firing squad in 1860—an inglorious end for a man who is now a national hero. All through the 1860s, quarrels among the coffee growers helped to put presidents in power and later depose them. Nevertheless, most presidents during these years were liberal and intellectual civilians. Despite the political instability of the decade, the country managed to establish a well-based educational system. This was a time when new schools were founded, European professors were brought over to design academic programs, and the first bookstores in San José opened their doors.

THE ATLANTIC RAILROAD AND UNITED FRUIT

By the mid-1800s, Costa Rica realized it needed an Atlantic port to facilitate coffee export to Europe. When Tomás Guardia declared himself Chief of State in 1871, he decided to build a railway to Limón. He contracted Henry Meiggs, a North American who had built railways in Chile and Peru. Meiggs went to England to secure loans for the project. He obtained 3.4 million sterling pounds, of which only 1 million actually arrived. These loans created the first foreign debt in Costa Rica's history.

Costa Rica's population wasn't large enough to provide the project with the necessary labor force, so thousands of Jamaican, Italian, and Chinese workers were recruited. After an optimistic start, it soon became evident that it was going to be a slow, dangerous, and costly process. Construction of the railroad claimed some 4000 workers' lives, cost the equivalent of $8 million and lasted 19 years. The jungle proved itself a formidable and deadly barrier.

Meiggs' nephew, Minor C. Keith, became the director a few years after the project started. The railroad he inherited was constantly beleaguered by severe shortages of funds, so he started experimenting with banana production and exportation as a way to help finance the project. When he realized that the banana business could yield very profitable results, Keith made a deal with the new president, Bernardo Soto, in 1884. In return for a grant from the Costa Rican government of 323,887 hectares of untilled land along the tracks, tax-free for 20 years, and a 99-year lease on the railroad, Keith would renegotiate the project's pending debts to England, and complete construction at his own expense.

By 1886, Keith had settled the financial problems with England. He spent the next four years laying the last 52 miles of track that climbed through the steep, treacherous valley of the Reventazón River. Relations between Keith and the labor force weren't good. In 1888, Italian workers organized the first strike in Costa Rica's history, demanding prompt payments and sanitary working and living conditions.

The railroad was completed in 1890. Until 1970, it was the only route from the Meseta Central to Limón. And, until the line was closed in late 1990, it was still the major means of transportation for many of the people who lived in the tiny towns it passed. Children took the train to school; it served as an ambulance for the sick and as a hearse for the dead.

After they finished the railway, many Italian workers settled in Costa Rica's highlands. Chinese workers settled in various parts of the country. The Jamaicans stayed on the Atlantic Coast and started working on the banana plantations that Keith established on his free acres. The development of banana plantations where there had once been jungles forced the native peoples to move up into the mountains.

In 1899, Keith and a partner founded the United Fruit Company. La Yunai, as it was called, quickly became a legendary social, economic, political, and agricultural force in many Latin American countries. Costa Rican author Carlos Luis Fallas describes work conditions on the steamy plantations in his book *Mamita Yunai*, and Gabriel García Márquez tells what it did to the imaginary town of Macondo in *One Hundred Years of Solitude*. Although Costa Rica was the smallest country where it operated, United possessed more land here than anywhere else. Costa Rica became the world's leading banana producer.

Keith ended up a very wealthy man and married the daughter of one of the presidents of Costa Rica. Most profits from the banana industry went to the foreign owners of the production, shipping, and distribution networks that made export possible.

United's peak year in Costa Rica was in 1907. By 1913 the company was facing serious problems. Panama disease had infected banana trees, and United's employees were protesting unfair working conditions. A 1913 strike was broken by the Costa Rican government—two strike leaders were chased into the plantations and killed.

United initiated a new policy: it would lease company land to independent growers and buy bananas from them. Tensions with workers grew; a 1934 strike led by two young San José communists, Manuel Mora and Jaime Cerdas, finally brought better working and living conditions. They maintained the original demands of 1913 and added to the list regular payment of salaries, free housing, medical clinics on plantations, and accident insurance. United wouldn't talk with the strikers, but the planters leasing land from United did, and convinced United to sign an agreement.

In the late 1930s, a new disease, *Sigatoka*, infected banana trees up and down the coast. In 1938, United decided to pick up and move west to the Pacific lowlands around Golfito, where banana remained king until violent labor conflicts and dwindling Pacific markets compelled the company to abandon its installations in 1985. Now bananas are again becoming big business on the Atlantic lowlands, as huge projects buy up land, cutting down whatever forest remains in their way and forcing small farmers out of the area.

LIBERALISM ARRIVES IN COSTA RICA

The 1880s saw an increasing split between a traditional, conservative church and a liberalizing state. The bishop of Costa Rica criticized the European ideas that were becoming popular with the elite and the politicians. The bishop was summarily expelled from the country in 1884, and in 1885 there was an official denouncement of an earlier church-state concord that had declared Catholicism the state religion. Public outcry at the government's treatment of the church was minimal.

The first truly democratic election, characterized by real public participation (male only), took place in 1889. Liberals saw it as the result of their efforts to educate and raise democratic consciousness in the people. In fact, their efforts worked so well that the public gave their overwhelming support to the liberals' opposition. Supporters of the liberals threatened not to recognize the new president, so 10,000 armed opposition members flooded the streets of San José. The liberals then demonstrated their firm commitment to democracy by recognizing the new, rightfully elected president.

Costa Rica's democratic tradition has endured until today, with only a few exceptions. One was in 1917, when the Minister of War and the Navy, Federico Tinoco, overthrew an unpopular president. Tinoco's brutal and repressive dictatorship lasted through 30 months of widespread opposition. Finally, Tinoco fled the country. A provisional president held office for a year until normalcy was reached, and Costa Rica resumed its democratic tradition with a fair presidential election.

ROOTS OF THE 1948 CIVIL WAR

In 1940, Dr. Rafael Angel Calderón Guardia was elected president. Calderón was a very religious Catholic who had studied medicine in Belgium and was convinced that the social guarantees available to Europeans should be instituted in Costa Rica. He initiated many social reforms that still exist today, including social security, workers' right to organize, land reform, guaranteed minimum wage, and collective bargaining. These reforms, plus the fact that he wanted to raise taxes, alienated him from the elite. However, he found support in the Catholic archbishop, Monseñor Victor Manuel Sanabria, and in Manuel Mora of the Costa Rican Communist Party.

Although Calderón enjoyed great popularity among the poor, many educated, middle-class Costa Ricans were suspicious of the alliance between the Church, the government, and the Communist Party. Calderón's most vocal opponent, José "Pepe" Figueres, also wanted to improve conditions for the poor, but he was adamantly opposed to communism. "Social revolutionaries and bourgeois conservatives," he declared, "you fight under the same flag: antagonism." Figueres felt that laissez faire capitalism created an arbitrary class division, pitting owners against their competition, and owners and workers against each other. In reality, he maintained, both management and workers are needed in order for production to take place, so they should have a cooperative relationship. He also was convinced that "in the large industrialized countries, sheltered in the idealists' camps, supposed redeemers set up their tents, only to become vampires of the weakest classes, extortionists of the privileged classes, and impediments to production."

After the 1944 presidential election, suspicions began growing that Calderón's party had manipulated the ballots in order to elect Calderón's successor, Teodoro Picado. The opposition fanned the flames of these suspicions until many citizens were convinced that Calderón and the communists were not going to relinquish power if their party lost the next election. When the police shot some demonstrators at an opposition rally in Cartago in July 1947, the opposition mobilized the shocked populace into a nationwide strike that shut down schools, banks and businesses for 12 days. The government responded by bringing 3000 banana union workers from the Atlantic coast to reinforce the 300-man army. The armed banana workers were stationed on street corners in the capitol. Because they were unaccustomed to the cool highland weather, the government gave them blankets, which they wore across their shoulders. The communist banana workers looked like stereotypical Mexican peasants with their blankets and their ammunition belts, so the *josefinos* called them "mariachis." That became a generalized derogatory term referring to Calderón and his allies.

The next presidential election in February 1948 was won by Otilio Ulate of the opposition party. But Calderón called the election a fraud, and a fire in the schoolhouse where the ballots were stored destroyed many voting records. The legislative assembly, controlled by Calderón's party, annulled the election. This was the final straw for Figueres and his allies, who had been preparing for this eventuality for months beforehand. He had already been training an army to fight for "electoral purity" and to attack what he called "Caldero-Communism." On March 12, 1948, Figueres took over the airport in San Isidro de El General, in the southern part of the country, and moved his troops north toward Cartago, east of San José. Figueres and his soldiers then captured the Atlantic port of Limón.

Through astute military planning and strategy, and widespread popular support, Figueres managed to bring Calderón's government to the bargaining table in just over a month. In a historic clandestine meeting, Catholic priest Benjamin Nunez negotiated an agreement between Mora of the Communist Party and Figueres in which Figueres agreed that he would implement Calderón's social guarantees if Calderón would honor the rightful election results.

Figueres took over the government for 18 months in order to formulate a new constitution. He gave voting rights to women and blacks, established an independent branch of the government to oversee elections, imposed an income tax, and nationalized the banking system. To neutralize opposition and to channel funds to social priorities like education, he abolished the army.

Figueres, a clear-eyed observer of history, saw that armies in Latin America had only sapped government resources and acted as tools of the elites to prevent positive change. He had also been impressed that the United States, newly in Cold War mode after its alliance with Russia in World War II, had begun to amass troops in Panama to come to the aid of his rebels who were thought to be fighting communism. Calderón and Mora, fearful of more bloodshed if the U.S. entered the fray, had been more receptive to negotiating an end to the hostilities because of this. Figueres reasoned that if the United States was so bent on policing its "backyard" against communist incursions, it wasn't really necessary for Costa Rica, a U.S. ally, to waste her limited resources on her own army.

After 18 months, Figueres turned the government over to Otilio Ulate, the rightful winner of the 1948 election. Since then, elections have happened each year without a hitch. A 70 percent voter turnout is considered apathetic in Costa Rica. In the U.S., voter turnout is usually around 50 percent.

In the years after 1948, Figueres and his fellow revolutionaries formed the National Liberation Party (PLN), which is a member of Socialist International. The Costa Rican government nationalized the electric, telephone, water, insurance, and health care industries, reasoning that only government-owned services would promote development at all levels of society. They also promoted Solidarismo, a cooperative bargaining arena for workers and business owners. Their audacious reforms ushered in an era of economic growth and upward mobility for many Costa Ricans, and by the 1960s a strong middle class was forming. This kept Costa Rica free of the civil unrest that plagued the rest of Central America in the 1970s and '80s, in which many countries became unfortunate pawns in the Cold War.

Figueres was elected president in 1953 and again in 1970. "Don Pepe" died on June 8, 1990, and was mourned by people of all political persuasions as a defender of Costa Rican democracy and development.

SINCE 1948

Costa Rica fortified its progressive social policies during the three decades following 1948, and enjoyed a gradual upward economic trend. The policy of the 1960s and 1970s was to try to become more self-sufficient agriculturally and industrially, which actually led to a heavier dependence on imported pesticides, fertilizers, raw materials, machinery, and oil. Costa Rica and many other Third World countries accepted large First World loans for infrastructure projects like bridges, hydroelectric dams, and roads. When the price of oil rose in the early 1970s, the economy could no longer do without it. Then coffee, banana, and sugar prices went down on the world market, the loans came due, and Costa Rica found itself entering the 1980s with its economy in shambles.

The instability of neighboring countries like Nicaragua and El Salvador impeded cooperation in the Central American Common Market and made Costa Ricans feel insecure. From 1978 to 1979, under President Rodrigo Carazo, northern Costa Rica served as a virtual base for Sandinista operations. Costa Ricans had no sympathy for the Somoza dynasty and were hopeful that the Nicaraguans could make a go of democracy. But after Somoza was deposed, the Sandinista arms build-up and Marxist-Leninist doctrine disillusioned many Costa Ricans. Although the government had an official policy of neutrality, PLN President Luis Alberto Monge (1982–1986) lent tacit support to the Contras, who were operating out of the northern jungles of Costa Rica.

Costa Rica elected a president in February 1986 from the younger generation of the PLN. Oscar Arias, an economist, lawyer, and author of several books on the Costa Rican economy and power structure, campaigned on the promise to work for peace in Central America. The first part of his task was to enforce Costa Rica's declared neutrality policy, and to stand up to the United States and the politicians within his own party who were supporting Contra activity in Costa Rica (such as the secret airstrip that figured in the Iran-Contra scandal).

As the world knows by now, Arias' untiring efforts to fulfill his promise won him the 1987 Nobel Peace Prize. While the peace process met with much opposition at home, plus skepticism and even ennui in the First World press, for many Central Americans it signified a coming of age—a chance to unite and shape their future in a new way. The first democratic elections in Nicaragua's history, held February 25, 1990, were largely a result of the peace plan and saw the Sandinistas defeated.

Rafael Angel Calderón Fournier, son of Rafael Angel Calderón Guardia (who "lost" the 1948 Civil War), succeeded Arias in 1990. Calderón Fournier was inaugurated as president 50 years to the day after his father assumed power. In 1994, José María Figueres, son of Don Pepe, took over from "Junior" Calderón, becoming one of the youngest presidents in history. Following in his father's footsteps, he initiated some truly novel policies, like the sale of "carbon-sequestering" bonds. He built on Costa Rica's reputation for having a well-educated populace to attract software giant Intel, which opened a 400,000-square-foot plant in April 1998 and promptly became the country's number-one exporter. Costa Rica's progressive labor codes have ensured that this has meant decent jobs, unlike the *maquiladoras* (sweatshops) NAFTA has produced in the Mexican border area.

As mentioned in the introduction, Costa Rica has been a world-leader in fostering the notion that forested areas perform a service for the planet, and that the owners of these areas (public or private) should be compensated for this service. In Costa Rica, 87 percent of the water for hydroelectric generation comes from protected forests. Replacing it with fossil fuel generation would cost $104 million. With money from a 15 percent fuel tax, the Figueres administration initiated the National Fund for Forest Financing, which pays landowners for the environmental services provided by their forests.

The 1998 election was won by a wealthy and well-educated economist and businessman, Miguel Angel Rodriguez. His administration allowed thousands of forest giants to be cut down in the Osa Peninsula and Talamanca. The government then announced plans to deregulate environmental building controls, and to abolish laws that halted building permits when archaeological sites were unearthed during construction projects. In general, the Ro-driguez administration did little to further the far-sighted environmental and social policies that have made Costa Rica famous.

As had previous administrations, Rodriguez implemented the "structured adjustment programs" recommended by international lending institutions for Latin America's developing nations; this has resulted in a strengthened macroeconomy but has not led to growth of the small businesses that make up 95 percent of Costa Rica's economy, so conditions for average Costa Ricans have actually gotten worse. Another thrust of the international bankers is to privatize much of Costa Rica's large public sector. While this cuts costs, it has caused some bitter strikes.

COSTA RICA TODAY

The 2002 presidential election was the first time a third party had a signifi-cant effect on electoral politics. Straight-talking candidate Otton Solis of the Citizen's Action Party, committed to combatting government corruption and formed only 14 months before the elections, won 26 percent of the vote. This forced a runoff election between the two major parties, National Liberation and National Unity (the present incarnation of Calderón's party), since neither of the traditional parties had won the required 40 per-cent of the vote to be elected. Abel Pacheco of National Unity eventually won the runoff; he is a psychiatrist who for many years was a respected tel-evision commentator.

During the previous presidential term, then-president Miguel Angel Ro-driguez (1998–2002) had granted Harken Oil (the company in which George W. Bush and Dick Cheney figured prominently) exclusive oil ex-ploration rights off Costa Rica's beautiful Caribbean coast. The area in-cludes a RAMSAR wetlands site, is recognized by the U.N. as a World Heritage Site, and is considered by The Nature Conservancy to be a critical bird migration area. Communities all over Costa Rica organized against the decision, and the Environmental Ministry also ruled against the drilling project, but Harken persisted. One of Abel Pacheco's first acts when he took office in May 2003 was to ban open-pit mining and oil exploration, ordering Harken to leave Costa Rica. In September 2003, the company filed for international arbitration in Washington, D.C., seeking to recover $57 billion in "lost potential" because it was prevented from drilling an es-timated 2.3 billion barrels of oil and 6 trillion cubic feet of natural gas. Fifty seven billion dollars is about four times Costa Rica's gross domestic product. The government insisted that Harken's lack of compliance with environmental measures gave Costa Rica grounds to terminate the contract, and that the dispute could be resolved in Costa Rican courts. Pacheco's firm stance caused the oil company to withdraw its arbitration request in October 2003.

Costa Rica and the U.S. have disagreed on several issues in recent years. Armyless Costa Rica does not receive conventional military aid, but the U.S. had been helping Costa Rica police and Coast Guard intercept drug shipments. However, the U.S. government has cut this assistance because Costa Rica supports the International Criminal Court. Ironically, cutting off aid to Costa Rica's police might increase drug shipments into the U.S.

Costa Rica also clashed with the U.S. over Costa Rica's membership in the Group of 21 during the dramatic World Trade Organization talks in Cancún, Mexico. U.S. negotiators of the Central American Free Trade Agreement (CAFTA) indicated that it would be to Costa Rica's advantage to withdraw from the controversial group of uppity developing countries if it wanted negotiations to go well, and Costa Rica gracefully withdrew. CAFTA was the cause of many demonstrations in 2003 and 2004 by workers from Costa Rica's nationalized industries.

The Costa Rican Electricity Institute (ICE) is seen as a key force behind the country's development for the past 50 years. Opening this government-owned monopoly to competition as CAFTA mandates is seen as a step backward. Costa Ricans don't want to see the success of their unique system thrown away for a one-size-fits-all economic scheme imposed from without.

Intel and other software companies are responsible for 25 percent of Costa Rica's GNP, and employ around 4300 workers. Over 130 software firms operate here, 77 percent Costa Rican–owned. Costa Rica has more software developers per capita than any other country in the world. However, tourism is still the top generator of foreign currency in this country, bringing in over $1.2 billion in 2002.

But with all this development, rural and urban poor people feel that their interests are being ignored, as public infrastructure, which they rely on heavily for health care and schooling, deteriorates. According to a 2000 United Nations study, 20 percent of Costa Ricans live in poverty. New nontraditional agro-industries promoted by the IMF and World Bank demand high startup and input costs, and are not labor-intensive; this shuts the small farmer out. As they become islands in an ocean of monocrop plantations owned by wealthy corporations, small farmers are being forced off land once granted them by government agrarian development institutions.

The biological corridor programs and related ecotourism projects mentioned throughout this book are designed to bring equilibrium back to the Costa Rican agricultural landscape.

Costa Rican currency has suffered regular devaluation over the last two decades. The annual per capita income is only $6650, and the gap between rich and poor is growing. Yet because of Costa Rica's national health care and social security systems, life expectancy is the same as in countries where income is four times that much, and health care is on par with that of industrialized nations.

Ticos, rich and poor, actively support their democracy. On election day they honk horns, wave party flags, dress up in party colors, and proudly display their index fingers dipped in purple indelible ink to show they have voted. Recently, 70 percent of the electorate turned out to vote, as compared to 20 to 50 percent in the United States. Children, wearing their party's colors, proudly volunteer to lead voters to the polls.

Costa Ricans' love for the beauty and freedom of their country is almost palpable. At 6 p.m. each September 14, the eve of their Independence Day, everyone drops what they are doing to sing the national anthem. In corner stores and homes across the country, everyone joins in. It's a rousing hymn in tribute to peace, hard work, and the generosity of the earth, but it's also a warning that if these things are threatened, Costa Ricans will "convert their rough farming tools into arms," as they did when William Walker tried to invade in the 19th century.

Costa Rica does not want the kind of tourist development that regards local people merely as a pool of potential maids, waiters, gardeners, laundresses, and nothing more. The traditional values of the small independent farmers who are the backbone of Costa Rican democracy could be lost in the process. Most Costa Ricans are proud to share the beauty of their land with visitors and know how to make foreigners feel at home.

Hopefully a new and exciting chapter is opening in Costa Rica's continuing challenge to keep its democracy vital and relevant, and to recognize a healthy environment as a basic human right. The rest of the world could benefit by keeping an eye on her progress.

TWO

The Ecological Picture

Costa Rica measures only 185 miles across at her widest point, but four mountain ranges divide her like a backbone. Mount Chirripó, at 12,000 feet, is the highest point in southern Central America. It is part of Costa Rica's oldest and southernmost mountain range, the Cordillera de Talamanca, which extends into Panama. The Central Volcanic Range is made up of volcanoes Turrialba, Irazú, Barva, and Poás. More than half of Costa Rica's 3.8 million inhabitants live in the Central Valley, whose fertile soil was created by the activity of these volcanoes over the last two million years. To the northwest is the Tilarán range, which reaches 5500 feet at Monteverde and includes the active Volcán Arenal. Farthest northwest, toward the Nicaraguan border, is the Guanacaste Range, which boasts five active volcanoes, including Rincón de la Vieja and Miravalles (now being used to generate geothermal energy). The most ancient rocks in the area are more than 100 million years old and occur in the "Nicoya complex," low mountains that crop up here and there along the Pacific.

Costa Rica may be one of the smaller countries in the Americas, but it boasts the most diverse selection of flora and fauna in the hemisphere. There are several reasons for this diversity: Costa Rica's topography ranges from the bleak, treeless paramo, 12,000 feet above sea level, to rainforests on the coasts only 50 miles away, with countless microclimates in between. Costa Rica's latitude contributes steady temperatures year-round, and abundant precipitation creates hospitable conditions for many forms of life. Perhaps most important is Costa Rica's position between the Americas: a land bridge between North and South, where migrating animals and plants meet. North American white-tailed deer sniff at South American brocket deer and northern rattlesnakes slide by southern bushmasters. There are animals here that have evolved nowhere else in the world: pacas and agoutis (cousins of guinea pigs), dantas (huge tapirs), and prehensile-tailed porcupines, to name a few. The ecology of Costa Rica is so complex and fascinating that this brief chapter should only be considered a very elementary and anecdotal survey.

ECOSYSTEMS

From high, dry mountains to verdant rainforests, Costa Rica is home to a wide range of ecosystems, a term used to describe a community of living organisms and their complex interactions with their environment. Following are descriptions of some of Costa Rica's more common ecosystems.

The **paramo**, related to the Andean ecosystem of the same name, covers the summits of Costa Rica's southern Talamanca mountain range. Just as the foliage is tough and small, which protects it from the elements and conserves energy, the animals that live here are mostly small rodents and tiny lizards activated by strong sun. Paramos originally were limited to the highest peaks of Costa Rica, but due to deforestation, this bleak zone is extending downward. There is paramo at Cerro de la Muerte, Chirripó, and the high mountain peaks in Parque Internacional La Amistad (visit through Dúrika Biological Reserve above Buenos Aires).

The highest rainforests, blanketing the slopes of the Continental Divide, are called **cloud forests** because they are nearly always veiled in clouds. Clouds pause momentarily at the Divide after ascending the Atlantic slope, and the forest soaks up their moisture. Scientists postulate that global warming is making the clouds rise higher over the divide, depriving cloud forests of their mist. They think that this subtle drying effect might be responsible for the disappearance of moisture-sensitive frogs and toads. These forests provide a crucial watershed for areas below. Monteverde is Costa Rica's most famous cloud forest. There are many others as well, some of which are easier to reach from San José: Los Angeles Cloud Forest, Bosque de Paz, Braulio Carrillo National Park, the reserve above Nacientes Palmichal, and the ancient oak forests on Cerro de la Muerte.

The Atlantic Coast and the Corcovado Peninsula are home to what most of us think of when we hear the word "**rainforest**": tremendously tall trees with vines twisting up their girth, hanging roots of philodendrons whose leaves are high above. Rainforest pilgrims may also visit the many reserves in the Sarapiquí and Gúapiles areas, like the Tirimbina Wildlife Refuge, Selva Verde, La Selva, and Rara Avis. The Heliconias Reserve, north of

Cañas on the road to Upala, is one of the most beautiful in the country. Carara and Manuel Antonio national parks are the most (over)visited rainforests in the country, due to their easy accessibility.

The characteristic that most differentiates tropical rainforests from their temperate counterparts is their diversity. Year-round warm temperatures and abundant rain have produced a plethora of species, each with a high degree of specialization. There are insects that blend in perfectly with the type of leaves they eat. Some of the most fragrant flowers only release their scent at night, to attract nocturnal, nearly blind bats.

The forest has several levels, from ground-covering ferns and mosses, to short bushes and tree ferns, to canopy species stunted by a lack of light, to shade-loving trees that reach a certain height and provide a mid-canopy, to the canopy trees, which, depending upon the life zone (determined by altitude and precipitation), can reach up to 180 feet in height. Seeds are eaten or unwittingly carried by birds or monkeys that travel through the forest and drop them along the way, often far from the mother tree. Many seedlings flourish in the shade at ground level. Species that demand much light will flounder in the relatively dark forest floor until an old tree dies or falls, and leaves a "light gap." At that point, the light-demanding species will shoot up until one reaches the canopy and fills the hole.

A true rainforest is evergreen: trees will never all lose their leaves at once. The **dry pacific forest** is deciduous, shedding its leaves during the severe dry season to conserve water. The canopy is significantly lower than in the rainforest. When the trees are bare, it is often easier to see wildlife here. Many of the animals that frequent the dry pacific forest are seasonal visitors from other ecosystems. Tropical dry forests occur only in Guanacaste. Santa Rosa protects a large tract, and Lomas Barbudal and Palo Verde are home to others.

Mangroves are found in intertidal zones at river mouths and estuaries where fresh water and saltwater meet. Comprising the various species of tree that are virtually the only flora that can live half the time submerged in salty water, the other half in nearly airless mud, the different types of mangroves (red, black, white, tea, and buttonwood) are actually from four unrelated families, each having developed ways of coping with these challenging conditions. They resist osmosis by maintaining a higher concentration of salt in their tissues than in the seawater, and secrete excess salt from their leaves or roots. To aerate, as well as to survive in a natural flood zone, mangroves have aerial roots with multiple buttresses. By preventing large predators from entering, their tangle of roots provides a habitat for many species of marine life at their most vulnerable stages of development. Baby oysters and sponges attach to the roots. Algae generated in the nutrient-rich mud is abundant food for young crabs, lobsters, shrimp, and barnacles.

Some types of mangroves gradually turn a wet intertidal zone into dry land. As their leaves drop onto silt collected in the roots, a layer of soil slowly develops. Eventually, the mangroves, which can't live outside their tidal habitat, are stranded on dry land and die. At the same time that this curious suicidal behavior occurs, however, unique floating seedlings with weighted bottoms are carried in the water until they can lodge in the mud. Because seeds germinate while still on the tree, they quickly take root, in a never-ending quest for new territory.

Some of the best areas to observe mangroves include the estuaries of the Pacific Coast, the Río Sierpe boat trip to Drake Bay, the Atrocha route between Golfito and Zancudo, the canals just north of Moín on the way to Tortuguero, and on Isla Chira in the Gulf of Nicoya.

Mangroves filter sediment-rich river water so that much clearer water flows into the ocean. In some areas off the coast, where the water is very clear, **coral reefs** develop. Coral reefs are animals, plants, and geologic formations all in one. They create habitats of rich biological gardens populated by life forms as diverse as those found in the rainforest, from unicellular organisms such as algae to fish like the damselfish. (The damselfish actually tends her garden, plucking undesirable sea grasses from her seascape.)

The coral structure is formed by unique plantlike animals that live within it, filtering water to obtain nutrients then excreting calcium carbonate, which becomes the coral skeleton. The coral reef itself breaks waves, creating a calm interior thick with sea grasses, and important nutrients for turtles, manatees, and other marine animals.

Manuel Antonio's third beach has calm waters and a lovely reef. The point at Cahuita has, too, although sediment carried downriver from banana plantations is diminishing its growth. The Manzanillo Reef south of Puerto Viejo has only recently been mapped, and we hear it is spectacular. We have had mixed reports about the reef in Bahía Ballena National Marine Park south of Dominical. One of the best places to dive and snorkel is Isla del Caño, 20 kilometers off Drake Bay, which has five coral platforms.

FLORA

Costa Rica is home to an incredibly diverse selection of flora, each type adapted for life in a particular ecosystem. At forest floors, the predominant color is green, but at eye level there are brightly colored and fragrant flowers. Especially common in rainforests are species of the heliconia flower—large red, yellow, or orange bursts of tropical exuberance. Fragrant orchids, too, are common here, as are a spectacular array of ferns. From the lowliest lichen to the towering ceiba tree, the Costa Rican landscape offers a rich display of plant life.

EPIPHYTES   Whether in the ghostly, fog-draped cloud forests or the towering lowland rainforests, branches and treetops look impossibly top-heavy, covered as they are with orchids, mosses, ferns, lichens, bromeliads, and other families of epiphytes (plants whose roots grasp tree branches and absorb their nutrients from leaf matter and water dripping off the canopy).

Among the tiniest epiphytes are the mosses found growing on leaf surfaces and the lichens clinging to tree bark. They are restricted to areas that are moist year-round. Because they can hinder a plant's ability to photosynthesize, many plants have developed a variety of techniques for getting rid of these pesky hangers-on. "Drip tip" leaves will drain water collected on them so that their surface is dry, making it difficult for mosses to colonize. Some trees slough off their bark regularly, shedding lichens as well.

Ferns are a diverse category of flowerless epiphyte. Notable species among the 800 types found in Costa Rica include the primordial-looking tree fern (an upright fern with prickly spines) and the resurrection fern, which dries and curls up during periods of drought, only to spring back to life with the return of the rains.

The 1500 species of orchids that are found in Costa Rica are the showiest epiphytes, with intricate and spectacular flowers. Orchids appear on every continent except Antarctica, but are most diverse in the tropics, where they range in size from half an inch to twenty-five-and-a-half feet. Because they do not have edible pollen to offer their pollinators, orchids rely either on an alluring strong scent or mimicry to deceive insects into believing they are something they are not.

Bromeliads are epiphytes that collect and store water in their tightly joined leaf bases, or trap tiny droplets in their hairlike trichomes. This water is rendered nutrient-rich when particles fall into it or when mosquitos and other insects that breed in it die and decompose there. The 170 species of bromeliads found in Costa Rica provide niches for up to 250 forms of life.

FLOWERS   Costa Rica offers a variety of flowering plants, many of which have developed very specific traits for survival. For instance, the angel's trumpet tree produces pendulous white flowers that open only at night and are just the right shape for a bat snout. They exude an almost dizzying smell. The aristolchia flower, which attracts one particular bat as its pollinator, mimics the genitalia of the female of that species of bat to attract the males. The dracontium flower depends on feces-loving flies as pollinators and has a distinct stench almost everyone recognizes.

TREES   The diversity of the tropical forest is evident in the trees that make it up. In just two and a half acres, there can be over 90 species of trees. Following are descriptions of just a few of the many unusual types of trees you may encounter during your visit to Costa Rica.

Coconut trees lean out over the beach to reach more sunlight and to drop their nuts where the waves will pick them up. Coconuts can float in the ocean for several months and land on another beach thousands of leagues away before they sprout. The infant plant is nourished by the rich coconut milk and meat, and once leaves emerge and photosynthesis begins, thousands of roots emerge from the nut and anchor the young tree to the beach. Biologists have observed this colonization process on new volcanic islands. Coconuts are what have made human habitation possible on otherwise inhospitable islands. New leaves grow and old ones are shed about once a month. So, in order to calculate the age of a coconut tree in years, count the number of leaves and leaf scars on a coconut tree trunk, and divide by twelve.

Recognizable by its prominent orange-red roots, the milk or cow tree is common in the rainforest of Corcovado National Park. Its Latin name is *Brosimum utile*, and useful it is. Through the trunk flows a drinkable white latex. The tree's sweet fruit is edible, and its wood is useful for construction. The indigenous people of the area used its bark to stay warm: they would cut a portion of bark from the tree, soak it, then dry it and beat it to make a warm, soft blanket.

Indio desnudo ("naked Indian," also known as the "sunburned gringo"), with bright orange bark, is another easily recognizable tree found mostly in dry Pacific forests. The leaves fall off during the dry season, but chloroplasts under the bark's surface allow photosynthesis to continue. Each tree produces a bounty of between 600 and 6000 fruits, which are savored by white-faced monkeys. When the monkeys accidentally drop fruit-laden branches onto the forest floor, collared peccaries eat them, too.

Considered sacred by Costa Rica's indigenous people, the ceiba or kapok tree is one of the fastest-growing trees known, climbing as much as 13 feet a year to a maximum recorded height of 198 feet. This makes it a prime pioneer, quickly colonizing fields allowed to regenerate. Its seed pods contain envelopes of cottony fibers that enclose the seeds. The envelopes are carried by the wind and eventually the seed falls out. Kapok fiber has long been used as stuffing for pillows, saddles, and clothing. The wood is too light for construction, but is used for canoes and coffins.

Strangler figs are parasitic tree-like plants that begin as epiphytes on a tree limb when a seed from a bird dropping takes root in a hospitable nook. Once the seedling is established, it sends roots that surround the host tree trunk in a close embrace, and branches reach to cover the upper branches of the host tree. The host tree eventually dies, probably not because of strangulation, but because the fig's branches block the host tree's light source. The Original Canopy Tour in Monteverde begins with a climb inside a hollow strangler fig tree.

FAUNA

As rich and varied as is Costa Rica's flora, you'll find the fauna that use it as a habitat equally diverse.

REPTILES AND AMPHIBIANS   Rainforest amphibians generally have toxins in their skin. The mildest poisons just taste bad, while the strongest can kill predators (including humans) by causing vasoconstriction, respiratory paralysis, hypertension, and other mortal conditions. The toxin may be ingested through the mucous membranes of the mouth or throat, or through the pores in the skin. The message: don't touch these guys. (Ironically, they may be the source of lifesaving antibacterial and antiviral compounds that scientists are still researching.) Big bullfrogs that are common near beaches can even shoot toxin a distance of up to six and one half feet, so be wary of them, too.

So named because indigenous warriors poisoned their arrow tips with its venom, the vermilion-colored **poison dart frog** spends its entire life high above the rainforest floor. Bromeliad water vessels serve as the frog's breeding grounds, protecting the developing tadpoles from predators. At the end of the two-month gestation period, an adult dart frog emerges from the plant shelter with a fully developed defense system: Its skin glands exude a poison that rolls off its back like drops of sweat. Any animal taking a poison dart frog into its mouth is poisoned. The frog's brilliant red color serves as warning.

Other toxic amphibians warn predators with "flash colors"—brightly colored legs or groin areas, which are revealed only when the animal jumps. This startles the predator, and might dissuade it from attacking.

Three kinds of **sea turtles** nest on Costa Rica's shores: the Pacific or olive ridley at Playa Nancite in Santa Rosa National Park and at Ostional near Playa Nosara; the green turtle at Tortuguero; and the leatherback at Playa Grande near Tamarindo, Tortuguero, the Pacuare Reserve near Parismina, and the Gandoca–Manzanillo Wildlife Refuge in Talamanca. We provide descriptions of these giant sea creatures and their nesting habits in the geographic chapters that cover their nesting grounds.

Two kinds of **crocodiles** are found in Costa Rica. The smaller ones, called caymans, which grow no longer than three feet, live in creeks, ponds, mangrove swamps, and beach lowlands. They are most common in the Corcovado area. What are commonly called crocodiles are the larger animals, reaching up to 13 feet in length. We have seen them lounging in the muddy banks of rivers in the Northern Zone, on the boat trip to Tortuguero, on the Río Sierpe, and at the Carara National Park near Playa Jacó.

SNAKES   Due to their camouflage and wariness of humans, you are not likely to see snakes in a brief visit to the forest, but it is worth knowing which ones are dangerous. Non-poisonous **boa constrictors** are long (reaching 18 feet in length), fat snakes with dark squares on a light brown or gray background. They sit and wait until a likely prey appears (they have been known to eat lizards, tanagers, opossums, young porcupines, deer, and even ocelots), and then they strike, impale the animal on their fangs, lift it, strangle it, then swallow it head first. Because they have few recorded predators, boas are believed to be at or near the top of the food chain. When a boa feels threatened, its body fills with air along its entire length, and it emits a deep, ghostly roar.

Of the 136 species of snakes in Costa Rica, 18 are lethal. **Fer-de-lance** *(terciopelo)* snakes are venomous residents of rainy jungles, large rivers, and overgrown fields. They are brown and black with a white "X" pattern running down their back, which make them almost impossible to see among the twigs and leaves. When disturbed, this aggressive six-and-a-half-foot-long snake bites anything that moves, and its bite can be fatal to humans. Its usual diet consists of mammals and birds. At Parque Viborana

in Turrialba, we observed snake expert Minor Camacho walking in a cage of angry *terciopelos*. When they prepared to strike, he stood completely still until they calmed down. Then he would take a step, they would rear their heads again, he would stand still again and they would relax. He did this several times, demonstrating how knowledge of this snake's behavior can keep people from getting bitten, and also keep snakes from being killed by fearful humans.

The dreaded **eyelash vipers** are so named for a visor-like scale that extends beyond their eyes. These snakes are small, less than three feet in length, and come in green, brown, rust, gray, or light blue, with a darker diamond pattern on the back, although some are gold, without the pattern. They hang in trees. Three to six people per year in Costa Rica die after being bitten by this highly venomous snake.

Costa Rica has its own species of **rattlesnake** as well, with stripes on its neck and diamonds on its back. They are mostly found in Guanacaste. Their venom can cause blindness, paralysis, and suffocation.

These are the poisonous snakes. You can look them in the eye at one of the country's many serpentaria. Hopefully, those will be the only snakes you will encounter on your trip. See "Health Precautions" in Chapter Three to find out what to do if bitten by a snake.

BIRDS   Costa Rica's most famous cloud-forest bird is the **resplendent quetzal**, a large, brilliant green bird whose males sport a two-foot-long wispy tail. Despite their size and bright colors, they are not easy to spot because they remain very still high up in the trees while tracking insects or small arboreal frogs and lizards. During their mating season from February to April, they are more visible. Quetzals cannot live in captivity, a poetic quality that has made them a symbol of freedom for the people of Central America. Quetzals migrate during the year to follow ripening fruits of trees in the avocado family.

Other birds that follow ripening fruits up and down the mountains include the **three-wattled bellbird**, which gets its name from its bell-like voice and the three wattles or wormlike pieces of skin that flop over its beak. This bird eats the same avocado-like fruits as the quetzal, and also migrates to much lower elevations after breeding in the cloud forest.

There is also the **bare-necked umbrella bird**, whose males are large and black with big fluffy pompadour headdresses and bright red featherless throats that they inflate to attract the much less ornate females. Females are usually much less conspicuous and camouflage their young while nesting.

Other, more notable birds include the liquid-voiced **oropéndolas**. These large, dull-colored birds with yellow tails weave long, sac-like nests on dead tree branches. Visitors from temperate climes enjoy sighting **parrots**, abundant in the tropics. Sixteen species of this raucous family inhabit Costa Rica, from tiny parakeets and parrotlets, to giant scarlet macaws. **Scarlet macaws**, which are monogamous and mate for life, used to live throughout the lowlands of Costa Rica, but massive deforestation and poaching have restricted the few remaining birds to Carara National Park and the Osa Peninsula. Our sharp-eyed guide, Modesto Watson, spotted a pair in Tortuguero in 1998, an encouraging sight.

Green macaws used to range through the entire Atlantic lowland region of Costa Rica, nesting in giant *almendro* trees. Until recently, these trees were left by lumbermen because their wood was too hard to process as lumber. However, new technology has been developed and the trees are being cut at an alarming rate. The habitat for green macaws has been reduced by 95 percent, and biologist George Powell estimates that only 25 to 35 nesting pairs remain on the northeastern plains. The International Union for the Conservation of Nature has been working to save the remaining birds and their habitat.

Of the 330 species of **hummingbirds** known to exist in the world, almost one-fifth are found in Costa Rica. These tiny nectar-eaters have unusual wings that can rotate at the shoulders, allowing them to fly in any direction or hover over a flower while they fit their beak into the floral tube and suck out the nectar. Almost any pink, red, or orange flower attracts hummingbirds. A great place to get to know hummingbirds is La Paz Waterfall Gardens on the eastern slopes of Poás volcano.

Among the many waterbirds frequenting Costa Rica are the **frigate bird** (pterodactyl-like with a six-and-a-half-foot wingspan, whose primitive body type makes landing and taking off difficult) and the six species of **kingfishers** (short-necked, large-headed, and sharp-billed divers who dwell at rivers and coasts).

About a quarter of Costa Rica's 850 species of birds are seasonal visitors from North or South America. They fly to the tropics to escape scarcity during harsh winters, making long, arduous journeys over land and sea. Among the most amazing feats is the first leg of the **ruby-throated hummingbird**'s annual trip south: a nonstop 500-mile flight over the Gulf of Mexico. The **raptors** (hawks, falcons, and eagles) fly over Costa Rica on their way south every October. Traditionally, they have sought temporary shelter in the Atlantic Zone. The Kekoldi indigenous tribe has built a raptor observation tower in the hills above Puerto Viejo de Talamanca. Birds that summer in North America and winter in Costa Rica include warblers, swallows, thrushes, finches, orioles, flycatchers, and tanagers.

Ornithologist Carmen Hidalgo offers these suggestions for birdwatchers: The best hours of the day to see most birds are before 8 a.m. and for an hour or two before sundown; use lightweight binoculars. In general, the best time of the year to see birds is in May, the beginning of the rainy season and nesting season for many species, but for aquatic varieties the end of the rainy season (November–December) is best.

Serious birders will want to bring *A Guide to the Birds of Costa Rica* (Gary F. Stiles and Alexander Skutch, Cornell University Press). Audio field guides are available online at http://birds.cornell.edu/shop/audioguides. A series of laminated cards with bird species for various areas of the country is available in most souvenir shops.

MAMMALS   Even though you must have a lot of patience and be accompanied by an experienced guide to see birds in the forest, they are still easier to observe than most other animals. Mammals such as the jaguar and the tapir are part of the hype that is attracting so many ecotourists to the rainforest. However, they are rarely seen by visitors because they flee from humans and are nocturnal.

Jaguars, the largest Costa Rican carnivores, are most common in areas where there has been little human penetration. Each jaguar adult requires a forest-covered hunting ground one hundred miles in size. As humans colonize their territories, the jaguars recede, crowding into areas too small for them. A reduced gene pool leads to weakened animals and mutations; this might eventually lead to their extinction. See the Introduction for a description of the Mesoamerican Biological Corridor, which hopes to link protected areas throughout Central America in order to create one unbroken reserve the length of the isthmus for large cats and other animals who need vast amounts of space to roam.

Huge vegetarian **tapirs** have long been considered one of the finest delicacies a Costa Rican hunter can bring home, so these mammals are also in danger of extinction. Currently, they can be found only where hunting has been prohibited. Their immense size does not prevent them from being swift runners. Their feet have an interesting adaptation that aids them when running through the muddy forest floor. Their feet spread out as they step down, then their toes draw together to make pulling out of the mud easier.

With a keen eye, you might see a **sloth** hanging from a tree limb. This animal's name is no coincidence—a sloth hardly moves. Most vegetarian animals must eat berries or nuts to generate the energy they need to survive. Sloths just eat leaves, so they need to carry out a low-maintenance lifestyle. They have little muscle tissue, compared to other animals. As much as they annoyed energetic explorers of the colonial period (Captain

William Dampier whipped a sloth to make it move—it wouldn't), they do have a perfect system worked out: their upside-down position hanging from tree limbs is ideal for scooping hanging leaves into their mouths. Algae-shrouded fur camouflages them in the treetops, and their meat does not taste good. When attacked by one of their few predators, their slow metabolism allows them to survive wounds that would kill other animals.

Monkeys are the most sociable forest dwellers. Intensely attached to their family group or troupe, they are among the most intelligent animals. There are four types of monkeys in Costa Rica. The diminutive, insect-eating **white-faced monkey** (*mono cariblanco*) inhabits the Caribbean lowland rainforest, Manuel Antonio National Park, Monteverde premontane forest, the Osa Peninsula, and the dry forests of Guanacaste. Large **howler monkeys** (*mono congo*), audible if not always visible throughout Costa Rica, are so named because their bellows resonate through the forest, making them sound like much more terrifying animals than the vegetarians they are. Blond-chested **spider monkeys** (*mono colorado*) have long, prehensile tails with a fingerprint-like imprint at the end, adapted for gripping. Their increased agility allows them to leap up to 30 feet. These monkeys love physical contact so much that they sleep in a big heap. Tiny **squirrel monkeys** (*mono tití*) live in the Pacific lowland area and are highly social, living in bands up to 30 strong. Often the first indication that monkeys are near is the sight or sound of branches bouncing as they jump from tree to tree.

Coatis (*pizotes*), which look like jungle raccoons with long, slightly bushy, monkeylike tails, are diurnal and easily seen in open areas. Agile in trees, they are competent ground dwellers as well. They live in every habitat in Costa Rica, and eat everything from fruit and mice to tarantulas and lizards. Females and young live in bands that can number 30 (this contributes to their being easy to spot); adult males are solitary.

Another community-oriented mammal is the pig-like **collared peccary**. Living in groups of 3 to 30, they greet one another by rubbing their heads to the scent glands near their tails, and sleep together to conserve heat. They have long hair covering their gray-black skin; a band of white rings their neck.

Some mammals that are receiving renewed attention in Costa Rica are dolphins and whales. Several species of **dolphin** are visible on both the Atlantic and Pacific coasts. Special dolphin-watching tours are offered in Drake Bay on the Osa Peninsula and in Manzanillo on the Caribbean. Those who have come to know and love the intelligent and friendly dolphin are noting a decrease in the populations and are becoming increasingly concerned that the "dolphin-safe" fishing methods used by tuna fish companies are not really allowing dolphins to escape. For more information, e-mail costacetacea@ hotmail.com or call 770-8012.

Humpback and pilot **whales** are visible off the Pacific coast, especially at Ballena National Marine Park in Uvita de Osa and in Drake Bay, where they come to give birth between mid-December and mid-April. Because the baby whales can't stay submerged for too long, the whales are easier to see here than in more northern climes. Humpback whales are shyer, while pilot whales seem to like people.

INTERACTIONS

Even more fascinating than the individual species in the forest is how they interact. Nature's most intimate and complex relationships involve what biologists call "mutualisms." In mutual relationships, each actor provides a necessary service for the other, and often neither can survive alone. Following are a few intriguing examples of nature's interdependencies.

Tiny tree frogs, which never touch ground, have one of the most intimate relationships with bromeliads. The female vermilion poison dart frog lays a few eggs in damp humus, but when they hatch she carries them on her back to her "nursery": bromeliad water vessels. In this secluded habitat, they develop virtually unthreatened. The mother visits daily, locating them easily because they wiggle their tails to make ripples in the water. She lays unfertilized, protein-rich eggs, which the tadpoles perforate and suck. Two months after birth, they are fully developed, two-centimeter-long adult frogs. The frogs' waste products decompose in the bromeliad's stored water, making absorbable nutrients for the plant.

Ants participate in some of the most complex and perfect mutualisms. One example is the azteca ant/cecropia tree relationship. Cecropias are medium-sized, weak-limbed rainforest trees. Azteca ants live in the hollow trunk and stems of the cecropia and obsessively scour the limbs for epiphyte seeds and seedlings, which they dump off the side. This act is crucial for the cecropia because the weight of epiphytes would break its limbs. Cecropias produce fat and protein-packed capsules at their leaf tips, which nourish the ants. Azteca ants appreciate sweet nectar, too, but since the cecropia doesn't produce flowers, the ants tend masses of aphids inside the tree. The aphids do not harm the cecropia, but produce a sweet honeydew, which the ants eat.

Sometimes a mutual relationship can appear quite exploitative. Cowbirds and *oropéndolas* have a very intricate relationship that puzzled scientists for many years until biologist Neal Smith, working at his research site in Panama, discovered what was really happening. *Oropéndolas* are bird artisans that craft long, sacklike nests which hang from bare-limbed trees in the forest. Cowbirds are parasitical, laying their eggs in *oropéndolas*' nests and then leaving the *oropéndola* to incubate and raise the cowbird hatchling. Although cowbird chicks do preen *oropéndola* chicks, cowbird chicks are aggressive and develop faster than *oropéndola* chicks and can deprive *oropéndolas* of food. Sometimes *oropéndolas* tolerate this, sometimes they don't. It wasn't until another threat to *oropéndolas* was discovered that the *oropéndolas*' decision-making process was revealed. *Oropéndola* chicks are born without a protective downy coat of feathers, and are particularly vulnerable to botflies burrowing into them and killing them. When wasps and bees are present in the area, they prevent a botfly population from developing. *Oropéndola* mothers allow the cowbirds to lay their eggs only if the nest is located in an area with no wasp or bee populations to control the botflies, so the cowbirds' preening is appreciated. If there are wasps or bees around, the *oropéndola* will chase away the cowbird mother or dump her egg out of the nest.

DEFORESTATION

The interactions of species that are so fascinating to observe in Costa Rica forests are a lesson for humans in how to live cooperatively with nature, rather than exploiting, exterminating, and controlling it. Despite the steps that the country has taken to conserve nature, it had one of the highest deforestation rates in Latin America in the late 20th century. Now, according to Environment Minister Carlos Manuel Rodriguez, deforestation is slowing and forest cover is increasing by about 5 percent per year. Although only about 15 percent of Costa Rica's original forest cover still stands, today about 45 percent of the country is covered in some kind of forest, including the 25 percent that is planted in tree farms, mostly of the foreign species gmelina and teak. Since 1999, more wood has come from these tree farms than from the nation's forest. But monoculture tree crops cannot support the biodiversity of rainforests, so many projects in the Mesoamerican Biological Corridor (see the Introduction) are reforesting with a variety of native species.

A green seal for bananas (ECO-O.K., known as "Better Bananas" in Europe) has been developed by the New York–based Rainforest Alliance and the Costa Rican Fundación Ambío, in collaboration with scientists, environmentalists, and banana growers. It gives a marketing incentive to growers who make the effort to protect workers and produce bananas away from rivers and with less dangerous pesticides. About 15,000 hectares of banana-cultivated land in Costa Rica has passed the test so far, including all of Chiquita's Costa Rica–based operations, and Chiquita has brought all of its Latin America plantations up to ECO-O.K. standards. Look for ECO-O.K. coffee, oranges, and chocolate, too (www.ra.org).

The Rainforest Alliance also has the Smart Wood Program, to certify wood products that were harvested from forests managed in compliance with environmentally sound principles.

There is still a long way to go before Costa Rica can be considered a true model for harmony between humans and nature, but many people are dedicating their lives toward this end.

TOURISM AND THE ENVIRONMENT

Costa Rica transformed itself from an agricultural to a tourism-based economy between 1985 and 1990, and development was poorly planned. Now that Costa Rica is a prime ecotourism destination, growth can no longer be allowed at the expense of environmental and community concerns. Several major tourist attractions are dealing with infrastructure problems brought on by the rapid growth of tourism

The Costa Rican Tourism Institute (ICT) has authored a 10-Year General Plan for Sustainable Tourism Development. The plan recognizes, for example, that the port town of Quepos, gateway to the famous beaches of Manuel Antonio, needs a wastewater treatment plant, a landfill, better bridges, and lifeguard towers on the beach. These improvements are not yet in place, so Quepos is having to make do. Similarly, hotels in Tortuguero are building more and more rooms in response to the demands of tourism wholesalers, without a viable system of waste disposal. The number of rooms in Tortuguero exceeds the number of people allowed on the beach to see the nesting turtles, setting the stage for overtaxing the unique natural resource that draws tourists there in the first place.

The ICT is promoting a 6.6 percent annual increase in tourism, aiming to double annual visitation to 2.3 million in 2012. However, in the hot, dry Guanacaste region, community activists are bringing a hotel complex before the Central American Water Tribunal, claiming that needed water resources are being drained by tourism development. Residents of Puerto Viejo on the Caribbean coast protest that the ICT plan wants to fill in a wetland in order to build more hotels.

The ICT spent $9.5 million on advertising, while the country's principal attractions—its national parks—are chronically under-funded for personnel and equipment. The small, principled hotels that have made Costa Rica famous as an ecotourism destination are often overlooked as the ICT promotes large beach hotels that bring tourists in greater volume. The lodgings we tell you about in this book are those that are doing their best to protect the environment and foster local economies while respecting local cultures.

HOW TO HELP

Fortunately, many Costa Ricans and international conservationists have good ideas about how to turn the tide toward restoration and preservation of the country's natural resources. Below, you can read about their efforts, as well as their suggestions for how you as a tourist can help.

VISIT COMMUNITY-BASED ECOTOURISM PROJECTS

As you can see from reading the Introduction, Costa Rica is making many efforts toward integrating sustainable agriculture, conservation and ecotourism. You can be part of this by spending time at small, locally owned reserves that are part of the Mesoamerican Biological Corridor. Almost everyone who consults me about planning their trip (www.keytocosta rica.com/costaricaconsults.htm) starts out wanting to go to Arenal volcano, Monteverde, Manuel Antonio, and Tortuguero. These places are beautiful, it's true, but they are over-visited. The community-based ecotourism projects are sometimes difficult to get to, but once you are there, you often have the whole place to yourself. If logistics are too complex, consider taking a tour with CONSERVacations (www.keytocostarica.com) or Cultourica (www.cultourica.com), or contact ACTUAR (e-mail: actuar@racsa. co.cr) or Simbiosis Tours (www.turismoruralcr.com). You'll bathe in waterfall pools, see birds and other wildlife, and be inspired by the dedication of these citizen conservationists. There is no better way to get to know the culture, support local communities and, in the long run, make tropical conservation work.

BE AN ETHICAL TRAVELER

Here are some simple guidelines for ethical ecotourism:
- Dispose of waste properly.
- Stay on trails.
- Ask permission before entering private property or indigenous reserves, and pay fees if required.
- Dress appropriately. In Costa Rica, this means no skinny dipping.

- Coral reefs, caves, and petroglyphs are easily damaged, so be careful not to touch them.
- Monkeys and other wild animals should not be fed because this alters their diet and behavior.
- Keep your distance from wildlife so that it is not compelled to take flight. Animal courtship, nesting, or feeding of the young should not be interrupted. Birds and their nests should be observed from a safe distance through binoculars, and nesting sea turtles should be observed only with a trained guide.
- Photographers should keep their distance. Leave foliage around nests, and be careful not to bother animals for the sake of a picture.
- Make sure that natural products you buy are commercially grown, and that archaeological artifacts are reproductions.
- Hire local guides. You'll see more, and you'll be supporting the local economy.

The year 2002 was the United Nations International Year of Ecotourism. Over 1000 delegates from 133 countries met in Quebec in May 2002 to draft guidelines for ecotourism to be used at the Johannesburg Summit on Sustainable Development in August 2002. Their final Declaration, which can be viewed at www.world-tourism.org/sustainable/ecotourism2002.htm, reflects a deep understanding of the importance and impact of ecotourism on rural communities: " . . . Ecotourism development must consider and respect the land and property rights, and, where recognized, the right to self-determination and cultural sovereignty of indigenous and local communities, including their protected, sensitive, and sacred sites as well as their traditional knowledge. . . . Many of these areas are home to peoples often living in poverty, who frequently lack adequate health care, education facilities, communications systems, and other infrastructure required for genuine development opportunity. . . . Small and micro businesses seeking to meet social and environmental objectives are key partners in ecotourism and are often operating in a development climate that does not provide suitable financial and marketing support for ecotourism. . . ." We strongly support this worldwide effort to make ecotourism a force for good.

ASK QUESTIONS

When you want to buy hardwood souvenirs or stay in a hotel built with precious woods, ask about the materials, and how the business has contributed to conservation and reforestation efforts. Most beautiful hardwoods are not "sustainably harvested" but are mined right from the rainforest. One rainforest tree can be used to make dozens of coffee tables or hundreds of bowls. Since the wood is much more valuable when used in this way, the hope is that its value will generate more respect. While it is not necessarily unconscientious to use endangered woods, those who use them should recognize their endangered status and contribute to efforts to reforest with these types of trees. If nothing else, your questions might sensitize the handicraft dealer or hotelier.

WRITE LETTERS

Tourism is Costa Rica's largest industry, and officials need to maintain the country's image as a tourist's eco-paradise. Letters from travelers worried about environmental destruction, unbridled growth of mega-tourism projects, and abuses by police or bureaucrats all serve to inform and pressure the government about these problems. Your experience in Costa Rica is of interest to policymakers. Write to the president of Costa Rica (Hon. Abel Pacheco, Presidente de Costa Rica, Apdo. 520, Zapote, San José; fax: 253-9078) or to the minister of tourism (Rodrigo Castro, Ministro de Turismo, Apdo. 777-1000, San José; fax: 223-5107). It's a good idea to send a copy of your letter to the media as well (*The Tico Times*: Apdo. 4632, San José; www.ticotimes.net, e-mail: ttimes@racsa.co.cr; or in Spanish, *La Nación*: Apdo. 10138-1000, San José; www.nacion.co.cr).

CONTRIBUTE MONEY

Visitors are important financial collaborators in the efforts of Costa Rican conservationists. Following is a list of some of the most active conservation groups at work here. If you are especially interested in a particular region of Costa Rica, and would like to help conservation or social projects in that area, ask around for local grassroots organizations. However, check out the reputation of the group and its leaders in the community before writing out your check.

APREFLOFAS (Asociación Preservacionista de Flora y Fauna Silvestre; phone/fax: 240-6087, cell phone for emergency reports: 381-6315; www.preserveplanet.org, e-mail: preserve@racsa.co.cr) organizes volunteers on weekend patrols of wilderness areas to report illegal hunting, fishing, and logging to the appropriate authorities. They support several community-based ecotourism projects.

Arbofilia (phone/fax: 240-7145; www.ticoorganico.com/arbofilia.htm, e-mail: arbofili@hotmail.com) works on fresh restoration in the Carara region. Their "Light and Joy" workshops develop a deep understanding of biodiversity while traveling from beach to mountains in the Carara Ecological Corridor.

CEDARENA (Centro de Derecho Ambiental y de los Recursos Naturales; 283-7080; www.cedarena.org, e-mail: cedarena@racsa.co.cr) seeks to make the environment a fundamental element within the legislative and judicial order. Their projects range from promoting biological corridors to better demarcating indigenous reserves, to legal regulation of hazardous materials. Thanks to their example and outreach, centers similar to CEDARENA have opened throughout Central America. Researchers will be interested in CEDARENA's publications on Costa Rica's environmental laws.

FECON (Costa Rican Federation of Environmental Groups; 283-6128, fax 225-7606; www.feconcr.org, e-mail: info@feconcr.org, e-mail: feconcr@racsa.co.cr) is a network formed to unify the forces in the Costa Rican environmental movement. They are the main environmental lobby in the legislative assembly working on deforestation, water, and energy issues. They also help grassroots organizations throughout the country channel reports of environmental abuse to the proper authority for legal action.

Fundación Iriria Tsochok (phone/fax 222-8958; e-mail: firiria@sol.racsa.co.cr) is a defense team made up of indigenous people and campesinos living in the Parque Internacional La Amistad. Their main concerns are to protect the people and the forests of La Amistad from agro-industrial expansion, mining, deforestation, and fires. So far they have been able to stall the creation of a coast-to-coast road crossing the Talamanca Mountains in the south of the country, and to halt a proposed oil pipeline; they're now working on community development projects.

Fundación Neotrópica (253-9462, fax: 253-4210; www.neotropica.org, e-mail: info@neotropica.org) promotes conservation and sustainable development in communities near national parks and other protected areas. Their *Editorial Heliconia* sells a wall-sized map of Costa Rica showing locations of all national parks, refuges, and reserves; Deidre Hyde's beautiful posters of the flora and fauna of each life zone (great souvenirs!); and photo-illustrated books on the national parks.

Grupo YISKI (297-0970, 236-3823, fax: 235-8425; e-mail yiskicr@racsa.co.cr) is a student-parent group that has done much to persuade Costa Ricans to recycle. They publish an informative booklet about garbage management, maintain a library, and travel to communities throughout the country to give workshops. Every two years they organize a Youth Conservationist Meeting for high school students.

VOLUNTEER

Volunteering opportunities exist all over Costa Rica. You'll find them outlined in the regional sections of the book, complete with websites and e-mail addresses. For links to environmental volunteer projects all over Costa Rica, check out FECON's website: www.feconcr.org.

There are three different turtle protection projects on the Atlantic Coast: **ANAI** in the Gandoca–Manzanillo Wildlife Refuge, the **CCC** in Tortuguero, and the **Reserva Pacuare** in Parismina. ANAI also takes volunteers at its experimental farm in Gandoca.

Caño Palma Biological Station, near Tortuguero, welcomes volunteers who are at least 18, fit, and able to adapt to remote field station conditions. Minimum stay is two weeks ($100/week, meals included). Volunteers assist researchers and help run the station, contributing to kitchen and yard work as well as research projects. During their free time, volunteers can enjoy the station's kayaks and hammocks.

In the Northern Zone, **Monteverde Institute** coordinates a number of volunteer projects ranging from trail maintenance to working in health clinics to organizing women's groups. Also in Monteverde, the **Centro Panamericano de Idiomas** includes volunteer work with its Spanish classes. At **Ecolodge San Luis**, people with a strong background in biology and ecology can receive room and board for helping with research and acting as nature guides.

In Guanacaste, volunteers can work protecting turtles at Playa Grande, Playa Langosta, or Santa Rosa (see ASVO, below).

In the Central Pacific, volunteers are needed at the **Karen Mogensen Reserve** and **ASEPALECO** on the Nicoya Peninsula. In Manuel Antonio, **Coope El Silencio** needs help with its macaw release and endangered orchid-raising projects.

In the Southern Zone, **Proyecto Campanario** and **Delfin Amor** are exciting projects in the Drake Bay area, working in rainforest ecology and cetacean research, respectively.

Volunteers almost always have to pay for their own room and board, usually $10-$15 per day, and usually have to make a definite time-commitment to the project they work on.

Through **ASVO** (Association of Volunteers for Service in Protected Areas; MINAE Building, Calle 25, Avenida 8-10; phone/fax 233-4989; www.asvocr.com), visitors at least 18 years old can donate support services to the severely understaffed national parks and reserves. Volunteers must adapt themselves to work in all kinds of weather, and they should be willing to do everything that a normal park ranger would do. Initiative and willingness to learn are more important than previous experience. Volunteers pay $14 per day to cover coordination from the central office, lodging, and food. Volunteers must also pay for their own transportation, but especially remote parks will provide rides from a nearby point. Volunteers should speak basic Spanish and provide two letters of reference from organizations abroad or from individuals in Costa Rica, a photo, and a copy of their passport. They must fill out an application form and have a personal interview before being formally accepted. You can choose from a list of parks that have requested volunteers.

NOTE: Sometimes it is possible to just walk up to a national park or reserve and volunteer without going through an organization. Try it!

There are several interesting projects in which you can learn about organic farming, sustainable living, permaculture and agricultural experimentation. Among them are **Finca IPE** (www.fincaipe.com) near Dominical, **The Ark Herb Farm** (239-2111; e-mail: arkherb@racsa.co.cr) in Santa Barbara de Heredia, **Finca La Flor** (534-8003; www.la-flor-de-paraiso.org, e-mail: asodecah@racsa.co.cr) in Paraiso de Cartago, **Punta Mona** (www.costarican adventures.com), and **Rancho Mastatal** (www.ranchomastatal.com) in the mountains between the Central Valley and the Pacific.

THREE

Planning Your Trip

CALLING COSTA RICA

In this book, Costa Rica numbers are listed without the country code, which is 506. To call Costa Rica from North America, dial 011, then 506, then the number.

SURFING THE WEB

There is a lot of information on the internet about Costa Rica, but nothing truly comprehensive, and not a lot about community-based ecotourism and other low-cost accommodations, so your trusty guidebook is not yet obsolete. Most websites charge the hotels that appear on them, so you will only see the hotels that have paid to be on that site. No website (so far) has as complete a rundown on hotels in an area in all price categories as we do in our book, so you only get a partial view of what is available. We have tried to list websites in the text whenever possible, so with the combination of our recommendations and the websites, you should be able to make very good choices. New websites are springing up every day, so if you want to find out more about a hotel that has no website in the book, type its name and "costa rica" after it, and you might well find it on the web. Here are some of the websites we think can be the most helpful in planning your trip:

www.keytocostarica.com, our website, has links to our favorite ecolodges, and reports on old and future family trips. If you would like our help with your travel plans, contact us at info@keytocostarica.com (fee). Please put "Costa Rica" in the subject of your e-mail.

www.costaricainnkeepers.com has information on inns and B&Bs in all price ranges.

www.costarica.com has good information on weather (with satellite images updated hourly), visas, what documents you need to get married in Costa Rica, how to bring your car with you, residency requirements, and much more.

www.centralamerica.com gives flight, car rental, and tour package information.

www.costa-rica-guide.com offers comprehensive travel-planning advice.

Some of the best sites are created by community-minded groups of tourism people from the areas you are interested in visiting, like **arenal.net**, **nosara.com**, **dominical-costarica.com, tamarindo.com**, **greencoast.com** (an excellent site about the Talamanca region on the Atlantic coast), and **nicoyapeninsula.com**. These websites usually put you in direct contact with the hotels, and the group that puts the website together provides quality control. It is best to look for such sites rather than going through a third-party website; you are more likely to get lower rates that way.

WHEN TO GO

In Costa Rica, the tourist season is December through April, which corresponds to the dry season. You can almost depend on clear, sunny weather, but there are occasional unseasonal storms from the north that can last for several days. The rainy season usually takes a while to get started in May, and often diminishes for a couple of weeks in June or July. The rains dwindle in December. (In Guanacaste, the only really rainy months are October and November.)

There are certain advantages to going during the off-season: The mornings are almost always clear and warm. The scenery is fresher and greener. The days are cooled by the rains, which can be a blessing, especially at the beach. The clouds usually clear in time for a magnificent sunset. Many hotels offer substantial discounts during the off-season, sometimes as much as 50 percent. All places are less crowded, more peaceful. Less harm is done to the ecosystems in the parks when fewer people come trooping through at one time.

You really need to plan ahead for Christmas week and the week before Easter. Hotel rooms are booked months in advance, and popular hotels are often booked several months in advance in the dry season. But during the rest of the year you can take a "let's just explore and see what happens" vacation, and you'll almost always find a place to stay. Airlines are usually booked far in advance from about December 10 to January 10, so make your plane reservations early if you want to go during that time. The same goes for the weeks before and after Easter.

CLIMATE

Given Costa Rica's latitude—between 8 and 12° north of the Equator—day length and temperature do not change drastically with the seasons. The sun rises around 5 a.m. and sets around 6 p.m. year-round. Temperature differences are experienced by changing altitude. The misty highlands are in the 10°–13°C (50°–55°F) range, while the Central Valley, at 3800 feet, averages 26°C (78°F). At sea level, the temperature is 30°–35°C (85°–95°F), tempered by sea breezes on the coast. Slight variations occur in December, January, and February, due to cold winds from the North American winter. These cooler temperatures bring on the dry season or "summer," as Central Americans call it, which lasts from December through April. Temperatures start to rise as the sun approaches a perpendicular position over Costa Rica. This causes increased evaporation and brings on the rainy season, or "winter," which lasts from May through November, except for a two-week dry season, a time called *el veranillo de San Juan* (the "little summer"), which occurs sometime in June or July.

Costa Rica's weather pattern is changing and is not as predictable as it used to be. Now there are many dry days during the "winter" and a few storms during the "summer." Here's a new rule of thumb: the more gloriously sun-drenched the morning during the rainy season, the harder it will rain in the afternoon. Conversely, on a cloudy morning there will be less evaporation, and thus a generally drier day.

The Atlantic Coast has always been an exception to the rule. Trade winds laden with moisture from the Caribbean approach Costa Rica from the northeast. As the moisture rises to the chilly heights of the Cordillera, it condenses into rain on the eastern slopes. For this reason, there is no definite dry season in the Atlantic zone, but the beaches tend to be sunnier than the mountains. Residents insist that the rainiest months in the rest of Costa Rica, September and October, are the driest on the Caribbean coast. Often you can see Arenal volcano best in September and October. In a similar phenomenon, trade winds from the southeast discharge their moisture against the mountains that separate the Osa Peninsula from the rest of the country. The Atlantic plains and the Osa both receive 150 to 300 inches of rain a year, compared to an average of 100 inches in the Central Valley.

One of the most surprising things for newcomers to the Central Valley is that it's not as warm as they expected. The truly hot months are at the end of the dry season, March and April. December, January, and February are usually rain-free, but the weather can be downright chilly, especially at night or if a wind is blowing. During the rainy season, May to November, the days tend to start out warm and sunny but cloud over by noon. The downpour usually starts around 2 or 3 p.m. and it can get pretty cold then, too. Usually a sweater and long pants are enough to keep you warm. When it rains, it *really rains*, but afternoon downpours are usually short-lived. If you go down in altitude from San José's 3800 feet, you'll be able to wear the kind of clothes you hoped you could wear in the tropics.

HOLIDAYS

Costa Rica has 11 official *feriados* (holidays) per year, and they are taken quite seriously. Do not expect to find government offices, banks, professional offices, or many stores open on *feriados*. Twice during the year, the whole country shuts down completely. These are *Semana Santa* (the week before Easter) and the week between Christmas and New Year's Day. Transportation stops totally on Holy Thursday and Good Friday, making Wednesday's buses very crowded. If you are on a tour or visiting during Holy Week, don't worry—gas stations will be open, and life will go on.

Easter week is the time to see picturesque religious processions in the countryside. There are large nonreligious parades in San José on Labor Day, Independence Day, and during Christmas week. *The Tico Times* (www.tico times.net) will tell you where the most interesting events are. It's best to avoid visiting the beach during Easter week because it's often the last holiday young Ticos have before school starts, and they're all there with their boomboxes.

Following is a list of Costa Rica's *feriados*:

January 1   New Year's Day
April 11   Anniversary of the Battle of Rivas
Holy Thursday through Easter Sunday
May 1   Labor Day
July 25   Annexation of Guanacaste Province
August 2   Our Lady of the Angels (Costa Rica's patron saint)
August 15   Assumption Day, Mother's Day
September 15   Independence Day
October 12   Día de la Raza (Columbus Day, Carnival in Limón)
December 24 and 25   Christmas Eve and Christmas Day

CALENDAR OF EVENTS

JANUARY

San José: Top junior tennis players from around the world compete in the week-long **Copa del Café**.

Santa Cruz: Tico-style bullfights and lively regional folk dancing are the main attractions at the **Santa Cruz Fiestas**.

FEBRUARY

Liberia: The **Liberia Festival** is held the last week in February, hosting Guanacastecan folklore, concerts, and horsemanship.

Monteverde: **Monteverde Music Festival** features Costa Rica's best classical, jazz, and folk musicians February to April.

Playa Chiquita: The **Music of South Caribbean Coast Festival** runs in February and March.

3San Isidro de El General: A cattle show, agricultural and industrial fair, and orchid show highlight this town's **fiestas**.

San José: The **Open-Air Festival** at the National Center for Culture offers free theater, concerts, and dance shows on weekends all month.

MARCH

Countrywide: **Holy Week** processions throughout the country. The best processions are at the Church of San Rafael de Oreamuno near Cartago, and in San Joaquín de Flores near Heredia.

San Antonio de Escazú: A parade of brightly colored carts and the blessing of the animals and crops mark **Día del Boyero** (Ox-Cart Driver's Day).

San José: March is a busy month in San José. You'll find the **National Orchid Show**, featuring more than 1500 species, as well as the **Bonanza Cattle Show**, the year's biggest event for cattlemen (but many visitors come for the Wild West fun of the rodeos and horseraces). An **International Arts and Music Festival** brings musicians and theater groups from all over the world to perform. The **Carrera de la Paz** marathon attracts as many as a thousand runners.

Ujarrás: The ruins of the first colonial church in Costa Rica, in Ujarrás, is the destination of a **religious procession**.

APRIL

Alajuela: Fiestas are held in honor of Costa Rica's national hero in this, his hometown, on **Juan Santamaría Day**.

MAY

Limón: May 1, celebrated as **International Labor Day** all over Costa Rica, is a day for picnics, dances, and cricket matches.

San Isidro: Any town of this name—and there are several—is likely to be celebrating **San Isidro Labrador** on May 15 (this saint's day) with festivities that include a blessing of the animals.

San José: The University of Costa Rica marks **University Week** with parades, dances, and cultural events. San Juan Day sees the running of the **Carrera de San Juan**, the year's biggest marathon.

JUNE

Countrywide: On June 29, **Saint Peter and Saint Paul's Day** is celebrated throughout the country. The third Sunday of the month is **Father's Day**.

JULY

Liberia: Fiestas and rodeos are the highlight of the celebration commemorating the **Annexation of Guanacaste** to Costa Rica in 1824.

Puntarenas: Don't miss the regatta of beautifully decorated fishing boats and yachts celebrating the **Fiesta of the Virgin of the Sea**.

San José, mountain and beach hotels: The **International Music Festival** features renowned artists from around the world in July and August.

AUGUST

Countrywide: **Mother's Day** is August 15 in Costa Rica.

Cartago: On August 2, the old capital is the destination of an annual national pilgrimage honoring Costa Rica's patron saint, the **Virgin of Los Angeles**, known for her miracles.

San José: **International Black Peoples' Day** is the focal point of **Semana Cultural Afro-Costarricense** (Afro–Costa Rican Culture Week), and features lectures, panels, and displays on black culture.

San Ramón: All the saints from neighboring towns are brought on a pilgrimage for **Día De San Ramón** in the town named for this saint. Fiestas follow the parade.

SEPTEMBER

San José: **Independence Day** is celebrated with parades in the capital and the rest of the country. The Freedom Torch is passed across the Nicaraguan border to relay runners who deliver it to the President in the old colonial capitol of Cartago at 6 p.m. on September 15. Children parade with homemade paper lanterns.

OCTOBER

Limón: The weeklong **Carnival** resembles Mardi Gras in Rio, with brightly costumed dancers parading through the streets all night, concerts, and general merrymaking.

NOVEMBER

Countrywide: From an **International Surf Tourney** to special services in honor of **All Soul's Day**, events take place all across the country this month.

DECEMBER

Countrywide: Christmas celebrations begin early in the month everywhere in Costa Rica, with music, special foods, *rompope* (eggnog), *chicha* (home-made corn liquor), and tamales. There are three annual **Christmas Bird Counts**, each in a different part of the country. Call La Selva (710-1515) for information, or watch for announcements in *The Tico Times*.

Boruca: See a re-creation of the struggle between the Indians and the Spaniards at the time of the conquest during the **Fiesta of the Diablitos**, held in this small Indian village near Buenos Aires in the Southern Zone.

Guanacaste: Nicoya is the site of **Fiesta de la Yegüita**, with a procession, foods made from corn, music, bullfights, and fireworks.

San José: December 15 is the start of **Las Posadas**, a Christmas tradition in which children, musicians, and carolers go door-to-door re-creating Mary and Joseph's search for lodging. The week between Christmas and New Year's Day offers San José's biggest celebration of the year. There are Tico-style bullfights, a giant parade with floats, and *El Tope*, a huge equestrian parade in the Sevillian tradition in which elegantly clad riders show off their purebred steeds. The fairground in Zapote turns into an amusement park. On New Year's Eve, a dance to welcome the new year is held in San José's Central Park. Choirs from around the country perform at the National Theater for the **Christmas Choir Festival**. The **International Dance Festival** is held the first two weeks of the month.

COMING AND GOING

ENTRY REQUIREMENTS

When traveling with a passport, citizens of the United States, Canada, and most Latin American and European countries are entitled to stay in Costa Rica for 90 days. They must enter the country with a departure ticket and a valid passport that does not expire within three months of their arrival in Costa Rica. In other words, if you enter Costa Rica on January 1, your passport must be valid until at least April 1. Citizens of some Latin American, Asian, African, and East European countries must obtain a visa from a Costa Rican consulate and pay a deposit upon entering the country, refundable when they leave. Check with the consulate nearest you for the latest information or see www.costarica.com/travel/visas.

Always carry your ID: While in Costa Rica, if you don't want to carry your passport with you, get a copy of it made. Don't go anywhere without identification. You can have your passport copy *emplasticado* (laminated) at various street stands in San José. You *will* need your passport to change money at banks.

EXIT AND EXTENDED VISAS

All tourists must pay an airport tax of $26 when they leave.

If you overstay your 30- or 90-day visa, you will have to pay an extra $20 fine upon departure.

You can stay legally by leaving the country for a few days after your first three months and coming back in with a new tourist visa. *Be sure that your passport is stamped as you re-enter Costa Rica.* If your passport is not stamped correctly on re-entry, your efforts to renew your visa will have been in vain. Don't depend on leaving the country every three months as a way to remain in Costa Rica. Immigration officials start becoming suspicious after you have done this three times. They could deport you. Longer stays are granted only to those applying for student visas or residency.

Be sure to confirm your departure flight 72 hours in advance.

Get to the airport at least two hours ahead of flight time. Flights are often overbooked.

TRANSPORTATION

AIRLINES SERVING COSTA RICA

LACSA, Costa Rica's international airline, is part of Grupo TACA, the alliance of Central America's airlines. It flies from San Francisco, Los Angeles, New York City, Miami, Orlando, Dallas, and Toronto.

American West, **American Airlines**, **Delta**, **United**, **Continental**, **US Airways**, and **Air Canada** have flights to Costa Rica with package connections to all major American cities. Discounted rates are offered several times a year, especially in the off-season.

You can fly to either Juan Santamaría International Airport (SJO) in the town of Alajuela, about half an hour west of San José, or to Daniel Oduber

Quiros International Airport (LIR) in Liberia, Guanacaste. The Liberia airport is only half an hour to two hours away from the beaches of Guanacaste, usually a five-hour drive from San José. As of this writing, airfares to Liberia are about $75 more expensive than to San José. Airlines with flights to Liberia are **American** out of Miami, **Continental** from Houston, and **Delta** from Atlanta. **British Airways**, the German airline **Condor**, Spain's **Iberia**, and the Dutch **Martinair** connect Costa Rica with Europe.

When I am planning a trip to Costa Rica, I go to Expedia.com or a similar online travel site and see which airline is offering the best deals, just to see what the field looks like. But I also get e-mails from airlines about current fare sales. Usually I find the cheapest rates on American (aa.com). If you are working with a travel agent, try to get one who is experienced in sending people to Costa Rica because there are many alternatives. I recommend **Earthroutes** (207-326-8635; www.earthroutes.com).

We've found some of the best rates at **www.centralamerica.com**. **Selva Mar** (771-4582; www.exploringcostarica.com, e-mail: selvamar@racsa. co.cr) is a Costa Rica–based travel agency that can also get you travel deals.

Whatever airline you take, book several months ahead if you are going during the dry season, especially for Christmas or Easter, and confirm your reservation 72 hours in advance because schedules sometimes change. Get to the gateway airport at least two hours before flight time. Check-in lines are lengthy and documentation checks and payment of airport taxes may take time.

CHARTER FLIGHTS   Any travel agent can give you glossy catalogs about charter flights to Costa Rica with all-inclusive stays at big fancy beach hotels. Charter flights usually only operate between December and May. Packages including airfare, room, and meals run from $920 to $1600 per week. You can take advantage of low charter rates without taking the rooms in order to visit smaller, more interesting lodges. **Sky Service** charters flights to Liberia from Toronto and Montreal, **Pace** from Atlanta, and **Northwest** from Minneapolis. You have to buy these tickets through travel agents.

LOCAL TRANSPORTATION

See Chapter Four for information on buses and car rentals.

DRIVING TO COSTA RICA

If you're driving, allow about three weeks from the time you enter Mexico until the time you reach Costa Rica, ten days if you don't want to sightsee on the way. Avoid the highlands of Guatemala and El Salvador, drive only during the day, and do not plan to camp. You may drive your car tax-free for up to six months as a tourist. You pay $40 when you enter the country and another $40 to renew your visa after three months. After that you have to pay taxes or pay to have the car stored.

SAMPLE ITINERARIES

Costa Rica offers thousands of places to visit during your vacation. These few sample itineraries are designed to accommodate particular interests, with as much efficiency in routing as possible. We've tried to include off-the-beaten track destinations in these suggestions. Combine several circuits for a longer vacation. These itineraries work best if you have your own car.

OLD ROUTE TO LIMÓN, WITH RAINFOREST

Day 1   San José
Day 2   Drive to Turrialba, go white-water rafting or visit a *trapiche* to see brown sugar made in the traditional way
Day 3   Drive from Turrialba to Talamanca
Day 4   Talamanca beaches
Day 5   Talamanca rainforests with ANAI or ATEC
Day 6   Rainforest visit in Sarapiquí or tour Tortuguero
Day 7   Back to San José

CENTRAL HIGHLANDS, NORTHERN ZONE, ARENAL, AND GUANACASTE BEACH

The most efficient way to include beaches, rainforests, and volcanoes.

Day 1   Central Valley hotel
Day 2   Early-morning visit to Poás and La Paz Waterfall Gardens; drive to Sarapiquí
Day 3   Rainforest visit in Sarapiquí
Day 4   Drive to Volcán Arenal
Day 5   Visit volcano and hot springs
Day 6   Drive to Guanacaste Beach
Days 7 & 8   Stay at beach
Day 9   Return to Central Valley

NICOYA PENINSULA AND GUANACASTE

A one-week rainforest and beach trip off the beaten track.

Day 1   Drive to Puntarenas, take a ferry to Playa Naranjo, continue to Lepanto. Ride horses to Karen Mogensen Reserve
Day 2   Hike in the reserve

Day 3	Hike down to Bridal Veil Falls, drive to Carrillo or Nosara
Days 4 to 6	Stay at beach
Day 7	Back to Central Valley

NORTHERN GUANACASTE AND ARENAL

Ten days with volcano, national park, and beach visits; a good route in the rainy season.

Day 1	From Liberia airport, drive to Rincón de la Vieja; camp or lodge nearby
Day 2	Rincón de la Vieja National Park or Buenavista water- slide
Day 3	Santa Rosa National Park
Day 4	Visit beaches of northern Guanacaste, like Bahía Junquillal Wildlife Refuge
Day 5	Camp at beach
Day 6	Visit Heliconias Rainforest in Bijagua de Upala, or Los Inocentes east of La Cruz
Days 7 & 8	Drive back through Cañas, Tilarán, and around Lake Arenal. Stay on the lake or near Volcán Arenal
Day 9	Visit volcano and Tabacón Hot Springs
Day 10	Back to Central Valley or San José

SOUTHERN ZONE

This area is still off the beaten track for most visitors, but tourism is defi- nitely increasing.

Day 1	San José; leave early afternoon for Copey, Mirador de Quetzales, or San Gerardo de Dota
Day 2	Drive south to San Isidro after a morning birding hike, drive east to San Gerardo de Rivas and Chirripó, or go west to visit the beaches of Dominical or Uvita
Day 3	Explore previous day's destination
Day 4	Continue south to Sierpe, take boat to Drake Bay
Days 5 to 7	Tour Isla del Caño, Corcovado, watch dolphins or whales
Day 8	Head back to San José

QUETZALS, BEACH, AND RAINFOREST

A multi-altitude loop in the Southern Zone.

| *Day 1* | Go to Palmichal de Acosta, a lovely mountain town about an hour south of the San José airport |

Day 2	Hike, visit local farms, see how coffee is processed
Day 3	Drive through the Los Santos area to Copey de Dota
Day 4	Look for quetzals in the morning, drive south across Cerro de la Muerte to San Isidro and then west to Dominical, and south again to Uvita
Day 5	Visit the beaches of Ballena National Marine Park
Day 6	Visit Isla Ballena or Isla del Caño, or go horseback riding
Day 7	Return to Central Valley via the coast, stopping to see the scarlet macaws and crocodiles at Carara National Park north of Jacó.

PACKING

Tourists are permitted to bring binoculars, two cameras, and electrical items that are for personal use only, like a small radio, a hairdryer, a laptop, a video camera, etc. The most important thing to remember is that the items should not be in their original boxes and not look too new. The government doesn't want tourists to "import" electronic items for resale.

In San José during the rainy season, people usually carry umbrellas—brightly colored *sombrillas* for women and black *paraguas* for men. In the mountains, a lightweight rain poncho is usually more convenient except for those who wear glasses. You'll be glad to have high rubber boots if you go hiking in the rainforest, especially in Corcovado or Sarapiquí. You can buy good ones in Costa Rica for under $7 at San José's Mercado Central and at provincial supply stores, and many places, like Monteverde, rent them to visitors for around $1. Bring boots from home only if you wear an especially large size. Along with your rubber boots, you must have a couple of pairs of fairly thick socks that extend up your calf beyond the tops of the boots. If you don't, the boots rub and irritate your skin, taking the fun out of your hikes.

When you go to the beach or rainforest, bring at least one shirt for each day. You're bound to get sweaty. Lightweight cotton or cotton-mix clothing is best, protected inside a plastic bag in case of sudden downpours. Even if you are going to the steamy lowlands, you often have to pass through high mountains to get there—Cerro de la Muerte on the way to the Osa, Braulio Carrillo or Vara Blanca on the way to Sarapiquí. You'll be happier if you have a windbreaker, long pants, and socks that can be peeled off as you get to lower altitudes.

Most hotels will let you store excess luggage while you venture off. You can usually fit everything needed for a trip to the countryside in a day pack. Start out with a bathing suit, lightweight pants, a cotton overshirt, socks, and running shoes. In addition, bring another bathing suit, two pairs of light-weight pants or shorts, extra socks, and shirts for each day. Bring something to sleep in, sandals, and a scarf, as well as insect repellent, a flashlight, a book, an umbrella or rain poncho, a towel, and toilet paper. Highly recommended: a lightweight, one-layer, hooded nylon windbreaker, especially the kind that folds up into a handy little pouch made out of the front pocket. This handy jacket takes up almost no room and can even be used as a pillow on the bus! If you are traveling during the dry season and not planning to spend a lot of time atop volcanoes, it's all you'll need to keep warm and to ward off occasional raindrops. If you are going to Irazú, Poás, Chirripó, or other high-altitude areas, you'll need a lined jacket and warm socks.

Things that are not made in Costa Rica are sold with a 100 percent import tax, and therefore are much more expensive here than elsewhere. Following is a list of items that you should bring with you:

Film and camera equipment
Binoculars
Pocket alarm clock or watch with alarm
Pocket calculator
Good walking shoes
Insect repellent
Sulfur powder (sprinkle on socks to deter chiggers)
Anti-itch ointment or After Bite
Water purifying device if you will be hiking long distances
Small first-aid kit

Contact lens solution
Birth control items
Vitamins
Earplugs
A universal plug for bathroom sinks
Beach towel
Washcloth
Your own cup
Flashlight
String and clothespins for hanging wash
Battery-operated reading lamp for late-night readers

ELECTRICITY

The electrical current used in Costa Rica is 110 volts, AC. The sockets are American-style, but budget places usually don't have a place for a grounding prong. American and Canadian appliances whose plugs don't have grounding prongs should work, but it's always a good idea to check with your hotel about the voltage *before* you plug anything in.

TRAVELING EXPENSES

Costa Rica is not as inexpensive for travelers as other Central American countries. Still, you can take a bus to anywhere in the country for under $8, meals cost from $3 to $10, and you can usually find decent hotels for under $50 for two people. If you are determined to spend as little money as possible, visit during the rainy season and take advantage of the off-season rates. You can also find clean and decent rooms with shared baths for under $12 almost anywhere. Fancy rooms at the beach are often $75 and up. Groceries cost about two-thirds as much as in the United States. According to Tourism Institute statistics, most visitors spend between $75 and $116 per day. However, two people can travel for about $25 a day each, including bus transportation, comfortable lodging (double occupancy), and restaurant meals. Camping out is cheaper still, but you have the inconvenience of hauling around equipment and making sure your tent is guarded at all times. Yet another advantage of visiting community-based lodges is their extremely reasonable prices—usually $25-$45 including meals and tours.

CURRENCY AND BANKING

The currency unit is the *colón* (¢). Bills come in denominations of ¢500 to ¢10,000, and coins from 5 to 100 *colones*. The exchange rate (check www. costarica.com for up-to-date rates) is around ¢450 per US$1. The *colón* "floats" against the dollar, so rates change gradually day by day.

CHANGING MONEY

Use U.S. dollars: Costa Ricans are usually happy to be paid in dollars because their currency is constantly being devaluated in comparison to the dollar. But the dollar is not the official currency. So while it is good to carry *colones,* don't worry if you run out. Just carry a calculator with you to make sure the person changing your dollars is giving you the right amount. Everyone knows the *tipo de cambio*, the rate at which dollars are being bought and sold on a particular day. The rate appears in the newspaper. If you are from a country other than the U.S., you will probably find it easier to buy U.S. dollars before leaving home than to try to exchange your currency for *colones* in Costa Rica. This might change if the U.S. dollar remains weak, though.

Traveler's checks: It is increasingly difficult to cash traveler's checks outside banks or big hotels. So don't forget to cash your traveler's checks when you are in large towns.

Before you get there: There is no advantage to trying to change dollars to *colones* before you get to Costa Rica.

At the airport: You can change money at the airport banks from 5 a.m. to 8 p.m. There are two ATMs there as well. Ask for the *cajera automática.*

CREDIT CARDS

Most, though not all, tourism businesses accept major credit cards. Visa seems to be the most widely accepted. There is often a 6 percent surcharge for credit card transactions.

In case your **American Express** card is lost or stolen, call 001-800-528-2121. They will authorize the San José offices to make you a new one. Call 0-800-011-0080 to have lost or stolen traveler's checks replaced.

The downtown Credomatic office (Calle Central, Avenidas 3/5; 295-9898 for 24-hour service) helps **MasterCard** and American Express clients in emergency situations and can negotiate emergency cash advances. For **Visa** cards, call 224-2631 or 224-2731. For lost or stolen Visa cards, call 0-800-VISA-911 or 410-902-8022 (call collect).

At your hotel: Hotels are authorized to change money and traveler's checks for their guests; sometimes their rates are less favorable than the bank rate, but only by a few cents on the dollar. Smaller hotels might not have enough money on hand to cash your checks; it's wise to carry $20 traveler's checks if you're planning to spend time in the countryside, and to check beforehand if they cash traveler's checks.

ATMs: Call or check online for ATM locations at your destination with **Cirrus** (800-424-7787; www.mastercard.com) or **PLUS** (800-843-7587; www.visa.com). Be sure you know your PIN, and find out your daily withdrawal limit before you depart. To protect themselves from theft, credit card companies sometimes limit the amount that can be withdrawn abroad. You can get the official exchange rate using an ATM, but remember that many banks impose a fee every time a card is used at an ATM in a different city or bank, and the bank from which you withdraw cash may charge its own fee. To add to the confusion, Costa Rican ATMs are often out of order.

In the provinces: It is possible to change money in towns other than San José. Often the provincial banks' process is faster. Even if you are not near a bank, certain hotels, tourist information centers, and *pulperías* (corner stores) usually provide this service for travelers. In fact, most places are glad to be paid in dollars, but you'll have better luck with cash than with traveler's checks.

Bring your passport: To change money or traveler's checks at banks, you must have your passport with you. They won't accept photocopies.

At San José banks: Banks are open from 9 a.m. to 3 p.m., and some branches stay open until 5 p.m. State-owned banks (Banco de Costa Rica, Banco Nacional de Costa Rica, Banco Popular, Banco de Crédito Agrícola) are more crowded. The many private banks such as Banex and Banco de San José are quicker, and the money-changing process is simpler. One exception is the *Operaciones Internacionales* department at the central offices of Banco de Costa Rica on Avenida Central, Calle 4. This second-floor office is devoted only to changing currency and is pretty efficient (open weekdays, 8:30 a.m. to 3 p.m.). On Monday, Friday, and any day following a holiday, the lines will be longer than usual.

On the street: Don't risk changing money on the street. A common changer's scam is to pretend to panic and run because "the police are coming"—before you have time to count the *colones* they give you. They're experts in folding bills so that the stack appears larger.

Special note for Canadians: All branches of **Banco de Costa Rica** (Avenidas 2/Central, Calles 4/6; 287-9000) and **Banco Nacional de Costa Rica** (Calles 2/4, Avenidas 1/3; 223-2166) accept cash or traveler's checks in Canadian dollars.

HEALTH PRECAUTIONS

INOCULATIONS

See your doctor before taking any foreign journey to be sure you're up to date on your regular vaccinations (tetanus, polio, measles, and so on). You probably won't need to get any special vaccinations or inoculations before traveling to Costa Rica, but it's a good idea to check for current recommendations by calling the **Centers for Disease Control** hotline in Atlanta at 877-394-9747, or visit www.cdc.gov/travel/camerica.htm. The only vaccination we have gotten in preparation for the trip is for hepatitis A. These shots must be given six months apart.

WATER

Water is safe to drink in most parts of Costa Rica, but if you feel safer drinking bottled water, it is sold in most supermarkets throughout the country. Responsible beach hotels usually provide bottled water for guests in their rooms. Don't be afraid to ask if it is safe to drink the water.

AMOEBAS AND PARASITES

Even though Costa Rica's water is good in most places, visitors traveling in the provinces sometimes have intestinal problems. If symptoms are persistent, they might be due to *amibas* or *giardia*. If you get a strong attack of diarrhea, it's wise to take a stool sample to a local lab to have it analyzed. Put it in a clean glass jar, and deliver it immediately, or just appear at the lab and they will give you the appropriate receptacles to take a sample then and there. Amoebas can't be found in samples that are a few hours old. Your results will be ready the same day, especially if you bring your sample before noon ($6-$8 in advance). If results are negative, take up to three samples. Sometimes the offending organisms are not found the first time. The most dangerous one is *entamoeba histolytica*. This can migrate to your liver and cause damage later.

It is not necessary to go to a doctor unless you want to. A pharmacist can give you the needed drug based on your lab results. We have not found that natural methods cure amoebas. Even if you get over your diarrhea, the organisms can still be doing damage to your system unless you've taken the proper medicine. Symptoms often show up as a tendency toward constipation and a feeling of depression and low energy. It's best to take the chemicals and be done with the bugs. Be sure to ask for the literature that goes with the medicine so you'll know about possible side effects.

To avoid bugs when traveling outside San José, stay away from drinks made with local water or ice, and fruits and vegetables that cannot be peeled.

DEHYDRATION

Dehydration can be a problem at the beach and other steamy lowland areas where you sweat a lot, and equally problematic if you suffer from excessive diarrhea or vomiting. Bring a drinking bottle of good water if you hike. The water in green coconuts (*agua de pipa*) is both pure and full of the very same minerals that you lose when you sweat or vomit. *Caldo*, a clear soup with vegetables and chicken or meat, can also help you regain lost liquid and salt, and it is one of the easier foods to get down when you're not feeling well.

DENGUE FEVER

The disease that has caused the most trouble in the last few years is dengue fever, a virus carried by mosquitoes. It begins with a sudden fever of 102° or higher that can last for as long as seven days. Acute pain in the head, muscles, joints, and eyes, and a rash on the chest and back can accompany the fever. You should seek medical treatment as soon as symptoms appear. People usually recover from dengue, but if you catch the disease twice it can be life-threatening.

MALARIA

Malaria is not a danger for most travelers to Costa Rica. According to the Ministry of Health, it only occurs in very isolated areas of the country, principally at the banana plantations in the Valle de la Estrella in inland Talamanca and near the Nicaraguan border in the canton of Los Chiles. If you are going to these areas, or just want to take precautions, you can pick up chloroquine at the Dispensary of the hospital San Juan de Dios in San José (Calle 14, Avenidas Central/6) or in any pharmacy. Sometimes doctors prescribe prophylactic doses of Lariam or Mephaquine, the trade names for mefloquine, which has been known to produce neuropsychiatric effects like panic attacks, convulsions, headaches, and visual and auditory hallucinations that persist months after the last dose. Find out more at www.geocities.com/thetropics/6913/lariam.htm. The CDC actually recommends chloroquine for visitors to Costa Rica. We have never taken any anti-malarial medication in the 30 years we have been visiting Costa Rica.

SWIMMING POOLS AND RIVERS

Look for any visible signs of pollution before you jump into a river or pool, and always be sure to wash well with soap and water after you come out. To avoid fungus infections in the ears, clean them with rubbing alcohol and a swab after swimming.

INSECTS

Mosquitoes can be a problem, even in breezy San José at night during the dry season. Natural repellents that have been tested to be effective for up to three hours against mosquitoes, sandflies, and *purrujas* are **Cactus Juice Skin and Insect Protectant** (877-554-5222; www.cactusjuicetm.com) and **Lemon Eucalyptus Repellent** (800-558-6614; www.wpcbrands.com).

Most hotels located where mosquitos are a problem have screened windows and/or mosquito nets.

On the Atlantic Coast, beware of **sandfly** bites that seem to become infected and grow instead of disappearing. This could be a sign of *papalomoyo* (Leishmaniasis), a disease that can be life-threatening if untreated. See a tropical disease specialist immediately.

Purrujas (no-see-ums) are perhaps the most aggravating of Costa Rican insects. They bite you without your even seeing or feeling them, then the bite itches for days. *Purrujas* like to hang out at the edge of the beach where the sand meets the trees. They seem to be more active at dusk. You can buy sulfur powder by the quarter kilo for very little money. Sprinkle it on your socks to discourage sandflies. That means you should wear shoes and socks on the beach for your sunset walk. Dusk is generally the time to apply insect repellent, too.

Eating lots of garlic and brewer's yeast tablets purportedly makes your blood unpalatable to mosquitoes, flies, and no-see-ums.

Some people have serious allergic reactions to **ant** bites. A person having an allergic reaction might begin to itch all over, then turn red and swell up. If that happens, get to a hospital as soon as possible. In the worst scenario, a person's throat swells up, causing asphyxiation. To avoid ant bites, wear closed shoes whenever you're in the jungle or on the beach.

Africanized bees have worked their way north from Brazil, and can attack humans with fatal results if the bees' nests are disturbed. Bee colonies are ten times denser in hot, dry areas than in rainforests. If attacked, run as fast as you can in a zigzag direction, or jump into water. Bees don't see well over distances. Never try to take cover; don't crawl or climb into a precarious position from which you cannot make a quick exit. Throw something light-colored over your head to protect your eyes and nose; keep your mouth closed. For more detailed information, contact the OTS (240-6696). If you know you are allergic to bee stings, talk with your doctor before you go to Costa Rica and carry the proper medication with you. You might want to buy a self-injector kit for bee stings, available in pharmacies in the U.S. with a prescription. This could save you if you can't get to a hospital fast enough.

SNAKES

Although not all snakes in Costa Rica are dangerous, a few are potentially deadly: fer-de-lance, eyelash vipers, bushmasters, and rattlesnakes. To recognize these snakes should you run across one in the wild, visit the Serpentarium in Turrialba, Monteverde, or Sarapiquí. If you are bitten, stay calm and head to the nearest health post for a series of antivenin shots. According to *The Tico Times*, you shouldn't waste time trying to suck the venom out cowboy-style; experts say it doesn't help. And definitely don't use a knife or razor to enlarge an opening in your skin: bleeding and risk of infection will only make matters worse. You have four hours to get to a clinic from when you were bitten before tissue loss sets in. To avoid bites, wear thick hiking boots (even when crossing streams) and do not touch branches or plants without looking first.

ACCOMMODATIONS IN COSTA RICA

How we list hotel rates: Our hotel rates are based on *double* occupancy (unless otherwise indicated) and *include* a 16.4 percent tax. Most hotels give their rates without the taxes, so amounts in this book might appear to be more than those stated in hotel advertising or on their websites. Prices change; although we try to be as accurate as possible, don't take it on faith that a hotel still charges what we said it charges—always ask. Rates will vary if you are alone or in a group, or if meals are included.

Reservations: Make reservations three months ahead at Christmas or Easter. Most hotels have fax or e-mail numbers. Some hotels require a deposit. Travel agents have told us that even if you have confirmed your reservation, you can still get bumped if you haven't sent a deposit.

Rates to expect: You can find clean, fairly comfortable rooms almost anywhere for $10 to $30 for two. Atmosphere costs more, getting you into the $50-$100 range. If you can afford them, there are plenty of places with great atmosphere, equipment, and service.

Noise pollution: Our main complaint about many hotels, even some expensive ones, is that you're often subjected to noise pollution from somebody's high-powered sound system. The usual source is a nearby dance hall or neighbors with a loud radio. A place can seem perfectly *tranquilo* when you arrive during the day; the thumping disco across the river only comes on at night. The best solution is to get up and dance. Places owned by foreigners are often quieter than places owned by Ticos, who regard loud music as *alegre*. The sounds of trucks and motorcycles rumbling by during the day might not be a problem, but it can keep you awake at night, so be aware of your hotel's distance from the road.

How many words for hotel are there in Spanish? We should clarify the meaning of various terms referring to lodging.

Hotels usually have more than one story, though not always. *Cabinas* are the most common form of lodging at the beach or in the mountains. They may be separate, or connected in rows or duplexes, roughly corresponding to what a North American would call a "motel." However, here *motel* refers to a small number of establishments, mostly on the southeastern side of San José, that couples use for clandestine romantic trysts. Motels rent by the hour. *Villas, bungalows,* and *chalets* are fancy cabinas, usually separate from one another. *Pensiones* and *hospedajes* are usually converted houses, and often serve family-style meals. A *posada* is an inn. An *albergue* is a lodge, usually in the forest or the mountains, and most often oriented toward ecotourism.

Youth hostels are also called *albergues* or, less commonly, *hostales*. Most of them are simply hotels and lodges that give substantial discounts to International Youth Hostel Federation members. If you are already a member, your card will be honored; otherwise, purchase one at **Toruma Hostel** (Avenida Central, Calles 29/31; 224-4085) in San José. Bring a photo. There are affiliated hostels in San José, Puerto Viejo de Talamanca, Liberia, Rincón de la Vieja and Guanacaste National Park, Monteverde, Jacó, and Puntarenas. The hosteling desk at Toruma can also arrange tours and transportation throughout the country. Often a cheap hotel is less expensive than a hostel.

Homestays offer the opportunity of a more authentic Tico experience. If you study Spanish in San José or at schools in beach or mountain locations, you can choose to live with a Tico family fairly inexpensively. See the listings for Spanish schools near the end of this chapter. **Bell's Home Hospitality** (225-4752; www.homestay.thebells.org, e-mail: homestay@racsa.co.cr) is another great way to hook up with Tico families and get comfortable accommodations in the $40-$50 price range. See their listing near the end of the San José chapter (Chapter Six). If you have young children, homestays might be a good alternative because many Tico homes have children of their own.

Discounts: Beach and mountain hotels often give discounts in the green season (May to November). Weekly and monthly rates are common as well.

House rentals: If you are staying in one place for a while, consider renting a house. See *The Tico Times* for listings, or ask at a local *pulpería*; www.greencoast.com lists inexpensive house rentals on the Caribbean coast, or see www.crvacationrentals.com or call 770-992-1374.

Shower temperature: We have four categories for telling you about water temperature in the shower when we describe a hotel.

Cold water means just that—no hot water. However, showers at places near the beach are often "solar-heated" naturally, and it sometimes feels good to take a cool shower instead of a hot one.

Heated water refers to an electric device that warms the shower water as it comes out of the showerhead. *Note:* These contraptions are usually set to come on when the water is turned on, but in some places you have to turn them on yourself. Check how yours works while you are dry and have your shoes on. You don't want to be fooling around with it while you are wet and barefoot in the shower. If there is too little water pressure, the little buggers become too hot and can burn out, so be careful. Usually they make for pretty limp, lukewarm showers.

Hot water refers to water heated by a hot-water tank.

Solar-heated water indicates the use of solar-heating devices, often something as simple as black tubing on the roof.

Natural ventilation refers to places at the beach that, because of their location or construction, take advantage of ocean breezes and don't need fans.

NOTES FOR SENIOR TRAVELERS

Older travelers will certainly be able to find good company, comfortable traveling conditions and lodging, with the assurance that excellent health care is available if they should need it.

Note: The bad condition of the sidewalks is a real problem in many towns, and much care must be taken by pedestrians.

Elderhostel (877-426-8056; www.elderhostel.org), which sponsors inexpensive and interesting trips for people 55 years of age or over, includes Costa Rica in its itinerary.

A tour company oriented toward travelers over 50 is Boston-based **Grand Circle** (800-597-3644; www.gct.com). Its Costa Rica trip rates are very reasonable. Its sister company, **Overseas Adventure Travel** (800-955-1925; www.oattravel.com), specializes in smaller groups of 16 people or less. A foundation arm of the company makes significant donations to nonprofit organizations in Costa Rica.

NOTES FOR TRAVELERS WITH DISABILITIES

In 1996, activists for disabled rights won a victory when legislation was enacted that guarantees education, social services, and jobs for all disabled people in Costa Rica. Public transportation is to be accessible to all people as is any new public construction. However, great laws aren't always implemented in Costa Rica.

Unfortunately, very little has been done to make access easier for people with disabilities and parents pushing strollers. Streets and sidewalks are often in deplorable condition, some curbs are more than a foot high, and many roads do not have sidewalks at all, forcing everyone into the street. Despite all this, several people with disabilities have told us that they felt conditions were better for them here than in the U.S. because of the climate, the relatively low cost of quality health care and hospitalization, and the low cost of maids and other helpers. Many neighborhoods do have sidewalks and downtown San José has some sidewalk ramps at intersections, but they are often too high to be helpful.

The **Instituto Internacional de Desarrollo Creativo** (771-7482; www. consult-iidc.com, e-mail: chabote@racsa.co.cr) uses the following three categories to classify tours and lodging:

1. *Adapted:* a person with a disability could use the installations without any help. The only place that fits this category is the **Hotel Real Comfort** in Santa Ana. All rooms have signs in Braille, and offer the choice between an adapted room with a bath or a rolling shower. A phone for deaf people is also available.

2. *Accessible:* no steps (ramped) and enough space to go everywhere without help: **Poás Volcano** and **InBio Park** in Santo Domingo de Heredia.

3. *Accessible with help*: one or two steps at the entrance, steep ramps, but enough space to get to bathrooms and rooms for a person in a wheelchair.

The following tourist attractions and hotels are in this third category:

SAN JOSÉ MUSEUMS   **Gold Museum** (steep ramp); **Museo Nacional** (one step in one of the exhibition rooms); **Museum of Costa Rican Art**, La Sabana Park (one step); the **Museum of Form, Space and Sound** (designed especially for blind and deaf people).

TOURS AND TOURIST ATTRACTIONS   **Café Britt**, Heredia; **Parque Central and church**, Heredia; **Zoo Ave**, La Garita; **Oxcart Factory** and souvenir shop, Sarchí; **Central Park and Basílica**, Cartago; **Lankester Gardens**, Cartago; **Irazú Volcano**, near Cartago; **Rainforest Aerial Tram**, Braulio Carrillo; **Tabacón Resort** (using the left-hand side entrance), La Fortuna; trails at La Selva, Sarapiquí, and **Arenal Observatory Lodge**, La Fortuna; **Restaurant Ram Luna**, above San José.

HOTELS   *Near San José:* **Casa Laurin B&B**, Escazú; **Bougainvillea**, Santo Tomás de Santo Domingo de Heredia (recommended); **Hotel Aeropuerto**, Alajuela (for proximity to airport); **Aurola Holiday Inn**, San José; **Best Western Irazú**, La Uruca (for proximity to shopping centers and restaurant); **Hotel Villa Zurquí**.

In provinces: **Hotel Occidental Tucano**, San Carlos; **Tabacón Resort and Lodge**, La Fortuna; **Centro Neotrópico Sarapiquís**, Sarapiquí; **Hotel Del Sur**, San Isidro de El General; **Hotel Mangaby**, Playa Hermosa, Guanacaste; **Hotel Espadilla**, Manuel Antonio; **Hotel de Lucía**, Monteverde; **Hotel Docelunas**, Jacó.

Many other places could be accessible, depending on the disability level of the travelers and their willingness to deal with obstacles, but are not up to North American standards. The IIDC (www.empowermentaccess.com) prepares personalized itineraries to answer the specific needs and interests of physically challenged travelers so that they can enjoy themselves. In 2001, they helped a group of blind people climb Mount Chirripó, the highest mountain in Costa Rica.

Vaya con Silla de Ruedas (phone/fax: 454-2810; www.gowithwheel chairs.com, e-mail: vayacon@racsa.co.cr) is a transportation and tour company with an ADA-approved van with elevator, three wheelchair stations, front and back air conditioners, and room for friends and companions. They custom-design trips to accessible places and their website has many links to other interesting sites for disabled travelers.

Otherwise it is best to get around by taxi. Taxi service is fairly reasonable, but you'll have better luck if you summon a taxi by phone instead of trying to hail one on the street. Taxi drivers seem to ignore the disabled if they have the opportunity to pick up others.

NOTES FOR TRAVELING WITH CHILDREN

Ticos love children. You won't get dirty looks for bringing them along— only smiles and a helping hand when needed. Both men and women seem to be naturally sensitive to the needs of children, whether it is to spontaneously help you lift them on or off the bus, or to include the kids in conversation. If you have a baby (especially a fair-haired one), be prepared to be stopped in the street while people admire your little treasure.

Entry/exit parental authorization letters: If you are traveling with a child 18 or under, one or both of whose parents will not be in the country, you must get a notarized letter from the absent parent(s) giving you permission to enter Costa Rica and take the child out of Costa Rica again. (Even if you are one of the parents, you need a letter from the other if he or she is absent.) If the child was born in Costa Rica, you must present a variety of documents, even if the child has a foreign passport. To check on these regulations, call the Costa Rican embassy nearest you. See www. costarica.com/embassy for a list.

What to bring: When preparing for your trip here, you should pack a junior first-aid kit with baby aspirin, thermometer, vitamins, diarrhea medicine, oral rehydration solution in case of serious dehydration, sunblock, bug repellent, tissues, wipes, and cold medicine. Nelson's homeopathic Hypercal cream is excellent for removing the pain of sunburn. After Bite is a roll-on medication that relieves itching and pain caused by bug bites.

Pack extra plastic bags for dirty diapers, cloth diapers for emergencies, baby sunscreen, a portable stroller and papoose-style backpack, a car seat if you plan to use a car, easy-to-wash clothes, swimsuits, a floppy hat to wear in the water, a life jacket, beach toys, and picture books relating to Costa Rica.

Travel tips: Try to plan a flight during your child's nap time, but feed a baby during take-off and landing to relieve pressure in the ears. If you are pregnant or breast-feeding, be sure to stay well hydrated during the flight. Bring everything you need on board—diapers, food, toys, books, and extra clothing for kids and parents alike. It's also helpful to carry a few new toys, snacks, and books as treats if boredom sets in.

Pace your trip so your child can adapt to all the changes in routine. Don't plan exhausting whirlwind tours, and keep travel time to a minimum. You'll be a lot more comfortable if you splurge on a rental car rather than taking buses, at least until your kids are over seven. Our seven- and nine-year-olds did great on bus trips. The thing that really bothered them was getting too hot, so we'd try to take early-morning or late-afternoon rides. Seek out zoos, parks, plazas, outdoor entertainment, and short excursions to amuse your child. Costa Rica's marketplaces are more fascinating to some children than museums. On the other hand, our kids didn't like the crowds, noise, hustle and bustle of San José at all.

Bathrooms are hard to find sometimes, and it is perfectly acceptable for little ones to pee in the bushes or even against a building if you are in the city. Disposable diapers are readily available for trips, but you won't find many places with changing tables. A portable changing pad comes in handy. People will help you find the best place to do what has to be done.

Activities: During the Costa Rican summer (January to March), the Ministry of Culture, Youth, and Sports (257-1433, 256-4139) sponsors many interesting courses for kids ages 7 to 15, ranging from art to dance to archaeology to astronomy. There are children's theater performances on Sundays and some arts-and-crafts stuff in the parks. Playgrounds, like Central American plumbing, seem to get trashed and ruined overnight. The Friday and Sunday editions of the daily *La Nación*'s *"Viva"* section and the "Weekend" section of *The Tico Times* list whatever is happening for children over the weekend.

One place most kids will enjoy is the **Parque Nacional de Diversiones** (open daily November through February, 9 a.m. to 7 p.m.; Wednesday to Sunday the rest of the year, 9 a.m. to 5 p.m.; 231-2001), a large, clean, and well-run amusement park in La Uruca, west of San José. It has many rides, including a small Ferris wheel, two rollercoasters, and the *Pacuare*, where six "rafters" in a round, inflatable boat go down a 150-foot slide into a tranquil lagoon. Expect to get wet. About $8.50 will entitle your kid to all the rides he or she can take in a day, as well as admittance to **Pueblo Antiguo**, a model of old-time Costa Rican life, where dance and theater performances are often held on weekends; actors wear traditional campesino attire and become the citizens of Pueblo Antiguo. All proceeds go to support the Children's Hospital. There are plenty of places to eat there, but they are all of the greasy fast-food variety, so bring your own snacks and juices.

The park is located two kilometers west of Hospital México, the large building you see on the left as you leave the western suburbs of San José heading for Puntarenas. To find it, you must get off the main highway at the Juan Pablo II rotunda and take the access road that runs parallel to the highway directly in front of the hospital. Or take the "Hospital México" bus.

San José converted its castle-like penitentiary into a well-designed **Children's Museum** (admission $2, children under 18 $1.50; open weekdays, 8 a.m. to 3 p.m.; weekends, 10 a.m. to 4 p.m.; at the extreme north end of Calle 4; 258-4929). There is a genuine airplane cockpit to play in, and a couple of flight simulators. Another large room has been turned into a rainforest. There are many other exciting interactive exhibits. (You have to cross a pretty bad neighborhood to get there, so spring for a cab.) You can read about the excellent Gold, Jade, Natural and Art Museums in the San Jose chapter.

Our favorite beaches for kids—those that are shady and have gentle waters—include: Bahía Junquillal Recreation Area and Carrillo in Guanacaste, Ballena National Marine Park in Uvita, and the third beach at Manuel Antonio (though it's a 20-minute walk through the park to get there). The beaches are beautiful and lined with palms in Talamanca, but the currents can be so strong that nothing more than wading or playing in knee-deep water is suggested. At low tide in Playa Chiquita (south of Puerto Viejo), Drake Bay, Dominical, Playa Santa Teresa, and Montezuma, there are tidepools that are fun for kids to play in.

To prepare your six- to twelve-year-olds, order *Let's Discover Costa Rica*, a bilingual, 64-page book full of activities like cut-out-and-assemble mobiles, mazes, and paint-by-number pictures, all woven into a story of intercultural friendship. Order at www.butterflyfarm.co.cr.

NOTES FOR WOMEN

Costa Rica is one of the safest countries for women travelers in Latin America, given its peaceful nature and well-developed tourism industry. Although domestic violence is, unfortunately, all too common, the sexual assault rate is much lower than in the U.S. However, as in any area, women traveling alone must use caution, especially at night. Be aware of which neighborhoods have a reputation for trouble. Take advantage of programs like **A Safe Passage** (365-9678; www.costaricabustickets.com, e-mail: rchoice@ racsa.co.cr), which has a link to tips from **The Women's Travel Club** (800-480-4448; www.womenstravelclub.com).

This is a country where machismo is still considered normal male behavior. An unaccompanied woman should disregard the flirtatious comments many Tico men will call out, such as *mi amor* (my love), *machita* (if you are a blond), or *guapa* (pretty). If they are farther away, they hiss as a woman passes by. It's annoying, but not dangerous. The best policy is to ignore them and keep walking.

Ticos can be compelling in their professions of eternal devotion. Whether they are married or single does not seem to have much to do with it. Take anything that is said with a grain of salt. Ticos often regard foreign women as easy conquests. But, as in most other Latin countries, they look for *la Virgen Purísima* when making a lasting commitment.

NOTES FOR MEN

Prostitution is legal in Costa Rica, and prostitutes are given medical tests on a regular basis. Some prostitutes have been found to be carrying AIDS. Prostitutes have been known to gang up on men in the street and rob them. There have also been cases of men being drugged and robbed after having invited women to their apartment or room—or just for a drink. Be careful, guys.

Sexual exploitation of minors has also become a problem in the last ten years, and Costa Rica has enacted severe laws to punish anyone caught paying or giving any kind of economic benefit to underage persons for sexual favors. Call Casa Alianza at 253-5439 or Patronato Nacional de la Infancia (PANI) at 800-226-2626 for more information.

Costa Rican women are known for their loveliness and intelligence. Ticas are also good at being *chineadoras*, i.e., taking care of men as if they were babies. Many foreign men have sought out Costa Rican women for relationships. Although we know of many successful intercultural marriages, we urge our readers to pay close attention to deeply ingrained cultural differences that can cause major communication problems when the idyllic glow wears off.

NOTES FOR TRAVELING WITH PETS

Dogs are not regarded with the same affection as they are in North America and Europe, and are used as guards rather than as pets. Most Costa Ricans are scared to death of dogs. If there is a rabies epidemic, government agents go around feeding poisoned meat to dogs, especially in the countryside. Several friends have lost pets in this way.

Another problem might be finding a temporary place to stay with your pet. In general, bed and breakfasts are more willing to take animals.

To learn the current requirements for bringing pets to Costa Rica, go to www.costarica.com and search for "pets."

NOTES FOR STUDENT TRAVELERS

If you are interested in adventure, plus the opportunity to understand the interface between conservation, community development, and ecotourism, or tropical biology and ecology, there could be no more interesting place to visit than today's Costa Rica. The community-based ecotourism projects, mentioned in the introduction and throughout the text, are inexpensive to visit, give you a real taste of the culture, and are small enough for you to really connect with people. You might be able to find a way to get credit for your stay. Many universities and colleges offer study/travel options in Costa Rica.

See "Accommodations in Costa Rica" section earlier in this chapter for details on youth hostels, and check out the study-abroad options near the end of this chapter. The U.S. **Peace Corps** and **Habitat for Humanity** also have projects here. See Chapter Two for volunteer opportunities.

NOTES FOR GAY AND LESBIAN TRAVELERS

Costa Rica continues to enjoy a steady increase in gay and lesbian visitors. This is in part due to the social tolerance exhibited here, at least when compared to other Latin American countries. But keep in mind, this is a small, mostly Catholic country and the gay lifestyle is primarily discreet in nature.

Gay rights have only recently been allowed out of the closet. After a 1995 police raid on the popular gay disco Deja Vu, the owners filed suit and, with a legal victory, opened the door for a more public gay rights movement. In 1999, protesters blocked the arrival of a bus of gay tourists who were headed for a festival in Manuel Antonio. After a lot of press coverage and apologies by key officials, the controversy faded away.

However, both gay and straight men are vulnerable to crime that can occur when they pick up people. In February 2003, Richard Stern, director of the Costa Rica–based Agua Buena Human Rights Association, issued a statement warning visiting gay men about the possible violence against gays in Costa Rica. "While 99 percent of all gay men in Costa Rica are honest and trustworthy, serious events have occurred in recent weeks which have motivated us to publish this warning." According to *The Tico Times*, a police spokesman estimated that 30 gay foreign men have been murdered in the last 15 years, and that the number of cases has increased since 2000. "Costa Rican men face the same risk, but often are more aware of their environment," said the police official. "Foreign men may be more adventurous and less careful." The main motive is robbery, according to the police. Victims are targeted in bars or parks known as "pick-up" spots. The assailant usually gains the trust of the victim over a few hours, days, or weeks.

Both Agua Buena and the Center for the Promotion of Human Rights in Central America recommend the following precautions:

• Avoid excessive consumption of alcohol or drugs when visiting nightspots.

• Avoid Parque Nacional and La Sabana park, which are very dangerous after dark.

• Use caution if someone approaches you or if you decide to invite someone to visit you. Meet their friends first and ask for home and work phone numbers. Make sure that numbers are valid before making further plans. If the person does not have a phone, don't go.

Gay and lesbian businesses are springing up throughout the Central Valley. (See Chapter Six for gay and lesbian bars and discos in San José.)

You shouldn't have any trouble in other areas of the country. When checking in to your hotel as a couple, you should both be at the desk so they know you're staying together. Managers get nervous when they see unknown people in their hotel. Once again, the best policy is to be discreet but not deceive. You might be more comfortable in the hotels or cabinas that offer a greater sense of privacy. Many couples are going to Costa Rica for their weddings. See costaricapages.com/gayweddings.

For hotels, **Colours** in the western suburb of Rohrmosher remains the city's most established exclusively gay/lesbian hotel. They have a similar hotel in Florida, and their U.S.-based travel agency (www.colours.net) can make reservations at Colours and throughout Costa Rica. **Hotel Kekoldi** is a midrange alternative in San José. They coordinate with Holbrook Travel in Gainesville, Florida, which provides quality natural-history travel to the gay and lesbian community (800-451-7111; e-mail: travel@holbrooktravel.com). They also have a branch at Manuel Antonio. Or try the inexpensive **Casa Agua Buena** (234-2411; www.aguabuena.org/casabuena/index.html) in San Pedro, San José's university district.

Most gay and lesbian travelers head for the Pacific beach of Manuel Antonio, where **Casa Blanca Hotel** (an exclusively gay and lesbian facility) is a favorite spot. La Playita, the tiny private beach just past the northern point of Manuel Antonio, is a gay and lesbian scene, especially during

Christmas and Easter holidays. It is not accessible at high tide. **Casitas LazDivas** (656-0295; www.lazdivaz.com) provides a gay and lesbian oasis on Playa Sámara in Guanacaste.

For up-to-date gay and lesbian information in English, go to www.gay-costarica.com/index2.html.

Uno en Diez (open Monday through Saturday, 9 or 9:30 a.m. to 9 p.m.; 258-4561; www.1en10.com) is an internet café, gallery, and gay information center on Calle 3, Avenidas 5/7, 400 meters north of the Plaza de la Cultura in San José.

SPECIAL WAYS TO VISIT COSTA RICA

NATURE TOURS

The following companies specialize in setting up nature tour packages. You can easily arrange nature tours when you get here, through your hotel, or through tour companies listed in this book. The Costa Rica–based companies will help you with the sometimes-complicated logistics of visiting exciting rural community tourism destinations.

COSTA RICA–BASED NATURE TOUR COMPANIES

ACTUAR
phone/fax: 228-5695
www.actuarcostarica.com
e-mail: actuar@racsa.co.cr
Tours and connections to community-based ecotourism.

Cultourica
249-1761, 249-1271
www.cultourica.com
e-mail: cultourica@expreso.co.cr
Low-cost nature tours that visit cooperatives and other community-based tourism projects, emphasizing community development and interactions with local people.

Selva Mar
771-4582
www.exploringcostarica.com
e-mail: selvamar@racsa.co.cr
Trekking and birdwatching, especially in the Southern Zone.

Horizontes
San José, CR
222-2022, fax: 255-4513
www.horizontes.com
e-mail: info@horizontes.com
Natural, cultural, and educational tours to all locations; hiking tours. Can arrange conventions, seminars. Tours to community-based ecotourism projects.

Simbiosis Tours
248-2538
www.turismoruralcr.com
e-mail: cooprena@racsa.co.cr
*Tours and connections to commu-
nity-based ecotourism.*

**U.S. and CANADA–BASED
NATURE TOUR COMPANIES**
Adventure Life
Missoula, MT
800-344-6118, 406-541-2677
fax: 406-541-2676
www.adventure-life.com
e-mail: info@adventure-life.com

Costa Rica Connection
San Luis Obispo, CA
800-345-7422, 805-543-8823
fax: 805-543-3626
www.crconnect.com
e-mail: info@crconnect.com

Forum Travel
Pleasant Hill, CA
800-252-4475, 925-671-2900
fax: 925-671-2993
www.foruminternational.com
e-mail: fti@foruminternational.com

Geo Expeditions
Sonora, CA
800-351-5041, 209-532-0152
www.geoexpeditions.com
e-mail: sales@geoexpeditions.com

Halintours
Austin, TX
phone/fax: 512-301-0655
halintours.tripod.com
e-mail: halintours@aol.com

Lindblad Expeditions
800-397-3348, 212-765-7740
www.expeditions.com
e-mail: explore@expeditions.com

Journeys
Ann Arbor, MI
800-255-8735, 734-665-4407
fax: 734-665-2945
www.journeys-intl.com
e-mail: info@journeys-intl.com

Natural Outings, Ltd.
Mansfield, ON, Canada
800-668-8911
www.naturaloutings.com
e-mail: info@naturaloutings.com

Preferred Adventures
St. Paul, MN
800-840-8687, 651-222-8131
fax: 651-222-4221
www.preferredadventures.com
e-mail: travel@preferred
adventures.com

Wildland Adventures
Seattle, WA
800-345-4453, 206-365-0686
fax: 206-363-6615
www.wildland.com
e-mail: info@wildland.com

LANGUAGE-LEARNING VACATIONS

Many people like the idea of learning Spanish on their Costa Rican vacation. The excellent language schools listed here offer a variety of experiences. Most schools arrange for students to live with Costa Rican families to immerse themselves in the language, but some have guesthouses where students can stay if they want more privacy. Most schools set up weekend sightseeing trips for participants. Intensive conversational methods are used for four to six hours a day in programs lasting from one week to several months. Students are placed according to ability. Programs cost an average of $400 to $600 per week, $1100 to $1500 per month, including room and board. Most schools give academic credit.

Spanish schools provide an excellent opportunity to learn about Costa Rican culture and often place students in volunteer activities so that they can practice what they have learned.

Many schools have urban and rural campuses so you can combine language learning with a beach or mountain vacation. We offer the most salient features below.

CENTRAL VALLEY

Alajuela:

Instituto de Cultura y Lengua Costarricense
458-3157, fax: 458-3214
www.institutodecultura.com
e-mail: corpcost@racsa.co.cr

Includes afternoon classes in Central American issues, Costa Rican art, literature, and history, in addition to Latin dance, music, and cooking. Volunteer placements.

La Guácima de Alajuela and Playa Sámara:

Rancho de Español
phone/fax: 438-0071
www.ranchodeespanol.com
e-mail: ranchesp@racsa.co.cr
One week at the beach during the four-week program. Special classes for children.

La Trinidad de Ciudad Colón:

El Marañon
249-1271, fax: 249-1761
www.cultourica.com
e-mail: cultourica@racsa.co.cr
Combines 30 hours of Spanish with an inexpensive six-day tour to community-based ecotourism destinations. Four routes to choose from.

Orosi:

Montaña Linda Youth Hostel and Spanish School
phone/fax: 533-3640
www.montanalinda.com
e-mail: info@montanalinda.com
Very inexpensive classes; students choose direction and set the pace.
Nice country town.

Santa Ana and San José:

Centro Lingüístico Conversa
221-7649, 256-3069, fax: 233-2418
in the U.S.: 800-367-SPAN
www.conversa.net
e-mail: conversa@conversa.co.cr
Six-acre hilltop campus with pool, volleyball, basketball, and tennis
courts, and plenty of hammocks. On-campus housing is in family suites
or six-bedroom lodge. Special program for retirees includes field trips,
cultural events, and fine dining. Take their entertaining online Spanish
test to determine your level.

BEACHES AND MOUNTAINS

Dominical and Turrialba:

Adventure Education Center
248-0147
in the U.S.: 800-237-2730
www.adventurespanishschool.com
e-mail: aecdominical@racsa.co.cr
Midweek and weekend adventures include kayaking, river rafting, mountain biking, and snorkeling trips. Medical Spanish. Special programs for
kids kindergarten to 13 years old.

Heredia and Playa Sámara:

Intercultura Costa Rica
260-8480, fax: 260-9243
in the U.S.: 800-205-0642
www.spanish-intercultura.com
e-mail: info@interculturacostarica.com
Classes include Latin dance, music, and cooking.

Jacó:

Escuela del Mundo (School of the World)
643-1064
www.schooloftheworld.com

e-mail: info@speakcostarica.com

Combines Spanish study with classes in surfing, art, and digital photography. Excellent photos on their website.

Manuel Antonio and San José:

Costa Rican Spanish Institute (COSI)

234-1001

in the U.S.: 800-771-5184

www.cosi.co.cr

e-mail: office@cosi.co.cr

San José–based teen summer program includes rollerskating, art, bowing, and movies.

Escuela de Idiomas D'Amore

777-1143, 777-0233

in the U.S.: 310-435-9897

www.escueladamore.com

e-mail: damore@racsa.co.cr

Stunning views from classrooms, two-week minimum, homestays in Quepos. Weekly field trips focus on social and environmental issues.

Centro de Idiomas del Pacífico

777-0805

www.cipacifico.com

e-mail: info@cipacifico.com

Alajuela campus has a pool, jacuzzi, tennis courts, and mini-apartments surrounded by gardens. Manuel Antonio campus has a small pool. Volunteer positions arranged.

Monteverde, San Joaquín de Flores de Heredia, and Playa Flamingo:

Centro Panamericano de Idiomas

265-6306

in the U.S.: 888-682-0054

www.cpi-edu.com

e-mail: info@cpi-edu.com

Special programs in Medical Spanish and Spanish in the Social Sciences. PADI certification is combined with Spanish at Playa Flamingo. Optional volunteer program; Monteverde campus students can volunteer in Habitat for Humanity and other community projects. Heredia students volunteer at a hospital, while Flamingo campus students volunteer teaching English.

Nicoya and Playa Sámara:
Instituto Guanacasteco de Idiomas
686-6948
www.spanishcostarica.com
e-mail: info@spanishcostarica.com
Never more than two students per class. Free tour after four weeks of classes.

Playa Grande, Arenal, and San José:
Kalexma Language Institute
290-2624, phone/fax: 232-0115
www.kalexma.com
e-mail: instructor@kalexma.com
In addition to inexpensive classes, they offer a four-week language and travel option, with one week near San José, one week at Arenal volcano, and two weeks at Playa Grande in Guanacaste for a minimum of five people.

Playa Santa Teresa and San José
**ICAI, Central American Institute
for International Affairs**
233-8571, fax: 221-5238
in the U.S.: 800-765-0025
www.educaturs.com
e-mail: icai@expreso.co.cr, info@isls.com
San José campus has cultural activities and kids' programs. Santa Teresa campus is right on a good surfing beach.

San Isidro de El General, Uvita de Osa, and Osa Peninsula:
SEPA
770-1457, fax: 771-5586
www.sabalolodge.com/sepa
e-mail: sabalo@racsa.co.cr
Volunteer placements; tours to Uvita and Corcovado.

Tamarindo:
WAYRA Institute
phone/fax: 653-0359
www.spanish-wayra.co.cr
e-mail: info@spanish-wayra.co.cr
Inexpensive. Housing with other students or with families.

SAN JOSÉ

Comunicare

281-0432, phone/fax: 224-4473

www.comunicarecr.com

e-mail: comunica@comunicarecr.com

In San Pedro, a ten-minute walk from the University of Costa Rica. Inexpensive courses for high school and college students, medical students, and tourists. Special three-week courses in Spanish and Environmental Studies, Central American Studies, or Women and Society in Central America, with field trips during the third week. Discounts with International Student ID.

Forester Instituto Internacional

225-3155, 225-1649, 225-0135, fax: 225-9236

in the U.S.: 800-444-5522

www.fores.com

e-mail: forester@racsa.co.cr

Special classes for children and teens, with excursions three days a week.

ICADS, Institute for Central American
Development Studies

234-1381, fax: 234-1337

www.icads.org

e-mail: icads@netbox.com

Four-week courses include studies in sustainable development, human rights, environmental issues, gender issues in Latin America, and indigenous and Afro-Caribbean culture in Costa Rica. Located in the quiet suburb of Curridabat on the east side of San José. Field trips to a women's cooperative, a medicinal plant farm, and an indigenous center. Volunteering in any of 40 placements.

ILISA, Instituto Latinoamericano de Idiomas

225-3155, fax: 225-4665

in the U.S. and Canada: 800-343-7248

www.ilisa.com

e-mail: spanish@ilisa.com

Spanish for fun, or for your career. Lectures on national parks, Costa Rican history, society, and culture. Special programs for families, doctors, educators, therapists, and psychologists. Nannies available for small children.

Instituto Costa Rica
phone/fax: 283-4733, 280-6622
www.intensivespanish.com
e-mail: iespcr@racsa.co.cr
The least expensive in San José. They cover socio-cultural, economic, historical, and political aspects of Costa Rica, and offer medical and legal Spanish.

Intensa
281-1818, 224-6353, fax: 253-4337
in the U.S. and Canada: 866-277-1352
www.intensa.com
e-mail: info@intensa.com
Their Spanish and Fine Arts program includes trips to the theater, symphony, and art museum, plus a Tortuga Island tour.

IPEE, Instituto Profesional de Español para Extranjeros
283-7731, fax: 225-7860
in the U.S.: phone/fax: 813-643-0416
www.ipee.com
e-mail: ipee@gate.net
Medical and business Spanish, Latin American literature. Located in Curridabat.

Mesoamérica
253-3195, fax: 234-7682
www.mesoamericaonline.net
e-mail: ourschool@mesoamericaonline.net
Their $60 one-day Survival Spanish course includes tips on customs and travel. Inexpensive.

STUDY PROGRAMS

Spanish, architecture and planning, women's studies, Latin American culture, politics, economics, literature, tropical biology, ecology, international relations, international business—you can study nearly anything in Costa Rica. There are several options for university-level students who want to spend a semester or a year here, as well as shorter seminars for nonstudents. All programs require advance planning, so start thinking about it early. Also, since there are two decidedly different seasons, choose your months according to your preferred weather.

Many of the projects listed here, as well as some of the Spanish courses above, provide opportunities for volunteering. This is a great and inexpensive way to see the real Costa Rica. There are other volunteer opportunities listed at the end of Chapter Two.

Associated Colleges of the Midwest, **Friends World College**, **University of California**, **University of Kansas**, and **State University of New York** are among the many universities that send students to Costa Rica. Your college probably does, too, or can coordinate with an existing program. Check out **www.studyabroad.com** for a complete list of options with handy links to each program's web page.

Students in the Spanish program at the **University of Costa Rica** (207-5634, fax: 207-5089; cariari.ucr.ac.cr/~filo/ingles, e-mail: aspaucr@le.ucr.ac.cr) may attend lectures and cultural events and interact with native speakers on campus. Beginner, Intermediate, and Advanced levels are offered in one-month to four-month sessions.

The **University for Peace** (205-9000, fax: 249-1929; www.upeace.org, e-mail: info@upeace.org), founded by the United Nations in 1980 and located on a beautiful tract of forested farmland in Villa Colón, southwest of San José, is the world's only truly international university. It offers master's degrees in International Law and Human Rights and Natural Resources and Sustainable Development, as well as short courses such as Peace and Socioeconomic Development.

Lisle Intercultural Programs (800-477-1538, fax: 512-259-0392; www.lisle.utoledo.edu, e-mail: lisle@utnet.utoledo.edu) welcome students, families, and elders to explore what it means to be a global citizen. Their tour ranges from rainforest reserves and beaches to agricultural cooperatives, and participants volunteer to help the communities they visit. Basic Spanish is helpful but not required. Academic credit is available through the University of Toledo.

The **Monteverde Institute** (645-5053, fax: 645-5219; www.mvinstitute.org, e-mail: mvi@mvinstitute.org) offers unique courses in which architects and planners, biologists, ecologists, and those interested in women's studies can use the Monteverde forests and communities as laboratories for practical, hands-on learning experiences. Professors can collaborate with the institute to create courses, or individuals can sign up on their own. The institute also coordinates volunteer work in the zone.

Proyecto Campanario (282-5898, fax: 282-8750; www.campanario.org, e-mail: campanario@racsa.co.cr) runs courses in Tropical Ecology for middle school, high school, and university students and teachers from its rainforest reserve on a beautiful cove in the Osa Peninsula. Students also participate in a service or conservation project in one of the nearby communities or at the reserve. Family conservation camps are also held during school vacations. It is hoped that by meeting and working together with the people of the area, students will gain an appreciation for the problems that face the tropics in general. Campanario also accepts volunteers.

The **Organization for Tropical Studies** (919-684-5774, fax: 919-684-5661, in C.R.: 240-6696, fax: 240-6783; www.ots.duke.edu, e-mail: nao@acpub.duke.edu) is a consortium of universities and research institutions dedicated to education, investigation, and conservation in the tropics. They offer "Tropical Biology: An Ecological Approach," a two-month lecture/field experience course, twice a year at their research stations in La Selva, Palo Verde, and Wilson Gardens, as well as undergraduate semester-abroad programs in Tropical Biology and Spanish Language and Culture, and shorter courses for Elderhostel groups and the general public. They also provide logistical support for dissertation research.

The **Institute for Central American Development Studies** (225-0508, fax: 234-1337; www.icadscr.com, e-mail: icads@netbox.com) was formed to educate first-worlders about Central America through hands-on experience in order to gain insight into current social and economic realities and their effect on women, the poor, and the environment. ICADS has a semester-abroad study program, including coursework and structured internship opportunities in Costa Rica and Nicaragua. One program is devoted solely to resource management and sustainable development. The internships allow students to give something back to the host society through service projects. There are fall and spring terms with credit. Noncredit summer internship placement is also available.

Costa Rica Rainforest Outward Bound (777-1222; www.crrobs.org, e-mail: info@crrobs.org) has students hike all the way across Costa Rica, learn kayaking, rafting, surfing, and Spanish, living with local families, and spending two days alone in the wilderness. Some programs include time in Nicaragua and Panama.

La Suerte and Ometepe Biological Field Stations (305-666-9932, fax: 305-666-7581; www.studyabroad.com/lasuerte, e-mail: lasuerte@safari.net) offer undergraduate and graduate studies in Primate Ecology, Ornithology, Rainforest Art, Medicinal Plant Ecology, and related subjects from their forest reserves in Costa Rica and Nicaragua.

Global Routes (510-848-4800; www.globalroutes.org, e-mail: mail@
globalroutes.org) is committed to strengthening global community by de-
signing four- to five-week community-service/cross-cultural-exchange programs for high school and college students.

DENTAL VACATIONS

You'd love to go to Costa Rica but you've got too many dental bills? Why
not get your dental work done here? The money you save could pay for your
ticket. Costa Rican dentists are well-trained and professional, and charge a
fraction of what you'd pay at home. For instance, a root canal costs about
$170 to $290, fillings cost about $25 to $40, crowns and bridges $230 to
$270. You can get recommendations at http://discoverypress.com/www.
board/wwwboard.html.

HEALTH VACATIONS

Costa Rica has some great places to go for relaxation and healing. They are
listed in the various geographical sections of the book.

In Alajuela, **Xandari Plantation Inn** (www.xandari.com) and the **Hotel Martino** (www.hotelmartino.com) are known for their spas. **Pura Vida
Spa** (888-767-7375; www.puravidaspa.com) in the mountains above Alajuela
brings yoga and growth workshops to Costa Rica and has week-long wellness packages.

In the Northern Zone, **Tabacón Resort and Spa** (www.tabacon.com),
at the base of Arenal volcano, offers thermal springs, massages, and mud
packs in a garden setting, as does **Montaña de Fuego** (www.montanade
fuego.com). The elegant **El Tucano** (www.occidental-hoteles.com) near San
Carlos has saunas and jacuzzis, and thermal and mud baths. **Sueño Azul
Resort** (www.suenoazulresort.com) in Las Horquetas de Sarapiquí, with its
yoga studio and spa, is the winter destination of the Omega Institute's
Holistic Studies Program.

On the Atlantic, **El Encanto B & B** (www.elencantobedandbreak
fast.com) has a quiet meditation room and an open-air yoga platform in the
midst of well-tended tropical gardens. **Samasati Nature Center** (www.
samasati.com) has twice-daily yoga classes in its large octagonal screened
seminar room surrounded by jungle. Their week-long retreats combine
yoga, massage, and trips to nearby beaches for swimming, snorkeling, and
dolphin watching.

In Guanacaste, **Nosara Wellness Service** (682-0360; www.nosarawell
ness.com) offers massage and physiotherapy as well as nutrition counseling

in Playa Nosara. **Nosara Yoga Institute** (www.nosarayoga.com) trains teachers, provides yoga vacations, and gives classes in its spacious center.

On the Nicoya Peninsula, the **Sano Banano** (www.elbanano.com) offers yoga and natural food on the beach in Montezuma. The serene yoga room at the **Flor Blanca Resort** (www.florblanca.com) at the north end of Playa Santa Teresa is watched over by hand-carved statues of deities from Indonesia.

The Southern Zone offers many opportunities to heal with diet and yoga. **The New Dawn Center** (www.thenewdawncenter.com), in the hills above San Isidro de El General, is devoted to teaching people how to grow and heal with plants. Their month-long courses include medicinal botany, naturopathy, massage therapy and holistic health care, permaculture design for ecological health gardens, agroforestry, and working with bamboo. They also offer a Spanish course. **Río Chirripó Retreat** (in the U.S.: 707-937-3775; www.riochirripo.com) is a small lodge near the base of Costa Rica's tallest mountain that offers yoga, raw food retreats, and workshops. In the hills above Uvita, south of Dominical, **La Cascada Verde** (www.cascadaverde.org) is a communal retreat center focusing on organic permaculture farming, cleansing diets, and body-mind healing. **Durika** is a spiritual community in the mountains east of Buenos Aires, the center of Costa Rica's pineapple growing region, on the border of La Amistad International Park. They offer meditation, vegetarian food, hydrotherapy, and bodywork.

Almost every lodge on the eastern Osa Peninsula has a yoga platform. The view from the open-air yoga studio at the **Luna Lodge** (www.lunalodge.com) in Carate is magnificent. South of Drake Bay, in Playa San Josecito, **La Guaria de la Osa Retreat Center** (www.osaretreat.org) gives seminars in ethnobotany and shamanic healing. **Chen Taiji International** (www.chentaijiinternational.com) offers personalized Tai Chi vacation packages, retreats, and training camps in Pavones, south of Golfito.

Homeopathy is practiced by doctors all over Costa Rica. The **Association for Homeopathic Research** (244-3145) maintains a list of qualified practitioners.

An increasing number of people are coming here for face-lifts, liposuctions, and other cosmetic surgeries that are not covered by regular health insurance. Experienced doctors, low prices, and luxurious post-op recovery facilities like Villa Plenitud (www.villaplenitud.com) make for a truly transformational experience. For more information, see **www.cocori.com/healthtourcr**.

GETTING MARRIED IN COSTA RICA

Although Costa Rica has been known as a honeymoon destination, more and more couples are coming here for their weddings or just to elope! Many hotels have become adept at wedding planning, and now Aimee Monihan, a certified wedding planner, has founded **Tropical Occasions** (377-6004; www.tropicaloccasions.com, e-mail: amonihan@tropicaloccasions.com) to help you plan yours. According to Monihan, weddings can cost from 25 to 40 percent less in Costa Rica, not counting travel. The legal procedures take about a month to coordinate, and the rest of the plans can be made by e-mail.

Many gay and lesbian couples are also having their commitment ceremonies in Costa Rica. See www.costaricapages.com/gayweddings.

FOUR

Once You Arrive: Getting Around in Costa Rica

LOCAL TRANSPORTATION

FROM THE AIRPORT

Taxi service into San José is about $13 per taxi. A bus (45 cents) goes into San José, but you can't take much baggage on it. A taxi to Alajuela from the airport should only cost $3-$7. If you have rented a car, vans will transport you to rental agency offices. Having the rental agency deliver the car to the airport involves a surcharge and is unnecessary because the offices are near the airport. Good B&Bs and hotels will arrange to have a rental car delivered to you the morning after you arrive in Costa Rica.

TAXIS

Taxis are relatively inexpensive by northern standards. Within towns and cities, drivers are supposed to use computerized meters, called *marías*. As soon as you get in the cab they should press a button and the number 265 should appear on the meter. Official rates in 2004 were ¢265 (60 cents) for the first kilometer and ¢115 (33 cents) for each additional kilometer; outside towns and cities, taxis usually have a set rate they charge to different destinations. They might even have a printed list that shows how much it costs to go from their home base to anywhere in the country. A taxi driver should be able to tell you how much he will charge before you get in the cab. It usually costs about $2.50 an hour for taxi drivers to wait for you. It is not customary to tip taxi drivers here.

A few taxi drivers do not use their meters or claim that they are broken. Legally, they must have a letter from the Ministerio de Obras Públicas y Transporte certifying that their *maría* does not work. If your *taxista* doesn't put the *maría* on, write down the driver's ID number, which should be clearly displayed in the window, and the license plate number and call 220-0102 to make a complaint. Keep your eye on the *maría* when you reach your destination. Some taxi drivers turn it off just before you get there and then charge you whatever they want.

There are many honest taxi drivers and many dishonest ones. Even if they overcharge you, their rates are very reasonable compared to other places. However, it's good to know your rights. If you are on a budget, watch out for taxis that are called for you by hotels. They charge more because they are on call for the hotel. They also justify charging more because many of them provide "special service," i.e., they speak English.

Most taxis are very well maintained. Taxi drivers cringe when passengers slam the doors shut because they feel it damages the car. One driver told us that he no longer stopped for foreign tourists because they usually slam doors. Ease the door closed, or let the driver do it for you.

Taxis can come in handy if you want to visit hard-to-get-to places but do not want the expense of renting a car. You can take an inexpensive bus trip to the town nearest your destination and hire a jeep-taxi to take you the rest of the way. Usually taxis hang out around the main square of any small town. It's best to ask several drivers how much they charge to make sure you are getting the going rate.

Taxis can be a lot cheaper than renting a car or taking a tour, especially if there are several of you. For instance, a tour to Volcán Poás with a travel agency usually costs $50 per person. You can hire a taxi in Alajuela to take you to Poás for $40 or $50 per *carload*—including the time spent waiting for you at the top.

CARS FOR HIRE

As an alternative to a taxi, your hotel can probably recommend a bilingual driver you can hire to show you around. Sometimes these drivers have vans that can hold up to seven people. In Monteverde, for instance, you can hire a van to take you to San José or Liberia for $100. You can divide the fee between the number of people in the van. Sometimes your hotel will find other guests who need the same service, and you can split the cost with them. Adobe Rentacar (www.adobecar.com) includes bilingual chauffeurs with their cars for $174/day. We know of two excellent waterfront guides who specialize in personalized tours: Enrique Dodero of Turismo Personalizado (www.costaricapersonaltours.com) and Miguel Pagan of Boritico Tours (262-7360, 359-2934; e-mail boriticotours@yahoo.com).

HITCHHIKING

Because bus service is widely available, most people prefer to take buses. Hitchhiking is rare. In the countryside, where bus service is infrequent or nonexistent, cars often stop to offer rides to people on foot.

BUSES

Since most Costa Ricans don't have cars, buses go almost everywhere. Most buses that travel between San José and the provinces have well-padded seats and curtains on the windows to shade you from the sun. Tall people, however, tell us that the bus seats are too cramped for their comfort. Fares rarely run more than $7 to go anywhere in the country. Some provincial buses are a bit rickety, but you won't find pigs and chickens tied to the roof, and most buses are fairly punctual. Buses from San José to the provinces are crowded on Friday and Saturday and the day preceding a holiday or three-day weekend. Likewise, it is difficult to get buses back to San José on Sunday, Monday, and the day following a holiday. This is especially true when trying to make connections to beach or mountain tourist destinations.

Many first-time visitors are reluctant to use the public bus system because of lack of Spanish, fear of being robbed, difficulty of getting to bus stops, etc. All those problems are addressed by **A Safe Passage** (441-7837, cell phone: 365-9678; www.costaricabustickets.com, e-mail: rchoice@racsa. co.cr), founded by Californian John Koger. For $15 ($25 for two), John will buy your bus tickets and deliver them to your Alajuela hotel, much closer to the airport than San José, with directions on how to get to the appropriate bus stops. You must let him know at least a week in advance so that you get reserved seats at the front of the bus, close to the driver, for increased security. His **Home Base** program includes airport pick-up, first and last nights at an Alajuela hotel, a bus ticket, and transportation to the bus stop, or your rental car and travel information ($89-$149/person, depending on quality of hotel; $124-$209 double). This service can give you an extra day of vacation if your flight arrives early. The Safe Passage website contains a list of bus departure times to destinations to the north and west of Alajuela. For groups of six or more, John will arrange transportation to the Caribbean as well, or set up shuttle service all over Costa Rica.

Some buses don't have buzzers or bells to tell the driver when you want to get off. When the bus gets close to your stop, shout *"¡La parada!"* or whistle loudly. If you are not sure where you should get off, ask the driver to let you know when he reaches your stop. Most drivers are very accommodating about letting people off right where they need to go. If you are traveling cheaply by bus, it's a good idea to bring as little with you as possible and leave most of your luggage at your hotel. Big suitcases are very inconvenient for bus travel. We have traveled for up to two weeks with just what we could fit in a day pack. Always keep your baggage at your feet rather than putting it in the overhead racks.

The second half of this book gives detailed information on transportation, including locations of bus stops and numbers to call to check schedules. English is usually not spoken. The best way to get to a provincial bus stop in San José or Alajuela is to hail an inexpensive taxi and have them deliver you there.

The **ICT** (Tourism Institute) (underneath the Plaza de la Cultura, Calle 5, Avenidas Central/2; 222-1090, 223-1733) keeps an updated, computerized list of bus stops and related information. Check bus schedules to provinces online at www.monteverdeinfo.com.

For those of you who are shy about taking public buses, **Gray Line Tourist Bus** (232-3681, 220-2126; www.graylinecostarica.com/grayline touristbus.html) runs daily air-conditioned buses to many destinations on the Pacific, the Northern Zone, and the Atlantic for $25 to $38 per person, with a 50 percent discount for kids. Your hotel can make reservations for you. Their main competition, **Interbus** (283-5573, in the U.S.: 800-748-8853; interbusonline.com), has buses to even more destinations and is very reliable. They offer a one-month Flexipass of four to ten transfers at a reduced rate.

PLANES

Because of Costa Rica's mountainous terrain, small aircraft are frequently used. A 35-minute flight can get you to Quepos and Manuel Antonio on the Pacific Coast, as opposed to a four-hour bus ride. **SANSA**, a government-subsidized airline, flies fairly inexpensively ($90-$150 roundtrip) to all corners of the country. **Nature Air** flights ($90-$190 roundtrip) cost a bit more than SANSA's but they're worth it for their increased reliability and convenience.

Children between ages two and eleven get a 25 percent discount on either airline. Nature Air and SANSA have a maximum luggage allowance of 12 kilos (25 pounds) per passenger. Nature Air will safely store excess luggage for you.

SANSA (221-9414, fax: 255-2176; www.flysansa.com) flights leave from a small terminal just west of the Juan Santamaría Airport. SANSA is part of Grupo TACA, the alliance of Central American airlines, along with LACSA. It is best to make reservations a few weeks in advance in the dry season.

Nature Air (220-3054, fax: 220-0413; www.natureair.com, e-mail: res ervations@natureair.com) uses the Tobias Bolaños Airport in Pavas west of La Sabana. They will pick you up at any San José or Central Valley hotel and deliver you to the airport ($6). They will also deliver you to your destination hotel. You need to arrive at the Pavas airport 45 minutes before your departure.

Adobe Rentacar (www.adobecar.com) will let you pick up or drop off your car for free at any hotel in the San José area or in Manuel Antonio, Liberia, Tamarindo, Playa Hermosa, Papagayo, Flamingo, Conchal, Ocotal, or Playa del Coco if you are renting for three days or more. This way you can drive there and fly back, or vice versa.

For the purpose of planning your itinerary, we have included the routes that were in effect in 2004. Some of these are condensed or combined in the green season.

DAILY ROUTES FOR SANSA (HIGH SEASON):

San José–Golfito–Coto 47–San José

San José–Golfito–San José

San José–Quepos–San José

San José–Liberia–San José

San José–Palmar Sur–San José

San José–Puerto Jimenez–San José

San José–Puerto Jimenez–Drake Bay

San José–Punta Islita–Sámara–Nosara–San José

San José–Sámara–Nosara

San José–Tamarindo–San José

San José–Tambor–San José

San José–Barra del Colorado–Tortuguero–San José

DAILY ROUTES FOR NATURE AIR (HIGH SEASON):

San José–Barra del Colorado–Tortuguero–San José

San José–Drake Bay–Carate–San José

San José–Puerto Jiménez–Golfito–San José

San José–Tambor–Punta Islita

San José–Tamarindo–Liberia–San José

San José–Nosara–San José

San José–Nosara–Carrillo–San José

San José–Quepos–Palmar Sur–Quepos–San José

San José–Quepos–Puerto Jimenez–San José

San José–Quepos–San José

Alfa Romeo Aero Taxi (phone/fax: 735-5112) is one of several compa-nies that has small planes available for charter. For a single-engine plane with room for three passengers you will pay about $275 per hour, plus $30 for landing and $40 for each hour the pilot waits for you at your destina-tion. A double-engine plane with room for five costs about $385 per hour of flight time. Check the Yellow Pages under *"Aviación"* for additional companies.

DRIVING IN COSTA RICA

CAR RENTALS

A car rental costs around $55 per day, $250-$300 per week, including in-surance and mileage (four-wheel drives are about $75-$100/day, $350-$400/week). The insurance has a $800 deductible, which you can waive by pay-ing $7 to $14 more. All major rental agencies have branches in Costa Rica. You're more likely to get a special rate if you book a rental car in your country of origin. You can often get a discount of up to 30 percent in the off-season. If you don't have an American Express, Visa, Diners Club, or MasterCard, you must leave a deposit of about $1000. Some agencies (Na-tional, Budget, Toyota, and Dollar, for example) allow you to decline their insurance if you have a gold credit card; Visa's gold card is the most com-monly accepted one. Find out what your credit card covers before you leave on vacation. If you are already here, reserve a car as far in advance as possible, especially in high season. Look under *"Alquiler de Automóviles"* in the phone book, or in the classifieds of *The Tico Times* for less expen-sive rentals.

To rent a car, you must be at least 21 years old, have a valid passport and driver's license, and a major credit card. You can rent a car at 18, but you must leave a double deposit. Some agencies charge more for people under 25 and won't rent to people over 75. Check websites for each com-pany's rules. Valid foreign driver's licenses are good in Costa Rica for three months.

Car rental agencies will provide transport from the airport to their nearby offices. Avoid having a car wait for you at the airport—there is of-ten a 12 percent surcharge for that. Better yet, take a taxi to your hotel and work with a company that will deliver the car to your hotel. Don't hassle with trying to navigate unfamiliar streets when you first arrive.

STREET ADDRESS SYSTEM

As you can see from the Downtown San José map in Chapter Six, San José's streets are laid out in a very logical system. Odd-numbered streets (*calles*) are east of Calle Central, even-numbered streets are west. Odd-numbered *avenidas* are north of Avenida Central and even-numbered avenues are south. So if an address is on Calle 17, Avenidas 5/7, it is in the northeastern part of the city.

However, most Ticos completely ignore the street numbering system. *Calles* and *avenidas* appear in the phone book, and that's about it. The accepted way to give directions is from *puntos cardinales* or landmarks. If you call for a taxi, you have to give the name of a church or a *pulpería* (corner store) or a well-known business (like Pollos Kentucky). Then you state how many *metros* you are from there and in what direction. *Cien* (100) *metros* roughly corresponds to one city block. These are some examples of typical ways of giving directions: *"De la pulpería La Luz, cien metros al norte y cincuenta al oeste."* ("From the La Luz grocery store, one block north and half a block west.") *"De la Iglesia La Soledad, doscientos al sur y trescientos al este."* ("From the Soledad Church, two blocks south and three blocks east.")

The absence of street signs complicates the issue, but the post office has ambitious plans to put signs on all streets and numbers on all houses. We will see if the Costa Ricans adopt the program or if they ignore it the way they ignore the already logical and efficient street numbering system.

A high clearance is more important than four-wheel drive, especially in the dry season. Regular cars can take you most of the places you want to go in Costa Rica, but you'll feel less paranoid if your chassis isn't scraping on the edge of a sudden pothole. Some rental companies won't even rent you a regular car if they know you plan to go to Monteverde, for instance. Some of the worst roads are the paved ones that have gone to potholes: they are more uneven and less predictable than a well-graded gravel road.

Note that all repairs must be okayed first with the main office, or you will not be reimbursed. According to Jim Corven's "Consumer Almanac" column in *The Tico Times*, "Stick shift is the norm in most rental cars; automatics are sometimes hard to get. Coupled with the lethal potholes and

PROVINCIAL RENT-A-CAR AGENCIES

Some car-rental agencies have branch offices in the provinces.
You could take a bus or plane and rent a car when you get there.
Branch offices are in:

LIBERIA
  Alamo 800-462-5266
  Avis 666-7585
  Dollar 668-1061
  Economy 231-5410
  National 666-5595
  Payless 668-1054
  Toyota 258-5797

TAMARINDO
  Alamo 653-0727
  Economy 653-0752
  Payless 653-0015

LA FORTUNA
  Alamo 479-9090
  National 777-3344

JACÓ
  Economy 643-1098
  National 643-1752
  Payless 643-3224

QUEPOS AND MANUEL
ANTONIO
  Alamo 777-3344
  Economy 777-5353
  Payless 777-0115

winding roads, these cars must endure conditions unseen elsewhere. Reduce your chances of a breakdown by checking the car out thoroughly before heading out. Do not assume the agency did it for you. Check the oil, water, brake fluid, tire pressure, air conditioner, lights, belts, and hoses while still in San José. Make certain there is a spare tire and jack. Also report any small nicks or dents on the surface. If you have any concern whatsoever, contact the agency for service. You will have far less chance of getting their understanding after you've driven the car for a couple of days and develop problems." He also points out that the insurance you pay covers damage to vehicles, but not your possessions within the vehicle. Make sure you return the car with a full tank of gas. The agency's rate may be four times as much as the gas would cost at a service station.

Renting a car makes exploring easier and is less time-consuming than taking the bus. However, if you get impatient driving roads riddled with potholes, washboards, or farm animals, or if crazy traffic makes you nervous, think twice about driving yourself. It is said that the more polite people are in person, the ruder they are behind the wheel. The impeccably courteous Costa Ricans are no exception. Passing on blind curves is common. Getting stuck behind an ancient truck overloaded with green bananas and climbing a two-lane highway at 5 mph is to be expected. Parking in the middle of the driving lane on a highway (often there is no shoulder) for repairs is the norm. Buses pull into traffic lanes without looking or signaling. Dividing lines and other road markings are ignored. And if you happen upon a pile of branches in your lane while feeling your way through the fog at night, *watch out*. Someone has broken down just ahead.

If you decide you want your own wheels, try to arrange to rent the car on the day you will be leaving San José for the provinces, because driving in San José is more hassle than it's worth. The car must be left in parking lots at all times to avoid theft. Driving in the city is like driving through a bee-hive, requiring a mix of finesse and aggressiveness. In San José and many other cities, most streets are one-way but are totally unmarked, so you have to guess if a street is one-way or not—and if it is, which way? Particularly tricky are streets that are two-way for a few blocks, then suddenly become one-way without any signs. Taxis or buses are much cheaper and easier for city travel.

If you do decide to rent a car, do not leave anything in it, even for a minute, unless it is in a well-guarded place.

You should be aware that Costa Rica has strict traffic laws with high fines for a variety of infractions. Booklets with all the points are available in the car rental offices, but if you always wear your seatbelt, go the speed limit (90 kilometers per hour on multi-lane highways, 40 to 80 elsewhere), pay special attention to school zones (where the speed limit drops to 25 kph), and watch for occasional signs or numbers painted on the road surface, you will probably be okay.

Policemen usually station themselves in the shade at the side of the road and flag down drivers. Certain policemen stop tourists for "speeding," and tell them they must appear in court at an inconvenient time in an inconvenient place, then offer to let them "pay on the spot" to avoid ruining their vacation. If a cop demands payment, you should refuse, and demand that he issue you a ticket ("*Hágame el parte, por favor*"). Officers are legally required to show their *carné* (ID card) on request, so if you feel you are being harassed or unduly pressured, get the ID number or at least the license plate number and report the officer to the Ministerio de Transporte, Operaciones Policiales (24-hour hotline: 222-9245, or 257-7795 ext. 2353 or 2354).

Here are some helpful vocabulary words:

despacio: slow

alto: stop

peligro: danger
ceda: yield
precaución: be careful

MAPS

Small yellow posts mark the distance in kilometers from San José on Costa Rica's highways, but these aren't enough to find your way around.

If you rent a car, you will be given a map. The ICT (Tourism Institute) has put out a new road map that includes the locations of most national parks, reserves, and wildlife refuges. Order it through the ICT offices, or pick one up at the ICT office under the Plaza de la Cultura. ITMB Publishing also puts out an excellent map that's available throughout Costa Rica. You can order it from amazon.com.

Even with a map, it's best to call a hotel at or near your destination and ask about current road conditions and travel times. A heavy afternoon rain can cause landslides, changing road conditions in a short time. Because of the unreliability of many roads, try to limit your driving to daylight hours. Hotels will also have current bus schedules.

Topographical maps can be purchased at **Librería Lehmann** (Calle 3, Avenidas Central/1), **Librería Universal** (Avenida Central, Calles Central/1), or the **Instituto Geográfico Nacional** (Avenida 22, Calles 9/11). Ask for *mapas cartográficos*. You'll be shown a little map of Costa Rica divided up into 20 x 30 kilometer sections. Indicate which sections you want. Maps show roads, trails, water sources including rapids, and contours at every 20 meters. They cost about $1.50 a section.

GAS

Gas costs about $2.50 per gallon, but is sold here by the liter, roughly equivalent to a quart. There are no self-service stations in Costa Rica.

ACCIDENTS

Costa Rica has one of the highest auto-accident mortality rates in the world, surpassed only by the United States. Thanks to long-time insurance agent Dave Garrett and *The Tico Times* for this updated information on what to do in case of an accident.

1. Do not move vehicles until you are authorized to do so by an official. This is very important. Let people honk their horns. Offer paper and pencils to witnesses to write their names and *cédula* numbers (legal identification).

2. Find out your location according to *puntos cardinales* or *señas,* i.e., *"300 metros al sur del antiguo higueron en San Pedro."* Call 911, 222-9330, 222-9245, or 800-012-3456 for a traffic official if one doesn't immediately appear. If it appears that the other driver has been drinking, ask the officer to give him or her an *alcoholemia* test.

3. Do not remove badly injured people from the scene. Wait for the Red Cross ambulance (call 911 or 128). Make no statements on the cause of the accident except to the official or a representative of the National Insurance Institute (INS), whom you can summon by calling 800-800-8000. If an inspector cannot come, they will give you a code number and you will have *three working days* to fill out an accident report at the nearest INS office (in Curridabat, Heredia, Alajuela, Cartago, Ciudad Neilly, Ciudad Quesada, Golfito, Guápiles, Liberia, Nicoya, Puntarenas, San Isidro, San Ramón, or Turrialba). Keep track of the code number, because it assures them that you called right after the accident. The insurance inspector often gets there sooner than the police. Pay attention to what he says about how to proceed with your claim. Do not make any deals with other people involved in the accident. If the INS finds out that a deal has been made, it will not pay a claim.

4. A tow truck is likely to appear on the scene, even if you haven't called for one, as towing services routinely monitor the police radio. You may even have more than one to choose from. Make sure your car gets to one of the 270 body shops authorized by the INS. Do not allow a tow truck operator to take your vehicle to an unauthorized body shop, because they do not do the paperwork that the INS requires.

5. Make a sketch of the area and the positions of the vehicles before and after the accident. Make note of the principal characteristics of the other vehicles involved, as well as the damage to your car and others. Avoid further damage by staying with your car.

6. You should report the accident to the police, even if it is insignificant, in every case. If you don't report it and get witnesses' names, things can get changed around and you may be accused of doing terrible damage and then driving away.

7. You will be given a citation by the police, telling you when and where to appear at the traffic court. Make sure you understand what it says before the police official leaves. It usually gives you ten working days to appear. A copy of this report must be presented to the INS (Avenida 7, Calles 9/11; 223-5800), along with your driver's

license, insurance policy, police report, and information about injuries and witnesses.

Foreign insurance policies are not effective in court and only the INS can provide local service for defense or adjustment of claims. Insurance is included in car rental fees unless you have declined and are using a gold-card policy.

ROAD TROUBLE

If you have a rented car, call the rental agency first in all cases, and they will tell you what to do. You can also dial 911.

If you are driving your own car, by law you should have fluorescent triangles to place on the road in case of a breakdown or accident as a warning to other vehicles.

Do not abandon your car, if you can avoid it. If you don't speak Spanish well, have someone explain your location in Spanish when you make the phone call. If a wrecker is needed, it can be called by Coopetaxi radios.

SAFETY AND THEFT

THEFT

Take precautions to avoid theft. So far, San José is much safer than most other cities, except for theft. The whole downtown area of San José has become a mecca for pickpockets and chain-snatchers. Other places to watch out for are Limón and Quepos. The zippered compartments of backpacks are excellent targets. It's best not to wear them downtown. Don't carry a lot of packages at once. Purses should be zippered and have short shoulder straps so that you can protect them with your upper arm. If you wear a waistpack, keep it under your shirt or jacket, or rest your hand on it when walking. Wallets and passports shouldn't be carried in your back pocket, and expensive watches, chains, and jewelry should not be worn. Unless you will need the original for banking, just carry a photocopy of your passport, specifically the pages with your photo and personal information and the Costa Rican entry stamp. Most hotels will keep your passport in their safety deposit box, and many now have safety boxes in each room. Before setting out for your destination downtown, check your route.

If, while on a bus or in a crowd, you feel yourself being jostled or pinched between several people at once, don't just be polite. Protect your purse or wallet and elbow your way out of the situation immediately. If you are driving downtown, keep your window rolled up high enough so that a thief can't reach in and grab your necklace, glasses, or watch. Don't leave

TOURISTS BEWARE!

Though San José is generally a safe city, it's not crime-free. Following are two scams to watch out for:

THE FLAT TIRE SCAM   Recently there are more and more reports of tourists picking up rental cars and finding after a few minutes that they have a flat tire. They stop by the side of the road to repair the tire. Friendly passersby offer help and end up robbing them, or robbers just swoop down on them without trying to be friendly. If you get a flat tire, just keep going until you get to a gas station or a place where there are a lot of people. Some agencies will deliver rental cars to your hotel.

THE SLIMY GOO SCAM   Tourists are walking down the street and someone squirts their clothes with slimy goo. Helpful onlookers appear with tissues and before they know it, the tourists' purses and wallets are gone.

tents or cars unguarded anywhere. Don't leave cameras or binoculars in sight of an open window, even a louvered one. A pole can be stuck in and they can be fished out. If you follow these precautions, you probably won't have any trouble. We've never been robbed on the street in our 30 years of living and traveling in Costa Rica. However, if you do have the misfortune of getting robbed, you might want to file a *denuncia* at the OIJ (Organismo de Investigación Judicial). There is one in most major towns and in San José at Avenidas 6/8, Calle 21. It is unlikely that they will investigate your robbery, but the document they type up and give to you can be presented to your insurance company. Take a Spanish-speaker with you. There is also a hotline (289-7486) for tourists who have been robbed.

EARTHQUAKES

These little surprises can make you question the very ground you walk on and remind you of the transience of being. The frequency of minor *temblores* (tremors) depends on the state of the tectonic plates Costa Rica sits on and can range from 40+ times a month to only once or twice. Most of them register less than 4.5 on the Richter scale and are barely perceptible. Those that register 4.5 to 6 can rock you but cause little damage.

If you happen to be caught in a big *terremoto* (earthquake), this is the official advice: Stay calm. Turn off electric appliances and extinguish cigarettes. Move away from windows or other breakables, or places where something could fall on you. Look for refuge under a desk or in a doorway. Don't lean against walls. Don't use stairs or elevators during the quake. Afterward, use the stairs, not the elevator. Leave the building you're in through the closest exit, as soon as possible.

BOMBETAS

If you hear two very loud explosions in rapid succession, don't run for cover—that's just the Tico way of celebrating momentous occasions. Usually the fireworks are from the neighborhood church, which is celebrating a Saint's Day, or are to announce events at a *turno* (town fiesta). In the case of a *turno*, the *bombetas* often begin at dawn and are fired off at regular intervals during the day, usually ending around 9 or 10 p.m. Sounding all the sirens in town is another way of expressing joy, as when the Pope or Tico astronaut Franklin Chang Diaz arrived in San José.

EMBASSIES AND CONSULATES

Many consulates are only open in the mornings. Following is a list of phone numbers for embassies and consulates in San José:

Austrian Consulate: Avenida 4, Calles 36/38; 255-3007, fax: 255-0767

British Embassy: Centro Colón; 258-2025, fax: 233-9938

Canadian Embassy: Sabana Sur; 242-4400

Dutch Embassy: Sabana Sur; 296-2933, fax: 296-2933

German Embassy: Rohrmoser; 232-5533

Guatemalan Embassy: Curridabat; 283-2555, fax: 283-2556

Japanese Embassy: Rohrmoser; 232-3787

Mexican Embassy: Los Yoses; 280-5690, 280-5701, fax: 234-9613

Nicaraguan Embassy: Barrio California; 256-4140, fax: 221-5481

Panamanian Consulate: Paseo Colón; 257-3241, fax: 257-4940

Swedish Consulate: La Uruca; 232-8549

Swiss Embassy: Centro Colón; 233-0052

United States Embassy: Pavas; 220-3939, fax: 232-7944, after-hours/ emergencies: 220-3127

United States Consulate: Pavas; 220-3050

HEALTH CARE

According to a 2000 United Nations study, Costa Rica holds first place in Latin America for development of preventive and curative medicine. It is ranked ahead of the United States among the 40 best health systems in the world. Many Costa Rican doctors have been trained in Europe and the United States, and the University of Costa Rica Medical School is considered one of the best in Latin America. A full seven percent of visitors to Costa Rica come here specifically for medical or alternative treatments. See "Health Vacations" at the end of Chapter Three.

If you are involved in an accident, you will probably be taken to a hospital or clinic that is part of Costa Rica's nationalized health care system. You will probably be treated for free.

The following private hospitals also have emergency medical, x-ray, laboratory, and pharmacy services available to foreigners: **Clínica Bíblica** (Avenida 14, Calles Central/1; 257-5252, emergencies: 257-0466), **Clínica Católica** (Guadalupe; 283-6616), **Clínica Santa Rita** (specializes in maternity care; Avenida 8, Calles 15/17; 221-6433). The new $40-million **Hospital CIMA San José** (208-1000), located on the highway to the western Central Valley town of Santa Ana, is more like a five-star hotel than a hospital. Its "suites" have separate living rooms with TV and minibar. It enjoys an interhospital agreement with Baylor Medical University in Dallas that allows its doctors to go there for training, and has the latest CAT scan equipment as well as neonatal and trauma units.

Many dentists are fluent in English. Services, such as crowns, fillings, and root canals, cost about half of what they would in the United States. Ask the United States Consulate or foreign residents for recommendations.

We've heard several glowing reports about **Villa Alegría Nursing Home** (393-2804, 433-8590; e-mail: info@costaricanursinghomes.com), formerly Golden Valley Hacienda. For a fraction of the price of its northern counterparts, Villa Alegría provides a warm, loving environment for its residents, as well as excellent health care. It is located one kilometer west of the church in Alajuela's Barrio San José.

TIPPING

A 10 percent service charge and a 13 percent tax are included in your restaurant bill, so it's not customary to tip unless you really feel like it. It is not customary to tip taxi drivers either. A nice thing about Costa Rica is that people aren't always standing around with their hands out—partly because of a tradition of equality and pride. We hope that these qualities survive the influx of massive tourism. You should tip airport porters about 500 *colones* (or $1) per bag. You would be surprised to know how little the staff at most hotels, including luxury hotels, earns (usually less than $200/month), so a little gratuity here and there for the maids who clean your room is certainly helpful. Some hotels leave envelopes in the rooms for this purpose.

Many times when you park your car a man will appear, point to his eyes, and point to your car. That means he will watch your car for you, and it's worth it, for the 200-300 *colones* you will give him when you return (more at night or for long periods of time). Even though it might appear that he is hired by the restaurant, nightclub, or other facility he is in front of, he is probably only working for tips.

When you pay with a credit card at restaurants, the waiter will often leave the "tip" and "total" spaces blank, even though a 10 percent gratuity has already been included. *Beware:* Unless the "total" space is filled in by the customer, any amount could be written in later.

One place where tips are not appropriate is at community-based eco-tourism lodgings, where staff and owners are the same.

BUSINESS HOURS

Costa Ricans tend to start the day early. You'll find that stores are generally open from 8 or 9 a.m. until 6 or 7 p.m., six days a week (most businesses are closed Sunday). Core banking hours are 9 a.m. to 3 p.m.; government offices are open from 8 a.m. to 4 or 5 p.m.

THE METRIC SYSTEM

Whether you're getting gas, checking the thermometer, or looking at road signs, you'll notice the difference: everything is metric. Costa Rica is on the metric system, which measures temperature in degrees Celsius, distances in meters, and most substances in liters, kilos, and grams.

To convert from Celsius to Fahrenheit, multiply times 9, divide by 5 and add 32. For example, 23°C equals [(23 x 9)/5] + 32, or (207/5) + 32, or 41.4 + 32, or about 73°F. If you don't have a pocket calculator along (but you probably should), just remember that 0°C is 32°F and that each Celsius degree is roughly two Fahrenheit degrees. Here are some other useful conversion equations:

- 1 mile = 1.6 kilometers. 1 kilometer = 3/5 mile
- 1 foot = 0.3 meter. 1 meter = 3 1/3 feet
- 1 pound *(libra)* = 0.45 kilo. 1 kilo = 2 1/5 pounds
- 1 gallon = 3.8 liters. 1 liter = about 1/4 gallon, or about one quart

TIME ZONE

All of Costa Rica is on Central Standard Time, which is six hours behind Greenwich Mean Time. During daylight saving time in the U.S. (early April to late October) Costa Rica is on Mountain Standard Time.

COMMUNICATIONS

While Costa Rica boasts more phones per capita than any other Latin American country, patience and perseverance are still key when dealing with the communications bureaucracies.

COUNTRY CODES

Throughout the text, Costa Rica phone numbers are listed without the country code, which is 506. Other country codes you may need are 505 for Nicaragua and 507 for Panama. To dial Costa Rica from North America, dial 011, then 506 and the number.

TELEPHONES

Most public phones now require that you use a "Servicio 197" telephone card. You can usually buy them for 500, 1000, or 3000 *colones* at a store located near the public phone. Ask for *tarjetas telefónicas*. You can also buy them at the airport when you arrive. They are handy to have in an emergency.

If you can't find a number in the directory, try dialing 113, the directory assistance line.

If your hotel room has a telephone, you can usually use it to call out on; charges will be billed to you when you leave, unless you have made the calls on a 197 or 199 card (see below). Some hotels offer free local calls.

Some car-rental agencies, like Dollar, Solid, and Economy, give free or discounted cell phones with their rentals ($.75/minute within Costa Rica, $2-$3 international). Because of Costa Rica's mountainous terrain, however, only 75 percent of the country has coverage.

INTERNATIONAL CALLS

Calling cards with 800 numbers don't work in Costa Rica. Keep in mind that the calling cards you use at home have very expensive rates when calling from Costa Rica. You can purchase a "Servicio 199" calling card for $10 or $20 at ICE that will allow you to make international calls from any touch-tone phone at the normal rates. You key in the number on the card, dial your number, and the amount of your call is deducted from the value of the card. International call rates are cheaper evenings and weekends. The exact times are found in any telephone directory. You can also buy "Servicio 197" calling cards, which allow you to make calls within Costa Rica from private or public phones. You can call home also on these cheaper 197 cards and ask friends and family to call you back.

If you have access to a private phone, direct dialing is easy from Costa Rica. The telephone directory has a list of codes for various countries. To dial the U.S. or Canada direct, for example, dial 001 first, then the area code and number.

To call person-to-person or collect, dial 175 and an operator will then come on the line. For international information, dial 124.

If you don't have access to a phone in San José, go to **Radiográfica** (open daily, 7:30 a.m. to 9 p.m.; Calle 1, Avenida 5).

FAX AND E-MAIL SERVICES

If your hotel lists a fax or e-mail number, they will usually accept a fax or e-mail for you. Many hotels make a point of offering free e-mail access to guests. Internet cafés are listed with the restaurants in the San José chapter and are found in tourist areas throughout the country.

MAIL

Mail letters from a post office. There are hardly any mailboxes on the streets, and they are seldom used. Provincial post offices are open weekdays 8 a.m. to 5:30 p.m., and Saturdays 8 a.m. to noon. Your hotel will mail postcards and letters for you.

Beware of having anything other than letters and magazines sent to you in Costa Rica. A high duty is charged on all items arriving by mail in an attempt to keep foreign merchandise from entering illegally. Receiving packages can mean two trips to the *Aduana* (customs office) in Zapote, a suburb of San José. The first trip is to unwrap and declare what you have received. The second one, that day or the following day, is to pay a customs charge on every item in the package before you can take it home. If the package contains food, medicine, or cosmetics, it must be examined by the Ministry of Health—a process that takes even longer. Usually anything that fits in a regular-sized or magazine-sized envelope will arrive duty-free.

There is a general delivery service (*Lista de Correos*). If you are planning to stay in Costa Rica for a while, you can rent a post office box (*apartado—Apdo.* for short), or have your mail sent to a friend's box, which is safer than having it sent to a street address. Many people are turning to private mail services. You can sign up with **Interlink** (296-4980, fax: 232-3979; www.interlink.co.cr, e-mail: sales@interlink.co.cr), which, for $15/month, gives you a post office box in Miami from which mail is delivered to you twice a week in Costa Rica. **Aerocasillas** (208-4848, fax: 257-1187; www.aerocasillas.com, e-mail: aerosjo@racsa.co.cr), a similar service, allows you to send or receive one and a half kilos of mail per month. **Mail Boxes Etc** (232-2950, fax: 231-7325; e-mail: mbeetc@racsa.co.cr) has a branch in Pavas, 300 meters east of the U.S. Embassy, with similar services, plus internet access, copying, printing and binding, office supplies, etc.

Courier services DHL (210-3838), UPS (290-2828), TNT (233-4993), and JETEX (293-0505) are all available in Costa Rica.

LAUNDRY

Many hotels have laundry services. Most cheaper hotels have large sinks (*pilas*) where you can wash your own clothes, or they can connect you with a person who will wash them for you for about $1 an hour. Beware of hotel laundry services that charge by the piece. We once spent over $10 on one load of laundry. Most provincial hotels will do your laundry for $5/load.

"TIQUISMOS"—
HAVING FUN WITH COSTA RICAN SPANISH

Ticos are amused and delighted when foreigners try to speak Spanish, especially when they include *tiquismos*, expressions that are peculiar to Costa Rican or Central American culture.

Not only the vocabulary, but the way you use words, is important. Spanish speakers use a lot of *muletillas* (fillers, literally "crutches") in their speech. They directly address the person with whom they are speaking more often than is done in English, and they do it in a way that English speakers might consider slightly offensive. It is common for women to be called *mamita*, *madre*, *mi hijita* (little mother, mother, my little daughter—all roughly corresponding to "honey"). Latins love to use salient physical characteristics as nicknames. Common ones are *gordo* (fatty), *flaco* (skinny), *macho* (Costa Rican for fair-skinned or fair-haired), *negro* (dark-skinned), *chino* (it doesn't matter if you're Asian or just have slightly slanting eyes, your name is Chino), *gato* (blue or green eyes). You need only be slightly *gordo* or *flaco* to merit those names. If you're really *gordo* or *flaco*, and people really like you, you get a special name like *repollito* (little cabbage) or *palito* (little stick). *Gordo* and *negro* are commonly used as terms of endearment, regardless of appearance. The feminine of all the above nicknames ends in -a instead of -o.

Younger Ticos and Ticas are usually called *maje* (pronounced "my") by their friends. This literally means "dummy," but figuratively is more like pal or buddy. It is used widely as a *muletilla*. *Majes* have various expressions of approval—such as the famous *pura vida* (great, terrific), *tuanis* (cool), and *buena nota* (groovy). *Mala nota* is ungroovy, *furris* is uncool, and *salado* means "too bad for you." Expressions of extreme approval are *qué bruto*, *qué bárbaro*, and disapproval, *qué horror*, or *fatal*, *maje*.

The above expressions are the slang of urban youth. However, all Ticos are aware of polite, courteous, and respectful forms of speech. They make their world more pleasant by using little expressions of appreciation. For example, if someone helps you in a store or on the street, you say, *"Muchas gracias, muy amable"* ("Thank you very much, you are very kind"), and they will say, *"Con mucho gusto"* ("With much pleasure").

It is customary in the morning to ask, *"¿Cómo amaneció?"* ("How did you wake up?") *"Muy bien, por dicha, ¿y usted?"* ("Very well, luckily, and you?") *"Muy bien, gracias a Dios."* ("Very well, thank God.")

When talking about a future event or plan, Ticos will often include *si Dios quiere* ("if God wants" or "God willing"): *"Nos vemos el martes, si Dios quiere."* ("We'll see each other Tuesday, God willing.")

If you are in the city and see someone on the other side of the street whom you know, you call, *"¡Adiós!"* In the countryside, when you pass someone on the road, it is customary to say *adiós* even if you don't know them. In these situations, *adiós* means hello. It is only used to mean good-bye when you're going away for good. Everyday good-byes are *hasta luego* (until then, until later), and the other person might add, *"Que Dios le acompañe."* ("May God accompany you.")

Giving a coin to a beggar in the street often earns you a special blessing: he or she will say, *"Dios se lo pague."* ("May God repay you.")

Although "now" and "in a little while" have very different meanings in English, here they can be expressed with the same word: *ahora*. Perhaps this is the linguistic root of the *mañana* attitude that so frustrates gringos. If you want to express the idea of "right away," you can emphatically use the word *¡ya!* keeping in mind that *ya* can also be used to mean already, later, and soon. Eskimos have 26 different words for snow. Latin Americans have the same words for many different time concepts, perhaps because time is not of such vital importance to their existence. It's what people love and hate about the tropics. Keep that in mind when dealing with the bureaucracy, or when deciding whether or not you have enough time to buy a cold drink when you've been told the bus is coming *ahorititica*.

Vos is a form of second-person-singular address used throughout Central America instead of *tú*. The verb form used with *vos* is made by changing the *r* on the end of an infinitive to *s* and accenting the last syllable. Thus with the verb *poder*, *"tú puedes"* becomes *"vos podés,"* and with *sentirse*, *"tú te sientes"* becomes *"vos te sentís."* Much to the consternation of their Spanish and South American friends, more and more Ticos use the formal *usted* for everyone, probably because it's easier and safer.

Other common Spanish fillers are terms like *fíjate*, *imagínate*, and *vieras que*, for which there are no real equivalents in English. Roughly, they could be translated as "would you believe" or "just think!" These expressions are used to give emphasis to what the speaker is saying. For example: *"¡Fíjate vos que no me dejaron entrar!"* ("Would you believe it—they wouldn't let me in!") Or you might say, *"Imagínese cómo me dió pena verla así."* ("Imagine how bad I felt to see her like that.")

Vieras is often used the same way we use "sure" in English: *"¡Vieras qué susto me dió!"* ("I sure was scared!" or, "You should have seen how it scared me!")

Achará is another particularly Tico expression and indicates regret at a loss: *"Fíjese que el perro comió mis begonias. Achará mis florecitas."* ("Would you believe it—the dog ate my begonias. My poor little flowers!")

When you come to someone's house, especially in the country, it is customary to stand on the ground near the porch and say *"¡Upe!"* as a way of letting them know you're there. When they ask you to come in, as you enter the house you say, *"Con permiso."* ("With your permission.") If they offer you something to eat, it is polite to accept. Giving makes people happy; if you don't let them give to you, it hurts their feelings. People will ask you about your family, whether you're married, how many children you have. Most can't quite grasp the idea of people not being married or not having children. When you're sitting and talking and finally no one can think of anything else to say, you say, *"Pues, sí."* ("Well, yes.")

Learn some of these expressions and practice them until you don't make any *metidas de pata* (literally, "putting your foot in it," or mistakes). Ticos will be glad to help you. If you do make a mistake, there is a word that is instant absolution: just say, *"¿Diay?"* It means, "Well, what can you expect?" or "What can be done about it?" As you get to know the Ticos, you'll find that this little word comes in very handy.

FRUITS AND VEGETABLES

Costa Rica produces an amazing abundance of fruits and vegetables. To get an idea of their beauty and variety, go to any of the Saturday- or Sunday-morning neighborhood *ferias del agricultor,* where streets are closed to automobiles while farmers sell their fresh produce. Bring your own shopping bags. Many suburbs of San José also have weekend street markets—Escazú, Guadalupe, Tres Ríos, and Zapote, to name a few.

Here are some tips on how to identify and choose the best produce:

A ripe **papaya** will always be slightly soft, but still firm. A too-soft papaya should be avoided. To find the perfect papaya, shoppers will surreptitiously stick their thumbnail into the skin to see if it is thin enough to be easily pierced. That also lets them see if the color is of an intensity that indicates ripeness. It is customary for papaya vendors to cut a triangular piece out of the papaya to show you its color. Some people are fans of the rounder *amarilla* or yellow-orange papaya. Others will swear that only the more elongated, red-orange *cacho* papaya is worthy of the name. You don't have to buy a papaya just because the vendor cut a piece out of it for you— at least Ticos don't.

Mangos should be slightly soft but still very firm, and red and yellow in color, although it's okay for part of them to be green. Reject any that have mushy spots. By far the most delicious are the large *mangas,* given feminine gender because of their voluptuous size. The neatest way to eat *mangas* is to slice them close around the flat oval seed to get two meaty halves. With the skin side down, score each piece into one-inch divisions without cutting through the skin (use a butter knife for this part). Now gently turn each half inside out, and you will have a bunch of delicious bite-sized pieces offering themselves to you. Ticos also love to eat green mangos sliced and sprinkled with lemon and salt. (Some people get a rash or irritation around their lips from eating mangos. This can be avoided by cutting off the part of the fruit nearest the stem, as the irritation is caused by the sap.)

Ticos judge the ripeness of a **piña** (pineapple) by giving it a slap. A good *piña* should sound firm and compact. The yellow pineapple is best for eating. The white pineapple is more acidic and is used in cooking and to tenderize meats. It produces a hollow sound when thumped. A green color on the outside does not necessarily mean the fruit is unripe. You should be able to pluck a leaf easily from the top of a ripe *piña.*

Sandías (watermelons) are considered sweeter if they produce a firm rather than a hollow sound. The best watermelons come from the hot coastal zones. One of the nicest parts of driving to the Pacific Coast is stopping at a fruit stand in Esparza or Orotina for a delicious *sandía.*

Don't make the mistake of a friend of ours who, on a hot San José afternoon, came home with what he thought was a delicious, red, juicy watermelon. "And what a bargain!" he said as he thirstily cut into the **chiverre**, only to find a mass of whitish spaghetti-like pulp. *Chiverre* (spaghetti squash)

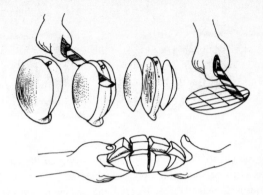

looks just like a watermelon from the outside. You'll see it sold on the roadsides during Semana Santa. Its pulp is candied with *tapa dulce* to make special Easter treats.

Melón (cantaloupe) is judged for sweetness by its firm sound, but a fragrant smell is the best indication of a fully ripe *melón*.

Moras (blackberries) are used in *refrescos* and ice cream. You have to liquefy *moras* in a blender, strain, and add sugar and water to the sour juice.

Four types of **limones ácidos** (sour lemons) grow here. The seedless *verdelio* is rare. The *criollo* is small, juicy, and greener. The *bencino* is more the size of a North American lemon but is green and has much less juice than the criollo. The *limón mandarina* looks like a bumpy tangerine, and is very sour and juicy; it's good for making lemonade. The **limón dulce** (sweet lemon) has a mild, slightly sweet flavor, and is said to be an appetite stimulant and general cure-all.

Guayabas (guavas) are plentiful in Costa Rica from September through November. Their pink fruit is used for jam or guava paste.

Similar to the *guayaba*, **cas** is a little round fruit whose tart tropical flavor is popular in *refrescos* and sherbets. Try the *nieve de cas* at Pop's, a local ice cream chain.

Tamarindo is a tart and sweet *refresco* made from the seed pod of the tamarind tree. You will see the orange-sized balls of brown tamarindo seeds and pulp at the markets. The seeds are put in hot water so the sticky tamarindo dissolves. Then sugar and cold water are added. The resulting light-brown *refresco* is somewhat similar in flavor to apple juice. Add grated ginger and lemon juice for a fine alcohol-free cocktail.

Granadillas (passion fruit) are yellowish-red and slightly larger than an egg. They have a crisp but easily broken shell. Inside are little edible seeds surrounded by a delicious, delicately flavored fruit, which is first slurped and then chewed. **Maracuyá** is a larger, yellower cousin of the

Pejibayes

granadilla, too tart to slurp, but delicious in a *refresco*. Its taste has been described as a mix between pineapple and tangerine.

Marañón is an unusual fruit. Its seed, the cashew nut, grows on top of it in a thick, rubbery shell. Don't try to bite open the shell; it's very bitter. Cashews must be roasted before they can be eaten; they are poisonous when raw. The ripe fruit can be eaten or made into a *refresco* or fermented into wine. The dried fruit is like a cross between a prune and a fig and is sold in supermarkets. You can make a quick and elegant dessert with half a dried *marañón* topped with a dollop of cream cheese and a cashew.

When you travel to Limón, you'll see several highway stands near Siquirres selling large, green, bumpy **guanábanas**. Inside these football-sized fruits, you'll find a sensuous surprise. Some spoon out the fibrous white flesh and eat it as is, but most people prefer it in *refrescos, en leche*, or *en agua*. Its English name, significantly less melodious, is soursop.

Avocados are called **aguacates**. They are usually a little less buttery and flavorful than their North American counterparts. They are soft when ripe, but if bought green can be left inside a paper bag to ripen.

Zapotes look like big brown avocados, and their texture is avocado-like, but their pulp is bright red-orange and sweet. Some places make *zapote* ice cream.

Fresh **coco** (coconut meat) can be found at fruit stands downtown. **Pipas** or green coconuts are popular with Ticos on hot days at the beach. They are sold whole, with a straw stuck through a hole in the outer shell so that the coconut water can be drunk.

The best way to get coconut meat out of its shell is to hack it open with a machete or a hammer, then heat the shells on the stove in a pan. This makes the meat shrink a little so it's easier to remove.

Pejibaye, a relative of the coconut, is one of Costa Rica's most unusual treats. *Pejibayes* grow in clusters on palm trees, like miniature coconuts. The part that you eat corresponds to the fibrous husk, while the hard *pejibaye* seed, when cracked open, reveals a thin layer of bitter white meat around a hollow core. The bright orange or red *pejibayes* are delicious boiled in salted water, then peeled, halved, and pitted and eaten alone or with mayonnaise. You'll see them sold on San José streets year-round. Their flavor is difficult to describe. They are not sweet, but more a combination of chestnut and pumpkin with a thick, fibrous texture. You can buy a *racimo* (bunch) of raw *pejibayes* at the Mercado Borbón and boil them up for parties, or you can buy them peeled and canned in the supermarkets to take home as souvenirs.

Palmito (palm heart) is another delicacy worth trying. It is sold raw at the *ferias* or tenderly pickled in jars or bags in the supermarkets. It is the succulent inner core of small palm trees. Even though whole trees must be cut so that you can savor *palmito*, the trees are cultivated as a crop, so are replaced.

As human nature would have it, the most highly prized fruits in Costa Rica are imported apples, grapes, and pears. They signify the advent of the Christmas season, and Ticos pay dearly for them. Recently though, highland Ticos have started to grow a good, sweet-tart variety of apple. You also might enjoy the native **manzana de agua**, a dark-red, pear-shaped fruit that is light and refreshing.

Mamones are little green spheres, which you can break open with your fingers or teeth to expose a large seed covered with a layer of fruit that tastes like a peeled grape. Be careful when small children eat *mamones* or *mamones chinos*. Because of their size and shape they can get stuck in their throats.

Mamón chino is the *mamón*'s exotic cousin, sporting a red shell with soft spines growing all over it. It resembles a fat, round, red caterpillar and has a larger grapelike fruit inside its outrageous shell.

When you slice a yellow **carambola**, the pieces look like five-pointed stars. It makes a delicious *refresco*.

Mamón chino and carambola

COMIDA TÍPICA (NATIVE FOOD)

Those who expect to find spicy food anywhere south of the border will be disappointed in Costa Rican cuisine. It is not spicy, but it is tasty. Except for being a little heavy-handed with the grease, Ticos have a wholesome high-fiber diet, with rice and beans included in every menu. Lunch is the big meal of the day, and many businesses still give two hours off at lunchtime so that people can take the bus back to mama's for a substantial *casado*. People often content themselves with soup and toast in the evening. Those who stay in Costa Rica develop a certain affection for the noble bean, and a good *gallo pinto* is a real delight. Ticos who want to spice up their food usually have a jar of tiny pickled red and yellow chilies on the table. Be wary of these: They are pure fire!

Sodas are small restaurants where you can get inexpensive snacks and light meals. They line San José's streets and fill the Mercado Central. Following are some of the foods you'll run across at *sodas* countrywide.

   arreglados—sandwiches, usually made of meat, on a tasty but greasy bun

   arroz con pollo—rice with chicken and vegetables

   cajeta de coco—delicious fudge made of coconut, *tapa dulce*, and orange peel

   casado—a plate of rice, black beans, cabbage and tomato salad, meat or egg, *picadillo*, and sometimes fried plantains

   ceviche—raw seabass cured in lemon juice with *culantro* (Chinese parsley) and onions—delicious

   chicharrones—pork rinds fried crisp and dripping with grease, sometimes with wiry hairs still sticking out

   chorreadas—corn pancakes, sometimes served with *natilla*

   cono capuchino—an ice cream cone dipped in chocolate

   dulce de leche—a thick syrup made of milk and sugar

   elote asado—roasted corn on the cob

   elote cocinado—boiled corn on the cob

   empanadas—corn turnovers filled with beans, cheese, or potatoes and meat

   gallo pinto—the national breakfast dish of rice and beans fried together

   gallos—meat, beans, or cheese between two tortillas

   guiso de maíz—fresh corn stew

   horchata—a sweet drink made of roasted ground rice and cinnamon

   masamorra—corn pudding

   melcochas—candies made from raw sugar

milanes and tapitas—small, foil-wrapped, pure chocolate candies, available in corner stores and restaurants all over the country. Beware: these delicious little things are addictive

natilla—sour cream, often more liquid than North American sour cream

olla de carne—literally "pot of meat," but actually a meat soup featuring large pieces of *chayote* (a green, pear-shaped vegetable that grows on vines), *ayote* (a pumpkin-like squash), *elote*, *yuca*, *plátano*, and other vegetables

palomitas de maíz—"little doves," or popcorn

pan bon—a dark, sweet bread with batter designs on top—a Limón specialty

pan de maíz—a thick, sweet bread made with fresh corn

patacones—fried, mashed green plantains, served like french fries with meals on the Atlantic Coast

patí—flour-based *empanadas* filled with fruit or spicy meat, sold on the Atlantic Coast

picadillo—a side dish of sautéed vegetables, often containing meat

plátanos—plantains. They look like large bananas, but cannot be eaten raw. Sweet and delicious when fried or baked. Also sold in a form similar to potato chips. A Central American staple

queque seco—pound cake

refrescos—cold fruit drinks. Most *refrescos* are made with a lot of sugar. If you order a *refresco* that is not made in advance, like *papaya en agua, papaya en leche*, or *jugo de zanahoria* (carrot juice), you can ask for it *sin azúcar* (without sugar) and add your own to taste. Similarly, an *ensalada de frutas* (fruit salad) might come smothered in Jello and ice cream. You can ask for it *sin gelatina, sin helados*

sopa de mondongo—tripe soup

sopa negra—soup made from bean gravy, with hard-boiled egg and vegetables added

tacos—a bit of meat topped with cabbage salad in a tortilla

tamal asado—a sweet cornmeal cake

tamal de elote—sweet corn tamales, wrapped in cornhusks

tamales—cornmeal, usually stuffed with pork or chicken, wrapped in banana leaves and boiled—a Christmas tradition

tapa de dulce—native brown sugar, sold in a solid form that looks like an inverted flower pot. It's grated with a knife or boiled into a syrup from which is made *agua dulce*, a popular campesino drink

torta chilena—a many-layered pastry filled with *dulce de leche*

tortas—sandwiches on bread rolls

tortilla—may mean the Costa Rican thin, small, corn tortilla, but also another name for an omelette

tortilla de queso—a large, thick tortilla with cheese mixed into the dough

yuca—manioc, a thick tuber, another staple of the Central American diet. *Enyucados* are *empanadas* made from a yuca-based dough

SOUVENIRS

You can fill your entire list with inexpensive souvenirs that benefit local conservation and humanitarian efforts, making your gifts meaningful conversation items. **ANAI** (224-3570) makes beautiful necklaces, earrings and belt buckles out of leatherback turtle shells that they find on the beach. The $5-$15 you pay goes directly to supporting their turtle protection projects in the Gandoca–Manzanillo Wildlife Refuge on the Caribbean coast. The **Damas Voluntarias** (228-0279) makes calendars and note cards featuring local artwork. Proceeds support needy children. The **Humanitarian Foundation** (249-1516) sells journals and traditional bows and arrows and other crafts from the Cabécar indigenous community. The **Sarapiqui Conservation Learning Center** (766-6482) offers a bilingual cookbook of Costa Rican dishes to support its after-school education programs.

Tiny *huacas*, copies of pre-Columbian jewelry representing frogs, lizards, turtles, and humanesque deities, are relatively inexpensive and make lovely necklaces, earrings, and tiepins. Authentic pre-Columbian artifacts cannot be taken out of the country, so don't believe anyone who tells you something is original. If it is original, the item has been stolen from an archaeological site.

The creative, bilingual coloring and activity book, *Let's Discover Costa Rica*, is the answer for the kids on your souvenir list. It is sold almost everywhere, or you can order it from A. Gingold, Apdo. 1-6100 Mora, Ciudad Colón, CR; fax: 249-1107; e-mail: agingold@racsa.co.cr.

David Norman's inexpensive Costa Rican **wildlife coloring books** are also good for kidshopping. Intelligently written, they tell about some of the animals you might encounter on a trip to Costa Rica. The drawings are so accurate that they can be used as guides to the animals. Look for the coloring books in gift shops or visit www.amerisol.com/costarica/shop/kids.html.

If you're staying for a while, avail yourself of the low prices and excellent work of local tailors and seamstresses. They make fine formal clothes, or can copy your favorite designs. The best way to find one is to ask well-dressed Ticos whom they would recommend.

You can buy freshly ground **coffee** or coffee beans at the Central Market, or at the airport in souvenir shops. It is usually ground fine for use in the *chorreador*, a filter bag that hangs from a wooden stand. Cafe Britt (800-462-7488; www.cafebritt.com) offers several gift packages featuring coffee, macadamia nuts, and chocolate-covered coffee beans, or an espresso-lover's kit including a grinder. Percolator grinds are available in supermarkets, where you'll find *Caferica*, a coffee liqueur, as well as dried bananas, coconut twirls, macadamia nuts, cashews, yummy Angel jams, fruit leathers, and pastes. *Tapa de dulce*, the native hard brown sugar, can be grated to add a rich flavor to baked goods or used on cereal and in coffee. We've heard of tourists who take home cases of **Salsa Lizano**, a tasty bottled sauce that Ticos love to sprinkle on their *gallo pinto*.

Souvenir shops all over the country carry souvenirs made from renewable resources by rural artisans. These include seed jewelry, carvings and boxes of plantation-grown wood, pencils made from coffee branches, and recycled paper notebooks and stationery.

The capital of Costa Rican **woodcraft** is Sarchí, about an hour northwest of San José (see the Central Valley chapter). Everything from salad bowls to rocking chairs to miniature ox carts (the rocking chairs fold, and the ox carts come apart for easy transport) can be purchased there. **Artesanía Napoleon** (454-4118), across from Fábrica de Carretas Joaquín Chaverri, will take care of mailing your purchases home for you. The capital of Costa Rican **leathercrafts** is Moravia, a suburb of San José, where there are a couple of blocks filled with souvenir shops near the main square. **Artesanía la Rueda** (235-8357), 100 meters south and 100 meters east of the Municipalidad in Moravia, will mail all your gifts for you.

If you are going to Monteverde, save some of your souvenir budget for **CASEM**, the women's crafts cooperative there, which specializes in embroidered and hand-painted clothing depicting cloud-forest wildlife. You'll see it on the right as you enter Monteverde.

Wicker, raffia, and woven palm-leaf items should be spray varnished when you get home. Don't be tempted to buy tortoise-shell or alligator-skin goods—they are made from endangered animals that are internationally protected. Customs officials at your home-country airport will confiscate those items.

See the "Souvenirs" section in the San José chapter for more on where to shop in the capital.

FIVE

The Outdoors

Costa Rica is an outdoor adventurer's paradise. From volcanoes and cloud forests to pristine beaches, this tropical wonder boasts breathtaking beauty. You'll find every imaginable activity—from birdwatching to bungee jumping. This is definitely the place to come to take that walk on the "wild side."

NATIONAL PARKS, RESERVES, AND WILDLIFE REFUGES

Costa Rica's 58 national parks, reserves, and wildlife refuges occupy approximately 12.5 percent of national territory and protect jewels of the country's rich but diminishing wilderness. The whole country is organized into ten mosaic-like "Conservation Areas." Each of these has as its nucleus one or more totally protected national parks or absolute reserves. These are buffered by forest reserves and "protected zones" where sustainable land use is supposed to take place. In these buffer zones, reforestation, forest management, ecotourism, and private conservation projects are promoted, bringing protected areas to 28 percent of Costa Rica's territory.

In some areas surrounding the national parks there are private reserves. Visitors to these wild areas can stay at small private lodges and tour the privately held land, seeing flora and fauna similar to that in the national parks; their money helps preserve these important buffer zones.

For information about national parks and reserves, call the National System of Conservation Areas (SINAC). For the English/Spanish phone line: dial 192 (7 a.m. to 7 p.m. daily) or 283-8004 ext. 110 and tell them which park you want to visit. They give information about camping facilities, availability of meals, nearby lodging, and transportation. Both telephone numbers can be used from outside Costa Rica by dialing 011 and the country code 506 first. Foreign visitors to the national parks pay $6 to $10 per person per day, children ages 6 to 12 pay $1.

All national parks, reserves, and refuges are indicated on the fold-out map at the back of this book. We describe each park, reserve, and refuge in our chapters on the various regions.

For specialized information on biodiversity in the protected areas, contact the Instituto Nacional de Biodiversidad (INBio, 507-8100; www.inbio.ac.cr), located in Santo Domingo de Heredia, 15 minutes northwest of San José.

INBioparque (open daily, 7:30 a.m. to 4 p.m.; 507-8000; www.inbioparque.org, e-mail: inbioparque@inbio.ac.cr; entrance fee $15, children under 12 $9, students $12) provides a thorough introduction to Costa Rica's national parks for first-time visitors, and showcases the work of INBio and its parataxonomists, who are trying to identify all the plant, insect, and animal species in Costa Rica. Along the paved, wheelchair-accessible trails, you can see examples of several native ecosystems, plus gardens of ornamental, medicinal, and aromatic plants and fruit trees, as well as exhibits of frogs, tarantulas, bees, ants, orchids, and butterflies. Guided tours last from two and a half to four hours, depending on visitors' interests and needs. A delicious typical breakfast or lunch can be enjoyed in their attractive cafeteria for $6 to $10. Their souvenir shop is full of nature-based books, CDs, and gifts. Family rates and transportation from San José are also available. It is located in Santo Domingo de Heredia, 400 meters north and 250 meters west of the Shell station.

HIKING

Although Costa Rica has been described as a Disneyland of ecological wonders, you must be aware that here you are dealing with Mother Nature in all her harsh reality. Every year several overconfident hikers get lost in Costa Rica's dense forests. For example, hikers were lost in unseasonal fog and rain for 11 days on Barva Volcano on the west side of Braulio Carrillo National Park. Their goal was a simple day hike around the crater lake, but landslides blocking the trails threw them off course. Two hikers became lost and died in the mountains of Talamanca in 1999, and in 2000 a Canadian hiker ignored signs telling him to keep on the trail and ended up sliding into the crater of Volcán Rincón de La Vieja, where he was stranded for four days with only a water bottle and a camera. Luckily, the volcano was in an inactive phase, and he was rescued. Costa Rica's famous parks are victims of the country's budget deficit, and trails are not maintained with the same rigor foreigners are used to. Tropical weather itself makes trail maintenance a full-time job.

The Red Cross gives the following recommendations for solo hikers:

- prepare for the worst
- tell someone where you're going and when you'll be back
- wear boots and layer your clothing
- carry a canteen, knife, flashlight with extra batteries, candy, dried fruit or granola bars, a compass, a map, a poncho or plastic in case you need to make a shelter, a first-aid kit, matches, a small piece of rubber and a candle (for lighting fires), and if possible a light sleeping bag
- pack everything in plastic bags
- don't touch anything without looking
- bring medications
- if you get lost, stay calm and work with other people in your group as a team

Always stay on the trail when hiking in mountainous areas. The hikers who have gotten lost for several days—and survived—have done so by drinking river water, eating palmito (the edible core of certain palm trees), and hunting wild animals. Rescuers recommend building a primitive shelter and tying a brightly colored cloth to it if you think anyone will come looking for you. If no one knows you are lost, following a river downstream is probably the best way to reach civilization.

CAMPING

Don't expect to find many well-organized campgrounds in Costa Rica. It's possible to camp in many places, but you often have to carry in your own water or make arrangements with local people to use their facilities. Most parks have camping facilities; most refuges and reserves don't. Detailed information can be obtained by calling the park information number, 192. The best source for current weather and road conditions, they will also take reservations if required. The main problems with camping are rain (it's better to come during the dry season if you plan to camp) and not being able to leave things in your tent unless there is someone around to watch it.

A good place to buy camping equipment in San José is **La Tienda de Camping** (Avenida 8, Calles 11/13; 221-9070). They sell Swiss Army knives, compasses, binoculars, first-aid kits, and battery-powered lanterns.

BEACHES

The Ecological Blue Flag program (Bandera Azul Ecológica) is an incentive for local communities to keep their beaches and rivers uncontaminated and clean. The 56 communities that earned the coveted Blue Flag in 2004 scored at least 90 percent on a test that covers microbiological purity of ocean water, safety of drinking water, beach cleanliness, garbage disposal, environmental education, and security. Beaches that score 100 percent and receive an AA rating have signage indicating areas with dangerous currents and have lifeguards during the high season. The AAA rating is reserved for those beaches that fill all the above requirements, have zoning plans, are accessible to disabled people, and have public bathrooms and showers. Only one beach, Playa Blanca at Punta Leona, gained this distinction.

Communities that depend on rivers for tourism can also win the Blue Flag if they pass tests on drinking water quality, waste disposal, signage, environmental education, availability of health care, water protection, and security.

Fifteen beaches within the National System of Conservation Areas were also awarded the Blue Flag in 2004. Among them were Manuel Antonio, Cahuita, Ballena Marine Park, Gandoca, Playa Grande, Barú, and Ostional. You can find a current list of Blue Flag beaches at our website, www.keyto costarica.com/blue-flag-beaches.htm.

BEACH SAFETY

Each year, hundreds of ocean bathers suffer serious near-drownings or death due to their ignorance about rip currents, a phenomenon found on wave-swept beaches all over the world—including Costa Rica. Ironically, these currents can be fun if properly understood—yet they are responsible for 80 percent of ocean drownings, or four out of every five.

What is a rip current? A rip current is a surplus of water, put ashore by waves, that finds a channel to drain and reach equilibrium. All rip currents have three parts: the feeder current, the neck, and the head. The feeder current is made up of water moving parallel to the beach. You know you're in one when, after a few minutes, you notice that your friends on the beach have moved down 30 to 50 yards, yet you thought you were standing still.

At a depression in the ocean floor, the current turns out to sea. This can occur in knee- to waist-deep water, and is where the "neck" begins. The current in the neck is very swift, like a river. It can carry a swimmer out to sea at three to six miles per hour, faster than a strong swimmer's rate of two to four miles per hour, and can move a person 100 yards in just a moment.

It's typical for an inexperienced swimmer to panic when caught in the neck, and it is here that most drownings occur.

What to do if you get caught in a rip current: If you're a weak swimmer, you should call for help as soon as you notice a current is moving you and making it difficult to get in toward land. Most drowning victims are caught in water just above waist level.

If you realize that you can't walk directly in, you should turn and walk sideways, leaping toward the beach with every wave, to let the water "push" you toward shore.

A crashing surf can throw you off balance, so it's dangerous to turn your back to it. Once off balance, a swimmer is unable to get traction on the ocean floor and can be dragged out five feet into deeper water with each swell. After a few swells you may be in over your head, and it becomes extremely important to float—by arching your back, head back, nose pointing in the air.

Floating conserves energy. The human body is buoyant, even more so in saltwater. Everyone should learn to float, because every minute you can salvage gives someone the opportunity to make a rescue.

Once you are no longer touching bottom and are in a rip, you should not fight against the current in a vain effort to get back to shore, for this is like "swimming up a river" and will sap your strength.

The rip current loses its strength just beyond the breakers, dissipating its energy and eventually delivering you to relatively calm waters. This area, known as the "head," may appear to have a mushroom shape when seen from the air, as debris picked up by the current is dispersed.

Here, the water is deep but calm. You can get back to shore by moving parallel to the beach in the direction of the bend of the current, and then heading toward shore at a 45-degree angle rather than straight in, to avoid getting caught in the feeder current again.

Where do rip currents occur? There are four types of rip currents: permanent, fixed, flash, and traveling:

Permanent rips occur at river mouths, estuaries, or by small streams, and can be quite wide. They also occur at finger jetties designed to prevent beach erosion, where the water's lateral drift is forced to turn seaward.

Fixed, flash, and traveling rips are caused by wind-generated waves.

Fixed currents, which appear only on long, sandy, surf-swept beaches, can move up or down the beach depending on shifts in the ocean floor, but they are generally stable, staying in one spot for several hours or even an entire day.

Flash, or *temporary*, *rips* are created when an increased volume of water is brought to shore from sudden wave build-ups. These currents can occur on a warm, sunny day, generated by distant storms whose waves do not lose their energy until they crash on a shore. The excess water build-up has no opportunity to drain and reach equilibrium while the unusually large and fast waves are coming in; a flash rip current therefore forms during a lull in wave action.

A *traveling rip current* is just what the name implies. You'll see it in front of you; then, five minutes later, it may have moved 15 yards up or down the beach. Traveling rips can move 30 yards in a minute. They occur on long, sandy beaches where there are no fixed depressions on the ocean floor.

How to spot a rip current: Some beaches, such as **Espadilla** at Manuel Antonio, **Playa Dominical**, **Jacó**, **Playa Grande** in Guanacaste, and **Playa Cocles** south of Puerto Viejo, are known to have rip currents and must *always* be approached with caution. The currents can be spotted by the trained eye by a brownish discoloration on the water's surface, caused by sand and debris; or there can be a flattening effect as the water rushes out to sea, making the surface appear deceptively smooth.

As a safety precaution, before you enter the ocean, throw a buoyant object like a coconut or a stick into the water and watch where the current carries it: this is the direction you will have to go before you can get back to shore. There is definitely one direction that is better than the other.

Rip currents aren't dangerous to people who understand them. The more you know about the ocean, the more fun it can be. Surfers use rip currents as an energy saver, since they provide "a free ride" out to sea just beyond the breakers. Good swimmers are encouraged to seek out rip currents under controlled conditions—and with experienced trainers. As long as you swim in the ocean, you might get caught in a rip current, so it's critical that you know how to get out of one. Following are some rip current rules of thumb:

- Weak swimmers should avoid surf-swept beaches.

- The safest beaches include Playas Rajada and Jobo near La Cruz, Bahía Junquillal Wildlife Refuge, Playa Hermosa in northern Guanacaste, Playas del Coco, Sámara, Carrillo, Bahía Ballena/Tambor, any beach on the Golfo Dulce between Puerto Jimenez and Golfito, any beach in Ballena National Marine Park in Uvita de Osa, and the third beach at Manuel Antonio.

- Be sure to ask at your hotel where it is safe to swim, and observe other swimmers. At certain beaches, playing in knee-deep water is the only water play recommended.

- Never swim alone.
- Always be prepared to signal for help at the earliest sign of trouble.
- After a long period in the sun, rest in the shade before swimming to avoid hypertension.

FISHING

Deep-sea sportfishing for sailfish, marlin, tuna, wahoo, and more than a dozen other species is very big in Costa Rica. Most of it is catch-and-re-lease. The most popular fishing areas are Guanacaste, Jacó, and Quepos on the Central Pacific, and Golfito and Drake Bay in the Southern Zone. Some claim that the world's best tarpon and snook fishing is in Barra del Colorado on the Atlantic. Tarpon can also be fished in Manzanillo (www.tarpon ville.com) on the southern Atlantic and in Caño Negro lagoon. Fresh water fishing for rainbow bass is good in Lake Arenal, Caño Negro lagoon, and Lago Hule in the Northern Zone. Trout can be fished in the Río Savegre, the Río Chirripó Pacífico, in Copey de Dota, and Cerro de la Muerte in the mountainous Southern Zone. You can find out everything you need to know about fishing from **Costa Rica Outdoors** (800-308-3394; www.costa ricaoutdoors.com, e-mail: jruhlow@racsa.co.cr).

OUTDOOR ADVENTURE SPORTS

When it comes to adventure sports, it is good to stick to companies with a reputation for safety. It is not a good idea to go for the cheapest tour. Michael Kaye, owner of Costa Rica Expeditions, one of the country's most experienced adventure outfitters, suggests a few questions you can ask to determine whether adventure companies really put safety first.

- Ask if they have written safety rules and policies. Safety is a matter of sticking to a set routine that has proved to minimize risk. If that routine has not been written down, you can be pretty sure that it will not be adhered to.
- Ask to speak to a guide. Ask her to mention a few of the most important rules. If she can't do it, you probably want to try another outfitter.
- Ask about cancellation policies. If you sense any hesitation on this, take a pass. Canceling trips when the conditions do not permit minimum margins of security is the most effective safety measure there is.

Among unsafe conditions that are most often overlooked are clients who have signed up for an experience that is too challenging for them. Under these circumstances, the trip should be changed or, if that is not possible, cancelled. Whether or not a person is suitable for an activity is the outfitter's—not the client's—decision. This may seem obvious, but the economic pressure not to cancel trips is strong, and many outfitters fail to train their guides to enforce clear cancellation policies in the face of client pressure.

After several deaths in the last few years, adventure tour operators have gotten together to formulate minimum safety requirements for rafting, zip-lining, rappelling, caving, mountain biking, scuba diving, surfing, and other adventure activities. For information on which tour operators are the safest, e-mail the Association of Adventure Tour Operators: aoadejecutiva@hot mail.com.

The dry season (December 15 to April 15) is the best time to come for hiking, biking, and horseback riding because creeks are dry and rivers are low. Less rain makes for better diving, too. Rappelling and caving are best when the rocks are dry.

SURFING

Costa Rica has become famous for its great waves. The Pacific, with its long point breaks, river mouths, and beach breaks, keeps surfers busy all year. Guanacaste is best in the windy season from January through May; the Central Pacific is best August through October. If they want to get serious, surfers go to the Atlantic from December through March, where waves from deep water break over the shallow reef, creating the perfect imitation of Hawaiian surf.

Alacrán Surf Tours (in the U.S.: 888-427-7769; www.alacransurf. com, e-mail: info@alacransurf.com) customizes surfing vacations that include friends and family. Their website has descriptions of 60 different surfing areas. Get the latest wave report at their website, or check out **www.crsurf.com**.

The nearest surfing beach to San José is **Boca Barranca**, between Puntarenas and Puerto Caldera, known for long waves at high and low tide. The water can be very dirty. About a half-hour to the south are **Playa Jacó** and **Playa Hermosa** (not to be confused with Playa Hermosa in Guana-caste), where an international surfing contest is held each year. These beaches have a large expatriate and Tico surfing community that provides services like board repairs, wave reports, surfing tours, and cabinas with surfers' discounts. The whole area between Jacó and **Playa Dominical** to the south has many excellent surfing spots. Parents of teens might want to check out Green Iguana Surf Camp (www.greeniguanasurfcamp.com) in Dominical.

Playa Pavones, south of Golfito on the Golfo Dulce, is said to have a left "so long you can take a nap on it," but we have heard that it's been inconsistent lately. The waves at **Playa Zancudo**, just to the north, are better for beginners. Across the Golfo Dulce, **Playa Matapalo** near the tip of the Osa Peninsula attracts surfers.

Playas Carrillo, **Nosara**, **Negra**, **Junquillal**, and **Tamarindo** in Guanacaste have areas for surfing, as well as swimming and snorkeling spots; Tamarindo and nearby beaches can be very crowded. **Corky Carol's Surf School** (682-0385) gives lessons in Nosara. **Playas Malpaís**, **Santa Teresa**, and **Coyote** on the west side of the Nicoya Peninsula are becoming known for their waves, and **Playa Cedros** on the east side of the Peninsula below Montezuma is good for beginners (see Central Pacific Zone chapter).

Playa Naranjo, in Santa Rosa National Park, is known for **Witch Rock**, where there are perfect tubular waves. The road to Playa Naranjo is very rough; rented Suzuki Sidekicks get stuck there regularly. If you drive there, get the car with the highest clearance you can. Surfing outfitters run trips from Tamarindo and other beaches by sea to Witch Rock. They *must* pay the $6/person park entrance fee even if arriving by sea. You can camp right on the beach.

Puerto Viejo, south of Limón, is famous for "La Salsa Brava," a challenging ride responsible for many a broken surfboard. Take it right. If you take it left, you may crash. It is usually up January to April and only for advanced surfers. Playa Cocles farther south is easier.

There are board-rental shops in Puntarenas, Jacó, Manuel Antonio, Limón, Puerto Viejo, and Cahuita ($10-$20/day). Used boards cost $160-$260. Many car-rental agencies and hotels give discounts to surfers, especially May through November.

Some airlines have restrictions and charges for carrying surfboards. Find out which are surfer-friendly at www.worldwideadventures.com/fees.htm.

Kite-surfing is one of the fastest growing new sports. There is a kite-surfing instructor in Salinas Bay, Guanacaste, near the Nicaraguan border (www.suntoursandfun.com).

SCUBA DIVING

Costa Rica is blessed with coral formations on both the Pacific and Atlantic coasts. The reefs off Manzanillo in the Gandoca–Manzanillo Wildlife Refuge are the healthiest on the Caribbean, partly because the area is far from a major river mouth. Diving operations in Guanacaste, spearheaded by Hotel El Ocotal, have put floating moorings near dive sites so that anchors will not damage the coral.

Inexpensive diving excursions and courses are available through **Aquamor** (www.greencoast.com/aquamor) in Manzanillo on the Talamanca coast. You'll find diving operations in Playa del Coco, Ocotal, Playa Hermosa,

Brasilito, Flamingo, and Tamarindo. In the Central Pacific Zone, look for divemasters in Punta Leona, Playa Jacó, and Manuel Antonio. Drake Bay on the Osa Peninsula in the Southern Zone is a mecca for divers because of the clear waters found off Isla del Caño. Because its waters are protected, there are more fish. Six or seven hotels offer diving there, and some go to Isla del Coco, 500 kilometers southwest of Costa Rica, which offers some of the best diving there is. **Undersea Hunter** (228-6613, in the U.S.: 800-203-2120; www.underseahunter.com) offers ten-day trips to the island.

KAYAKING AND CANOEING

Various companies and hotels along both coasts rent kayaks and offer sea kayaking trips. We mention them in the regional chapters. Kayaks are quite stable, and first-timers can feel safe and get a rush when exploring with a good guide. The gentle waters of the Golfo Dulce on the east side of the Osa Peninsula lend themselves to peaceful sea kayaking. See the Puerto Jimenez and Golfo Dulce sections of the Southern Zone chapter. **Caves and Waves** (787-0036) can lead you through the natural tunnels in **Ballena National Park** south of Dominical. The dolphins of the Caribbean know well the kayaks and guides of **Aquamor Adventures** (759-0612; www.greencoast. com/aquamor.htm, e-mail: aquamorl@racsa.co.cr) based in the Gandoca–Manzanillo Wildlife Refuge south of Puerto Viejo de Talamanca. **Escondido Trek** (735-5210; www.escondidotrek.com) specializes in sea kayaking on the Golfo Dulce side of the Osa Peninsula.

Vermont-based **Battenkill Canoe Ltd.** (in the U.S.: 800-421-5268; www.battenkill.com) leads canoe tours to Yorkín in the Bribrí indigenous lands of Talamanca, and to rivers in the Northern Zone. See the Tortuguero section in the Atlantic Coast chapter for info on *cayucas*. Florida-based **Canoe Costa Rica** (732-350-3963; www.canoecostarica.com) leads customized five- to ten-day trips all over Costa Rica.

WHITEWATER SPORTS

Rafters, canoers, and kayakers flock to Costa Rica for its exciting rivers. Rivers are rated Class I (still water) to Class VI (waterfalls). Most whitewater rafting tours are Class II (easy) to Class V (very advanced). Class II is the way to go if you want to relax and spot birds and wildlife. Class III is good for family fun and thrills; Class III guides must have at least six months of training at a well-known guide school. Class IV rapids are long, very turbulent, and constricted, and require paying close attention to the instructions of an experienced guide. Make sure that rafts, life jackets, paddles and helmets are in excellent condition. River classification can change depending on water level.

In the Northern Zone, the Sarapiquí and Toro rivers offer both Class II and Class IV rapids. Guanacaste's Corobicí River is Class II. Near Manuel Antonio are the flowing Río Naranjo and the more complex Savegre. The Río General near San Isidro in the Southern Zone has Class III and IV rapids. Most rafters come to Costa Rica for the Pacuare (near Turrialba, about two hours east of San José), known for its scenic gorges, primary forest, wildlife, and Class III and IV rapids. Hopefully it will be made into a national park soon.

Wear closed-toed yet lightweight shoes like old sneakers. Bring sunblock and a swimsuit. Leave your passport, money, and fragile equipment behind because you *will* get wet.

The Río Pacuare is considered world-class by sportspeople and ranked one of the five best rafting rivers by the Discovery Channel. In addition to their one-day rafting trips, **Ríos Tropicales** (233-6455; www.riostropicales. com) offers four-day trips that include a whitewater paddle to its lodge on the Pacuare, with ziplines over the river and hiking to jungle waterfalls. They also run sea kayaking trips to Curú on the Nicoya Peninsula, with camping on a deserted beach and paddles to nearby islands. Kayaking the quiet canals of Tortuguero and rafting on the Río General are also on their menu. **Aventuras Naturales** (225-3939, in the U.S.: 800-514-0411; www.toenjoynature. com) also has a jungle lodge on the Pacuare with a canopy tour. Their tenday tour takes you to the Monteverde canopy tour, biking at the base of Arenal volcano, rafting on the Río Sarapiquí, kayaking in Tortuguero, and rafting on the Pacuare. **Costa Rica Expeditions** (257-0766; www.costarica expeditions.com) can take you to many destinations, but it has its own quality lodges in Monteverde, the Osa Peninsula, and Tortuguero.

In Turrialba, **Serendipity Adventures** (in the U.S.: 877-507-1358; www. serendipityadventures.com) specializes in rafting trips for families and other groups. **Costa Rica Ríos** (556-9617, in the U.S.: 888-434-0776; www. costaricarios.com) offers canoe and kayak instruction and certification, as does **Tico's River Adventures** (556-1231; www.ticoriver.com).

In Manuel Antonio, **Iguana Tours** (777-1262; www.iguanatours.com) and **Amigos del Rio** (www.amigosdelrio.com) offer trips down the Savegre and Naranjo rivers. In the Northern Zone, **Aventuras de Sarapiquí** (766-6768; www.sarapiqui.com) rafts the Río Sarapiquí. **Aguas Bravas** (761-1123, 292-2072, 296-2626; www.aguas-bravas.co.cr) rafts the Sarapiquí, Toro, and Peñas Blancas rivers, and runs mountain bike and horseback tours. You can usually book whitewater rafting tours through your hotel.

Do not be disappointed if your trip is cancelled due to too-high or toolow water levels. Six people have died in rafting accidents in the past four years, and companies should err on the side of caution.

BIKING

Mountain-biking is one of the fastest-growing sports among Costa Ricans. Most of the hotels in the Rincón de la Vieja area of Guanacaste have bikes for rent and bike trails on their property or between their lodges and the national park. International biking superstars come each November to participate in the annual **Ruta de los Conquistadores Race** (225-8186; www.adventurerace.com), which starts in Puntarenas, climbs Volcán Turrialba, and ends up on the Caribbean coast. You can take a tour along the same route at a more relaxed pace. **BiCosta Rica** (380-3844, 446-7585; www.bruncas.com/bicostarica.html, e-mail: bicostarica@bruncas.com) organizes mountain-bike tours lasting from one day to one week all over the country. **Coast to Coast Adventures** (280-8054; www.ctocadventures.com, e-mail: info@ctocadventures.com) also offers hiking, biking, sea kayaking, and rafting tours. There are rental places in Puerto Viejo de Talamanca, La Fortuna, Sámara, and Jacó. Watch out for high winds during the dry season if you are biking in Guanacaste.

BUNGEE JUMPING AND PARAGLIDING

Bungee jumping has come to Costa Rica. Thrill-seekers jump from a 265-foot abandoned bridge near the Grecia exit on the highway to Puntarenas. **Tropical Bungee** (phone/fax: 248-2212, cell phone: 383-9724; www.bungee.co.cr) offers this ultimate adrenaline rush as well as rock climbing and paragliding.

HOT-AIR BALLOON RIDES AND ULTRALIGHTS

Floating in a hot-air balloon will give you a hawk's view of the Costa Rican countryside. The one-and-a-half-hour tours begin at daybreak and depart from Volcán Arenal, Naranjo, and Turrialba. **Serendipity Adventures** (558-1000, fax: 558-1010, in the U.S.: 877-507-1358; www.serendipityadventures.com, e-mail: info@serendipityadventures.com) specializes in custom adventures for families, couples, and groups of friends or co-workers. Trips include breakfast and transportation from your hotel.

The Flying Crocodile (656-0413; www.flying-crocodile.com, e-mail: flycroco@racsa.co.cr), specializing in ultralight flying trips, is run by a German pilot just north of Playa Sámara.

TREETOP EXPLORATIONS

Inspired by biologist Donald Perry's explorations of the rainforest canopy and his subsequent Rainforest Aerial Tram (Chapter Nine), there are now many opportunities for visitors (who don't suffer from vertigo) to ascend into the treetops, either to sit on an observation platform, or to zoom from tree to tree using a cable-and-pulley system. According to *The Tico Times*, out of the 80 or so canopy tours that exist in Costa Rica, only a handful meet the international safety standards formulated by the Association for Challenge Course Technology (www.acctinfo.org). The Association of Adventure Operators is trying to set standards that all can agree on.

The Original Canopy Tour (phone/fax: 257-5149; www.canopytour. com) has sites at Termales del Bosque hotsprings near San Carlos in the Northern Zone, at Monteverde (645-5243), at Hacienda Guachipelín, near Rincón de la Vieja, and most recently at the isolated **Pacuare Lodge**, reachable only by the Aventuras Naturales whitewater rafting trip. **Albergue de Montaña Rincón de la Vieja** (661-8198; www.rincondelavieja lodge.com) has a similar cable-and-pulley system on its property. The one at **Buena Vista Lodge** is very long and also has a waterslide. Near Lake Arenal, **Lago Coter Eco Lodge** (257-5075) offers its own version of the canopy tour, along with **Hotel Villablanca** (228-4603; www.villablanca-costarica.com), near San Ramón in the Central Valley. The Manuel Antonio versions are called **Canopy Safari** and **Dream Forest Canopy Tour**. One of the most famous is the **SkyTrek** (www.skytrek.com) in Monteverde. Prices for these tours range between $40 and $80.

Monteverde Preserve, the **SkyWalk** (also in Monteverde), **Arenal Hanging Bridges** (253-5080; www.puentescolgantes.com), the **Rainmaker Reserve** north of Manuel Antonio, **Reserva Los Campesinos** inland from Manuel Antonio, the **Tirimbina Reserve** in the Northern Zone, and **Heliconias Rainforest Reserve** in Bijagua de Upala north of Cañas all have bridge systems suspended above the canopy so that you can walk instead of zip.

Corcovado Lodge and Tent Camp (222-0333, fax: 257-1665; www. costaricaexpeditions.com) has a platform 120 feet off the ground, located

an hour's hike from the Lodge. Also in the Osa, **Bosque del Cabo** (www. bosquedelcabo.com) has an observation platform you get to on a zipline, as does **El Remanso** (www.elremanso.com). In Dominical, **Hacienda Barú** (787-0003; www.haciendabaru.com) has a tree platform easily accessible from the road and the Flight of the Toucan canopy adventure, which is interspersed with natural history hikes. **Selva Bananito Lodge** (253-8118; www.selvabananito.com), in Limón Province, teaches you how to climb into the canopy with a secure system of ropes, harnesses, and ascenders. **La Isla Botanical Gardens** (www.greencoast.com) in Puerto Viejo de Talamanca also has an observation platform in a tree.

ATVs

ATV tours have become popular lately, and they are probably fun and a good way to get into the beautiful back country, but we are prejudiced against them because of the noise and the seeming invasion they make into small rural communities where most people can't afford such toys.

JET SKIS

We don't like jet skis for the same reasons we don't like ATVs, but more so. According to Harry Pariser of the *Adventure Guide to Costa Rica*, jet skis account for 40 percent of all boating injuries. They traverse shallow and sensitive waters where boats would usually not go. They cause injury and death to manatees and other marine wildlife, and discharge up to one third of their gas and oil into the water. And they are noisy.

HORSEBACK RIDING

Most beach and mountain resorts rent horses, and we mention them throughout the book. Most noteworthy in the Northern Zone are the famous horseback ride between Monteverde and Lake Arenal (we recommend that you don't do it in the rainy season or that you take the drier and flatter Lake Trail, which is easier on people and horses) and the trip to Río Celeste. In Montezuma, **Finca Los Caballos** specializes in high-quality equine experiences. **Brisas del Nara** (www.tourbrisasnara.com) takes you to mountain waterfalls inland from Manuel Antonio, as does **Don Lulo's**, inland from Dominical and Rancho La Merced in Uvita de Osa. For a beautiful down-home Costa Rican experience, rent a horse from Don Concho of **Poor Man's Paradise** (www.mypoormansparadise.com) to explore the beaches south of Drake Bay in the Osa Peninsula.

Make sure that the rented horses are not tired and do not have sores or swollen places. Give them plenty of opportunity to drink water during the trip and don't leave them standing in the sun. If you feel horses or any other animals are being mistreated, you can report it to the Asociación Humanitaria para la Protección Animal de Costa Rica (267-6374, 267-7158, fax: 267-7296; www.animalsheltercostarica.com, e-mail: refugio@infoweb.co.cr) in Los Angeles de San Rafael de Heredia.

Be sure to wear long pants when you ride, or you'll end up with sore, irritated skin on your legs, and check yourself for ticks afterwards.

SOCCER

Costa Ricans are very sports-minded. There isn't a district, town, or city where *fútbol* (soccer) isn't played. Much to the Ticos' delight, Costa Rica's national team made it into the World Cup in 2002—the second time in their history. It's said that Costa Ricans learn to kick a ball before they learn to walk! There are teams all over the country in every imaginable category, including all ages and both sexes, although only men play on the major teams. If you want to experience the Ticos' love for this sport firsthand, attend a Sunday soccer match. Be aware that Ticos can get pretty crazy at these games. During the final games of the 1993 national championship at the Cartago stadium, a bad call was made. Fans cut through the chain-link fence and streamed onto the field in the middle of the game. A riot ensued. The referees fled, the national guard was called to the scene, and the game was terminated. In the next week, the Cartago team went to the Supreme Court to demand retribution for this "violation of their human rights" (no joke). After tempers cooled, the teams had a private game with no spectators, and Heredia was declared the national champion. The whole episode gave Tico men something to discuss in the backs of buses for months.

TENNIS

Many upscale beach and mountain hotels, like El Ocotal, south of Playas del Coco, and Villa Serena in Playa Junquillal, have tennis courts. Both are in Guanacaste. Often courts are lighted at night because it's too hot to play during the day.

RUNNING

There are many marathons during the year, including the one sponsored each April by the **University for Peace**. The **Hash House Harriers** (www.costaricahhh.com), a worldwide organization devoted to running and beer-drinking, also meets here once a week. Call 290-2704 or 838-5357 for information.

SIX

Getting to Know San José

In 1821, after learning that Guatemala had declared its independence from Spain, Costa Rica began creating its own form of self-government. During this process, General Agustín de Iturbide, self-proclaimed emperor of Mexico, sent word urging immediate annexation to his empire. The citizens of the older cities of Heredia and Cartago were in favor of annexation, but the more liberal residents of Alajuela and San José saw de Iturbide's demand as imperialist and chose independence. A short civil war ensued; it was won in 1823 by the *independistas*, who moved the capital city from Cartago to San José.

Today San José is a noisy, bustling city—the economic, political, and cultural center of the country. If you have come to Costa Rica to get close to nature, you will probably want to get out of San José as fast as possible. Set in the middle of the Central Valley, surrounded by high mountains, it is battling the demons of its rapid growth: congested one-way streets filled with too many cars, buses, and taxis belching black diesel smoke into the mountain air; a lack of jobs for all the country people who have given up on working the land and are trying their luck in the city; increasing petty theft.

On the upside, San José still ranks as one of the safer cities in the Western Hemisphere and has much less violent crime than most U.S. cities. Foreigners enjoy the city's springlike climate, the availability of high-quality cultural events like National Symphony concerts and international music, dance, theater, and film festivals, and the relaxed life in suburban areas like balmy Rohrmoser, Escazú, and Santa Ana to the west, and Moravia, Curridabat, and brisk San Ramón de Trés Ríos to the east. Great places to dine are also plentiful in San José, as you'll see in this chapter. Modern supermarkets and shopping malls have largely taken the place of the Mercado Central, but Saturday morning farmers markets held in the streets of different neighborhoods still provide a folksy tone and a fairlike atmosphere. And Costa Ricans are almost always friendly and polite, ready to take a moment off for a joke or to help you find where you're going.

Here are some tips for while you're in the city:

- When crossing streets in downtown San José, always look over your shoulder at the cars coming from behind you. In practice, the pedestrian does not have the right of way. Drivers love to whip around corners whether or not people are trying to cross.

- When a traffic light for oncoming cars changes from green to yellow or red, do not take it to mean that the cars will stop. Look at the cars, not the light. When you see that the cars have stopped, run across real quick. This habit is easily developed because another characteristic of San José is that traffic lights are hung so that pedestrians cannot see them. *Buena suerte.*

- Street numbers are attached to the sides of buildings near intersections. Not all corners have them, but keep looking and you're bound to find one.

- To ask directions, you don't have to use a lot of fancy Spanish. It is acceptable to say "*¿Para* [name of your destination]?", like "*¿Para* Heredia?" or "*¿Para la* Coca Cola?", and the person you ask will point you in the general direction. We've found it's best to ask people who look like they drive, and it's best not to ask people standing in front of bars.

- If you're driving downtown, keep your window rolled up high enough so that a thief can't reach in and grab your purse, necklace, or watch. Better yet, don't even try to drive downtown unless you think of driving as a competitive sport.

See a description of the street address system in Chapter Four.

A WALKING TOUR

The following tour can take several hours to a full day, depending on how involved you get.

We will start out at the **Correo Central** (223-9766), or Central Post Office, on Calle 2 between Avenidas 1 and 3. The entrance is in the middle of the block. Stop by for an espresso, a latte, or a coffee milkshake at **Café Tostadora La Meseta** (open Monday through Saturday, 9 a.m. to 7 p.m.), a charming internet café hidden behind the post office boxes in the former guards' headquarters. Philatelists will be interested in the commemorative stamp department on the second floor. Also on the second floor is a museum of old telephone and telegraph equipment as well as historic stamps and photos.

Walk two blocks west on Avenida 1 and you're at the **Mercado Central**, entering through the flower section. The market is a crowded, bustling maze of shops, restaurants, and produce stands covering the whole block between Avenidas Central/1 and Calles 6/8. Although there are quite a few more sedate places to buy souvenirs, at the Central Market you can get a glimpse of the lives of everyday Costa Ricans. Everything from hammocks to leather goods to fresh fish to mangoes is sold there. Of special interest are the stands where herbs are sold, labeled with their medicinal uses. It's easy to get quite disoriented in the market, but try to come out at the southeast entrance on Avenida Central and start walking east again. (If you don't like crowds, skip the market.)

Between Calles 6 and 4 on Avenida Central, you'll pass **La Gloria**, Costa Rica's largest department store. Across from that is the huge black marble **Banco de Costa Rica**. Their second floor has a special department for efficiently changing traveler's checks. They exhibit local artists' work on the ground floor. You can also take an elevator to the eighth floor to get a bird's-eye view of the city.

Continuing on Avenida Central and looking left on Calle 4, you'll see one of San José's monuments to its democracy: a group of bronze campesinos stands humbly but solidly looking up at some unseen authority, waiting to be heard. The large building beside them is Costa Rica's **Banco Central**.

East of Calle 4, Avenida Central has been made into a pedestrian mall, so you'll have a little more room to walk. This is San José's busiest commercial section, with shops and restaurants vying for your attention on either side of the street.

In two blocks, look to the left on Calle Central and you will see **La Casona**, a two-story wonderland of souvenirs. Half a block ahead on Avenida Central is **Librería Universal**, where you can buy anything from electronic appliances to art supplies, as well as books and stationery. It sells large-scale maps, which are helpful for hiking.

Look to your left at the intersection of Calle 1 and Avenida Central. Three blocks north is **Radiográfica** (open daily, 7:30 a.m. to 9 p.m.; 287-0489), where you can make international phone calls, check your e-mail, or send and receive faxes.

You are still on Avenida Central. In the next block you'll see **Librería Lehmann**, another great bookstore. Next you'll come to the **Plaza de la**

Cultura on Avenida Central, Calles 5/3. The eastern half of the plaza is full of children chasing pigeons and feeding them popcorn, and the center is often the stage for street comedians, concerts, and fairs. Since this is a prime tourist area, beware of pickpockets.

Cross the plaza to the famous **Teatro Nacional** (National Theater). In 1890 the world-renowned prima donna, Adelina Patti, appeared with a traveling opera company in Guatemala, but could not perform in Costa Rica because there was no appropriate theater. In response, newly rich coffee merchants financed the construction of a theater with a tax on every bag of exported coffee. Belgian architects were called in to design and supervise the building, and the metal structure was ordered from Belgian mills. Painters and decorators were brought from Italy, along with that country's famous marble. The Teatro Nacional was inaugurated in 1894 with Gounod's *Faust* and an opening-night cast that included singers from the Paris Opera. A source of cultural pride, the theater was made into a national monument in 1965. Extensive restoration work has renewed its beautiful ceiling paintings and sumptuous decor. The **Café del Teatro Nacional**, to the left as you enter the building, has changing art exhibits and specializes in exotic coffee combinations and desserts featuring Café Britt, of the famous Coffee Tour in Heredia. Take a moment to see the incredibly alive bust of Joaquin Gutierrez, one of Costa Rica's great modern writers, outside on the north side of the theater.

Down the grassy steps on Calle 5 is the information center of the **Instituto Costarricense de Turismo (ICT)**, or Tourism Institute, to the left. It's open Monday through Saturday, 9 a.m. to 1 p.m., 2 p.m. to 5 p.m.; 222-1090. There, too, is the entrance to the plaza's excellent underground exhibition rooms, which feature changing shows, as well as the famous pre-Columbian **Gold Museum** (open Tuesday through Sunday, 10 a.m. to 4:30 p.m.; 243-4202; www.museodelbancocentral.org; admission $5, children and students $1). This little gem features shimmering displays of over 2000 gold artifacts crafted by the Diquis master goldsmiths, who once inhabited the southwestern part of the country. Next to it is the **Coin Museum**, with a well-presented overview of the history of money in Costa Rica.

In a small plaza one block to the south, on weekday afternoons, you might be lucky enough to see San José's version of the Buena Vista Social Club—*La Nueva Marimba de San José,* a group of retired musicians who play just for the fun of it. Passersby stop to dance, and you can, too.

Back at the Gold Museum, head north (left) on Calle 5. In a block you'll pass two upscale crafts stores: **Atmósfera**, on the corner to your right, and **Suraska**, on your left at the corner of Avenida 3. They feature

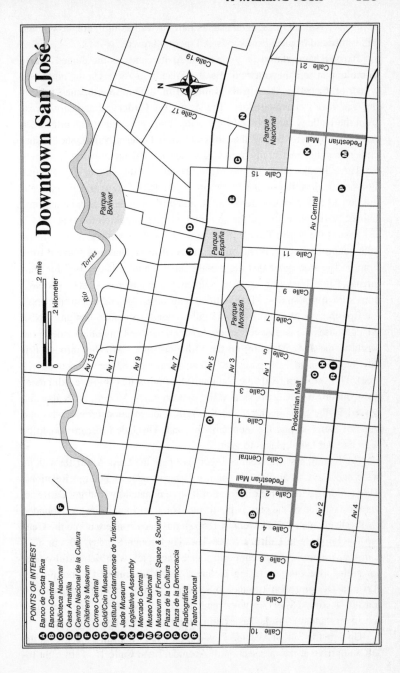

Downtown San José

POINTS OF INTEREST

- Ⓐ Banco de Costa Rica
- Ⓑ Banco Central
- Ⓒ Bibiloteca Nacional
- Ⓓ Casa Amarilla
- Ⓔ Centro Nacional de la Cultura
- Ⓕ Children's Museum
- Ⓖ Correo Central
- Ⓗ Gold/Coin Museum
- Ⓘ Instituto Costarricense de Turismo
- Ⓙ Jade Museum
- Ⓚ Legislative Assembly
- Ⓛ Mercado Central
- Ⓜ Museo Nacional
- Ⓝ Museum of Form, Space & Sound
- Ⓞ Plaza de la Cultura
- Ⓟ Plaza de la Democracia
- Ⓠ Radiográfica
- Ⓡ Teatro Nacional

excellent wood carvings, ceramics, and art, as well as furniture, bowls, and boxes made of tropical hardwoods. All merit a browse.

Parque Morazán is on your right. At its center is the domed **Music Temple**, purportedly patterned after Le Trianon in Paris. On the northwest corner of the park is the **Aurola Holiday Inn**, with mirrored panels reflecting San José's changing skies. The **Amir Art Gallery**, diagonally across from the Holiday Inn, sells oils and watercolors by Costa Rican artists. On Avenida 7, directly behind the Holiday Inn, is **Galería Namú**, showcasing authentic indigenous crafts from Costa Rica and Panamá.

Three blocks north of the Music Temple is the entrance to **Parque Bolívar**, the location of San José's **zoo** (open daily, 9 a.m. to 4:30 p.m.; admission $1.50). Monkeys, crocodiles, and birds live there, as well as some felines. At the beginning of the zoo is an interactive exhibit for kids.

East of the Music Temple is the green **Escuela Metálica**, a turn-of-the-20th-century school building built entirely of metal that was shipped from France. The story goes that the prefabricated school was destined for Puntarenas, Chile, but was mistakenly delivered to Puntarenas, Costa Rica. Next comes **Parque España**, which is filled with venerable and beautiful trees.

Continue to Avenida 7 and the tall National Insurance Institute (INS), which houses the largest collection of American pre-Columbian jade in the world in the **Jade Museum** on the 11th floor (open Monday through Friday, 8:30 a.m. to 3:30 p.m.; 287-6034; admission $2, children under 12 free). This museum rivals the National Museum in its extensive exhibits of pre-Columbian jade, gold, stonework, and ceramics. Modern art is also displayed in the outer gallery, and the 11th-floor location provides a good view of San José and the mountains beyond. The Jade Museum should be high on your list of places to visit.

Continuing east on Avenida 7, you will pass the **Casa Amarilla** with its wide stairways. It houses the country's Department of Foreign Relations. This building and the park in front of it were donated by Andrew Carnegie. On the east side of the park is the former National Liquor Factory, founded by President Juan Rafael Mora in 1856. It has been converted into the **Centro Nacional de la Cultura** (open Tuesday through Sunday, 10 a.m. to 5 p.m.), an impressive museum and theater complex with delightful places for sitting, walking, or taking pictures. The **Museum of Contemporary Art and Design** (open Tuesday to Saturday, 10 a.m. to 5 p.m.; Sunday, 10 a.m. to 4 p.m.; 257-9370; www.madc.ac.cr; admission $3, kids free, free for all on Sunday), inside, has exciting exhibits from all over the world.

Up a gentle hill on Avenida 7, you'll pass the Mexican Embassy on the left and arrive at the intersection of Avenida 7 and Calle 15. Turn right toward the **Biblioteca Nacional** (National Library). On its western side is the **Galería Nacional de Arte Contemporáneo** (open Monday through Saturday, 10 a.m. to 1 p.m., 2 p.m. to 5 p.m.), which often has good exhibits. Across the street is the other entrance to the Centro Nacional de la Cultura.

The library faces the largest of San José's city parks, **Parque Nacional**. In the center of the park is the massive and beautiful **Monumento Nacional**, which depicts the spirits of the Central American nations driving out the despicable *filibustero* William Walker. The statue was made in the Rodin studios in France and shipped to Costa Rica.

One hundred meters east of the library, in the old train station, is the wheelchair-accessible **Museum of Form, Space and Sound** (222-9462), with sculptures, musical instruments, and historical exhibits, all made to be touched.

Across the street from the park you will see a statue of **Juan Santamaría**, the national hero, holding aloft his torch. The elegant, white Moorish **Legislative Assembly** building he fronts houses the Costa Rican Congress.

Two blocks south of the Parque Nacional, on the Jimenez Oreamuno pedestrian walkway, is the **Museo Nacional** (open Tuesday through Sunday, 8:30 a.m. to 4 p.m.; 257-1433; www.museocostarica.com; admission $4, students and children under ten free), housed in the former Bellavista Fortress. There are bullet holes in the turrets from the 1948 civil war. Inside are a lovely courtyard and large exhibits of indigenous gold and ceramics, religious objects, colonial furniture, and art. Definitely worth a visit.

The museum overlooks the **Plaza de la Democracia**, built by the Arias administration to receive visiting presidents during the historic Hemispheric Summit in 1989. Here you will see a statue of former president Don Pepe Figueres, hero of the 1948 civil war, and the abolisher of the Army. His human stance and expression show that the citizens of this very small country know their leaders well. The plaza is usually full of tented market stalls selling jewelry, clothing, hammocks, wood crafts, and more.

CREATIVE ARTS

Costa Ricans are well known for their interest in culture and the arts. The Ministry of Culture stimulates activity by sponsoring theater, choral music, opera, dance, literature, poetry, art, sculpture, and film.

The **International Festival of the Arts**, held every other year in the fall, showcases national actors and musicians one year, and international artists the next. The 2004 festival featured theater, dance, and music groups from Ecuador, Israel, Colombia, Mexico, Spain, Brazil, Nicaragua, Taiwan, and Canada; and performers in all categories from Costa Rica. Tickets sell out early. Get more information at www.festivaldelasartes.com, e-mail: fest art@racsa.co.cr, or by calling 223-6361 or 223-6961.

MUSIC

Costa Rica's National Youth Symphony was inaugurated in 1972 by ex-President Figueres' famous quote: "We need to concern ourselves not only with the standard of living but the quality of life as well. Why have tractors without violins?"

Many of the young musicians trained in the Youth Symphony have graduated to participate in the National Symphony, which performs in the **Teatro Nacional** (Avenida 2, Calle 3; 221-5341) on the Plaza de la Cultura. Internationally famous guest directors and soloists are often featured. Entrance fees are kept low so that people at all economic levels may enjoy the concerts. The least expensive seats are in the *galería* section, which is up three flights of stairs through an entrance on the east side of the theater. The *butacas* are in the first tier of boxes above the *luneta* (orchestra) section. The *palcos* (box seats) are on the second tier. The symphony season starts in March and ends in December. Call or check the newspapers or the sign out front for current show times. Also see www.entretenimiento.co.cr.

Teatro Melico Salazar (Avenida 2, Calle Central; 221-4952), across from the Parque Central, is slightly less grandiose than the Teatro Nacional, but often hosts performances by famous international musicians as well as the **National Youth Symphony** (236-6669), the **National Lyric Company** (222-8571), the **National Choir** (236-5396), and the **National Dance Company** (222-2974).

The world-renowned **International Music Festival**, presented each summer since 1990, has been compared to the Aspen and Salzberg music festivals. Tickets are sold through Credomatic (224-6266, fax: 234-6208).

Costa Rica has a number of gifted folk singers and musicians who regularly perform at some of the bars and theaters listed below. Look for posters around town or announcements in *The Tico Times* for concerts by some of the country's most creative contemporary performers: **Cantares** researches the history of Costa Rican music from all over the country, and writes songs with an ironic political twist; **Luis Angel Castro** sings *nueva trova* and calypso; **Canto América** adds to Afro-Caribbean rhythms with trumpets and flutes; **Adrián Goizueta** combines heartfelt lyrics with political statements and a great Latin beat; **Manuel Obregón** brings magic to the piano; and the very popular violin, guitar, and percussion group, **Editus**, which recently won a Grammy award for back-up work with Rubén Blades, has a New Age yet distinctly Latin tilt to its sensitive compositions. All of these musicians have produced CDs that make great souvenirs, and most of them can be heard at the music festivals in Monteverde (see the Northern Zone chapter) and Playa Chiquita (see the Atlantic Coast chapter). Highly recommended.

THEATER

Ticos are great actors. Even if you don't understand Spanish, it might be worth it to go to the theater to see the creativity that they bring to the stage. The English-speaking community also puts a lot of energy into its **Little Theater Group**, which presents musicals and comedies several times a year. Check *The Tico Times* for performance and audition information.

FILMS

North American movies dominate the film scene here, and are usually shown with Spanish subtitles. Check schedules in *The Tico Times* or *La Nación*. First-run movies are about $3-$5.

The **Sala Garbo** (Avenida 2, Calle 28; 222-1034) features excellent international films with Spanish subtitles. Next door, the **Teatro Laurence Olivier** offers films, plays, and concerts, as well as a gallery and coffee house. Take the Sabana–Cementerio bus and get off at the Pizza Hut on Paseo Colón. The two theaters are one block south. You can walk to them from downtown in 25 minutes.

The **University of Costa Rica** in San Pedro runs an excellent, cheap international film series during the school year (March to December), Wednesday through Friday nights. The movies are shown in the auditorium of the Law School. Check current listings in *The Tico Times* or call **Cine Universitario** (207-4717).

ART

The Ticos converted their former air terminal into the **Museum of Costa Rican Art** (open Tuesday through Saturday, 10 a.m. to 4 p.m.; Sunday, 10 a.m. to 2 p.m.; 222-7155; www.crc.co.cr/musarco; admission $5). This tastefully done museum displays the work of the country's finest painters and sculptors, as well as international exhibits. Located in La Sabana at the end of Paseo Colón.

Following local tradition, the National Liquor Factory downtown has also been converted to an impressive art center. FANAL (Fábrica Nacional de Licores) has become **CENAC** (Centro Nacional de la Cultura), a major gallery and theater complex (open Tuesday through Sunday, 10 a.m. to 5 p.m.; Avenida 3, Calles 15/17; 257-9370; admission $3, free on Sunday).

Galería Namu (open daily, 9:30 a.m. to 6:30 p.m.; Avenida 7, Calles 5/7; 256-3412) specializes in indigenous and women's art from around the country. The gallery hopes to give a forum to these artists so they may earn the recognition they deserve, and has already presented their beautiful artwork at galleries in New York.

See "A Walking Tour" above for some of San José's many public galleries. Check *La Nación* and *The Tico Times* for exhibits at the galleries downtown. The Centro Cultural Costarricense-Norteamericano and the Alianza Francesa (see below) have monthly art exhibits. Their openings are a wonderful place to meet people and enjoy free wine and *bocas*.

NIGHTLIFE

While long-term residents and native Ticos often gripe about a lack of nightlife, there's plenty to do after dark in San José. Besides dozens of theaters and cinemas, night owls can sample a wide variety of bars, discos, and all-night cafés.

The area bordered by Calle 4 on the west, Avenida 9 on the north, Calle 23 on the east, and Avenida 2 on the south is the heart of downtown nightlife in San José. Of course, you should use common sense when walking around: keep your purse close to you; don't act drunk and out of control; and be extra-alert on deserted streets. Some of the nightspots listed here are in San Pedro, a ten-minute bus ride from downtown.

BARS

Most bars offer a traditional *boca*, or small plate of food, along with your drink. *Ceviche* (raw fish "cooked" in lime juice), fried fish, chicken wings, little steaks, and rice and beans are common *bocas*; they are usually free. You'll find a variety of local beers, and most are pretty good. We recommend Imperial, Pilsen, or the more expensive, locally brewed Heineken.

At **Cafe 83 Sur** (open Tuesday through Saturday, 6 p.m. to 2:30 a.m.; Sunday, 6 p.m. to midnight), live deejays spin hip-hop and rhythm and blues. The decor is Arabic/Indonesian. Reasonably priced food is served as well. Located 100 meters south of the Nicaraguan Embassy.

Caccio's (100 meters east and 200 north of the San Pedro Church, near the railroad tracks; 223-3261) is a popular college bar, with two-for-one beers on Tuesday and Saturday, and free pizza *bocas* from 8 to 10 on Thursday night.

Cafe Expresivo (Avenida 9, Calles 31/33; 224-1202) has live *trova*, *boleros*, an open mic, and dancing. Shows start at 8 p.m.

Chelles (open daily, 24 hours; 221-1369) doesn't have much atmosphere, but if you're a people watcher, you'll enjoy hanging out here. Probably because it remains open all the time, Chelles has become a landmark. You'll see actors, musicians, and dancers from the National Theater there having a midnight snack. You'll see middle-aged Costa Rican men amusing each other with toothpick tricks. You'll be asked to buy wilted roses from intriguing old ladies and persistent young boys. There are free *bocas* with every drink. Chelles is at Avenida Central, Calle 9. *Overpriced.*

El Cuartel de la Boca del Monte (open weekdays, noon to 2 p.m., 6 p.m. to 3 a.m.; Saturday and Sunday, 6 p.m. to 3 a.m.; Avenida 1, Calles 21/23; 221-0327) is one of the most popular singles bars in San José. The *bocas* aren't free, but they're good, and the music is live. *Pricey.*

Jazz Café (open daily, 6 p.m. to 2 a.m.; make reservations at 253-8933 after 2 p.m.; $5 cover) is a restaurant/bar/art gallery on the main street of San Pedro, where you can hear Costa Rica's top live jazz bands, rhythm and blues, New Age, world beat, reggae, and Latin American music. The Café seats 200 and has shows five nights a week. Internationally famous jazz musicians play there at least twice a month.

El Pueblo, in Barrio Tournón near the entrance to the Guápiles Highway, is a huge maze of Spanish Colonial–style alleyways and tiled roofs. You can spend hours wandering around there, getting lost and spending money. **Los Balcones** (open daily, noon to 2 p.m., 5 p.m. to 2 a.m.) features live music, from Latin fusion to Andean to *nueva trova* to jazz. The music starts at 9:30 p.m., Monday through Thursday, and 8:30 p.m., Friday and Saturday. There is a small bar where you can hear authentic Argentinian tango, a sushi bar, a skating rink, and three discotheques. **Lukas** (open daily, 11:30 a.m. to 2:30 a.m.; 233-8145) is a popular place to go for a moderately priced late dinner or snack. At the **Cocina de Leña** (open daily, 11:30 a.m. to 11 p.m.; 255-1360), you can eat native Costa Rican dishes in an authentic campesino atmosphere, for twice the price of the Mercado Central. There are many more restaurants and nightclubs at El Pueblo to try out, as well as boutiques, galleries, and offices. Most nightspots have a cover charge, especially on weekends and holidays. El Pueblo is located north of downtown, across from the Villa Tournón. Walk, taxi, or take a Calle Blancos bus.

DISCOTHEQUES

Costa Rica's discos are not haunted by the specter of John Travolta, but are lively places to work on losing those rhythmic inhibitions. While some specialize in salsa and merengue, many mix in a fair selection of reggae and U.S. pop for those whose hips and footwork are not up to snuff.

While partner dancing is a novelty in the United States, it has a long tradition and a set of rules down here. The more serious salsa discos and salons try to encourage a sense of style and frown upon T-shirts and sneakers. Women who go alone or in groups should expect and be prepared for relentless pickup attempts. Women do not usually invite men onto the floor.

If you're not familiar with Latin music, here are some brief descriptions. *Salsa* is fast, lively Latin dance music. *Merengue* is similar, but basically Dominican with slightly less fancy footwork. *Cumbia* is Colombian, basic 4/4 dance music, and is also lively. *Boleros* are slow romantic ballads. *Rancheros* are a North Mexico version of country music. *Reggae* is mellow Jamaican music, with the words often in English. *Soca* is fast Caribbean dance music, a cross between merengue and reggae. Some places play Spanish-language rap, sometimes called *Punta*.

Cocoloco (in El Pueblo; 222-8782) attracts an older crowd. The emphasis here is on dancing, despite the small floor. Upstairs, **Gravity** has open-air dancing with a younger crowd.

Tobogán (223-8920) is 200 meters north and 100 meters east of La Republica newspaper near El Pueblo.

La Plaza (just across from El Pueblo; 233-5516) has a large dance floor and attracts a young, lively crowd.

Risas (Avenida Central, Calle Central; 223-2803) is a reasonably priced disco with two levels, five bars, and a spacious dance floor.

At **Salsa 54** (Calle 3, Avenidas 1/3; 233-3814), it's worth the cover just to watch some of Costa Rica's best dancers strut their stuff on the raised stage.

GAY/LESBIAN NIGHTLIFE

For women, good *salsa/merengue* and a management that has supported many causes over the years make **La Avispa** (closed Monday; Calle 1, Avenidas 8/10; 223-5343) the first stop on a nightlife tour of San José. Men are welcome there, too, especially on Tuesday. It features three dance floors, a snack bar, pool tables, big-screen TV, and lots of local flavor. La Avispa attracts mostly locals and is popular as the country's first lesbian-owned bar.

For men, **Deja Vu** (Calle 2, Avenidas 14/16; 223-3758) is probably the hottest dance bar in Latin America, with pop, alternative, and techno music. It features a café, a quiet bar, a souvenir shop, and two large dance floors.

On Saturday you'll usually find high-quality dancers and drag shows. Deja Vu attracts a younger, more upscale crowd than La Avispa. The management has invested thousands of dollars and many hours of work in support of gay and lesbian causes.

Al Despiste (open Tuesday through Saturday, 6 p.m. to 2 a.m.; Sunday, 5 p.m. to 10 p.m.; across from Mudanzas; 283-7164) has candle-lit poetry readings on Tuesdays, *trouva* on Wednesdays, and karaoke on Fridays.

Check current listings on www.gaycostarica.com.

RESTAURANTS

COFFEE SHOPS

Below are some of the best places we've found to eat a quick meal or have a cup of coffee. They are all rather pricey by Tico standards, but at any of them you can eat lunch for less than $5 and have coffee and a pastry for under $2.50. The traditional Tico way to serve coffee is in two separate pitchers, one filled with strong black coffee and the other with steaming hot milk. You can mix them to suit your taste. Many establishments have stopped this practice for economic reasons, but Giacomín has retained the tradition. Decaffeinated coffee is available only in those restaurants that serve Café Britt, Costa Rica's export-quality coffee. As an alternative to coffee, most places only offer black or chamomile tea, although many excellent herbal teas are manufactured here. You can always bring your own and ask for a pot of hot water at restaurants. Incidentally, the concept of smoking and nonsmoking areas in restaurants is just being introduced. If it matters to you, stick to vegetarian restaurants.

Azafrán (open daily, 9 a.m. to 7 p.m.; 296-6107) makes delicious sandwiches, lasagna, cannelloni, and desserts. The food can be ordered to go, and they will deliver. Their *torta Azafrán* has to be one of the best cakes of all time. Located in Rohrmoser in the Plaza Mayor Mall.

Boston Bagel Café (open Monday through Saturday, 7 a.m. to 6:30 p.m.; 232-2991) has the best bagels we've tasted here or in the U.S. They come in 12 flavors, and the café serves them with pastrami, four flavors of cream cheese, and other delicacies. Located on the road to Pavas across from La Artística, and in San Pedro in the Plaza Calle Real next to Rosti-Pollo. Recommended.

Bagelmen's (open Monday through Friday, 7 a.m. to 9 p.m.; 224-2432) offers a wide variety of bagel sandwiches and snacks. There's a branch on Avenida Central in Barrio La California east of downtown, one in Escazú at Galerías San Rafael, and another in Curridabat across from the Indoor Club.

Many friends have recommended **Café de Artistas** (open Monday through Saturday, 8 a.m. to 6 p.m.; Sunday, 8 a.m. to 4 p.m.; 100 meters south of Plaza Rolex in Escazú; 288-5082) for fantastic breakfasts, gourmet lunches, and Sunday champagne brunch (sometimes with live music), all in a bohemian café ambiance created by international art on the walls, antique furnishings, and a book exchange.

Café Heliconia (open Monday through Saturday, 8 a.m. to 8 p.m.; 288-0707), next door to Café de Artistas, is in the patio of El Tallercito, a ceramic and mosaic gift shop. Soups, salads, crepes, sandwiches, and pasta are on the menu in a very colorful and charming atmosphere.

In Barrio Amón, **La Esquina del Café** (open daily, 11 a.m. to 7 p.m.; Avenida 9, Calle 3 bis; 258-2983) is a small, quiet café with an in-house coffee roaster and grinder. Connoisseurs will be delighted by the gift-size packets of coffee from the country's different microregions. They offer an inexpensive lunch special that includes coffee and dessert.

Giacomín (open Monday through Saturday, 8 a.m. to noon, 2 p.m. to 7 p.m.; 234-2551) has an upstairs tea room; it's a nice place to enjoy coffee and Italian-style pastries or homemade bonbons. It is next to the Automercado in Los Yoses, with a branch in Escazú (open Monday through Saturday, 10 a.m. to 7 p.m.; 228-1893), in downtown San José (50 meters north of Fischel; 221-5652), and in Santa Ana at the Automercado (203-5312).

Café Ruiseñor (open Monday through Friday, 7 a.m. to 9 p.m.; Saturday and Sunday, 10 a.m. to 5:30 p.m.; 225-2562) is a lovely place that serves delicious pastries and light meals made with pure, healthful ingredients. It has some outdoor tables. Located in Los Yoses, 150 meters east of Automercado—a 20-minute walk from downtown toward San Pedro.

INTERNET CAFÉS

Internet cafés are constantly popping up in San José. Here are some of the more interesting ones:

Browsers (open Monday through Saturday, 9 a.m. to 8 p.m.; 228-7109; www.browsers.co.cr), in the Plaza Colonial shopping center in Escazú, has a pleasant art-deco atmosphere and serves as a gallery for local art.

CyberCafe Las Arcadas (open daily, 7 a.m. to 11 p.m.; 233-3310) is a popular spot for tourists, who can people-watch at their indoor or outdoor tables in the Las Arcadas building in front of the National Theater.

Another downtown café with 20 computers is the **Internet Club** (open daily, 24 hours; 221-7927), 25 meters north of the Caja on Calle 7, Avenidas Central/2.

San Pedro's **Internet Café** (open daily, 24 hours; 224-7382) is a smoky, late-night hang-out with computer games. It's not much on atmosphere but has quick and dependable service.

INEXPENSIVE EATERIES

The **Mercado Central** (Avenidas Central/1 and Calles 6/8) is filled with inexpensive places to eat—many of them, like the Marisquería Ribera, recommended for good food. The only problem with the market is that the restaurants are usually so crowded, you don't feel you can sit down and relax. Go in the late afternoon when things are winding down so you aren't competing with hundreds of hungry workers on their lunch hour.

For dessert, visit **Las Delicias**, on the southeast corner of the Mercado. There the Mora family sells only one flavor of ice cream, a blend of cinnamon, cloves, vanilla, and nutmeg, invented by their great-grandfather in 1901. You can enjoy it with *barquillos* (cookie straws) or in the famous Costa Rican "fruit salad" with canned fruit and Jello.

Our favorite hole-in-the-wall place is the **Soda Amón** (Calle 7, Avenidas 7/9), where you can get a delicious *gallo pinto con huevo* for about $2, and a great *casado* for about $3. It has been there forever, always with the same humble, friendly Tico hosts. Recommended.

La Gauchada (200 meters south of Canal 7; 232-6916) in Sabana Oeste serves piping hot Argentinian *empanadas* with a variety of fillings, including vegetarian.

Kontiki Caribeña (open daily, 11:30 a.m. to 10 p.m.; 224-6848), in the southeastern *barrio* Zapote, has tasty Caribbean cuisine. It's on the north side of the Zapote bull ring, 250 meters west of the PriceSmart.

Don Wang (open daily, 8 a.m. to 10 p.m.; 233-6484) has become famous for its *dim sum* but has an extensive Cantonese, Szechuan, and Pekinese menu as well. Three or four of their plump Chinese dumplings cost under $2. Don Wang is on Calle 11, Avenidas 6/8.

Besides the Mercado Central, you'll find the highest concentration of inexpensive *sodas* in **San Pedro**, the neighborhood bordering the Universidad de Costa Rica. After lunch, you can browse in the area's many bookstores or stroll the shady campus. To get there from San José, catch one of the buses that leave from Avenida 2, Calles 5/7/9. The bus (15 cents) should say "La U" or "San Pedro" in its front window.

Il Pomodoro (open Tuesday through Sunday, noon to 11 p.m.; in San Pedro north of the church and also 100 meters south and 100 meters east of the church, 224-0966; and in Escazú, 100 meters east of the U.S. Embassy residence, 289-7470) has thin-crust pizzas and inexpensive pasta dishes. Popular with students and professors.

By the way, if you must, Pizza Hut, Burger King, McDonald's, Kentucky Fried Chicken, and Taco Bell all have branches here. They are fast, but not as cheap as local places. The best thing about them is that they usually have clean, easy-to-find bathrooms—a boon in downtown San José.

VEGETARIAN RESTAURANTS

All of the restaurants listed here are inexpensive, offering prix-fixe lunches for under $3.

Bio Salud (234-2475), in the Plaza del Sol shopping center in Curridabat, is a health food store with a vegetarian café and a resident herbalist.

Isla Verde (open daily, 11 a.m. to 11 p.m.; 296-5068), located 300 meters west of the U.S. Embassy in Rohrmoser, is a Chinese restaurant with vegetarian selections.

Shakti (open Monday through Friday, 8 a.m. to 7 p.m.; Saturday, 10 a.m. to 5 p.m.; Calle 13, Avenida 8; 222-4475) serves generous, inexpensive, high-quality vegetarian meals. Their *plato del día* has soup, salad, a main course, and a fruit drink for $2. Recommended.

Tin-Jo (open daily, 11:30 a.m. to 3 p.m., 5 p.m. to 10 p.m.; 257-3622) certainly has the most interesting vegetarian menu in town, though it is not known as a vegetarian restaurant. Meat-free Chinese, Thai, and Indian dishes, as well as delicious sushi, are served in a quiet environment with classical music. On Calle 11, Avenidas 6/8.

Comida para Sentir (open Monday through Friday, 10 a.m. to 6 p.m.; 224-1163) is a small, organic, macrobiotic joint popular with students. It's located 125 meters north of the San Pedro church near the train tracks.

Vishnu (open Monday through Saturday, 7:30 a.m. to 9:30 p.m., Sunday, 9 a.m. to 7:30 p.m.; 222-2549) gives inexpensive, generous servings. It's crowded at lunch—get there early. There are five locations: Avenida 1, Calles 1/3; Calle 14, Avenidas Central/2; Calle 1, Avenida 4; Avenida 6, Calles 7/9; and in Heredia, 75 meters south of Fresas.

You can order organic produce at 232-2643 or 393-5314 and pick it up at distribution points in Escazú, Rohrmoser, and San Pedro. Supermarkets **Automercado**, **Mas x Menos**, and **Mega Super** sell tofu, brown rice, and soy products.

MODERATE TO EXPENSIVE RESTAURANTS

San José has many excellent restaurants. In the following list you will find many French, Italian, and Chinese places, but don't overlook those that specialize in Spanish, Korean, or Japanese cuisines. See the Central Valley chapter for excellent restaurants in a mountain setting less than an hour's drive from the city.

Moderate means that most entrées are under $8. *Expensive* indicates that entrées are $8 to $15. Wine can really increase the total price of a dinner, since wines in Costa Rica are imported and expensive. All restaurant bills include a 10 percent tip and a 15 percent tax. Tipping is not customary but is certainly appreciated, especially when the service is good.

Since getting around in San José is such a hassle, especially at dinnertime, we have arranged the following restaurants according to neighborhood:

DOWNTOWN/BARRIO AMÓN   **Aya Sofya** (open Monday through Saturday, 11 a.m. to 10:30 p.m.; 221-7185) delights its patrons with stuffed grape leaves, shish kebab, and a wide variety of Turkish specialties in Barrio California (Avenida Central, Calle 21). *Moderate.*

Bakea (open Tuesday through Saturday, noon to midnight; 221-1051) is *the* place to go for French fusion-style food. It's housed in a restored mansion in Barrio Amon at Calle 7, Avenidas 9/11. *Moderate.*

Café Mundo (open Monday through Friday, 11 a.m. to 11 p.m.; Saturday, 5 p.m. to 11 p.m.; Avenida 9, Calle 15; 222-6190, 233-6272), owned by a young Chicago chef, offers a reasonably priced, healthy menu featuring "Costa Ricanized" international dishes. There's also espresso and a nice selection of desserts. *Moderate.*

Fleur de Lys (open Monday through Saturday, 6:30 p.m. to 9:30 p.m.; Calle 13, Avenidas 2/6; 223-1206) specializes in Costa Rican cuisine. The restaurant is in the courtyard of the hotel of the same name, half a block from the Plaza de la Democrácia. *Expensive.*

Goya (open Monday through Friday, 11:30 a.m. to 11 p.m.; Saturday, noon to 9 p.m.; Avenida 1, Calles 5/7; 221-3887) has great Spanish food and pleasant service. *Moderate.*

Tin-Jo (open daily, 11:30 a.m. to 3 p.m., 5 p.m. to 10 p.m.; Calle 11, Avenidas 6/8; 221-7605) is a friendly, creative Asian restaurant that serves spicy Szechuan, Thai, Indian, and Indonesian dishes. The kitchen accommodates vegetarians. Recommended. *Moderate.*

LOS YOSES/BARRIO ESCALANTE   **Jurgen's Grill** (open weekdays, noon to 2:30 p.m., 6 p.m. to 10:30 p.m.; Saturday, 6 p.m. to 10:30 p.m.; call for reservations: 283-2239) offers classy European cuisine and attentive service in an intimate atmosphere. It's 300 meters north of Subaru in Barrio Dent. *Expensive.*

Le Chandelier (open Monday through Friday, 11:30 a.m. to 2 p.m., 6:30 p.m. to 10:30 p.m.; Saturday, 6:30 p.m. to 10 p.m.; 225-3980) offers fancy French cuisine. From Spoon in Los Yoses, 100 meters south, 100 meters east, and 100 meters south. *Expensive.*

L'Île de France (open daily, 6 p.m. to 10 p.m.; 283-5812) offers excellent traditional French cuisine and superb service. Even if you think you can't afford a full meal, stop in for a glass of wine and a delicious *crema de mariscos* and finish it off with a light, airy *parfait glace de maracuya*. But get there early—the place fills up with loyal patrons. Located in the relaxing garden court of the Hotel Le Bergerac, 50 meters south of the *"primera entrada Los Yoses." Expensive.*

Restaurant and Pub Olio (on Avenida 5, Calles 33/35, 200 meters north of Bagelman's; 281-0541) is a hip tapas bar that also serves Mediterranean main dishes. Generous servings. *Moderate.*

SAN PEDRO/CURRIDABAT **Ambrosia** (open Monday through Saturday, 11:30 a.m. to 10:30 p.m.; Sunday, 11 a.m. to 4 p.m.; 253-8012) is a quiet place for lunch, tea, or dinner, serving both vegetarian and nonvegetarian fare. All specialties are named after Greek deities. Located in the Centro Comercial de la Calle Real in San Pedro. *Moderate.*

Masuri Sushi (280-5522) is famous for perfectly prepared and presented Japanese cuisine. It is located in the Plaza Cristal shopping center in Curridabat.

Marbella (open Tuesday through Saturday, 11 a.m. to 3 p.m., 6:30 p.m. to 10:30 p.m.; Sunday, noon to 5 p.m.; across from the Banco Popular; 224-9452) is an elegant Spanish restaurant that serves a diverse assortment of meat dishes unusual in Costa Rica—rabbit, lamb, and veal, for example. *Expensive.*

Ponte Vecchio (open Monday through Saturday, noon to 2:30 p.m., 6 p.m. to 10:30 p.m.; 200 meters west of San Pedro church, 25 meters north; 283-1810) offers intimate, attentive service and is a good place to propose marriage. Chef/owner is a New York City transplant and prepares the best Italian food we've tried in San José. Recommended. *Expensive.*

PASEO COLÓN/SABANA/PAVAS **Casa Luisa** (open Monday through Saturday, noon to 3 p.m., 6 p.m. to 11 p.m.; 296-1917) is a family-run restaurant with lovingly prepared Catalán cuisine. Make reservations for this popular restaurant, especially if you want the house specialty, *paella.* It's in Sabana Sur, 400 meters south of the Contraloría, and 40 meters east. *Moderate.*

Flor del Loto (open Monday through Friday, 11 a.m. to 3 p.m., 6 p.m. to 11 p.m.; Saturday, 11 a.m. to 11 p.m.; 232-4652) serves delicious Hunan and Szechuan Chinese specialties. On the north side of the ICE (pronounced "ee-say") building, Sabana Norte. *Moderate.*

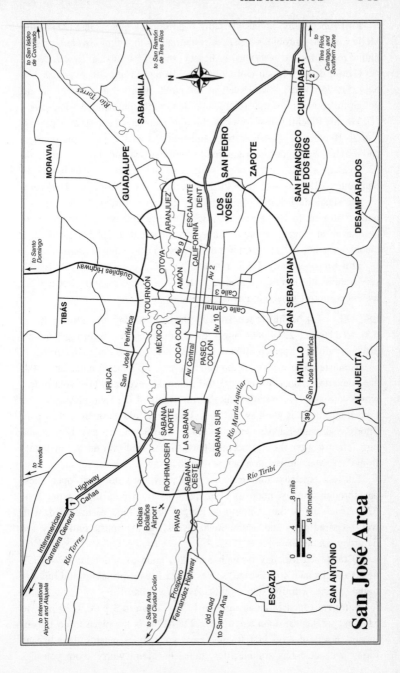

San José Area

Fuji (open daily, noon to 3 p.m., 6 p.m. to 11 p.m.; 232-8122) is the Meliá Comfort Corobicí's Japanese restaurant, with tatami-covered, private dining rooms for six. Near the northeast corner of La Sabana. *Expensive.*

Grano de Oro (open daily, 6 a.m. to 10 p.m.; Calle 30, Avenidas 2/4, No. 251; 255-3322) is an excellent restaurant with a varied menu, in the delightful courtyard of the Hotel Grano de Oro. Recommended. *Moderate.*

Machu Picchu (open Monday through Saturday, 11 a.m. to 3 p.m., 6 p.m. to 10 p.m.; 222-7384) features authentic Peruvian *ceviche,* pisco sours, and *anticuchos.* A good introduction to Peruvian seafood. Located on Calle 32, Avenida 1, 125 meters north of Paseo Colón, with another branch in San Pedro, 125 meters south of the Ferretería El Mar (283-3679). *Moderate.*

La Masía de Triquell (open Monday through Saturday, 11:30 a.m. to 2 p.m., 6:30 p.m. to 10:30 p.m.; 296-3528) serves Spanish and international cuisine in an elegant colonial atmosphere. Located in Sabana Norte, 175 meters west and 175 meters north of the Nissan dealership. *Expensive.*

Shil La (open daily, 11:30 a.m. to 3 p.m., 6 p.m. to 10 p.m.; 296-1808) serves authentic Korean cuisine as well as sushi and sashimi. Located 25 meters north of Cemaco in Pavas. *Moderate.*

ESCAZÚ **Taj Mahal** (open Tuesday through Sunday, noon to 3 p.m., 6 p.m. to 11 p.m.; 228-0980) offers East Indian cuisine, featuring tandoori and curry dishes. Located 800 meters west of Paco in Escazú. *Moderate.*

Monastere (open Monday through Saturday, 7 p.m. to 11 p.m.; 289-4404) is a converted chapel. Waiters dressed as monks reverently take your orders while you gaze out over the shimmering lights of the Central Valley. The French cuisine is as good as the view. They have live music after 8:30 p.m. Thursday through Sunday. Take the old road to Santa Ana past Escazú and turn left just after the Multicentro Paco. Signs lead you up the mountain from there. Make reservations a few days in advance. *Expensive.*

For less expensive dining with a great view, try **Valle Azul** (open Tuesday through Sunday, noon to 11 p.m.; Monday, 5 p.m. to 10 p.m.; 254-6281), high above San Antonio de Escazú on the Pico Blanco road, with well-prepared pasta and international dishes and live music on Friday and Saturday. *Moderate.*

Q'tal (open Monday through Saturday, noon to midnight; 289-9335), next to McDonald's in Escazú, serves Costa Rican specialties and international cuisine, with live music on Fridays. *Moderate.*

Samurai (open Monday through Friday, noon to 3 p.m., 6:30 p.m. to 11 p.m.; weekends, noon to 10 p.m.; 228-4124) is the place to go for authentic Japanese food in Escazú. Leave your shoes outside their private rooms with cushions around a low table, but don't worry about you legs falling asleep—there are pits under the tables for leg room. It's 500 meters south of the Cruce on the main road to San Rafael de Escazú, with another branch in the Centro Comercial Plaza Itskazu (288-0202). *Moderate.*

LODGING

You will find lodgings scattered throughout metropolitan San José; see "San José Lodgings by Neighborhoods" on pages 148–49 for an overview of the city's neighborhoods. In addition to the accommodations below, you may want to check the listings in the following chapter, which covers the Central Valley area. The towns of Alajuela, Heredia, and Santa Ana are closer to the airport than San José and may be good places to stay on your way in and out of Costa Rica.

UPPER-RANGE HOTELS

For what you'd spend in a lackluster roadside motel in the States, you can get elegant accommodations in San José, with excellent service, attentive tour-planning information, and great restaurants. Double-occupancy room rates for these hotels range from $70 to $120; some offer luxurious, pricier suites as well. In our opinion, you can get all the luxury you need in this price range, and personalized service as well. All these hotels accept children. Amenities include private baths, hot water, and, unless indicated, cable TV and phone. If you come in the Green Season, most of them give discounts.

Le Bergerac (ceiling fans, internet access; Calle 35, Avenidas Central/8; $80-$120, including breakfast; children under 12, $10; 234-7850, fax: 225-9103; www.bergerachotel.com, e-mail: bergerac@racsa.co.cr) is quiet and distinguished, with sunny, landscaped grounds. Several rooms have private gardens. The elegant French restaurant L'Île de France is in the garden courtyard. Recommended.

The **Bougainvillea** (ceiling fans, some bathtubs, pool, restaurant, bar; $90-$120; 244-1414, fax: 244-1313; www.bougainvillea.co.cr, e-mail: info@bougainvillea.co.cr) is filled with Costa Rican and pre-Columbian art. Its quiet grounds have a pool, a conference room, a sauna, and tennis courts. Each room's private balcony overlooks the beautiful gardens or San José. The Bougainvillea name is associated with superb service and an excellent restaurant. Located 15 minutes from downtown in Santo Tomás de Santo Domingo de Heredia; microbuses provide a shuttle service between the hotel and San José. Recommended.

Britannia (ceiling fans, bathtubs, air conditioning, cable TV, bar; $100-$130; Calle 3, Avenidas 9/11; 223-6667, fax: 223-6411; www.hotelbritannia

costarica.com, e-mail: brittania@racsa.co.cr) is a remodeled mansion in Barrio Amón, with high ceilings, spacious rooms, and a reasonably priced restaurant in the cool, former wine cellar.

Don Carlos (wheelchair-accessible, ceiling fans, restaurant, bar; $70-$100, including breakfast; children under 12 free; Calle 9, Avenida 9, No. 779; 221-6707, fax: 255-0828; www.doncarloshotel.com, e-mail: hotel@doncarloshotel.com) is a well-run hotel in a pleasant historical neighborhood within walking distance of museums. It is filled with Costa Rican art, has a sun deck, a gym, and a souvenir shop, and shows tour videos. Guests are greeted with a special Don Carlos cocktail, and they have free access to e-mail services. Recommended.

Located on a quiet downtown street, **Fleur de Lys** (fans, most with bathtubs; $80-$170, including breakfast; children under 12 free; Calle 13, Avenidas 2/6; 223-1206, fax: 257-3637; www.hotelfleurdelys.com, e-mail: florlys@racsa.co.cr) is a faithfully renovated mansion that has comfortable sitting areas on each floor as well as atriums. Rooms are graced by original works of art by Costa Rican painters and sculptors. There is also an excellent restaurant and pleasant porch-side bar. Near the National Museum. Recommended.

Hotel 1492 (cable TV, phones; $70-$80, including breakfast; children under 5 free, children 5-12, $5; 2985 Avenida 1, 300 meters east of the Cine Magaly; 256-5913, fax: 280-6206; www.hotel1492.com, e-mail: contact-us@hotel1492.com) is a lovely small hotel in a Spanish-style house on a quiet residential street east of downtown. The walls are hung with gorgeous paintings of tropical flora, painted by the original owner of the house, artist Amalia Jimenez Volio. Rooms are quiet and well-appointed, and three different breakfast menus are served in the garden. Guests are greeted in the evenings with wine and cheese. Seniors might especially like this hotel because it is all on one level. Pets are also welcome. Recommended.

Grano de Oro (ceiling fans, bathtubs, hot tubs, bar, all rooms nonsmoking; $100-$290; Calle 30, Avenidas 2/4, No. 251; 255-3322, fax: 221-2782; www.hotelgranodeoro.com, e-mail: granoro@racsa.co.cr) is an elegant restored mansion located in a quiet neighborhood, yet close to restaurants, theaters, and shops. It has comfortable furnishings, deluxe baths, one of the best restaurants in the city, jacuzzis, and a sunny garden patio. If you have to stay in San José, this is the way to go. Highly recommended.

Hotel Jade (ceiling fans, cable TV, pool, bar; $80-$100, including breakfast; 250 meters north of the Subaru dealership; 224-2455, fax: 224-2166;

www.hotelboutiquejade.com) has spacious rooms in peaceful Barrio Dent, near San Pedro. A comfortable place for business travelers.

María Alexandra (kitchen, air conditioning, cable TV, pool, bar; $80-$100; 228-1507, fax: 289-5192; www.mariaalexandra.com, e-mail: apartotel @mariaalexandra.com) is quiet and very clean, featuring washing machines, a sauna, a gym, and an excellent restaurant. It is located in Escazú, west of San José.

Secure and centrally located downtown, **Hotel Santo Tomás** (private bath, hot water, ceiling fans, some bathtubs, cable TV, phone, pool, nonsmoking; $70-$100; Avenida 7, Calles 3/5; 255-0448, fax: 222-3950; www. hotelsantotomas.com, e-mail: info@hotelsantotomas.com) is in a beautifully remodeled old home with many nice touches. A solar-heated swimming pool and jacuzzi are set in an open courtyard beside the gym and the elegant international restaurant/bar. The rooms are back off the street, a real boon in noisy downtown San José. Breakfast, internet access, and tour planning are included in the rates. Airport pickup on request. Recommended.

Torremolinos (pool, restaurant, ceiling fans, air conditioning; $80-$120; Calle 40, Avenida 5 bis; 222-5266, 222-9129, fax: 255-3167; www. occidentaltorremolinos.com, e-mail: torrehtl@racsa.co.cr) is a large, quiet hotel near Paseo Colón and La Sabana.

BED AND BREAKFASTS

Bed and breakfasts are a growing trend in Costa Rica and can be found both in the city and the country. Even though there are many other hotels that include breakfast in their rates, the distinguishing characteristic of bed and breakfasts is that they are small and have a homelike atmosphere, usually with the owner in residence. All of the establishments listed below pride themselves on the personalized service they give to their guests in tour planning, car rentals, etc. Most will provide lunch and dinner on request and offer kitchen privileges. They range from basic to luxurious, with a wide variety of amenities, listed in each description. For pleasant B&Bs in San José and throughout Costa Rica, see www.costaricainnkeepers.com. To call Costa Rica, dial 011-506, then the number

Ara Macao (private bath, heated water, table fans, cable TV, some refrigerators; $40-$60; 233-2742, fax: 257-6228; www.hotels.co.cr, e-mail: aramacao@hotels.co.cr) is very clean, with pleasant, sunny upstairs rooms, and a nice eating area. Near the National Museum in Barrio California, 50 meters south of the Pizza Hut.

SAN JOSÉ LODGING BY NEIGHBORHOOD

DOWNTOWN   Downtown hotels are convenient for sightseeing and mobilizing for day trips but can be noisy, and the central city is badly polluted. We define "downtown" as the area between Avenida 7 and Avenida 12, Calle 20 and Calle 15. The cheaper hotels are west of Calle 2, in an unsavory section. The hostels are on the east side, in a much nicer neighborhood.

Upper-range: Fleur de Lys; Hotel Santo Tomás
Mid-range: Diplomat; Europa Centro
Inexpensive: Bienvenido; Cocorí; Gran Hotel Centroamericano; La Posada de Don Tobias; Musoc; Pensión de la Cuesta (B&B)
Hostels: Casa León; Casa Ridgway

BARRIOS AMÓN, OTOYA, AND ARANJUEZ   Most hotels in San José's historic northern neighborhoods are restored turn-of-the-20th-century homes with high ceilings and enclosed court-yards. Barrios Amón, Otoya, and Aranjuez are safe, quiet (except for the city's ubiquitous traffic noise), and close to downtown restaurants, shopping areas, and museums.

Upper-range: Brittania; Don Carlos; Raya Vida (B&B)
Mid-range: Aranjuez; Casa Morazán; Hotel Rincón de San José; Kap's Place

PASEO COLÓN   This area, on the Paseo (Avenida Central between Calle 14 and Calle 42) and the two or three blocks north and south of it, is convenient for travelers who are coming from or heading west on the Interamerican Highway—stay here and you can avoid crossing town. Many car rental agencies have their offices here. Several fine restaurants are also in this area.

Upper-range: Grano de Oro; Torremolinos
Hostels: Gaudy's Backpacker's

EASTERN BARRIOS   Barrios Escalante, Dent, and Los Yoses are elegant embassy areas east of downtown toward San Pedro.

Casa de las Tías (no children under 12; private bath, hot water, ceiling fans, all rooms nonsmoking; $60-$90; 289-5517, fax: 289-7353; www.hotels.co.cr/casatias.html, e-mail: casatias@kitcom.net), an ample wood-paneled house, sits at the end of a quiet street in Escazú. Each room is decorated

Upper-range: Hotel Jade; Le Bergerac

Mid-range: Apartotel Los Yoses; Ara Macao (B&B)

Hostels: Costa Rica Backpackers; Toruma

SAN PEDRO AND CURRIDABAT   This University area bustles with students during the March–December academic year, and is packed with good, inexpensive restaurants and nightspots. Buses leave San Pedro frequently for the ten-minute ride downtown.

Mid-range: Ave del Paraíso; D'Galah

Inexpensive: Casa Agua Buena; Condo Casa 43; Maripaz (B&B)

SANTO DOMINGO   One of the area's best hotels is in the quiet residential neighborhood of Santo Tomás de Santo Domingo:

Upper-range: Bougainvillea

PAVAS, ROHRMOSER, AND LA SABANA   The hotels in sunny, upscale Pavas and Rohrmoser, or ringing the green La Sabana, are convenient to the park.

Upper-range: Colours (B&B)

Mid-range: Apartotel La Sabana; El Sesteo; Sabana (B&B); Tennis Club

ESCAZÚ   This small village nestles in a valley to the southwest of San José. The road leading into town is lined with strip malls and high-rises, but once you get into the village center and its nearby hills, Escazú regains its traditional campesino feel. Many B&Bs are here; walkers will enjoy their proximity to beautiful country roads.

Upper-range: Casa de las Tías (B&B); Casa Laurin (B&B); María Alexandra; Posada El Quijote (B&B)

Mid-range: Las Golondrinas (B&B); Pico Blanco; Pine Tree Inn; Tapezco Inn; Villa Escazú

Hostels: Friendly Hostel

with mementos of the owners' sojourns in Latin America as part of the foreign service. Airport pickup ($15) is available.

Casa Laurin (internet, use of kitchen, pool, jacuzzi, sauna; $50-$90; 289-4198, fax: 288-0380; www.costa-rica-bed-and-breakfast.com, e-mail:

lauring@racsa.co.cr) is located in Bello Horizonte de Escazú. Rooms are comfortable and spacious. Ginette Laurin, the attentive French-Canadian owner, creates a congenial atmosphere among guests and serves gourmet breakfasts near the lush gardens. Call or check the website for directions, or Ginette will send a taxi to pick you up at the airport. Recommended.

Colours (private bath, hot water, fans, CD players, cable TV, jacuzzi, pool, restaurant, bar; $100-$130, including breakfast; 150 meters west of Farmacia Rohrmoser; 296-1880, 232-3504, fax: 296-1597, in the U.S.: 877-932-6652, 786-428-0208; www.coloursoasis.com, e-mail: colours@travel base.com) is a gay guesthouse in Rohrmoser. They welcome lesbian travelers as well as men. Special trips and social events are planned throughout the year that cater to visitors and the Tico community. Owned by a Florida travel agency, they can plan your whole vacation, booking gay-friendly hotels and travel agents for side trips. Discounts for longer stays and cash payment.

Built on the lower slopes of an orchard, **Las Golondrinas** (private bath, heated water, kitchen; $40-$50; phone/fax: 228-6448) is a small private cabin with secure parking, located about two kilometers above the church in San Antonio de Escazú (call for directions). The friendly owners take advantage of their farm's fruits in season, and serve all sorts of jams and juices. It's best to have a car when staying here.

Maripaz (shared or private bath, hot water, table fans on request, all rooms nonsmoking; $20-$40; 300 meters south and 100 to the east of the *antiguo higuerón*; phone/fax: 253-8456, 397-3435; www.bedandbreakfast costarica.com, e-mail: maripaz@racsa.co.cr) is located in a friendly Costa Rican home in San Pedro. Convenient for those visiting the University of Costa Rica or the area's many nongovernmental organizations.

Located west of Parque Nacional, near museums and galleries, **Pensión de la Cuesta** (shared bath, heated water, some table fans, shared kitchen, e-mail service, cable TV in living room; $20-$40; Avenida 1, Calles 11/15; phone/fax: 255-2896, 256-7946; www.suntoursandfun.com, e-mail: lacuesta @suntoursandfun.com) has eight rooms (some rather dark) in an interesting old building—the rooms are filled with paintings and creative touches. The fun will be in hanging around with other guests in the light-filled living/ dining room.

Posada El Quijote (private bath, hot water, ceiling fans, phone, cable TV; $70-$100; call for directions; 289-8401, fax: 289-8729; www.quijote. co.cr, e-mail: quijote@quijote.co.cr) is a family home with great views of the Central Valley and a comfortable sitting room with a fireplace. The fruit tree–filled yard has sitting areas with tables and benches. In Bello Horizonte de Escazú.

Raya Vida (internet, cable TV, private bath, hot water, all rooms non-smoking; $110-$120; Calle 15, Avenidas 11/13; 223-4168, fax: 223-4157; www.rayavida.com, e-mail: rayavida@costarica.net) is in a very elegant and delightfully quirky house located at the end of a quiet street in Barrio Aranjuez. There are many unusual and artistic touches such as a small patio with fountain and a mirrored reading room. Every seventh night is free.

Sabana (private bath, heated water, fans, cable TV, internet access; children under 12 free; $50-$70; 100 meters north, 25 west and 175 north of the Chicote Restaurant; 296-3751, phone/fax: 232-2876; www.costaricabb. com, e-mail: go@costaricabb.com) accepts kids and provides a babysitting service. Rooms are small.

MID-RANGE HOTELS

Hotel rates have gone down quite a bit in San José. You can get very pleasant lodgings for about half of what you would pay at home. A double room in these hotels ranges from $30 to $70, and they offer a wide variety of amenities. Some of these hotels are downtown; ask for a room off the street if you like quiet. When we say "TV" in this category, we mean just local-channel TV; cable TV is indicated when available. Many places in the B&B section have similar rates, as do homestays (see below). Be sure to look there, too. All rates include taxes. Don't forget to ask for off-season discounts. If you want to call a hotel directly, dial 011 and Costa Rica's area code, 506.

Aranjuez (solar hot water, shared refrigerator; shared bath, $20-$30; private bath, cable TV, $30-$40; children under 8 free; Calle 19, Avenidas 11/13; 256-1825, fax: 223-3528, in the U.S: 877-898-8663; www.hotelaranjuez.com, e-mail: info@hotelaranjuez.com) comprises several old-fashioned houses linked together in Barrio Aranjuez. There are sitting areas scattered throughout the hotel where people can gather and talk, and quiet gardens in the back. The Aranjuez is popular because of its low rates and the many services it offers—like free local phone calls, free e-mail, and discounts on tours—so make reservations well in advance. A generous buffet breakfast is included in the rate.

Ave del Paraíso (heated water, cable TV; $40-$60, including breakfast; 350 meters north of the Fuente de la Hispanidad, San Pedro; phone/fax: 225-8515, 253-5138, fax: 283-6017; www.hotelavedelparaiso.com, e-mail: apar aiso@racsa.co.cr), owned by a Polish-Tico family, is homey and quiet. A five-minute walk from San Pedro's many inexpensive restaurants and bars, this hotel borders the western side of the Universidad de Costa Rica's campus.

Located across from the University of Costa Rica campus in San Pedro, **D'Galah** ($40-$50; $50-$70 with kitchen; rates include breakfast; in front of the Facultad de Farmacia; phone/fax: 280-8092, 280-7506; e-mail: dgalah@racsa.co.cr) is a quiet place offering a pool and sauna, a jacuzzi, mud baths, and massage.

The **Diplomat** (private bath, hot water, phone, restaurant, bar; $20-$40; Calle 6, Avenidas Central/2; 221-8744, 221-8133, fax: 233-7474; e-mail: huillas@racsa.co.cr) is a clean, well-run, centrally located hotel with a good restaurant.

Europa Centro (cable TV, free internet, air conditioning, some bathtubs, indoor pool, restaurant, bar; $60-$70, including breakfast; Calle Central, Avenidas 3/5; 222-1222, fax: 221-3976; www.hoteleuropacr.com, e-mail: info@hoteleuropacr.com) is a distinctive European-style hotel with a light and airy atmosphere. Ask for an inside room.

Kap's Place (private bath, hot water, ceiling fans, cable TV, phone, kitchen privileges; $30-$70; 221-1169, fax: 256-4850; www.kapsplace.com, e-mail: kapsplace@racsa.co.cr) is in quiet Barrio Aranjuez. Comfortable rooms are off a common living/dining area, and there are hammocks in a covered patio. More rooms are across the street. Located at 1142 Calle 19, between Avenidas 11 and 13.

Casa Morazán (private bath, hot water, air conditioning; $40-$50, including breakfast; Calle 7, Avenidas 7/9; 257-4187, fax: 257-4175; www.casamorazan.com, e-mail: anakeith@racsa.co.cr) is the converted home of Minor Keith, of Atlantic Railroad fame. Rooms are spacious and stylish. The double-paned windows keep out most of the street noise.

Pico Blanco (private bath, hot water, some refrigerators, pool, bar; $50-$60; suites, $70-$80; 228-1908, 289-6197, fax: 289-5189, in the U.S.: 916-862-1170, fax: 916-862-1187; www.picoblanco.com, e-mail: frontdesk @picoblanco.com) is a mountain hotel with a great view, friendly atmosphere, clean, charming rooms, and a restaurant. In San Antonio de Escazú, eight kilometers west of San José.

The **Pine Tree Inn** (private bath, hot water, ceiling fans, cable TV, phones, pool; $50-$60, including breakfast; 289-7405, fax: 228-2180; www.hotel pinetree.com, e-mail: pinetree@racsa.co.cr) has a very helpful staff and is within walking distance of many of Escazú's best restaurants. It is located in the exclusive Barrio Trejos Montealegre in Escazú, 200 meters north and 100 meters west of Rostipollo.

Hotel Rincón de San José (ceiling fans, some bathtubs, cable TV; $50-$60; Avenida 9, Calle 15; 221-9702, fax: 222-1241; www.hotelrinconde sanjose.com, e-mail: info@hotelrincondesanjose.com) is comfortable and elegant. Wallpaper and handmade furniture enhance the interior.

Apartotel La Sabana (air conditioning, cable TV, phone, pool, kitchen; $50-$100, including breakfast; 220-2422, 296-0876, fax: 231-7386; www. apartotel-lasabana.com, e-mail: info@apartotel-lasabana.com) is a sunny complex on a quiet street near La Sabana, with clean, carpeted rooms, a laundromat, and a sauna.

Near the Sabana is the tropical oasis **El Sesteo** (ceiling fans, cable TV, pool, laundromat, conference room; without kitchen, $50-$60; with kitchen, $60-$100; rates include breakfast; 200 meters south of La Sabana McDonald's; 296-1805, fax: 296-1865; www.sesteo.com, e-mail: sesteo@racsa.co. cr). The rooms and apartments surround the unheated pool, the hot tub, and the lush garden. It's a great place to stay with kids, and there is a nice view of the hills from the buffet-breakfast area. Recommended.

The small, two-story **Tapezco Inn** (private bath, hot water, table fans, cable TV, phone; $50-$60, including breakfast; just south of the Escazú church; 228-1084, fax: 289-7026; www.tapezco-inn.co.cr, e-mail: camtapez @racsa.co.cr) is in downtown Escazú.

Tennis Club (air conditioning, cable TV, pool, restaurants, bar; $40-$80, including breakfast; 232-1266, fax: 232-3867; www.crtennis.com, e-mail: crtennis@racsa.co.cr) comes complete with tennis courts, a gym, a sauna, three pools, a bowling alley, playgrounds, and two restaurants. Located on the south side of La Sabana. A good value.

Villa Escazú (private bath, hot water, kitchen; $275/week; phone/fax: 289-7971; www.hotels.co.cr/escazu, e-mail: vescazu@hotels.co.cr) rents studio apartments by the week and offers lots of peace and quiet on its beautiful grounds. In Escazú, west of San José (call for directions).

Apartotel Los Yoses (ceiling fans or air conditioning, cable TV, pool; $50-$100, children under 12 free; 225-0033, 225-0044, fax: 225-5595; www.apartotel.com, e-mail: losyoses@apartotel.com) is very clean. Their larger apartments can accommodate big families or groups, and they have a babysitting service. In Los Yoses, on the main thoroughfare 100 meters west of the Fuente de la Hispanidad. A good value.

INEXPENSIVE HOTELS

These run $7-$30, double occupancy. Almost all are downtown in the midst of traffic noise and gas fumes. We wouldn't want to be in most of these neighborhoods at night. Most of these rooms are basic but clean. If you want to enjoy San José's museums and nightlife, it might be more fun to splurge on something in the mid-range section or stay at one of the hostels or homestays (see below). Most of these hotels are close to the Coca Cola and the bus stops for Guanacaste, Manuel Antonio, Monteverde, and the Zona Sur, but a taxi within San José only costs $1-$2, so you don't have stay in this area in order to get to the buses on time. Don't forget that there are cheap places to stay in Alajuela and Heredia in case the idea of San José doesn't appeal to you, and most buses stop in Alajuela. To call the places below directly, dial 011-506 and the number.

Located one block from the Mercado Central, **Bienvenido** (private bath, heated water, shared refrigerator, restaurant; $20-$40; Calle 10, Avenidas 1/3; phone/fax: 233-2161, 221-1872) is large, clean, friendly, and well-run. Most rooms are off the street, yet are light and fairly well-ventilated. They change traveler's checks.

Condo Casa 43 (no children under 13; rooms $20-$30; apartments $50-$70, $275-$350/week; 224-4395, 825-1012; www.1-costaricalink.com, e-mail: rafaelenriquez2003@hotmail.com) is a new building on a quiet street in San Pedro, 300 meters east of the Lourdes Church and near three universities.

If you plan to stay in San José for a week or more, **Casa Agua Buena** (no children under 14; shared bath, kitchen, washing machine, cable TV, phone; $60-80/week, $160-$250/month; phone/fax: 234-2411; www.agua buena.org/casabuena, e-mail: rastern@racsa.co.cr) is an inexpensive option. Guests share three houses in the pleasant Lourdes section of San Pedro and do their own cooking and cleaning. Gay-friendly.

Close to bus stops, **Cocorí** (private bath, hot water, TV; $10-$20; Calle 16, Avenida 3; 233-0081, fax: 255-1058; e-mail: hotelcocori@racsa.co.cr) has clean, light rooms but is not in a good neighborhood. Make sure you get an inside room. A good value.

Gran Hotel Centroamericano (private bath, hot water; $20-$30; Avenida 2, Calles 6/8; 221-3362, fax: 221-3714; e-mail: ghcmejer@racsa.co. cr) has good wheelchair access and an inexpensive cafeteria.

Clean and well-run, with a friendly staff, **Musoc** (shared or private bath, heated water, shared refrigerator; $10-$20; Calle 16, Avenidas 1/3; 222-9437, 223-3388, fax: 232-4373) is located next to the Coca Cola bus station.

La Posada de Don Tobias (private bath, hot water, TV; $12-$20; 258-3162, phone/fax: 233-8754; www.monteverdeinfo.com/tobias, e-mail: hp tobias@racsa.co.cr), 550 meters north of Parque La Merced, is clean, friendly, and near many provincial bus stops.

HOSTELS

Although neither very private nor luxurious, hostels offer visitors a congenial atmosphere, with ample opportunities for meeting student and budget travelers. The managements of these hostels go out of their way to make guests feel welcome and comfortable. Both dormitory-style and private rooms are available.

Costa Rica Backpackers (shared bath, heated water, pool, internet access, lockers, kitchen, and laundry facilities; dorm rooms, $9/person; private rooms, $20/person; Avenida 6, Calles 21/23; phone/fax: 221-6191; www.costaricabackpackers.com, e-mail: info@costaricabackpackers.com) is a hostel near the National Museum. A swimming pool and a tropical garden with hammocks are not your usual hostel amenities, but they have them. No curfew.

The Swiss-run **Casa León** (heated water, shared kitchen; in dormitory-style rooms with shared bath, $10/person; private rooms with shared bath, $20-$30; with private bath, $30-$40; Avenida 6, Calle 13; 222-9725; e-mail: casa_leon_sa@hotmail.com) is in a clean converted home with good mattresses.

Casa Ridgway (heated water; no smoking; shared bath; $10-$12/person; Avenida 6 bis, Calle 15; 222-1400, 255-6399, fax: 233-6168; www.amigosparalapaz.org, e-mail: friends@racsa.co.cr) is a small *pensión* that helps to support the Quaker Peace Center next door. It has a convivial atmosphere, kitchen and laundry privileges, and dormitory-style bunks in some rooms. Make reservations in advance—it is often full. Rooms with private baths will soon be available.

Gaudy's Backpacker's (dorms, $7/person; private bath, heated water, $20-$30; Avenida 5 between Calles 36/38, north of Paseo Colón; 248-0086; www.backpacker.co.cr, e-mail: gaudys@backpacker.co.cr) has courtyards with plants and hammocks, internet access, and shared kitchen facilities.

Headquarters of the Costa Rica Youth Hostel Network, **Toruma** (hot water, all rooms nonsmoking; $10/person, including continental breakfast; $8 with IYHF card; Avenida Central, Calles 29/31/33; 234-8186, 224-4085; www.hicr.org, e-mail: recajhi@racsa.co.cr) is in an attractive remodeled mansion close to downtown. Men stay on one side, women on the other. All dorm-style rooms share baths. There are only two private rooms ($20-$30). Cable TV, free internet access, a tourism center, guarded parking, communal kitchen, international phone service, and car rentals are among amenities.

In the ritzy suburb of Escazú, the only hostel we've heard of is the **Friendly Hostel** (in dorms or private room, $15/person, including breakfast; 228-5280; www.friendlyhostelcr.com, e-mail: mactabash@racsa.co.cr). It's on the second story of a modern building in San Rafael de Escazú, 50 meters west of Super Saretto.

HOMESTAYS

This is a good way to get to know the local people and to practice your Spanish. To find a compatible family, call the language schools, look for signs at the University of Costa Rica, or use one of the contacts below. Be prepared for a lot of hospitality. If noise bothers you, check first to see if your family leaves the TV or radio on all the time. Amenities run the gamut and depend on the household you choose.

Bell's Home Hospitality (shared or private bath; $30-$50; 225-4752; fax: 224-5884; www.homestay.thebells.org, e-mail: homestay@racsa.co.cr) matches you with a compatible Costa Rican family. Breakfast is included in the rates; dinner is $7 extra. Owners Vernon and Marcela Bell are excellent hosts and very generous with helpful information. Highly recommended.

Sra. Soledad Zamora (phone/fax in Spanish: 224-7937) and her sister **Virginia** (225-7344) specialize in connecting longer-term renters with inexpensive rooms (Spanish speaking only). Rates are $300/month, including breakfast, dinner, and laundry service.

MISCELLANEOUS INFORMATION

SOUVENIRS

Moderately priced souvenirs can be found at the government crafts cooperative, **Mercado Nacional de Artesanía** (Calle 11, Avenida 2 bis, behind the Soledad Church), as well as in the **Mercado Central** (Avenidas Central/1, Calles 6/8), **La Casona** (Calle Central, Avenidas Central/1), and **Souvenir** (Avenida 1, Calle 11). One of the most charming, complete, and inexpensive souvenir shops, called **Annemarie's** (Calle 9, Avenida 9), is in the converted home of one of Costa Rica's ex-presidents, now the Hotel Don Carlos. You can see indigenous crafts at **Galería Namu** (Avenida 7, Calles 5/7).

If you have a little more money to spend, visit **Atmósfera** (Calle 5, Avenida 1), **Magia** (Calle 5, Avenidas 1/3), **Suraska** (Calle 5, Avenida 3), or **La Galería** (Calle 1, Avenidas Central/1), where more artistic items are sold, including the innovative woodwork of two North Americans, **Barry Biesanz** and **Jay Morrison**. Biesanz specializes in exquisitely crafted bowls and boxes, which the Costa Rican government gives as gifts to foreign dignitaries because they bring out the true beauty of native hardwoods. You can tour Barry's workshop and showroom, and stop for a *refresco* overlooking his wife Sarah's herb garden and pond in Escazú. Call 289-4337 for directions (www. biesanz.com). Morrison's creative hardwood furniture is displayed at Magia and also at his showroom, **Tierra Extraña** (282-6697), in Piedades de Santa Ana. Faced with the dilemma of using precious hardwoods in danger of extinction for their work, both Biesanz and Morrison have reforested farms with the varieties they use, and Barry sells hardwood saplings at his showroom.

If you don't want to spend money, don't even think of visiting **Angie Theologos' gallery** (225-6565) of irresistible, one-of-a-kind jackets and vests. The individually designed, lined jackets are crafted from Guatemalan textiles. Each one is a work of art. By appointment only. The gallery is in La Granja de San Pedro, east of San José.

BOOKS, NEWSPAPERS, AND MAGAZINES

English-language newspapers and magazines, including *The New York Times, Wall Street Journal, Miami Herald, Time,* and *Newsweek,* are sold throughout the metropolitan area. **Downtown**, there's the Candy Shop (Plaza de la Cultura), Hotel Aurola Holiday Inn (Parque Morazán), Automercado (Calle 3, Avenidas 3/5), Librería Francesa (Calle 3, Avenidas 1/Central), Seventh Street Books (Calle 7, Avenidas 1/Central), and Librería Lehmann (Avenida Central, Calles 1/3). **East of town** check out Revistas y Más (west of Muñoz & Nanne in San Pedro) and Staufer's (Plaza del Sol in Curridabat). On the **west side** there's Periódicos Americanos (across from the Hotel Corobicí in Yaohan's shopping center).

The Mark Twain Library (open Monday through Friday, 9 a.m. to 7 p.m.; Saturday, 9 a.m. to noon; 225-9433) of the Centro Cultural Costarricense-Norteamericano in Barrio Dent has the latest newspapers and a special room for watching CNN. They also have computers for internet access. Francophiles can visit the **Alianza Francesa** (open weekdays, 8:45 a.m. to 11:45 a.m., 3 p.m. to 7 p.m.; 222-2283) on the corner of Calle 5 and Avenida 7, behind the Hotel Aurola Holiday Inn in San José.

The best source of local news in English, **The Tico Times** (258-1558, fax: 233-6378; www.ticotimes.net, e-mail: info@ticotimes.net; $1) is published Friday and available at the above places and at many hotels. Winner of the Interamerican Press Association award for distinguished service to the community, as well as other prestigious awards, *The Tico Times* offers a well-researched synthesis of weekly events in Costa Rica and Central America. It is without comparison in its coverage of local environmental and political issues and gives an excellent rundown of cultural activities. See their online edition for up-to-the-minute news and facts.

With a convenient central location, **Seventh Street Books** (Calle 7, Avenidas 1/Central; 256-8251), run by two U.S. expatriates, boasts many shelves of contemporary English-language fiction and an excellent selection of books on tropical ecology and travel. They also buy and sell used books.

Mora Books (open 11 a.m. to 6:30 p.m.; in the Omni Building, Avenida 1, Calles 3/5; 255-4136) offers a wide selection of used books, CDs, DVDs, comics, and magazines. They will buy or trade English and German books.

The **Librería Internacional** (300 meters west of Taco Bell in Barrio Dent; 253-9553) is a large trilingual (Spanish, German, English) bookstore with special selections of travel books, esoterica, art, and children's books, as well as a good fiction collection. It has branches in Rohrmoser (100 meters west and 25 south of El Fogoncito Restaurant) and in the Multiplaza in Escazú (201-8320). Its popular discount cousin **LibroMax** (800-542-7662) has branches at the Plaza de la Cultura, at the Outlet Mall and Mall San Pedro, in downtown Heredia, and in the Real Cariari Mall in Alajuela.

For books in Spanish, **Macondo** (on the outside perimeter of the UCR campus, across from the main *Biblioteca*) in San Pedro has an exhaustive collection of fiction and academic works. Many other small bookstores in that neighborhood sell interesting books as well. The grand *librerías* **Lehmann** (Avenida Central, Calles 1/3) and **Universal** (Avenida Central, Calles Central/1) carry translations of U.S. bestsellers.

MEETING PLACES

The **Friends' Peace Center** (open Monday through Friday, 10 a.m. to noon, 1:30 p.m. to 6 p.m.; Calle 15, Avenida 6 bis; phone/fax: 233-6168; e-mail: friends@racsa.co.cr) in San José is a training center for conflict resolution, and addresses issues involving human rights, community development, and ecology. It provides meeting space, activity coordination, a library, and educational programs, and hosts a weekly Quaker meeting. The staff of the center is made up of both Central and North Americans, most of them volunteers.

A variety of clubs meet regularly in San José and the Central Valley, including the Women's Club, Bridge Club, Newcomer's Club, Republicans Abroad, Democrats Abroad, American Legion, La Leche League, Rotary, Christian Women's Club, Canada Club, Coffee Pickin' Square Dancers,

AA, OA, the English-Spanish Conversation Club, Ultimate Frisbee Club, and the Women's International League for Peace and Freedom. Current hours and numbers are often listed in *The Tico Times*.

SUPERMARKETS

Name-brand products from the U.S. are flooding Costa Rican markets. Because they are imported, they are very expensive. Right next to them on the shelf will be a comparable locally made product for half the price.

The **Más x Menos** supermarkets are open daily 8 a.m. to 8 p.m. Ask at your hotel for the nearest one. The **Automercado**, less crowded, cleaner, and more expensive than the Más x Menos, is also open all day. On the east side, **Muñoz y Nanne** in San Pedro is famous for its produce.

MUSEUMS

Most of the downtown museums are mentioned in our walking tour at the beginning of this chapter or in the Creative Arts section. The Children's Museum is mentioned in the "Traveling with Kids" section in Chapter Three. A living museum is the **Pueblo Antiguo** (231-2001, phone/fax: 296-2212), a theme park of Costa Rican history and cultural traditions at the Parque Nacional de Diversiones in La Uruca, two kilometers west of the Hospital México. The park re-creates the city at the turn of the 20th century, as well as a rural town and a coastal village. Professional actors take you into the past in the **Vivencias Costarricenses** tour (weekends from 10 a.m.), in which they trace the roots of Costa Rican traditions and democracy in an entertaining one-hour presentation. Friday and Saturday nights from 6:30 to 9 p.m. you can enjoy a typical dinner and folkloric show, **Noches Costarricenses**, with a historical view of Costa Rican dance and music. Wheelchairs and baby strollers are available at the entrance. Kids will enjoy the amusement park on the same property. Proceeds from Pueblo Antiguo fund the local children's hospital.

ORCHIDS AND INSECTS

Orchid lovers should plan to visit during March when the **National Orchid Show** (223-6517, 224-4278) is held at the Antigua Aduana on Calle 23. Butterfly enthusiasts will enjoy the **Insect Museum** (open Monday through Friday, 1 p.m. to 4:45 p.m.; 207-5318, 207-5647; www.insectos.ucr.ac.cr; admission $1.50) run by the University of Costa Rica's Facultad de Agronomía. It is located on the University of Costa Rica campus in San Pedro, in the basement of the Artes Musicales building.

LA SABANA

San José converted its former international airport into a metropolitan park with sports facilities. The National Gymnasium is on the southeast corner of the former airfield, the National Stadium on the northwest corner. A small lake, which had been filled in, is now restored, and the Air Terminal Building has become the National Art Museum. Residential districts have been built on three sides of La Sabana (which means "the savannah").

With jogging and walking paths; an Olympic swimming pool (open weekdays, 6 a.m. to 1:30 p.m.; 223-8730); tennis, volleyball, and basketball courts; and soccer and baseball fields, La Sabana is a favorite recreation area on weekends and a training ground for runners and joggers during lunch hours (showers are provided). There's a hill for kite flying and lots of trees for shady relaxation. People fly-cast in the lake. To get there, take the Sabana–Cementerio bus. Warning: La Sabana can be dangerous at night.

SEVEN

Central Valley and Surroundings

Costa Rica's Central Valley, or Meseta Central, is a large, fertile plateau surrounded by high mountains. Seventy percent of the country's population lives in this region, which centers around the towns of Alajuela, Heredia, and Cartago, as well as the city of San José. As you leave the more densely populated areas and drive toward the valley's western edge at San Ramón, or wind down through spectacular scenery to its eastern edge at Turrialba, you'll see large fields of sugarcane and corn.

Exploring the highlands leading to the volcanoes Poás, Barva, and Irazú, you will see hills full of coffee bushes, flower plantations, and dairy farms. People enjoy the varying climates of the Central Valley, ranging from year-round summer in the lower western towns of Alajuela, Santa Ana, and Villa Colón, to year-round spring at higher elevations.

A few years back, it was impossible to find lodging anywhere but in San José, but pleasant accommodations have sprung up all over the Central Valley. Since the Juan Santamaría International Airport is much closer to Alajuela and Heredia than to San José, it's possible to stay in or near these towns, avoiding the noise and pollution of the capital city.

You no longer need to go into San José to catch a bus to the provinces. Most of the direct buses to major tourist destinations like Playa Jacó, Guanacaste, Volcán Arenal, Manuel Antonio, and Monteverde pass through Alajuela on their way west, about 25 minutes after they leave San José. They do not go to the bus stations at the west side of Alajuela, but to a bus stop called *parada la Radial*, 100 meters north of the big Mas x Menos grocery store near the airport. The Soda Nandayure, which sells snacks at the bus stop, has a list of the buses that pass each day. There are usually plenty of

161

seats on the morning buses from Sunday through Thursday, but it's safer to go to the San José terminals if you're leaving on a Friday or Saturday, or during holidays.

With advance notice, **A Safe Passage** (441-7837, cell phone: 365-9678; www.costaricabustickets.com, e-mail: rchoice@racsa.co.cr) will buy your bus tickets ($15 for one, $25 for two) for you in San José and deliver them to your Alajuela hotel. The Safe Passage website contains a list of bus departure times from Alajuela to destinations to the north and west. This is a great service, well worth the price.

ALAJUELA AREA

Although only 20 kilometers from San José, **Alajuela** is 200 meters lower and considerably warmer. It is full of shady parks. Weekdays, old-timers sit in the Parque Central and entertain each other by thinking up nicknames for passersby. Sundays, the park fills with families, ice cream vendors, street entertainers, and kiosks selling balloons. The **Juan Santamaría Museum** (open Tuesday through Sunday, 10 a.m. to 6 p.m.), housed in the former jail one block north of Parque Central, features relics of the 1856 rout of William Walker.

The **Zoo Ave Wildlife Conservation Park** (open daily, 9 a.m. to 5 p.m.; 433-8989; www.zooave.org, e-mail: info@zooave.org; admission $9, children $1), 15 minutes west of Alajuela, houses the world's most comprehensive exhibit of Costa Rican wildlife, while also breeding and releasing more native species than any other zoo in Latin America. All the animals at Zoo Ave were former pets, or injured or confiscated wildlife. They are now healthy and living in a beautiful jungle environment, and are released to the wild whenever possible. If you missed seeing monkeys or crocodiles on your trip, you can catch plenty of them here. Birders visit Zoo Ave to familiarize themselves with the calls of the birds they want to see. There are even two male quetzals! Highly recommended. See their website for volunteer opportunities.

GETTING THERE: *By Bus*: Take an Alajuela bus to the end of the line. Then take a Dulce Nombre or La Gorita bus, or take a taxi (about $3 from Alajuela).

By Car: Drive five minutes west of Juan Santamaria airport on the Pan American Highway. Take the exit just after the large Zoo Ave sign. Cross a small bridge after the exit, and continue 2.5 kilometers east. You will see the entrance on your left.

The park-like **Butterfly Farm** (open daily, guided tours at 8:30 a.m., 11 a.m., 1 p.m., and 3 p.m.; 438-0400, fax: 438-0300; www.butterflyfarm. co.cr, e-mail: info@butterflyfarm.co.cr) is devoted to raising live butterflies

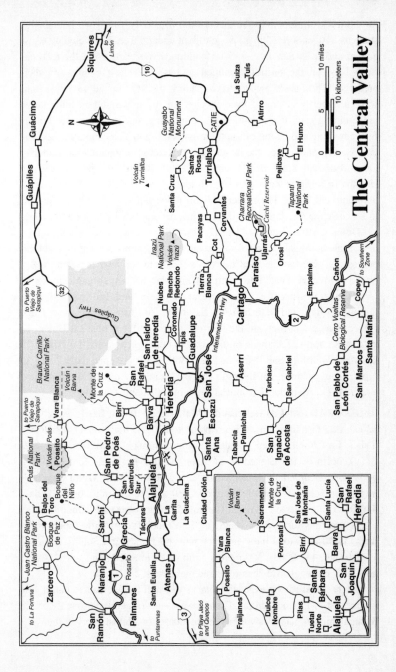

The Central Valley

for exhibit in Europe. On the entertaining Butterfly Tour (two hours; $15, students $10, children 5 to 12 $7, children under 5 free; $25 including transport to and from San José, $15 for children), you learn about the relationships between the beautiful winged insects, their host plants, and their predators. The farm's owners have made it possible for all visitors to observe a butterfly emerging from its chrysalis by presenting an informative video during each tour. Visitors on the morning tour may even see butterflies emerging and taking off on their maiden flight. You can stay as long as you want to photograph the butterflies. You can also combine the Butterfly Farm Tour with Café Britt's famous Coffee Tour ($70, children $50) in Heredia or a trip to Zoo Ave ($60, children $45). Both tours include transportation and lunch. The Butterfly Farm is located southwest of the airport in La Guácima de Alajuela on the left, just beyond Los Reyes Country Club.

Doka Coffee Tour (449-5152; www.dokaestate.com, e-mail: info@dokaestate.com) takes you through the Vargas family's farm and coffee-processing plant on the road to Poás volcano to see how they "put every ounce of love we have" into creating their prize-winning, organically fertilized, shade-grown coffee. Tours are at 9:30 a.m. and 1:30 p.m. Monday through Friday, and 9:30 a.m. on Saturday. You can sample their Three Generations brand brew on the tour or at their coffee shops: **La Luisa**, 12 kilometers north of Alajuela on the road to Poás volcano, and **La Hilda**, 15 kilometers north of San Pedro de Poás. Both shops are open daily 7 a.m. to 5 p.m. They also run **La Begonia** (open 11 a.m. to 7 p.m.; closed Sunday; 442-9846) in Alajuela, four blocks south of La Agonía Church.

RESTAURANTS **Las Delicias del Maiz** (433-7206) in Barrio San José, a $3 cab ride from downtown, is great for homemade traditional Costa Rican dishes. **La Chocita** (open Monday through Saturday, 7 a.m. to 3 p.m.; 442-7179), north of the Cathedral, is recommended by locals for cheap and good *comida típica* for breakfast or lunch. **Restaurante Mixto Vegetariano** (open Monday through Saturday, 7:30 a.m. to 7 p.m.; closed Sunday; 440-0413), upstairs on Avenida Central, 50 meters west of Parque Central, offers generous servings of veggie or Tico food. **TacoMiendo** (open weekdays, 11:30 a.m. to 9 p.m., until 11 p.m. on Friday and Saturday; closed Wednesday; 442-9003), 300 meters north of Perimercado on Calle 4, serves hot, mild, or veggie Mexican food and margaritas.

There are always inexpensive places to eat at the Mercado Central, one block west of Parque Central. There are also lots of good, reasonably priced roasted chicken places as well as internet cafés on almost every corner. The

Pavo Real (441-3274), on the road into town, is a good place for Chinese food; they have an international menu as well.

For nightlife, the indoor/outdoor **La Jarra Garibaldi** (441-6708) on the west side of town offers quality service, with live music and dancing on Wednesday, Friday, and Saturday. **El Mirador Bar-Restaurant** (open daily, noon to 11 p.m.; 441-9347), six kilometers north of town in Sabanilla, has fantastic valley views and karaoke on Wednesdays.

The **Herradura** (239-0033, fax: 239-2292), a resort lodging located on the highway to the airport, has three dining options. One of its restaurants, the **Sakura**, serves authentic Japanese cuisine, and includes a sushi bar. **Restaurant Sancho Panza** specializes in Spanish cuisine. The Herradura also has a 24-hour **coffee shop**. Pricey.

LODGING   There are a variety of accommodations in or near Alajuela. This is a convenient place to stay your first or last night in Costa Rica, much closer to the airport (about a $3-$6 cab ride to any of the hotels shown on the map) than San José, with less to worry about in terms of street safety. The only reason to stay in downtown Alajuela is the abundance of cheap, friendly hotels in the $10-$15 per person range, most of which are in converted older homes. If you are not on a budget, stay in one of the beautiful hotels that dot the hillsides around Alajuela.

Budget Hotels: **Hotel Mango Verde** (private or shared bath, heated water, communal kitchen; shared bath, $10/person; private bath, $15-$30; 441-7116, phone/fax: 443-5074; e-mail: mirafloresbb@hotmail.com) is owned by a friendly Tico family. It's pretty basic but has a spacious area in the back near the garden with hammocks and communal kitchen. It's on Avenida 3, 50 meters west of the Juan Santamaria Museum.

One block east, on Avenida 3 across from the Museum, **Hotel Los Volcanes** (shared bath, heated water, $30-$40; private bath, $40-$50; 441-0525, fax: 440-8006; www.montezumaexpeditions.com/hotel.htm, e-mail: losvolcanes@racsa.co.cr) has polished the tile floors of a fine old house. Ask for the quieter rooms behind the garden in back. Rates include breakfast, free local calls, and internet access. Their special package includes airport pickup and transportation to or from Montezuma (see Chapter Eleven) for $45 to $70, depending on the type of room you have.

Vida Tropical (shared bath, heated water, fans, communal kitchen; $20-$40, including breakfast; children under 12 free; phone/fax: 443-9576; www.vidatropical.com, e-mail: reservations@vidatropical.com) is a friendly guesthouse in a quiet residential neighborhood. In addition to a hearty gourmet breakfast, they provide free internet access and airport pickup, and give a Survival Spanish course ($50/session, $60 for two) that includes excursions into Alajuela to shop, take buses, etc. It's one block east and 3 blocks north of the Alajuela Hospital. There are only six rooms, so make reservations in advance.

A couple of blocks north of Parque Central on what's called Calle Ancha, across from the Corte, **Pensión Alajuela** (heated water, ceiling fans; shared or private bath, cable TV; $30-$40; phone/fax: 441-6251; www.pensionalajuela.com, e-mail pension@racsa.co.cr) is a good deal. The cramped lobby has a satellite TV, bar, internet access, and kitchen for guests. Behind that is an open-air patio. There are murals of iguanas, dolphins, and birds in each room, giving the place a funky charm. The staff offers good advice on getting around.

La Guaria Inn (private bath, hot water; $30-$40, including breakfast; phone/fax: 440-2948; e-mail laguariahotel@netscape.net) is centrally located, and the owner is full of helpful information. It's 100 meters south of the Cathedral and 125 meters east.

The German-owned **Hotel La Trinidad Puesta del Sol** (private bath, hot water; $20-$30, including breakfast; 441-1249, phone/fax: 441-3259; www.hotellatrinidad.com, e-mail: hoteltrinidad@com), located in a quiet neighborhood, is where a lot of foreign residents of Costa Rica stay when they are in the San José area. It's clean, friendly, has a cooking area for guests, and the price is right. It's in Alajuela's Barrio La Trinidad, 100 meters south and 300 meters west of the supermarket. Recommended.

Hillside Hotels: In the villages surrounding Alajuela there are several more hotels, with more pastoral settings than those in downtown Alajuela.

About a kilometer down the road to Tuetal is **Hotel Pura Vida** (private bath, hot water; $70-$110, including breakfast; phone/fax: 441-1157; www.puravidahotel.com), a friendly B&B with bungalows in a hillside garden. Two bungalows have two bedrooms. Owners Berni and Nhi are welcoming hosts; Nhi makes delicious dinners for guests, using her Chinese grandmother's recipes, having fun with local fruit (homemade pineapple ginger sorbet), and decorating everything with flowers. Their website has a wealth of information. Airport pick-up included. Recommended.

The American-owned **Las Orquideas Inn** (private bath, hot water, ceiling fans, some with air conditioning, pool; $60-$100; children under 5 free, children 5-12, $5; larger suites, $115-$150; breakfast included; 433-9346, fax: 433-9740; www.orquideasinn.com, e-mail: info@orquideasinn.com) is on the road to San Pedro de Poás, about three kilometers northwest

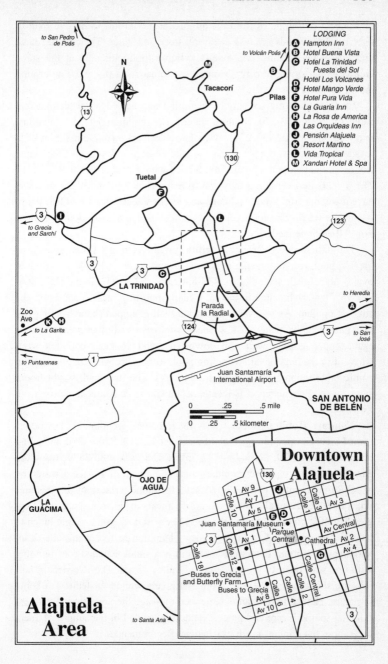

LODGING
- Ⓐ Hampton Inn
- Ⓑ Hotel Buena Vista
- Ⓒ Hotel La Trinidad Puesta del Sol
- Ⓓ Hotel Los Volcanes
- Ⓔ Hotel Mango Verde
- Ⓕ Hotel Pura Vida
- Ⓖ La Guaria Inn
- Ⓗ La Rosa de America
- Ⓘ Las Orquideas Inn
- Ⓙ Pensión Alajuela
- Ⓚ Resort Martino
- Ⓛ Vida Tropical
- Ⓜ Xandari Hotel & Spa

of Alajuela (ten minutes from the airport) at the turnoff to the old road to Grecia. The grounds are lush, with tall trees and vines. Their domes have kitchens, sunken baths, and small skylights for looking up at the stars. Guests gather in the Marilyn Monroe bar to eat roast pig and sing around the player piano.

La Rosa de America (private bath, hot and heated water, ceiling fan, cable TV, pool; $60-$70; children under 5 free, children 5-11, $8; breakfast included; phone/fax: 433-2741; www.larosadeamerica.com, e-mail: info@la rosadeamerica.com) is a great place to land when you first get off the plane. Rooms are set around a beautifully tended garden that attract lots of birds. The owners do everything they can to help orient you and make sure you have a smooth trip. Free local calls and internet access are provided. It's in Alajuela's Barrio San José, "*de La Mandarina, cien metros al sur y cien al este.*" Recommended.

The Italian-owned **Resort Martino** (private bath, hot water, phone, cable TV, pool, restaurant, spa, gym, free airport pickup $180-$250; children over 3, $15; breakfast included; 433-8382, fax: 433-9052, in the U.S.: 866-272-7477; www.hotelmartino.com, e-mail: martino@racsa.co.cr) is on the edge of opulent. As you work out in the well-equipped second-floor gym, you gaze out the plate-glass windows at trees. A Roman steam bath, a sauna and massage await you downstairs, and you can complete your workout in the large, oval swimming pool. Rooms are well appointed, with comfortable indoor and outdoor sitting areas. The one- and two-bedroom suites have kitchenettes. It is located in La Garita de Alajuela, across from Zoo Ave.

Xandari Hotel and Spa (hot water, natural ventilation, lap pools, heated jacuzzi, open-air gym; children under 12 $10; $200-$300, including breakfast; 443-2020, fax: 442-4847, in the U.S.: 800-686-7879; www.xan dari.com, e-mail: paradise@xandari.com) is a dream of a place. Created by a California architect and his artist wife, the stone terraces of the spacious villas overlook Alajuela. Guests can order meals made with spices and veggies from the hotel's organic gardens. They will pack you a picnic lunch to take on the trails leading through their plantation to five waterfalls. Xandari's spa is unique: Each massage room is a small thatched-roof building with one wall open to the gardens and valley views. The two-person hot-tubs are sheltered by the cozy room, yet give a wonderful feeling of being in nature. Helene Faivre, an experienced massage therapist from Montreal, runs the spa with care and grace. Xandari is located in the suburb of Taca-cori, about ten minutes north of Alajuela. Recommended.

With a spectacular 360-degree view of rippling coffee fields and the Central Valley below, the U.S.-owned **Hotel Buena Vista** (private bath, hot water, phone, TV, pool, restaurant; $80-$130, including airport pickup and breakfast; 442-8605, phone/fax: 442-8701, in the U.S.: 800-506-2304; www. arweb.com/buenavista, e-mail: bvista@racsa.co.cr) offers comfortable, carpeted rooms with balconies. It's in the small town of Pilas, five kilometers north of Alajuela.

Siempreverde B & B (private bath, hot water; $50-$60, including a hearty breakfast; 449-5134; www.siempreverdebandb.com, e-mail: info@ siempreverdebandb.com) is on the Vargas family's extensive coffee farm. Rooms have views of the plantations, and tree-lined paths lead you to even more incredible vistas. It's best to have a car if staying here. It is located ten kilometers north of the Alajuela courthouse; turn left at the San Isidro high school on the way to the Poás volcano.

Large Hotels near the Airport: On the General Cañas highway to the airport, about 20 minutes from San José, there are several major hotels.

The **Hampton Inn** (private bath, hot water, air conditioning, cable TV, pool, free local calls, wheelchair access, free airport shuttle; $110-$120, including breakfast; extra bed, $8; 443-0043, fax: 442-9532, in the U.S.: 800-426-7866; www.hamptonhotel.co.cr, e-mail: hamptoninn@grupomarta.com) offers a lot to its guests. Despite being two minutes from the airport and on a major highway, it seems quiet inside. They encourage their guests to "think green" by providing recycling bins in each room and composting restaurant waste to fertilize the hotel's gardens. Recommended.

The **Meliá Cariari Conference Center and Gold Resort** (air conditioning, cable TV; $190-$570; 239-0022, fax: 239-2803, in the U.S.: 800-336-3542; www.solmelia.com, e-mail: cariari@racsa.co.cr) offers an 18-hole, par-71 golf course, tennis courts, three swimming pools, a children's play area, exercise classes, a sauna, riding horses, a casino, bars, restaurants, a 1000-person convention center, and bus service to the airport. The **Villas de Cariari** ($500-$700/week; $1600-$2400/month; 239-1003, fax: 239-1341) are apartments with daily maid service near the Cariari hotel complex.

Another large-scale resort and convention center is the 232-room **Herradura** (cable TV, pool, restaurants; $140-$160; suites, $260-$930; children under 12 free; 239-0033, fax: 293-2713, in the U.S.: 800-832-0474; www. hotelherradura.com, e-mail: reservaciones@hotelherradura.com). Sauna and shiatsu massage, a business center, a large auditorium and nine meeting rooms, a golf course, and tennis courts are among the amenities. In back of its new wing, which has views of the mountains, is a wonderland of swimming pools: one is fed by a waterfall, another has four jacuzzis in it, another laps serenely on a sand-like beach, inviting you to swim up to the bar. The Herradura is also on the highway to the airport roughly 20 minutes from San José and has frequent bus service into town for guests.

The **Marriott Hotel and Resort** ($220-$580, including breakfast; 298-0000, fax: 298-0033; www.marriott.com) in San Antonio de Belén, just south of the airport, is built in the style of a colonial coffee hacienda. The stone arches, wrought-iron balconies, tiled roofs and mosaic staircases, the spacious courtyard, carved furniture and tapestries, and the small chapel are a welcome relief from the boring or pretentious architecture of most large hotels. The Marriott has four restaurants, 15 conference rooms, and a convention center. Add to this the pools, gymnasium, sauna, jacuzzi, tennis courts, golf-practicing course, an amphitheater, and a heliport, and you've got one of the most luxurious hotels in Costa Rica. A taxi from the airport takes 5 to 15 minutes. The Marriott also has its less-expensive Courtyard Hotel on the Prospero Fernandez Highway. Recommended.

GETTING THERE: By Bus: In San José, buses leave continuously for Alajuela (Avenida 2, Calles 12/14).

By Car: Take Paseo Colón west from San José to the General Cañas Highway and watch for the Alajuela signs before the airport. The trip takes about 20 to 45 minutes, depending on traffic.

SANTA ANA LODGING   On the south side of the airport, in the sunny, warm outlying area of Santa Ana, are three fairly new hotels:

Hotel Alta (private bath, hot water, fan, air conditioning, phone, cable TV, pool, jacuzzi, sauna, gym; $180-$215; 282-4160, fax: 282-4162, in the U.S.: 888-388-2582; www.costaricatravelplanners.com, e-mail: hotlalta@racsa.co.cr) is a special place to stay because of its innovative yet harmonious architecture, blending Moorish arches, wooden balconies, and tiled roofs with clean, contemporary spaces to create an elegant mix of old and new. The hall leading down to the restaurant is reminiscent of a street in Barcelona's old Gothic Quarter. Local art graces the walls. The hotel's **La Luz Restaurant** is known for fine gourmet dining. When we were there, Thursday was New Orleans night with Cajun cuisine and live jazz. Their all-day Sunday brunch features Costa Rican nouvelle cuisine. With a pristine, tiled pool, state-of-the-art gym and outdoor hot tub, and views of the Santa Ana Valley, the Alta is an experience to be savored. Recommended.

Albergue El Marañón (shared bath, solar hot water; $30-$60; private bath, $50-$60, including breakfast; apartment, $90; phone/fax: 249-1761, 249-1271; www.cultourica.com, e-mail: info@cultourica.com) is a pleasant

B&B owned by a German-Tica couple that also runs a language school for individuals or groups. Their tour company, Cultourica, takes guests to community-run ecotouristic projects. There is a shady garden with hammocks strung beneath the fruit trees and a great view. El Marañón is located next to the church in Barrio La Trinidad, on a back road between Piedades and Ciudad Colón. It's about 20 minutes from the airport. Recommended.

Paraíso Canadiense (private bath, hot water, phone, ceiling fans, cable TV, kitchens, pool; $50-$60; weekly, $225-$250; monthly, $520-$600; 282-5870, fax 282-4981; e-mail: lynandre@racsa.co.cr) is quiet and secure, right off the highway in a rather sterile industrial sector in Pozos de Santa Ana. Apartments rent by the week or by the month. The hotel hosts a steady flow of Canadian snowbirds in winter months. Their restaurant has a creative menu and live music on weekends.

The following towns offer country lodgings within an hour of the airport. Don't try to find these places by yourself after dark (5:30 p.m.) when you are fresh off the plane.

ATENAS

Fifteen minutes west of La Garita de Alajuela on a winding road is the sunny coffee-growing town of Atenas.

On the right, just before you reach the town, **Las Molas** displays a large variety of excellent souvenirs at reasonable prices in an elegant setting. It's a great place to take a break (nice bathrooms!) on your way back from the coast. At the entrance to town is the impressive **Monumento al Boyero**, commemorating the struggle of oxen and their drivers as they brought coffee and sugarcane down to the Pacific port of Puntarenas for export. As many as 800 oxcarts per day would rumble through Atenas in the 1800s on the trip to the Pacific, and the sturdy oxcart was often both ambulance and hearse in surrounding villages. The iron monument was inaugurated in 2003 with a visit from 400 teams of oxen from all over the country. Due to Costa Rica's rough terrain, the oxcart is still the vehicle of choice in many farm areas, and oxcart parades take place yearly in San José and San Antonio de Escazú.

The central square of Atenas is to your left off the main road as you travel west. **K'puchino's** (open daily, 8 a.m. to 11 p.m.; 446-4184; e-mail: elarimateo@hotmail.com) is a state-of-the-art internet café on the square, with high-speed DSL connections, travel information, and car rentals. They run a shuttle to Playa Jacó on weekends ($10). Spanish cuisine is the specialty of the café, featuring steak, good salads, and vegetarian dishes. **Mirador el Cafetal** (open weekdays, 7 a.m. to 6 p.m.; 446-4361), four winding kilometers west of Atenas, is a charming place to stop for gourmet coffees, fruit daiquiris, *comida típica*, warming soups, or artistic souvenirs and crafts while enjoying views of the lush forested hills.

Off the main road, in Santa Eulalia de Atenas, is the comfortable **El Cafetal Inn** (private bath, hot water, ceiling fans, pool; no smoking inside; $90-$130, including breakfast; 446-5785, fax: 446-7028; www.cafetal.com, e-mail: cafetal@cafetal.com); its owners, an English-speaking Colombian-Salvadoran couple, are helpful and warm hosts. All rooms have expansive views of the Central Valley. Guests can walk to a nearby waterfall, or pick coffee from October through February. If you are coming from the airport on the Interamerican Highway, take the Grecia exit. After less than a mile, take the first left, which will take you underneath a bridge on the Interamerican. Follow the winding road for three miles. El Cafetal will be on the right.

In nearby Rosario de Naranjo, **Vista del Valle Plantation Inn** (private bath, hot water, ceiling fans, some kitchens, pool, jacuzzi; $160-$190, including breakfast; phone/faxes: 451-1165, 450-0800, 450-0900; www.vista delvalle.com, e-mail: frontdesk@vistadelvalle.com), one of the most beautiful B&Bs we've seen. It sits on a coffee and citrus farm, on the edge of a forested 500-foot-deep gorge that is a protected nature reserve. For this reason you might not want to stay there with small children. A little road leads to the river below and a 300-foot waterfall. Private cottages are furnished in a simple, elegant Japanese style and surrounded by lovingly tended gardens. Some overlook the reserve, as does the poolside dining area. Most have outdoor showers and private sun-bathing patios. Suites in the main building have balconies and views. One cottage is "wheelchair friendly." Don't try to find this place at night. The turnoff is just after the Rafael Iglesias bridge, going west on the Interamerican Highway. From there, it's five kilometers on a gravel road. Signs mark the way. Highly recommended.

Also see sections on Grecia and Heredia for more hotels within half an hour of the airport.

ACOSTA

The mountains to the south of San José have not been opened to tourism like those to the north. The Acosta region is a good place to get a sense of rural Costa Rica. ✿ **Nacientes Palmichal** (private bath, heated water; $20-$30/person, including meals; 418-4335; www.nacientespalmichal.com,

LIVING CULTURE IN THE HILLS

The hillsides surrounding the Central Valley are full of tradition. You can learn to make bread in an adobe oven, visit local potters, see how sugarcane juice is pressed and boiled to make delicious *tapa de dulce,* visit local schools, try on the gigantic *papier maché* masks that local dancers wear for fiestas, learn how the Quitirrisí Indians weave baskets and hats from the fibers of the *estococa* plant, eat delicious local food, and experience the process of toasting, grinding, and savoring coffee in the back yard of the lady who picked it.

✿ **El Encanto de la Piedra Blanca** (228-0183; www.codece. org, e-mail: codececr@racsa.co.cr) in San Antonio de Escazú, and **Nacientes Palmichal** (418-4335; www.nacientespalmichal.com, e-mail: sanjoserural@racsa.co.cr) in Palmichal de Acosta can set these tours up for you, or contact **ACTUAR** (228-5695; www.ac-tuarcostarica.com, e-mail: actuar@racsa.co.cr), the umbrella organization for community tourism. John Goldberg of **Real Places, Real People** (810-4444; www.realplaces.net) arranges one- to three-day cultural tours in the Central Valley. All these tours offer a fun way to see the real Costa Rica.

e-mail: sanjoserural@racsa.co.cr) is a cloud forest reserve and lodge about an hour south of the airport, dedicated to the conservation of the many rivers and streams that spring from these mountains and give life to the valley below. The chalet-style lodge is 3.3 kilometers beyond the village of Palmichal de Acosta, with its pretty church and humble mountain charm. Rooms have two bunk beds each and private baths. There is a restaurant for guests and a meeting room. The community's reserve (4000 to 4650 feet above sea level) protects one of the few remaining cloud forests in this area, and offers both easy and strenuous trails and horseback riding. To emphasize its reason for being, part of the river that runs in back of the lodge has been channeled into little waterfalls in front so that you hear the sound of rushing water from all the rooms. Near one of the waterfalls is a plaque with their motto: "The Creator will fulfill the dreams of those who love Creation."

Palmichal is a model for sustainable living. Through the lodge, you can visit family farms that raise pigs and chickens and use the manure in biodigestors. The odorless methane gas from the biodigestors is piped into the house and supplies all the family's cooking needs. You can tour the coffee-processing plant and see how the berry-like pulp of the coffee beans is transformed into organic fertilizer. The lodge will pick you up at the airport, so it's a great option if your plane arrives fairly early and you like the idea of waking up in the countryside. The lodge is very inexpensive and ideal for groups. Recommended.

San Ignacio de Acosta is a larger town about half an hour east of Palmichal, where **Redatour** (281-1969, 410-1025; www.costaricarural tourism.org, e-mail: acsolcr@racsa.co.cr), an association of over a hundred local families, offers homestays, horseback riding, Spanish classes, and guided hikes to the local hot springs (the hike lasts several hours and must be arranged in advance). **Grupo de Giras** (410-0029; e-mail: grugiras@ racsa.co.cr) is a group of local women who offer massage, energy balancing, organic herbal teas, and dietary counseling with herbs and natural foods. Their spotless health center in San Ignacio is a mecca for those who want to cure themselves of chronic diseases or learn to live a healthier lifestyle. Their organic herbal teas make excellent souvenirs.

This area can be a gateway to the Southern Zone. The roads that lead east from these towns through the Los Santos region are well-paved and the countryside is beautiful. In two hours you can be in El Empalme on the Interamerican Highway south of Cartago, saving you the hassle of driving through San José with its traffic jams. For more about Los Santos, see the Southern Zone chapter.

GETTING THERE: Private transportation from the airport to Nacientes Palmichal costs about $10. If you are driving, take the highway to Ciudad Colon, and take the road toward Santiago de Puriscal. There is a Café Palmichal sign at the turnoff to the left for Tabarcia and Palmichal. From the center of Palmichal, ask directions for San Ignacio.

GRECIA

The Grecia area offers many possibilities for day trips, by itself or including La Garita and Volcán Poás. Grecia was voted the cleanest town in Latin America, and its citizens take pride in maintaining that reputation. From its airy red metal church with delicate wooden filigree altars to the well-kept homes of its farmers, it still exudes the goodness and simplicity that many other parts of the Central Valley have lost. We enjoyed the chicken roasted over a wood fire at **Pollo a la Leña**, on the south side of Parque Central. **Soda El Oasis**, on the southwest corner of Parque Central, is a clean and pleasant family-style restaurant with attentive service, reasonable prices, and an ample menu. **Coopevictoria** (494-1866; www.coopevictoria.com), the local sugar cane and coffee cooperative, will take you on a tour of its installations, as well as the attractions listed below.

In the village of Poró, five minutes east of Grecia, is the **Mundo de las Serpientes** (World of Snakes) (open daily, 8 a.m. to 4 p.m.; 494-3700; www.snakes-costarica.com; admission $11, children $6, children under 7 free), in which snakes from all over the planet are exhibited in outdoor concrete habitats. The young Austrian owners give a fascinating hour-long guided tour. They also breed endangered species for release into the wild.

In the sunny village of Rincón de Salas, 20 minutes west of the airport, is **Posada Mimosa** (private bath, solar-heated water with back-up, ceiling fans, pool; $60-$70, including breakfast; two-bedroom cottage with cable TV and kitchen, $120-150; phone/fax: 494-5868; www.mimosa.co.cr, e-mail: mimosa@mimosa.co.cr), owned by Tessa Borner, author of the no-nonsense guide, *Potholes to Paradise: Living in Costa Rica—What You Need to Know*, and her husband Martin, who does fascinating research on organic agriculture with his Tico neighbors. The grounds have beautiful tropical gardens and fruit trees. Almost half of the farm, descending to a stream below, is protected primary forest. Comfortably furnished rooms in the main house open onto a shady corridor. There are beautiful views of the Central Valley from here. Martin has set up different stations of "gym equipment" made from branches and rocks, designed to give every muscle in your body a workout.

GETTING THERE: By Bus: An hourly bus goes to Grecia from the Coca Cola.

By Car: Head west on the Interamerican Highway past the airport and turn right at the well-marked Grecia intersection. To get to Posada Mimosa, go two kilometers toward Grecia, then turn right and go three kilometers to the first crossroads at the village of Rincón de Salas. Turn right again, and go two blocks to Posada Mimosa. Their yellow signs will guide you.

SANTA GERTRUDIS AND LOS CHORROS   Sugarcane and coffee are the main crops in the Grecia area. A winding road through the hills to the northwest takes you to **Los Trapiches** (open Tuesday through Sunday, 8 a.m. to 5 p.m.; 444-6656; admission $2), where on Sunday you can see how *tapa de dulce*, the flavorful hard brown sugar of Central America, is made. A waterwheel activates the huge gears of a venerable Victorian cane press, imported more than a century ago from Aberdeen, Scotland. The cane juice is collected in enormous *pailas* (cauldrons) set into a brick vault in which a fire is built. As the liquid boils, it reaches different stages of consistency until it is ready to be poured into the flower pot–shaped molds. At one point the sugar can be whipped into different forms, called *sobado*. It is quite an interesting process to see, and you can spend the day there, picnicking or eating *comida típica* in the restaurant. There are swimming pools and a small lake for boating. Ticos love to go there on weekends, and there is live music on Sunday afternoon. Call before you go to make sure the *trapiche* is operating. To get there, drive three blocks past the church in Grecia and turn left onto Route 13, winding through the hills on paved roads to Santa Gertrudis Sur, following the Los Trapiches signs. A bus from the main terminal in Grecia—the Grecia–Poás bus—leaves hourly.

A few kilometers south of Los Trapiches, **Los Chorros** ("the jets"; 444-6332; admission $4) are two beautiful waterfalls, about 75 feet high. Numerous smaller jets of water pour from the rock cliffs between them. Rickety bridges hang over the river and there are several covered picnic areas. On weekends locals flock there to picnic and swim in the pools, but you'll have the place to yourself during the week. You pay the admission at a little building downhill from a small sign that indicates the entrance. There is also another entrance through a coffee field farther up the road to Santa Gertrudis.

Getting to the waterfalls requires a ten-minute hike along a well-maintained trail through a wooded gorge. At the entrance, take the lower trail straight to the river, or opt for the high trail and then veer left to the *mirador* for the overlook above the falls. The two trails meet at the main picnic area near the falls, so you can go in one way and come out the other. Only 20 minutes from Alajuela, this is an easy and delightful way to find relief on a hot day. The waterfalls come down with such force that a refreshing mist permeates the air at their base.

GETTING THERE: By Bus: If you don't have a car, you can take buses as far as Santa Gertrudis or Tácares and then walk. A taxi from the Tácares church only costs $1.50. An interesting day trip for those who like to hike might be to take the bus to Santa Gertrudis from Grecia, hike to Los Chorros, continue walking to Tácares, then bus it back to Alajuela from there.

By Car: If you're coming from Los Trapiches, continue south along the gravel Santa Gertrudis–Tácares road for about 15 minutes until the road descends from the hills and makes a sharp right. Here you will see the gated entrance to a quarry on your left. During the week you can drive through the gate, veer left at the bottom of the hill, and park at the entrance to Los Chorros. The gate is closed on Sunday, so you have to leave your car in the makeshift lot outside and walk five minutes to the entrance.

If you're coming from Alajuela, drive west on the Grecia road about 15 kilometers to Tácares. Turn right just past the Tácares church and bear left for three kilometers until the road makes a sharp left into the hills. You'll see the large gate on your right.

SARCHÍ

The small town of Sarchí is the home of Costa Rica's traditional brightly painted ox carts. You can watch artisans creating beautiful wooden bowls, plates, furniture, and walking sticks decorated with animals and birds. With the influx of tour buses full of souvenir-hungry tourists, the main road through Sarchí has become pretty tacky. Although you can buy the same items in San José and Moravia, if you have a lot of wooden crafts on your gift list it is nice to go right to the source. The most inexpensive place to buy crafts is at the cooperative, on the right at the west end of town. In the center of town, the **Plaza de la Artesanía** is a pleasant place to shop for souvenirs. There are many different shops, and a restaurant serves *comida típica*.

GETTING THERE: By Bus: Take the hourly Grecia bus from the Coca Cola. In Grecia, connect with the Alajuela–Sarchí bus. You can catch the latter bus in Alajuela, but it takes a long, roundabout route to Grecia.

By Car: To get to Sarchí, take the Grecia exit off the Puntarenas Highway, 30 minutes west of San José. When you get to Grecia, turn left behind the church, left again (circling the church), then right for three blocks. The road going diagonally to your left is the road to Sarchí.

BOSQUE DE PAZ   Serving as a biological corridor between Poás and Juan Castro Blanco National Parks, **Bosque de Paz** is a pristine forest sanctuary owned by a Costa Rican family, about an hour due north of Sarchí near the town of Bajos del Toro. Well-maintained and -marked trails through the 3000-acre reserve range from a mild one-kilometer loop to a six-kilometer half-day trek to waterfalls. Quetzals nest here between December and February, orchids bloom most exuberantly in April, and troops of monkeys can be spotted all year. It is a favorite stop for Audubon Society birding tours. Your hike will most likely be accompanied by the flutelike song of the jilguero (black-faced solitaire). Iridescent purple hummingbirds flit around their feeders.

Bosque de Paz Lodge (private bath, hot water; $95/person, including meals and entrance to the reserve, by reservation only; 234-6676, fax: 225-0203; www.bosquedepaz.com, e-mail: info@bosquedepaz.com) has comfortable, spacious rooms whose simple design blends with their beautiful natural surroundings. Genuine Costa Rican country food is served in the restaurant.

GETTING THERE: From Sarchí, follow signs directly north on a paved, winding road to Bajos del Toro. The entrance to Bosque de Paz is located to the left on the road that connects Bajos del Toro with Zarcero. It is less complicated to get there from Zarcero, although the road is rough. Take the road beside the Zarcero church for 15 kilometers to Bosque de Paz. The drive has stunning views of the ancient oak forests of Juan Castro Blanco National Park. We drove it at the

View with sombrilla del pobre.

height of the rainy season with no problem (four-wheel drive recommended). Juan Castro Blanco is not set up for visitors, but Bosque de Paz encompasses the same kind of glorious high-altitude forest.

If you are continuing from here into the Northern Zone (west to Volcán Arenal or east to Sarapiquí), drive through Bajos del Toro and down to Río Cuarto in the San Carlos plains. The road was built by ICE, the Costa Rican electric company, to transport workers and materials to build a large hydroelectric plant, so it is well-paved the whole way down.

VOLCÁN POÁS NATIONAL PARK

Poás is one of the few active volcanoes on the continent that is accessible by a good road. The 37-kilometer trip from San José is marked by beautiful scenery, with lookouts over the Central Valley. The famous Café Britt is served at **Cafe Botos** in the park's visitors center, along with sandwiches, pizza, and a variety of delicious pastries.

The main crater of Poás is one and a half kilometers wide and 300 meters deep. There is a hot, sulfurous lake at the bottom. Active fumaroles are visible from the lookout point above the crater. A 20-minute uphill hike takes you to another lookout over jewel-like Botos Lake, which fills an ancient crater.

Volcán Poás is coming out of an active phase, apparently part of a 40- to 45-year cycle. The volcano spewed a 4000-meter column of water and mud in 1910, sending ash as far as Puntarenas. Lava flow increased also in 1953. In May 1989, Poás shot ash a mile into the air, but still it is quiet compared to other volcanoes, such as Arenal and Irazú. Its last eruption was in 1994.

Scientists believe that Poás has a relatively open passage from its magma chamber to its huge crater, so it lets off steam more easily than other volcanoes and doesn't build up the pressure that causes large eruptions. Nevertheless, it is under close observation, and the park is sometimes closed to visitors because of sulfur gas emissions from the crater, which combine with steam to make sulfuric acid. The Seismological Network of the University of Costa Rica has a geochemical weather station at Poás. It detects the emission of hydrogen sulfide gas—often a predictor of eruptions and earthquakes.

Volcán Poás National Park (open daily, 8 a.m. to 3:30 p.m.; call 192 or 283-8004 ext. 110 for information; admission $7, students with ID and children $1) protects the headwaters of several rivers, which feed the Río Tárcoles to the southwest and the Río Sarapiquí to the north. While the active crater is full of subtle, moonscape colors, the rest of Poás is intensely green, with a great variety of wildflowers, bromeliads, ferns, mosses, and lichen. One of the most interesting plants there is the *sombrilla del pobre* (poor man's umbrella), which has thick, fuzzy leaves up to two meters in width, designed to trap airborne algae. Hummingbirds are among the 26 species of birds most easily seen along the road or on the trails. Quetzals, the famed sacred birds of the Maya, also frequent Poás. Don't miss the 20-minute hike along Sendero de la Escalonia that connects the upper parking lot to the picnic area farther along the main road. It's a green mossy tunnel through a shaggy cloud forest.

The average temperature on misty Poás is 50 degrees, dropping as low as 22 and climbing as high as 70, so it is important to dress in layers. It can be very windy. Bring rain gear. If you arrive too late in the day, clouds will be covering the crater, so the earlier you go the better. When it's clear, you can see Poás on the horizon to the northwest of San José. If you can't see it, it's probably too late to go. You can ask at the admission booth whether the crater is visible or not. If you are driving, be sure to get gas before you go up because there are few gas stations along the way. There is one in Poasito.

LODGING AND RESTAURANTS NEAR POÁS **Mirador y Cabinas Quetzal** (private bath, heated water; $30-$40; 482-2090), located near Poasito, is a gift shop and restaurant with four plain but comfortable rooms below it. The view from the guest rooms' large windows is a patchwork of cultivated fields, towns, and forest—an almost dizzying perspective of the Central Valley. Recommended.

The road to Poás is lined with strawberry plantations and restaurants. Be sure to stop at **Chubascos** (442-2280), one of the nicest places we know for native Costa Rican food. It is set in a hillside garden with covered outdoor tables. If it's windy, brightly colored tablecloths lend a welcoming touch to the indoor dining area. Native *olla de carne* (beef and vegetable soup) and *sopa de ayote* (pumpkin soup) are delicious and warming. The freshly handmade *tortilla aliñada con olores* is served with beans, sour cream, and salsa. Yummy *refrescos* are made from local strawberries and blackberries. It's about 16 kilometers (20 minutes) above Alajuela. Recommended.

Jaulares (open weekdays, 10 a.m. to 10 p.m.; Friday and Saturday, 10 a.m. to 2 a.m.; Sundays, 10 a.m. to 6 p.m.; 482-2155) is a large, rustic bar/restaurant at the intersection of the road from Alajuela with the road from San Pedro de Poás on the way to Poás National Park. It's a happening place after 9 on Friday and Saturday nights, when city musicians come to play *trova*, *boleros*, world music, jazz, salsa, and rock. They have rustic cabins in the back with small fireplaces (private bath, heated water; $10/person).

Another highly recommended eatery is **Las Fresas** (open daily, 9 a.m. to 11 p.m.; 482-2620, fax 482-2587; www.lasfresas.com, e-mail info@las fresas.com), owned by an Italian family, where the pizzas are baked in a wood-heated brick oven. The steak at this elegantly cozy restaurant has received rave reviews. Las Fresas rents rooms (private bath, hot water; $30-$40) in hexagonal buildings covered on the outside with lava rock. Coming down from the volcano, you'll see many signs for Las Fresas on the road to San Pedro de Poás. It's about five kilometers below Fraijanes.

At Poasito, there's a six-kilometer road going east to **Vara Blanca**, along the Continental Divide on the pass between Poás and Barva volcanoes. **Villa Calas** (private bath, heated water, restaurant; with kitchen, $30-$40; without kitchen, $20-$30; 482-2222) is a series of cute, two-story A-frame bungalows with fireplaces, located on the left as you leave Poasito on the road to Vara Blanca.

Half a kilometer west of the junction with the Heredia–Sarapiquí road, at Vara Blanca (16 kilometers from Poás), is the turnoff for **Poás Volcano Lodge** (hot water; shared bath, $60-$70; private bath, $80-$90; suites, $100-$140; breakfast included; 482-2194, fax: 482-2513; www.poasvol canolodge.com, e-mail: poasvl@racsa.co.cr), an imposing English manor house 6175 feet above sea level, with cozy rooms and a sunken fireplace in the living room to take the chill out of the air. About one kilometer off the road on a lush dairy farm, this bed and breakfast is especially suited for hikers and birders who like to roam the countryside. There are trails through the forested sector of the farm. The manager can connect you with neighbors who run horse tours through the mountains. To get there by bus, take the Río Frio–Sarapiquí bus from the Terminal Atlántico Norte and get off in Vara Blanca (see below).

There is a gas station in Vara Blanca. Next door, **Restaurant Vara Blanca** is recommended for generous servings of local food and friendly service.

LA PAZ WATERFALL GARDENS   Just about ten minutes (six kilometers) north of Vara Blanca, **La Paz Waterfall Gardens** (open 8:30 a.m. to 3:30 p.m.; admission $21, students with ID and children 12 and under $10; 225-0643; www.waterfallgardens.com) are really worth seeing. Sturdy, non-slip steel bridges and stairways have been built right next to a series of rushing waterfalls, higher tiers of the famous La Paz waterfall that can be seen a few kilometers down the road. To walk next to such power and feel safe is rare, but when you add the incredibly exuberant cloud forest vegetation around the misty waterfalls, and the ozone in the air, this is a truly exhilarating experience. If that weren't enough, there is a huge butterfly observatory and a hummingbird garden where large charts help you identify the jewel-like iridescent creatures flitting around their birdfeeders, seemingly oblivious to visitors. The hike can take as long as you like, but can be done in an hour. It goes downhill, and a mini-bus picks you up at the end and brings you back to the entrance where you can enjoy a *comida típica* buffet ($9). Highly recommended.

There is nothing ordinary about the **Peace Lodge** (private bath, hot water, jacuzzi, cable TV; $220-$400, including breakfast; children 12 and under, $20; www.waterfallgardens.com). The private stone terrace of each villa has a hot tub with jacuzzi, from which you can gaze out over the billowing forest during the day, or stargaze at night. The focal point of the huge garden/bathrooms is a stone waterfall showers and another hot tub. The bedroom has king or queen-sized beds, a gas fireplace, cable TV and a sound system. The two-story Monarch, their honeymoon suite, has a kitchenette and more fireplaces in the bathroom and in the sleeping loft. Recommended.

TOURS   Many companies, including this hotel, will arrange tours that include the Waterfall Gardens as well as Poás volcano and the Doka coffee plantation, or canopy tours and river rafting, or Arenal Volcano and Tabacón hot springs.

GETTING THERE: By Bus: A bus to Volcán Poás leaves daily at 8:30 a.m. from the Tuasa station across from Parque de la Merced in San José (Avenida 2, Calles 12/14; 222-5325). It stops at the Tuasa terminal near the Alajuela central market around 9 a.m. Buses leave from Alajuela's Parque Central on Sunday at 8:30 a.m. Get there early to reserve yourself a seat. The bus from San José arrives at the volcano around 11 a.m. Check with the driver for return time. Many tour companies offer day trips to Poás for between $30 and $60 per person, but a taxi from Alajuela to Poás costs about $50 per taxiload (including waiting and return trip) and a taxi from San José costs about $60. Ask at your hotel for reliable *taxistas,* or call the Alajuela taxi company at 443-3030 or 443-3535. To go to the Waterfall Gardens, take the 6 a.m. or noon Río Frío bus (256-8963) from Calle 12, Avenida 9 in San José.

By Car: Take the Alajuela turnoff from the General Cañas (Interamerican) Highway. It goes past Alajuela's Central Park. Stay on the same road until you get to Fraijanes Lake and Chubascos. About one and a half kilometers beyond the restaurant, you will connect with the road from San Pedro de Poás, which leads to the volcano. If you are near Heredia, take the Barva–Birrí road to Vara Blanca and turn left for six kilometers, then right at Poasito. If you are in Grecia, take the back road to Alajuela through Tácares, turn left at Hotel Las Orquídeas to get to San Pedro de Poás, and continue on to the volcano. You can make a nice circular route, entering through Alajuela, and returning through Vara Blanca and Heredia, with a detour at the waterfall gardens, six kilometers north of Vara Blanca. We highly recommend the Vara Blanca–Heredia route, especially for coming down; it is still beautiful and undeveloped, whereas the faster road from Alajuela has become too crowded and a lot of the beautiful farmland on that route is covered with gray screening that protects berry and flower agroindustries.

If you start out early, you can get to Volcán Arenal by way of Poás and the waterfalls. Continue north of the waterfalls to San Miguel, where you take a very sharp left to go west to La Fortuna by way of Aguas Zarcas and Muelle. To visit Sarapiquí get from the waterfalls to the volcano in about three hours. Or turn right in the center of Aguas Zarcas, and left at the next blinking light. To visit Sarapiquí, continue north from San Miguel to La Virgen de Sarapiquí, about an hour north of the waterfalls. See the Northern Zone chapter.

HEREDIA AND SURROUNDING TOWNS

Just west of Alajuela, **Heredia** has retained a friendly, small-town atmosphere. Its colonial 1796 **church** has a pretty facade and a peaceful garden. Here, too, is the Universidad Nacional that has a substantial student population. There are band concerts Sunday mornings in the music temple in **Parque Central**.

In the **Mercado Florense** (300 meters south and 50 meters west of the church) there's an inexpensive place to have a good seafood lunch. You'll also find some nice, clean restaurants behind the Mercado Central, across from the buses. **Vishnu Mango Verde** (open weekdays, 9 a.m. to 6:30 p.m.; Saturday, 9 a.m. to 5 p.m.; 237-2526) is a vegetarian restaurant downtown on Avenida Central, Calle 7. Servings are generous and inexpensive. **Fresas** (262-5555), near the University, has a great lunch menu, and serves *bocas* at its bar. **Le Petit Paris** (closed Sunday; 262-2564) serves crêpes and French cuisine in its garden near the university.

Wander over to **The Literate Cat** (262-5206), a homey used bookstore on the second floor of Plaza Heredia, where you can browse for books in several languages, with soft classical music in the background.

Located about 750 meters north of Colegio Santa Cecilia in Heredia, **Apartotel Vargas** (private bath, hot water, fans, TV, kitchens, parking; $30-$60; e-mail vago@hotmail.com) offers clean, fully equipped apartments on a quiet street. The upper rooms are lighter. Laundry facilities and airport pickup are available.

The stucco highrise **Hotel Valladolid** (private bath, hot water, air conditioning, hairdryers, phone, cable TV, kitchen; $70-$80, including breakfast; Calle 7/Avenida 7; 260-2905, fax: 260-2912; e-mail: valladol@racsa.co.cr) hosts dignitaries visiting the Universidad Nacional as well as tourists who seek urban luxury in a small-town atmosphere. From the topfloor jacuzzi, sauna, and solarium there are 360-degree views of the Central Valley, and at sunset, the Pacific Ocean is a bright sliver on the horizon.

Hotel Verano (shared bath, cold water; $12-$20; 237-1616), up three flights of stairs on the west side of the market in Heredia, is clean, friendly, and inexpensive.

GETTING THERE: By Bus: Buses to Heredia leave every five to ten minutes from Calle 1, Avenidas 7/9 in San José, 5:20 a.m. to 10:30 p.m. (through Tibás), and from Avenida 2, Calle 12 every 5 minutes (through La Uruca).

By Car: From downtown San José, you should have a good map and ask for detailed instructions. From the General Cañas Highway there are good signs from the turnoff near the airport.

BARVA DE HEREDIA   The town of Barva, two kilometers north of Heredia, is one of the oldest settlements in the country. Its historic church and the houses near it have been restored.

The Museo de Cultura Popular (open weekdays, 9 a.m. to 4 p.m.; weekends, 10 a.m. to 5 p.m.; 260-1619; www.ilam.org/cr/cr.html; admission $1.50) in Santa Lucía de Barva, just outside of Barva, is a colonial-era Central Valley dwelling that has been carefully restored to showcase the best of traditional design. The seven stages of *bahareque*, or reinforced adobe construction, are demonstrated, and the cool house is proof that this is a practical technique in hot climates. Adobe construction without reinforcement has been illegal in Costa Rica since 1910, when an earthquake toppled many adobe houses, killing the people inside. The fruit tree–shaded *solar* (yard) is decked with traditional children's playground equipment: a plank seesaw, rope-and-stick swings, and homemade stilts. A *soda* serves economical and delicious *comida típica* on Sunday, and a little crafts shop sells inexpensive children's toys. By car, follow the signs that start on the road to Barva from Heredia. Otherwise, take the bus 25 meters north of the Heredia high school gymnasium.

Maker of Costa Rica's excellent export-quality coffee, **Café Britt** (open daily, 9 a.m. and 11 a.m; 277-1600, fax: 238-1848; www.coffeetour. com, e-mail: info@cafebritt.com; $27, including transportation from your hotel; by reservation only; discounts for children under 10 and students) has an educational tour of its operations, including a lively show about coffee's vital role in forging Costa Rican democracy, featuring professional performers and multimedia entertainment. Their **Teatro Dionisio Echeverría** also features weekly concerts by some of Costa Rica's finest musicians, as well as innovative plays and cinema. After the tour, visit **Café Don Próspero**, where local delicacies are used to create dishes like macadamia chicken, accompanied by an extensive fruit and salad bar, and finished off by gourmet coffee and pastries. You can also combine the coffee tour with a trip to the Butterfly Farm in La Guacima de Alajuela ($70 including transportation and lunch). To get there, continue uphill from McDonald's in Heredia, turn left at the first stop sign and right after the 500 meters, then follow the Coffeetour signs on the road to Barva. Recommended.

On the Barva–Santa Barbara road, Spanish *paella* master Vincent Aguilar prepares personalized *paellas* and other Valencian specialties at **La Lluna de Valencia** (open Friday and Saturday, noon to 10 p.m.; Sunday, noon to 5 p.m.; phone/fax: 269-6665). His restaurant has become a gathering place for the international NGO crowd. He has revived the tradition of *la tertulia*, where people get together to discuss literature and ideas. The restaurant is located 50 meters from Pulpería La Máquina in San Pedro de Barva.

La Rosa Blanca (private bath, hot water, pool, concierge service, non-smoking; $210-$320, including breakfast; children 3 to 12 half-price; 269-9392, fax: 269-9555; www.fincarosablanca.com, e-mail: info@fincarosa blanca.com) is near Santa Barbara de Heredia. Each room has a theme, and the architecture and handcrafted furnishings are full of fantasy and delightful, creative touches. The honeymoon suite features a tower room with a 360-degree view and a bathroom painted like a rainforest, with the water for the bathtub bubbling out of a rocky waterfall. Gourmet dinners are available for guests only. Airport pickup can be arranged. They have received the highest possible score of all hotels participating in the Certification for Sustainable Tourism of the ICT. Recommended.

SAN RAFAEL AND MONTE DE LA CRUZ   The mountains above Heredia are full of evergreen forests and pastureland. It's exhilaratingly chilly year-round, and a bright, sunny day can turn into a rainy one in minutes, especially after noon. From these mountains you can see the sun glinting off the Gulf of Nicoya in the west. A hike to **Monte de la Cruz Recreation Area** (open daily, 8 a.m. to 4 p.m.; admission 75 cents) gives you an incredible panorama of the entire Central Valley and beyond. Take a picnic lunch, an umbrella, and a sweater. This large, well-maintained park has a slick basketball court, plenty of playground equipment, a soccer field, covered picnic tables, and trails permeated with the smell of evergreens. Many Ticos go there on Sunday. A restaurant is open 11 a.m. to midnight.

The road from San Rafael de Heredia forks at the entrance to Monte de la Cruz. If you take the left fork, in about one kilometer you will arrive at the **Hotel Chalet Tirol** (hot water, bathtub, electric heating; $100-$110; children under 12 free; 267-6222, fax: 267-6373; www.chalet-tirol.com, e-mail: apereira@chalet-tirol.com). At 1800 meters (5900 feet), the hotel is surrounded by a private cloud forest reserve that borders Braulio Carrillo National Park. The older rooms are charming two-story, vine-covered cabins with handpainted Tyrolean designs, and the newer, larger rooms are in a cement building. Their **Salzburg Café Concert** features international musicians. The hotel's private reserve is a great place for a hike, and you can warm up with hot chocolate and pastries on the second floor of the Chalet's restaurant.

Añoranzas (open Wednesday through Saturday, noon to 11 p.m.; Sunday, noon to 6 p.m.; 267-7406), down a road on your left from the main road four kilometers above San Rafael, specializes in *comida típica* and has play equipment for kids.

For nightlife in this area, follow the Bosque de la Hoja road to the left just above Añoranzas to **Refranes B.B.Q.** (closed Wednesday; 267-6076), an atmospheric restaurant specializing in meats and fish served with a variety of tropical sauces. Their charming, candlelit bar features live music on weekends. A cheery fireplace and decorative tiles add to the warmth. They also rent rooms with and without kitchens. **El Mesón de la Cruz** (267-6727), 600 meters east of the Convento de la Cruz, is a quiet restaurant whose tasteful architecture and fireplace create an intimate feeling. The owners take pride in cooking for and waiting on their guests. Try their yummy, creative crêpes and salads.

The nearby **Wolfgang Lodge** (private bath, hot water, cable TV; $40-$80, including breakfast; low weekly rates; 267-6363, fax: 267-6464; www.wolfganglodge.com, e-mail: hotel@tucantico.com) is a friendly, inexpensive B&B with ample open space around the lodge. Helpful owners Carlos Lobo and his wife will arrange horseback riding and birding tours in the area, and make you feel at home.

If you take the road behind the pretty church of San Rafael and cross four bridges (4.5 kilometers), you will see the turnoff on the right for **Restaurante Rincón Suizo** (open Wednesday through Sunday, noon to 10:30 p.m.; 268-3302), which has been recommended for excellent European cuisine in a charming Swiss atmosphere. Just down the hill is **Debbie King's Country Inn** (private bath, hot water; $60-$70; with kitchen, $80-$90; breakfast included; 288-3084; e-mail: debbiecr@racsa.co.cr), a homey B&B set on a working coffee and fruit farm. The cute apartments with kitchens are good for families.

GETTING THERE: By Bus: Buses for this area leave from one block south of the Mercado in Heredia. For Monte de la Cruz and Chalet Tirol, take the San Rafael "Monte de la Cruz" bus, which leaves hourly during the week and every half-hour after 8 a.m. on Sunday (60 cents). The terminus is at a fork in the road, one kilometer from Chalet Tirol (left) or from Monte de la Cruz (right). The bus goes all the way to Monte de la Cruz on weekends.

By Car: Monte de la Cruz and Chalet Tirol are about 35 minutes from San José by car. Take the San Isidro exit to the left about 14 kilometers down the Guápiles Highway right after the Restaurant Las Orquídeas. When you reach San Isidro, turn right uphill in front of the church and go two kilometers to Concepción (ignore any previous Concepción signs). Continue a few minutes more to San Rafael, and again turn right uphill at the church, to reach the road that goes through Los Angeles to Monte de la Cruz. If you are staying in Alajuela, ask for directions from your hotel.

VOLCÁN BARVA

On the western edge of Braulio Carrillo National Park (see below) is Volcán Barva (closed Monday; admission $6). This ancient volcano, on whose slopes Heredia and its neighboring villages roost, offers a good heavy-duty hike through pastureland and, near the top, cloud forest. You usually must walk about four kilometers from where the road gets too bad for most vehicles, and then it's an hour's hike from the park entrance to the 2900-meter-high Laguna Barva, a forest-rimmed green lake in the old crater. The vegetation is vibrant and full of birds. The other, smaller Laguna Copey is a more difficult hour-long hike from the turnoff for Laguna Barva. The Copey trail crosses the divide from the Pacific side to the very moist, muddy Atlantic side. This trail is lined with flowering bushes and huge, primordial *sombrilla del pobre* plants, making it a pretty walk. Try to go early in the day so you can see the views from the trail to Copey. Allow five to six hours at the park if you wish to hike it all. Since there are 2000-year-old trees in the cloud forest surrounding the old crater, scientists surmise that the volcano has been dormant for at least that long. However, vulcanologists have been noticing some volcanic activity in the pass between Barva and Volcán Irazú, and speculate that Barva will act up again soon.

Quetzals are sometimes visible here. They migrate to forests more than 3600 feet above sea level, where they nest in the hollows of the tallest and oldest trees. Males and females share the incubation of eggs and the feeding of hatchlings. The females sit on the eggs at night and at midday, and the male sits with his beautiful green tail hanging out of the nest during the rest of the day. Also heard on Volcán Barva is the black-faced solitaire, which has been compared to the nightingale for the sweetness and delicacy of its song.

Note: Not a year goes by without some overconfident hiker getting lost in this area. The lucky ones are discovered by search parties or follow a stream down to the Atlantic plains. Be sure to take food, water, warm clothes, a flashlight, raingear, plus camera and binoculars. Do not stray from the trail. The forest is too dense and the terrain too hilly for you to navigate on your own. Know that the best strategy is to sign in at the ranger station and tell them which trails you will use. If you get lost, stay put, rig a brightly colored shelter, and drink water from the cups formed in bromeliads.

Tamarak (private bath, hot water, kitchen; $50-$60; 396-4847, 228-6050; www.tamarack.es.vg, e-mail: tamarakcr@yahoo.com) is a charming, two-story wooden chalet with deck, set in a forest about 600 meters beyond **Restaurante Sacramento**. Meals at Tamarak can be arranged for $15 extra per person, or you can buy eggs and tortillas from the neighbors. **Restaurante La Campesina**, three and a half kilometers above Paso Llano, serves tasty, wholesome country food at outdoor tables overlooking the valley, as does Restaurante Sacramento.

El Ranchito (open Thursday through Sunday; 266-1081) in Paso Llano serves Tico favorites grilled on a wood stove. A bit farther down the road, rustic **Chago's** is popular on weekends for good *bocas.*

In the rainy season, the road beyond Sacramento is impossible for regular cars. Even when we visited in the height of the dry season, it was in such poor condition that we had to leave our vehicle and walk the remaining three kilometers to the park entrance. Some four-wheel-drive trucks were navigating the rutty, rock-filled road, however. Every once in a while, the Park Service smooths out the road, so check on road conditions before going (192 or 283-8004 ext. 110). Even if you can't make it to the park, the scenery around Sacramento is worth the trip.

GETTING THERE: By Bus: To climb Volcán Barva, you should catch the 6:20 a.m. San José de la Montaña–Paso Llano bus from the west side of the Mercado in Heredia. (Later buses leave at 11 a.m. and 4.p.m. Check schedules at 237-5007.) At Paso Llano (Porrosatí), you'll see signs for the park entrance eight kilometers uphill to the left. It's a steep uphill walk. The crater lake is 2.6 kilometers beyond the entrance. Be sure to make it back for the 5 p.m. Paso Llano bus to Heredia. A taxi from Heredia to the park entrance costs about $30.

By Car: Follow the road north of Heredia through Barva. Take the right fork north of Barva to lovely San José de la Montaña, with its peaceful church and charming country houses. Continue five kilometers beyond it and turn right at the signs for Braulio Carrillo. In a few hundred meters you'll arrive at Paso Llano. Turn left. The road after San José de la Montaña has quite a few potholes. Four-wheel drive is not necessary, but the steep road requires a powerful engine.

BRAULIO CARRILLO NATIONAL PARK

The founding of Braulio Carrillo National Park in 1978 represented a compromise between ecology and development. Environmentalists were concerned that the opening of a highway between San José and Guápiles would result in the ecological disasters that accompanied the opening of other roads in Costa Rica: indiscriminate colonization and deforestation. The government agreed to make 80,000 acres of virgin forest surrounding the highway into a national park.

The Guápiles Highway, opened in May 1987, made Braulio Carrillo the national park most accessible by car. The scenery is inspiring. Hopefully, it is an education in itself for all the motorists who pass through it on their way to the Atlantic coast—mountains of untouched rainforest as far as the eye can see. And just 50 years ago, most of Costa Rica looked like that!

In order to hike the trails accessible from the highway, you must stop and pay the entrance fee ($6) at the visitors center (1.8 kilometers after the tollbooth if you're coming from San José, or 500 meters after the tunnel if you're coming from Limón). While you're there, ask which trails are accessible and patrolled at the moment. The forest is constantly evolving—trees frequently fall and block paths. It can be risky to try a trail that the rangers don't have resources to take care of. We took a lovely, solitary two-and-a-half-hour hike on the trail right near the visitors center. Views were as beautiful as the more crowded cloud forests in the country, but, unfortunately, loud semi-trailer truck noises competed with the flutelike song of the *jilguero* and probably chased other animals much deeper into the forest. The trails in Braulio Carrillo are usually muddy and steep, so wear appropriate shoes and bring rain ponchos.

GETTING THERE: By Bus: Take the hourly Guápiles bus from the terminal Caribe ($1.50) and ask to be let off at the Oficina de Parques Nacionales, 1.8 kilometers after the *peaje* (tollbooth).

By Car: The trip from San José is about 20 minutes on the Guápiles Highway.

Note: Avoid the *miradores*, the scenic lookout points along the highway—especially the ones that are out of view of the main road. Tourists have been robbed at these places, and the park does not have enough personnel to guard them.

CARTAGO AND VOLCÁN IRAZÚ

Though **Cartago** was the birthplace of Costa Rican culture and the capital for 300 years, many of its historic buildings were destroyed in the earthquakes of 1823 and 1910. The 1910 quake prevented the completion of a cathedral in the center of town. The **ruins** of that church have been made into a pleasant garden, but it's closed indefinitely because of fears of earthquakes. On August 2 every year, thousands of Costa Ricans walk from all over the country to Cartago in honor of *La Negrita*, the Virgin of Los Angeles, who appeared to a peasant girl in 1635. She has become Costa Rica's patron saint, and her shrine is surrounded by offerings from grateful pilgrims whom she has miraculously cured. Tiny metal arms, legs, hearts, and other charms decorate the walls inside **La Basílica de Nuestra Señora de Los Angeles**, an imposing structure on the east side of town. Pilgrims collect water from a spring in back of the church, then go down to the basilica's basement to touch the rock where the virgin repeatedly appeared.

Museo de Cultura Indígena Kurietí (open 9 a.m. to 5 p.m.; closed Tuesday; 573-7113; admission $1.50, with guided tour in Spanish) is the labor of love of Don Angel Ramirez. Don Angel has worked to preserve indigenous tombs and has exhibits about traditions, legends, cooking, and medicinal plants. Coming from San José, pass the main Cartago exits and turn right at El Quijongo, continuing about four kilometers to Tobosí del Guarco.

GETTING THERE: By Bus: Buses to Cartago leave often from Calle 5, Avenidas 18/20 (233-5350) in San José. It's a half-hour trip and the bus lets you off in the middle of bustling downtown. Walk east to the ruins and the basílica.

By Car: Just follow Avenida Central east of San José through the suburbs of San Pedro and Curridabat. That will put you onto the Autopista Florencio del Castillo (50 cents toll), part of the Interamerican Highway, which leads to Cartago.

PARQUE NACIONAL VOLCÁN IRAZÚ   Volcán Irazú (open daily, 8 a.m. to 3:30 p.m.; admission $7, children under 12 $1) is 32 kilometers north of Cartago. On a clear morning, the trip up its slope is full of breathtaking views of farmland, native oak forests, and the Central Valley below. The craters are bleak and majestic. On March 19, 1963, the day John F. Kennedy arrived in Costa Rica on a presidential visit, Irazú erupted, showering black ash over the Central Valley for the next two years. People carried umbrellas to keep the ash out of their hair, roofs caved in from the weight of piled-up ash, and everything was black. Since then the volcano has been dormant, but there were a few tremors in 1991. Gases and steam are emitted from fumaroles near the sulfurous lake that recently formed in the crater, and in January 2004, seismologists noted that the lake suddenly turned bright blue. It is said that you can see both the Atlantic and the Pacific from Irazú's chilly 3432-meter (11,260-foot) summit. This is true on occasion, but often the Atlantic side is obscured by clouds. You can get plenty of exercise there, hiking along the rim of the crater from the *mirador*. Irazú is at high altitude, so you might experience fatigue and lightheadedness.

As you get toward the top of Irazú, you'll see some magical old oak trees covered with lichen and bromeliads. The mossy pastureland there is a good place for a picnic. If you want to try to catch the view of both oceans, you must go early. Bring warm clothes and rain gear. There are clean rest-rooms at the top and a restaurant and souvenir shop offering soup, *tamales*, and gourmet coffees. Rain ponchos are available for rent.

On the way to or from the volcano in the town of Cot, be sure and stop at **Restaurant 1910** (open daily, 11 a.m. to 9 p.m.; phone/fax: 536-6063). Their plentiful and varied buffet includes delicious salads and excellent Costa Rican and international entrées (about $10 including dessert). You can eat indoors or out. Be sure to look at the historical photographs on the walls—1910 was the year of the earthquake that destroyed Cartago. Recommended.

Another good place to go for a day hike is **Area Recreativa Jiménez Oreamuno** (also known as Parque Prusia), a reforestation project started after the 1963 eruption. It's about halfway up the west side of the volcano, eight kilometers west of Tierra Blanca, near Prusia. The hike to the forest is very beautiful, through steep hills covered with oak and pine. Once there, you'll find trails and picnic tables. To get there, take Route 8 to Tierra Blanca and ask for directions from there.

GETTING THERE: By Bus: Buses to Irazú (551-9795, 272-0651; $4.50 roundtrip) leave Saturday and Sunday at 8 a.m. from Avenida 2, across from the Gran Hotel Costa Rica in San José. You can also catch this bus at the Cartago ru-ins at 8:30. The bus leaves Irazú at 12:15 p.m., arriving in San José at 2 p.m. Other days you have to drive or take a tour.

By Car: Take the Interamerican Highway east to the Taras Intersection, two kilometers before the entrance to Cartago. There's a nondescript three-pronged monument there. Go straight, then take the first left (there's no sign). The road signs after that are pretty good. Stay on the main road, veering left at the large statue of Christ. A taxi from San José should cost about $40 for one to four peo-ple. A taxi from Cartago costs about $20.

OROSI VALLEY

In just a few hours you can visit an amazing variety of sites on a trip to the Orosi Valley, south of Cartago. The trip can be as quick as an hour or as long as a couple of days. Following is a description of a circular route from Cartago.

Two blocks after the Basílica in Cartago, make a right, then a left onto the main road that leads to Paraíso.

Six kilometers after Cartago, you will pass the turnoff on the right for **Lankester Gardens** (open daily, 8:30 a.m. to 4:30 p.m.; 552-3247; admis-sion $5), which display the hundreds of varieties of orchids and bromeliads for which Costa Rica is famous. The wheelchair-accessible labyrinthine gardens are run by the biology department of the University of Costa Rica.

Orchids are abloom all year, but the best show is between February and May. They also have a butterfly garden. Recommended.

Next you'll come to the town of **Paraíso**, which is about seven kilometers from Cartago. Drive through town until you see the park, where you turn right. Continue straight down this street, which becomes a narrow country road. Before descending into the valley, you will come to **Sanchiri Lodge** (private bath, hot water; $30-$40, including breakfast; fax: 533-3873; www.sanchiri.com, e-mail: sanchiri@racsa.co.cr), a row of individual wooden cabins on a hillside, each with a balcony and great view. A wooded glen has hiking trails. The family that runs the lodge has been on the land for five generations. There is a restaurant (open daily, 7 a.m. to 8 p.m.) with reasonably priced *comida típica*. Recommended.

Continue on to the **Mirador de Orosi**, a well-tended public park and picnic ground with another great view. It's easy to miss the entrance on the right after Paraíso, but the place is definitely worth a stop. An intimidating flight of steps goes uphill at the entrance, but you can take a path to the left, circle around by the *mirador*, and end up at the top without losing your breath.

Once you get to the floor of the valley, you will soon arrive at the town of **Orosi**. It has a colonial **church** whose beautiful wooden altar and shrines were carved with a special grace. This is one of the few churches in Costa Rica that has survived enough earthquakes to preserve its original atmosphere. A small museum of colonial religious history, **Museo Franciscano** (open daily, 9 a.m. to 5 p.m.; admission 75 cents, children 25 cents) is next door.

There are two thermal swimming pools/recreation areas in town: **Balneario Termal Orosi** (open daily, 7:30 a.m. to 4 p.m.; admission $1.25), southwest of town, and **Los Patios** (open Tuesday through Sunday, 8 a.m. to 4 p.m.; 533-3009; admission $1.50), two and a half kilometers beyond Orosi. The pools are lukewarm, reputed to be medicinal, and full of kids and their families. Both have picnic areas and restaurants, and Balneario Termal Orosi has a basketball court and soccer fields. This is a worthwhile stop if you have young children. Weekdays are more tranquil here.

Near the Balneario Termal Orosi is **Montaña Linda** (shared bath, heated water, shared kitchen; dormitories, $6.50/person; private room, $10.50/person; camping, $4/person in their tent, $3/person in your own tent; kitchen for guests, $1; meals, $2-$5; 533-3640, fax: 533-2153; www.montanalinda.com, e-mail info@montanalinda.com). This friendly youth hostel offers a variety of services: laundry, bike and horse rentals, weddings, and an inexpensive language school with an emphasis on conversation. A five-day intensive course costs $99, including a dormitory room and two meals a day. A homestay is $5 extra per night. Staying here gives you a chance to be part of the life of this lovely little town. Now there is **Montaña Linda B&B** (private bath, hot water; $40-$50, including breakfast), a homey guesthouse with a nice view. Guests can use the kitchen and laundry facilities. To get there, ask to be let off the Orosi bus at Super Anita Numero Dos, the local supermarket, then walk back half a block to Bar La Primavera. Turn left at the bar and go two and a half blocks.

The locally owned **Cabinas Media Libra** (private bath, hot water, TV; $30-$40; 533-3838, fax: 533-3737; www.orosilodge.com/medialibra, e-mail: medial@racsa.co.cr) are clean and loaded with amenities. The second-floor rooms look up to hills covered with a patchwork of coffee and bananas. The cabinas are 200 meters past the plaza and 25 meters to the right.

The **Orosi Lodge** (private bath, hot water, ceiling fan, kitchenette, TV; $50-$60; children under 12 free; phone/fax: 533-3578; www.orosilodge.com, e-mail: ccneck@racsa.co.cr), next to the Balneario Martinez on the east side of town, has verandas with stunning views of the Irazú and Turrialba volcanoes and a charming **Art Café** serving good home-cooked meals and decorated with local art work. You can also check your e-mail there.

As you no doubt will notice, Orosi is a fertile coffee-growing region. When we drove this circuit in January, we passed groups of young coffee pickers strolling home after a day in the fields. Costa Rican coffee farmers use the labor of kids on vacation from school and housewives getting some fresh air. Coffee fields are hot and full of stinging bugs, but coffee picking is also an opportunity to stray from daily routine, spend time with friends and neighbors, and bring in some supplemental cash. The pickers we saw after their day's work looked refreshed and jubilant.

TAPANTÍ NATIONAL PARK   After you pass the coffee plant, you can take a right and drive ten kilometers over gravel roads (about 30 minutes) to Tapantí National Park (283-8004 ext. 110; admission $6). Make sure you bear left at the church after the electric plant; there's no sign. Tapantí protects the rivers that supply San José with water and electricity. It's a great place for birdwatching (black-faced solitaires, hawks, guans, to name a few) and river swimming. There are three trails, one a short trek to the Río Grande, another to a swimming hole, and another a two-kilometer circuit.

Tapantí has just been incorporated into Costa Rica's twenty-sixth national park, which bears the unwieldy name of **Tapantí–Macizo de la Muerte**. By connecting tiny Tapantí to the 52,000-hectare Río Macho forest reserve, the new park extends to Chirripó National Park, which then connects to Parque International La Amistad, making a total of 75,696 protected hectares. This is an important step toward the goal of forming a

Mesoamerican biological corridor so that species can migrate between Mexico and South America without interruption.

The nearby **Kiri Lodge** (private bath, heated water; $30-$40, including breakfast; 533-2272; e-mail kirilodge@hotmail.com) has trout ponds, picnic huts, and a restaurant that will cook your catch. The family-run lodge has its own reserve. Since hiking and birdwatching in Tapantí are best early in the morning, it's a convenient place to spend the night. If you are traveling without a car, it's a pleasant (albeit long) nine-kilometer hike, or you can hire a jeep-taxi in Orosi ($6 one way).

One kilometer from the Río Macho, the road to Tapantí passes the entrance to **Monte Sky** (by reservation only; 231-3536, 228-0010; www.intnet. co.cr/montesky, e-mail: montesky@intnet.co.cr; admission $10, including tour), a private reserve whose Costa Rican owner considers a spiritual retreat. The reserve stretches over 536 mountainous hectares; 80 percent is primary forest. Trails lead to waterfalls and mountain peaks. You can have lunch in the rustic farmhouse, located about half a kilometer uphill from the parking lot. There are also camping platforms in the forest. Taxis from Orosi will charge $5-$6 each way to Monte Sky. The road is passable with any type of vehicle, but those with low ground clearance should drive slowly to avoid rocks.

Back on the main circuit, as soon as you cross the Río Grande de Orosi on a narrow suspension bridge, you will see a driveway to the left for the **Motel Río Palomo** (private bath, heated water, some with kitchen, pools; $20-$30; 533-3128, phone/fax: 533-3057), which has a huge, tour group–size restaurant (open daily, 8:30 a.m. to 5 p.m.), and has traditionally been the place for a fresh-fish lunch.

CACHÍ LAKE As you circle **Cachí Lake**, you'll see the entrance to **La Casona del Cafetal** (open daily, 11 a.m. to 6 p.m.; 533-3280) on the left. This open-air restaurant has a creative menu featuring trout, crêpes, and a wide range of coffee specialties made with coffee grown on the farm. They have a breakfast buffet on Sunday morning, after which you can take a refreshing stroll on lakeside trails. Near the restaurant you can see the work of self-taught woodcarver José Luís Sojo, whose massive creations are made from wood he has salvaged from the rivers or otherwise found. Each one of his pieces has a story and a message. Definitely worth seeing.

Several kilometers later, continuing around the Cachí reservoir, you'll see the **Casa del Soñador** on your right. This whimsical, sculpture-filled house built by the late sculptor Macedonio Quesada is also worth a stop. His sons, Hermes and Miguel, fashion melancholy campesino and religious figures out of gnarled coffee roots. Some are for sale at moderate prices. Hermes can take you to see local petroglyphs.

Soon after is the **Cachí Dam** and the left-hand turnoff for **Ujarrás**, a small agricultural town in a peaceful setting, home to the ruins of Costa Rica's oldest church, **Nuestra Señora de la Limpía**.

GETTING THERE: By Bus: Take the Cartago bus from San José (Calle 5, Avenida 18), which leaves every 10-20 minutes for the 40-minute trip. Ask to be let off at Las Ruinas and walk to the Orosi bus stip on Calle 6, Avenida 1 (leaves every hour on the hour weekdays and every half-hour on weekends; 45 minutes to Orosi). The Orosi bus passes Mirador Sanchiri and goes through Orosi (but get off at the park in Orosi if you want to hire a taxi for Tapantí).

TURRIALBA AREA

Whitewater, still water, rafting, kayaking, canoeing, canyoning, hiking, biking, horseback riding, canopy tours, birding—there is hardly any adventure or naturalist sport that cannot be done in **Turrialba**. It is also the site of Costa Rica's most developed archaeological site, Guayabo National Monument. Definitely off the beaten track, Turrialba has a life of its own beyond tourism, and its residents are open and friendly to visitors. The area offers many possibilities for an interesting day or weekend trip.

As well as offering individual canyoning or rafting tours, most of the companies mentioned below will take you on multiday adventures combining rafting, canyoning, hiking biking, sea kayaking, and surfing. **Loco's Tropical Tours** (556-6035; www.whiteh2o.com, e-mail: riolocos@whiteh 2o.com) has been recommended by readers. **Costa Rica Ríos** (434-0776; www.costaricarios.com, e-mail: info@costaricarios.com) offers a week of adventures, including rafting, biking, camping on the Pacuare, canyoning, and surfing on the Caribbean. **Aventuras Naturales** (225-3939, fax: 253-6934; www.toenjoynature.com) guides you on a Class III/IV trip to their **Pacuare Jungle Lodge**, which features individual bungalows nestled in the rainforest with a gourmet restaurant on the Pacuare river and a **canopy tour**. You can only reach it by raft—there are no roads.

Ríos Tropicales (233-6455; www.riostropicales.com), one of Costa Rica's premier rafting companies, also has a lodge and zipline in its rainforest reserve on the Pacuare.

Don't be disappointed if your river-rafting company calls off your trip because it has been raining. Sometimes *cabezas de agua* can develop when water becomes dammed behind fallen trees upriver and then releases with life-threatening power. Low water levels can be dangerous as well. Prudent companies will call off their trips when they see a potential for these conditions.

Oddly enough, some of the rapids in the mighty Reventazón that made Turrialba famous have disappeared under Costa Rica's newest and largest hydroelectric dam, **Lake Angostura**, which flooded the valley southeast of town in May 2000. Before the valley was flooded, ICE, the national electricity institute, conducted an exhaustive archaeological study of the dam area, unearthing 42 distinct pre-Columbian sites. You can learn about regional archaeology at the **Omar Salazar Obando Regional Museum** (open Tuesday through Saturday, 9 a.m. to noon, 1 p.m. to 4 p.m.; 558-3615; admission $2), located at the University of Costa Rica's Turrialba campus east of town.

The world-famous Pacuare is threatened with being dammed as well. Environmentalists and the rafting industry are trying to have the Pacuare declared Costa Rica's next national park.

If it's hot, you might want to take a dip at **Balneario Las Américas** (admission 75 cents), two large pools for kids and adults that have a bar/restaurant. You'll see signs for it on the main road, on the east side of town.

Turrialba is the home of **CATIE** (Centro Agronómico Tropical de Investigación y Enseñanza; 556-6431, fax: 556-1533; www.catie.ac.cr, e-mail: postmaster@catie.ac.cr). Established in the 1940s, it is one of the five major tropical research and education centers in the world. Its fascinating Botanical Gardens are open weekdays 7 a.m. to 4 p.m. Call Lorena Barrantes at 558-2450 to arrange a tour.

Over the past 30 years, CATIE has been a major force in helping rural farmers in remote places, from Bolivia to Nicaragua, find added value and market niches for their goods, like organic coffee, chocolate, and bananas.

Birders will find the purple-crested gallinet and other rare waterfowl around the lagoon at CATIE. There is a trail from behind the administration building to the Río Reventazón for more birdwatching. By car, drive toward La Suiza and Siquirres, four kilometers from Turrialba. A taxi charges about $2, and La Suiza buses leave hourly from the main terminal in Turrialba.

Located on CATIE grounds, the **Adventure Education Center** (556-4609, in the U.S. and Canada: 800-237-2730; www.adventurespanish school.com) is one of Costa Rica's most dynamic language schools. With campuses in Turrialba, Dominical, and La Fortuna, near Arenal volcano, the school offers a serious language program in regular, medical, and business Spanish plus many opportunities for adventure and cultural exchange.

Spanish by the River (www.spanishbythesea.com) is a language school located five kilometers from the center of Turrialba, in the middle of a coffee field with a beautiful view of Volcán Turrialba. They serve delicious breakfasts on their wide balcony and have inexpensive accommodations at the school (shared room, $6; private, $10). They can also arrange lodging with local families. In addition to medical Spanish and business Spanish, they give a six-hour Spanish Survival course for travelers. Children's programs are also offered. Students can volunteer to teach English at the orphanage or seniors' home, in CATIE's gardens, or with local environmental organizations.

At **Finca Orgánica Patio de Aguila** (556-7661, 354-6315), you'll see the results of one family's commitment to sustainability. The Contreras family raises rabbits, pigs, and cows, uses their manure in a biodigestor to produce cooking gas, treats what is left with worms to make organic fertilizer, raises tilapia, and produces organic coffee, bananas, and medicinal plants. They are located in Colorado de Turrialba, minutes from downtown.

✿ **El Copal** (shared bath, heated water; $20-$30, including meals; 535-0047, Spanish only) is a 190-hectare rainforest reserve in El Humo de Pejibaye, south of Turrialba. The quiet reserve is great for birding, and has a rustic but clean and comfortable lodge run by members of the sugarcane producers' cooperative. The best part of staying there is the *trapiche* at the entrance to the reserve, where you can see how sugarcane is pressed, boiled, and molded into the flavorful hard brown sugar (*tapa de dulce*) that is an integral part of campesino life. Take the Pejibaye/El Humo bus near the central bus station in Turrialba. It leaves at 10 a.m., noon, and 3:30 p.m. Check schedules at 556-2919. From El Humo, it's a six-kilometer walk to the lodge. If you have a four-wheel-drive car, the trip from Turrialba takes about an hour and a half. Make reservations several days in advance.

Parque Viborana (open daily, 9 a.m. to 5 p.m.; cell phone: 538-1510; e-mail: viborana@racsa.co.cr; admission $5), a 20-minute drive from downtown Turrialba in the village of Pavones, is one of the country's model wildlife rehabilitation and educational centers. Owner Minor Camacho worked in the venom extraction laboratories of the University of Costa Rica for over two decades before moving back to this area; he knows as much as anyone in the country about snakes. He is a man with a mission: to teach people about snake behavior so that they can avoid being bitten and thus avoid killing snakes. For instance, we learned that snakes are likely to be out the day after several days of heavy rains because they want to dry out in the sun (see snake section in Chapter Two). Exhibits here include well-designed terrariums for Costa Rica's most dangerous serpents and a large walk-in cage for nonvenomous boa constrictors. Don Minor has planted his small farm with flowers and trees that attract birds, and many species that had disappeared from the sugarcane-monopolized landscape are beginning to come back to his land. Recommended.

RESTAURANTS **La Hulera** (open 7 a.m. to 5:30 p.m.; closed Sunday; 556-2025), on the east side of town is a favorite with the river guides for inexpensive but interesting local food. After your adventure, **Betico Mata's** has great *bocas* and beer, **La Garza** is known for huge *casados* and good service, and the friendly **Soda Aguirre** is popular and inexpensive. **El Conde del Marisco** (556-5029), 100 meters west of the northwest corner of Parque Central, offers Peruvian ceviche. **Don Porfi's** (556-9797) above Santa Rosa is also a favorite with locals for seafood.

The charming and folkloric **Turrialtico** (open daily, 7 a.m. to 10 p.m.; 538-1111, fax 538-1575; www.turrialtico.com) is high on a hill about eight kilometers east of town. The spacious open-air dining room has a magnificent view of the valley. Native food is the specialty. Above the restaurant are comfortable rooms (private bath, heated water, playground equipment; $50-$60, including breakfast; www.turrialtico.com, e-mail info@turrialtico.com) with the same great view. Enjoy their orchid collection, which blooms in March and April.

La Posada de la Luna, west of the church in Cervantes, halfway between Turrialba and Cartago, serves *comida típica* and homemade desserts. Diners are surrounded by cases full of antique memorabilia: Spanish swords, pre-Columbian artifacts, Japanese *netsuke*—you name it, they've got it.

LODGING The **Hotel Wagelia** (private bath, hot water, phone, some with table fans, some with air conditioning, TV, refrigerator; $80-$90, including breakfast; 556-1566, fax: 556-1596; e-mail: hotelwagelia@racsa.co.cr), at the entrance to Turrialba, 150 meters west of the central park downtown, has clean, small rooms and a restaurant that offers an elegant menu with reasonable prices. Just outside of town in a more suburban setting is **Hotel Geliwa** (private bath, heated water, cable TV, refrigerator, ceiling fans, pool, conference center; $80-$90, including breakfast; 556-1142, fax: 556-1029; www.wagelia.com/geliwa, e-mail: hotelgeliwa@racsa.co.cr).

The best budget place to stay is the **Hotel Interamericano** (shared or private bath, hot water, TV; $20-$30; 556-1142; www.hotelintercontinental.com, e-mail: hotelint@racsa.co.cr). As one reader put it: "A gem...very well run, with a caring, helpful, socially responsible management…a good value." It is centrally located, has guarded parking, and a place to hang your wet equipment and store gear. Its structure was recently reinforced to make it earthquake proof. The rooms are painted cheerful colors and comfortable rockers enhance the sitting area. Recommended.

The nicest place to stay in this area is **Guayabo Lodge** (private bath, hot water; $80-$90, including breakfast; 538-8492, phone/fax: 556-1628; www.guayabolodge.com, e-mail: reservaciones@guayabolodge.com). From its perch on the slopes of Turrialba volcano, only half an hour from the center of town, mountain and valley views delight the eye. The hotel is designed with European grace by the Dutch owner, with a sunny dining area, and cozy sitting area with sofas and a tile-decorated fireplace. The rooms are charming and comfortable. Breakfasts include delicious European baked goods. Recommended.

Volcán Turrialba Lodge ($75/person, including all meals and tours; phone/fax: 273-4335; www.volcanturrialbalodge.com, e-mail: info@volcan turrialbalodge.com) is near the top of the Turrialba volcano; their special feature is a descent into the dormant volcano's crater. Turrialba is the only volcano in Costa Rica where such a descent is possible. Access is only via four-wheel drive; they can provide transportation from San José.

Located on a curve in the Reventazón river, **Casa Turire** (private bath, balcony, cable TV, phone, pool; no children under 8; $150-$280; 531-1111, fax: 531-1075; www.hotelcasaturire.com, e-mail: turire@racsa.co.cr) is a unique art deco–style hotel. The elegant lodge overlooks Lake Angostura, the new dam in the flooded valley south of town. Here you'll find a pool, tennis court, kayaks, and a fancy international restaurant. The very well-appointed rooms are reached by a wide staircase leading up from a spacious covered courtyard. Comfortable sitting and game rooms complete the amenities. The hotel also offers local tours. It is 15 minutes southeast of Turrialba.

Catering to birders, naturalists, and photographers, **Rancho Naturalista** (private and shared bath, hot water, good mattresses; 297-4134, fax: 297-4135, in the U.S.: 888-246-8513; www.ranchonaturalista.com, e-mail: info@ranchonaturalista.com) sits high in the hills above Tuís, east of Turrialba. There are nature trails through their private virgin rainforest reserve, the habitat of four species of toucans, the snow-capped hummingbird, and many other bird and butterfly species. The comfortable lodge overlooks the wide valley, and there are three separate cottages, one with two bedrooms. The restaurant's creative cookery is a special attraction. They specialize in week-long birding packages, combining Rancho Naturalista with birding sites in Monteverde, Sarapiquí, Tortuguero, and Drake Bay. Prices run from $850 to $1500/person/week, including meals, transportation, and tours.

GETTING THERE: By Bus: Buses leave San José hourly for Turrialba from Calle 13, Avenidas 6/8 (556-4233; $1.25). The trip takes an hour and a half.

By Car: The traditional route is through Cartago and Paraíso, then winding through sugarcane fields into Turrialba, about one and a half hours total from San José. There is also a delightful, paved back road that starts slightly south of the town of Cot on the slopes of Volcán Irazú, skirts Volcán Turrialba, and passes through the towns of Pacayas and Santa Cruz before arriving in Turrialba itself. This route takes less than two hours from San José.

GUAYABO NATIONAL MONUMENT

Guayabo National Monument (open daily, 8 a.m. to 3:30 p.m.; admission $4, children under 12 $1), on the slopes of Volcán Turrialba, is considered the most significant archaeological site in Costa Rica. It offers a glimpse into the harmony between people and nature that existed in pre-Columbian times. Birds abound in the ruins, which are set in premontane rainforest and dotted with the guava trees that give the town its name. *Oropéndolas* (related to North American orioles) hang their sacklike nests from tree branches. Water sings its song in ancient aqueducts.

Archaeologists have excavated only the central part of a 10,000-inhabitant city that existed from 1000 B.C. to about A.D. 1400. The exposed area is composed of circular mounds, which were the floors of large buildings raised to keep them dry; paved sidewalks, some of whose stones are decorated with petroglyphs; a large stone carved with stylistic representations of two Indian gods: the jaguar, god of the forest, and the crocodile, god of the river; a system of covered and uncovered aqueducts that still functions well; and the oldest bridge in Costa Rica, a flat rock, now broken in several places, which crosses one of the aqueducts. Several roads radiate from the center of the town. Spot excavations verify that some of them extend at least eight kilometers. It is thought that Guayabo was an important conduit between the Aztec and Maya peoples of the north and the Incas of the south.

There are many mysteries about the civilization that inhabited Guayabo. No one knows why the people left (just before the *conquistadores* discovered Costa Rica), nor why Spanish explorers never found or never kept records of finding the site. Yet the peace and beauty that reign in Guayabo echo a wise and gentle people.

From the *mirador*, you can see green grassy mounds and stone sidewalks nestled within the rainforest. Hawks and vultures swoop and sail in front of the striking four-layered backdrop of mountains. Across the road from the site, behind the campground, a steep trail leads down to the fast-flowing Guayabo River, where you can sit bathing your feet and looking for birds. You can also walk up the road past coffee and sugarcane fields for views of the green Guayabo valley.

Park personnel orient visitors when they arrive, then give them a pamphlet to do a self-guided tour. Bring rain gear.

GETTING THERE: By Bus: From Turrialba, two buses a day (11 a.m. and 5 p.m., Monday through Saturday) leave the main bus terminal for Guayabo. They return at 5:30 a.m. and 12:50 p.m. On Sunday, the bus leaves Turrialba at 9 a.m. and returns at 4 p.m. so locals can spend the day up at the monument.

By Car: From Turrialba, follow the signs off the main highway through downtown, crossing the river on the old steel bridge. Stay on the main road until you see the sign indicat-

Oropéndolas

ing a left to the Park. It's a 19-kilometer trip and takes about 40 minutes. The road is paved except for the last four kilometers.

From San José you can choose to take the above-described back road from San José to Turrialba, via Pacayas and Santa Cruz. There's a short cut to Guayabo National Monument. Watch for a steep left down a gravel road a few kilometers after Santa Cruz at the Pulpería Arca de Noe. Drive approximately six kilometers on this road, then take a right. From here it's only four kilometers to Guayabo. If you want to drive back to San José this way, drive through the park until you reach a T intersection, make a left, then drive until you reach the paved road, where you make a right.

EIGHT

The Atlantic Coast

A trip to the Atlantic coast in Limón Province offers a chance to enjoy this area's wild beauty and the distinct culture that characterizes it. Much of the region is a jungle-covered lowland that is skirted by a coastline dotted with beautiful white- and black-sand beaches, where turtles come to nest and monkeys and sloths hang out in the trees. The tall Talamanca mountains force migrating birds from North America to fly over the narrow strip of land to the south of Puerto Limón. The Nature Conservancy has named the Talamanca area a birding hot spot, with as many as three million raptors (hawks, kites, falcons, eagles, vultures) touching down during their spring and fall migrations. The birds' presence indicates a healthy ecosystem. You can visit and participate in many fascinating projects combining bird-friendly agriculture, conservation, community development, and eco-tourism when you choose this region, and you can get in plenty of swimming, snorkeling, surfing, and fishing, too. People who want to avoid touristy atmospheres will enjoy the slow-moving rhythm of life in the Talamanca area.

Tortuguero, several hours by boat north of Limón, is unique in Costa Rica because of its jungle-lined canals and the famous green-turtle nesting season from July to October, but you can also observe the less numerous leatherback turtles nesting all up and down the coast from mid-February to mid-June.

Barra del Colorado, near the Nicaraguan border, has become famous as a sportfishing destination, but it also has a turtle beach and lovely canals, and is one of the largest wildlife refuges in the country.

Limón is the least populated province in Costa Rica and is unique in its mix of ethnic groups. Afro-Caribbean peoples migrated to the Atlantic coast in the 19th century to fish, work on the railroad, and farm cacao and coconut, and they now comprise roughly a third of the province's population. A variety of English dialects are spoken here, including an elegant Jamaican English and a patois called *mekatelyu*. "What happen" (pronounced "whoppen") is the common greeting. Instead of saying *"adiós"* when they pass each other, people say "all right" or "okay." For a fascinating history of the region, read Paula Palmer's *What Happen*, in which elders of the black community tell their life stories (see "Recommended Reading" in Chapter Thirteen).

A relatively large population of indigenous Bribris and Cabécars inhabits the rainforests of Talamanca. They try to maintain their traditional lifestyle in harmony with nature. Limón also has many Chinese residents whose relatives immigrated in the 19th and early 20th centuries.

PUERTO LIMÓN

The people of Puerto Limón, Costa Rica's Atlantic port, are making great strides in improving the appearance of their town for the 400,000 tourists that arrive each year on cruise ships between October and April. Near the cruise ship landing, **Parque Vargas** is pleasant with its towering palm trees. The street going west from the park has been made into a pedestrian boulevard with restaurants and souvenir shops. On the east side of the park, you can take a refreshing walk along the sea wall.

The **Festival of Black Culture** (Festival de las Flores de la Diáspora) is celebrated during August, culminating in Black Culture Day, August 31. Most events are held in the **Black Star Line Cultural Center**, which was built in 1911 as a shipping office by Marcus Garvey (founder of the United Negro Improvement Association, one of the largest African-American organizations in history). The Center is still managed by the Limón chapter of the UNIA.

Limón's biggest celebration is **Carnaval**, held in October near El Día de las Culturas, the Costa Rican version of Columbus Day. Brightly costumed *Limonenses* parade to the rhythm of drums, tambourines, maracas, and whistles. The *comparsa* groups practice their dance steps all year in preparation for the festival, which has been held since 1949. You're part of the parade, too, drawn in by the irresistible Afro-Caribbean beat. The ten-day festival includes concerts, fireworks, and local food. Make sure you reserve a hotel room in advance.

Isla Uvita, a small island off the coast of Puerto Limón, is purported to be the place where Christopher Columbus landed on September 18, 1502, on his fourth and final trip to the new world. A half hour hike takes you around the island. A new dock is being built to make landing easier amidst the coral reefs surrounding it.

Stevedores load containers of bananas and pineapples onto huge freighters at **Moín**, a few kilometers to the north. Moín is where independent boatmen dock for trips up the canals to Tortuguero.

RESTAURANTS   **Mr. George's** (open Sundays; 795-3045), on the beach road north of Moín, is a favorite with locals for rice and beans on Sundays. It's on the left, marked only by a small sign announcing "*Se vende* rice and beans." Inside the gate, outdoor tables made cheerful with bright, patterned oil cloth are filled with happy diners enjoying plentiful servings of chicken or meat with the coconut-laced Limonese specialty at very reasonable prices. Just down the road, a friend recently saw about 50 sloths in the trees near the beach.

Bar Restaurant Placeres (795-1335) is a pleasant open-air restaurant on the road to Playa Bonita for seafood and *comida típica*. **Bar and Restaurant Quimbambu** (795-4850) on Playa Bonita serves delicious grilled fish at tourist prices.

The fanciest place to dine is the hillside **Restaurante El Faro** (open daily, 10 a.m. to 1 a.m.; 758-2269, 758-2159), with an international menu featuring seafood and meats (under $15). The view from El Faro makes Limón look like a romantic Mediterranean seaport, a flattering angle for this town.

LODGING   Across from the northeast corner of the *mercado* is the **Hotel Acón** (private bath, hot water, air conditioning, TV, phone; $30-$40; 758-1010, fax: 758-2924), with a restaurant and a big disco on the second floor. Ask for a room off the street. If you can get a room facing the sea, you will find the freshly remodeled **Park Hotel** (private bath, wall fans, air conditioning, hot water, cable TV, phone; $50-$60; 798-0555, fax: 758-4364; e-mail: irlixie@racsa.co.cr) very pleasant. It's located a block north of Parque Vargas.

You might prefer to stay at one of the comfortable hotels north of Limón on the road to Moín, a short ride from downtown. From the *mercado*, drive straight north until you reach a T intersection, then turn right and follow the road that winds along the coast through Playa Bonita to Moín, finally intersecting with the main highway back to San José. Buses leave frequently from the Radio Casino bus stop, a block north of the *mercado*.

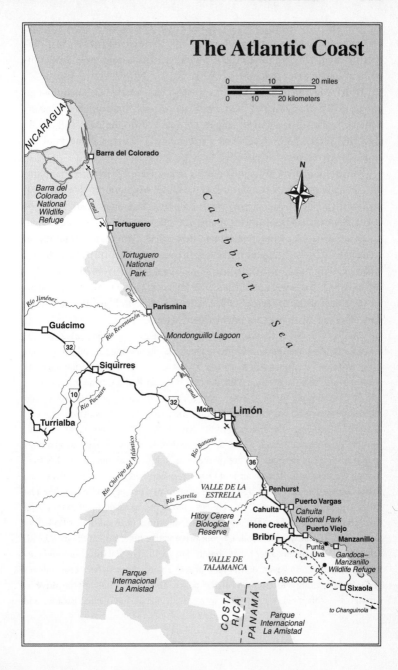

The Atlantic Coast

The first hotel along this road is the **Hotel Oasys del Caribe** (private bath, unheated water, fans, pool, cable TV; $20-$30; 795-0024, fax 795-3591; e-mail: moyso@racsa.co.cr), which has cute, clean, individual cabinas and an open-air restaurant.

Hotel Maribú Caribe's (private bath, hot water, air conditioning, phone; $70-$90; 795-4010, fax: 795-3541; e-mail: maricari@racsa.co.cr) white, circular, thatch-roofed cabinas are perched on the only cliff in the area, and the complex resembles a tribal fort. The cabinas and pool are spotless, the restaurant overpriced, the view terrific.

About a kilometer away, without the ocean view but in a luxuriant jungle setting crossed by several trails, is the **Hotel Matama** (private bath, hot water, air conditioning, phone, pool; $50-$60, including breakfast; 795-1123; www.matama.com). The rooms are clean and tastefully decorated. Tours are available, and the restaurant here offers Caribbean specialties on weekends. Across the street is the smaller-scale **Cocorí** (private bath, hot water, ceiling fans; $40-$50, including breakfast; 795-1670, fax: 795-2930), which has some apartments with kitchens, as well as a breezy open-air restaurant. Both of these establishments are close to Playa Bonita—quite dangerous for swimmers but popular with surfers.

GETTING THERE: By Bus: In San José, the buses for Limón (221-2596; $3) leave hourly from the Terminal Caribe at the north end of Calle Central. Buy tickets in advance for a weekend or holiday trip. To get to the area north of Limón, on the road to Moín, take the Moín or Villa del Mar bus near Radio Casino in Limón.

By Car: Driving to the Atlantic coast is fairly easy and enjoyable, unless you get behind a long line of trucks heading for the port. It takes about two and a half hours from San José. The first part of the drive is through the mountains of Braulio Carrillo National Park. It's hard to believe that when it's raining cats and dogs in San José, it can be clear and hot on the other side of those mountains. It's true, though, especially in September and October, usually the heaviest months of the rainy season. The reverse is true as well. Limón can be very wet during the rest of the country's dry season. Try to go early in the day to avoid fog and rain. And if it has been raining a lot, ask around about landslides in Braulio Carrillo before you set out. If you want to break up your drive with a hike, stop at the park headquarters, 1.8 kilometers after the tollbooth. They will give you directions and current information. However, do not stop or leave your car anywhere else (thieves are common along the highway in the park). The second half of the drive is through the Atlantic lowlands, past towns with names like Cairo, Boston, and Liverpool.

TORTUGUERO NATIONAL PARK

Tortuguero National Park protects a unique series of natural inland waterways that are home to freshwater turtles; river otters; crocodiles; sloths; howler, spider, and white-throated capuchin monkeys; toucans; *oropéndolas*; parrots; morpho butterflies; and many other species. In addition, it is known as one of the world's richest fishing grounds for tarpon and snook. Manatees also inhabit the canals. Some scientists claim that manatees are distant relatives of the elephant. These shy creatures and a related species, the dugong, are said to have given rise to the legend of the mermaid. When frightened, they can stay underwater for as much as half an hour, but usually they stop grazing on aquatic plants and seaweed long enough to surface every 10 to 15 minutes. That is when they become vulnerable to the propellers of the dozens of motor boats that ply the canals. For more information, see www.savethemanatee.com.

Tortuguero is the largest nesting area in the Western Hemisphere for the green sea turtle. These turtles return to Tortuguero every two to four years to mate offshore and dig their nests. Although their feeding grounds can be as far away as Florida and Venezuela, none of the thousands of green turtles tagged in Tortuguero has ever been found to mate at any other beach. Green turtle nesting season is from July to mid-October. Their flipper marks look like tractor treads, showing up as wide black lines on the beach at night.

Tortuguero has been famous for its turtles (as a source of meat, shells, and eggs) since the 1600s, when the Spanish set up cacao plantations on the Atlantic coast. Turtles were valued as a meat source on early ships because they would stay alive if they were kept out of the sun and sprinkled with water. Turtle soup became a delicacy in England around the end of the

Green sea turtle

1800s. Large-scale turtle export from Tortuguero started in 1912, and by the 1950s, the green turtle faced extinction.

Long-term biological research on the green turtle, started by the Caribbean Conservation Corp. (CCC; 709-8091, 224-9215, in the U.S.: 800-678-7853; www.cccturtle.org, e-mail: ccc@cccturtle.org) in 1954, has helped greatly in understanding and preserving this species. Dr. Archie Carr, the founder of CCC, wrote an entertaining and informative book, *The Windward Road* (which you can find at the CCC website), about his wanderings in search of the green turtles' nesting ground, which finally led him to Tortuguero. Thanks to international interest in Carr's work, Tortuguero was declared a national park in 1970 by the Costa Rican government.

Today Tortuguero is the premier center for turtle monitoring in the world. Despite this, it is estimated that poachers still get 80 percent of the turtle eggs in the area. The government has pledged more personnel to help during resting season.

Tortuguero is also one of the four areas in the world most frequented by the critically endangered leatherback turtle. Leatherbacks arrive in much fewer numbers than the greens, numbering only 137 in the 2003 season (February to July). Unlike the green turtles, leatherbacks do not return to the same beach to lay their eggs, so turtle protection groups up and down the coast are cooperating to monitor them. The leatherback population on the Pacific coast has diminished 90 percent in the last decade, mainly due to fishing practices that trap and kill turtles along with whatever fish boats are trying to catch. Turtles are safer on the Atlantic coast because shallower water makes fishing more difficult.

When we were in Tortuguero in March, we saw two huge *baulas* (leatherback females) laboriously digging holes in the soft brown sand by the light of the full moon. Witnessing this age-old ritual left us with a deep respect for the primordial instincts of all creatures, including humans.

The turtles lay about 100 eggs at each of several nestings per season. The eggs incubate for approximately 60 days, then the baby turtles bite through the rubbery shells and clamber out of the nest, heading straight for the ocean, which they try to reach before dawn. Once they hit the water, their instinctive navigational powers direct them to the open sea. Research has shown that turtle hatchlings are attracted to the light reflected off the sea. When researchers block their view of the sea and set up a light source in another direction, the turtles head toward it.

The CCC's biological field station and **Natural History Visitors Center** are at the north end of Tortuguero village. In addition to beautiful pho-

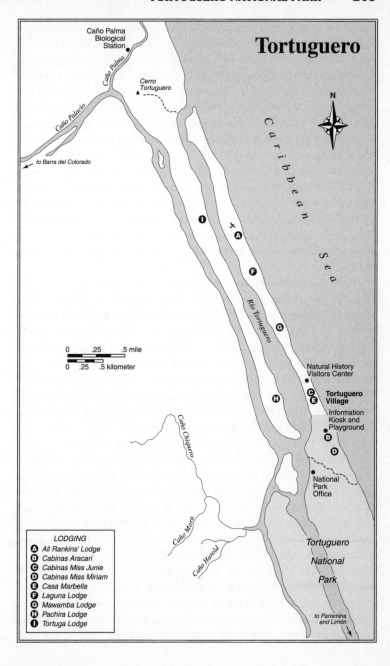

Tortuguero

Caño Palma
Biological
Station

Cerro
Tortuguero

Caño Palma

Caño Palacio

to Barra del Colorado

Caribbean Sea

N

Río Tortuguero

0   .25   .5 mile
0   .25   .5 kilometer

Natural History
Visitors Center

Tortuguero
Village

Information
Kiosk and
Playground

National
Park
Office

Caño Chiquero

Caño Mora

Caño Harold

Tortuguero

National

Park

to Parismina
and Limón

LODGING
A All Rankins' Lodge
B Cabinas Aracari
C Cabinas Miss Junie
D Cabinas Miss Miriam
E Casa Marbella
F Laguna Lodge
G Mawamba Lodge
H Pachira Lodge
I Tortuga Lodge

tographs and interpretive material on the area's wildlife, the center features a lifesize model of a mother turtle laying her eggs, and shows an excellent video about sea turtles. Naturalists are available to answer questions and tell you about volunteer programs. The center also sells T-shirts, books, laminated field guides to the birds of Tortuguero, and other wildlife gifts. You can adopt a turtle in Tortuguero or through www.cccturtle.org. Proceeds help fund the CCC's conservation programs. The visitors center is open from 10 a.m. to noon and 2 p.m. to 5:30 p.m. Monday through Saturday, and 2 p.m. to 5 p.m. Sunday. Admission to this excellent small museum is about $1. You can adopt a turtle in Tortuguero or through www.cccturtle.org.

In the information kiosk near the playground at the center of Tortuguero village, there is a fascinating exhibit on the cultural history of the area, illustrated by Deirdre Hyde. To learn more about the human inhabitants of Tortuguero, where they came from, and how they made their living for so many years before tourism discovered the area, read *Turtle Bogue* by Harry LeFever.

Caño Palma Biological Station (381-4116; admission $2; $40/person, including meals) near Cerro Tortuguero, eight kilometers northwest of the village, is another research facility founded in 1991 by the Canadian Organization for Tropical Education and Rainforest Conservation (COTERC: in Canada: 905-831-8809, fax: 905-831-4203; www.coterc.org, e-mail: info@ coterc.org). The station preserves 40 hectares of tropical lowland forest home to monkeys, jaguars, sloths, margays, anteaters, tapirs, river otters, caimans, toucans, green parrots, hawks, and poison-dart frogs. Their Partners in Preservation Project protects wildlife habitat through animal sponsorship for as little as $15. They have volunteer programs ($100/week) and educational programs for high school and undergraduate students.

The area north of Limón, like most of the Atlantic coast of Nicaragua, is a water-based society. All travel is by boat. In 1974, a series of canals was built to connect the natural inland waterways between Limón and Barra del Colorado, thus allowing coastal residents to get to Limón without the hazards of sea travel. In 1979, the government established a twice-weekly launch service up the inland waterway, but due to mechanical difficulties, the flat-bottom boat stopped running. The difficulty of getting in and out of Tortuguero has begun to wear on local residents, who see boatloads of tourists zooming up and down the canals while they can't afford to travel (some community-minded hotels and tour operators take local people to Limón when there is space on their boats). It also means that they must pay higher prices for food because local *pulpería* owners have to pay high prices for transport. In January 1996, the Municipality of Pococi, a town inland from Tortuguero, paid for the clearing of a road bed through at least one and a half kilometers of national park land, ending seven kilometers from the village. The road project was stopped by the government and a suit was filed against the municipality. Locals began using the road again, especially in the dry season, and in March 1999 Environment Minister Elizabeth Odio ordered a ten-foot deep ditch dug across the road bed. Protesters began filling in the ditch by hand until the government sent park officials to guard it. Local people who have benefitted from tourism realize that building a road will threaten the pristine conditions in which wildlife thrives, but they also see that their families cannot afford transportation as it now stands.

LOCALLY GUIDED TURTLE WALKS   Recognizing that no conservation effort can succeed without full support from the human community, the CCC, in partnership with the National Parks Service, has trained local people as turtle guides. Young men and women are learning a new way to make their living from the town's unique natural resource. They have formed a cooperative and take small groups (ten people) onto the beach to see the turtles in their peak nesting season from July to October. The guides are familiar with the stages of the nesting process; they only let people approach once the mother turtle is so fully absorbed in laying her eggs that the observers' presence will not disturb her. Turtle taggers are also at work on the beach, and visitors must retreat to about 30 feet away from the turtles while the tagging is going on.

The turtle walks are undertaken in two shifts, at 8 p.m. and at 10 p.m. Only 200 people are allowed on the beach at one time, so the guides queue early to buy permits for night tours. You can hook up with a guide during the day at the main dock, at the information kiosk, or through your hotel, and arrange to meet at 8 p.m. or at 10 p.m. Guided turtle walks cost $10. Park admission costs $7, or $10 for three days and two nights (709-8086). Most package-deal hotels do not include the turtle tours in their rates because the tours only take place July 1 through October 15.

Tortuguero has become so popular that now the number of hotel rooms exceeds the number of people who can be allowed on the beach to observe turtles. We don't know how this situation will be resolved.

TOURING BY BOAT   One way to enjoy the exuberant vegetation and abundant wildlife of Tortuguero's canals is to rent a *cayuca*, or dugout canoe (about $5/hour, three hours for $15/person with a guide). Tino, Castor, Reynaldo Hooker, Chico Torres, and Bill Sambola are some of the villagers who rent out *cayucas*. (They also serve as guides.) *Cayucas* are quite stable and easy to paddle. Paddle around for awhile to see if your dugout is the right size for you and make sure it is of solid, one-piece construction and not caulked together. Check also that it has a plastic bailer. Miss Junie at the north end of town rents nice fiberglass canoes ($10 for the morning) and the Paraiso Tropical Souvenir shop rents bicycle canoes for $9/hour.

You have to pay $7 admission to the park at the administration office, just south of the village, (709-8091) before you set off in a *cayuca*. The main waterway of the park is inland from the canal that comes from Moín. Paddle south. You will see smaller waterways branching off that you can explore. If you go out without a guide, ask where the currents are most gentle. The current in the Río Tortuguero can be quite strong.

To make your boat trip more comfortable, bring the following:

Thick-soled athletic shoes	Lightweight long-sleeved
Socks	and short-sleeved shirts
Insect repellent	Towels
Sunblock	Lunch in waterproof bags
Broad-rimmed hat	Drinking water
or visored cap	Swiss Army knife
Umbrella for sun or rain	Flashlight
Lightweight plastic poncho	
or picnic cloth for rain	

Most lodges use electric motors to reduce noise that disturbs the quiet beauty of the jungle streams and four-stroke engines to reduce pollution. Make sure you tour the canals in quiet boats. **Daryl Loth** (tortuguero_s.tri pod.com), an enthusiastic Canadian expat, enjoys giving educational tours ($15 for three hours) of the area, emphasizing not only wildlife observation but insight into the community. You'll find him at Casa Marbella across from the Jungle Shop. **Ross Ballard** is another Canadian who specializes in botanical tours.

FISHING   **Elvin Gutierrez** has a small Boston whaler for fishing trips. **Modesto Watson** (phone/fax: 226-0986; www.tortuguerocanals.com, e-mail: fvwatson@racsa.co.cr) takes up to four people fishing for $50.

CAMPING   Camping is allowed in the park, but remember that Tortuguero has one of the highest annual rainfalls in the world: more than 200 inches a year. *Terciopelo* (fer-de-lance) snakes are not uncommon on land, especially at night. There is a nature trail on the narrow piece of land between the large canal and the sea. It is a bit less swampy in the dry season.

Note: If you want to go swimming, Tortuguero is not the ideal place. The beach offers very little shade, has rough, dangerous surf, and is frequented by sharks.

LODGING AND RESTAURANTS   Many people splurge on a tour to Tortuguero because the logistics seem difficult. But it is quick, easy, and cheaper to fly there on SANSA or Nature Air and stay in one of the hotels in the village. Compare $50 and 20 minutes by air with $40-$45 by bus, taxi, and boat from San José through Limón and Moín (six hours travel time). If you want to return via the canals, it is easier to arrange boat transportation *from* Tortuguero than *to* it. The boat trip up the canals from Moín takes about three to five hours, depending on the condition of the canals, and is noisy and boring for some. It is worthwhile if you have a good guide.

Note: There is no bank in Tortuguero, and many local hotels and guides do not take credit cards or traveler's checks, so be sure and change money before you get there. Some shops and restaurants will take credit cards if you make a purchase, but they don't have the cash flow to handle money changing. There are public phones in Tortuguero that you can use with a 197 phone card.

There are several inexpensive hotels in the village. **Cabinas Miss Miriam** (private bath, heated water, fans; $10-$20; 709-8107, 844-7974) are in two locations: on the north side of the soccer field and near the beach in the neighborhood south of the soccer field. The lodging is clean and secure. They will also arrange transport and tours. Miss Miriam has restaurants at each location, serving delicious Caribbean dishes. Groups should make reservations.

On the south side of the soccer field, beyond the information kiosk and the playground, is **Cabinas Aracari** (private bath, cold water, wall fans; $12-$20; 709-8006), nice, clean cabinas surrounded by a garden with native fruit trees: mango, avocado, water apple, and cashew. There are bars on the windows, a thoughtful touch for travelers' peace of mind. The owner, Doña Bachi, who lives behind the cabinas in a blue house, is the essence of down-home motherliness. Recommended.

Casa Marbella (private bath, solar hot water, fans; $30-$50; 709-8011, 392-3201; casamarbella.tripod.com, e-mail: safari@racsa.co.cr) has nicely designed, comfortable rooms with great breakfasts and a communal kitchen for guests, in the heart of Tortuguero right on the water across from the

Catholic church. It is owned by nature guide Daryl Loth and his family. Recommended.

At the northern end of the village are **Cabinas Miss Junie** (private bath, hot water, ceiling fans; $30-$40, including breakfast; 771-0684, 709-8102; www.iguanaverdetours.com, e-mail: turtle@racsa.co.cr). Each room has its own pastel color theme, with walls and bed linens that blend harmoniously. The tiled bathrooms are impressive. Miss Junie's offers a three-day, two-night tour package for $200/person that includes bus/boat transportation from San José, lodging, meals, and a canal tour. Miss Junie gained fame over the years as the cook at the CCC, and now has her own restaurant. If you want to sample her cuisine, you must let her know in advance so that she can give your meal the preparation it deserves. Recommended.

When the CCC puts radio transmitters on the turtles, it gives each turtle a catchy name and includes the villagers in the events around the turtle's release. A few years back, one of the turtles was named in honor of Miss Junie. Unfortunately, the reptilian "Miss Junie" swam up to Nicaragua and wound up in someone's stew pot. After the researchers found out what had happened and recovered the transmitter, the CCC put out press releases to draw attention to the plight of green turtles in the Caribbean. The real Miss Junie and her kin were phoned for weeks by people expressing their sympathy for poor Miss Junie, who had been captured and eaten in Nicaragua's Miskito Cays. The transmitter was attached to another turtle, Miss Junie 2, who luckily did not suffer the same fate as her predecessor, at least during the life of the transmitter.

All Rankins' Lodge (private bath, heated water, fans; $49/person, including meals; 795-2556, 815-5175, 709-8101; www.greencoast.com/all rankin, e-mail: willis@racsa.co.cr), about one and a half miles north of Tortuguero village near the airstrip, has simple, rustic but comfy cabins and serves generous meals in its dining room on the lagoon. The setting is extremely tranquil, except for when the planes arrive in the morning. Durham Rankin and his wife Tomasa Gonzalez were among the first families to settle the area that became Tortuguero village back in the late 1940s. They fished and farmed and brought up their brood of seven when Tortuguero was an unknown outpost. The whole family worked with Dr. Archie Carr and the CCC on the sea turtle research and monitoring that eventually led to the creation of the national park. Willis Rankin runs the lodge, he and brother Danny run transport from Moín to Tortuguero ($55 roundtrip) and tour services ($5/hour), and are both excellent naturalist guides along with brothers Alonso and Eddy.

La Casona (open 9 a.m. to 9 p.m.; closed Saturday) is an excellent restaurant on the north side of the soccer field. They cook, with a light touch, delicate fish, chicken a *l'orange*, vegetarian dishes, and banana pancakes for breakfast. La Casona is also the town's bakery. Recommended.

There are several souvenir shops in the village. **El Paraíso Tropical**, an unmistakable purple building that you can see from the water, has many things that you'd find in souvenir shops in San José, and not many locally made articles. The **Jungle Shop**, a few houses to the south, has better-quality, more interesting, and more tasteful things for sale, as well as cold drinks, and donates a percentage of its profits to the local school.

LARGE HOTELS   All of these lodges offer two- and three-day packages that include food, lodging, tours of the canals via motorboat, and ascent of Cerro (Mount) Tortuguero. Most tours include bus and boat transportation between San José and Tortuguero, and all offer an air transport upgrade. Tour prices range between $180 and $380.

Mawamba Lodge (private bath, hot water, ceiling fans, pool; 293-8181, fax: 239-7657; www.mawamba.com, e-mail: mawamba@racsa.co.cr) has pleasant cabinas and a large, airy dining room that serves very good food. Just one kilometer north of Tortuguero village on the ocean side of the canal, it's one of the three lodges from which you can walk to the village or the ocean. There is a large, fanciful pool with a waterfall, near a bar where tropical drinks are served. With its air-conditioned conference room and resident multilingual biologist, it's a good setting for seminars or small conventions. The rustic cabinas blend in with the environment in a way that some large hotels do not. The three-day package is $262/person double occupancy, children 5-11, $131.

Next door, **Laguna Lodge** (private bath, hot water, ceiling fans, swimming pool with jacuzzi; cell phone: 225-3740, fax: 283-8031; www.laguna tortuguero.com, e-mail: info@lagunatortuguero.com) is owned by the brother of the owner of Mawamba, a noted Costa Rican poet and author. They have a huge shell-shaped gift shop/conference room/internet café and their pool has an island where you can spot red-eyed frogs. There is also an open butterfly garden. The three-day package is $249/person.

Tortuga Lodge (private bath, heated water, ceiling fans; 257-0766, 222-0333, fax: 257-1665; www.costaricaexpeditions.com, e-mail: costaric@ expeditions.co.cr) is two kilometers from the village across the canal from the airstrip. Tortuga Lodge was the first nature lodge in this area. Architecturally, it has expanded in a tasteful, harmonious way and maintains its tradition of excellent service. A riverside dining room adds a special tone to the atmosphere. The pool has an environmentally friendly purification system that doesn't irritate the eyes. Definitely the most expensive lodge in the area, but very nice. Three-day packages cost $379/person double occupancy.

Pachira Lodge (private bath, hot water, ceiling fans; $80/person, including meals; 256-7080, fax: 223-1119; www.pachiralodge.com, e-mail: paccira@racsa.co.cr), located on the canal to Barra, across from the village, is decorated in a traditional Caribbean style, with many attractive touches. A three-day package costs $251 to $445/person double occupancy, depending on the type of transportation used.

GETTING THERE: The nonprofit **Tortuguero Information Center** (833-0827, 709-8011; e-mail: safari@racsa.co.cr), located across from the Catholic church in Tortuguero village, is the most complete source of up-to-date information about independent travel to Tortuguero. They have internet access, and can connect you to low-cost tours and lodging. Because transportation options change frequently, it's best to communicate with them when planning your trip. Since there are no roads to Tortuguero, most visitors arrive in expensive, all-inclusive packages, but less expensive, independent travel is perfectly feasible.

Many independent operators offer transport out of Moín. Competition can be fierce and some of these have been known to mislead visitors who have prearranged travel agreements with other operators in order to steal their business. Some reliable and safe operators offering tours and transport are **Tropical Wind** (Sebastian Torres, 798-6059; and Alexis Soto, 758-4297), **Willis Rankin** (795-2556, 815-5175), and **Danny Rankin** (386-3972). All are particularly adept at spotting wildlife along the way. They charge $50-$55 roundtrip, $30 one way, and depart from Moín at 10 a.m. Take the 6:30 a.m. Limón bus from the Caribe terminal in San José (buy your ticket a day early in high season), then a $5 taxi from Limón in order to get to the JAPDEVA (hap-DAY-vah) dock on time.

The boats to Tortuguero stop more often to see wildlife than the returning boats, so going up takes around four hours and coming back around three hours. Returning boats leave Tortuguero around 10 a.m., getting you to Moín around 1 p.m.

If you haven't made arrangements with one of the boats above, you can just arrive at the JAPDEVA dock. The boat owners in Moín have formed a cooperative and there is a loose rotation organized to give all the captains a chance to take people to Tortuguero. You will have to negotiate a price. There is bargaining power in groups, so try to pair up with someone before arriving at the docks. Prices run about $50-$70/person, or $200 per boat roundtrip.

A last-minute possibility is to call one of the large hotels mentioned above after 5 p.m. the day before you want to arrive in Tortuguero. If they have space available, you can be picked up at one of the San José hotels on their route at 7 a.m. the next morning. Tell them you only need a ride to Tortuguero village ($45-$100 one way, including breakfast).

There are several other ways to get to Tortuguero:

By Boat: Modesto and Fran Watson offer flexible tours in their canopied Riverboat Francesca (two days/one night from San José, including lodging and meals, an early-morning tour of the national park, and a turtle walk in season; $175-$190; three days/two nights can be arranged; phone/fax: 226-0986; www.tortuguerocanals.com, e-mail: fvwatson@racsa.co.cr). Modesto has an eagle eye for animals and pointed out caimans, toucans, an osprey, jacanas, basilisk lizards, monkeys, sloths, a pair of scarlet macaws (a rare sight on the Atlantic coast), a roseate spoonbill, freshwater turtles, and lots of waterbirds on our trip up the canals. They also use a quiet, fuel-saving four-stroke motor. Recommended.

By Rental Car and Boat: Take the Braulio Carrillo highway towards Limón, leaving no later than 6:30 a.m. You will see the exit to Moín a few miles before you get to Limón. Exit to the left. Go past the oil refinery and under the only train bridge. You will see an entrance immediately on your left to a gravel road that leads to the JAPDEVA docks. These are before you get to the huge international freight docks. If you've crossed a bridge, you've gone too far. You will have to pass through a security gate. Just say "Tortuguero" and the guards will direct you to the dock. People there will show you where to park your car. The compound has 24-hour guards. You should tip them a couple of dollars per night spent in Tortuguero upon your return. See above for boat information.

By Rental Car to Cano Blanco Marina: There are some enigmatic signs saying "Tortuguero National Park" on the highway near the town of Siquirres. These are referring to the Cano Blanco Marina, which most of the big lodges use. Although there may be many boats there, most captains are under strict orders not to take any passengers that are not part of a tour package. Don't get stranded here. Only use this route if you have specific travel arrangements. For more details about this route, call the Tortuguero Information Center, above.

By Public Bus or Rental Car and Boat through Cariari: This can be the cheapest way to get to Tortuguero, but it is also the most complicated, uncomfortable, and changeable. Take the 9 a.m. direct bus to Cariari (about $2) from the Caribe terminal in San José. For independent travel, the recognized public route from Cariari is through "La Pavona," served by a bus that leaves from the local route terminal behind the Cariari police station. Touts will offer to sell transport and tours upon your arrival in Cariari, but your choices are greater once you arrive in Tortuguero. For current details and driving instructions to La Pavona, contact the Tortuguero Information Center, above.

By Air: Nature Air ($66 one way; 220-3054, 296-2316; www.natureair.com, e-mail: reservations@natureair.com) flies to Tortuguero every morning at 6:15

a.m. SANSA ($60 one way; 221-9414; www.flysansa.com, e-mail: info@flysansa. com) leaves for Tortuguero daily at 6 a.m. If you are visiting Tortuguero on your own, this might be a quick and easy way to travel at least one way. SANSA provides boat transportation to the village ($2.50). For boat transport to the Tortuguero airstrip, call Victor Barrantes at the SANSA office (709-8055, 709-8112) in Tortuguero the day before you will need a ride.

PARISMINA

Parismina is a small fishing village about halfway between Limón and Tortuguero. It is known in fishing circles for the **Río Parismina Lodge** (private bath, hot water, ceiling fans and air conditioning, pool; package deals only; phone/fax: 710-7564, in the U.S.: 800-338-5688; www.riop.com, e-mail: fish@riop.com), a luxury fishing resort set in 29 acres of tropical gardens, with nature trails in the forest behind the lodge. Rates run from $1850 for Saturday through Tuesday to $2950 for a week of fishing. Fishing is good year-round, but the seas are usually calmest March to May and August to October.

MONDONGUILLO LAGOON   About half and hour by boat south of Parismina is Mondonguillo Lagoon, where the Pacuare River runs into the sea. The area is protected by the private **Pacuare Matina Forestry Reserve**. The beach is one of the most frequented leatherback nesting beaches in the Caribbean. Two projects are based here to protect the leatherbacks and other nesting turtles.

On the north side of Mondonguillo Lagoon is a field station run by the U.K.-based **Endangered Wildlife Trust** (233-0508, 233-0451, 841-8599; e-mail: fdezlaw@tracsa.co.cr). They have a satellite station at the northern end of the six-kilometer stretch of beach that they monitor from early March to the end of September. Visiting researchers also stay at the station. Volunteers pay $120/week for room and board. **Ecology Project International** (www.ecologyproject.org) has a package that includes whitewater rafting on the Pacuare, a visit to Selva Bananito Reserve, and four days of turtle monitoring in the Pacuare Reserve. Tourists can arrange visits to the station for a minimum of two nights ($65/person/night, including meals).

On the south side of the lagoon is the Costa Rican–owned **Estacion Tortugas** (253-2260, 355-2784), which monitors the beach south of the lagoon from March to August. **Ecoteach** (www.ecoteach.com) brings groups to this station each year.

BARRA DEL COLORADO

Barra del Colorado, at the northeast end of Costa Rica, is a sleepy, rainy, car-free town occupying opposite banks near the mouth of the Río Colorado. The west bank of the river has the poverty-stricken village, the east bank has the expensive lodges. There is excellent fishing in the river, nearby canals, and the Caribbean Sea. All of the hotels here specialize in fishing.

Tarpon season is from January to June and September to December. Snook run from October to January and also in May. The rainy season on the Atlantic Coast is unpredictable, so bring a good windbreaker and sweatshirt. The lodges usually provide raingear. The beach in Barra is too rough for swimming, snorkeling, or scuba diving, but it is a nesting ground for sea turtles from July through September.

The **Barra del Colorado National Wildlife Refuge**, at 92,000 hectares, is the second largest in Costa Rica. If you fly to Barra, you'll see its importance. Everywhere between the Central Mountains and the Atlantic Coast, the land looks like an animal whose pelt has been shaved in large patches. Bright green spots littered with fallen trees finally give way to the beauty of the rich coat of billowing dark-green treetops extending north into Nicaragua. It is a great relief to see that this one expanse of virgin forest has been saved. SINAC (National Conservation Areas System) operates on a shoestring budget, with ten poorly equipped guards to patrol this huge area and to keep its monkeys, sloths, jaguars, and birds safe from hunters and loggers.

Because Barra is traditionally known as a fishing area, it is less crowded with naturalists than nearby Tortuguero, but its lagoons and streams offer just as many opportunities to commune with nature, often in a less regimented way, at least at this point. Researchers estimate that the reserve has 700 different kinds of orchids. You can get a three-day pass that is good for Barra as well as Tortuguero for $10 at the MINAE offices in Barra or Tortuguero.

LODGING   **Tarponland Lodge** (private bath, heated water, ceiling fans; $25/person, including meals; 710-2141, 710-1271, cell phone: 818-9921), right on the airstrip, is the only Tico-owned place in Barra. The basic rooms are not bad, and they have a funky swimming pool. Fishing trips cost $275 per person. Owner Guillermo Cunningham Aguilar also does natural history trips to beautiful Caño Nueve.

The **Río Colorado Fishing Lodge** (private bath, hot water, ceiling fans, air conditioning; $1500-$1800 for six days and five nights, including three days of fishing, transportation, and licenses; 232-8610, fax: 231-5987, in the U.S. and Canada: 800-243-9777; www.riocoloradolodge.com, e-mail: tarpon@riocoloradolodge.com) was one of the original lodges that gave Barra del Colorado its name as a world-class fishing destination. The lodge is a survivor from the days before Costa Rica got fancy, when fishing places at the beach were simple and shabby but had a certain charm. As do most other lodges in Barra, it has a bar with a free happy hour, cable TV, and VCR, and a ten-person hot tub with jacuzzi. The fishing fleet is outfitted with sonar fish finders, radios, and skilled guides. The lodge offers a two-day non-fishing tour that leaves San José for an early-morning trip to Poás volcano, then heads to Puerto Viejo de Sarapiquí to board a riverboat for a four-hour cruise northeast to the Río San Juan, which borders Nicaragua and flows into the Caribbean at Barra del Colorado. After a night at the lodge, the tour continues down the canals and back to San José. From July to September, the tour stops in Tortuguero on the return, to try to catch a glimpse of a leatherback or green turtle nesting. Call for scheduling information.

The best Barra accommodations are at the **Silver King Lodge** (private bath, hot water, ceiling fans, air conditioning; packages from $1935 to $2642; phone/fax: 381-1403, in the U.S.: 800-847-3474; www.silverking lodge.net, e-mail hal@silverkinglodge.net). Each spacious room has two huge orthopedic mattresses, real closets, and a large bathroom with plenty of hot water. Rates include food, beverages, flights to and from lodge, guides, boats, and laundry service—a real boon in Barra's wet weather. The gourmet food is excellent and plentiful, and the staff is friendly. The most memorable part of our stay there was the green-lighted hot tub with jacuzzi, followed by a very good massage—the perfect end to a cool, misty day of buzzing around Barra in speedboats. They also have a swimming pool with a waterfall. Their fishing fleet is as well-equipped as the rest of their operation. One of their guides took us on a heavenly jungle float at his farm.

A few minutes more down the waterway is the homey **Casamar** (private bath, hot water, ceiling fans, free bar, free laundry, VCR room; packages run from $1325 to $2675, not including flight to lodge; 710-6592, in the U.S.: 800-543-0282; www.casamarlodge.com, e-mail: info@casamar lodge.com), with well-designed, comfortable duplex cabinas. Mango trees shade the grounds; howler monkeys provide the sound effects. For non-anglers, there are guided nature walks on the reserve.

GETTING THERE: Most of the lodges in this area have tour packages that include transportation from San José.

By Air: SANSA has daily flights to Barra (6 a.m.; $60 each way; 221-9414, fax: 255-2176; www.flysansa.com). Nature Air also flies daily at 6:45 a.m. ($66 one way; 220-3054; www.natureair.com). See Chapter Four, "Local Transportation—Planes," for reservation procedures and policies.

The people of Barra del Colorado go in and out by way of Puerto Lindo and Cariari. Check for current schedules at the Tortuguero Information Center (833-0827; e-mail: tortuguero_info@racsa.co.cr). Don't go to Barra without reservations.

TALAMANCA REGION

When we first went to Talamanca in 1975, there was no road. We took a two-hour train ride from Limón to Penhurst on the Río Estrella, where we were met by a man in a dugout canoe who ferried us across the river to a rickety bus. Then it was another hour on a dirt road to Cahuita, a small village where horses grazed on the grassy paths between houses. That has all changed now that there are roads. Cahuita's grassy paths have become dusty streets, and the people of Talamanca find themselves thrust uneasily into the 21st century. During the 1980s and '90s, it seemed that independent farming and fishing were giving way to a tourism-based economy. But Talamancans have seen that tourism is a fickle industry: If you sell the farm to build cabins, and then bad weather or a negative news report cause tourism to dry up, you are left with nothing. So, although tourism is thriving in this area, Talamanca is also the center of intense collaboration between local farmers and conservation organizations to grow and market organic cacao, bananas, and medicinal plants. The Bribri and Cabecar indigenous people are an integral part of this effort, and are slowly opening up to tourism in a way that is harmonious with their values.

Naturalists and birders love the because 88 percent of the land in Talamanca is protected: the pristine beaches of Cahuita National Park and Gandoca–Manzanillo Wildlife Refuge, the rainforests that the Bribri and Cabecar tribes have preserved for centuries, and the wild mountains of La Amistad International Park, covering the central part of southern Costa Rica and stretching into Panamá. Together, they form the **Talamanca-Caribe Biological Corridor**. To find out more about this experiment in conservation, sustainable agriculture, community development, and ecotourism, contact the Biological Corridor office (272-2400, 271-0149; e-mail: corrbiol@racsa.co.cr).

The beaches are uncrowded, and the weather, from February to April and in June, September, and October especially, can be beautiful in contrast to the afternoon rains in the rest of Costa Rica. Because of community efforts, five beaches in the area have been awarded the prestigious "Bandera Azul Ecológica" for cleanliness. They are Playas Puerto Vargas and Blanca in Cahuita and Playas Cocles, Chiquita, and Uva south of Puerto Viejo.

At the Pacific beaches, the local culture takes second place to a tourist milieu created by highland Ticos and foreigners of all nationalities. Talamanca, however, is still terra incognita for most Ticos, so local culture remains intact. Life on the Atlantic coast is definitely laidback. Because of this, it is a great place to relax. There are a few places that offer air conditioning and hot water, but service everywhere is generally very slow. When going to a restaurant, bring along some snacks to eat while you're waiting, or dance with your waiter or waitress.

Single women should know that they could become targets for hopeful gringa-chasers, who see them as possible trust funds or at least a good time for a weekend. Most of these guys are gentlemanly enough to accept a flat "no." Also, if you look slightly bohemian you might be offered coke or crack, which are taking their toll on the local youth. Be aware that there are lots of narco-police on duty. Many tourists have gotten into trouble for their naivete. Security has improved in Talamanca, but it is generally not a good idea to walk alone at night in solitary areas.

CAHUITA AND CAHUITA NATIONAL PARK

The town of **Cahuita** is a 45-minute drive or a one-hour bus ride down the coast from Limón. The Playa Blanca entrance to Cahuita National Park is two blocks south of the bus stop. The first 400 meters of this beach can be dangerous to swim in. The currents can be very strong and unpredictable. Green and red flags are placed along the beach to indicate which areas are safe for swimming. The waves are gentler near the point. When we were last there, the sea was as placid as a bathtub and many bathers were enjoying the water. Cahuita celebrates its *carnaval* the last ten days in November. Playa Blanca and Puerto Vargas beaches have the Blue Flag.

Cahuita National Park (open daily, 6 a.m. to 5 p.m.; 755-0302) is the primary reason that Cahuita has become the tourist destination it is. The park was established to protect the coral reef that extends 500 meters out from Cahuita Point. This underwater garden is home to 123 species of tropical fish, as well as crabs, lobsters, shrimp, sea anemones, sponges, black and red sea urchins, and sea cucumbers. Try not to touch the coral while you explore its nooks and crannies.

Dissatisfied with the way the park was being administered in the early 1990s, the citizens of Cahuita decided to administer the park in conjunction with the government. Your donation at the Playa Blanca park entrance goes toward upkeep and security, the school, and other community projects.

Cahuitans are proud of the way they have managed the park. The usual $6 park entrance fee is required at the Puerto Vargas entrance to the south.

To reach the reef, simply take a shady, scenic hike down the nature trail that starts from the Playa Blanca entrance to the national park. It runs between the beach and the jungle, and is a good place to see wildlife. Tanagers, iguanas, sloths, and white-faced and howler monkeys are common along the trails. The freshwater rivers and estuaries are good places to spot caimans and herons. It's four kilometers by trail from the park entrance to the point and another three kilometers to the Puerto Vargas area of the park, where the campgrounds are. We don't recommend camping in the park.

Roberto Tour (755-0092), at the corner of the entrance road and the main street, has been recommended for snorkeling and dolphin-watching tours. **Cahuita Tours** (755-0232, phone/fax: 755-0082; e-mail: exotica@racsa.co. cr) can take you to the reef. (If it has been raining and the water is cloudy, it's not worth going out.) They can take you to Bocas del Toro, Tortuguero, Hitoy Cerere Biological Reserve, or the local indigenous reserves. They

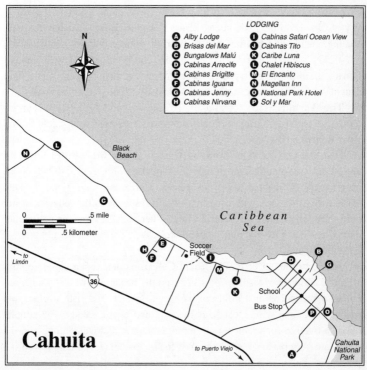

LODGING

A Alby Lodge
B Brisas del Mar
C Bungalows Malú
D Cabinas Arrecife
E Cabinas Brigitte
F Cabinas Iguana
G Cabinas Jenny
H Cabinas Nirvana
I Cabinas Safari Ocean View
J Cabinas Tito
K Caribe Luna
L Chalet Hibiscus
M El Encanto
N Magellan Inn
O National Park Hotel
P Sol y Mar

Black Beach

Caribbean Sea

0   .5 mile
0   .5 kilometer

to Limón

Soccer Field

School

Bus Stop

Cahuita

to Puerto Viejo

Cahuita National Park

also rent snorkeling equipment and binoculars; lead scuba and sportfishing expeditions; change traveler's checks; connect you with Western Union; and rent bikes. They're on Cahuita's main street, half a block from the Guardia Rural.

North of Cahuita is long, beautiful **Black Beach**. The water laps the grassy shore at high tide; low tide is the right time to swim or walk along the beach. Surfers like this black-sand beach, but currents can be strong, so be careful. At the entrance to Black Beach are the police station, post office, and surf and boogie board rentals.

RESTAURANTS **Miss Maudy's Food Stand** (open weekends, 11 a.m. to 9 p.m.), near the entrance to the park, is famous for Caribbean-style stews in hearty broth spooned onto coconut-flavored rice and beans. Her down-home cooking comes in generous portions and is accessible for any budget.

Roberto's, on the main street at the entrance to town, is a good place for fresh fish. **Restaurant Relax** (closed Tuesday; 755-0322) is good for pizza and seafood. It has a lively bar and is located near the main bus stop. We have received rave reviews of nearby **La Fé** (open daily, 8 a.m. to 9 p.m.). A few blocks down the main street, across from the Salón Comunal, the welcoming, candle-lit **ChaChaCha Restaurant** (dinner only; closed Tuesday; 755-0232) features seafood, tenderloin, and Tex-Mex cooked with French-Canadian *savoir faire*. Try their Black Magic Woman dessert, made with chocolate chip ice cream, coffee liqueur, and cinnamon. Recommended.

The World is Yours (open daily, 10 a.m. to 9 p.m.; 755-0409) is an internet café serving Caribbean food and pizza. It's across from **Ciclo Safari Bike Rental** on the main street.

One block to the right from the Guardia Rural, **Miss Edith** (open all day Monday to Saturday; open only for supper on Sunday; 755-0248) cooks up a storm, ladling out tasty, down-home Caribbean food—jerk chicken, spicy curry, fish soup with coconut milk. In response to the requests of her customers, she includes vegetarian fare in her menu, as well as native medicinal teas such as bay rum, *guanabana* leaves, *sorosi*, and lemongrass—good for what ails you.

At the beginning of Black Beach, **Café Bluspirit** (open daily, noon to 10 p.m.; closed Wednesday; 755-0122), on the beach, is owned by a Cahuitan who specializes in Caribbean barbecue, lobster, and fish in pineapple sauce; his Italian wife specializes in pasta and exotic salads. The simple, clean, attractive design of the restaurant is unique and welcoming, and the prices are very reasonable. They serve fresh piña coladas in a hollowed-out pineapple shell with a straw!

Sobre la Olas (closed Tuesday; 755-0109), also on the beach, has been recommended for great Italian seafood, but only when the Italian owner/chef is in the kitchen.

Nearby, **The Pastry Shop** (755-0275) bakes cinnamon rolls, cakes, and breads, and sells coffee, takeout only. Try the lemon bake.

The road that intersects 100 meters later will take you to the main highway. At the intersection is the Swiss-owned **El Cactus** (open 6 p.m. to 10 p.m.; closed Monday; 755-0276), which specializes in pizza, pastas, and barbecue, has been recommended by many visitors. They will deliver to any hotel in the area.

At the next corner, one and a half kilometers from the bus stop, are **Chao's Paradise** (755-0421), famous for soup and Caribbean cuisine, and the **Reggae Bar**, which serves vegetarian fare. Here a road will take you inland to several European-owned places: **Restaurant and Cabinas Brigitte** (private bath, heated water, fans; $20-$30, including breakfast; 755-0053; www.brigittecahuita.com, e-mail brigittecahuita@hotmail.com) has cute little rooms and an internet café (open all day for breakfast and snacks). Bike rentals and laundry service are also available. Brigitte offers beach, mountain, and moonlight horseback rides, suitable for all, including children.

La Casa Creole, near the Magellan Inn, serves delicious French Creole and seafood dishes for dinner by candlelight.

LODGING   Many of the cabinas in town are mom-and-pop establishments, with families erecting a few rooms in their back yards. While not the most deluxe accommodations, they are clean, with friendly owners. Staying at one of these places is a good way to give direct support to a

community trying to raise its standard of living while maintaining its cultural values. The first few places are right at the entrance to the national park.

National Park Hotel (private bath, hot water, ceiling fans; $20-$40; with air conditioning, satellite TV, kitchen; $50-$60; 755-0244, fax: 755-0024; www.cahuitanationalpark.com) is at the park entrance next to one of the most popular eateries in town, the **National Park Restaurant** (open daily, 11 a.m. to 9:30 p.m.). These nice rooms have the best views in town.

The **Sol y Mar Restaurant**, across the road, offers hearty breakfasts and local specialties, and also has spacious, clean cabinas (private bath, heated water, table fans; $12-$20; 755-0237, fax: 755-0238). The upstairs rooms have balconies with views. Recommended. They are owned by the family of Walter "Mr. Gavitt" Ferguson, Cahuita's famous calypso composer, whose songs often contain humorous commentary on the issues of the day. If you run into Mr. Gavitt at the restaurant, you might be able to buy one of his tapes or CDs.

Follow a trail to the left, bearing left, to the Austrian-owned **Alby Lodge** (private bath, heated water, mosquito nets, table fans; $30-$40; phone/fax: 755-0031), individual thatch-roofed A-frames with hammocks on the porches in a peaceful, parklike setting. There are lots of nice details here that will make your stay more comfortable, like mosquito coils and broom and dustpan provided in each room, as well as communal kitchens. Bring a flashlight. Recommended.

Another fun-loving French-Canadian place is **Cabinas Jenny** (private bath, heated water, ceiling fans, mosquito nets; $15-$30; 755-0256; e-mail: jennys@racsa.co.cr). Overlooking the sea, this breezy two-story building has good mattresses and internet access.

One block north, also near the sea, is **Brisas del Mar** (private bath, heated water, wall fans; $20-$30; 755-0011). The clean, simple rooms are in the backyard of an older local couple, with hammocks on the porches.

Cabinas Arrecife (private bath, heated water, wall fans; $20-$30; 755-0081), around the corner from Miss Edith's, are shady and quiet. There's a small *soda*. The owner claims you can fish for snapper off the reef in front. Bikes and snorkels are available for rent.

There are cabinas and restaurants up and down the Black Beach road. If you stay at the lodgings that are farther along the road, you should either enjoy walking, rent a bike, or have a car. Remember that it's not advised to walk along this road at night. As you leave Cahuita and walk north on the Black Beach road, the first sign is for **Cabinas Tito** (private bath, cold water, table fans; $10-$20; 755-0286; www.cahuitacabinastito.com, e-mail: cahuitacabinastito@yahoo.com). These are very clean little houses with porches run by friendly owners. The road can be muddy; check before driving in. Behind Tito's, the **Caribe Luna** (private bath, heated water, wall fan, some kitchens; $20-$40; 755-0417; www.disimob.com/caribe luna, e-mail: caribelanguage@racsa.co.cr) has new cabins that can be combined to sleep up to eight people comfortably in three bedrooms. Kitchens can be included. The Barcelonan owner gives Spanish lessons and offers internet access from 4 to 8 p.m.

El Encanto (private bath, hot water, ceiling fans; $50-$60, including breakfast; phone/fax: 755-0113; www.elencantobedandbreakfast.com, e-mail: encanto@racsa.co.cr) is a comfortable bed and breakfast run by a friendly French-Canadian couple. Lovingly tended gardens, a quiet meditation room, an open-air yoga platform, and delicious breakfasts add to the charm of this enchanting place. They also rent a house ($140). Recommended.

Cabinas Safari Ocean View (private bath, heated water, wall fans; $20-$30 with or without kitchen; 755-0122) are brand-new cabins right on the beach with hammocks on the beach side. There are Cabinas Safari in downtown Cahuita, too, in a less attractive setting.

Inland from Chao's Paradise is **Cabinas Iguana**. There are natural wood rooms (shared bath, heated water, mosquito nets, pool; $20-$30; private bath, refrigerator, $30-$40; 755-0005, fax: 755-0054; www.cabinas-iguana.com, e-mail: iguanas@racsa.co.cr) with porches and two houses (private bath, heated water, ceiling fans, mosquito nets, kitchens; one bedroom, $40-$50; three bedrooms, $50-$60). A clean swimming pool is in a secluded setting at the back of the property. The helpful Swiss owner runs a multilingual book exchange in the office; he will pick you up at the bus stop. They also offer kayak tours down the Sixaola river. Recommended.

Cabinas Nirvana (private bath, heated water, fans, mosquito nets; some kitchens, pool; $30-$40; four-person apartment, $50; 755-0110; e-mail: nirvana99@racsa.co.cr), on the right at the end of the road, is a nice place for families, with kitchens, hammocks on the porch, and a pool.

Bungalows Malú (heated water, ceiling fans, refrigerators, some with air conditioning; $30-$40; phone/fax: 755-0114) are artistically designed cabinas that incorporate driftwood and stone into the furniture and have porches with overhangs and benches. The owner is an Italian artist whose paintings also decorate the rooms. Her mama serves up Italian home-cooking in their open-air restaurant during the high season.

From here on, the establishments are farther apart.

The **Chalet Hibiscus** (private bath, hot water, wall fans, pool, some with kitchens; $40-$120; 755-0021, fax: 755-0015; e-mail: hibiscus@racsa.co.cr) offers one- and two-bedroom bungalows with ocean views and chalets that sleep six to ten.

An elegant option at the end of the road is the **Magellan Inn** (private bath, hot water, ceiling fans, pool, some with air conditioning; $80-$100; phone/fax: 755-0035; e-mail magellaninn@racsa.co.cr). The carpeted rooms are quiet, the Canadian hosts are attentive, and the garden setting is serene.

GETTING THERE: By Bus: Direct buses leave San José's Caribe terminal (Transportes MEPE, 257-8129) for Cahuita at 10 a.m., 1:30 p.m, and 3:30 p.m.

The ride takes three to four hours. Buses return to San José at 7 a.m., 9:30 a.m., 11:30 a.m., and 4:30 p.m.

From the bus terminal (754-1572) 100 meters north of the *mercado* in Limón, buses leave for Cahuita (90 cents) at 5 a.m., 8 a.m., 10 a.m., 1 p.m., 2 p.m., and 4 p.m.

If you are staying at one of the hotels on Black Beach, you can get off at the first or second entrance to Cahuita and walk from there (not recommended at night). The first two entrances take you several hundred meters to the Black Beach road, and the last leads half a kilometer to the center of town.

Buses leave at 7 a.m. and 3:30 p.m. from Cahuita to Puerto Viejo and Manzanilla, returning at 8:30 a.m. and 5:30 p.m. Buses also leave every three hours for Puerto Viejo and Sixaola.

Interbus (www.interbusonline.com) has air-conditioned buses that leave San José daily for Puerto Viejo ($25). They will drop you off at your hotel.

By Car: From Limón it's pretty much a straight shot down the coast. Turn south at the first intersection as you arrive in Limón; there's a Texaco plant at the intersection. It's 45 minutes from there to Cahuita. Close to Cahuita the road is riddled with potholes, so drive carefully. Cahuita is about half a kilometer off the main highway; the first two marked entrances take you to the Black Beach area and the last takes you to the center of town.

AROUND CAHUITA   Ten kilometers north of Cahuita is the bird-filled **Estrella River delta**, with narrow waterways similar to those near Tortuguero. This area is a flyway for migratory birds and a haven for waterfowl like herons, kingfishers, *jacanas*, and *gallinules*. It also has been featured on the Discovery Channel for the **Sloth Rescue Center** ($12). You can combine an informative tour of the Rescue Center with a short canoe trip for under $25, or you can relax with four hours of birdwatching as you glide silently down the canals, followed by a delicious breakfast ($30). Luis and Judy Arroyo, proprietors of a comfortable bed and breakfast here, have worked hard to protect what is now a private wildlife sanctuary encompassing the delta. **Aviarios del Caribe Lodge** (private bath, hot water, table fans, laundry service; $70-$110; shared bunkbed rooms, $22/person, including breakfast; phone/fax: 750-0775, fax: 750-0725; www.ogphoto. com/aviarios, e-mail: aviarios@costarica.net) has large rooms downstairs and a screened-in library/dining room upstairs for relaxing between your canoe expeditions. Even if you don't stay here, take the canal tours, which start at 6 a.m. Recommended.

Selva Bananito Lodge and Preserve (private bath, solar hot water, natural ventilation; $110-$120/person, including meals; $25 for kids 4 to 11; 253-8118; www.selvabananito.com, e-mail: conselva@racsa.co.cr), named one of the Top Ten Ecolodges in the World by *Outside Magazine* (March 2003), is the place to go if you want a real wilderness experience. Originally a farm owned by a German family, it is now a wilderness preserve at the foot of the Talamanca mountains, offering excellent birding and canopy explorations with rope and harness. The lodge is run in complete harmony with nature, thus there is no electricity, but each of the spacious, nicely designed cabins is provided with flashlights and gas lamps. The rooms have wide verandas with hammocks for star-gazing at night. Candles grace the flower-adorned tables in the dining room to provide a warm and cheery atmosphere for people to exchange ideas while enjoying meals. Jurgen and Sofia Stein are a charming brother and sister who run the lodge and guide the canopy activities. Three-day, two-night packages are offered for $330-$350/person, including roundtrip transportation from San José. Recommended.

GETTING THERE: The entrance to Selva Bananito is 27 kilometers north of Cahuita and 20 kilometers south of Limón. You must have four-wheel drive to get to Selva Bananito yourself. If you have a regular car, you can leave it at the village of Bananito, a few kilometers inland from the entrance, and they will come and pick you up. The hour-long trip from the highway involves fording several rivers and can be confusing. They will send you a map before you set out.

Hitoy Cerere Biological Reserve (reservations: 283-8004 ext. 110; admission $6; food and lodging possible with prior reservation) is definitely off the beaten track. For hardy explorers, there are beautiful views, clear streams, waterfalls, and lots of birds to see, including some lowland species that are hard to find elsewhere due to deforestation. The nine-kilometer Espavel trail has the best primary-growth forest. You have to take a Valle de la Estrella bus from Limón to get to Hitoy Cerere, which winds its way into the banana plantations. Get off at Finca 12, the end of the line. Jeep-taxis there will take you ten kilometers farther and leave you at the entrance. They will return to pick you up at an agreed-upon time and can take you back to Cahuita if you want (one and a half hours; $30). Try to arrange a ride with park personnel for the cheapest rates. Samasati Nature Retreat (below) arranges tours to Hitoy Cerere. You will need four-wheel drive for the last 14 kilometers if you drive yourself.

Samasati (private bath; $90-$110/person, double or triple occupancy, including meals; 224-1870, 800-563-9643, fax: 224-5032; www.samasati. com, e-mail: samasati@samasati.com) is a private 250-acre rainforest reserve in the hills between Cahuita and Puerto Viejo. You can swing in a hammock on the porch and gaze out over acres of forest to the blue Caribbean. Rooms in the guesthouse (shared bath; $70-$90/person, including meals) do not have the views, but are cozy. Everyone shares the view and the congenial atmosphere at the open-air restaurant where delicious vegetarian meals are served buffet-style. An energetic movement meditation to music gets your energy flowing in the morning, and yoga classes and bodywork will soothe you after a day on the nature trails. Samasati is located ten kilometers south of Cahuita, then 800 meters inland on a gravel road, then uphill about ten minutes (four-wheel drive needed—they will meet you below if you don't have a car). Take the 6 a.m. Sixaola bus or the 10 a.m. or 1:30 p.m. Puerto Viejo buses from the Caribe station at the north end of Calle Central in San José (257-8129) and ask to be let off at the Samasati sign in Hone Creek.

A group of local women have an organic banana farm and medicinal plant garden near Samasati. They offer attractive cabins in the middle of the jungle. Ask in Hone Creek for ✿ **La Asociación de Familias Productoras El Yüe**, or call Rosa Emilia Cruz at 750-0380.

✿ **Casa Calateas** (shared or private bath, cold water; $20-$30/person, including meals; 751-0046; e-mail: luisaz@costarricense.cr) is a rustic lodge overlooking the forest in the village of Carbón Dos, just inland from Cahuita. This locally owned project offers horseback rides, visits to local farms and waterfalls, and a chance to experience nature and rural life. It's a great place for birding, and the country cuisine is excellent. To get there, take the first road to the right after the Puerto Vargas entrance to Cahuita National Park. Go four kilometers on this narrow country road until you see a sign for the lodge on your right. You'll need four-wheel drive.

PUERTO VIEJO

Puerto Viejo is 19 kilometers south of Cahuita on paved road. A boom in tourism has taken place in the last few years and a plethora of restaurants and discos have opened in town; new hotels have sprung up along the road south to Manzanillo. Fortunately, the development is low-density, leaving most of the forest standing. The pristine beaches are some of the most beautiful in the country. Puerto Viejo can also be a base for excursion into the Bribri and Cabécar indigenous territories.

Puerto Viejo on the web: Almost all our favorite places in this area have websites on **www.greencoast.com**, which promotes "responsible and organic tourism." You can also get quite a bit of information at **www.puerto viejo.net**.

Culture: The Puerto Viejo area is home to at least three different cultures: the English-speaking black farmers who grew cacao and coconut until a blight in the early 1980s ruined the cacao harvest; the indigenous people of the Bribri and Cabécar tribes who live in the foothills; and the Spanish-speaking immigrants who came to the area in search of land. Because the Talamanca region was so isolated from the rest of Costa Rica until recently, many of its cultural traditions are still alive.

Check with Miss Sam or Miss Isma to find out when they are going to bake journey cakes; then get there on time because a line forms and locals and keyed-in tourists snap them up quick. Also check out the small bakery run by Mr. Patt.

Miss Dolly makes bread with coconut milk, which is good with her home-made guava jam. You can buy ginger biscuits, pineapple rolls, plantain tarts, *patí* and *pan bon* from other bakers, just ask any resident. Doña Guillermina cooks family-style in her home.

Services: To learn more about the area, plan to stop by the office of the **Talamancan Ecotourism and Conservation Association** (ATEC) (phone/fax: 750-0188, 750-0191; e-mail: atecmail@racsa.co.cr), across from Soda Tamara in "downtown" Puerto Viejo. There you can buy *Taking Care of Sibö's Gifts* ($7), in which the people of the Kekoldi reserve explain their way of life and their commitment to conserving nature. It also has a bird list of the area. ATEC is the local communications center, with a public phone and fax machine and internet access. They sell stamps and phone cards for the public phones in front of the office. They also have a spring water dispenser where you can fill your water bottles. It's usually open weekdays 8 a.m. to 9 p.m., with some variations on weekends. There are several other internet cafés on the main street. There is also a public phone at Manuel León's *pulpería*.

Hotel Los Almendros will change dollars for you. The Girasol will do your laundry and change your traveler's checks. There's no bank in town.

There is a **medical clinic and doctor** at the Hone Creek *cruce,* five kilometers from Puerto Viejo.

Bull (750-0112), Delroy (750-0132), and Mr. Spence (750-0008) are the main taxi drivers in town. Bull usually meets the bus in his gray-and-maroon Trooper.

Turtles: **ANAI** (750-0020; anaicr.racsa.co.cr) at the Puerto Viejo turn-off in Hone Creek coordinates leatherback turtle observation tours during the February 15–June 15 nesting season. They need committed volunteers for their programs in Barra de Hone Creek, north of Puerto Viejo, and in Gandoca, south of Bribri.

Birds: The ✿ **Kekoldi Indigenous Reserve** now features a **birdwatching tower** on a hill overlooking Puerto Viejo. Talamanca is one of the best places in the world to observe hawks, eagles, vultures, and kites during their spring and fall migrations. Tours to the **Wak Ka Koneke** (Earth Protectors) towers can be arranged through ATEC. The four- to five-hour climb includes a visit to the Kekoldi iguana farm. There you can buy *Mi Libro de Historias Bribris*, in which tribal storyteller Juanita Sanchez recounts and illustrates Bribri legends.

Organic tourism: ATEC will put together customized tours with local guides based on your interests ($15 for a half day, $25 for a full day), including early-morning bird walks, snorkeling at coral reefs, and dolphin-watching. There are both Spanish- and English-speaking guides. Ask for Harry Hawkins, who specializes in medicinal herbs and Afro-Caribbean culture, or Martín Hernandez, who leads wildlife walks and ocean diving tours in Punta Uva. Tino Grenald of Manzanillo is the expert on the Gandoca–Manzanillo refuge, and Gloria and Lucas Mayorga (Spanish) or Alex Paez, Edward Stewart, and Mauricio Salazar (English) take people to the Kekoldi Indigenous Reserve, including the birding tower and the iguana farm. Traditional meals can be arranged. Willis Rankin takes visitors to Tortuguero ($50). *Note*: Only authorized guides are allowed to lead tours within the Kekoldi reserve. All the guides recommended by ATEC and ANAI have official ID cards.

ATEC will also lead you on a seven- to ten-day transcontinental hike through unmarked traditional trails in the Talamanca mountains of Amistad International Park, or to the indigenous village of Yorkín. See www.green coast.com for details. Don't attempt to do these hikes without a guide. Two independent hikers died in these mountains in 1999.

Along the stretch of beach before you get to town is the entrance to the **Tropical Botanical Garden** (open Friday through Monday, 10 a.m. to 4 p.m.; 750-0046; $2.50, $8 with guided tour; www.greencoast.com/garden. htm), where black pepper, tropical fruits, and spectacular flowering plants are grown. Colorful frogs live among the bromeliads. You can sample fruits and spices from all over the world, or take a walk on a rainforest loop trail. Wear sturdy shoes for the two-and-a-half-hour tour. To get there, walk 500 meters inland from the sign on the beach road, then bear to your right, following the signs.

Canopy tours: **Terraventuras** ($40; 750-0426; e-mail: terraventuras@ hotmail.com) has an eight-platform, 1200-meter canopy tour in Hone Creek, just north of Puerto Viejo.

Water sports: The area outside the reef in Puerto Viejo has become famous in surfing lore as **La Salsa Brava**. The waves are world-class from December to February. Another season opens up in June and July. During the high season, surfers on their way out often sell their boards to new arrivals. This avoids the tremendous hassle of taking surfboards on the plane or bus. Some surfers hire a taxi or truck to haul their gear from Limón ($25-$30). This is cheaper than renting a car in San José, and most of the good waves are an easy walk from Puerto Viejo. La Salsa Brava is definitely not for neophytes.

In June, September, and October the sea is calmer and better for snorkeling and swimming. Nonsurfers will be able to enjoy Puerto Viejo a lot more in these months. Everything is less crowded, and the weather is generally beautiful. As in most good surfing areas, rip tides are common; ask about conditions before swimming. If caught in a riptide, don't try to swim against it—swim parallel to the beach and the tide will eventually bring you back in. (See "Beach Safety" in Chapter Five.)

Sea kayaking and snorkeling rentals are available from **Atlántico Tours** in Puerto Viejo and **Aquamor** in Manzanillo. Aquamor also runs inexpensive scuba diving tours and gives a PADI certification course.

Horses and bicycles: Other activities you can do on your own in the area include walking the beach trail between Puerto Viejo and Manzanillo, or renting a bike to pedal the flat, coastal road between these two towns. Being on a bicycle, even if you have rented a car, seems like the best method of locomotion in the area. A bike can provide just enough breeze to keep you cool. Atlántico Tours and Tabú near the bus stop rent bikes, but you have to get there early. To rent horses, ask around for Don Antonio or Don Jesus.

Note for drivers and bicyclists: Do as the locals do and get off your bike to cross the small bridges along the beach road. It's very easy to lose your balance on the sandy concrete surface, and there are no railings to keep you from falling into the rocky river below. If you are driving, do so slowly: the bridges are unmarked and you can be on them before you know it. Also, locals ride without reflectors, becoming another hazard.

Insects: Whether you will be bothered by mosquitos depends on the climatic conditions and the location and design of your hotel. Many hotels now offer mosquito nets. Check when you make reservations. If there are mosquitos, they will only bother you at night. Worse than mosquitos are no-see-ums in the sand, which bite your ankles around dusk. And watch out for mean biting ants in the grass. Bring a good insect repellent.

Water: Have bottled water in your hotel to brush your teeth with and drink at night. Many hotels supply drinking water for guests. Make sure the bottle is filled before you settle in.

Art: Across the street from Cabinas Guarana, **Galería Luluberlú** (open 1 p.m. to 9 p.m., open all day in high season; 750-0394) showcases the intricate, beautiful work of prolific French mosaic artist, Luluberlú. She also exhibits high-quality indigenous art and crafts. Recommended.

RESTAURANTS   If you want a taste of the culture, stop by **Miss Sam's** front porch restaurant, two blocks inland from the main street. Her fluffy rice and beans are served with a delicious cabbage *curtido* at rock-bottom prices. Recommended.

Soda Isma (open daily, 8 a.m. to 9 p.m.; 750-0579) on the main street serves rice and beans, whole fish in Caribbean sauce, and *rondon*, a flavorful fish stew made with coconut milk (order in advance). Several breakfast spots are across from the bus stop. **Café Red Stripe** serves homemade ice cream. Or try the homemade bread and jam at German-owned **The Place** (open 7 a.m. to 10 p.m.; closed Thursday; 750-0195). Or look for the Dutch-owned **El Café Rico** (open 8 a.m. to 8 p.m.), across the street from Casa Verde, where generous servings of delicious food are served all day.

Our favorite place to eat in Puerto Viejo is **El Loco Natural** (open Thursday through Sunday from 6 p.m.; 750-0263). If you are tired of *comida típica* and have a hankering for something truly exotic, try their artistically presented Guayanese fusion of East Indian and Caribbean flavors, accompanied by tropical coconut concoctions. With bossa nova on the sound system and live music after 8:30 p.m., this is a very happening scene. Recommended.

Stanford's Restaurant El Caribe is famous for fresh seafood. Their disco is jumping Thursday through Sunday. **La Salsa Brava**, just beyond Stanford's, serves seafood with a Spanish touch.

Travelers craving Italian cuisine will have no problem satisfying their taste buds in Puerto Viejo. **Amimodo** (open noon to 4 p.m., 6 p.m. to 10:30 p.m.; closed Wednesday; 750-0257) just south of town, offers authentic pastas and Italian-style seafood like lobster ravioli, gracefully served in their lovely open-air restaurant. **Caramba** (closed Wednesday; 750-0527), right in town, serves calzones, sandwiches, and pizza. **El Café Viejo**, down the street, has tasty Italian food. The **Lotus Garden** (open 3 p.m. to 11 p.m.; 750-0232) serves sushi made by a Japanese chef.

Ask when fresh fruits and vegetables are delivered to Puerto Viejo. You can buy them from the delivery truck as it makes its rounds or at the vegetable stands near the bus stop and at the Parquecito.

LODGING   If you make a left at Pulpería Violeta instead of veering right to Puerto Viejo, you'll drive along an intensely black beach. After about

300 meters you'll come to the following beach establishments, which we recommend for their simplicity, tranquility, reasonable rates, and proximity to the sea. **Chimuri Beach Cottages** (private bath, heated water, kitchens, mosquito nets; $30-$50; $225-$315/week; 750-0119; www.greencoast. com/chimuribeach, e-mail: chimuribeach@racsa.co.cr) are simple, campesino houses with porches and hammocks. Ask about their jungle cabins on the edge of the Kekoldi reserve.

Just down the road is **Chalet Luna Mágica** ($50-$60; $700/month; 750-0115; e-mail: comander@racsa.co.cr), a house for four with an ocean view and a lovely private garden in front. The owner, Silvana Comino, also does energy-balancing bodywork.

The next cabinas are in Puerto Viejo proper. Therre are many others, but these are our favorites in town. See the next section for beach cabins south of Puerto Viejo.

The Italian-owned **Cabinas Guarana** (private bath, heated water, ceiling fans; $20-$30; 750-0024; www.cabinasguarana.com, e-mail: guarana@ racsa.co.cr), one block inland from El Coco Natural and half a block to the left, have light, pleasantly decorated rooms with hammocks around a garden courtyard. The dense garden gives a sense of privacy to each room. There is a shared kitchen for guests. Recommended.

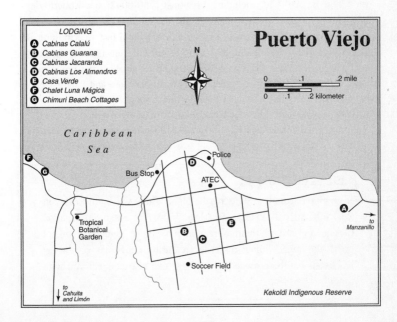

Across from the **Pan Pay**, a good place for breakfast, are the new, locally owned **Cabinas Los Almendros** (private bath, heated water; $30-$40; with refrigerator, air conditioning, TV; $60-$70; 750-0246, phone/fax: 750-0246; e-mail: flchwg@racsa.co.cr). These cabins are well-run and have a money-changing service.

Nicely furnished and decorated, the **Cabinas Jacaranda** (shared or private bath, heated or cold water, table fans, mosquito nets; $12-$30; 750-0069; www.puertoviejo.net/jacaranda/homes.htm) have bright mosaic walkways and a garden gazebo.

One of our favorite places in town is the Swiss/Tica-owned **Casa Verde** (heated water, ceiling fans, mosquito nets; with shared bath, $20-$30; with private bath, $30-$40; 750-0015, fax: 750-0047; www.greencoast.com, e-mail: casaverde@racsa.co.cr), famous for its very clean and nicely decorated rooms. One small house has its own kitchen but shares a bath ($30-$40). There is a massage *rancho*, or you can venture behind the cabins to see the poisonous-frog collection. Laundry service, secure parking, money exchange, and a coffee shop are among the many services offered at the Casa Verde. Recommended.

As you leave town, set back from the road on the right, is **Cabinas Calalú** (private bath, hot water, ceiling fans, pool, mosquito nets, some with kitchens; $30-$40, including breakfast; 750-0042; www.puertoviejo.net/calalu/menu.htm, e-mail: calalu@puertoviejo.net). The thatch-roofed cabins are surrounded by trees. Guests can eat breakfast overlooking the **butterfly garden** (open 8 a.m. to 4 p.m.; $5 for non-guests) or at the pool.

GETTING THERE: By Bus: MEPE (Caribe terminal, at the north end of Calle Central; 257-8129) runs buses daily between San José and Puerto Viejo (6 a.m., 10 a.m., 1:30 p.m., 3:30 p.m.; $7). The ride is about four hours.

A bus leaves Puerto Viejo for Manzanillo at 7 a.m. and 4 p.m.

From the Talamanca bus stop in Limón (100 meters north of the *mercado*, 754-1572), a bus leaves every other hour between 6 a.m. and 6 p.m. ($2.35). You

---

LET ATEC DO IT

If you have trouble contacting the place where you want to stay in Puerto Viejo, call ATEC (750-0188, 750-0191; e-mail: atecmail@racsa.co.cr) and ask them to transmit a message. Remember, do not go to this area without reservations during Christmas or Easter; weekends can be crowded, too. ATEC can also connect you with tours.

can also take the Manzanillo bus (6 a.m., 2:30 p.m.; $2.85), which passes through Puerto Viejo and follows the coastal road south of Puerto Viejo through Cocles and Punta Uva. Get there early to buy a ticket. You can check these schedules at ATEC or www.greencoast.com.

Interbus (283-5573, 800-748-8853; www.interbusonline.com) has air-conditioned buses that leave San José daily at 8 a.m. for Puerto Viejo ($25). They will drop you off at your hotel. They will also take you to Puerto Viejo from Siquirres, La Fortuna, and Sarapiquí ($38).

By Car: From San José, the trip to Puerto Viejo takes three and a half to four hours, depending on the number of trucks on the highway to Limón. From Limón, it is about an hour to an hour and a half (depending on road conditions) to Puerto Viejo. When you reach Hone Creek there is a *cruce*, where the road curves to the right toward Bribrí and the Panama border, and the road straight ahead continues six kilometers to Puerto Viejo.

Note: Cars and buses are often stopped by the Guardia Rural and checked for Panamanian contraband as they leave Talamanca, so be sure to carry your passport and have all immigration documents in order.

BEACHES SOUTH OF PUERTO VIEJO

Lovely hotels and cabinas are scattered all along the 15-kilometer road between Puerto Viejo and Manzanillo. Most of them are within the Gandoca–Manzanillo Wildlife Refuge. We list them in appearance north to south. Most of them are clustered around **Punta Cocles** (four kilometers from Puerto Viejo), **Playa Chiquita** (five kilometers from Puerto Viejo), and **Punta Uva** (seven kilometers from Puerto Viejo). Punta Uva is gorgeous and has the best swimming. All of these shady beaches, especially Playa Cocles, have strong currents; pay attention to signs on the beach directing you to the most secure areas (November through February are the most dangerous months). All three have won the coveted Bandera Azul Ecológica award for cleanliness of water and sand. These are the kind of places to stay if you're looking for tranquility and less contact with village (and disco) life than you would get in Puerto Viejo. Since there are *pulperías* and restaurants dotting the coast, you won't have to return to Puerto Viejo for meals. Four buses a day travel this road, and some hotels offer shuttle bus or boat service into town.

The Playa Chiquita Lodge hosts the **Music Festival of the South Caribbean Coast**, several weekends of concerts by Costa Rica's most lively jazz, calypso, ska, and reggae musicians. There's also poetry, cinema, dance, and theater presentations, and workshops on drum-making, Afro-Caribbean dance, and permaculture. Definitely worth catching if you're in the area in February or March. For more information, call Wanda Paterson (750-0408, fax: 750-0062; www.playachiquitalodge.com).

RESTAURANTS   There is an organic **farmer's market** (every Saturday at 10 a.m. at the corner of Shawandha Lodge) that features homemade cheeses and baked goods. **El Rinconcito Peruano**, on the right after the soccer field, doesn't look like much but locals tell us their seafood preparation is truly sophisticated. The best restaurant in the area is **La Pecora Nera** (750-0490), where the enthusiastic owner and chef, Ilario Giannoni, rhapsodizes about what he can make for you and how he will do it. You can watch his every move through a window that looks into the kitchen, easily visible from all the tables. Pricey.

Elena's Bar and Restaurant on Playa Chiquita offers seafood and tasty sandwiches. The atmosphere is dominated by whatever is on their satellite TV. **Selvin's**, at Punta Uva, is the place to go for authentic Caribbean cooking (including fresh lobster) in a relaxed, friendly atmosphere.

LODGING   The Italian-owned **Escape Caribeño** (private bath, heated water, ceiling fans, refrigerators, air conditioning, TV, mosquito nets; $40-$60; phone/fax: 750-0103; www.greencoast.com/escapec.htm, e-mail: es capec@racsa.co.cr) has tidy cabinas with porches and hammocks set in a garden across the road from the beach, and beach cabins designed to catch the sea breezes. All manner of beautiful birds flock to the bird feeders outside their welcoming breakfast *rancho*. They also rent a two-room house with kitchen.

Rocking J's (750-0657; www.rockingjs.com), right on the beach, seems to be the place to stay for young people, with your choice of dorms, tents, or hammocks all under $7/person, and $20 for private rooms. Communal kitchen, laundry, and bike and snorkeling rentals—they've got it all.

The beachfront **Apartments Agapi** (private bath, hot water, fans, mosquito nets, hammocks, kitchens; $30-$50; 750-0446), 800 meters south of town, are a good value. The second-floor rooms have balconies with a nice view of the water.

A kilometer and a half south of Puerto Viejo, **Cariblue** (private bath, heated water, ceiling fans, mosquito nets, pool; $80-$90, including breakfast; with kitchen and room for seven, $190-$200; 750-0035; www.cari blue.com, e-mail: cariblue@racsa.co.cr), owned and managed by a friendly Italian couple, is set back from the road in a tranquil, park-like setting. The individual wooden bungalows sleep up to six, and are private and polished, with nice touches like hammocks on the porches and creative mosaics in the bathrooms. They have a great restaurant featuring Italian specialties and seafood. Recommended.

Azania Bungalows (private bath, heated water, pool; $70-$80, including breakfast; 750-0540, fax: 750-0371; www.azania-costarica.com, e-mail: info@azania-costarica.com) are two-story, thatched-roof cabins set in a jungly garden. The high roof, cross ventilation, and screened windows keep them cool and fresh inside, and there are many nice decorative touches, including hammocks on the porch. Each cabin sleeps four.

Set in a lush five-acre garden with a pond and resident sloths, **La Costa de Papito** (private bath, hot water, ceiling fans; $40-$60; kids free; 750-0080; www.greencoast.com/papito.htm, e-mail: costapapito@yahoo.com) offers individual wood bungalows with good mattresses. Their spacious porches with hammocks, surrounded by lush greenery, make this a true tropical paradise. Bike, snorkel, and surf equipment rentals are available. A good value. Recommended.

Aguas Claras (private bath, hot water, ceiling fans, kitchens; $50-$170; $270-$815/week; 750-0131, fax: 750-0368; www.aguasclaras-cr.com, e-mail: aguasclaras@racsa.co.cr) has cute gingerbread cottages of different sizes in a parklike garden. These are some of the most charming accommodations at the beach, with open-air kitchens and living rooms built in a colorful Caribbean style. Good for families or groups. The path to the beach is through an arbor of ancient trees; a shallow tidepool forms there at low tide. Recommended.

Six kilometers south of Puerto Viejo is the German/Tica-owned **Playa Chiquita Lodge** (private bath, heated water, ceiling fans; $50-$60, including breakfast; children under 12 free; 750-0062, fax: 750-0408; www.playachiquitalodge.com, e-mail: wolfbiss@racsa.co.cr), which organizes the yearly Music Festival of the South Caribbean Coast. The connected cabins are nicely designed and are shaded by exuberant vegetation. The seemingly secluded beach, down a path from the cabinas, has three tide pools where kids can enjoy themselves at low tide.

Across the road, the elegant, tranquil **Shawandha Lodge** (private bath, heated water, natural ventilation; $100-$110, including breakfast; 750-0018, fax: 750-0037; www.shawandhalodge.com, e-mail: shawandha@racsa.co.cr) comprises several thatch-roofed A-frames set in the forest. Each large, half-moon bathroom is adorned with a different fanciful tile mosaic. A 200-meter path leads directly to Playa Chiquita. Their spacious, open-air restaurant features French-tropical cuisine.

The Italian-owned **Villa Paradiso** is a well-stocked grocery store on the right. They also rent inexpensive cabins (private bath, heated water, fans; $20-$30; 750-0322).

About one kilometer farther down the road on the left are **Selvin's Cabinas** (shared or private bath, cold water, mosquito nets; $7-$12; with kitchens, $15-$20; house, $50; 750-0664). **Selvin's Restaurant** (closed Monday and Tuesday during peak season; open weekends only during the low season) is one of the best in the area and specializes in fish and lobster dinners. They serve the local dish of rice and beans on weekends. The basic cabins are a boon for budget travelers since they are a short walk from the most beautiful part of the beach at Punta Uva. Recommended.

Itaitá Villas, also near Punta Uva (private bath, hot water, fans, kitchens; $120-$130; 750-0414, 229-0950; e-mail: labvaco@rasa.co.cr), are two-room cabins with Caribbean-style gingerbread details.

Casa Viva (private bath, hot water, kitchens; $70-$100, two-night minimum; $450-$600/week; 750-0089; www.puntauva.net, e-mail: puntauva@racsa.co.cr) is right on the best part of Punta Uva. These lovely, handcrafted, two-bedroom houses have wide verandahs strung with hammocks, fully equipped kitchens, and are placed well apart from each other amidst beautiful tropical gardens. Recommended.

Two kilometers south of Selvin's, a road on the left takes you to the small community at **Punta Uva** and to some good picnic/parking spots at the beach. This is not as scenic or as swimmable as the beach near Selvin's.

Almendros y Corales Lodge Tent Camp (private bath, cold water, table fans; $60-$70/person, including two meals; 272-2024, 272-4175, fax: 272-2220; e-mail: almonds@racsa.co.cr) is right in the middle of the Gandoca–Manzanillo Wildlife Refuge (see page 241). Elevated, screened-in huts, with vinyl Boy Scout tents permanently erected inside, complete with beds, cabinets, bathrooms, and a table and chairs, are scattered throughout the mostly intact jungle, connected by a boardwalk. The walkway leads to the beach. When we stayed there, howler monkeys were right over our cabin in the morning. They have a rather tame zipline tour and a one-and-a-half- kilometer nature trail with stops at an orchid garden and frog habitat. The Costa Rican owner has recreated a Bribri Indian village there, more picturesque than the real villages because it's not real. All these attractions are designed for cruise ship customers so they can feel like they have been in the jungle during their 12-hour stop in Costa Rica. The entrance is beyond Las Palmas by a few hundred yards.

MANZANILLO

Seven kilometers beyond Punta Uva is the small fishing village of Manzanillo. The **Gandoca–Manzanillo Wildlife Refuge** protects a nine-kilometer beach where four species of turtles lay their eggs, including the giant *baula* (leatherback). The turtles' main nesting season is February 15 through June 15.

Just offshore and within easy snorkeling distance, the varied corals of the **Manzanillo reef** look like brains, stars, lettuce, cacti, flowers, and cups. Their tunnels, channels, nooks, and crannies are home to sponges, lobsters, eels, sea stars, and amazing tropical fish. The many beaches of the area are lined with coconut palms. Monkeys, sloths, parrots, butterflies, frogs, and wild felines like jaguars live in the lush forest of the refuge.

In the southern part of the refuge, the Gandoca River estuary is a nursery for tarpon; manatees, crocodiles, and caimans are also seen there. Dolphins, as well as pygmy, sperm, and pilot whales, are often present offshore.

Get information about the refuge and pay the $6 admission fee at the turquoise-and-white gingerbread-style MINAE headquarters. Always go with a guide when you explore the jungle here.

ATEC offers tours from Manzanillo to Punta Mona and Gandoca through the reserve with **Florentino Grenald** (750-0191; www.greencoast.com), a local community leader with a great sense of humor. He can arrange dol-

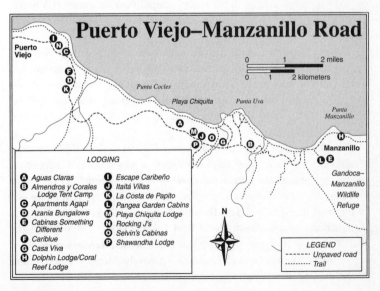

Puerto Viejo–Manzanillo Road

Puerto Viejo

Punta Cocles

Playa Chiquita   Punta Uva

Punta Manzanillo

Manzanillo

Gandoca–Manzanillo Wildlife Refuge

0   1   2 miles
0   1   2 kilometers

LODGING

Ⓐ Aguas Claras
Ⓑ Almendros y Corales Lodge Tent Camp
Ⓒ Apartments Agapi
Ⓓ Azania Bungalows
Ⓔ Cabinas Something Different
Ⓕ Cariblue
Ⓖ Casa Viva
Ⓗ Dolphin Lodge/Coral Reef Lodge
Ⓘ Escape Caribeño
Ⓙ Itaitá Villas
Ⓚ La Costa de Papito
Ⓛ Pangea Garden Cabins
Ⓜ Playa Chiquita Lodge
Ⓝ Rocking J's
Ⓞ Selvin's Cabinas
Ⓟ Shawandha Lodge

N

LEGEND
- - - - - Unpaved road
········· Trail

phin watching, medicinal-herb walks, and bird- or insect-watching trips on foot or horseback, depending on your interests. Tino is building some cabins; ask him about them. The ✿ **Guías MANT** (759-0964; e-mail: grenald60@ hotmail.com) office in Manzanillo can connect you with Tino and other well-qualified guides.

Aquamor (759-0612; e-mail: aquamor@racsa.co.cr) rents kayaks and snorkeling equipment, and offers inexpensive kayak tours, scuba diving, and PADI certification. The owners, siblings Greg, Katrina, and Shawn Larkin, are the founders of the **Costa Rica Cetacean Institute** (www.costa cetacea.com), which works with MINAE to protect dolphins. They are trying to get the refuge extended to include the newly mapped reef and dolphin area offshore. Their love and respect for dolphins is reflected in their dolphin tour: these wonderful creatures are not chased, but allowed to approach boats out of their own curiosity. If conditions are right, you can swim with them. Aquamor has also set up buoys in shallow water that you can tie your kayak to so that you can explore the reefs as long as you want. They welcome committed volunteers, especially those experienced with boats.

Manzanillo Tarpon Expeditions (www.tarponville.com) does catch-and-release fishing, and involves local guides who have been active in getting gill nets out of the marine reserve.

Locals gather in **Maxi's Bar** to play dominos, and tourists flock there for the Caribbean cuisine in the breezy second-floor restaurant. **La Selva**, at the entrance to town, is also good and has faster service. **Miss Marva** also cooks for visitors in her home.

Pangea Garden Cabins (private bath, heated water, ceiling fan, mosquito nets; $30-$40, including breakfast; 759-9024; www.puertoviejo.net/ pangea.htm, e-mail pangea@racsa.co.cr), 200 meters inland from Aquamor, is a friendly place to stay. **Cabinas Something Different** (private bath, hot water, fans, refrigerator, direct TV; $30-$40; 759-9014), next door, are a good value.

The **Talamanca Dolphin Foundation** (759-9115, 759-0612; www.dol phinlink.com, e-mail: info@dolphinlink.com) works to further dolphin research and sustainable community development in Manzanillo. They have two comfortable houses on a small, shady beach, 200 meters beyond the end of the road. The four-bedroom **Dolphin Lodge** ($1000-$1400/week) sleeps eight and the three-bedroom **Coral Reef Lodge** ($800-$1200/week) sleeps four. It is rare to find such nicely situated beach houses. Recommended.

Between Manzanillo and Gandoca, on lovely Monkey Point, **Punta Mona** (614-5735; www.puntamona.com) is a 30-acre organic farm and educational retreat dedicated to setting an example of sustainable living through permaculture. Volunteers can get experience in many aspects of permaculture (minimum one-month time commitment; $200/month for room and board). Short-term guests are welcome to stay for $20/person, including meals. It's accessible by a 1.5-hour hike five kilometers south of Manzanillo (guide strongly recommended because of swampy areas), or by arranging for a boat to take you there in 15 minutes. You can meet their captain, Bako, at Maxi's.

GETTING THERE: By Bus: Buses leave Limón at 6 a.m. and 2:30 p.m., passing through Puerto Viejo at 7:30 a.m. and 3:30 p.m. to continue on to Manzanillo (check exact times at ATEC). They can drop you off at your hotel of choice. Buses leave Manzanillo for Puerto Viejo and continue to Limón at 5 a.m., 8:30 a.m., and 5 p.m., and will pick you up if you wait on the road outside your hotel.

By Car: If driving, pay special attention to the bridges along the road. Some are on curves, some are in great need of repair, all are narrow. Careless drivers have drowned.

BRIBRÍ

Bribrí, a nondescript town between Cahuita and Sixaola on Panama's border, is the gateway to the isolated territories of the Bribrí and Cabécar tribes. Try the delicious garlic fish at **Restaurant Zamia** (open Monday through Saturday, 11 a.m. to 10 p.m.; 751-0133), in the middle of town. You must drive through Bribrí to get to Gandoca, San Miguel, Bambú, Shiroles, Amubrí, or any other village in the Bribrí territories.

GANDOCA, SAN MIGUEL, & BUENA VISTA

The Blue Flag beach at ✿ **Gandoca**, on the southern end of the Gandoca–Manzanillo reserve, is the nesting ground for four kinds of sea turtles. The leatherback season is between February 15 and June 15. Dedicated volunteers help protect the turtles, patrolling the beach at night and moving nests if they might be disturbed. Contact ANAI (224-6090; e-mail: anaicr@ racsa.co.cr) if you would like to be part of this effort. ANAI also accepts volunteers on its experimental farm in Gandoca.

Accommodations in Gandoca are nothing fancy, but staying there after a turtle tour might be preferable to the long trip back to Puerto Viejo. The friendly **Cabinas Orquidea** (private bath, cold water; $7-$12; 837-4079) are almost on the beach.

Deep in the forest behind Gandoca in San Miguel is a remote, primary forest reserve owned by ASACODE (Asociación Sanmigueleña de Conser-

ADVENTURE REPORT: YORKÍN RIVER TRIP

We awoke early to a hearty campesino breakfast at Las Calateas, our lodge in the hills near Cahuita, owned by a cooperative from the village of Carbon Dos. Soon we met Benson Venegas, director of ANAI and our tour leader for the day. ANAI was one of only seven organizations worldwide to win the 2002 Equator Prize, recognizing their efforts in conservation and poverty reduction over the last 25 years. Benson accepted the award at the Johannesburg World Summit in August 2002. We were lucky to have him as our guide to the Bribrí indigenous territories.

He took us to the Bribrí town of Bambú, where we crossed a wide river in a dugout canoe, and started hiking, through lush tropical countryside, toward the isolated village of ✿ Yorkín. We hiked past a country school, where kids were playing soccer, and Benson got soccer-loving Dan involved in the game. He made a goal!

Soon we heard the voices of two men from Yorkín, almost yodeling over the crest of the next hill. They had come to take us on the next leg of our trip in their dugout. The water in the river was low, after a long dry season, and we were going against the current. Our boatmen strained every muscle in their bodies to keep us from running aground on the rocks, maneuvering the boat with the help of strong poles and their life-long knowledge of the river. Finally we reached Yorkín, where we swam in the delightful river, accompanied by several village kids who kept our kids entertained. We walked to the Casa de las Mujeres for a delicious lunch, which included fresh *palmito*.

The cacao tree is sacred to the Bribrí tribe. In their mythology, the cacao tree was made from the sister of their creator Sibu. Cacao farming is being revived in Talamanca. The women showed us a fresh cacao pod, and let us suck the fruit around the

vación y Desarrollo), a small farmers' association. They are dedicated conservationists who experiment with reforestation of native trees and harvest hardwoods selectively from their forest, dragging out the tree trunks with water buffalo for the lowest impact possible. Besides being ecologically conscious, they are economically wise as well, processing the wood seeds. They showed us how the seeds are dried and fermented, then toasted and ground to make the bitter hot chocolate favored by the Bribrí. Their organic banana and palm heart plantations are also cultivated in harmony with the forests that cover half of their territory.

Tourism is handled in a way that fits in with the Bribrí culture: when tourists visit, everyone in the association helps with transportation, cooking, serving, and cultural presentations. They also donate the food that is served and divide the income.

After the presentation came one of the highlights of the trip for me. Bernarda Morales, head of the Stibraupa Women's Group, asked us about ourselves and what we thought of their project. One member of our group said that visiting Yorkín and seeing the conservation efforts there gave her hope for the future of the planet, whereas before she had been very pessimistic. Another person said that he could see that the values he grew up with in the city were not necessarily the best ones, as he had formerly believed. We were all glad to be there in that moment of sharing.

Going downstream in the dugout was quite a bit faster than going up because the current was with us. We bounced through some rapids before joining the bigger river and arriving again in Bambú. From there we traveled to Shiroles, where we stayed at the ✿ Finca Educativa (373-4181), a well-appointed lodge and educational center that also runs trips to Yorkín and other villages like Amubri and the Cabécar village of Cachabri, where a local shaman shares his knowledge of healing with medicinal herbs.

To visit Yorkín, call ATEC (750-0191; e-mail: atecmail@ racsa.co.cr), ANAI (750-0020, 253-7524; e-mail: anaicr@racsa. co.cr), or ACTUAR (228-5696; www.actuarcostarica.com, e-mail: actuar@racsa.co.cr).

themselves to offer the more expensive finished product directly, bypassing middlemen. Easiest access is from Finca 96, a town off the Bribrí–Sixaola road, but hikes in from Manzanillo can be arranged as well.

The ✿ **CASACODE Lodge** (shared bath, cold water, mosquito nets; 835-6819; e-mail: kumarycr@yahoo.com) in the middle of the reserve offers simple accommodations for groups. The community wants visitors to see the beauty and problems of the area; they present legends, plays, and dances for their guests.

GETTING THERE: By Bus: Take the bus to the border at Sixaola, then take a taxi to ASACODE or Gandoca.

By Car: You have to go to Bribrí and continue through banana plantations to Finca 96, where you turn left for Gandoca. After the bridge over Caño Creek, turn left and go two kilometers to get to ASACODE (four-wheel drive only), or go straight to get to Gandoca. The trip takes about an hour and a half from Puerto Viejo.

If you really want to get off the beaten track, ✿ **Buena Vista** ($40-$50/person, including meals; 750-0136; e-mail acodefo@hotmail.com) is for you. This isolated lodge, located in the hills west of Bribrí at 1650 feet above sea level, offers a panoramic view of the Sixaola river. It is an adventure to get to on foot, horseback, or, in the dry season, by jeep. Besides hikes to local waterfalls, they can take you on a four-day trek ($580/person) into the Bribrí and Cabécar indigenous territories or to hot springs on the Panamá border ($140). Most excursions require a minimum of six people.

NINE

The Northern Zone

Costa Rica's Northern Zone extends from the Atlantic plains in the east to the San Juan River on the Nicaraguan border in the north, and to Lake Arenal and the Tilarán mountain range in the west. More and more visitors include a visit to the Northern Zone's towering rainforests and the spectacular Arenal volcano in their itinerary.

During the 1980s and '90s, this zone was the scene of large-scale deforestation. Primary forest gave way to orange, banana, and pineapple plantations. At first, the *almendro* tree (a primary food source for the endangered great green macaw, or *lapa verde* in Spanish) was left standing in the fields because its wood was too hard to cut. But as logging technology progressed during the 1990s, the *almendros* began to fall, and the *lapa verde* began to disappear.

Biologists found that the foraging areas for pairs of green macaws with eggs or nestlings did not overlap. They found that each pair needs about 550 hectares of nesting territory and that a minimum of 50 mating pairs was required to guarantee short-term survival of one subpopulation of the species, as long as there were occasional genetic interchanges with other subpopulations. These subpopulations form a metapopulation, which, according to geneticists, must be around 500 breeding pairs in order to remain genetically healthy. So the amount of land they would need to protect the great green macaw: 550 hectares per pair times 50 pairs per subpopulation, times 10 for a 500-pair metapopulation = 275,000 hectares plus migratory habitats.

Because so much logging had occurred in Costa Rica already, the amount of land needed to preserve the species had to extend beyond the

Costa Rican border to the Indio-Maíz Biological Reserve across the San Juan River in Nicaragua. These extensive forests are now threatened by illegal logging and clearing.

The endangered *almendro* and the endangered *lapa verde* are the justification for the San Juan–La Selva Biological Corridor, which would connect the Indio–Maíz Reserve on the Nicaraguan side of the Río San Juan with La Selva Biological Reserve in Puerto Viejo de Sarapiquí to the south, extending to Barra del Colorado National Wildlife Refuge to the east and to Braulio Carrillo National Park in the Central Valley. The 30,000-hectare Maquenque National Park is proposed for this area, but a tight budget has prevented the Costa Rican government from buying the land.

Ecotourism is definitely on the agenda for San Juan–La Selva. Currently the inhabitants work at seasonal agricultural or logging jobs. Only 12 percent of the proposed Maquenque National Park has soils suitable for agriculture. The scarlet macaw draws tourists to Carara National Park on the Pacific and to the Osa Peninsula. The resplendent quetzal draws visitors to Monteverde, Los Santos, and Cerro de la Muerte. Hopefully, due to habitat protection by the San Juan–La Selva Biological Corridor, the endangered great green macaw will survive, the *almendro* trees will flourish, and they will bring economic growth and well-being to the inhabitants of this area.

To find out more, consult the Tropical Science Center website (www.cct.or.cr/lapa) and the Friends of the Great Green Macaw (www.greatgreenmacaw.org). There are plenty of volunteer opportunities with this exciting project.

ON THE WAY TO SARAPIQUÍ

On your way to Puerto Viejo de Sarapiquí, as you descend from Braulio Carrillo National Park, you'll see a sign on your right for the **Rain Forest Aerial Tram** (open daily from 6:30 a.m. to 3:30 p.m., by reservation only); make reservations two days in advance, by phone or online. Rates are $49.50 for walk-ins; $24.75 for children over five and card-carrying students (children under five are not allowed on tram); $78.50, including breakfast or lunch and transportation from your hotel, kids and students $53.75, from San José; 257-5961, fax: 257-6053, in the U.S.: 866-759-8726; www.rainforesttram.com, e-mail: oficina@rainforesttram.com. Six-person gondolas, hanging from a 1.3-kilometer cable, glide silently through the forest at heights ranging from three feet off the ground to mid-canopy to 120 feet. The ride lasts 80 minutes. This sedate guided tour is an inform-

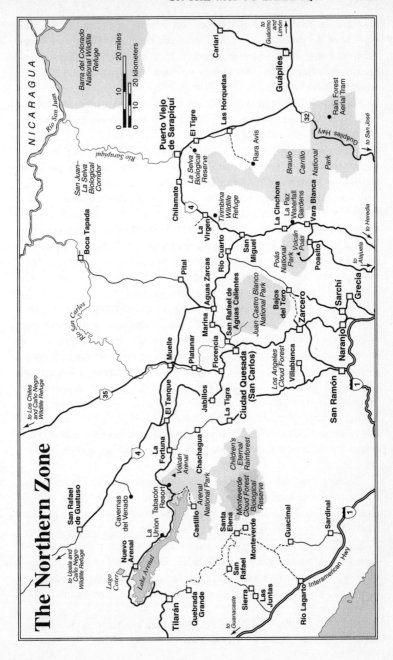

The Northern Zone

ative and easy introduction for those short on time or endurance and who don't need the thrills of the canopy tours and hanging bridges. The Aerial Tram now has attractive **cabins** (private bath, hot water; $80/person, including meals and tram ride) to stay in. They also make special arrangements for disabled access.

Rancho Roberto (open daily, 7 a.m. to 10 p.m.), at the turnoff to Sarapiquí, is a nice place to stop for a meal. Their ample menu includes delicious grilled tilapia and good *bocas*.

Back when people were first learning of the destruction of rainforests worldwide but didn't know what to do about it, Amos Bien, an ecologist and former manager of La Selva, had a brilliant idea. He decided that the best way to convince people not to cut down rainforests was to demonstrate that it was economically viable to conserve them through tourism and sound land management. The result of Amos Bien's efforts is the now-famous **Rara Avis**, a 1500-acre forest reserve near the small village of Las Horquetas. Through its excellent tours, visitors get a short course in how the rainforest works, why it is being cut down, and how it can be restored—without feeling that they have been in school.

Various accommodations are available at **Rara Avis** (764-3131, fax: 764-4187; www.rara-avis.com, e-mail: raraavis@racsa.co.cr), Costa Rica's original rainforest lodge. The comfortable, eight-room **Waterfall Lodge** and the more secluded **River Edge Cabin** (private bath, hot water; no electricity; $60-$80/person, double occupancy) are both close to a gorgeous three-tiered waterfall. The River Edge Cabin is especially designed for birdwatchers. Their casitas (shared bath, cold water; $40-$50/person, double occupancy) are more rustic but still comfortable. Prices include three hearty meals, guided tours, and transportation from Las Horquetas. Discounts for children, residents, students, hostel card–holders, and researchers are available.

Because transportation to Rara Avis is difficult, you need to make reservations. You must arrive by 8:30 a.m. in Las Horquetas, which is 15 kilometers north of the Guápiles Highway on the Río Frío–Puerto Viejo road. At 9:30 a.m. a tractor-pulled *chapulín* leaves Las Horquetas for Waterfall Lodge, 15 kilometers away. (Don't attempt this adventure if you have a bad back.) The trip takes three hours. It is impossible to get to Rara Avis any other way, except by horse (available through Rara Avis), which takes longer and involves walking the last three kilometers because the road is covered with logs.

GETTING THERE: By Bus: Take the 7 a.m. Río Frío bus from the Terminal Caribe in San José. A car from Rara Avis will meet you at the bus.

By Car: Las Horquetas can be approached from San José, Arenal volcano or Límon. See details at www.rara-avis.com.

To the left, just outside the town of Horquetas, is the 48-room **Sueño Azul Resort** (private bath, hot water, ceiling fans, pool, hot tub; $100-$110; children 12 and under free; 764-4244, fax: 764-3129; www.sueno azulresort.com, e-mail: info@suenoazulresort.com), winter headquarters for the Omega Institute's Holistic Studies program. Located on a 1200-acre ranch and forest reserve with a lake and lush gardens, this peaceful place has a yoga studio and spa offering a variety of healing treatments and is only 90 minutes from San José.

SARAPIQUÍ

Some of the country's best ecotourism experiences, like Rara Avis, Selva Verde, Tirimbina Wildlife Refuge, and La Selva, are seeing the importance of their decision to preserve rainforests through tourism and scientific research. In the 1990s, it seemed like they were becoming islands in a sea of banana plantations, with their attendant heavy use of fertilizers and pesticides. But these lodges are also leaders in community involvement, offering education and training opportunities for local residents as well as tourists. The result is a community ready to stand up for conservation and ready to embrace the San Juan–La Selva Biological Corridor.

Puerto Viejo de Sarapiquí is the major town in the region, and was Costa Rica's main port in colonial times. Boats embarked from here to cruise down the wide Río Sarapiquí, north to the Río San Juan, which forms Costa Rica's border with Nicaragua, and from there to the Atlantic. During the 1980s, the years of Contra activity in northern Costa Rica, the area was closed to tourists, but now ecotourism thrives in this region.

Grass Roots Expeditions (www.tierrahermosa.com, e-mail: alex@andrea cristina.com) offers backcountry trips to less-visited places, guided by naturalist and environmentalist Alex Martinez. One ten-day tour visits Volcán Poás, La Paz Waterfall Gardens, and the forests and rivers of Sarapiquí, continuing on to Tortuguero via the Río San Juan, then down to Limón. The tour ends with trips to the indigenous reserves and beaches of Talamanca.

Aventuras del Sarapiquí (766-6768; www.sarapiquí.com, e-mail: miguel@sarapiquí.com) leads rafting, kayaking, hiking, and mountain biking tours throughout the Northern Zone, as does **Aguas Bravas** (292-2072, fax: 229-4837; www.aguasbravas.co.cr). Aguas Bravas also runs a nature camp for 10- to 17-year-olds that features hiking, horseback riding, rope courses, rappelling, mountain biking, and rafting. In La Virgen, the **Jardín**

de Serpientes (adults $6; children $3; 761-1059) has over 40 local and exotic snake species.

LA SELVA   This 1516-hectare research station and biological reserve of the Organization for Tropical Studies (OTS) has brought fame to Sarapiquí because of its enormous variety of tropical plants and animals. In an effort to secure the large hunting territories needed by jaguars and pumas, Braulio Carrillo National Park was extended to meet it, forming a corridor from Volcán Barva (2500 meters above sea level) to the lowlands (30 meters) at La Selva. More than 470 species of birds either live in or migrate to La Selva from the highlands, including toucans, *oropéndolas* (golden orioles), tinamous, and umbrella birds. Almost 350 different species have been observed there in a single day by the Audubon Society Birdathon. Research and education are the reserve's top priorities. Over 1600 articles, theses, and books have resulted from research done at La Selva.

One of the many courses offered at La Selva is not for biologists but for the world's decisionmakers: government and business leaders who need to balance economic development with the use, management, and conservation of nature.

Groups or individuals can roam La Selva's 57 kilometers of well-kept trails through primary and secondary forest, and its arboretum. The best way to visit is to stay overnight at **La Selva** (shared or private bath; $60-$70/person, including meals and one half-day tour; children 6 to 12, $21; call the San José office at 240-6696, fax: 240-6783, in the U.S.: 919-684-6724; www.ots.ac.cr, e-mail: reservas@ots.ac.cr). There are also some nice houses with kitchens. La Selva rents bicycles and kayaks to guests.

You can also go on half-day tours ($26/adult, $11/children 6 to 12) that leave daily at 8 a.m. and 1:30 p.m. A cafeteria-style lunch is $9 extra. Call the station at least a day ahead for reservations (766-6565, fax: 766-6535; e-mail: nat-hist@sloth.ots.ac.cr). Some of the trails are wheelchair accessible.

La Selva is about five kilometers east of Puerto Viejo; look for the sign opposite the Lapa Verde restaurant. From that turnoff it is about two kilometers to the main administration building. A taxi will charge about $3.25 to La Selva from Puerto Viejo, or you can take any bus from Puerto Viejo to Río Frío or San José via the Guápiles highway and walk from the main road.

TIRIMBINA   The **Tirimbina Wildlife Refuge** (adults $10; guided tour $15; children under 14 $8; www.tirimbina.org) is one of the most beautiful rainforests we've seen. The University of Wisconsin and the Milwaukee Museum have taken pains to make access to the reserve as unobtrusive as possible. A long hanging bridge over the wild Sarapiquí River separates the reserve from the 21st century, and from there on it's just you and nature on seven well-maintained trails, one of which goes to a waterfall. A bridge in the heart of the reserve lets you walk beside the forest canopy. You can enter through the Centro Neotropico or at the Tirimbina's own entrance to the right in La Virgen de Sarapiquí. Recommended.

PUERTO VIEJO LODGING AND RESTAURANTS   The town of Puerto Viejo has several hotels. **Mi Lindo Sarapiquí** (private bath, heated water, ceiling fans; $20-$30; 766-6281, fax 766-6074) is next to the soccer field. It is a newer building with bright, sunny rooms upstairs and good food and service in the restaurant below.

El Bambú (private bath, hot water, ceiling fans, air conditioning, cable TV, phones, pool, security boxes, guarded parking; $60-$70, including breakfast; children under 12 free; 766-6005, fax: 766-6132; www.elbam bu.com) is comfortable and airy, with good mattresses. Downstairs you'll find a bar and restaurant built around a stand of giant bamboo.

Andrea Cristina Bed & Breakfast (private bath, heated water, table fans, small kiddy pool; $30-$40, including breakfast; children under 12 free; phone/fax: 766-6265; www.andreacristina.com, e-mail: alex@andreacristina. com), owned by one of Sarapiquí's foremost environmental activists, Alex Martinez, who is also a naturalist guide. The grounds are shady and quiet; its quaint A-frame and cottage rooms have a European flavor, with outdoor tables and hammocks. Special rates for families. Recommended.

Ara Ambigua (private bath, heated water, ceiling fans; $30-$40; children under 12 free; 766-6281, 393-5021; www.tourism.co.cr/hotels/ara_ ambigua) is a great, inexpensive place for families. It's back from the main road so it's quiet, and has a pool, volleyball court, a small lake for fishing, and plenty of green areas and trails. Their restaurant, La Casona, is open 11 a.m. to 10 p.m. daily. Recommended. To get there, go to the cemetery of Barrio La Guaria, west of Puerto Viejo, and go north 400 meters.

There is a budget hotel four kilometers west of Puerto Viejo on the road to Chilamate at **Cabinas Yacaré** (shared or private baths, cold water, table fans, restaurant; $7-$12; 766-6691)—clean and simply decorated. Take a Cristo Rey bus from Puerto Viejo to get there. They leave every 45 minutes.

West of Puerto Viejo **Selva Verde Lodge** (private bath, hot water, ceiling fans; $60-$70/person, double occupancy, including meals; children under 12 free, 12- to 15-year-olds half price; 766-6800, fax: 766-6011, in the U.S.: 800-451-7111; www.selvaverde.com) in Chilamate, five minutes by car west of Puerto Viejo, is a complex of covered walkways leading to a riverside dining room, an open, airy lounging area with hammocks and a conference room. Its comfortable cabins are raised on pillars to jungle (and bird's-nest) level. Guests may roam trails in the secondary forest reserve. You must go with a guide to visit the butterfly garden ($5) and the primary forest reserve. Early-morning birdwalks are offered for guests, and three- to four-hour walks with naturalist guides leave at 8:30 a.m. and 1:30 p.m. Both guests and nonguests can join the hikes for $15 per person, including boots.

Selva Verde's owners, long concerned with the well-being of the local community, have established the **Sarapiquí Conservation Learning Center** (766-6482; www.learningcentercostarica.org), with the only library in the area, a day-care center, and English and environmental education classes. Guests and their children can participate in recycling, tree planting, composting, research, and art projects with the community children. Selva Verde Lodge is unique in providing opportunities for tourists to interact with locals. Volunteers are also welcome for a minimum of six months. They live with local families and receive a stipend to cover living expenses.

La Quinta de Sarapiquí Country Inn (private bath, hot water, ceiling fans, pool; $50-$60; children under 12 free; 761-1300, 761-1052, fax: 761-1395; www.laquintasarapiqui.com, e-mail: info@laquintasarapiqui.com), on the Río Sardinal one kilometer off the main Puerto Viejo–La Virgen road, has lush gardens that attract a variety of birds. Guests can visit their butterfly garden, ride horseback, or fish in their tilapia pond for free. Their restaurant serves delicious, country-style food with fresh vegetables from their organic garden.

La Quinta's museum houses a vast collection of moths, butterflies, beetles, and other insects. The iridescent creatures are displayed in geometric patterns, or arranged on velvet to highlight their jewel-like colors. There you can learn about insect camouflage, mimicry, parasitism, prey–predator relationships, and other tropical biology topics. While you are at La Quinta, ask to see the paper crafts that the owner Beatriz Gamez makes with local schoolchildren out of pineapple fiber.

Centro Neotrópico Sarapiquís (private bath, ceiling fans, phones, internet connection; $90-$100; children half price; meals $25/day; 761-1004, fax: 239-2738, 761-1415; www.sarapiquis.org, e-mail: magistra@racsa.co.cr) is a beautiful ecolodge on the banks of the Río Sarapiquí, patterned on a 15th-century pre-Columbian village. The restaurant terrace overlooks the river and the Tirimbina rainforest reserve. A digital telescope brings guests closer to the stars. Their research and education center attracts students from all over Costa Rica. The use of solar energy and natural waste-water treatment make this a truly ecologically sound project.

During construction, workers discovered pre-Columbian tombs (adults $7; children 8 to 16 $3) that you can now see next to a petroglyph garden

White-faced monkeys (mono cariblanco) are one of four types of monkeys *that make Costa Rica's forests their home.*

Right: Of the 136 species of snakes in Costa Rica, 18, including the eyelash viper, are lethal.

Below: The poisonous dart frog spends its entire life high above the rainforest floor.

Left: The three-toed sloth's upside-down position is ideal for scooping hanging leaves into its mouth.

Right: Mosses, ferns, lichens, and other epiphytes grasp tree branches and absorb their nutrients from leaf matter and water dripping off the canopy.

Below: Caymans live in creeks, ponds, mangrove swamps, and beach lowlands.

Right: Elephant beetle.

Below: Leaf-cutter ant.

Right: The Catarata La Fortuna is so powerful that swimming is not possible beneath it.

Above: Day breaks through the morning clouds along one of Costa Rica's many beautiful beaches.

Below: Its remote location, tremendous rainfall, and variety of unique habitats make Corcovado National Park an ecological treasure.

Left: The exuberant red, yellow, or orange bursts of the heliconia flower are a common rainforest sight.

Below: Costa Rica is an outdoor adventurer's paradise—definitely the place to take a walk on the "wild side."

Above: Verdant farmland blankets the agriculturally rich area around Lake Arenal in the Northern Zone.

Below: Fiery-billed aracaris, which make their homes in old woodpecker holes, sometimes gather berries from the ground.

Three species of herons, the tiger heron among them, inhabit the lowlands of Costa Rica.

at the entrance to Centro Neotrópico. The **Museo de Culturas Indígenas Dra. Maria Eugenia Bozzoli** (adults $12; children under 10 free; 761-1418), named after one of Costa Rica's foremost anthropologists, highlights the culture of the country's living indigenous tribes, with exhibits on healing practices, music, dress, and celebrations.

GETTING THERE: By Bus: Buses to Puerto Viejo de Sarapiquí leave several times a day from the Caribe terminal in San José. The 6:30 a.m., noon, and 3 p.m. buses travel the scenic route above Heredia. The trip takes a little over three hours. Hourly buses take the Guápiles Highway through Braulio Carrillo and turn north to Las Horquetas, La Selva, and Puerto Viejo, where they end. This trip takes only an hour and a half. You will have to change buses or get a taxi to go to Chilamate or La Virgen if you take the latter route. Be sure to take the bus to Puerto Viejo de Sarapiquí, not Puerto Viejo de Talamanca. Check schedules at www.monteverdeinfo.com.

Aguas Bravas (766-6574, 292-2072) offers transfers from Sarapiquí to La Fortuna. Also, check out Interbus (283-5573; www.interbusonline.com) for private bus routes all over Costa Rica.

By Car: A scenic route above Heredia winds around the northeast side of Poás Volcano to the northern plain and passes through La Virgen, Chilamate, and Puerto Viejo before reaching La Selva. (Don't go this way if you tend to get carsick.) It is one of the most beautiful rides you can take, passing by the amazing La Paz Waterfall Gardens, with vistas of the forests of Braulio Carrillo to the east. This route takes two and a half hours from Heredia, all on paved road. To combine this trip with a visit to Poás, go straight instead of turning right at the gas station in Vara Blanca, travel about six kilometers to Poasito, and follow signs to the national park. You should be at Poás in about 20 minutes. Recommended.

A quicker, less winding route is along the Braulio Carrillo Highway from San José. Turn left on the road to Puerto Viejo after you descend out of Braulio Carrillo National Park. The road to Puerto Viejo from the turnoff is smooth, wide, and virtually straight, taking you through cow pastures and oil palm plantations and passing Las Horquetas, the entrance to Rara Avis, and Sueño Azul on its way to La Selva and Puerto Viejo.

You can get from Volcán Arenal to Puerto Viejo in under two hours, avoiding San Carlos, if you turn left at El Tanque, eight kilometers out of Fortuna, then take the turnoff to Muelle (Route 4), following signs to Aguas Zarcas and turning right at each turn. At Aguas Zarcas, 23 kilometers west of San Carlos, turn left to San Miguel, and left again to La Virgen, Chilamate, and Puerto Viejo, all on paved roads.

Sixteen kilometers south of the Nicaraguan border, **La Laguna del Lagarto Lodge** (shared bath, heated water, ceiling fans; $50-$60; private bath, $60-$70; meals $30/day; www.lagarto-lodge-costa-rica.com, e-mail: info@lagarto-lodge-costa-rica.com) is a prime birdwatching spot, with 350 species sighted, including the endangered green macaw. The comfortable rooms sit on a hill overlooking a lake filled with orchid-draped dead trees. You can paddle in a canoe through this rather eerie waterway into the rainforest. Ten miles of trails lead through 500 hectares of primary rainforest. Also offered are horseback rides and a three-hour boat ride up the Río San Carlos to the Nicaraguan border. The lodge is remote, and you should probably have four-wheel drive to get there by car. See their website for current travel recommendations by car or bus.

ON THE WAY TO VOLCÁN ARENAL

There are three ways to get to Volcán Arenal from the Central Valley. One is through Naranjo and Zarcero. Another is through San Ramón. Another is to visit Poás volcano, La Paz Waterfall Gardens, and Sarapiquí, returning to San Miguel to go to Aguas Zarcas and La Fortuna. There are interesting things to do on each route to break up your trip.

ZARCERO

Zarcero is one of the most charming Costa Rican towns, perched on the hills that divide the Central Valley from the San Carlos plain. At 1700 meters above sea level, its climate is fresh and invigorating. Its ruddy-cheeked inhabitants are famous for their peach preserves and homemade white cheese. In the past few years Zarcero has become the organic farming capital of Costa Rica, thanks to guidance from a Japanese volunteer from that country's version of the Peace Corps.

Hotel Don Beto (463-2509) offers tours to these organic farms and dairies, as well as waterfall rappelling on the Río Toro, horseback riding or hiking in nearby Juan Castro Blanco Natural Park, and El Chayote Reserve.

But Zarcero's real claim to fame is the fancifully sculpted **topiary garden** in front of its picturesque little church: bushes shaped into gigantic green rabbits, a bullfight, a couple dancing, a monkey riding a bicycle, ox carts, and elephants. The topiary garden has been lovingly pruned by Don Evangelista Blanco, who says that God has been telling him what to sculpt for the last 37 years. He has posted little signs throughout the park with sayings like "You have doubted God, and yet he lives inside you." You can buy postcards at the park that help fund this unique effort. When we were there, a huge rainbow guided us down the country roads above Zarcero to the town plaza, then remained in a perfect arc directly over the church.

Just before you reach Zarcero coming from San José, there is a group of restaurants and stands selling cheese, candied fruit, and flowers. If you want to stop for something to eat, the restaurants here are better than those in Zarcero itself. **Doña Chila's** is open 24 hours. **Rancho Típico Zarceño** is nice, too. On the north side of the Zarcero church is the homey **Hotel Don Beto** (shared or private bath, heated water; $30-$40; 463-2509, phone/fax: 463-3137; www.donbeto.com, e-mail: info@donbeto.com).

GETTING THERE: By Bus: Buses leave hourly from San José for San Carlos from the Atlántico Norte station (255-4318) on Calle 12, Avenida 9, passing through Zarcero an hour and a half later. It's easy to catch a bus back to San José, or on to Volcán Arenal.

By Car: Zarcero is an hour and a half from San José. Take the Naranjo–Ciudad Quesada exit off the Interamerican Highway to Puntarenas.

SAN CARLOS

Ciudad Quesada is a bustling commercial center in the San Carlos plain of central Alajuela Province, one of Costa Rica's most agriculturally productive zones. The countryside is a vibrant green with pastoral, rolling hills. Ten minutes to the east, in San Rafael de Aguas Calientes, are three ways to visit the local hot springs.

Termales del Bosque (460-4740, fax: 460-1356; www.termalesdelbosque.com, e-mail: termales@racsa.co.cr; admission $4, children 6 to 12 $3) is a great place for the travel-weary to stop on their way to La Fortuna. After a short hike through this 100-hectare forest reserve, you arrive at a series of thermal pools of different temperatures next to a rushing stream. There is a stone sauna cantilevered over the river, a place to change with showers and lockers, a little building for massage and mud treatments, and a rustic bar. Everything has been left as natural as possible, so you bathe under the canopy of the trees. Don't spend more than 20 minutes in the warm baths before immersing yourself in the river to cool off. Up near the road is a restaurant, a **canopy tour** ($45; five platforms, three traverses, and a rappel; www.canopytour.com/termales.html) and clean, comfortable rooms (private bath, ceiling fans; $50-$60, including breakfast and access to trails and hot springs). It's seven kilometers east of San Carlos in San Rafael de Aguas Calientes on the road to Aguas Zarcas. Recommended.

On the other side of the Río San Rafael, set back from the road in forest shade, sits **Hotel Occidental Tucano** (private bath, hot water, some bathtubs, air conditioning, cable TV, phones; call for rates; children under 12 free; 460-6000, fax: 460-1692, in the U.S. and Canada: 800-858-2258;

www.occidentaltucano.com, e-mail: occhr@racsa.co.cr). El Tucano offers mini-golf, tennis courts, and tours. Its elegant European-style spa, graced with marble fountains, offers massage, hydrotherapy, and mud treatments. The natural warm mineralized waters of the area are channeled into a swimming pool. Jacuzzis, a sauna, a gym, a beauty salon, and a gift shop full of Italian bath and beauty products complete the luxurious scene. This 90-room hotel also has a conference center.

If you are worried about the dangers of Tabacón Hot Springs at the foot of Volcán Arenal, this is a very safe alternative. You can visit the hot springs for the day for about $8.

Parque de Recreación y Conservación de la Naturaleza (open Wednesday to Sunday, 8 a.m. to 4 p.m.; 460-0891), right across the river from El Tucano, provides access to the same warm river for $2. Access to the river is a one-kilometer hike from the entrance.

GETTING THERE: By Bus: San José–San Carlos buses ($1.50) leave almost every hour, 5 a.m. through 6 p.m., from the Atlántico Norte station on Calle 12, Avenida 9. It's a three-hour trip. Try to get a Directo bus—it makes fewer stops. Take any of the buses from the Ciudad Quesada terminal (Río Frío, Puerto Viejo, San Miguel, Pital, Venecia, or Aguas Zarcas) to get to the three places above.

By Car: Take the Naranjo exit, about an hour down the General Cañas Highway from San José, and continue north through Zarcero to San Carlos. Signs in Ciudad Quesada will direct you to the Aguas Zarcas road just north of the cathedral. San Rafael de Aguas Calientes is about ten minutes away. To stop here on your way from Sarapiquí to La Fortuna, just follow signs from San Miguel to Aguas Zarcas, going straight through town until you get to El Tucano and Termales del Bosque.

SAN RAMÓN

Another way of getting to Volcán Arenal from the Central Valley is through the agricultural town of **San Ramón de Alajuela**. This medium-sized, non-touristy town is home to **Don Pedro's Cigars** (447-0093; e-mail cigar@ costarricense.cr), a learn-how-to-roll-your-own Cuban-and-Tico-owned cigar store, a **Butterfly Farm** with hundreds of blue morphos, the western campus of the University of Costa Rica, and some Tico-style *balnearios*. Their *feria del agricultor* (farmer's market) on Saturdays is huge and worth going to for inexpensive fresh fruits and vegetables. Farmer's markets are held on Saturday all over Costa Rica, even in San José. The town's saints day, August 31, is celebrated with religious processions.

The **San Ramón Museum** (open weekday afternoons), next to the plaza in the old Municipal Palace, features a replica of a campesino home from the turn of the 20th century and recounts local history, from pre-Columbian times through local efforts to fight William Walker to the rise of famous native sons like former President José Figueres.

The **José Figueres Ferrer Historic and Cultural Center** (closed Sunday; 447-2178; www.centrojosefigueres) has exhibits about the 1948 civil war and hosts concerts and theater productions.

Hotel La Posada (private bath, hot water, refrigerator, TV, CD player; $50, including breakfast; 445-7359, fax: 447-3131; e-mail: johotel@racsa.co.cr) has pleasant rocking chairs on its front porch from which to observe life in this Costa Rican town. Well-appointed and reasonably priced.

Angel Valley Farm (shared bath, heated water; $25/person, $80/two; breakfast and dinner included; 447-4684; e-mail ranchos@racsa.co.cr) is a five-room B&B with a great view in Los Angeles Sur, five kilometers north of San Ramón on the road to La Fortuna. It's on a 100-acre coffee, sugar cane, and fruit farm. They offer horseback riding and mountain biking.

GETTING THERE: San Ramón is about one hour west of San José on the main road between San José and Puntarenas. Buses leave every half hour from the Puntarenas terminal (Calle 16, Avenidas 10/12; 222-0064).

LOS ANGELES CLOUD FOREST   North of San Ramón is the Los Angeles Cloud Forest, a private reserve owned by ex-President Rodrigo Carazo. The 2000-acre sanctuary is easily accessible for a day trip from San José—a good alternative for those who don't want to make the long, arduous trip to Monteverde. The almost two-kilometer trail is paved with wood covered with chicken wire, a simple and practical way to prevent slipping. Two-hour tours ($24/person) are led by an excellent naturalist, and birding tours ($24) begin at 6 a.m. daily.

Hotel Villablanca (private bath, hot water, bathtub and showers with handholds; $110-$120; two-room honeymoon bungalows, $130-$140; two-room family bungalows, $180-$190; all rates include breakfast; 461-0301, fax: 461-0302; www.villablanca-costarica.com, e-mail: information@villa blanca-costarica.com), next to the reserve, consists of 48 *casitas*, charmingly decorated in the style of traditional campesino houses, each with its own fireplace, and a large central lodge where hearty Costa Rican meals are served. Bunk bed lodging for students ($30) includes meals and entrance to the reserve. The highlight of Villablanca is the chapel, whose vaulted ceiling is covered with beautiful hand-painted tiles. The tiles depict religious figures as well as tropical flora and fauna, interspersed with the words of the rosary. The large windows of the chapel look out on greenery. It would be a great place for a wedding. Horses and mountain bikes can be rented. This is a suitable destination for seniors, and is a stop on Elderhostel tours. Recommended.

Ecco Colonia (private bath, hot water; $70-$130, including breakfast; 222-2333; www.eccocolonia.com, e-mail: eccocolonia@racsa.co.cr), owned by a Tica/gringo family, has a wide variety of accommodations, some of which sleep four to seven. Several rooms have outdoor hot tubs that can be fired up for $10. Our favorite was the screen house, set in the middle of the jungle, screened on all sides, with an observation deck on top. Other rooms have a distant volcano view when the weather is clear. Four-wheel drive is necessary to get there. The entrance is at Restaurant Los Lagos on the left, about halfway between San Ramón and La Fortuna.

Chachagua Rain Forest Hotel (private bath, hot water, ceiling fans, restaurant; $90-$100; 239-6464, fax: 290-6506; www.chachaguarain foresthotel.com) is a comfortable mountain ranch about half an hour south of La Fortuna, two kilometers off the main San Ramón–La Fortuna road. Trails lead through a private forest reserve, and horseback tours around the farm are possible. A stream passes between the spacious, wood cabins and the open-air restaurant; it is channeled into a shallow, cement-bottomed pool that is especially good for kids. It's a nice getaway for families. The access road needs four-wheel drive in the rainy season.

GETTING THERE: From the main highway's entrance to San Ramón, follow the main street through town, where good signs for Villablanca will direct you to the La Tigra road (200 meters west of the hospital). Villablanca is 45 minutes from San Ramón, all on a paved road. The entrance to Ecco Colonia is 45 minutes to the north on the La Tigra road. Chachagua is another half hour beyond that. As you leave San Ramón, a winding road branches off to the right from the La Tigra road and takes you to Zarcero.

CAÑO NEGRO WILDLIFE REFUGE

Caño Negro Wildlife Refuge comprises the Río Frío and Caño Negro Lake, which grows and shrinks seasonally. The wetland refuge was created to protect the diverse aquatic birds that live and breed there including the northern jacana, which builds its nest on lily pads; the endangered *jabiru*; black, long-necked, and sharp-billed anhingas; and roseate spoonbills, the only pink birds in Costa Rica. Caño Negro is home to the country's largest colony of olivaceous or neotropical cormorants, glossy black birds that fish in groups then dry out their wings in the sun. Birding is best between January and April. Sloths, iguanas, and three types of monkey inhabit the trees on the shores of the Río Frío; you will probably see caimans and turtles, and maybe even the gar fish, a prehistoric relic with a caiman-like snout and a hard exoskeleton. Fishermen are enthusiastic about the lake because of the tarpon, snook, rainbow bass, machaca, and drum that abound there. Park rules prohibit fishing from April through July.

The village of **Caño Negro** is within the refuge, right on the western side of the lake. It still has not been impacted by tourism, because most of the tours that say they are going to "Caño Negro" actually go to the bustling border town of Los Chiles, 19 kilometers northeast of the village, where a fleet of canopied tourist boats takes people to the eastern edge of the refuge, but not inside it, so they won't have to pay the park entrance fee ($4). Here we have the dilemma of ecotourism. Because it has been "left out" of the tourist boom, the village and the shimmering lake have the pure, untouched feel of the Costa Rica of 20 years ago, without the plethora of billboards and "tourist info centers" that plague places like La Fortuna. The mayor and the park director are trying to open the area to tourism in a principled way. We hope this tiny village can avoid the pitfalls that have transformed other sleepy little towns into tourist traps. Refuge staff have been working to involve residents in conservation and protection activities; they participate in maintaining turtle and caiman nurseries and a butterfly garden, which you can visit near town. The park office can set you up with a guide.

There are a couple of *sodas*, and rustic lodging at **Albergue Caño Negro** (shared bath, cold water, mosquito nets; $10-$20; 461-8442), whose informative owner, Don Alvaro Arguedas, offers wildlife observation boat rides through the reserve and fishing trips. Take repellent.

The **Caño Negro Natural Lodge** (private bath, hot water, ceiling fan, air conditioning, pool, jacuzzi; $100-$110, including breakfast; 471-1426, fax: 265-4561; www.canonegrolodge.com, e-mail: natural@racsa.co.cr) is a new Italian-owned lodge offering fishing and birding tours. Their airy, attractive restaurant has an international menu for both meat lovers and vegetarians.

Besides the main dock, the **Salón El Danubio Azul** is a popular restaurant/bar serving good fresh fish. **Soda La Palmera** is good for breakfast and lunch.

GETTING THERE: By Car: There are two ways to get to Caño Negro. Take Route 4 northwest from El Tanque to San Rafael de Guatuso (**Rancho Ucurín**, on the left just beyond Guatuso is a good place to stop for lunch). Drive 25 kilometers (half hour) north of Guatuso to the small town of Colonias de Puntarenas and take the marked gravel road to the right for another 26 kilometers (an hour and a quarter drive). Because there are a lot of potholes and many speed bumps between Guatuso and Colonias, it's probably better to take the Los Chiles road—Route 35 north from Muelle. Seven kilometers before you get to Los Chiles, a National Park sign indicates the road to Caño Negro on the left. It's 19 kilometers (1 hour) on a pretty good gravel road from there.

CAVERNAS DEL VENADO   The Cavernas del Venado (cell phone: 284-9616) are alive with thousands of bats, cave fish, crickets, and spiders. Located an hour's drive north of La Fortuna, they are more accessible than the caves of Barra Honda (see the Guanacaste chapter), but are not for the faint-hearted. To explore them, you must wade through a rushing underground river, which is only knee- to ankle-high in dry season, but rising as high as a meter in the rainy season. At some points, you must crawl on your hands and knees. Guides accompany visitors on the hour-and-a-half tour ($6/person). Kids are welcome as long as they don't get too scared of the river or the dark. Boots, flashlights, face masks, and helmets are included in the admission, as well as soap and showers for after the hike. It's important to bring a change of clothes. The caves were closed for two months in 1998, after several visitors came down with histoplasmosis, a fungus infection that affects the lungs, causing flu-like symptoms, which can be transmitted by exposure to bat droppings. Studies have shown that the incidence of histoplasmosis within the caves is low, but now the Ministry of Health requires wearing protective gear and showering afterwards. Hotels and tour agencies in La Fortuna, an hour away, offer excursions to the caves, or you can drive there yourself. Call ahead in order to have a guide waiting for you when you get there—otherwise you might have to wait for him.

On the way to the caves, **Cabinas Las Brisas** (shared bath, cold water; $7-$12) is a clean and inexpensive place to stay in the nice little town of Venado.

GETTING THERE: By Bus: A bus leaves Ciudad Quesada at 2 p.m. for Venado, arriving at 4:30 p.m.

By Car: It's better to approach from the east, as all but the last two kilometers before the caves are paved. The approach from the west, on Lake Arenal, is entirely unpaved and sometimes disappears in the middle of a cattle pasture. For the paved road, drive north from El Tanque towards San Rafael de Guatuso about 30 minutes. Turn left at a turnoff marked Jicarito. From there it's 15 minutes to the picturesque village of Venado. The driveway to the caves is marked by a sign on the right, on a gravel road 2 kilometers beyond Venado.

VOLCÁN ARENAL

Volcán Arenal is the quintessential volcano. Its perfectly conical shape emerges from Alajuela's gentle green hills. From time to time, loud explosions are heard, a gray, brown, orange, or blue mushroom cloud of gases and steam billows out of the top, and you can watch the ejected boulders as they bounce down the slopes. Although the volcano is capable of inspiring intense fright and awe in visitors, inhabitants of nearby **La Fortuna de San Carlos** and the dairy farms at the volcano's base seem to live with relative peace of mind.

Arenal was dormant until the late 1960s, and the only people who suspected that it was a volcano were those who had scaled it and found a crater and steam vents at the top. But few listened to them, until a series of earthquakes began shaking the area late in the evening of July 28, 1968. The following morning, Arenal blew, sending out shock waves that were recorded as far away as Boulder, Colorado. All damage occurred roughly five kilometers west of the volcano, where people were knocked down by shock waves, poisoned by volcanic gases, and struck by falling rocks. Lava flows eradicated the town of Pueblo Nuevo, and by the end, 78 people had died. Three new craters formed during the explosion.

Arenal is most impressive at night—in the dark, bursts of fire and red-hot rocks sometimes shoot hundreds of feet into the sky. Incandescent material cascades down the slopes, especially on the north/northwestern side. In the daytime, you only see steam and hear the volcano's terrible roar. There are explosions every few hours during Arenal's active phases, but it can go for months without activity. Very often the volcano is shrouded in clouds and it's hard to see anything—even if it's active. When we were there in November 2001, we only caught glimpses of the volcano, but did manage to get some great pictures when it was clear. In November 2003, we couldn't see the volcano at all. If you see the volcano, take your pictures right away.

Note: Although the volcano is not dangerous at a distance, it is very perilous to climb. One tourist was killed and another burned in July 1988 when they hiked too near the crater, foolishly trusting Arenal's placid appearance between explosions. If they had seen it explode before climbing, they probably would never have begun. They also unwittingly risked the lives of 15 Costa Rican Rural Guards and Red Cross workers who heroically searched the volcano to retrieve the body of its victim. The volcano is not safe to scale even part-way. There are steam vents and abysses, and lava sometimes descends quite far down the side. *Do not climb this volcano.* Even observation areas can be deadly. On August 23, 2000, a tour guide and a tourist were fatally burned when a sudden pyroclastic avalanche of hot gases, rocks, and mud opened up on Arenal's northeast slope above Los Lagos. This was the strongest eruption since 1968. The guide and his tourists were in an area previously regarded as safe when the avalanche traveled toward them at 80 kilometers per hour. Just stay completely off the volcano and you'll be fine. For updates on current volcanic activity, see www.arenal.net/arenal.htm.

ATTRACTIONS   Between La Fortuna and Lake Arenal, there are a few spots worth checking out:

The **Catarata La Fortuna** is a beautiful waterfall five and a half kilometers from the town of La Fortuna. If you have the time, it's a nice walk. There are two ways to get there. At the back of the church you'll see a sign pointing south to the La Fortuna–San Ramón road. Go one kilometer toward San Ramón and turn right up a country lane. The entrance to the waterfall is four kilometers from there, negotiable in a regular car. Or you can stay at Cerro Chato Lodge or La Catarata (see below) and walk or ride horseback two or three kilometers. There is a parking lot and information office at the entrance (open daily, 8 a.m. to 4 p.m.; admission $6). If you want to walk down to the bottom of the falls, keep to the right on the ravine trail. The trail has steps built into it at the steepest parts, and there are guardrails. The force of the waterfall is such that swimming is not possible. There is a place to swim if you take a trail to the left near the bottom of the falls. Don't try this hike if you have high blood pressure, asthma, or diabetes. The hike is an exhilarating workout—it took us about 45 minutes to descend and huff and puff back up again.

Dedicated hikers will enjoy the steep two-and-a-half-hour climb to **Cerro Chato**'s blue-green crater lake. Cerro Chato is a dormant volcano southeast of Arenal.

There are two choices for enjoying the **thermal waters** that spring out of the volcano. However, you should be aware that the area was the site of a 1975 hot avalanche deposit (the ongoing source of heat for the thermal waters) and vulcanologists consider the location hazardous and at risk for future hot avalanches. In fact, during stronger-than-usual explosions on May 5, 1998, and October 25, 1999, lava flowed to within 500 meters of Tabacón. Four hundred tourists and employees were evacuated, but business was back to normal within 48 hours. Another blast on September 5, 2003, sent lava to the north/northeast. With that in mind, you can die happy at **Tabacón Resort** (open daily, noon to 10 p.m.; $17/person, children under 9 $10; children under 4 free). Here a stream is channeled into a veritable thermal wonderland: 12 pools of varying temperatures and depths; one waterslide; benches tucked under waterfalls; jacuzzis and individual tubs. There is a great **restaurant** (open daily, noon to 10 p.m.) with a creative and varied menu including vegetarian dishes and a great volcano view. The place seems a bit hectic out front, especially when you see all the tour buses parked there (all cars and buses must park facing out toward the road for quick evacuation), but there is plenty of room once you get onto the lushly landscaped grounds to find your own little stream and a steaming hot waterfall to massage your shoulders. There are several cold pools and showers to cool off in. The management recommends that you alternate hot with cold water every 15 minutes to avoid high or low blood pressure. Two paramedics are employed by the resort.

We loved the mud wrap experience at Tabacón's **Iskandria Spa**. Your massage therapist rubs your body with a thin layer of warm, gritty volcanic mud. You are then wrapped in a large sheet of plastic and covered by a hot towel. Your therapist might burn incense as you relax into the warmth, feeling the mud drawing toxins out of you as it dries. After half an hour you are unwrapped, given a towel, and led down a path to a private, warm stream that flows into a swimming hole, where you skinny-dip to swim off the mud. Bliss! Prices range from $20 for a mud mask or pedicure to $148 for the Rain Forest Life treatment. Shiatsu, reiki, and yoga are also offered.

Across the street you'll find the budget thermal springs **Las Fuentes** (open 10 a.m. to 10 p.m.; admission $7), with the same water but in a creek that's terraced into sandy-bottomed pools. There are picnic areas with grills, a *soda*, and changing rooms with showers on the nicely landscaped grounds.

Ecotermales La Fortuna ($14) is a peaceful alternative to Tabacón, in a safer location. There are hot pools and waterfalls, a bar serving delicious tropical fruit smoothies, and attractive dressing rooms and lockers. It's great to go there after a day of hiking. Ask for directions at Las Brasitas Mexican restaurant on your right as you leave La Fortuna heading toward the volcano.

Tabacón's **Canopy Tour** runs between Tabacón Lodge and Las Fuentes. It is pretty close to the main road so it's not a real nature experience. The 90-minute tours ($45, students $35, children $25) leave at 8 a.m., 10 a.m., 2 p.m., and 4 p.m.

To get to the hot springs from La Fortuna (if you don't have a car), take the 8 a.m. bus to Tilarán. The driver will let you off at any of the hot springs or parks. A taxi to Tabacón costs about $5.

Three kilometers beyond the springs, as the road curves around the volcano, you'll come to a turnoff on the left to **Arenal National Park** (open daily, 8 a.m. to 3:30 p.m.; phone/fax: 461-8499). The guard station is two kilometers down a bumpy dirt road. If you pay the entrance fee ($6/person), you can visit their four-kilometer "Los Tucanes" trail, which leads through the area devastated by the 1968 eruption. Visits can only be made with an experienced, certified guide and in groups no greater than ten people at a time. In our opinion, you don't gain anything by being on the volcano. It is more interesting to observe from a distance. A taxi from La Fortuna to the park costs about $12.

Arenal Hanging Bridges (admission $20; with transportation from your hotel and guide, $40; open daily, 7:30 a.m. to 4:30 p.m.; 479-8362, fax: 479-9686; www.hangingbridges.com) is a series of six well-constructed bridges spanning lush forest ravines. The bridges allow for sweeping views of the dramatic terrain as well as close-ups of sensuous tropical leaves as they sprout and howler monkeys moving through the trees. If you want to learn about the variety of life forms that crowd into every square foot of tropical nature, take this hike with an experienced guide (two to two and a half hours, depending on how many questions you ask). When we were there, it was drizzling all day, but that just seemed to enhance the rainforest experience. The circle of trails that connects the bridges has only one steep climb and is suitable for people of all ages. This is rainforest viewing at its best, very much like the Skywalk in Monteverde. Their **Restaurant Los Puentes** (open daily, 8 a.m. to 8 p.m.) has a view of the lake and volcano. The entrance is to the right immediately after you cross Arenal Dam.

The same family who started the famous Monteverde SkyTrek and Sky-Walk have opened **Arenal Rainforest Reserve** ($60; 645-5238; www.arenal reserve.com, e-mail: info@skytrek.com), with a zipline, hanging bridges, trails, waterfalls, and the **Skytram**, a motorized funicular. In my opinion, these motorized rides lead to an unnecessary Disneyfication of nature. The project is to the west of the volcano, near the village of El Castillo.

Advertised as the "rapid transit system," the **horseback ride to Monteverde** has become very big business in La Fortuna. The real rapid transit system is the **taxi–boat–jeep ride**, which boats you across Lake Arenal and up the Río Chiquito to a jeep that transports you on steep, bumpy roads to Monteverde. That trip takes about three hours ($25). Otherwise, you have to drive or take a bus around the north side of Lake Arenal to Tilarán, and then take the very bad Tilarán–Santa Elena road or go down to the Interamerican Highway south to the Lagarto entrance and travel an hour and a half uphill from there.

However, there are horse trails between El Castillo, on the south side of the lake, and Mirador San Gerardo, a lookout point 13 kilometers from Monteverde from which you can see the volcano. The horseback ride can be done in four hours. A taxi then drives you to your Monteverde hotel. People have told us that this trip, although beautiful and enjoyable, is hard on the horses and can be scary for some. It is probably not appropriate for children under nine.

It's best not to do the horseback trip on the Mirador trail if it has been raining. The mud is too deep and slippery and the river crossings can be dangerous because of flash floods. The Lake Trail ride offered by **Desafío Expeditions** (479-9464; www.monteverdetours.com, e-mail: desafio@racsa.co.cr) and other companies is a three-and-a-half-hour horseback trip on a flat, non-muddy trail on the south side of Lake Arenal to the Río Chiquito, where you are picked up by a jeep and transported in another hour and a half to Monteverde. The tours cost $65 one way and include a fruit snack, but be sure to get some breakfast before you go. Wear long pants on the ride to avoid chafing. The companies will take your bags and cars up to Monteverde ($35) if you don't mind someone you don't know driving your rental car. We would be interested in hearing feedback about this trip from our readers. E-mail us at info@keytocostarica.com.

Other tours offered in the area include a volcano and hot springs night tour, horseback riding to the Catarata La Fortuna, waterfall rappelling, mountain biking in the National Park, a boat tour of the Caño Negro Wildlife Refuge, boating and fishing on Lago Arenal, and a visit to the Cavernas de Venado. **Desafío** and **Aguas Bravas** (479-9025; www.aguas-bravas.co.cr, e-mail: info@aguas-bravas.co.cr) offers whitewater rafting on the Toro, Peñas Blancas, and Sarapiquí rivers ($44-$75).

Note: Because there are so many hotels in La Fortuna, the competition is fierce. Hotels often send people to meet the buses and convince tourists to go one way or the other. Don't be swayed by these people. They also will try to sell you tours, but never accept a tour from someone who doesn't have an office and a business permit in case something goes wrong and you need somewhere to go to complain.

Renting a bike is a good way to get mobile if you don't have a car in this area. It's a hilly but lovely ride from La Fortuna west to the springs and the lake. Bikes are for rent at **Ciclo Cali**, on the left as you head west leaving Fortuna. You can rent scooters at **Pura Vida Tours**. If you lack stamina, taxis are relatively cheap and plentiful ($5) from Fortuna to the hot springs. Hotel Don Manuel (see below) has a free shuttle.

There are a number of internet cafés in La Fortuna. **Destiny Tours** (open daily, 7 a.m. to 9 p.m.), across from Sunset Tours, does digital photo processing.

LA FORTUNA RESTAURANTS   These are some of our favorite places to eat in La Fortuna: **El Jardín** is right on the main street near the bus stop. Their *plato del día* is cheap and comes lightning fast. **La Nena**, 100 meters east and set back about 20 meters from the main road, serves generous helpings of good, inexpensive food. Their lunch costs less than $3. **Soda La Parada**, across from the bus stop at Parque Central, is popular with tourists. **La Choza de Laurel**, on the main road after the church, offers an international menu with lobster and *lomito* in a friendly atmosphere with

FAMILY ADVENTURE

Despite the hokey name, **Sunset Tours' Safari Float** (479-9800, fax: 479-9415; www.sunsettourcr.com, e-mail: sunsettours@racsa.co.cr.) offers relaxation, wildlife viewing, and the chance to meet a Costa Rican farm family. A bus takes you 20 minutes east of La Fortuna to the beautiful green Río Peñas Blancas, where you float silently in inflatable rafts. Our guides pointed out sloths, howler monkeys, and many birds. Even though it was the rainy season (June), only a light shower sprinkled us along the way, and we soon dried off in the warm breeze. After an hour and a half of gentle floating, we stopped and climbed up a trail carved into the riverbank to Don Pedro's *finca*. Don Pedro is a sprightly nonagenarian who has lived by the river all his life. He canoes and walks to get into town, lives without electricity, and seems to like it that way. Our tour guides revered him as a symbol of everything that is important in the Costa Rican character. Don Pedro was offered a fortune for the remaining virgin forest on his farm, and refused to sell. His daughters, Anita and Mayo, served us their homemade cheese with tortillas, delicately fried *plátanos,* coffee, and other treats. We stopped by the kitchen to thank them as we left and they embraced us and gave us a fragrant gardenia to sniff on the way back. It was a memorable afternoon. The trip can be taken in the morning or the afternoon, although our guides told us that wildlife are more visible in the afternoon. Be sure to take a camera and binoculars. Don Pedro supplies rubber boots if you want to hike in his rainforest reserve. Other companies offer the Safari Float with a picnic lunch, but only Sunset Tours visits Don Pedro's farm.

brightly colored oilcloth tablecloths. Service is excellent and meals are served with style. **Las Brasitas**, 250 meters west of the park, has Mexican food and a volcano view. **Rancho La Cascada**, a large thatch-roofed restaurant across from the football field, is the most elegant restaurant in town, but seems to cater mostly to tour groups. **Heladería La Fortuna** has a good ice cream parlor a few doors down, across from the plaza. **Hotel Pizzería and Spaghettería Vagabondo**, one and a half kilometers beyond La Fortuna on the left, just after Cabinas Rossi, serves genuine Italian food, and their rooms are very nice too (private bath, hot water, cable TV; $30-$40; 479-9565; e-mail: vagabond@racsa.co.cr). For a flavorful, well-prepared meal on your way to or from the hot springs or the volcano, visit the large, thatch-roofed **La Pradera** (open daily, 11 a.m. to 11 p.m.; 479-9167), three kilometers west of La Fortuna. **El Novillo**, on the left just before Tabacón Lodge, is the place to go for grilled meats.

LA FORTUNA LODGING   *Budget Hotels ($10-$30):* The following lodgings are clean, inexpensive, decent places for budget travelers in the town of La Fortuna. Unless noted, all have private baths, heated water, and fans. Most offer secure parking lots. They appear in order, east to west:

One block south of the gas station, **Cabinas Mayol** (private bath, hot water, pool; $20-$50; 479-9110) has a pool for adults and one for kids, good water pressure in the showers, good mattresses, and nice gardens, with the sound of the Río Burió in the background. Recommended.

Half a block east, **Cabinas Monte Real** (private bath, heated water, fans, some air conditioning; $30-$40; 479-9357) has large, quiet rooms, a garden, and guarded parking.

One block west, **Las Colinas** ($20-$30; phone/fax: 479-9305; www. lascolinasarenal.com, e-mail: hcolinas@racsa.co.cr) is a three-story hotel whose front rooms have volcano views.

Las Tinajas ($20-$30; 479-9308; e-mail: mcastro@racsa.co.cr) is very clean and has nice furnishings.

Mid-range Hotels ($30-$90): These are some of the nicest accommodations in La Fortuna, listed from east to west. All have good mattresses, new furnishings, and views of the east (non-active) side of the volcano:

Cabinas La Rivera (private bath, heated water, ceiling fan, communal kitchen, pool; $30-$40, including breakfast; 479-9048; www.costarricense. cr/pagina/cabinaslarivera, e-mail: cabinaslarivera@costarricense.cr) is one of the best places to stay in La Fortuna. It's located at the end of a quiet street and has peaceful gardens that attract brightly colored euphonies and tanagers, as well as hummingbirds and toucans. Sixty species of birds have been sighted amidst the orchids, heliconias, and fruit trees. From the Banco Nacional at the eastern entrance to town, go right 100 meters, right again 400 meters, and left 50 meters. Recommended.

Las Cabañitas (private bath, hot water, bath tubs, ceiling fans, pool, restaurant; $90-$110; children under 12 free; 479-9400, 479-9343, fax: 479-9408; www.cabanitas.com), a few hundred meters east of town, across the road from the gas station, are comfortable, tile-roofed *casitas*.

Villa Fortuna (private bath, hot water, fans, pool, air conditioning, refrigerator; $50-$60; phone/fax: 479-9139) has spacious cabins with porches and rocking chairs in a large, bird-filled yard. It is on the right as you approach town, just beyond Las Cabañitas.

Guacamaya (private bath, hot water, air conditioning, small refrigerator; $40-$50; children under 10 free; 479-9393, fax: 479-9087; www.cabinas guacamaya.com, e-mail: info@cabinasguacamaya.com) has grown from a couple of cabins in the owners' backyard to a row of comfortable, modern guest rooms.

The best thing about **San Bosco** (private bath, heated water, ceiling fans, some cable TV, with air conditioning; $40-$50; 479-9050, fax: 479-9109; www.arenal-volcano.com, e-mail: fortuna@racsa.co.cr) is the observation deck above the hotel. This is a cool, shaded place to sit and contemplate the great green pulsing giant. Apartments for groups are available ($80-$100). They have a pool, jacuzzi, and gym.

If you take a left at the road to San Ramon, you'll come in about a kilometer to the road to Catarata La Fortuna. On this road, **Cabinas La Catarata** (private bath, heated water, ceiling fan, kitchen; $30-$40; 479-9753) have two separate rooms, are very reasonably priced, and have a good view of the inactive side of the volcano. Recommended.

Two more of our favorite places are down a dirt road to the south, one and a half kilometers west of La Fortuna. Located at the base of the volcano, both have the advantage of being at a slightly higher altitude than La Fortuna and are thus cooler. They are also off the main road enough to avoid sounds of grinding gears that are audible from almost all of the previously mentioned hotels. Both provide easy walking access to the Catarata La Fortuna. **Cerro Chato Lodge** (hot water, ceiling fans; shared bath, $15-$30; private bath, $30-$40; breakfast included; 479-9494, 479-9575, cell phone: 384-9280, fax: 479-9404; www.geocities.com/cerrochatocr, e-mail: cerrochato@racsa.co.cr) has tidy grounds and offers a two-night tour for couples, families, or groups that includes transportation to and from San José, visits to Grecia, Sarchí, Zarcero, Tabacón, the La Fortuna falls, a night tour of the volcano and lake, meals, and lodging (about $225/person).

Owner Miguel Zamora is involved in many ecological community-development projects in this area. He provides transportation from your hotel in San José, Alajuela, or Liberia for $30.

✿ **Catarata Lodge** (private bath, hot water; $40-$50, including breakfast; phone/fax: 479-9522, fax: 479-9168; www.cataratalodge.com, e-mail: catarata @racsa.co.cr) is a lodge run by a cooperative of campesinos. Their cabinas are quiet and comfortable and the downhome breakfast included in their rates will last you all day. This hotel also has a great place to camp ($2/tent).

To get to the above two places, go one and a half kilometers west of La Fortuna. Take a dirt road on the left just before Cabinas Rossi and go another one and a half kilometers, bearing left. You might need four-wheel drive in the rainy season.

A number of cabinas have sprung up along the road that skirts the northeast side of the volcano. They have good volcano views, but not of the nighttime lava flows, which in early 2004 were on the north and northwestern side (check www.arenal.net for up-to-date information). All have private bath, heated water, and fans: **Hotel Sierra Arenal** ($30-$40; 479-9751; www.infoarenal.com/hoteles), **Cabinas Mary** ($20-$30; 479-9734), **Hotel Arenal Rossi** (air conditioning, TV, refrigerator, telephone, pool, scooter rentals; $50-$70; with room for 7, $120-$130; 479-9023; www.

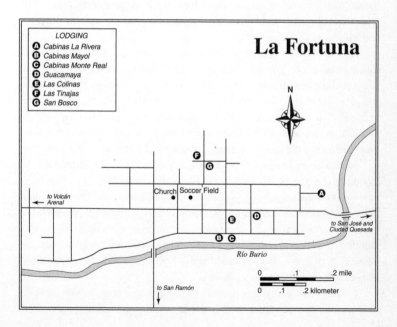

LODGING
Ⓐ Cabinas La Rivera
Ⓑ Cabinas Mayol
Ⓒ Cabinas Monte Real
Ⓓ Guacamaya
Ⓔ Las Colinas
Ⓕ Las Tinajas
Ⓖ San Bosco

La Fortuna

N

to Volcán Arenal ←

Church Soccer Field

to San José and Ciudad Quesada

Río Burio

0   .1   .2 mile
0   .1   .2 kilometer

to San Ramón ↓

hotelarenalrossi.com), **Villas Vilma** (cable TV, gardens, terraces; $50-$60; 479-9215; www.infoturistica.com/hospedajes/vilma, e-mail: villasvilma@ racsa.co.cr), **Hotel and Restaurant La Pradera del Arenal** (air conditioning, cable TV, private terrace, international restaurant; $30-$50; 479-9597).

A nice option located one and a half kilometers off the main road is **Lomas del Volcán** (private bath, hot water, ceiling fan, refrigerator; $80-$90, including breakfast; children under 10 free; 479-9000, fax: 479-9770; www.lomasdelvolcan.com, e-mail: lomasrm@racsa.co.cr). It has comfortable individual bungalows with private terraces and a sweeping volcano view.

Hotels with Views of the Volcano's Active Side: Because volcano watching is best at night, we recommend getting a hotel with a view of the active side of Arenal. (You can see a map of the active side at www.arenal.net/ arenal-costa-rica-map.htm.) These hotels are listed below. Since they are six to nine kilometers from La Fortuna, you will probably want a car if you plan to stay here.

Volcano Lodge (private bath, hot water, ceiling fans, air conditioning, pool; $90-$100, including breakfast; children under 12 free; 460-6080, fax: 460-6020; www.volcanolodge.com, e-mail: volcanolodge@racsa.co.cr) features comfortable rooms with volcano views and an outdoor, warm-water jacuzzi where you can soak your travel-weary muscles while watching lava ooze down the side of Arenal. Their **Restaurant Arenal** is decorated with lush tropical murals and built around a giant fish tank. It features Costa Rican cuisine with a modern flair.

Arenal Paraíso Resort and Spa (private bath, hot water, ceiling fans, refrigerator, pools, jacuzzi, phones, cable TV; $70-$80; with glassed-in balcony and air conditioning, $100-$110, including breakfast; children under 12, $6; 460-5333, fax 460-5343; www.arenalparaiso.com, e-mail: arenalpa@racsa.co.cr) has trim wooden cottages with porches. Some rooms are wheelchair accessible. Their spa offers a variety of treatments from mud masks to reflexology. **Arenal Paraíso Steakhouse** is on the property.

Montaña de Fuego Resort and Spa (private bath, hot water, fans, air conditioning, direct TV, phones; $100-$130; 460-1220, fax: 460-1455; www.montanadefuego.com, e-mail: monfuego@racsa.co.cr) has 42 cabins with glass-enclosed porches and its own exclusive restaurant, **Acuarelas**. It boasts a spa with a jacuzzi, a swimming pool, and ten massage rooms with jungle views. A conference room and another restaurant complete their extensive installations. Both Arenal Paraíso and Montaña de Fuego have forest reserves and offer tours on horseback.

Cabinas Los Guayabos (private bath, hot water, fans; $40-60 for up to five people; 460-6644) has simple cabinas with great volcano views from their back porches. There is a hill between these two places at the volcano, so although they are on the volcano side of the road, they are considered safe "at this time, as far as we know," according to vulcanologists. Two other options in this area are **Cabinas Fuego Arenal** (private bath, heated water, cable TV, phone, some air conditioning; $70-$90; 460-4692) and **Erupciones Inn** ($60-$70 for up to four, including breakfast; 460-8000).

Another two kilometers toward Lake Arenal is **Tabacón Lodge** (air conditioning, cable TV, pool; $185-$310, including breakfast and access to Tabacón resort; 256-1500, fax: 221-3075, in the U.S.: 877-277-8291; www.tabacon.com, e-mail: sales@tabacon.com), a luxury hotel across from the famous hot springs. Hot water is piped into the tubs, showers, and swimming pools from the springs. Many of the 73 rooms and 9 suites have terraces with a close-up view of the volcano. The price includes unlimited access to Tabacón and a fantastic breakfast buffet.

Continuing around the volcano, you come to the entrance of the National Park on the left. Go two kilometers to the park headquarters. In two more kilometers, you'll climb a steep hill across from the south side of the volcano to arrive at the **Arenal Volcano Observatory** (hot water; with volcano views, $120-$150; without views, $90-$100; budget rooms with shared bath and common sitting room with fireplace, volcano view from porch, $60-$70, including breakfast; children under 11 free; 290-7011, 692-2070, fax: 290-8427; www.arenal-observatory.co.cr, e-mail: info@arenal-observatory.co.cr). Five rooms and one nature trail are wheelchair-accessible. This site was chosen by Smithsonian vulcanologists who wanted a safe vantage point from which to study the volcano's activity. There is a small museum with a seismograph monitoring current action. When there is an eruption during the day, you are close enough to see boulders bouncing down the sides of the volcano, but if there are no eruptions, you are better off viewing the incandescent lava flows on the northwest side at night. The climate at the lodge is cool and fresh, and there are tours and self-guided hikes to a nearby waterfall and to Cerro Chato, a dormant volcano. A bouncy hanging bridge leads to the newer luxury rooms with volcano views. The lodge has an attractive spring-fed pool and three five-person jacuzzis nestled below the cabins. If you cannot afford to stay, $2 will get you a day's access to the trails and a seat on the restaurant's well-appointed viewing deck. Birding is great there. Though the road to the entrance is bumpy, the steep road up to the lodge from the entrance is paved.

Before you get to the observatory entrance, there is a turnoff to the right for the hilltop **Linda Vista del Norte** (private bath, hot water; $60-$70, including breakfast; suites, $90-$100; 692-2090, fax 692-2091), a family-owned restaurant and hotel with a fantastic view of the volcano *and* the lake. Some of the rooms don't face the volcano, so request one that does; the restaurant terrace provides great views for all. *Casados* at the restaurant are well prepared and feature tilapia raised in Lake Arenal. Linda Vista offers a five-hour horseback and hiking trip to the volcano ($20/person) or to a large natural reserve on the family farm.

On a hill west of Linda Vista, you can see the cabins of **El Castillo Dorado** (private bath, hot water; $40-$50, including breakfast; 383-7196; e-mail: cabinitaselcastillo@racsa.co.cr). Amenities include a pool table and kayak rentals. To get there, drive through the town of El Castillo and look for the entrance uphill on the right.

GETTING THERE: By Bus: From San José, buses (255-4318; $4) leave the Atlántico Norte terminal for La Fortuna every day at 6:15 a.m., 8:40 a.m., and 11:30 a.m., returning at 12:45 p.m. and 2:45 p.m. From Ciudad Quesada you can catch a La Fortuna bus at 5 a.m, 8 a.m., 12:15 p.m., and 3:30 p.m. (1 hour). From Monteverde or Santa Elena, catch the 7 a.m. bus to Tilarán (3 hours). In Tilarán, catch the San Carlos bus at 12:30 p.m. It will drop you in La Fortuna (4 hours). To get to Monteverde from La Fortuna, take the 8 a.m. bus to Tilarán (4 hours), have lunch in Tilarán, then board the 12:30 bus for Santa Elena (3 hours; $2).

Gray Line buses (232-3681; www.grayline.com) will take you to La Fortuna from San José, Monteverde, and most Pacific or Atlantic beaches for $25 to $38. Interbus (283-5573; www.interbusonline.com) reservations can be made by your hotel.

Your hotel can arrange a taxi, boat, and jeep to Monteverde ($25/person). The trip takes three hours—that's faster than the horseback ride.

By Car: A direct road connects La Fortuna with San Ramón de Alajuela. From San José, follow the Interamerican Highway west and turn north at San Ramón, 55 minutes west of San José. Follow the signs for Villablanca through town, then north along the lovely La Tigra road. This road borders a reserve that protects a beautiful rainforest southeast of Monteverde and conserves the water supply for the town of San Ramón. It ends right in La Fortuna. Alternate routes are: through Naranjo, Zarcero, and Ciudad Quesada; through Heredia, Varablanca, San Miguel, and Aguas Zarcas; or from Monteverde or Guanacaste by way of Tilarán and Lake Arenal. All of them are beautiful drives. La Fortuna is about three and a half hours from San José.

Car Rentals: Alamo, National, and Poás Rentacar have offices in La Fortuna.

LAKE ARENAL

Lake Arenal is a large reservoir at the foot of the volcano. The original Laguna Arenal was the source of a river whose waters flowed east to the Atlantic. Dams built for a hydroelectric energy plant enlarged the lake and diverted the waters. Now they flow from the northwest side of the reservoir to irrigate Costa Rica's dry Pacific coast.

Many people enjoy boating and fishing on the lake. The lake also offers the best windsurfing conditions in the country, if not in all of Central America. The lodges on the west side of the lake specialize in windsurfing and rent equipment.

Even though crocodiles are not native to Lake Arenal, at least 14 local residents swear they have seen them in the lake over the past two years, according to an article in the *Tico Times* (January 16, 2004). The presence of these large, dangerous reptiles has not been documented on film, but it is probably best not to swim in the lake until more is known.

LODGING   Lake Arenal's eastern and northern banks are flanked by a road that passes by all the lodgings listed below. It's easiest to have a car if you want to stay at one of these places.

After La Unión, the road around the lake has some unpaved and pot-holed patches until you hit Nuevo Arenal. The road is a great way to connect Volcán Arenal, Sarapiquí, and Tortuguero with Monteverde and the beaches and parks of Guanacaste. Be sure to call ahead and check on its condition before setting out.

The lake is dammed at its southeastern tip, 20 kilometers from La Fortuna. Just north of the dam, **Arenal Lodge** (private bath, hot water; without view, $70-$80; with view, some with kitchens, $130-$180, including breakfast; 253-5080, fax: 253-5016; www.arenallodge.com, e-mail: info@arenal lodge.com) is a comfortable place, high on a hill two and a half kilometers from the main road. There is a lovely view of Volcán Arenal from the dining room and most guest rooms. A library with leather chairs and a fireplace, an outdoor jacuzzi, and a pool table contribute to the clubby atmosphere; there's also a mountain bike tour. Fishing trips on the lake are a specialty.

Sixteen kilometers to the west, in La Unión de Arenal, **Toad Hall** (open daily, 8 a.m. to 5 p.m.; 692-8020, fax: 692-8001) is a nontraditional general store with a fabulous selection of local and national handicrafts (Cecilia Figueres' fanciful ceramics, hand-sewn dolls made by a local campesina, indigenous masks, and spears, to name a few). There is a used-book nook and a delightful restaurant that has outside tables overlooking the lake and a healthy menu featuring organic vegetables, fruit drinks and smoothies, and espresso. Recommended.

NUEVO ARENAL

Nuevo Arenal was founded by ex-inhabitants of the old Arenal when that town was submerged by the lake in the 1970s. It is cool and breezy there.

Most locals are afraid to swim in the lake; there have been several drownings, usually due to the victim not knowing how to swim or being inebriated.

Restaurante Lajas is neat and clean and open for breakfast and lunch. They serve Argentinian specialties and have an internet café.

Two kilometers down the road (and only two kilometers before Nuevo Arenal) is **Villa Decary** (private bath, hot water, ceiling fans; $90-$100; with kitchen, $110-$120; one-bedroom bungalows with kitchen and a great view of the lake, $130-$140; fax: 694-4330, cell phone: 383-3012; www. villadecary.com, e-mail: info@villadecary.com), with large, clean, comfortably furnished rooms whose balconies overlook the lake below. Within moments of our arrival we saw seven species of small, jewel-like birds. About a hundred meters from the hotel a troop of howler monkeys sojourned by the lake, oblivious to our presence. Rates include breakfasts with homemade preserves. No credit cards. Recommended.

We spent an unforgettable morning with Gordo from **Establo Arenal** (694-4092). He takes you up to a ridge where you can see heart-shaped Lago Coter on one side and Lake Arenal on the other. He sings *rancheros* as he rides along, and embodies the joyful sprit of the *vaquero guanacasteco*. Another great horseman is Lucas (694-4357).

You should treat yourself to a meal at **Tramonti** (open Tuesday through Sunday, 11:30 a.m. to 3 p.m., 5 p.m. to 9:30 p.m.; 694-4282; located in a subdivision accessible from the southern entrance to town), whose Italian owners bake their pizza in traditional wood-burning ovens.

Tom's Pan (open daily, 8 a.m. to 4 p.m.; 694-4547) is a great German bakery and café featuring pretzels, blueberry cheesecake, baguettes, and croissants. Hearty wienerschnitzel, goulash, sauerbraten, and delicious sandwiches loaded with fresh veggies complete the menu. They rent a homey cabin (private bath, heated water; $40-$50, including breakfast) with huge windows in their garden. Recommended. It's on the right as you enter Nuevo Arenal.

Up the street, **Texas Bill** rents kayaks and bicycles at his gift shop.

Another favorite is **El Caballo Negro** (open daily, noon to 8 p.m.; 694-4515) on the right, three kilometers west of Nuevo Arenal. This open-air restaurant in a garden setting features hearty European and vegetarian home cooking using organic ingredients. The owner and her triplet daughters have rescued many animals, and the girls sell their artwork to pay for the animals' upkeep. They also run an excellent gift shop featuring ceramics. Recommended.

Chalet Nicholas (private bath, hot water, table fans; $60-$70, including breakfast; nonsmokers only; phone/fax: 694-4041; www.chaletnicholas.

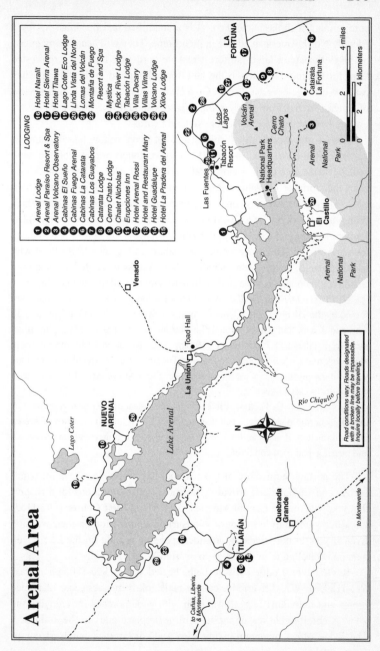

Arenal Area

LODGING

1. Arenal Lodge
2. Arenal Paraíso Resort & Spa
3. Arenal Volcano Observatory
4. Cabinas El Sueño
5. Cabinas Fuego Arenal
6. Cabinas La Catarata
7. Cabinas Los Guayabos
8. Catarata Lodge
9. Cerro Chato Lodge
10. Chalet Nicholas
11. Erupciones Inn
12. Hotel Arenal Rossi
13. Hotel and Restaurant Mary
14. Hotel Guadalupe
15. Hotel La Pradera del Arenal
16. Hotel Naralit
17. Hotel Sierra Arenal
18. Hotel Tilawa
19. Lago Coter Eco Lodge
20. Linda Vista del Norte
21. Lomas del Volcán
22. Montaña de Fuego Resort and Spa
23. Mystica
24. Rock River Lodge
25. Tabacón Lodge
26. Villa Decary
27. Villas Vilma
28. Volcano Lodge
29. Xiloe Lodge

Road conditions vary. Roads designated with a broken line may be impassable. Inquire locally before traveling.

com, e-mail: nicholas@.racsa.co.cr) is a small bed and breakfast run by a friendly North American couple in their home. They will accompany guests on hikes through a large rainforest reserve bordering their own reforested farm for birding, or down to the lake for fishing and birdwatching. They can also arrange horseback trips. On a clear day, you can see a distant view of Volcán Arenal from every room. Visitors should like dogs because the owners have several Great Danes. No credit cards.

Lago Coter Eco Lodge (private bath, hot water, ceiling fans; children 6-12 free; 440-6768, fax: 440-6725; www.ecolodgecostarica.com, e-mail: ecolodge@racsa.co.cr) has individual cabins with lake and volcano views from their private balconies ($80-$90) and comfortable hotel rooms ($60-$70). They offer two-day, one-night packages including meals, horseback riding, and kayaking for $120-$130 per person. In addition to an eight-platform canopy tour ($50), hiking, horseback riding, water sports, and volcano trips are offered. The lodge's rainforest nature trail is completely lined with wooden planks, so you won't slip and slide. Access to the lodge's site on a small mountain lake is via a three-kilometer gravel road in good condition.

GETTING THERE: By Bus: All of the lake lodgings and Nuevo Arenal are served by the Tilarán–Ciudad Quesada bus, which leaves Ciudad Quesada at 6:30 a.m. and 3 p.m. and passes through La Fortuna around 8 a.m. and 5 p.m. It returns from Tilarán at 7 a.m. and 12:30 p.m. You can ask to be let off anywhere along this route. More frequent buses from Tilarán to Nuevo Arenal stop at all the hotels in the northwestern section of the lake. From Nuevo Arenal you can get a taxi to places east of town.

By Car: From La Fortuna, drive around the volcano, then bear right to skirt the lake's northern shore. The full distance from La Fortuna to the town of Arenal is 47 kilometers. It takes an hour to an hour and a half to drive, given the curves and possible bad road conditions.

The northwestern shore of Lake Arenal has become a mecca for windsurfers and kiteboarders, providing the most stellar conditions for this sport that you will find in Central America. **Tico Wind Surf Center** (692-1153; www.ticowind.com) has a lot of windsurfing information on their website. Even if you do not windsurf, consider spending a night on the lake if you plan on encircling it on your way to or from Volcán Arenal.

Rock River Lodge (private bath, heated water; $50-$80; phone/fax: 692-1180; www.rockriverlodge.com, e-mail: rokriver@racsa.co.cr) has nice rooms and individual bungalows, both with wide porches for enjoying the view. A comfortable restaurant/bar with a fireplace adds to the ambiance. The lodge offers mountain-biking trips and can arrange windsurf equipment rental.

Xiloe Lodge (private bath, heated water; $12-$20; with kitchen, $30-40; 692-1101) rents small cabins. Its **Restaurante Equus** (open Wednesday through Friday at 4 p.m. to 9 p.m.; Saturday and Sunday, 11 a.m. to 11 p.m.) features barbecued chicken. They have dances every weekend.

The rooms at **Mystica** (private bath, hot water; $60-$70, including breakfast; 692-1002; www.mysticalodge.com) are comfortable and have delightful artistic touches. The flowering vine–covered porches have distant views of the volcano across the lake. Their restaurant serves breakfast from 7:30 a.m. to 9:30 a.m. From 12 p.m. to 9 p.m. they offer Italian home cooking, including homemade pasta, fresh salads, and excellent pizza, enlivened by fresh tomatoes and herbs grown in their garden.

The largest hotel on the western shore is the sports-oriented **Hotel Tilawa** (private bath, hot water, ceiling fans, pool, tennis court; $50-$90; apartments with lake view and fireplaces, $90-$100; 695-5050, fax: 695-5766; www.hotel-tilawa.com, e-mail: info@hotel-tilawa.com). Their **Windsurf Center** on the banks of the lake, a kilometer away, offers both guests and walk-ins windsurf equipment rental. They also rent kiteboards and provide a safe place to learn this exciting sport. Their spacious restaurant is adorned with unique frescos patterned on the Palace of Knossos in Greece, and has a terrific view of the lake. They rent kayaks, and offer on-site massage as well as their own microbrewery, the **Tilawa Brew Pub**.

Soon you will see signs for Tilarán to the right and Tronadora to the left. If you are on your way to Monteverde or Guanacaste, turn right to go into Tilarán.

TILARÁN

Fifteen minutes beyond the lake is the clean, pleasant mountain town of Tilarán, with its streets full of cowboys and churchyard trees full of songbirds.

Leaving Tilarán through Quebrada Grande on the road to Monteverde, you can see three sources of non-fossil-fuel energy: the large white windmills that catch the wind off Lake Arenal to the northeast, the three fumaroles at the Miravalles geothermal plant to the north, and the candy-striped surge tank of the Arenal hydroelectric plant. The Costa Rican government is committed to finding alternative sources of energy by the year 2020. On a clear day you can also see four volcanoes from this site: Tenorio, Miravalles, Rincón de la Vieja, and Orosi.

Hotel and Restaurant Mary (private bath, hot water, table fans, cable TV; $20-$30; 695-5479) offers second-floor rooms with big windows overlooking the park. Their restaurant has good *sopa negra*.

Cabinas El Sueño (private bath, heated water, direct TV; $20-$30; 695-5347), half a block from the northwest corner of the park, has a nice interior garden and sitting area. **Hotel Naralit** (private bath, heated water, ceiling fans, cable TV, carpeted; $20-$30; 695-5393), across the street from the cathedral, has some quieter rooms off of the street. **Hotel Guadalupe** (private bath, heated water, wall fans, TV; $20-$30; 695-5943), one block south of the cathedral, is very clean with a nice atmosphere. All of the above hotels have guarded parking.

GETTING THERE: By Bus: It's a four-and-a-half-hour trip to Tilarán from San José (Calle 14, Avenidas 9/11; 7:30 a.m., 9:30 a.m., 12:45 p.m., 3:30 p.m.; 222-3854; $6). If you are traveling to Tilarán from Monteverde, catch the 7 a.m. bus from the cheese factory (a two-and-a-half-hour trip on bumpy but passable roads). You can continue on to La Fortuna by connecting in Tilarán to the 12:30 p.m. San Carlos bus. The bus from San Carlos to Tilarán passes through La Fortuna around 8 a.m., arriving in Tilarán around 11 a.m. You can continue to Monteverde on the 12:30 p.m. Santa Elena bus.

By Car: From the Interamerican Highway, turn into Cañas and continue 22 kilometers up into the mountains on a good paved road.

From Monteverde: Passable gravel roads connect Tilarán with Monteverde. In the rainy season, ask first about the best route and current road conditions. A high-clearance vehicle is necessary.

From La Fortuna: It's a pleasant two-hour drive, longer with stops at the attractions along the shores of Lake Arenal. The road conditions are not great between the volcano and the town of Arenal, but regular cars can make it. Between Arenal and Tilarán the road is in good shape.

MONTEVERDE

During most of the two-hour ascent east from the Interamerican Highway to Monteverde, you climb through deforested, eroded pastures. This would be Costa Rica's future without conservation: unbridled tree-cutting and cattle-grazing until nothing is left but dust in the dry season and mudslides in "winter." When you arrive at the misty heights of Monteverde, you see the other possibility, which, thanks to the work of a growing number of conservationists, has become reality. Here the land is still productive for farmers and, with large patches of forest untouched and thick windbreaks between pastures, there's plenty of moisture and less erosion.

The road from the Interamerican Highway to Monteverde is graded but unpaved. Monteverde residents, in an attempt to protect the simple, friendly lifestyle that has made their community such a special place, have fought against paving the road, believing that easier access would ruin the peaceful ambiance of the area. Many communities in Costa Rica have developed tourism quickly over the last few years because they desperately need the business, but often much is lost in the process. Despite the bad roads, Monteverde receives over 200,000 visitors a year and is in danger, like Manuel Antonio and Tortuguero, of being loved to death.

A group of Alabama Quakers who felt that Costa Rica's disarmament policy was in line with their pacifist tradition started dairy farming in Monteverde in the early 1950s. Visiting biologists found the cloud forest above their community rich in flora and fauna, and the Quakers, along with the Tropical Science Center, had the foresight to make it a reserve.

Monteverde is not a place you can visit in one day. You need a day for travel and recovery each way, plus at least two days to visit the Monteverde Reserve and other nearby attractions.

What to Bring: Bring rain gear (a lightweight rain poncho works well, or an umbrella if you wear glasses), long-sleeved shirts and long pants, preferably made of material that dries quickly, and good socks. Most hotels rent rubber boots. Be sure to dress in layers for the trip up and down. You forget when you are in cool, windy Monteverde how swelteringly hot you'll be by the time you get to the Interamerican Highway.

Arranging tours: The Association of Tour Operators of Monteverde (ATOM, 645-6565) facilitates logistics between many of the tourist attractions in Monteverde. It is less expensive to buy tickets from them than to arrange tours through your hotel. You can buy tickets for the Frog Pond, the Cheese Tour and Coffee Tour, the Skywalk, Skytrek and Serpentario, Monteverde Reserve, Santa Elena Reserve, La Estrella Horseback Tours, the Butterfly Garden and the Natural Wonders Tram, Walk and Ride. Tickets to any of the above tours are also available at the offices of any ATOM member. Discounts increase if two or more tours are purchased together. ATOM's central office is in Santa Elena between the Salon Parroquial and the Tienda Vitosi.

Guides: The Monteverde Guides Association is made up of experienced naturalists who can greatly increase what you see and what you learn in the rainforest. You can see the range of their expertise at www.cloudforestalive.org/tour/guide_bios.htm.

Helpful websites: www.monteverdeinfo.com, www.monteverdetours.com. Research biologists have placed cameras to monitor wildlife activity in the Monteverde Reserve. See live QuetzalCams, BatCams, and HummingbirdCams at the Live eTours section of www.cloudforestalive.org.

VOLCANO VIEWING FROM MONTEVERDE   Although many people
make a circuit from Volcán Arenal to Monteverde, it is not widely known
that you can see the volcano from the hills north of Monteverde. Part of the
reason for this is that clouds on the rainy Atlantic slope often obscure the
view. But when it is clear, the view of the volcano behind the forested
slopes of the Children's Eternal Rainforest is awe-inspiring. We know of
four places from which you can see this lovely sight: by hiking to the observation tower of the Santa Elena Reserve or the San Gerardo station in
the Bosque Eterno, or by walking or driving (four-wheel drive is necessary) to Mirador San Gerardo or the Hotel Vista Verde. The latter two are
about a 45-minute drive from Monteverde. More information below.

SANTA ELENA FOREST RESERVE   The 765-acre Santa Elena Forest
Reserve (open daily, 7 a.m. to 4 p.m.; phone/fax: 645-5390; www.monte
verdeinfo.com/reserve, e-mail: rbnctpse@racsa.co.cr; admission $9, stu-
dents $5), located six kilometers northeast of Santa Elena, has 12 kilome-
ters of trails, with one leading to an 11-meter observation tower that
overlooks forest canopy; on clear days, you have a view of Arenal Lake
and Volcano. Arrange for guides ($15) beforehand through your hotel, or
by calling 645-5693. You can rent boots there. Owned and maintained by
the Santa Elena high school, this reserve helps to fund courses in environmental education, biology, language, and tourism. The Santa Elena Forest
Reserve is an inspiring, community-run effort that should be a model for
conservationists trying to integrate sustainable development with wilderness preservation. It is usually less crowded and bureaucratic than the
Monteverde Preserve. Volunteer opportunities are available. The reserve
has a *soda* (open daily, 7 a.m. to 4 p.m.) and small local crafts shop. The
reserve's information office is located on the left before the high school in
Santa Elena. A jeep leaves the Banco Nacional in Santa Elena several times
a day for the Santa Elena Reserve (make reservations by calling 645-5236,
645-5390; $2 each way). It also passes by the SkyWalk and can leave you
three kilometers from Mirador San Gerardo (see below). A taxi from Santa
Elena should cost about $7.

MIRADOR SAN GERARDO   On the way to the Santa Elena Forest Reserve, a fork to the left leads three kilometers to the private 100-hectare reserve at **Mirador San Gerardo** (phone/fax: 645-5087, 645-5354, cell
phone: 661-8000; www.monteverdesangerardolodge.com, e-mail: miradorq
@racsa.co.cr), famous for its spectacular views of Arenal Lake and Volcano during the dry season and its waterfall trails. Lodging is also offered

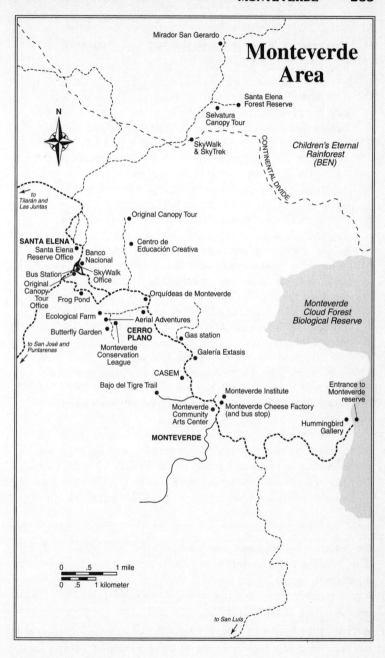

Monteverde Area

Mirador San Gerardo

Santa Elena Forest Reserve

Selvatura Canopy Tour

SkyWalk & SkyTrek

CONTINENTAL DIVIDE

Children's Eternal Rainforest (BEN)

to Tilarán and Las Juntas

Original Canopy Tour

Centro de Educación Creativa

SANTA ELENA

Santa Elena Reserve Office

Banco Nacional

Bus Station

Original Canopy Tour Office

SkyWalk Office

Frog Pond

Orquídeas de Monteverde

Monteverde Cloud Forest Biological Reserve

Ecological Farm

Aerial Adventures

CERRO PLANO

Butterfly Garden

Gas station

to San José and Puntarenas

Monteverde Conservation League

Galería Extasis

CASEM

Bajo del Tigre Trail

Monteverde Institute

Entrance to Monteverde reserve

Monteverde Community Arts Center

Monteverde Cheese Factory (and bus stop)

Hummingbird Gallery

MONTEVERDE

N

0   .5   1 mile

0   .5   1 kilometer

to San Luís

ZIPLINES AND RAINFOREST WALKWAYS

It seems like many people think that Monteverde is the only place you can do the famous canopy tour. Although zipline tours started in Monteverde, the industry, which is a pretty low-impact way to earn money while preserving forests, has made its way into the farthest corners of the land. The Original Canopy Tour started in Monteverde in 1997 and was later awarded a patent for the idea by the Costa Rican government. It then tried to shut down the other 80 or so canopy tours in Costa Rica, with little success.

There are now three major zipline tours in Monteverde, several hanging bridge walkways, and an electric tram.

For the **Original Canopy Tour** you are strapped into a harness, then you take a short hike through the forest until you come to a hollow strangler fig; you climb up inside it to reach a platform at its top. Your harness is then attached to a pulley system on a steel cable, and you zoom among the treetops to another platform 75 feet above the ground. There you climb a tower to another platform and zoom off again. After a few more zooms you rappel down the last tree. Our seven-year-old was afraid to cross the first time, so a guide went across with her; the next crossings she did by herself. The kids loved this trip. The Canopy Tour office is in Santa Elena across from Super La Esperanza. They provide transportation to the Cloud Forest Lodge, where the tour takes place (645-5243, phone/fax: 257-5149; www.canopytour.com; $45; student and child discounts).

The **SkyTrek** ($40; www.skytrek.com) is a much longer and higher cable ride. You have to be at least ten years old to go. It is even more thrilling than the Original Canopy Tour, up to 2525 feet long and 416 feet high toward the end of its 11 cables. Our kids loved this one, too, when they were 11 and 13. The Skytrek office

(hot water; individual rustic cabins for up to six with private bath, $60-$70). Meals in the restaurant are moderately priced. The owners also offer a horseback ride to Volcán Arenal ($65/person). It's a scenic and unique way to travel between these two popular destinations. Don't expect to enjoy this trip during the rainy season.

✿ THE CHILDREN'S ETERNAL RAINFOREST   Children from all over the world have been inspired by the efforts of a group of Swedish fourth-

is in "downtown" Santa Elena across from the bank, but the reserve itself, which protects 563 acres of forest, is on the road to San Gerardo, a 20-minute ride from Santa Elena.

The **SkyWalk** (open 7 a.m. to 4 p.m.; 645-5238; www.skytrek. com, e-mail: info@skytrek.com; admission $15, children $6) is for those who aren't quite up to a zipline. It is a two-and-a-half-kilometer walk through a series of easy, well-maintained trails that lead to six narrow bridges with cyclone fencing on the sides, suspended as much as 120 feet above the ground, surrounded by gorgeous forest. As with any wildlife tour, you should go early in the morning if you want to see animals. During the high season, visitors can hire bilingual guides ($12). The hike takes about an hour and a half at a leisurely pace. SkyWalk and SkyTrek provide transportation for $1.

Selvatura (645-5929; www.selvatura.com) claims to out-zip the SkyTrek with 14 platforms and two miles of cable ($35, including transportation from local hotels) and an eight-bridge forest walkway that's good for late-afternoon birding ($15). Located at the turnoff to the Santa Elena reserve, Selvatura also has butterfly and hummingbird gardens, and displays the famous Jewels of the Rainforest insect collection, containing over one million arthropods, including incredible silver- and gold-colored beetles. Their **La Casona Restaurant** serves international cuisine.

People with limited mobility, small children, or fear of heights might like **Natural Wonders** (645-5960; e-mail natural wonders@racsa.co.cr; $15), covered gondolas that glide on a mile of metal rails suspended over the forest on towers up to 36 feet high. The slow-moving ride takes about an hour. There is a guided forest walk as well. It's in Cerro Plano on the way to the Ecological Farm.

graders who organized the first Children's Rainforest campaign in 1987, in response to a presentation at their school by a biologist who talked about growing deforestation in the Monteverde area. Since then, schoolchildren and adults from 44 countries have raised money to buy more than 56,000 acres of rainforest on the Atlantic slope to the east of the Monteverde Cloud Forest reserve. This land, now the largest private reserve in Costa Rica, is called the Children's Eternal Rainforest (Bosque Eterno de los

Niños, or BEN) in honor of the children of the world who have helped protect this special place. So far, 707 species of birds, reptiles, and mammals
have been identified in the BEN, representing over half of all species found
in Costa Rica.

Two rustic stations in the forest offer lodging for groups of students or
tourists. The **Poco Sol Station** (dorms with shared bath or rooms with two
bunks and private bath), 2350 feet above sea level and accessible from La
Tigra, south of La Fortuna, is near a waterfall, hot mineral springs, and a
mountain lake, with excellent hiking and wildlife observation opportunities. You can hike there in two days from Monteverde, or drive 13.5 kilometers from the BEN office on the La Tigra road (four-wheel drive only).
The **San Gerardo Station** (private bath, cold water), at 4000 feet above
sea level, offers a breathtaking view of Arenal Volcano and Lake Arenal. It
can be reached in a two-hour downhill (3.5 kilometers) hike from the Santa
Elena Forest Reserve. The station has comfortable bunkbeds and sleeps
four to a room. The trails, and the chances of seeing the volcano, are best
in the dry season. Highly recommended for those who enjoy hiking. Contact Poco Sol (468-0148, phone/fax: 468-0260; e-mail acmtigra@racsa.co.
cr) or San Gerardo (645-5200, fax: 645-5104) for reservations. Groups of
six or more pay $34/person. For less than six people it's $45/person. All
rates include meals. Student discounts are available. Each station can be
rented as a whole for retreats and workshops.

The only section of the Children's Rainforest currently open to walk-in
visitors is the **Bajo del Tigre Trail** (open daily, 8 a.m. to 5 p.m.; Sunday 9
a.m. to 4 p.m.; admission $6, students with ID $3, including trail map). The
entrance is down a side road on the right about 100 meters past Stella's
Bakery and CASEM as you enter Monteverde—watch for the sign. Our favorite is the Murciélago trail, which goes along the canyon's edge. Bajo del
Tigre has a **Visitors Center**, with a spectacular view of the Gulf of Nicoya,
and a **Children's Nature Center**, designed to help kids discover the wonders of a tropical mountain rainforest.

The **Monteverde Conservation League** (645-5003, fax: 645-5104;
www.acmonteverde.com, e-mail: acmmcl@racsa.co.cr) administers BEN.
Besides ongoing projects in environmental education, reforestation, protection, and biological research, the League, through its Forests on Farms and
Continuous Forest programs, have planted over 700,000 trees as windbreaks and to protect streams as well as to link patches of Pacific and Atlantic coasts. The Monteverde Conservation League has been a real pioneer
in the promotion of biological corridors that will ensure the continued exis-

tence of habitats for migratory birds and butterflies. Donations for the League's important work are welcome.

MONTEVERDE CLOUD FOREST BIOLOGICAL RESERVE   At Monteverde Cloud Forest (field station open daily, 7 a.m. to 4 p.m.; reservations: 645-5122; e-mail: montever@cct.or.cr; admission $12, students with ID $6, children under six free; $1.50 boot rentals), you can walk along the well-maintained trails with a map available at the field station. But we recommend taking at least one guided tour, as you will be shown wonders that your eyes alone would probably never catch. Call 645-5122 or e-mail montever@cct.or.cr to arrange a two-and-a-half to three-hour guided tour (starts at 7:30 a.m.; $15 plus entrance fee) the night before you want to visit the reserve. The guided hike, given by naturalists with years of experience in the cloud forest, includes a slide show of amazing wildlife photographs by Michael and Patricia Fogden, and helps support the reserve. The reserve's tours are done in groups of ten people. Your hotel can help you arrange a private tour, but it won't include the slide show. If you don't take the reserve's guided walk, but want to see the slides, you can reserve a presentation between 10 a.m. and 3 p.m. (admission $3, minimum of four people).

In order to protect the forest, only 150 people can be in the reserve at one time. If you'd like to miss the crowds, avoid the peak hours of 8 a.m. to 10 a.m. The least crowded months are between May and December, although it is rainier during that time, and the quetzals are less active. If you want to arrive at dawn for good birding, ask for permission by e-mail or phone (645-5122; e-mail: monteverde@cct.or.cr) and tell them which trails you will take.

Quetzals feed on the tiny, avocado-like fruits of *aguacatillo* trees. They are most visible in the early morning from January through June, especially during the mating season from February to May, but we talked to happy tourists who had seen them in November and December, too. Now you can see quetzal nesting activity monitored every half hour at www.cloudforest alive.org.

Behind the ticket office, there is a souvenir shop and a small **restaurant** that opens at 7 a.m. for breakfast and serves sandwiches, fruit drinks, and a very good vegetarian *casado* for lunch. Bathrooms are across the road. The Fogdens' slideshow is shown next door to the famous Hummingbird Gallery, on the right as you leave the reserve. The guided nature walks depart from there. Bring your bird book—eight hummingbird species are easily identifiable at the gallery's bird feeders. Seventeen species have been recorded over the years. In addition to the beautiful fauna and flora, other highlights of a hike in the reserve are a cascading waterfall, a *mirador* with stunning views of the area, and a 328-foot-long suspension bridge spanning the forest canopy.

If you like to live in nature, you'll enjoy hiking to the **rustic shelters**, El Valle, Eladio's, and Aleman, within the reserve. The lodges have bunk beds with foam padding and gas stoves. The largest lodge, Eladio's, sleeps 22 people and is five hours from the entrance. El Valle and El Aleman sleep ten people each and are two and three hours from the entrance, respectively. Hikers must bring food and bedding. You can stay at the lodges for $3.50-$5 per night, plus the daily entrance fee. Volunteers who want to help with trail maintenance can stay at the Reserve Field Station ($15/person, including meals; 645-5122, fax: 645-5034; www.cct.or.cr, e-mail: montever@cct.or.cr; two-week minimum). Volunteers can visit the shelters for free

GETTING THERE: The reserve is a lovely one-hour uphill walk from "downtown" Monteverde; farther from most hotels. Only La Colina, Fonda Vela, Mariposa, and the Trapp Family Lodge are within 20-30 minutes' walk from the entrance. A bus ($1) leaves Santa Elena at 6:30 a.m. and picks up passengers all the way through Monteverde to the reserve, where it arrives at around 7 a.m. It returns to Santa Elena at 11 a.m. and makes the run again at 1 p.m., returning to Santa Elena at 4 p.m. Taxis to the reserve cost $5 from Monteverde.

RESERVA SENDERO TRANQUILO   Reserva Sendero Tranquilo (645-5010) is the uncrowded 200-acre private reserve of the Lowther family. Visitors must go with one of their excellent bilingual guides (reservations required; $20/person, including entrance fee). Visitors are usually pleased with the amount of wildlife they see in the leisurely three- to four-hour hike. Recommended.

FROGS, BUTTERFLIES, AND ORCHIDS   Beautiful, strange frogs used to live in the cloud forest. The golden toad, once endemic to the Monteverde area, was remarkable for its color and the poison glands behind its ears, but it has not been observed since 1989 and is feared to be extinct. Biologists believe that global warming has caused a general drying trend in the cloud forest, depriving the frogs of the gentle mists that were vital to their existence. The best place to see frogs now is the **Frog Pond** (open daily 9 a.m. to 8:30 p.m.; 645-6320, fax: 645-6318; www.ranario.com, e-mail: ranariomv@racsa.co.cr; admission $8, students $6), a fascinating 45-minute guided tour of Costa Rica's most beautiful frogs and toads. The project aims to study the amphibians, and is dedicated to preventing their extinction. It's open at night so you can see the many frogs that are more active after dark. The entrance fee can be used twice on the same day. It's on the road between Santa Elena and Monteverde Lodge. Recommended.

The **Monteverde Butterfly Garden** (open daily, 9:30 a.m. to 4 p.m.; admission $8, students $6, children $3; 645-5512) is a biodiversity center dedicated to teaching the world about insects. Their four butterfly gardens represent different habitats. They have exhibits on live insects, a leaf-cutter ant nest under glass, a medicinal plant trail, and a Bug Theater. Guides give a fascinating explanation of the habits of each species, with ample botanical information as well. To get there, follow the small butterfly-shaped signs that start across from the Hotel Heliconia in Cerro Plano. Take the dirt road to the right 600 meters, turn left, then go another 300 meters.

Orquídeas de Monteverde (645-5510; admission $5, students $3) exhibits more than 430 species of orchids near the home of Monteverde's leading orchid expert, Gabriel Barbosa. Visitors are presented with magnifying glasses so they can observe *Platystele jungermannioids,* the world's smallest flower. At least 40 orchid species will be in bloom at any given time in the garden, located in Cerro Plano, next to Johnny's Pizza.

HORSES   Horseback riding is a great way to get around in Monteverde. **Meg's Stables** (645-5052; www.stellasbakery.com) offers a two-hour trail ride on local back roads, ending with a climb 40 feet up inside a strangler fig tree ($20-$30). The horses are tame and child-sized saddles are available. Meg's four-hour Waterfall Tour is for the hardy and adventurous. You ride to a local farm in San Luis Valley, then hike to the base of a huge waterfall, where you can swim and cool off ($50).

The **Tucán Valley Tour** (645-5479; $25) takes you past local farms and forests.

EDUCATION, ART, AND MUSIC IN MONTEVERDE   The **Monteverde Institute** (645-5053; www.mvinstitute.org, e-mail: mvi@mvinstitute.org) offers courses in tropical biology and conservation, sustainable development, political economy, sustainable design, public health, Spanish, and Costa Rican culture. These courses are complemented by research and community programs. They also place volunteers in reforestation programs, reserve maintenance, and local ESL programs.

The **Monteverde Music Festival** (www.mvinstitute.org; admission $12, children free), held at the Monteverde Institute at 6 p.m. from February to April, is a wonderful chance to hear some of Costa Rica's best musicians. Concerts range from classical string quartets and brass ensembles to New Age, jazz, Afro-Caribbean, and folk groups. Don't miss it.

The Centro Panamericano de Idiomas' **language school** (645-5448; www.cpi-edu.com, e-mail: info@cpi-edu.com) is located on the road into Monteverde, just before the gas station. Staying with local families is part of the program, and volunteer work can be arranged in Monteverde or at their Heredia or Flamingo beach campuses.

Marco Tulio Brenes' **Galería Extasis** (open daily, 9 a.m. to 6 p.m.; 645-5548) is nestled in the forest down a road to your left as you enter Monteverde. Using only wood from fallen trees, this local sculptor elaborates on the work already done by insects and fungi; his pieces follow the natural form and beauty of the wood. His three-story gallery features the work of many up-and-coming Costa Rican artists.

Across from Hotel El Bosque, **Paseo de Stella** (645-5419, 645-5052) combines an **art gallery**, showcasing the latest creations of stained-glass crafter Meg Laval and other local artists, with a cozy Argentinian-style **café and chocolate shop** owned by Argentinian chef extraordinaire Susana Salas. She makes savory pies, big organic salads, and daily specials like *mole de pavo* and crepes. Downstairs is a live **bat exhibit**, managed by Chiropteran expert Dr. Richard Laval. The exhibit is an opportunity to learn about these important but misunderstood mammals. Even though bats are main pollinators and seed dispersers in the wild, they are extremely elusive and seldom seen. Bats are kept in a reversed day-night cycle to allow visitors to see them actively "going about their business."

For arts and crafts, be sure to stop by **CASEM**, a cooperative of local women who make beautiful embroidered and handpainted clothing and souvenirs portraying quetzals, golden toads, and other cloud-forest flora and fauna. It's located on the right next to the food co-op as you enter Monteverde. Across the street and down a side road, **Bromelias Books and Café** (645-6272) offers natural history books, crafts, and organic food in a tasteful atmosphere.

Just beyond the bridge to the right of the cheese factory is the **Monteverde Community Arts Center** (645-5053 ext. 112), where you can learn anything from batik to book-binding. A four-hour class costs about $40. Their **gift shop** includes jewelry, ceramics, clothing, candles, and paintings by local talent. The center also promotes environmentally friendly technology, and features a very artistic composting toilet with a stained-glass window!

Patricia Maynard's **Hummingbird Gallery** (open daily, 8 a.m. to 4:30 p.m.; 645-5030), near the entrance to Monteverde Reserve, exhibits Michael and Patricia Fogden's photographs from around the world. The Fogdens spend months at a time with sloths, frogs, snakes, insects, and birds, trying to get just the right shot. You'll never see better wildlife pho-tographs. The framed photographs are not for sale, but slides and postcards are. The gallery sells beautiful Guatemalan textiles, locally made batiks, woodcrafts, ceramics, jewelry, tapes and CDs, posters, books, T-shirts, and Sarah Dowell's excellent watercolors.

Chunches (open Monday through Saturday, 8 a.m. to 6 p.m.; 645-5147), in the village of Santa Elena, could be the best-stocked bookstore in rural Costa Rica, with a great selection of literature in Spanish and English for children and adults, naturalist books, art, international newspapers and magazines, educational games, office supplies, and very useful topographi-cal maps. It's also a **laundromat** ($5/load, washed and dried) and serves espresso, popcorn, and fresh-squeezed orange juice.

The **Centro de Educación Creativa** (phone/fax: 645-5161; www.cloudforestschool.org) is a bilingual school whose main focus is en-vironmental education. Children maintain organic gardens, a recycling cen-ter, compost bins, a native tree nursery and a trail system, and study in the rainforest itself. With more than half the students on scholarship, the school welcomes volunteers and stateside collaborators.

You can learn a lot about Monteverde online at **www.monteverdeinfo. com**, run by the owner of the Pensión Santa Elena. He will also help you make reservations and travel arrangements.

CHEESE AND COFFEE The famous **Monteverde Cheese Factory** (open Monday through Saturday, 7:30 a.m. to 4 p.m.; Sunday, 7 a.m. to noon) sells cheddar, jack, gouda, and other cheeses. You can also buy ice cream, fresh milk, and *cajeta* (delicious milk fudge) there. An observation room off the store allows you to watch the workers as they go about mak-ing cheese in the factory's huge vats.

The **Monteverde Cheese Tour** (645-7090; www.crstudytours.com; adults $8, students $6) lets you learn about the cheese-making process, from when the milk is brought to the cheese factory to the formation of the different varieties of the famous Queso Monteverde. Meanwhile, you will learn about the history of the Quaker settlers who started the cheese plant, and how it evolved into a cooperative that benefits the entire community. You will also see how the protein-rich residuals from the process are used to feed pigs instead of being poured into the river as they used to be. This inexpensive and entertaining tour is given at 9 a.m. and 2 p.m. every day except Sunday at the cheese plant.

The **Monteverde Coffee Tour** (645-7090; www.crstudytours.com; adults $15, students $12) starts at the coffee roaster at **Café Monteverde**, next to the food coop. From there you travel to the San Luis Valley while learning about the history of the area. In San Luis you tour **Finca La Bella**, where 24 families cultivate coffee. Here you will learn about the role of agriculture in Monteverde's development, and how Fair Trade coffee benefits local farmers. You'll see the whole coffee process from bush to cup. The tour ends with coffee tasting. The tour is given daily at 8 a.m. and 1 p.m.

INTERNET ACCESS   Many hotels offer internet access for guests. The Hotel Camino Verde on Santa Elena's main street has computers for rent, as does the wilder Pensión Santa Elena. **Tranquilo Communications** (open daily, 10 a.m. to 8 p.m.; 645-6782), 100 meters before the supermarket at the entrance to town, has ten computers in a laidback setting, decorated by the artwork of local artist and community leader, Patricia Jiménez.

HOTELS AND RESTAURANTS

The Monteverde area is made up of several small communities. **Santa Elena**, the bustling commercial and transportation center of the area, is the first town you come to on the road from the Interamerican Highway. Most of the budget accommodations are here, but some nice, quiet hotels are as well, like the upscale Monteverde Lodge and the helpful, affordable Arco Iris. North of Santa Elena, in the communities of **Cañitas** and **San Gerardo**, there are inexpensive rural lodgings, like Miramontes, Mirador San Gerardo, and Eco-Verde Lodge. South of Santa Elena on the four-kilometer road to Monteverde is the community of **Cerro Plano**, where most of the hotels are located. There are only six hotels in the community of Monteverde itself. There are accommodations in each area for all budgets. At the lowest end, campers can pitch their tents at La Colina Lodge (www.lacolina lodge.com) and use their facilities for $5. If you're tempted to do this, be aware that temperatures are low and wind and precipitation are high most of the year. *Note:* Christmas and Easter are booked months in advance.

NEAR GUACIMAL   Before you get to Santa Elena, near the village of Guacimal in a climate that is lower and thus somewhat drier and sunnier than Monteverde's, is **El Sol** (private bath, hot water, bathtubs, kitchens, pool, sauna; $70-$100; 645-5838; fax: 645-5042; www.elsolnuestro.com, e-mail: imoinoc@racsa.co.cr). It is the project of Elizabeth, an artist and healer from Germany, her husband and chef Ignacio from Spain, and their charming teenage son Javier. Their two cabins are built of local teak with great attention to detail and wonderful views of the hills from their private porches. The larger one sleeps five. Ignacio cooks in Mediterranean, Central American and German style with plenty of options for vegetarians. Guests can come for the day to enjoy their wood-heated sauna, a swim in their lovely pool, an energy bodywork session, and a hike, or take a more adventurous trip to a waterfall. Javier enjoys entertaining kids.

SANTA ELENA   Many of the *pensiones* here will cook for you and make you box lunches, or you can eat at **Morpho's Cafe** (open daily, 9 a.m. to 9:30 p.m.; 645-5607), upstairs across from the supermarket, where freshly squeezed fruit and vegetable juices and gourmet coffees complement an extensive menu. They are known for their gringo-style hamburgers with all the fixings. They sometimes show sports events and movies. If you just want a snack, stop at **Chunches** around the corner from the bus stop. **El Marquéz** (open Monday through Saturday, noon to 10 p.m.; 645-5918) across from the bank serves fresh seafood, *bueno y barato*.

The main landmark in Santa Elena is the **Banco Nacional** (National Bank), where you can change money or cash traveler's checks (bring your passport). Directions are given from there. All the hotels below arrange transportation to La Fortuna.

The locally owned **Camino Verde** (shared bath, heated water, $5/person; private bath, $8-$10/person; communal kitchen; phone/fax: 645-5916; www.monteverdeinfocenter.com, e-mail reservations@monteverdeinfo center.com), across from the bus stop, is a clean, no-nonsense hotel with many small rooms off a central corridor. They provide internet access, laundry service, and change dollars daily from 6 a.m. to 9 p.m.

Three hundred meters uphill from the Banco Nacional are two sets of cabins owned by brothers. Spiffy **Cabinas Don Taco** (private bath, heated water; $20-$30, including breakfast; 645-5263, fax: 645-5985; www.cabinas dontaco.com, e-mail: cab_don_taco@racsa.co.cr) has views of the Gulf of Nicoya from both the breakfast room and the new individual cabins. Don Taco originated the "rapid-transit" system from Monteverde to La Fortuna (see "Getting There," below). **Cabinas Marín** (heated water; shared bath, $7-$12; private bath, $12-$20, including breakfast; 645-5279) are clean rooms behind the family's house.

Back in town, **Pensión Santa Elena** (shared bath, shared rooms, $5/person; private bath, heated water, $7-$15/person; suite for six, $40; community kitchen; 645-5051, fax: 645-6060; www.monteverdeinfo.com/pension.htm, e-mail: pension@monteverdeinfo.com) is a maelstrom of activity, presided over by its garrulous French-Canadian owner, Jacques Bertrand, who has a wealth of information about the area. He changes traveler's checks and offers inexpensive internet access, international phone and fax service, and laundry service ($2). Some rooms are near the street, others are in back of the garden. His wife rents "Sabine's Smiling Horses." They are the headquarters for the Interbus shuttle service.

Pensión El Tucán (heated water; shared or private bath; $15-$20; 645-5017, fax: 645-5017), 100 meters south of the Banco Nacional, has pleasant rooms above a very clean **soda** featuring delicious fruit smoothies and native food.

Up a side street to the left, on a grassy hillside, is **Arco Iris Eco-Lodge** (private bath, hot water; $50-$70; bunk beds, $30-$40; 645-5067, fax: 645-5022; www.arcoirislodge.com, e-mail: arcoiris@racsa.co.cr), a circle of private cabins set in beautifully landscaped grounds. You can birdwatch right on the property from nature trails near a small creek. Internet access and international phone and fax service are also offered, as well as same-day laundry service. Guests were raving about their German breakfast buffet. Recommended. A three-minute walk from downtown Santa Elena toward Monteverde.

On the same side street, **Pensión Colibrí** (private and shared baths; $5-$12/person; 645-5682), run by an accommodating local family, serves great breakfasts.

Monteverde Lodge (hot water, bathtubs; $150-$160; 645-5126, fax: 257-1665; www.costaricaexpeditions.com) is located on a road to the right at the entrance to Santa Elena. The lodge, built especially to accommodate tour groups from Costa Rica Expeditions, is spacious, beautifully designed, and comfortable. It features an indoor atrium with a large jacuzzi. The grounds include a botanical garden with charming rock pathways and benches to relax on and take in the view. A multimedia slide show incorporating sounds of the rainforest is shown several times a week ($5). A trail from the grounds leads, in about 15 minutes, to the **Finca Ecológica** (645-5554; adults $7, students $5; night tour, $14 including guide), which features guided nature walks and twilight hikes to spot nocturnal wildlife.

Just before you get to Santa Elena, going left after the toll booth, is a growing neighborhood with several hotels. **Tina's Casitas** (shared bath, $10-$15; private bath, hot water, $20-$40; house, $40-$50; 645-5641, 645-5648; www.tinascasitas.de, e-mail: tinas_casitas@hotmail.com) are rooms around a stone patio with an open-air communal kitchen. There is a view of the Gulf of Nicoya on clear days and of the Monteverde mountains. Tina has a reforestation project that plants trees that supply food for the bell bird. She needs volunteers from May to September. Down the street is the lovely **Hotel Claro de Luna** (private bath, hot water; $40-$60, including breakfast; phone/fax: 645-5269; e-mail: clarodelunamv@hotmail.com), with charming chalet-style architecture and a very attractive breakfast area with a distant view of the Gulf.

Farther along on this street are two budget options: **Cabinas Kelly** (shared bath, $5/person; private bath, $10/person; 645-6104, 645-5933) and **Cabinas Sol y Luna** (shared bath, $5/person; private bath, $10/person; 645-5629), each with clean, spacious rooms.

SAN GERARDO AND CAÑITAS **Cabanas Capulin** (private bath, hot water, kitchen; $30-$40; 645-5285) are on a hill overlooking the Gulf of Nicoya, 400 meters north of the soccer field in Santa Elena on the way to the SkyTrek. The cabins are on the diary farm of the hospitable Torres Leiton family. Their son Jose Manuel is a licensed nature guide.

One and a half kilometers above Santa Elena, on the way to the Sky-walk and Santa Elena Forest Reserve, **Sunset Hotel** (private bath, hot water; $30-$40, including breakfast; 645-5048, phone/fax 645-5228) is nicely landscaped and has fantastic views of the Gulf of Nicoya. There are bird-watching trails on their 35-acre reserve. The beautiful, glassed-in restaurant serves moderately priced dinners to non-guests (who must make reservations). Some readers really enjoyed their stay here.

About six kilometers farther down this beautiful but bumpy road, three kilometers beyond the SkyWalk, is the turnoff to **Hotel Vista Verde** (private bath, hot water, restaurant; $70-$100; 380-1517, 200-5225, fax: 645-6178; www.vistaverdelodge.com, e-mail: vistaverde@racsa.co.cr), with an incredible view of Arenal Lake and Volcano from each room (if the weather is clear) and a nearby waterfall with swimming hole on their private reserve. You should have four-wheel drive to get to these two places.

In Cañitas, on the road to Tilarán, **Miramontes** (private bath, hot water; $40-$70, including breakfast; 645-5152, fax: 645-5297; www.swisshotel miramontes.com, e-mail: miramont@racsa.co.cr) has a fine restaurant (open 1 p.m. to 8:30 p.m.) serving Swiss, French, Italian, and Costa Rican specialties and homemade strudel. Their wood-paneled rooms are comfortable and reasonably priced.

Nestled in a private cloud forest reserve six kilometers from Santa Elena, **Albergue Eco-verde** (shared or private bath, hot water; $30-$40; 645-5948, fax: 645-6396; www.turismoruralcr.com, e-mail: cooprena@ racsa.co.cr) is a project initiated by a local campesino association. Quetzals frequent the old-growth forest around the lodge, and trails lead to *miradores* where you can see Volcán Arenal. Accommodations are rustic and country cooking is served in their restaurant. You need four-wheel drive to get here, or take a taxi from Santa Elena. Call for directions—getting there is not a simple process.

CERRO PLANO   Along the winding road between Santa Elena and Monteverde Cloud Forest Biological Reserve are most of the area's hotels. There is usually enough friendly traffic to try hitching, at least part of the way. Taxi service from this area to the Monteverde reserve costs about $6 and can be worth it if you want to conserve your energy for hiking, or you can take the bus (see "Monteverde Cloud Forest Biological Reserve," above).

About a kilometer off the road, nestled in a hilly forest, is the **Cloud Forest Lodge** (private bath, hot water; $70-$80; 645-5058, fax: 645-5168; www.cloudforestlodge.com, e-mail: info@cloudforestlodge.com). Its reserve is where the Original Canopy Tour takes place; lodge guests receive a discount. There is plenty of good hiking right around the lodge. Look for the turnoff on the left, almost one kilometer outside Santa Elena. The lodge has a stunning view of the Gulf of Nicoya and beautiful old-growth forest.

With large, comfortable rooms featuring either sunset-view terraces or fireplaces, **El Sapo Dorado** (private bath, hot water; $100-$120; 645-5010, fax: 645-5180; www.sapodorado.com, e-mail: elsapo@racsa.co.cr) is one of the area's finest hotels. Their Fountain Suites have a separate bedroom for families. A five-kilometer self-guided nature trail behind the hotel circles through a private cloud forest reserve. Their gourmet restaurant, open to the public, serves generous helpings of fantastic food and sinful desserts in an elegant setting, with excellent service. The carefully prepared cuisine is low in fat, sugar, and salt, and covers all tastes, from steak to vegetarian dishes to pizza for the kids. There is internet service for guests. Recommended.

Along the main road as you approach the community of Cerro Plano is **Johnny's Pizzería** (open daily, 11:30 a.m. to 9:30 p.m.; 645-5066). Johnny's offers a salad bar and crispy, wood stove–baked pizzas, with some ingredients coming from the backyard vegetable garden.

On the street that leads to the Monteverde Butterfly Garden, **Restaurant Sofia** (open daily, 11:30 a.m. to 9:30 p.m.; 645-7017) is livening up the Monteverde cuisine scene with *nuevo Latino* recipes like roasted plantain and sweet potato soup, plantain-crusted sea bass, beef tenderloin with roasted red pepper and cashew sauce, shrimp with green mango, and seafood chimichangas. Their bar serves creative cocktails like mango-ginger *mojitos*. The restaurant is located before DeLucia as you go down to the Ecological Farm. Sofia's has been highly recommended by locals. Next door, **Heladería Sabores** (open daily, noon to 9 p.m., Sunday 1:30 p.m. to 9 p.m.; 645-6174) serves 11 flavors of locally made ice cream.

Down the same street, the **Restaurant De Lucía** (open daily, 11 a.m. to 9 p.m.; 645-5337) serves light lunches; dinner specialties are steak and fish filets, which are displayed raw so you can see how fresh they are—you pick the one you want. Their delicious hors d'oeuvres feature freshly made tortillas, salsa, and guacamole. **De Lucia Inn** (private bath, hot water; $50-$60, including breakfast; 654-5976, fax: 645-5537; www.costa-rica-monte verde.com, e-mail: delucia@racsa.co.cr) has comfortable rooms across the street from the restaurant, within easy walking distance of the Monteverde Butterfly Garden, Aerial Adventures, and the Ecological Farm. Two of the rooms are wheelchair accessible.

The nearby **Nidia Lodge** (private bath, hot water, bathtubs; $60-$70; 645-6082; www.flormonteverde.com, e-mail: flormonteverde@racsa.co.cr) is owned by local naturalist guide Eduardo Venegas and his family. The quiet, comfortable wooden rooms have garden views, and the restaurant serves seafood and *comida típica.* Eduardo can take you anywhere you want to go.

The **Flor de Vida** (open daily, 7 a.m. to 9 p.m.; 645-6081) on the main road serves good, healthy vegetarian food in a nice atmosphere.

About 100 meters farther along the main road, you'll find a road to the right, which leads to two of the most basic and inexpensive hotels near Monteverde. **Manakin Bed and Breakfast** (shared or private bath, heated water; $10-$30/person; phone/fax: 645-5080, fax: 645-5517; e-mail: mana kin@racsa.co.cr) offers clean rooms and private cabins, some with kitchens. We have heard good reports about the filling breakfasts served there. Next door is **Pensión El Pino** (shared or private bath, heated water, laundry sink; $10-$20/person; phone/fax: 645-5130), a small rooming house next to the owners' home. Meals are served on request. For $1 extra they will take you to the Monteverde reserve.

The beautifully landscaped **Hotel de Montaña Monteverde** (private bath, hot water; $70-$120; 645-5046, fax: 645-5320; www.monteverde mountainhotel.com, e-mail: info@monteverdemountainhotel.com) has a sauna and jacuzzi overlooking the Gulf of Nicoya, a restaurant, some homey wooden cabins with forest views, other rooms with Gulf views (their newest deluxe rooms have two-person bathtubs), and a private re-serve with nature trails.

On the left is the entrance to **Cabañas Los Pinos** (private bath, hot wa-ter, kitchen; one bedroom, $30-$40; two bedrooms, $40-$60; three bed-rooms, $70-$90; 645-5252, phone/fax: 645-5005; www.lospinos.net, e-mail: info@lospinos.net), offering cabins in a peaceful setting—a good value. The kitchens and separate bedrooms make them great for families.

The **Belmar** (private bath, hot water; $80-$100; 645-5201, fax: 645-5135; www.hotelbelmar.com, e-mail info@hotelbelmar.com) has beautiful views, comfortable rooms, and a good restaurant. Its entrance is uphill from the gas station on the left. They offer a package deal including the famous Calypso Tour from Puntarenas.

Albergue Bellbird (shared bath, $8; private bath, $10/person; 645-5518, phone/fax: 645-5026) caters to student groups with prices as low as $22/day, including breakfast. They are on the left near the language institute.

As the main road drops into a valley, you'll find the **Bar La Cascada** (open daily, 6 p.m. to 1 a.m.), with a nice view, lots of wood and windows, and moderate prices. It is the area's only disco; they often have live bands.

At this point, you still have not arrived in the community of Monteverde, and when you do you might not realize it because Monteverde is not what we usually think of as a town. Most houses are back in the woods where you don't see them, and are connected by footpaths. Monteverde residents are more likely to be receptive to tourism if their privacy is respected, so please pay attention to gates, fences, and posted signs.

MONTEVERDE   On the right as you enter Monteverde, **El Bosque Lodge** (private bath, hot water; $30-$40, including breakfast; 645-5158, 645-5221, phone/fax: 645-5129; www.monteverdecostarica-info, e-mail: bosquelodge@racsa.co.cr) is a bargain in its price range. Rooms are clean and comfortable, set in a quiet garden behind the reception building. **Restaurant Tramonti** (645-6120) next door specializes in pizza, pasta, and salads with authentic Italian flavor.

A few meters down the road are three cooperatively owned businesses: the well-stocked **Food Co-op**, a **coffee co-op**, and **CASEM**, the crafts cooperative. Also here is **Stella's** (open daily, 6 a.m. to 6 p.m; www.stellas bakery.com), a bakery/coffee shop full of delicacies we are not used to finding in Costa Rica: apple pie, brownies, strudel. Fresh, organic produce from the greenhouses out back appears in their salads, and you can construct your own sandwich.

Moon Shiva (open daily, 10 a.m. to 10 p.m.), 50 meters down a side street from Stella's, beneath Bromelias Art Gallery, has a nice atmosphere, good food, live music on weekends, and movies twice a week.

Out on the road again, you'll see the cheese plant up ahead, marked by a sign with a big silver cow's head between two mountains. To the left is the **Monteverde Institute**. The road turns right and crosses a bridge. On the other side of the bridge is the **Community Art Center** and gift shop.

The road turns right again, leading to **La Colina Lodge** (hot water; shared bath, $30-$40; private bath, $40-$50; full breakfast included; 645-5009, phone/fax: 645-5580; www.lacolinalodge.com, e-mail: lacolina@ hotmail.com). This is the remodeled Flor-Mar, one of the first lodges in

Monteverde, now more open, yet welcoming, with a fireplace downstairs and comfortable rooms upstairs, some with balconies. The managers, a knowledgeable Spanish ornithologist and his wife, will help you arrange all your Monteverde activities and, with prior notice, will prepare Mediterranean meals for guests, specializing in Lebanese and Moroccan cuisine. Camping is $5/person. Recommended.

A few hundred meters up the hill toward the reserve is the **Hotel Fonda Vela** (private bath, hot water; $90-$110; 257-1413, 645-5125, fax: 645-5119; www.fondavela.com, e-mail: fondavel@racsa.co.cr), which has lovely large rooms, some with views and balconies, a **restaurant** with a large, dramatic design and huge windows, and a cozier dining room with a fireplace.

Situated across the road is the simple **Hospedaje Mariposa** (private bath, heated water; $30-$40, including breakfast; 645-5013; e-mail: rafa vargas@costarricense.com), a good value for its close proximity to the Monteverde reserve.

The **Trapp Family Lodge** (private bath, hot water; $70-$80; 645-5858, fax: 645-5990; www.trappfam.com, e-mail: trappfam@racsa.co.cr) is only a 15-minute hike from the reserve. Its spacious wooden rooms with balconies have views of the treetops. It's probably best to have a car to stay here.

All of the above hotels will bag breakfasts and lunches for birders and hikers, and prepare vegetarian meals on request. Laundry services, horse rentals, transportation to the preserve, and tours to nearby points of interest are also available through the hotels. See Monteverde Cloud Forest Biological Reserve section above for information on staying in or volunteering at the reserve.

SAN LUIS   Only 45 minutes by horseback or car from all the attractions in the Monteverde area, the **San Luis Ecolodge and Research Station** (645-8049, 645-8051, fax: 645-8050; www.ecolodgesanluis.com, e-mail: reservations@ecolodgesanluis.com) is a working farm and biological reserve in the scenic San Luis Valley. Guided hikes, hands-on laboratory and field activities, reforestation, birdwatching, and fiestas with the San Luis community are some of the activities you can get involved with here. Three types of lodging are offered: a dorm-style converted milking barn (shared bath, hot water; $50-$60/person); bungalows (private bath, hot water; $60-$70/person); and lovely secluded rooms ($80-$90/person) about a kilometer from the main lodge, with balconies overlooking the forest and valley and the sound of a rushing stream in the background. Well-qualified volunteers can earn room and board as naturalist guides (five-month minimum); interns pay $450/month (three-month minimum). All rates include meals and activities. Children 7 to 12 pay $30, under 7 free. Recommended.

Homestays are possible at **Finca La Bella** ($10-$15; 645-5053; www.mvinstitute.org, e-mail: jcriado@mvinstitute.org), a 49-hectare community farm in the San Luis Valley. Visitors can stay from a couple of days to a couple of months with welcoming local families, milking goats, picking coffee (December and January), and helping in the schools or on the farm. You can also tour the area for a day. Recommended.

GETTING THERE: By Public Bus: Direct buses leave the Terminal Atlántico Nortel in San José (Calle 14, Avenida 9; 222-3854; $5) every day at 6:30 a.m. and 2:30 p.m., leaving Monteverde for the return trip at these same hours. Buy tickets in advance. You will get to Santa Elena before you get to Monteverde, so if you aren't staying in Santa Elena, just stay on the bus and ask the driver to let you off at your hotel. The bus does not go beyond the Cheese Factory, so if you are staying at La Colina, Fonda Vela, Mariposa, Trapp Family Lodge, or the Monteverde Cloud Forest Biological Reserve, make arrangements to be picked up. Beware of theft on this bus, especially on the way up. Make sure your large luggage gets safely into the luggage compartment underneath the bus and keep valuables with you at all times. We have heard many stories of someone who poses as a bus employee, and tells vulnerable-looking tourists that they may not keep their backpacks with them, but must store them in another place. Later their backpacks are gone. This said, we have ridden this bus many, many times and have never had any problems. The warning is to keep you alert, not to discourage you from taking this most economical way of reaching Monteverde. This bus is full of interesting people, and often the four- to five-hour trip passes very quickly if you get into a good conversation. The last time we took this bus it broke down and we chose to pay for a taxi to San José instead of waiting for it to be fixed.

Note: Seats on the Monteverde–San José bus are reserved. You can get on a nearly empty San José–bound bus at the Cheese Factory without a ticket, but you will have to get off and purchase one when the bus arrives at the Santa Elena bus station. If there are a lot of people that have already bought tickets ahead of you, you may end up without a seat—not a pleasant experience.

A daily bus from Puntarenas to Santa Elena leaves Puntarenas (bus stop on the oceanfront, one block from the San José–Puntarenas terminal) at 2:15 p.m., turns off the Interamerican Highway at Río Lagarto around 3:30 p.m., and arrives in Santa Elena around 5:30 p.m. If you are coming from the north, any San José–bound bus will let you off at Lagarto, where Monteverde-bound buses pass around 3:30 p.m. and 5:30 p.m. It's also pretty easy to hitchhike from Lagarto. If you are coming from Manuel Antonio, take the 10:30 a.m. Quepos–Puntarenas bus to connect with the Puntarenas–Santa Elena bus. The bus returns from Santa Elena at 6 a.m.

If you are coming from the Arenal area, you can catch an 8 a.m. bus in La Fortuna to Tilarán (3 hours). Eat lunch in Tilarán and then catch the bus for Santa

Elena at 12:30 p.m. (2 hours; $2). To do this in the opposite direction, catch a bus at the Cheese Factory for Tilarán at 7 a.m., then get on the Tilarán–San Carlos bus at 12:30 p.m. (it passes through La Fortuna).

Check bus schedules at www.monteverdeinfo.com or www.monteverdetours. com; make reservations through your hotel.

By Private Bus or Taxi: As you can tell from the above description, getting to Monteverde on public buses can be done, but if you're not sure of your Spanish or have a limited time frame, you are not going to want to get involved in the intricacies of busmanship. You might want to consider spending $20 to $40/person to take one of the private bus or taxi services to Monteverde. Most of them have family or group rates: Turiverde (645-5568; www.monteverdeinfocenter.com), Pension Santa Elena (645-5051; www.monteverdeinfo.com), or Interbus (283-5573; www.interbusonline.com). Many hotels offer special transportation deals, too. For instance, Hotel Sapo Dorado offers Land Rover or van transport from Monteverde to many beach destinations.

By Taxi, Boat, and Jeep: Don Taco (645-5263, 645-5985, 812-4780) will pick you up at your La Fortuna hotel, take you on a 25-minute boat ride across Lake Arenal, then take you in his jeep for a bumpy two-hour drive uphill to Monteverde (and vice versa). He leaves Monteverde daily. This is the fastest way to get to or from Volcán Arenal ($25/person). Mirador San Gerardo (645-5087, 381-7277) also performs this service, as do several tour agencies in La Fortuna and Monteverde.

By Car: Most people turn off the Interamerican Highway at Río Lagarto, about a half-hour north of the Puntarenas turnoff, but the Sardinal turnoff, about 15 minutes farther south on the Interamerican, has been paved until Guacimal, so it's the current route of choice. Go uphill from Sardinal or Lagarto for one and a half to two hours. **Base Tres** is a friendly bar at Lagarto where you can stop for a drink or a snack before you start up. If you are going directly to San Luís and don't want to stop in Monteverde, turn right at the covered bus stop about 12 kilometers before you reach Monteverde, and descend into the San Luis Valley.

If you have four-wheel drive, you can travel by car from Tilarán to Monteverde by way of Quebrada Grande, San Rafael, Cabeceras, and Santa Elena. During the rainy season, the Tilarán–Santa Elena bus can make it through when cars can't. The trip takes two hours. Check with your hotel on the best route to take before setting out.

TEN

Guanacaste Province

Guanacaste was a separate province of Spain's Central American empire until 1787, when it was given to Nicaragua. In 1812, Spain made Guanacaste part of Costa Rica so Costa Rica would be large enough to be represented in the colonial government, which ruled from Guatemala. After independence, both Costa Rica and Nicaragua claimed Guanacaste. *Guanacastecos* were divided, too. Liberians, whose founders were Nicaraguan cattle farmers, wanted to join Nicaragua. Nicoyans were in favor of joining Costa Rica. Nicoya won in a vote, and an 1858 treaty declared Guanacaste part of Costa Rica. Costa Ricans celebrate annexation of Guanacaste on July 25.

Guanacaste's long period of autonomy, sizeable indigenous population, and geographic isolation from the Meseta Central have contributed to make it a unique province in Costa Rica. Many "Costa Rican" traditions originated here. The people, dark-skinned descendants of the Chorotega Indians, are possibly closer to their cultural and historical roots than are other Costa Ricans, and there is a special campesino richness in their friendly manner.

Most of Guanacaste has been converted into pastureland for beef production. The deforestation of the region has altered its climate and ecosystems, causing occasional droughts. But Guanacaste is beautiful nonetheless. Brahma bulls lounge under the graceful, spreading shade trees that gave the province its name. The brilliant yellow blossoms of the *corteza amarilla* dot the plains in February, and in March the light red blossoms of the *carao* (carob tree) brighten the landscape. The waters of Guanacaste's beaches are clear and gentle, and the dry climate helps keep mosquitos to a minimum.

We enjoy Guanacaste more in the rainy season, when its trees still have their leaves, and a pale green tints the savannas. It is clean and lush then, like the rest of Costa Rica. It doesn't usually rain a lot in Guanacaste until September or October, and often there is just an hour of rain late in the day.

When you stop for *refrescos*, be sure to try some typical Guanacastecan grain-based beverages: *horchata* (rice), *resbaladera* (barley), and *pinolillo* (roasted corn) are all sweet, milky drinks. *Tamarindo* is made from the sticky fruit found in the pod of the tamarind tree. If you're prone to iron deficiency, buy a bottle of *miel de carao*, the iron-rich syrup made from the carao tree's pods. It doesn't taste too good, but it's very effective.

LAS JUNTAS DE ABANGARES

Las Juntas de Abangares, the old gold-mining capital, is a historic part of Costa Rica that is just beginning to open up to tourism. From 1884 to 1931, its mines attracted workers and gold seekers from all over the world. Now it is a quiet town in the foothills of the Tilaran range, a nice place to get a sense of rural Costa Rican life. Also, unlike most of Guanacaste, it is mountainous, with a cool climate.

The **Eco Museo** (closed Monday; 662-1340; admission $2) has trails through tropical dry forest to the top of an old gold mine built into the beautiful Río Abangares. The old mine structure bears a striking resemblance to a Mayan ruin rising out of the forest. To get there, turn right at the **Monumento a los Mineros** in front of the historic **Caballo Blanco Cantina** in Las Juntas, which has a good collection of turn-of-the-20th-century artifacts, and marks the road to Monteverde. Go four kilometers to a fork in the road, where there is a sign. The entrance is three kilometers to the right. It is a nice, shady walk from town. Taxis (about $3.50) and horses can also be hired in Las Juntas.

LODGING AND RESTAURANTS   The best place to eat in Las Juntas is **Los Mangos**, across from the church—though it lacks *ambiente*. **La Golo-sina**, around the corner from the Caballo Blanco, is a good and inexpensive *soda*. Locals have recommended **Restaurant Hi Lam Mung** for Chinese food. There are two inexpensive, clean places to stay in Las Juntas: **Cabinas El Encanto** (private bath, cold water, ceiling fan, guarded parking; $7-$12; 662-1016) are nicely decorated. They are on the road to Monteverde, 50 meters after the Monumento a los Mineros. **Cabinas El Cayuco** (private bath, cold water, ceiling fan, pool, restaurant, guarded parking; $12-

$20; 662-0868) are plainer but still a good value. They are 50 meters to the left of the Monumento a los Mineros as you are leaving town.

GETTING THERE: By Bus: Las Juntas is about three hours (145 kilometers) from San José. Direct buses leave at 10:45 a.m. and 5:10 p.m. from Calle 12, Avenidas 7/9 in San José ($2; 256-8598). If you're going by car, the turnoff is clearly marked on the Interamerican Highway. Las Juntas is only an hour from Puntarenas and 30 minutes from Cañas, so you could make it your base for exploring this area.

A bus leaves the cheese plant in Monteverde every morning at 5:30 a.m. It goes through Santa Elena, arriving in Las Juntas at 7:15 and at the Interamerican Highway at 7:30. There you can hail a bus going north to Liberia or to the Nicaraguan border, hail one going south to San José, or stay on the bus and get to Puntarenas at 8:30 a.m. The return bus leaves from Puntarenas at 1 p.m., arriving in Las Juntas around 3 p.m. and in Monteverde at 5 p.m. From Guanacaste, get off the Interamerican Highway at the Las Juntas turnoff (named "la Irma" after a restaurant there) and take a taxi ($3) into town.

By Car: From San José or Liberia, get off the Interamerican Highway at the well-marked Las Juntas sign. If you are coming from Monteverde, it is better to use the Lagartos exit. Even though there is a road between Monteverde and Las Juntas, it is not as well-maintained as the Lagartos road. The bus makes it, but it can be hard for cars.

CAÑAS AND RÍO COROBICÍ

Cañas is a busy, hot town where you might stay en route to somewhere else. If you're en route to Guanacaste, it is more pleasant and cheaper to stay in Las Juntas (see above). Fifty meters from the Interamerican Highway (turn in at the Hotel El Corral), the **Nuevo Hotel Cañas** (private bath, hot water, ceiling fans, air conditioning, cable TV, phone; $40-$50; 669-0039; e-mail: hotelcanas@racsa.co.cr) has light-filled rooms around a swimming pool.

It's worth traveling two and a half kilometers north to the peaceful **Capazurí** (private bath, cold water, ceiling fans; $30-$40, including breakfast; phone/fax: 669-6280; e-mail: capazari@racsa.co.cr), whose name means "deer" in the indigenous Chibcha language. Rooms are simple; despite some highway noise, it has a nice family atmosphere. Be sure to ask Don Jorge, the friendly owner, about his fascinating role in the Civil War of 1948. Camping is permitted in the groves near the main house ($4/person).

Four kilometers north of Cañas on the Interamerican Highway is **Safaris Corobicí** (phone/fax: 669-6191; www.nicoya.com, e-mail: deanhouse@rmisp.com), which offers raft trips down the smooth Corobicí

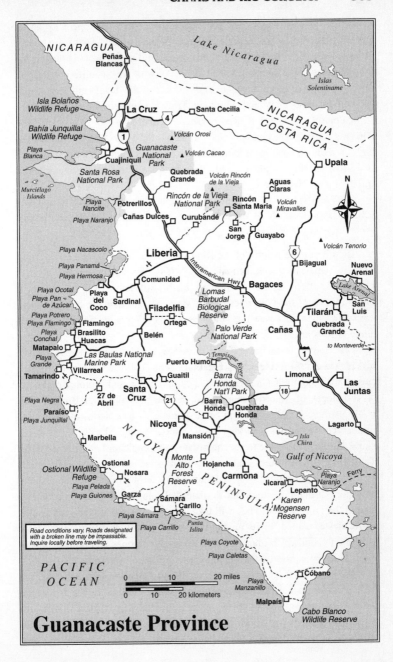

Guanacaste Province

Road conditions vary. Roads designated with a broken line may be impassable. Inquire locally before traveling.

River. Two-hour trips are $37 per person, three-hour trips are $45, and a half-day tour costs $60 (children under 14 half-price). These are scenic floats on which the guide does all the work, and are good for breaking up the monotony of a long trip to the coast. As with any wildlife observation tour, you will see more if you go early or late in the day. Bring a swimsuit, hat, camera, binoculars, and sunscreen. Trips run between 7 a.m. and 4 p.m.

Right on the Corobicí River **Rincón Corobicí** (669-1234, fax: 669-0303) is also a cool, pleasant place to stop—for a few hours or the whole day. Its Swiss-owned restaurant specializes in beef and seafood, and there is a souvenir shop, a playground, clean baths, a small campground, and a trail along the riverside.

GETTING THERE: Buses leave every two hours between 8:30 a.m. and 4:45 p.m. to Cañas ($3; Calle 16, Avenidas 3/5; 222-3006; 3.5 hours). By car, Cañas is about three hours from San José, right off the Interamerican Highway.

Three kilometers north of the Río Corobicí crossing, a road on the right heads to Upala between **Tenorio** and **Miravalles** volcanoes. We spent a memorable afternoon driving through this beautiful area. It is undeveloped, but the views of the volcanoes as you approach and then cut between them are spectacular. Just past the volcanoes, Lake Nicaragua and the Solentiname Islands are visible to the north.

The view is even better from ✿ **Albergue Heliconias** (private bath, heated water; $45, including breakfast; 466-8483; www.turismoruralcr. com, e-mail: cooprena@racsa.co.cr), a community-based ecotourism project on the slopes of Volcán Tenorio, just outside the village of Bijagua. The rainforest here is gorgeous. You can experience it on a series of suspended bridges connected by well-kept trails, similar to the SkyWalk in Monteverde. Birders flock here to see the ornate hawk eagle and many other birds. They have simple rooms and a **restaurant** specializing in *comida típica.* You can take a fairly easy one-kilometer hike through their private reserve, or a more difficult one up to the dormant volcano's crater, which becomes a lake in the rainy season. They will take you to Tenorio National Park and its **Río Celeste**, named for its unique blue color, which probably comes from volcanic minerals. A bit farther upstream are hot springs and boiling pots of mud. This trip is offered for a much higher price in La Fortuna.

Just north of Bijagua is the turnoff to **La Carolina** (shared or private bath, solar hot water; $50-$60, including meals; children under 5 free, under 12 half price; 380-1656; www.lacarolinalodge.com, e-mail: info@la carolinalodge.com), a working dairy farm/cattle ranch. The old hacienda has been converted into a guest house, where visitors enjoy down-home campesino cooking and hospitality. Hammocks are strung across the wide back veranda. One large room sleeps seven. The river below has a swimming hole and a natural jacuzzi. The horses accommodate riders of all experience levels. Hikes to hot springs, mudpots, waterfalls, and the Río Celeste are a 20-minute drive away in Tenorio National Park (admission $6).

Getting there: A few kilometers after Cañas, take the nicely paved Route 6 heading toward Upala. Drive 35 kilometers to Bijagua, and turn right at signs for Albergue Heliconias. The lodge is 2 kilometers down a dirt road from the town.

To get to La Carolina, drive about 5 kilometers north of Bijagua. You will see a sign on your right about 100 meters past Bar Mirador. Turn right and follow a gravel road to the village of San Miguel. Follow signs to the lodge, 1 kilometer from there. They provide transportation from the Liberia airport ($75). A taxi from Bijagua to the lodge costs about $12.

BAGACES AREA

Bagaces is a sunbaked town halfway between Cañas and Liberia. It is the gateway to Palo Verde National Park and the area around Volcán Miravalles.

PALO VERDE NATIONAL PARK

In addition to being a resting spot for 60 migratory and 200 native birds, such as the black-bellied whistling chick and the blue-winged teal, **Palo Verde** (admission $6) has 15 different types of habitat for mammals, amphibians, and reptiles, many of which can be observed relatively easily. During the dry season, animals stay near the few permanent springs in the area, one of which is only 100 meters from the park's administration building and campsite. There you can see peccaries, armadillos, jaguarundis, coatis, deer, and monkeys. The best observation spot for birds is in the swamp across from the OTS headquarters. The best months to go are January, February, and March.

Palo Verde is on the east side of the mouth of the **Tempisque**, Guanacaste's major river. Stretching along the banks of the river is a plain that floods during the rainy season and dries to a brown crisp in the dry season. Away from the river rise bluffs dotted with limestone cliff outcrops. The park administration is set in an old hacienda at the base of the bluffs; a couple of trails begin there and go up to lookout points.

Palo Verde became known as an important bird refuge when it was still a large cattle ranch. When it was granted park status, the cattle were removed. Over the years, vegetation formerly grazed by the cattle started to grow up and overrun the wetlands. The cattle were recognized to have become a natural part of the ecosystem and were reinstated selectively. This practice, along with other techniques, has resulted in the restoration of Palo Verde's wetlands. Cattle are also an important element in reducing fire hazards, since they eat vegetation that makes the park prone to fires. Being able to graze their cattle in the park helps local campesinos, who in turn do fire prevention work.

The **Organization for Tropical Studies** has a research station one kilometer before the park administration. Each room has a bunk bed and a reading lamp (though lamps attract insects at night). Food is plentiful and good. Arrangements must be made as far in advance as possible through OTS in San José ($50-$60/person, including food and orientation; children $20; half-day visits $15; 240-6696, fax: 240-6783; www.ots.ac.cr/eu/palo verde, e-mail: reservas@cro.ots.ac.cr). OTS can arrange transportation by taxi from Bagaces to their station.

Camping is allowed in the park, or you can stay in the park's **visitors center** (shared bath, cold water; $25, including meals). Even though there is potable water, bring water, a flashlight, and insect repellent for either facility. Make reservations in advance through the **Tempisque Conservation Area** office in Bagaces (open weekdays, 8 a.m. to 4 p.m.; 671-1062, 671-1290; e-mail: yolandar@ns.minae.go.cr), which directs all the parks and reserves in the region. The office is right on the Interamerican Highway, next to the Bagaces gas station.

GETTING THERE: Turn left at the gas station in Bagaces, north of Cañas. The park administration is 30 kilometers (one hour) from there. Signs mark the way. A taxi from Bagaces costs about $25. There is a small building at the entrance to the park, and some housing for personnel beyond it, but don't get off there because it's about eight more hot, dry kilometers to the administration building.

Palo Verde's **Isla de Pájaros**, in the Río Tempisque, is an important nesting ground for many showy waterbirds, including the roseate spoonbill, glossy ibis, anhinga, and several species of egrets and storks. One of the most pleasant and interesting ways to visit Isla de Pájaros is through Loma Larga (www.turismoruralcr.com), a community tourism experience based in the village of Bolsón, at the head of the Tempisque river. An old-fashioned cart will take you to the river, where you embark on a two-hour tour to Isla de Pájaros in a canopied boat. You can also see how village women make paper from rice and sugar cane, visit the children's greenhouse of native trees, eat delicious native food, and experience true Guanacastecan culture. Make reservations in advance at 651-8036, 651-8152, or through Simbiosis Tours (248-2538; e-mail: cooprena@racsa.co.cr).

Be aware that tour boats should remain 50 yards from the island and no one should try to startle the birds into flight because that endangers their nestlings.

GETTING THERE: You get there from the other side of Palo Verde. Instead of entering the park from Bagaces, follow the Interamerican Highway north to Liberia, turn left, and continue to Filadelfia, where you turn left again to Bolsón. You can also get there by crossing the Tempisque bridge and continuing through Nicoya and Santa Cruz to Filadelfia, where you turn right to Bolsón.

Just north of Palo Verde, **Lomas Barbudal Biological Reserve** (671-1290; e-mail: act@minae.go.cr; admission $6) has the most diverse tropical dry forest in this area as well as birds, monkeys, waterfalls you can hike to, and rivers with pools you can swim in shaded by graceful trees. Lomas Barbudal is at its best in March when the *corteza amarilla* trees are totally abloom with yellow flowers. Be careful here if you are sensitive to bees and wasps. Stop by the Tempisque Conservation Area office next to the gas station in Bagaces before heading out. Camping is allowed in the reserve, which is open only during the dry season. Bring your own food and water. Soon after passing Bagaces on the Interamerican Highway, heading north, there is a dirt road on the left for the reserve. After six kilometers on the dirt road, you'll come to the entrance. There is a picnic area near the river with bathrooms and drinking water.

LIBERIA

Liberia, the historic capital of Guanacaste's beef industry, is taking its place as the site of Costa Rica's second international airport. Most major U.S. airlines have flights to Liberia's Daniel Oduber Quirós International Airport, making it much faster and easier to reach Guanacaste's famous beaches. The city is unique in Costa Rica for its distinct colonial feel. Many of the old houses are made of adobe, the traditional building material of this hot, dry area, and have orange tile roofs, which help keep the temperature cool inside. You'll notice that some of the corner houses have a door on each side of the corner. This is known as the *puerta del sol*. The door on the east side lets in the morning sun, while the door on the south side lets in the afternoon sun. Liberia is bright and hot, so bring a hat or use your umbrella.

A small museum dedicated to the *sabaneros*, Guanacaste's cowboys, the **Casa de Cultura** (open Tuesday through Saturday, 8 a.m. to noon, 2 p.m. to 5 p.m.; 665-0135), three blocks south and one block east of the church, is also a very helpful tourist information center.

Tourists can make international phone calls at **ICE** (open weekdays, 7:30 a.m. to 5 p.m.; Saturday, 8 a.m. to noon), 50 meters south of the Banco Nacional on the right.

RESTAURANTS   **Las Tinajas**, on the main square, has pleasant outdoor tables where you can drink beer and munch *bocas* on hot Liberian afternoons. **Los Comales**, 100 meters north of the park, serves *comida típica*.

Restaurante Romanesca Jauja, two blocks toward town from the highway on the main boulevard, serves gooey Italian food in a pleasant, open-air ambiance. Seventy-five meters south of Bancredito, **El Café** (open weekdays, 10 a.m. to 6 p.m.) serves wine, French cheeses, sandwiches, and homemade tarts and *gateaux*, and runs a book exchange in air-conditioned comfort.

Pizza Pronto, one block toward town from the Casa de Cultura, has a wood-fired clay oven and a pleasant garden atmosphere. **Cafe Gourmet Morpho**, (666-8063) serves light lunches and sweets and displays local art. Not to be missed is **Café Europa** (668-1081), a German bakery and café on the left, two kilometers past the airport, near two large souvenir stores.

LODGING   There are gas stations on each corner where the main road to Liberia intersects the Interamerican Highway. (They are the surest places to get fuel on holidays.) At this intersection are **Hotel Boyeros** (private bath, hot water, air conditioning, phone, pools, conference center, restaurant open 24 hours; $40-$50; 666-0995, fax: 666-2529; www.hotelboyeros.com, e-mail: hboyeros@racsa.co.cr) and **Hotel El Bramadero** (pool; with fans, air conditioning; $40-$50; 666-0371, fax: 666-0203; www.accommodations.co.cr, e-mail: bramadero@racsa.co.cr), which has quieter rooms in the back away from the pool. **Restaurant Bar El Bramadero** serves Tico-style meats and seafood. **Hotel El Sitio** (private bath, hot water, air conditioning, pool, cable TV, gym, restaurant; $70-$80, including breakfast and airport pickup; 666-1211, fax: 666-2059; e-mail: htlsitio@racsa.co.cr) has huge concrete walls around its spacious, shady grounds, making for a peaceful environment despite its proximity to the highway. It is now part of the Best Western chain.

The **Hotel La Siesta** (private bath, cold water, air conditioning, TV, security boxes, pool, restaurant; $40-$50; 666-0678, fax: 666-2532; e-mail: hotellasiesta@hotmail.com) is clean and quiet.

The quiet neighborhood south of the central church has several good options for budget travelers in converted historical homes. All offer guarded parking. **Hotel Liberia** (private bath, cold water, fans; $12-$20; phone/fax: 666-0161; e-mail: hotelliberia@hotmail.com) has quiet rooms in the back, a souvenir shop, and a bar/restaurant, as well as internet access. It is half a block south of the church. The **Posada del Tope** (shared bath, cold water, ceiling fan, kitchen privileges, TV; $10-$20; phone/fax: 666-3876; e-mail: hottope@racsa.co.cr), one block south, is in an impressive historic building, but the rooms are not that great. Still, the owners are friendly and the price is right. **La Casona** (shared bath, cold water, ceiling fans, some air conditioning; $10-$20; 666-2971; e-mail casona@racsa. co.cr), another block and a half to the south, has nice tiled bathrooms, cable TV in the lobby, and e-mail service for guests.

Note: During the dry season, you need to make reservations for all Liberia hotels.

GETTING THERE: By Bus: Buses leave the San José Pulmitán station at Calle 24, Avenidas 5/7 ten times a day (256-9552; $2.75). Buses connect Liberia with Playa del Coco, Playa Hermosa, Puntarenas, Bagaces, Canas, La Cruz, and the Nicaraguan border. Schedules are clearly marked at the municipal bus station, five blocks north and two blocks east of the main entrance to Liberia. Pirate taxi drivers have been known to tell tourists that the posted bus schedules are wrong: always check with the bus companies.

Note: Buses from Liberia to San José may be stopped for passport checks, so bring at least a copy of your passport and make sure your visa is in order.

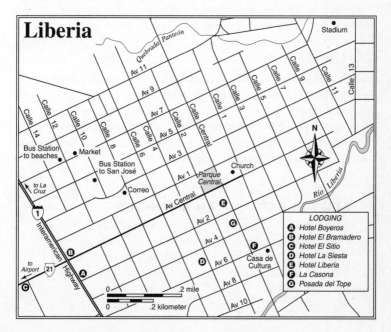

Liberia

LODGING
- **A** Hotel Boyeros
- **B** Hotel El Bramadero
- **C** Hotel El Sitio
- **D** Hotel La Siesta
- **E** Hotel Liberia
- **F** La Casona
- **G** Posada del Tope

By Car: Take the *autopista* north from San José. You can take a circular route through Liberia, Santa Cruz, and Nicoya, the gateways to the Guanacaste beaches, and come back on the Tempisque bridge. Roads are paved along that circular route, making it a two-hour trip by car from Liberia to the bridge.

By Air: SANSA flies to Liberia from San José every day ($142 roundtrip; 221-9414, 666-0017, fax: 255-2176; www.flysansa.com). Nature Air flies daily to Liberia three times a day by way of Tamarindo ($160 roundtrip; 220-3054, fax: 220-0413, in the U.S.: 800-235-9272; www.natureair.com).

Now you can fly to the Daniel Oduber Quirós International Airport just outside Liberia. The Liberia airport is only half an hour to two hours away from the beaches of Guanacaste, usually a five-hour drive from San José. As of this writing, airfares to Liberia are about $75 more expensive than to San José. Airlines with flights to Liberia are American out of Miami,·Continental from Houston, and Delta from Atlanta. Sky Service has charter flights to Liberia from Toronto and Montreal, Pace charters from Atlanta, and Northwest from Minneapolis. There are also charter flights to Liberia from Oakland, Dallas, Cleveland, Newark, and Boston. See Chapter Four for additional information about reservations and flight itineraries.

BEACHES NEAR LIBERIA

These popular beaches are good for water sports. The new, 23-platform **Witch's Rock Canopy Tour** (666-7546; e-mail: witchsrockcanopytour@ hotmail.com) is located in this area, as well as the 10-platform **Congo Trail Canopy Tour** (666-4422).

PLAYA DEL COCO   The most centrally located of the beaches near Liberia, Playa del Coco's waters are filled with small craft. The brown beach is not that great, but if you love being *near* the beach, there are some very pleasant and affordable accommodations here. (Virtually all the hotels in this area offer substantial off-season discounts.) It also has a large and involved community of international residents.

LIBERIA RENT-A-CAR AGENCIES

Alamo Rent A Car (668-1111), Elegante (668-1054), National Car Rental (666-5594), Sol (666-2222), and Toyota (666-8190) have car rental agencies in Liberia and provide transportation to and from their offices for customers. Make advance reservations in the dry season.

There is a **doctor** (380-4125, beeper: 225-2560) available 24 hours a day in Sardinal, the town before you get to Coco.

Local sailboats offer a four- to five-hour cruise, including a stop at a deserted beach for lunch and a swim, and frequent turtle and dolphin sightings. The afternoon cruises return at sunset. Snorkeling gear is included. Call Doña del Mar (383-0352), El Velero (672-1017), and Jessica Anne (672-0012).

A couple of scuba diving operations offer day and overnight trips, PADI certification, airfills, equipment sales, and boat charters for surfing or fishing trips. **Mario Vargas Expeditions** (670-0351) is located on the right as you enter town. **Deep Blue** (670-1004) has its office in the Hotel CocoVerde. **Rich Coast Diving** (670-0176; www.richcoastdiving.com) has also been recommended.

Hotel y Spaghetería Pato Loco (private bath, hot water, ceiling fans; $40-$60; 670-0145; www.costa-rica-beach-hotels-patoloco.com, e-mail: patoloco@racsa.co.cr), on the left as you enter town, is run by an Italian-Dutch couple. The food is great and very reasonably priced. Their candlelit restaurant, **L'Angoletto di Roma**, is open 6 p.m. to 9 p.m., closed Thursday. They also rent two-room apartments.

For pizza and seafood, **Señor Pizza** (open daily, 11 a.m. to 11 p.m.; 670-0532) is popular. It's on the left as you come into town. One reader gave us rave ratings about **Papagayo**, next to the bank. The Mexican-style restaurant, **Tequila**, a block and a half before the beach, and the Cajun-style **Louisiana Bar and Grill** have been recommended. **Chile Dulce** (open 12:30 p.m. to 10 p.m.; closed Tuesday; 670-0465), across from Hotel Coco Verde on the main street, serves healthy, low-fat sandwiches, salads, and natural drinks..

In the heart of the action and right on the beach are the relatively clean **Cabinas El Coco** (cold water, fans; $20-$30; with air conditioning, $30-$40; 670-0276, 670-0110, fax: 670-0167). The sound of the waves muffles the noises from the neighboring disco, but not completely. Less expensive and noisier rooms are in back. Ask for a breezier and quieter front room on the second floor. This place has been spruced up and gets our vote for the Quintessential Funky Beach Hotel and Restaurant in Playa del Coco.

Turn right (north) off the main road, about 150 meters before the beach, to reach some of Coco's quieter lodgings. In 800 meters, on the left, you'll come to the peaceful, beachfront **Vista Mar** (private bath, hot water, ceiling fans, some air conditioning, TV, pool, breakfast; $50-$60; 670-0753; www.beach-hotels-in-costa-rica.com, e-mail: hvistamar@racsa.co.cr). The

Canadian manager really takes care of her guests, and has set up hammocks in the courtyard garden. Only room #9 has an ocean view, but to be this close to the beach is rare in this area.

Soon after, on the right, you'll come to **Villa del Sol** (private bath, hot water, ceiling fan, some air conditioning, kitchens, cable TV, pool; $60-$70; $360-$450/week; in house, including breakfast, $40-$60; phone/fax, 670-0085; www.villadelsol.com, e-mail: info@villadelsol.com), attractive, light-filled rooms with kitchens for up to four guests, and smaller, well-ventilated rooms upstairs in the owner's home. The pool area is relaxed and tranquil and the beach is just a block away. The personable French-Canadian owners are very helpful and knowledgeable about the area. They also rent beach houses by the week or month. Recommended.

Back in town, **Cabinas Catarino** (private bath, cold water, fan, shared kitchen, free laundry; $10/person; 670-0156), across from Tequila, enthusiastically welcomes guests and is one of the cheapest places in town.

Overlooking Playa del Coco, about a ten-minute drive from the beach, is **Rancho Armadillo Estate** (private bath, hot water, ceiling fans, air conditioning, cable TV, gym, pool; $120-$130, including breakfast and use of kitchen; two-bedroom suites that sleep up to four, $160-$170; 670-0108, fax: 670-0441; www.ranchoarmadillo.com, e-mail: info@ranchoarmadillo.com). Guest rooms are in comfortable replicas of Guanacaste-style *casonas*. And best yet, the setting in the hills above the beach features a beautiful view and cooling breezes. The owners are avid star gazers. Guests can observe the stars while floating in the pool, or with the owners' telescopes. They have counted 56 bird species in their reserve, and have a nesting pair of laughing falcons.

GETTING THERE: By Bus: Buses leave San José (Calle 24, Avenidas 5/7; 222-1650; five-hour trip) every day at 8 a.m. and 2 p.m., returning from Playa del Coco at 8 a.m. and 2 p.m. Buses leave Liberia (222-1650) for Playa del Coco (one-hour trip) four times a day, returning one hour later.

By Car: Playa del Coco is about half an hour southwest of Liberia. Turn right at Comunidad. If you are coming from Santa Cruz, beware of some large green road signs that indicate Playa del Coco to the left by way of San Blas. Stay on the main highway to Comunidad because the San Blas road is unpaved.

Gray Line (270-2126; www.graylinecostarica.com) runs a shuttle to Coco, Ocotal, and Hermosa from San José for $25 one way. Arrangements must be made in advance through your hotel. Interbus (283-5573; www.interbusonline.com) will also take you there.

PLAYA OCOTAL   Playa Ocotal, a Blue Flag beach, is a shady cove four kilometers (a 40-minute walk or ten-minute drive) south of Playa del Coco, with a cup-shaped valley that is quickly filling up with luxury homes.

Perched high on a hill above the beach, **El Ocotal** (hot water, ceiling fans, air conditioning, phone, cable TV, refrigerator; $140-$275; children under 12 free; airport pickup in Liberia, $35; 670-0321, fax: 670-0083; www.oco talresort.com, e-mail: elocotal@racsa.co.cr) is the most elegant hotel in the area. Its beachfront pool and tennis courts make it nice for families. Couples will prefer the hilltop rooms with another two pools, outdoor jacuzzi, and stunning views. The more expensive suites have their own jacuzzis. They offer scuba-diving packages and have taken the trouble to put buoys at their dive sites to prevent damage caused by anchors. On their snorkel trips or sunset cruises, you can often see dolphins and, from December through April, pilot and humpback whales. Their four honeymoon packages include a picnic on a secluded beach and massages at Fusion Massage Natural Spa (see below). Recommended, though not recommended for people who have difficulty walking (the steep walkways have no railings).

On the way to Playa Ocotal, you'll see signs for **Villa Casa Blanca** (private bath, hot water, ceiling fans, air conditioning, pool; $90-$100, including breakfast; honeymoon suites with jacuzzis, $130-$140; condo, $160-$170; 670-0518, phone/fax: 670-0448; www.informationcostarica. com, e-mail: vcblanca@racsa.co.cr), a charmingly decorated and well-run bed and breakfast. They rent kayaks and horses, organize diving and snorkeling trips, and are very helpful. Recommended.

We've heard good things about **Fusion Massage Natural Spa** (670-0914).

GETTING THERE: You'll need to walk or take a cab to Ocotal from Playas del Coco ($4), or take the Gray Line bus (see above).

PLAYA HERMOSA With gentle waves and several beachfront hotels, Playa Hermosa, nine kilometers north of Playa del Coco, is a Blue Flag beach that offers activities for the whole family. **Bill Beard's Diving Safaris** (phone/fax: 672-0012, in the U.S.: 877-853-0538; www.diving-safaris.com, e-mail: diving@racsa.co.cr), mentioned as the #2 diving operation in the Indo-Pacific Region in *Scuba Diving Magazine,* has its headquarters here, and sets up diving and adventure packages through all the hotels in the area. They offer morning and afternoon excursions to two local dive sites every day, and offer NITROX and PADI certification courses. They are inside the Condovac complex, near the beach.

A new attraction here is one of the fastest-growing water sports in the world: **kite-boarding**, where your feet are strapped to a surfboard and you glide silently, powered by the wind, holding on to a kite 30 meters above you. You can jump up to 10 meters and land again, using the kite as a parachute. A pleasant and resourceful young Italian, Nicola Bertoldi, teaches the sport, and gives tours of the area. He also rents sea kayaks, bikes, and windsurfing, surfing, snorkeling, and fishing equipment. His inexpensive **studio apartments** in Condominiums Villa Hermosa on the main road are a very good deal (private bath, hot water, kitchenette, ceiling fans, air conditioning, pool; $20-$30; 396-4853, phone/fax: 672-0218; www.suntours andfun.com, e-mail: bertoldi@racsa.co.cr).

Down the first road on your left as you enter Playa Hermosa is **Villa del Sueño** (private bath, hot water, ceiling fans, pool; $60-$110; kids under 12 free; phone/fax: 672-0026; www.villadelsueno.com, e-mail: delsueno@ racsa.co.cr), with spacious rooms designed for good cross-ventilation. The gracious, friendly French-Canadian owners get together in the evenings and play music for guests. Their restaurant serves delicious meals at fair prices. They arrange personalized tour itineraries and airport pickups, and also run **El Oasis**, with attractive, air-conditioned one-bedroom and efficiency apartments ($130-$200; children under 12 free; weekly rates) with pool, gardens, and European balconies. Recommended.

A steep drive uphill to the left will take you to **La Finisterra** (hot water, ceiling fans, pool; $70-$80, including breakfast; phone/fax: 672-0227; www.finisterra.net, e-mail: finisterra@hotmail.com), a windy bistro (open 2 p.m. to 10 p.m.) with a great view that features a reasonably priced menu including pork medallions in apple and brandy sauce, and kebabs in tsatziki sauce. Rooms are upstairs. Call ahead to get a lift up the hill.

Right on the beach is the well-known **Hotel Playa Hermosa** (private bath, hot water, ceiling fans; $30-$40; phone/fax: 672-0046; e-mail: visani @racsa.co.cr). The screened rooms have been spruced up by the Italian owners, and the gardens surrounding the Italian restaurant are pretty.

Aquasport (672-0050) rents snorkeling gear, kayaks, windsurfers, pedal boats, beach paraphernalia, waterskiing boats, and canoes. They run snorkeling and fishing tours throughout the area. In addition to its sports facilities, Aquasport has a restaurant serving excellent seafood dinners, and a well-organized grocery store.

About 100 meters north of Aquasport on the beach is **Hotel El Velero** (private bath, hot water, ceiling fans, air conditioning, restaurant and bar, pool; $80-$90; 672-0036, phone/fax: 672-0016; www.costaricahotel.net, e-mail: elvelerocr@yahoo.com), a two-story villa with balconies, red-tiled corridors, and breezy, spacious rooms. They rent a sailboat for diving and snorkeling, and have a volleyball court. They have barbecue night once a week, with live marimba music in high season.

Ginger (open 5 p.m. to 10 p.m., closed Monday; 672-0041) serves only fun food, like appetizers and desserts. The Cordon Bleu chef and owner thinks it's more interesting that way. Their popular fish tacos are much more than a taco: seared tuna and pickled ginger on a crispy tortilla. Other menu items include grilled tenderloin skewers with oyster sauce and warm spinach salad with caramelized onions and mushrooms. For dessert, try the chocolate banana tart, served on a macadamia crust with chocolate truffle cream and custard and bananas on top. The restaurant is located 200 meters south of Condovac.

PLAYA PANAMÁ Playa Panamá, with usually gentle waters and tide-pools full of sea urchins, used to be the end of the road, the best place for camping and being alone. However, for more than 20 years the Costa Rican Tourism Institute, which owns the property, has been plotting to create a fun-in-the-sun resort area, the Golfo Papagayo Project.

Unfortunately, this region, covered in tropical dry forest, presents a grey, leafless landscape in the dry season, making the Guanacaste sun seem even hotter than it is. A little farther south and a little farther north, the landscape is greener and less forbidding. A whole lot of watering will have to be done to make this area as attractive as its southern neighbors, and water has always been scarce in Guanacaste.

If you go sailing, windsurfing, or use Hobie cats in this area or anywhere in Guanacaste, be aware that it can suddenly become extremely windy, especially after noon. We've heard comments from readers who have gotten into dangerous situations because they were not warned about this.

The several megaprojects in Papagayo are "all-inclusive"—meals, transportation, and services are put together into one package. Tourists are flown in to Líberia, bused to their resort, fed there, and bused out to various tours until it is time to get on the plane again. It's the perfect hygienic vacation, without the messiness of being in a "foreign country." You can find out about Giardini de Papagayo, Costa Smeralda, El Nakuti, Fiesta Premiere Resort, and Allegro Papagayo in the glossy tour books available at North American travel agencies. But because you are reading this book, you are probably interested in lodging that does not put a strain on local water resources, so we won't go into this area any further.

GETTING THERE: By Bus: Take the Empresa Esquivel bus from Calle 12, Avenidas 5/7 (666-0042; five-hour trip) for Playas Hermosa and Panamá at 3:20 p.m., returning at 5 a.m. From Liberia ($1), there are five buses daily. Interbus (283-5573; www.interbusonline.com) and Gray Line (232-3681) will get you there for $25-$30.

By Car: Playas Hermosa and Panamá are a few minutes north of Playa del Coco. Signs indicate the turnoff to the right as you approach from Liberia. Roads are well paved until Playa Panamá. There is a gas station along the way, after you pass the turnoff for Sardinal. A taxi from San José costs about $150, from Liberia $35, from Playa del Coco to Playa Hermosa $5.

BEACHES NEAR BELÉN

Some of Costa Rica's most famous beaches are accessible from the small highway town of Belén. This area attracts sun worshipers, sportfishing enthusiasts, and surfers, and is home to increasing numbers of U.S. expatriates, who have formed colony-like communities with English-language newsletters, bilingual schools, softball teams, and stores stocked with U.S. foods.

Flamingo is the ritziest. The sand there is whiter (less volcanic) than at many other beaches. Surfers like Playas Negra, Avellana, and Grande.

The beaches at Brasilito, Potrero, and La Penca are calm and the best for children. Many sportfishing operators anchor in Flamingo and Tamarindo. Because the land near the beaches is largely deforested, naturalists do not usually enjoy this part of Guanacaste, except for turtle observation at Las Baulas National Marine Park on Playa Grande (which we don't recommend because the turtles are disappearing) and mangrove exploration in the estuary between Tamarindo and Playa Grande.

BRASILITO AND CONCHAL   Brasilito is a small town on a gray-sand beach that is no great shakes. The area is dominated by **Meliá Playa Conchal Beach and Golf Resort**, with its 308 deluxe bungalow suites, lavish baths, a par-72 golf course, expansive free-form pool, tennis courts, health club, five restaurants, four bars, casino, discotheque, and conference center for up to 600 people. This hotel is at the center of a controversy over its plans for expansion. A federation of 13 small coastal communities brought a suit against the hotel before the Central American Water Tribunal, fearing that the water needed for the hotel's new swimming pools, gardens, and condominiums will threaten their own water supply. The tribunal decided that water sources for the community must be guaranteed before further expansion can take place. Guanacaste is not the place to take long, luxurious showers on your vacation.

We often heard local residents singing the praises of **Spaghettería Il Forno** (654-4125), a reasonably priced Italian restaurant set back from the road on the right as you enter Brasilito.

Right in town is the **Hotel Brasilito** (private bath, cold water, ceiling fans; $30-$40; 654-4237, fax: 654-4247; www.brasilito.com, e-mail: hotel @brasilito.com), a nice old wooden building with an attractive open-air restaurant right on the beach and a couple of rooms overlooking the ocean. They can arrange boat, diving, and horseback riding trips, and offer internet access. Their restaurant **Perro Plano** (open 7:30 a.m. to 10 p.m.; closed Monday) serves Indian-style shrimp sandwiches and summer salads with white cheese, watermelon, and marinated onion for lunch, and exotic specials like Kerala fish curry or wasabi tuna for dinner.

Between Brasilito and Flamingo, the sophisticated Belgian restaurant **Les Arcades** (open daily from 6 p.m.; 654-4385) serves crepes and escargot in its air-conditioned dining room or on the garden-view terrace.

Leaving Brasilito, you'll pass the **Camarón Dorado** on the left, a somewhat pricey restaurant that's known for its seafood.

FLAMINGO   Five minutes north of Brasilito is the entrance to **Playa Flamingo**. One of Costa Rica's most exclusive beaches, Flamingo sports its own landing strip. **The Edge Adventure Company** (open daily, 7 a.m. to 4 p.m.; 654-4946; e-mail: theedge@racsa.co.cr), at the entrance to Flamingo, offers sportfishing, kayaking, snorkeling, bike rentals, diving, and PADI certification. **Costa Rica Diving** (654-4148; www.costarica-diving.com, e-mail: coridive@racsa.co.cr) offers underwater cameras to record sightings of stingrays, mantarays, turtles, and schools of tropical fish. Their office is next to the Hillside Café. Big hotels rise up on a point beyond the beach, but Flamingo itself is a beautiful, untouched curve of white sand, lined with shady trees, one of the nicest beaches in the area. It flies the ecological Blue Flag. Since the coastline belongs to everyone in Costa Rica, you can enjoy the beach without staying in Flamingo. A good reason to visit Flamingo is the well-run **Centro Panamericano de Idiomas** (265-6213, in the U.S.: 888-682-0054; www.cpi-edu.com), which places students with local families in Flamingo and nearly Playa Potrero.

Economy Rentacar has an office in Flamingo (654-4152). The nearest **airports** are Tamarindo (20 minutes) and Liberia (45 minutes).

Marie's (654-4136) is popular for California-Mexican and seafood specialties. We had a terrific breakfast at the **Hillside Café** (open daily, 8 a.m. to 10 p.m.; 654-4228), owned and run by an excellent gringa cook who makes breakfast and lunch all day, plus flavored iced coffees, tropical smoothies, homemade ice cream, and gourmet desserts. It's on the hillside veranda just before Marie's. **Pleamar** (654-4521) on the beach at the entrance to Flamingo is known for good seafood.

In addition to its standard rooms, the **Flamingo Marina Resort** (private bath, hot water, air conditioning, fans, satellite TV; $90-$100; 290-1858, 654-4141, fax: 654-4035, in the U.S.: 800-276-7501; www.flamingo marina.com, e-mail: tickledpink@flamingomarina.com) offers suites that have their own terraces with jacuzzis and bars ($160-$170) and pristine oceanfront apartments for four ($210-$330). This hotel overlooks the marina and bay, is 300 meters from the main beach, and has a restaurant, the **Sunrise Café**, a conference center, and a pool. They provide roundtrip shuttle service from the Tamarindo ($10) or Liberia ($15) airports.

PLAYA PAN DE AZÚCAR   This pretty Blue Flag beach offers some shade, a rocky area for snorkeling, and a sandy area for swimming. It's 15 minutes (five kilometers) north by car from Playa Potrero, on a winding unpaved road; no problem for regular cars.

One of the oldest lodgings in the area, the recently remodeled **Hotel Sugar Beach** (private bath, heated water, air conditioning, ceiling fans, pool, satellite TV, phones; children under 12 free; $120-$200; with kitchen and room for 8 to 12 people, $400-$700, $2300-$4300/week; 654-4242, fax: 654-4239; www.sugar-beach.com, e-mail: sugarb@racsa.cr.co) has spacious rooms and pleasant grounds on a rise overlooking the sea. There is a great view from the restaurant/bar, and the beach itself has beautiful markings in its hard, walkable sand. There's also a 25-foot boat for charter trips and sports equipment.

GETTING THERE: By Bus: Direct buses from San José leave the Tralapa station (Calle 20, Avenida 5; 223-5859; $8; six-hour trip) at 8 a.m. and 10 a.m.

Interbus (283-5573; www.interbusonline.com) and Gray Line (232-3681; www.graylinecostarica.com) have air-conditioned buses from many other points to these beaches.

Buses leave the Folclórico station in Santa Cruz for Flamingo at 6:30 a.m. and 3 p.m., passing through Brasilito (680-0545).

From Playas del Coco, Hermosa, or Panamá, take a returning bus from your beach and get off at Comunidad (also called Tamarindo Bar) where the road from Coco meets the road from Liberia. There you can intercept a Santa Cruz or Nicoya bus. In 15 minutes you'll be in Belén, where at least seven buses a day stop on their way to Playas Brasilito, Flamingo, and Potrero.

There is no bus service to Playa Pan de Azúcar.

By Car: If you're traveling by car, you'll see the turnoff for the beaches about a block after you pass the plaza of Belén. A winding road leads to the village of Huacas, where you turn off to the right. Turn right again after about 200 meters to go to Playas Flamingo, Brasilito, Potrero, and Pan de Azúcar. The trip from Belén to Brasilito, the closest beach, takes about 45 minutes by car or an hour by bus, and is on paved road. The road is unpaved after Playa Flamingo, as is the road to Playa Grande. There are a couple of gas stations in Filadelfia, about halfway between Comunidad and Belén. If you like exploring by car, take the unpaved 16-kilometer "Monkey Trail" between Playas del Coco and Playa Potrero, passable only in the dry season with four-wheel drive. Coming from Coco, turn right at the Congo Trail Canopy Tour sign on top of the bus stop just past the turnoff to Playa Hermosa.

Note: If you are snorkeling anywhere in northern Guanacaste, beware of the *Pelamis platurus*, a small, thin sea snake with yellow and black stripes whose venom is lethal in 15 to 30 minutes and has no antidote. Fortunately, they have a very small mouth in which their teeth are set far back and, like most animals, won't bother you if you don't bother them. There have been no reports of fatal run-ins with this snake in Costa Rica, but it does live here, and we would think twice about snorkeling with children in this area.

LAS BAULAS NATIONAL MARINE PARK AND PLAYA GRANDE

The *baula* (leatherback) sea turtle is the largest reptile in the world, around five feet in length, some weighing over a ton. **Playa Grande** has been known as the fourth-largest nesting site in the world for leatherbacks, but in the October-to-February nesting season in 2003–2004, only 155 females came to lay their eggs, down from 1365 per season in 1988. Although scientists are blaming the diminishing numbers on irresponsible fishing practices, recent studies have shown that the presence of humans does indeed affect turtle reproduction. The thin line of light on the ocean horizon guides turtle hatchlings as they scramble towards the sea, and the illumination of human development, either on the beach or in the hills behind it, can confuse them, preventing them from reaching the water before their limited energy stores are depleted. Peaceful Playa Grande is the scene of a battle to protect the venerable and voiceless turtles' right to nest where their instincts demand. For more information, see www.leatherback.org.

Playas Langosta and Ventanas, the Tamarindo Estuary, and Playa Grande form **Parque Nacional Marino Las Baulas**. National marine parks protect the first 50 meters of land beyond the high-tide line. The exact status and coverage of these areas is in dispute, partly because the government has not paid for the expropriated lands that were made into the park. Buying the land behind Playa Grande would cost at least $5 million, money that the impoverished parks department doesn't have.

That point aside, since the area is officially protected, turtle watching is more regulated than it used to be. In the old days, excursion buses from the Central Valley would bring fun-loving Ticos who would ride on the mother turtles' backs. Instead of 150-plus people gathering around a nesting turtle, observers of this primordial ritual must now go with guides from the local community.

We recommend a visit to **El Mundo de la Tortuga** (opens at 4 p.m. from October through March; 653-0471; $5, children under 10 free), the leatherback turtle museum in Playa Grande, near the park entrance. This lovely project gives you earphones with recordings in English, Spanish, French, or German to guide you through an award-winning presentation on the leatherbacks, their life cycle, and the challenges they face.

Park personnel seem to think that the presence of tourists on the beach keeps poaching down. They also believe that tourism helps locals to earn a living as guides, and thus leads them to value the turtles more. Call MINAE (the Park Service) in Playa Grande (653-0470) to reserve a place for turtle tours ($6 park entrance, $7 for local guide; October 20 to February 15 only). The time of the turtle tours is determined by the phase of the moon and the hour of high tide. Signs are posted each day with the new time. Radio-carrying guides roam the beach until they spot a turtle. They alert the group guides, who then round up their flock of 15 or fewer, and the group walks down the beach to observe the nesting turtle. Sometimes you have to walk for a kilometer or more at high tide, so expect to get your feet wet. It is preferable to wear dark colors to make you invisible and long pants to protect you from bugs. When we were there last, the presence of our group striding along the beach trying to reach "our" turtle caused two mother turtles who were emerging from the surf to turn around and go back. Once you reach your turtle, you might have to wait awhile until she is ready to be observed. During the egg-laying process, because of the scarcity of turtles, your group might have to move away from the turtle you are watching and share it with another group. The observation ends when the mother turtle starts camouflaging her nest by throwing sand over it with her flippers; the leatherbacks can be distracted during this part, and observers can get a face full of sand. At Tortuguero or Ostional, you can watch the camouflage process, too, because the turtles are smaller and less powerful.

Note: Sometimes you will wait up to four hours for the tour to begin, and maybe there won't be any turtles. If you come to Playa Grande in a rental car, you don't have to pay your $13 entrance and guide fee until a turtle is actually spotted. If you come on a tour from Tamarindo ($30), you can only get a partial refund because the transportation costs have to be covered. It is safe to leave rental cars at park headquarters in Playa Grande.

Before becoming a national park, Playa Grande had already established a reputation as a favorite spot for surfers because of its long waves (avoid September, October, and late May). As is true with most beaches that are good for surfing, Playa Grande is not good for swimming. Playa Grande should not be considered a recreational beach. Camping is not allowed.

Note: If you are staying in Playa Grande, it is possible to walk along the beach during the day and catch a river taxi over the estuary to Tamarindo. Be aware, however, that the park is closed at night because of the turtles, so you will not be able to walk back to Playa Grande at night.

Hotel Las Tortugas (private bath, hot or heated water, fans and air conditioning, pools, jacuzzi; $60-$125; 653-0423, fax: 653-0458; www. cool.co.cr/usr/turtles, e-mail surfegg@cool.co.cr) has been designed to have the least possible negative effect on nesting turtles, with no ocean views toward the south and no lights shining on the beach. Recently, the turtle-viewing season has been shortened because of the diminishing number of turtles. Even if tourists are staying at this hotel on Playa Grande, they cannot watch the turtles before October 20 or after February 15.

Our favorite place in this area is **Casitas Linda Vista** (private bath, hot water, ceiling fans, kitchens; $60-$130; phone/fax: 653-0474, in the U.S.: 530-477-0996; www.tamarindo.com/kai, e-mail: helentvl@jps.net), three separate *casitas* nestled on a hillside. The upper house sleeps eight and has a view of the beach. The other two have the same clean, simple design. They are a five-minute walk from Playa Grande, 300 meters to the right at the entrance to Playa Grande Village. Recommended.

GETTING THERE: By Bus: The 10 a.m. San José–Flamingo bus (Calle 20, Avenida 1/3; 221-7202; $5.20) stops in Matapalo first. Buses leave Santa Cruz for Matapalo at 11 a.m. and 2:45 p.m. (2:45 p.m. only on Sunday; 680-0545), returning at 5:30 a.m. to Santa Cruz. From Matapalo you'll have to either walk or take a taxi 6 kilometers to Playa Grande.

By Car: Go straight on the gravel road going west from Huacas instead of turning right (north) for Brasilito and Flamingo. At the end of the soccer field in Matapalo, turn left for Playa Grande. It's about 15 minutes along a bumpy gravel road. If you're coming from Tamarindo, go to Villareal, turn left to Huacas, and go left again, then follow directions above.

TAMARINDO

Tamarindo is a wide, white-sand Blue Flag beach with a large estuary—a favorite with surfers. The safest swimming area is south of town, in front of the hotel Capitán Suizo. Tamarindo is a very happening place, with lots of good restaurants, nice hotels, activities, and service.

Leatherback turtles nest at Tamarindo (as well as Playa Grande to the north) from October to March. As they scramble to the ocean from late December to May, many baby turtles have been inadvertently crushed by beachgoers because it is hard to see the hatchlings in the dry, loose sand high up on the beach. Be sure to walk near the waterline, where it is easier to spot them.

Local guides can take you on mangrove/estuary tours to look for monkeys and crocodiles and, in season, to observe nestling turtles. Call Parques Nacionales (653-0470) in Playa Grande to set these up.

Agua Rica Diving Center (phone/fax: 653-0094; www.tamarindo. com/agua) will take you out to see the turtles while they are still in the water. They offer full SSI certification as well as a "resort course." They do night dives, snorkeling, and sail and dive cruises. **Pacific Coast Dive Center** (653-0267) at the entrance to town is a little less expensive.

Housed in a large thatch-roofed rancho on the road to Playa Langosta, **Iguana Surf** (653-0148; www.tamarindo.com/iguana, e-mail: iguanasurf@ aol.com) rents surfboards, boogieboards, Hobie cats, and sea kayaks, and has a surfing school. They offer snorkeling tours by kayak or boat to a nearby island. They can also take you to the Langosta estuary, south of Tamarindo, and have a surf taxi to nearby Playas Negra and Avellanes, favorites with surfers. Their tour and surf shop on the main road next to Cabinas Marielos has daily information on tides, surf conditions, and rip currents. There are several surf schools—even one especially for girls.

Tamarindo has three life guards. The community raises funds for them at the Turf n' Surf Festival at the end of July with a golf tournament at nearby **Hacienda Pinilla** and a surfing competition. There is a chapter of the Surfrider Foundation in Tamarindo. Find out what they are doing at www.surfridercostarica.org.

Other activities that people enjoy in this area are: horseback riding (653-8041; e-mail: kaydodge@racsa.co.cr) along the old cowboy trails; a boat tour of the **Río Tempisque**, which skirts Palo Verde National Park (653-0044); the **Cartagena Canopy Tour** (675-0158), though people say that the one at Buena Vista, north of Liberia, is more exciting; and golfing at **Hacienda Pinilla**. You can easily get to the Witch's Rock Canopy Tour near Playa del Coco.

You can study Spanish in Tamarindo at **Wayra Language School** (653-0359, fax: 653-0059; www.spanish-wayra.co.cr, e-mail: spanishw@racsa. co.cr), on the road to Playa Langosta. They offer three- and four-day survival courses as well as one- to four-week courses, and teach Latin dancing in the evenings. The owners will arrange housing for students.

Tamarindo has a **24-hour medical emergency center**: Call Dr. Hermes Quijada (680-2222) or the Clinica Villareal (653-0736).

You'll see real estate offices and internet cafés on seemingly every corner. One that offers a lot of services is **Interlink** (653-0605), which has administered telephone services in the high season, receives and mails letters and packages, lets you connect to the internet in five-minute intervals, and offers the cheapest laundry service in town—you have to leave your laundry early, pick it up the next day by noon. Speaking of laundry, **Mariposa Laundry**, located just before Iguana Surf, will do yours in two hours if you get there between 8 a.m. and noon. They charge by the kilo and use biodegradable products. There is a coin-operated laundry at **Punto.com**, a shopping center across from the Tamarindo Resort. Punto.com also has a homemade ice cream shop and an internet café.

The **Banco Nacional** on the left just before Tamarindo Diriá is a good place to change money. So is **Vista Villas**.

Alamo (653-0727), Economy (653-0728), Elegante (653-0015), and Budget (654-4381) have **car rental agencies** in Tamarindo. The Budget office, located in the Tamarindo Vista Villas, rents **cell phones**.

RESTAURANTS   On the right as you enter Tamarindo you'll see the **Panaderia de Paris** (open daily, 6 a.m. to 6 p.m.) for your morning croissants. **Cocodrilo**, next door, serves French cuisine. Croissants and Italian bread are available at the **Supermarket Tamarindo 2001**.

Frutas Tropicales, on the left just after the entrance to town, is reasonably priced, simple, clean, and very popular. Open all day. They also have clean cabinas in the back (private bath, heated water, ceiling fans, cable TV; $20-$30; 653-0041).

The Swiss-owned **Refugio del Moro** next to Cabinas Marielos serves fish with tropical fruit sauces, seafood, meat, and good pizza. Three-course dinner specials run about $8 including a glass of wine.

The Italian-owned **Al Bacio** on the main street near the supermarket is a great place to go for a quick lunch. A varied selection of sandwiches, salads, pastas, quiches, lasagna, gnocchi, and fruit smoothies have made it famous.

La Caracola, in a backyard across a side street from Fiesta del Mar in "downtown" Tamarindo, serves good, inexpensive local food in a friendly atmosphere.

Nogui's (closed Wednesday; 653-0029), just on the beach around the bend, offers moderately priced salads, sandwiches, grilled meats, and seafood, with sundaes for dessert. **Bar y Restaurante Zully Mar** (653-0023) is one of the original restaurants on the beach. It's a great place to go for a hearty breakfast or lunch and to get the lay of the land.

At the turnoff for Playa Langosta and set back from the street is the **Lazy Wave**, offering surfer haute cuisine. Nearby, the **Shark Bite Deli** makes great gourmet sandwiches and tantalizing brownies. We heard that **La Pachanga** (closed Sunday; 653-0079) down the street has a good chef.

They serve delicious lomito in red wine sauce, stuffed calamari, and curried shrimp, and have great desserts. **Stella's** (653-0127), farther down, offers Thai food and pizza.

Locals tell us that **Bruno's** is the best place to go for pizza. It's located on the corner of the road to Langosta. Farther down this road, next to Wayra Language School, **Taco Stop** has Mexican food—the best quesadillas in town.

Gecko's (653-0334), the famous restaurant at Iguana Surf, on the road to Playa Langosta, is popular for breakfast, lunch, and dinner. Make reservations.

The hotel **Capitán Suizo** serves excellent international cuisine. **El Jardín del Edén**'s Italian owners personally supervise their poolside restaurant, serving perfect homemade pasta and tender lobster. Recommended.

LODGING   Formerly an active fishing village, Tamarindo is now the site of many hotel development projects. All hotels offer substantial off-season discounts; off-season usually means May to mid-November. You can find out a lot more about most of the places listed below on the Tamarindo website, www.tamarindo.com.

The owner of the well-run Hotel Santo Tomás in San José rents out **The Surf House** (heated water, kitchen; $140-$210, minimum three nights; 255-0448, fax: 222-3950; www.thesurfhouse.com, e-mail: info@hotelsanto tomas.com), which sleeps up to ten in its three bedrooms. It's right on the beach. The entrance is across from Cabinas Pozo Azul. Guests have use of a canoe for estuary explorations, as well as boogieboards.

As you enter Tamarindo, you'll find the **Vista Villas** (private bath, hot water, air conditioning, ceiling fans, kitchens, cable TV, VCR, pool; $110-$250, including breakfast; 653-0118, fax: 653-0115; www.tamarindovista villas.com, e-mail: tamvv@racsa.co.cr), large apartments with views that sleep four to eight. The apartments have special closets for your surfboard. They rent water-sports equipment and have on-site surf instructors. **Hotel El Milagro** (private bath, hot water; with ceiling fans, $50-$60; with air conditioning, $80-$100, including breakfast; 653-0042, fax: 653-0050; www.elmilagro.com, e-mail: elmilagro@elmilagro.com) offers several rows of cabinas. Restaurant customers can use the pool.

A five-minute walk up the hill from El Milagro is the charming, tranquil, Italian-owned **El Jardín del Edén** (private bath, hot water, cable TV, refrigerator, ceiling fans, air conditioning; some kitchens, $140-$60, including breakfast; kids 5 to 12, $15; 653-0137, fax: 653-0111; www.jardin deleden.com, e-mail: frontdesk@jardindeleden.com). These stuccoed, tile-roofed rooms and apartments have a distinct Mediterranean feel. The upper rooms have views; the lower ones have larger terraces and garden views. There are pools (one with a swim-up bar) and a jacuzzi. The restaurant serves delicious lobster with European flair. A 100-meter footpath leads to the beach. Recommended.

Back on the main beach road is **Cabinas Marielos** (private bath, cold and heated water, ceiling fans, some air conditioning; $30-$60; phone/fax: 653-0141). Doña Marielos takes pride in her place, from the fine wood-work on her newest cabins to the aura-cleansing ylang-ylang trees in the gardens and her orchid collection. She offers many guest services: safety deposit boxes, laundry service, a pleasant communal kitchen, guarded parking, and surfboard rentals. Recommended.

One of the cheapest places is **Villa Amarilla** (private bath, heated wa-ter, fans, some air conditioning, refrigerator, communal kitchen; $20-$40, including breakfast; 653-0038; e-mail: carpen@racsa.co.cr), next to Super Las Palmeras and right on the beach. The European owners have ham-mocks in the garden for guests.

The **Tamarindo Diriá** (private bath, hot water, air conditioning, ceiling fans, satellite TV, phone, refrigerator; $130-$170, including breakfast; 258-4224, phone/fax: 653-0031; e-mail: salestno@racsa.co.cr) offers spacious new rooms, some with ocean views and balconies, and older, smaller rooms near its gracious lobby filled with indigenous art, and its poolside restaurant. The hotel has shady grounds, tennis courts, a game room, and a casino (open in high season).

Cabinas Zully Mar (private bath, cold water, ceiling fans, some air conditioning; $40-$60; 226-4732, fax: 286-0191, phone/fax: 653-0140; e-mail: zullymar@racsa.co.cr) are in "downtown" Tamarindo, where the road ends in a clutch of bar-restaurants on the beach. Zullymar has been trans-formed from a row of dark cabinas to a grandiose structure resembling an Italian villa. The dank old rooms still exist, but the new rooms are lighter and airier, and have balconies.

On a quiet side street is **Villas Macondo** (private bath, solar hot water, communal kitchen; $30-$40; with cable TV and air conditioning, $50-$60; with one or two bedrooms, cable TV, and kitchen, $80-$100; 653-0812; www.villasmacondo.com, e-mail: info@villasmacondo.com). Readers have sent enthusiastic comments about the friendliness of the young German owners, the great swimming pool, the private terraces with hammocks, the good showers, the quality mattresses, and the reasonable prices. To get there, go left at the restaurant Al Bacio.

If you turn left at the hotel Zully Mar and right at the Y in the road beyond Tamarindo Resort, you'll be on the Calle Real, the road to Playa Langosta, where European and North American beach-lovers have built some of the nicest places in Tamarindo. The friendly **Casa Cook** (private bath, hot water, ceiling fans or air conditioning, kitchens, cable TV, pool; one-bedroom cabinas, $180-$190; 653-0125; www.tamarindo.com/cook, e-mail: casacook@racsa.co.cr) on the right has one-bedroom apartments on the beach that sleep four. They welcome families.

Farther along on the right is the comfortable **Capitán Suizo** (653-0353, fax: 653-0292; www.hotelcapitansuizo.com, e-mail: capsuizo@racsa.co.cr), with rooms (private bath, hot water, ceiling fans or air conditioning, refrigerator, phone; $140-$170; children 4 to 12, $5), larger bungalows ($200-$210), and an apartment ($450-$460). The multilevel hotel is built around lush gardens and has a relaxed but sophisticated atmosphere. Their lovely pool is great for children or people with sensitive skin because it is shaded from the sun by large, lovely trees. First-floor rooms have air conditioning; the second-floor rooms have fans and ocean views and are less expensive. Recommended.

La Casa Sueca (private bath, hot water, ceiling fans, kitchens; $80-$90; phone/fax: 653-0021; www.tamarindo.com/sueca, e-mail: vikings@racsa.co.cr), just around the corner from the Capitán Suizo, has charming, spacious rooms with kitchens and offers monthly rates.

Two of our favorite places in Tamarindo are near the end of the road: **Sueño del Mar** (private bath, hot water, ceiling fans; $140-$160; with kitchen, $170-$190; matrimonial suite, $190-$200, including breakfast; no children under 12; phone/fax: 653-0284; www.sueno-del-mar.com, e-mail: innkeeper@sueno-del-mar.com) embodies what the owner most liked of the many architectural styles she encountered in her travels. You'll find double-thick adobe-style walls and uniquely sculpted Bali-style open-roof showers, to name just a couple of the wonderful features. The hotel is on rocky Punta Langosta, at the extreme south end of Tamarindo's beach. (From Capitán Suizo it is five more minutes south; take a right at Villa Alegre.) This charming hotel used to be alone on the beach, but now it is overshadowed by houses on either side.

Villa Alegre (private and shared baths, hot water, ceiling fans or air conditioning; $120-$140; one-bedroom villa with kitchen, $200-$210, including breakfast; 653-0270, fax: 653-0287; www.tamarindo.com/alegre, e-mail: vialegre@racsa.co.cr) is an oasis of peace and tranquility. Behind its high white walls, the friendly, helpful owners have created a spacious yet welcoming retreat with a lovely pool and rooms furnished with fabric and art from their worldwide adventures. Their gourmet breakfasts, served on the terrace, are memorable, as is the stretch of Playa Langosta that fronts the villa. Group rates are available for small workshops or seminars. Some rooms are wheelchair accessible. Recommended.

Back to the Y at Tamarindo Resort: veering left will get you to **Bella Vista Village Resort** (private bath, heated water, ceiling fans, kitchens, pool; $90-$110; phone/fax: 653-0036; www.tamarindo.com/bella, e-mail: belvista@racsa.co.cr), owned by a down-to-earth California couple. The resort comprises cylindrical, two-story efficiency *ranchos*. Each *rancho* accommodates four to five people. The upper *ranchos* have ocean views.

GETTING THERE: By Bus: Empresa Alfaro buses to Tamarindo leave San José (Calle 14, Avenida 5; 222-2666; $6) daily at 11 a.m. and 3:30 p.m. (six-hour trip), returning at 3:30 a.m. and 5:45 a.m.; on Sunday, there is another return bus at 12:30 p.m. instead of the 3:30 a.m. bus. Buy tickets early, especially on weekends and holidays. The Alfaro bus stop in Tamarindo is across from Tamarindo Resort (open Monday through Friday, 8:30 a.m. to 3:45 p.m.).

Buses leave Santa Cruz for Tamarindo daily at 9 a.m., 11:45 a.m., 2:30 p.m., and 4 p.m. Check schedules at 680-0401. You could also take the San José–Santa Cruz bus (6 a.m., 10 a.m., 1:30 p.m., 3 p.m., 5 p.m.) and then a taxi to Tamarindo (about $25).

Interbus (283-5573; www.interbusonline.com) and Gray Line (220-2126; www.graylinecostarica.com) have daily air-conditioned buses to Tamarindo from many locations, including San José, La Fortuna, and Manuel Antonio. Both cost about $25. Make reservations through your hotel.

By Car: If you are coming from Santa Cruz, drive north to Belén and turn left. If you are coming from points north, turn right off the main highway at Belén. A winding road leads to the village of Huacas, about 25 kilometers away; there you turn left for Villareal (14 kilometers), just five minutes from Tamarindo. This route is paved all the way into Tamarindo. If you are coming from Flamingo or Conchal, turn right at Centro Comercial Las Americas in Huacas.

There are several car rental offices in Tamarindo, Economy (653-0728), Alamo (653-0727), and Elegante (653-0015), so you could fly or take a bus on the arduous drive from San José, and rent a car for exploring Guanacaste, where the driving is much easier.

By Air: SANSA (221-9414, fax: 255-2176; www.flysansa.com; $71 one way, $142 roundtrip) has four flights daily to Tamarindo from San José. The SANSA office is on the right as you enter Tamarindo, next to Super Las Palmeras. Nature Air (220-3054, fax: 220-0413; $80 one way, $160 roundtrip) flies to Tamarindo from the Pavas airport near San José three times a day. Check schedules at www.natureair.com. Ask your hotel to arrange transportation from the airstrip (about $3). See Chapter Four for reservation information.

SANTA CRUZ

Santa Cruz is the home of much of Costa Rica's folklore. The music depart-ment of the University of Costa Rica has a special branch there, devoted to researching and celebrating traditional songs, dances, and instruments.

Just a 15-minute drive from Santa Cruz, through the beautiful hill country that is the heartland of the Nicoya Peninsula, are the villages of ✿ **Guaitil** and **San Vicente**, where local artisans have revived the art of Chorotega-style pottery making. With little use of a wheel, they recreate every known original design from native clay and natural paints and colors. Pieces range in price from $2 to $30. The pottery is displayed at the local shop and in front of homes. Stop for a chat with the artisans, and you'll feel the warmth and goodness of the Costa Rican campesino. Of interest on the road to Guaitil is ✿ **Casa del Sol** (open Monday through Saturday, 9 a.m. to 4 p.m.; 681-1015; e-mail: soldevida@racsa.co.cr), where local women use solar ovens and water heaters. They go all over the country teaching other women how to build solar ovens. Food that is slow-cooked in a solar oven doesn't stick or burn, retains more flavor and nutrients, and leaves the cook free to do other things, as well as saving energy. Santa Barbara buses leave Santa Cruz for Guaitil every two hours; to drive there, head towards Nicoya and take the left after you cross a bridge leaving Santa Cruz. Recommended.

Coopetortillas (open daily, 3 a.m. to 6:30 p.m.; 680-0688), 250 meters south of the church, is our favorite place to eat in Santa Cruz. It has grown from a tortilla factory to a popular restaurant featuring typical Guanacaste food. We don't know if you get emotional about huge hand-patted tortillas made from freshly ground corn, but this is a rare treat in Costa Rica, and well worth the $2 they charge for a hearty breakfast of *gallo pinto* with eggs and *café con leche.* The place looks unattractive from the outside, but the primal smell of wood smoke will lead you inside, where *señoras* in lovely pink aprons take you back into the kitchen area to show you the pots on the huge cement woodstove so that you can pick what you want to eat. This restaurant is a cultural experience in itself. Highly recommended.

Jardín de Luna (open daily, 11 a.m. to 3 p.m., 5:30 p.m. to 11 p.m.; 680-0819) on the north side of the Parque Central is the best we found of the plethora of local Chinese restaurants.

There is an open-air **farmers' market** at Plaza los Mangos on Saturday mornings and under the trees on the block behind the church on Monday mornings. Another block south is the **hospital**, which offers 24-hour emer-gency care.

LODGING   Hotels in Santa Cruz are not that exciting. Try to plan your time so you can get to the beach before nightfall (5:30 p.m.). **Hotel Diriá** (private bath, hot water, air conditioning, table fans, TV, phone; $40-$50; 680-0080, fax: 680-0442), at the entrance to Santa Cruz near the highway, is the fanciest option in town, a large hotel whose rooms enclose gardens and pools.

Close competition comes from **Hotel la Calle de Alcalá** (private bath, hot water, air conditioning, phones, local TV, pool, restaurant; $50-$60; 680-0000, fax: 680-1633), a fancy hotel one block east of the Tralapa bus stop in Santa Cruz. They don't have reading lamps and the air conditioners are noisy, but there is room service.

Hotel La Pampa (private bath, cold water, TV; with fans, $20-$30; with air conditioning, $30-$40; 680-0586) is clean and attractive, 50 meters west of the southwest corner of Plaza Lopez. A good value.

Cabinas Permont (private bath, cold water, ceiling fan or air conditioning; $12-$20; 680-0425) is a very clean establishment by the highway on the southeast side of town. Look carefully for the sign; it's on the left as you leave Santa Cruz for Nicoya.

GETTING THERE: By Bus: Ten daily Tralapa (221-7202) and Alfaro (222-2750) buses go to Santa Cruz (half a block west of the Coca Cola; 222-2666; $5; five-hour trip; buses leave hourly from Liberia and Nicoya for Santa Cruz).

By Car: Santa Cruz is about four hours from San José. Crossing the Tempisque river on the Puente La Amistad (the Friendship Bridge donated by the Taiwanese government in exchange, it is said, for the right to overfish Costa Rican waters). The bridge is about 25 kilometers west of the Limonal turnoff on the Interamerican Highway.

Guaitil is 12 kilometers east of Santa Cruz and 19 kilometers northwest of Nicoya. The road is paved between Santa Cruz and Guaitil, unpaved between Guaitil and Nicoya.

BEACHES NEAR SANTA CRUZ

This area gives more of a sense of Costa Rican rural life than the more populous beaches farther north. The hotels are just as nice—quieter and often more reasonably priced than in nearby Tamarindo, and not that much harder to get to. With off-season discounts, prices can be half of those listed here.

PLAYA JUNQUILLAL

This wide, almost deserted Blue Flag beach can have high surf and strong rip currents, but when we were there recently, the waves were calm and the sense of tranquility was pervasive, compared to Tamarindo. Horseback riding, surfing, kayaking on the estuary, and dolphin tours are available. At the southern and northern ends are tidepools big enough to snorkel in. Leatherback turtles lay their eggs at Junquillal from October to March, with greater activity from November to January. **Paradise Riding** (658-8162) offers horseback rides in the hills or on the beach ($25-$50).

The Canadian-owned **Iguanazul** (private bath, hot water, ceiling fans, pool; $80-$90; with air conditioning, $100-$110, including breakfast; 658-8124, fax: 658-8235; www.iguanazul.com, e-mail: info@iguanazul.com) is one kilometer north of Playa Junquillal on a cliff overlooking the ocean. You can rent surfing equipment, kayaks, and horses here. This isolated 24-room hotel could be rented as a whole for a retreat. To get there, turn right at the arched Iguanazul entrance and go one kilometer toward the beach. Their website has excellent directions for cars.

Next door is a real boon for campers, **Camping Los Malinches** ($5/person; phone/fax: 658-8429, 683-0264). Owned by a cultured Costa Rican gentleman who taught for many years in California, it has a lovely view from its shady campsites, and the cleanest bathrooms and showers we've seen at any Costa Rican campground. Although you have to hike for a kilometer to get to the campsite from the road, once you are there it's a short walk to the great restaurant at Iguanazul. In front of Los Malinches and Iguanazul the beach is mostly rocky tidepools, but sandy Playa Blanca is just 200 meters north.

Just before arriving in Junquillal, you'll pass the lovely **Guacamaya Lodge** (private bath, hot water, ceiling fans, pool; $50-$60; 658-8431, fax: 658-8164; www.guacamayalodge.com, e-mail: alibern@racsa.co.cr), which has attractive screened rooms and a Swiss restaurant on its hilltop perch. They also rent a two-bedroom house for $140 a night. A good value.

Arriving in Junquillal proper, you'll come first to **El Malinche** (shared bath, cold water, table fan; $7-$12; 658-8114), the cheapest place to stay. Owners Doña Aydee and Don Pedro also have a little grocery store (open daily, 7 a.m. to 7 p.m.) and serve as the public phone. Next door, the German-owned **Hotel Hibiscus** (private bath, heated water, ceiling fans; $40-$50, including breakfast; phone/fax: 658-8437; adventure-costarica.com/hibiscus, e-mail: hibiscus@adventure-costarica.com) has well-designed and -decorated bungalows. Their **restaurant** serves seafood and French and German cuisine. Across the street, with gardens leading to the beach, is **La Puesta del Sol** (658-8442), an attractive Italian restaurant serving handmade pasta and gelato. We've heard that their pricey, authentic Italian cuisine is worth a trip to Junquillal.

Hotel Playa Junquillal (private bath, heated water, fans; $30-$40; 658-8432, in the U.S.: 888-666-2322; www.playa-junquillal.com, e-mail:

hotel@playa-junquillal.com), right on the beach, has simple but clean rooms, friendly management, and a classic Tico beach restaurant that's the local hangout, open 8 a.m. to 10 p.m., with live music and dances every Saturday night.

Our favorite place in Junquillal is **Hotel Villa Serena Land Ho** (private bath, hot water, ceiling fans, some air conditioning, tennis court, pool; $50-$70; 658-8430, in the U.S.: 800-671-7757; www.land-ho.com, e-mail: info@land-ho.com), run by the owners of the famous Cape Cod restaurant, Land Ho. The hotel's **restaurant** looks out over the tranquil beach and serves delicious food. Costa Rican art and sculpture grace the walls. The rooms are quiet and comfortable. A poolside spa offers European facials, mud and seaweed wraps, and massage.

GETTING THERE: By Bus: A bus leaves the market in Santa Cruz for Junquillal at 10:15 a.m. and 5 p.m., arriving two hours later. A direct Tralapa bus (Calle 20, Avenidas 3/5; 221-7202; $4.50) leaves San José at 2 p.m. and returns at 5 a.m. The trip takes five and a half hours. Or take any San José–Santa Cruz bus and get a taxi to Junquillal.

By Taxi: A taxi costs $30-$40 from Santa Cruz or Tamarindo.

By Car: To reach Junquillal from Tamarindo by car, continue south 18 kilometers to the 27 de Abril crossing. Turn right onto an unpaved road and go another 12 kilometers. Turn left at Paraíso. The hotels are four kilometers from there. If you are coming from Liberia, it is faster to take a turnoff to the right just before you reach Santa Cruz (follow the signs). If you are coming from Nicoya, turn left after you cross the same small metal bridge as you leave Santa Cruz. From there, it's 19 kilometers to 27 de Abril. Turn left and proceed as above. Santa Cruz to 27 de Abril is paved; the other roads are not. You'll feel a lot better if you have a sturdy car with high clearance on these bumpy roads.

By Air: See Tamarindo section for flight information. A taxi from Tamarindo to Junquillal costs about $35 and takes about 45 minutes.

PLAYA NEGRA

Just north of Playa Junquillal, Playa Negra has been a secret destination for surfers for many years. This beach was featured in *Endless Summer II*, and is known for its hollow right barrel. The beach itself is quite pretty, with lovely shade trees all along the coast.

Within walking distance from the beach, **Pablo's Picasso** (cold water; with private bath and wall fans, $7-$12/person; air-conditioned rooms with kitchens, $40-$50; 658-8158; www.pablosplayanegra.com, e-mail: pablos cr@hotmail.com) is a lively surfer spot; the restaurant serves gringo food. Camping is allowed ($4/tent). On the beach, **Hotel Playa Negra** (private bath, hot water, ceiling fans, restaurant, pool; $70-$80; 658-8034, fax: 658-8035; www.playanegra.com, e-mail: playaneg@racsa.co.cr) has well-designed circular bungalows, a circular swimming pool, and a breezy circular restaurant on the beach. **The Secret Spot Bakery** (658-8083) serves muffins, cakes, and pizza at night.

GETTING THERE: By Bus: No public transportation goes all the way to Playa Negra. See the Junquillal bus directions and get off in Paraíso, where you can hitch, hire a taxi, or walk the rest of the way (about five kilometers).

By Car: For Playa Negra, drive to Paraíso as described in the "Getting There" section for Junquillal. In Paraíso, turn right (instead of left for Junquillal) and drive along the gravel road. In 15 minutes you will be at Playa Negra. It's best to have four-wheel drive in the rainy season, and a high clearance at any time of year.

NICOYA

While Liberia is the transportation and commercial capital of Guanacaste, Nicoya is the cultural capital. Its church (open daily, 8 a.m. to noon, 2 p.m. to 6 p.m.), dedicated to San Blas, was built in 1644 and is an adobe monument to the austere faith of the Spanish colonists. Next to it is a lovely, shady square abloom with flowers.

Café Daniela, an open, airy restaurant on the main thoroughfare one block from the park, has freshly baked goods, pizzas, and ice-cold *refrescos*, plus a full Tico menu, including a vegetarian *casado* and carrot juice. **El Presidente**, 25 meters east of the plaza, serves generous portions of tasty fried fish and Chinese food. We counted 11 Chinese restaurants in Nicoya.

An Italian couple has refurbished the town's art-deco cinema on Parque Central and converted it into **Un Dulce Momento** (open daily, 10 a.m. to 10 p.m.; 686-4585), serving homemade pastas and 40 varieties of pizza.

LODGING   A reader has recommended **Cabinas Tempisque** (private bath, heated water, air conditioning, refrigerator, cable TV, pool; $30-$40; 686-6650) modern, comfortable rooms in a garden setting, located two kilometers before Nicoya on the road to Santa Cruz.

In town, **Las Tinajas** (private bath, cold water, ceiling fans, some air conditioning; $10-$20; 685-5081), next to the Plaza de la Anexión supermarket, has some rooms off the street that might be quieter than other places in town.

The **Pensión Venecia** (shared or private bath, cold water, table fans; $7-$12; 685-5325), across from the church, is clean and basic with a nice airy sitting area.

Hotel Curime (private bath, hot water, pool; ceiling or table fans, TV, air conditioning, refrigerators; $50-$60; 685-5238, fax: 685-5530), south of town on the road to Playas Sámara and Nosara, has a recreation complex, including a large pool, tennis, volleyball and basketball courts, a playground, and a restaurant.

About 15 minutes down the road to Sámara, **Albergue Matambú** (private bath, hot water, air conditioning, cable TV, phones; $60-$70; 685-1049; www.matambu.com, e-mail: info@matambu.com), owned by a French/Tica couple, offers an international open-air restaurant, attractive rooms, and a creatively designed swimming pool with jacuzzi and areas for kids and adults. It's only 20 minutes from Playa Sámara, but it would be the perfect place to stop if you need a break on your trip to Nosara. Non-guests can use the pool (adults $4, kids $1.50).

GETTING THERE: By Bus: Buses to Nicoya leave San José from Empresa Alfaro (Calle 14, Avenida 5; 222-2160, 222-2666, 223-7685; $5) eight times a day. You must buy tickets in advance.

By Car: Take the Interamerican Highway and look for signs for the Tempisque bridge right after the turnoff for Las Juntas, at Limonal. The bridge is about 25 kilometers to the west. Cross the bridge and follow the signs to Nicoya.

Coming from Liberia, it's about 20 minutes from Santa Cruz to Nicoya on the paved road and an hour on the scenic old road that passes through Santa Bárbara and Guaitil. Buses run hourly between Santa Cruz and Nicoya.

✿ MONTE ALTO FOREST RESERVE   Monte Alto is a community-based conservation effort near the town of **Hojancha**, a cool, coffee-growing region in the hills southeast of Nicoya. In response to increasing water shortages, the community banded together in 1992 to buy 290 hectares of land, which they have left untouched. Mother Nature has already begun the regenerative process that will insure the survival of the Río Nosara and thus the community itself. Hojancha won the WHO Healthy Community Prize in 1998. Visitors can hike within the reserve and stay at the lovely wooden **lodge** (shared bath, cold water; $20-$30/person, including meals; 659-9347; e-mail: montealto92@tcrra.es) the community has built. You can bring your own picnic, or call in advance and they will cook for you. A small visitor's center displays old farm implements and has pictures of the animal and bird species in the area. The 500-meter Orchid Garden Trail has 67 varieties of orchids (best between December and February). There is a meeting room, a barbecue, and a cabin for families. During their annual April celebration, they run the old *trapiche* to show how sugar is made. They have a couple of short loop trails, and a steep two-kilometer climb to a *mirador* where you can see both sides of the Nicoya Peninsula. Recommended.

GETTING THERE: By Bus: A bus leaves San José (222-2160, Calle 14, Avenida 5) for Hojancha at 2:30 p.m. daily, returning at 7:30 a.m. There is also bus service from Nicoya.

By Car: The 14 kilometers from Nicoya to Hojancha are scenic and the road is nicely paved. The six kilometers from Hojancha to the reserve are best done with four-wheel drive, especially in the rainy season. There are four small streams to cross. Be sure to arrive before sundown so people can easily direct you to the reserve. Everyone in the community knows where it is.

NOSARA, SÁMARA, AND CARRILLO

NOSARA

Playas de Nosara, one of the only ecotouristic beaches in Guanacaste, is an international community with many North American and European residents who have set aside half their land as a wildlife reserve and park. The Nosara Civic Association governs the community and so far has been successful in keeping out large developers. You won't find many hotels right on the beach here because the residents respect and obey Costa Rican laws concerning development within the Maritime Zone, unlike many other more touristy beaches in the country. The maritime zone fronting four kilometers of beach is protected by the forest service. Nosara is a short drive (in dry season) from the ✿ **Ostional Wildlife Refuge**, which protects an important olive ridley turtle nesting ground (see page 340). Because of these reserve areas, Nosara is generally much greener than the rest of Guanacaste. No hunting has been allowed there for decades, so birds and wildlife are plentiful. It is common to see coatimundis, armadillos, howler monkeys, and even the jaguarundi, a cat that looks black from a distance but actually has a gray diamond pattern on its fur. Parrots, toucans, cuckoos, trogons, and pelicans are also easily observed. Humpback and gray whales can be seen offshore during the winter months. The beaches have community-maintained shelters for picnicking and camping.

Note: Bring a flashlight for walking around at night.

Playa Pelada is a small, S-shaped beach. Its volcanic outcrops house tidal pools and a blowhole that sends up a surprising shower and spray during high tide. There are coral reefs and tidepools on **Playa Guiones** that are good for snorkeling and safe for children at low tide. Surfing is best at Guiones and at the mouth of the **Nosara River**. Both beaches have the Blue Flag.

Canoeing or kayaking on the Río Nosara and through the mangroves on Ostional, moonlit horseback rides on the beach or to a local waterfall, and fishing and snorkeling trips are available through **Boca Nosara Tours**

(682-0610, fax: 682-0182; www.holidaynosa.com, e-mail: carinos@racsa. co.cr). **Iguana Expeditions** (www.iguanaexpeditions.com, e-mail: jungle joe33040@yahoo.com) takes you kayaking on jungle rivers or to Pink Island, trekking to waterfalls, and gives Spanish and surfing lessons. Surfing lessons are offered at **Corkey Carol's Surf School** (682-0385).

Nosara Wellness Services (682-0360, fax 682-0084; www.nosarawell ness.com, e-mail: info@nosarawellness.com) provides individualized health plans, including yoga and bodywork performed by Swiss and Austrian therapists.

We used to recommend that you rent a car to visit Nosara, but if you stay at a hotel in the Bocas de Nosara beach area, you'll be in walking distance of Swiss, French, Italian, and Costa Rican restaurants, and might not need a car. Ask your hotel if they can pick you up at the airport or at the bus stop. Most hotels can arrange for you to pick up a rental car in Nosara for a $40-$50 service charge.

You can rent **bikes** at Tuanis in Nosara Village, or at the local bike shop by the soccer field.

First we describe the lodgings and restaurants closest to Playa Guiones, then we move northward to those close to Playa Pelada and inland, to the village of Nosara. (This is the order in which you will find them if you drive in from Nicoya.) You'll find a good map of the area at www.nosara. com, as well as information on **house rentals**.

There are no banks in Nosara, but many hotels will take Visa cards. The closest banks are in Nicoya. There is a health clinic on the far side of the airstrip. The police station is next to the post office in Nosara village.

LODGING AND RESTAURANTS Near the southern end of Playa Guiones, **La Dolce Vita** (open daily, 11 a.m. to 11 p.m.; 682-0107) is worth the hike (or drive) from where you are staying. They serve gourmet Italian pizza, pasta, and seafood.

Housed in an airy, elegant mansion with a sea view, **Nosara Yoga Institute** (682-0071, fax 682-0072, in the U.S.: 866-439-4704; www.nosara yoga.com, e-mail: yogacr@racsa.co.cr) is dedicated to professional training for teachers and practitioners in the fields of yoga and bodywork. Their large yoga studio is on the left as you enter Nosara. Yoga classes are open to the public.

The Bocas de Nosara area has several friendly places near the beach. The first is **Café de Paris** (682-0087, fax: 682-0089; www.cafedeparis.net, e-mail: info@cafedeparis.net), which bakes French bread and croissants for its poolside restaurant (open daily, 7 a.m. to 11 p.m.). Their well-designed, light and airy rooms (private bath, hot water, ceiling fans, air conditioning, pool; $50-$60; with kitchen and hammocks, $70-$120; three-bedroom villas with ocean views, $130-$140) offer a variety of configurations for families and groups. An excellent value.

Down the street is a mini-mall with an internet café, laundromat, snack bar, and ice cream store. A few hundred meters toward the beach is **Villa Taype** (private bath, hot water, pool, restaurant, disco/bar; with ceiling fans or air conditioning, $90-$100; bungalows that sleep six, $130-$140; breakfast included; phone/fax: 682-0280, fax: 682-0187; www.villataype.com, e-mail: info@villataype.ocm), with landscaped grounds, two pools, tennis courts, and many activities for the whole family. They house the Budget car rental agency. Around the corner is Wind and Sun Massage.

Harbor Reef Lodge (private bath, hot water, ceiling fans, air conditioning, pool; $80-$90; with kitchens, $100-$130; 682-0059, fax: 682-0060; www.harborreef.com, e-mail: harborreef@racsa.co.cr) offers well-designed guest rooms with many amenities, some with private porches. Meals are served in the tastefully decorated restaurant. There is a supermarket next door. They also rent houses that sleep six to ten ($150-$180; three-night minimum).

Back on the main road, **Giardino Tropicale** is an open-air Italian restaurant surrounded by tropical gardens. Their pizza is baked in a wood-fired oven. They also rent spacious new rooms and smaller older ones (private bath, solar hot water, air conditioning, refrigerator, lap pool; $50-$90; 682-0258, fax: 682-0353; www.giardinotropicale.com).

From Giardino, follow signs to **Casa Romántica** (private bath, hot water, ceiling fans, refrigerator, pool; $70-$80; including breakfast; phone/fax: 682-0019; www.hotelcasaromantica.com, e-mail: casroma@racsa.co.cr). This small Swiss-owned hotel is where the international community goes when they want a special meal by candlelight. Delightful salads, filling Swiss, Italian, and seafood specialties, delicious desserts, and fine wines make up the menu. Next door, **Casita Romantica** has comfort-

Coatimundi

able rooms with kitchens ($90-$100; $10 more for air conditioning). Both are recommended.

The nearby **Condo Canadiense del Sol** (private bath, hot water, fans, pool, kitchens; $70-$190; 682-0350; www.condocanadiense.com, e-mail: reservations@condocanadiense.com) consists of one-bedroom apartments, simply furnished and secure, that sleep five; the gardens and pool are quiet. They give substantial green-season discounts.

The main road winds around a bit after the pizzeria, then you come to **Rancho Congo** (private bath, hot water, ceiling fans; $30-$40, including breakfast; phone/fax: 682-0078; e-mail: rcongo@infoweb.co.cr) on the left, a pleasant B&B owned by Monika Theil. The porch is strewn with hammocks and the gardens are beautifully tended.

The **Gilded Iguana** (682-0259) is famous for its Black Panther cocktail, named after the local jaguarundi. It also rents rooms (private bath, hot water, fans, refrigerators; $40-$80) 200 meters from the beach, and offers sportfishing, sea kayaking, and horse rentals.

Heading toward Playa Pelada, the following lodging is within a five-minute walk from the beach. Perched on a hill, with breezy balconies, original artwork on the walls, and ocean views, **Almost Paradise** (private bath, hot water, wall fans; $40-$50, including breakfast; kids under six free; phone/fax: 682-0173; e-mail: gnosara@web.de) is a homespun hotel owned by Gerlinde, a charming former reporter and producer on German TV. They have a great restaurant (serving salad, soup, and Thai chicken and fish) with a sunset view and a hillside garden with fruit trees that attract a variety of animals.

Vista del Mar (private bath, hot water, fans, some air conditioning, pool, access to kitchen; $40-$60, including breakfast; 682-0633; www.lodgevistadelmar.com, e-mail: g_ottley@yahoo.com) has a unique setting high in the hills, with a great view over the forest, down to Playas Pelada and Guiones. Birds and monkeys visit the trees surrounding the lodge, which borders the private Amigos de Nosara Reserve. The hospitable owner is a triathlete who coaches the local swimming team. Guests can work out in the 25-meter lap pool. Rooms are simple and comfortable. A local cook is available to prepare fresh seafood while guests enjoy unforgettable sunsets. Recommended.

At the summit of a rocky hill, with a terrific view of the meandering Nosara River and the beaches north of Nosara, is **Lagarta Lodge** (private bath, hot water, ceiling fans, pool; $50-$80; 682-0035, fax: 682-0135; www.lagarta.com, e-mail: lagarta@racsa.co.cr). This secluded, peaceful

Text continued on page 343.

ADVENTURE REPORT: TURTLE WATCHING AT OSTIONAL WILDLIFE REFUGE

The sunset from Lagarta Lodge was magnificent—delicately colored clouds billowed over the misty mangroves and beaches that stretch for miles north of Nosara. We could see at sunset that the Nosara and Montaña rivers were swollen from previous rains. Playa Ostional lay across those rivers. In the dry season it's easy to ford the rivers with four-wheel drive, but in November there was a risk that even the sturdiest SUV could become a boat.

Around 9 p.m. we got the word that the rivers were down and we could go. We drove in the darkness down the narrow winding road from the lodge, and then north from Nosara. When we got to the first river, a man with a strong flashlight met us. We parked and he guided us across the river on a hanging bridge. We all loaded into a cattle truck for a breezy drive down country roads to another river, which we forded in the truck, reaching the village of Ostional in about 20 minutes.

The refuge office was alive with young people from the village. They took our $6 entrance fee and introduced us to our guide José, an intelligent and very well-informed high school senior.

Just five days before, there had been a huge *arribada*, with an estimated one MILLION olive ridley sea turtles (*lepidochelys olivacea*) arriving over several days. Their name comes form their olive-colored shell, which measures about 30 inches long. Turtles nest at Ostional year-round, but the *arribadas* are more predictable from July through December. The turtles generally land at night, but during an *arribada* they start arriving around 2 p.m. and keep coming until 7 the next morning.

Even though the *arribada* had past, we saw five turtles at different stages in their nesting process. They dug holes about 20 inches deep on the beach and deposited about 100 eggs each. They then covered their nests and camouflaged the spot by spreading sand over it with their flippers.

The first *arribada* occurred at Ostional in 1959 and has happened regularly since then, usually occurring during the last quarter of the moon. As scientists studied the turtles, they found that eggs laid by the first wave of turtles were often excavated by turtles that arrive later, or by the strong surf at high tide. If excavated eggs are left to rot on the beach, they can contaminate healthy eggs as well.

Turtle eggs are thought to have aphrodisiac properties, and are a favorite *boca* at Costa Rican bars. The scientific studies mentioned above served as the basis for Ostional to become one of the only communities in the world where turtle eggs are harvested and sold in a sustainable way. Since 1987, the Integral Development Association of Ostional (ADIO) governs the harvesting and marketing of the eggs, and hires a biologist to monitor the health of the turtle population. Each of ADIO's 240 members is allowed to collect eggs for 10 to 15 hours during the first 36 hours of each *arribada*. After that, it is their responsibility to protect the nests.

When the turtles hatch, 40 to 55 days after the eggs are laid, women and children from the community accompany the baby turtles as they clamber toward the sea at dawn, protecting them from dogs and birds. Tourists can accompany them.

Olive ridley turtle

Seventy percent of the income from the sale of turtle eggs is distributed among ADIO's working members. The other 30 percent goes to beach protection and patrol, scientific research, scholarships, and support of the community's schools, health center, sports teams, churches, and environmental education and social welfare programs.

During our tour, it started raining again and we were pretty wet by the time it was over. We got back in the truck and rode to the river we had easily forded a few hours before. It was too high to cross, even for the monster cattle truck. But by then the skies had cleared. The few remaining clouds had been given silver linings by the rising moon.

In the dark, on a country road, we entered a true Costa Rican moment, where there is nothing else to do but be where you are. We all got to know each other a little better as nature's timetable took over and we waited for the river to go down.

VISITING OSTIONAL   Olive ridleys seem to be much more stable and plentiful than the critically endangered leatherbacks at Playa Grande, where numbers have dwindled from 1340 in 1990 to only 69 in 2002 (find out more at www.leatherback.org), compared with 500,000 to a million per month at Ostional.

Any hotel in Nosara can arrange a turtle tour for you, or you can arrange it yourself by contacting ADIO (682-0470; e-mail: adiotort@rasa.co.cr). Be sure to pay the $6 entrance fee and go with a local guide ($12-$15).

As in all turtle tours, it is best to wear dark colors and bring a large umbrella or a lightweight poncho. Don't use flashlights—the guides will have lights covered with red cellophane. No pictures can be taken, but there are photos, slides, and postcards of the turtles for sale in the ADIO office. Vehicles, camping, and campfires are not allowed on the beach.

GETTING THERE: It takes about 2.5 hours to drive to Ostional from Santa Cruz, about 3 hours from Tamarindo, on bumpy roads. It's only 25 minutes from Nosara if the rivers are low enough to cross; check with local people before setting out.

private reserve descends to the river, and nature trails lead at low tide to the turtle beach at Playa Ostional. Their Sunday barbecue and seafood fondue is legendary. Make reservations. Look for signs at the foot of the hill as you leave Nosara. They will pick you up at the Nosara airport if you don't have a car ($5).

NOSARA VILLAGE   The village of Nosara is about five kilometers inland from the beaches. There are a gas station and a couple of food markets in town, and disco dancing on Saturday nights. Also in town is **Rey de Nosara Spanish School** (682-0215; www.reydenosara.itgo.com, e-mail: reinaldo@infoweb.co.cr), with a shady outdoor classroom overlooking the river. **Tuanis Tours** (682-0265) on the plaza takes people to see the *arribadas* at Ostional.

As you approach town from the beaches, you will first come to **Cabinas Chorotega** (shared or private bath, some hot water, ceiling fans; $12-$20; air conditioning, $15-$30; 682-0142), a friendly, very clean place with a patio perfect for evening conversations with other guests. There is a restaurant next door.

GETTING THERE: By Bus: A direct bus from San José leaves the Alfaro terminal (Calle 14, Avenida 5; 222-2750; $8) at 6 a.m. daily, returning at 12:30 p.m. Buy tickets a day in advance. Interbus (283-5573; www.interbusonline.com) will also take you to Nosara from almost anywhere in Costa Rica. From Nicoya, a bus leaves daily at 1 p.m., returning at 6 a.m. Check schedules at 682-0236. The trip from Nicoya to Nosara takes about two hours by bus.

By Car: From Nicoya, follow the road southwest toward Sámara and Nosara. After about 30 kilometers, you will come to a Y intersection. Veer right and continue another 27 kilometers (about an hour) on a bumpy gravel road to Nosara. Most of the bridges on this route are in good repair, but there may be a couple of small streams to ford. You can also take the coastal road that connects to the first road about halfway between Samara and Nosara. The only thing that slowed us down was a herd of cattle that surrounded us, but that is what gives Guanacaste its charm. Be sure to ask about road conditions before setting out. A high-clearance vehicle is necessary. The San José–Nosara trip takes four to five hours by way of the Tempisque bridge.

By Air: SANSA flies to Nosara (221-9414, fax: 255-2176; www.flysansa. com; $66 one way) daily. Nature Air also has daily flights (220-3054, fax: 220-0413; www.natureair.com). Ask your hotel to arrange transportation from the airport. If you fly into Oduber International Airport in Liberia, you'll be two and a half hours from Nosara by car. Adobe Rentacar will deliver a car to you at the Nosara airport for no charge (www.adobecar.com).

PLAYA SÁMARA

Playa Sámara is a large half-moon bay with shallow, gentle waters. It's popular with swimmers and windsurfers, and is a favorite weekend destination for Costa Ricans during the dry season. The five-kilometer beach is protected from riptides and sharks by a barrier reef. There are a lot of things to do in Sámara. You can explore the coast and the hills with **Bike Costa Rica**; watch dolphins, ride horses, or learn to sea kayak with **Tio Tigre Tours**; fish with **Alexis and Marco Boat Tours**; go diving and snorkeling with **Pura Vida Dive Center**; learn Spanish at **Intercultura Language School**; or zip through the treetops with **Wing Nuts Canopy Tour**. You can explore all these options at www.samarabeach.com.

Tropical Latitude (656-0120; e-mail: travelcenter@samarabeach.com) is a dependable tourist information center and internet café in the center of Sámara. They also rent bikes, conduct nature tours by bicycle, and can help in travel planning.

The Flying Crocodile (383-0471, fax 656-0483; www.flying-crocodile.com, e-mail: flycroco@racsa.co.cr), run by a German pilot with an excellent safety record, takes people flying in ultralights in the dry season. His family also has very nice cabins (private bath, hot water, ceiling fans, pool; $40-$60; children under 12 free) near Bahía Montereyna, a mostly deserted beach with open-air cooking facilities for guests. They also rent cars, motorcycles, and bikes. To get there, turn left at the large gas station on the coastal road about 25 minutes north of Sámara.

Because it is now easily accessible (only 40 minutes from Nicoya on a good paved road), Sámara is quickly becoming crowded with new hotels and vacation homes. Make reservations if you want to visit on a weekend between December and April. Substantial discounts are available in the green season.

Ananas Café, at the entrance to town, serves breakfast, lunch, ice cream, and tropical juices. Down the first road to the right (on the road to Playa Carrillo) is the popular **Casa Paraíso**, where Ana, the chef/owner, cooks a range of seafood specialties, as well as excellent pastas and *comida típica*. She rents clean, simple rooms behind the restaurant (shared or private bath, heated water, fans; $20-$40, including breakfast; www.samarabeach.com, e-mail: paraiso@samarabeach.com).

Sámara's international community provides appetizing dining possibilities: **El Lagarto** serves up tasty barbecue on the beach; **Al Manglar** offers fresh, homemade Italian food and pizza; and the **Art Café** serves French cuisine with Caribbean flavor. **Soda Sheriff Rustic**, on the beach next to the police station, serves generous portions of Tico food.

A nice budget option in this area is the Italian/German-owned **Entre Dos Aguas** (private bath, hot water, ceiling fans, pool; $30-$40, including breakfast; phone/fax: 656-0641; www.samara.net, e-mail: entredosaguas@ racsa.co.cr), a unique bed and breakfast on the right as you enter Sámara, before you get to the Cangrejal road. They make creative use of rocks and shells in the spacious bathrooms, and also rent bikes.

Just off the road from Nicoya, at the first left-hand turn (down the Puerto Carrillo road), **Belvedere** (private bath, hot water, table fans, air conditioning, refrigerator, pool; $30-$50, including breakfast; with kitchen, $60-$70; 656-0213; www.samarabeach.com, e-mail: belvedere@samara beach.com) has small neat rooms downstairs from the owners' lodgings, two apartments, and an outdoor jacuzzi. Rising three stories on the hill that backs the town, the imposing **El Mirador de Sámara** (private bath, hot water, fans, kitchens, pool; $90-$100; children under 12 free; 656-0044, fax: 656-0046; www.miradordesamara.com, e-mail: mdsamara@racsa.co.cr) has large, comfortable apartments and views of the coast from the restaurant.

The Quebecois-owned **Casa del Mar** (hot water, ceiling fans; with shared bath, $20-$40; with private bath, some with air conditioning, $30-$50; breakfast included; 656-0264, fax: 656-0129; www.casadelmarsamara.com), down the street from the Super Sámara, is a tranquil and clean establishment. Down the street is **Casa Valeria** (private bath, hot water, kitchen for guests; $20-$60; 656-0511, fax: 656-0317), with rooms near the street and nice little bungalows right on the beach.

Heading toward Playa Carrillo, beachfront accommodations are accessible both from the beach (keep your eyes open for signs) and the parallel road that passes by the Belvedere and Mirador de Sámara.

Casitas LazDívaz Bed and Breakfast (private bath, hot water, ceiling fans; $50-$70, including breakfast; 656-0295; www.lazdivaz.com, e-mail: lazdivaz@hotmail.com) offers three cabinas, one with a full kitchen, designed by one of the owners, a German architect. She and her partner (from the U.S.) serve generous breakfasts in their beachfront *rancho* and provide shady hammocks. They fly the rainbow flag. To get there, turn left on the Carrillo road at the entrance to Sámara, turn right at the road adjacent to the parking lot of the Hotel Las Brisas, turn left at the beach, and you'll see the cabins in about 50 meters.

In Barrio Matapalo, named for a magnificent strangler fig tree that has been designated a national monument, **Villa Stephanie** (private bath, heated water, ceiling fans, kitchen; $20-$30; 656-0411) has two inexpensive apartments and rooms 50 meters from the beach.

GETTING THERE: By Bus: A direct bus from the Alfaro terminal in San José serves Sámara daily at 12:30 p.m. and 6:15 p.m., returning at 4:30 a.m. and 8:45 a.m., except on Sundays when it returns at 1 p.m. (Calle 14, Avenida 13; 222-2666; $7). It's a five-hour trip. Buy tickets several days in advance for three-day weekends. Empresa Rojas buses (685-5352) leave the Nicoya bus station for Sámara at 6 a.m., 10 a.m., 12 p.m., 3 p.m., 4:20 p.m., and 5 p.m.; the 10 a.m., 12 p.m., and 3 p.m. buses continue to Carrillo so you can get off at hotels along the beach. They return from Sámara at 5:30 a.m., 6:30 a.m., 7 a.m., 8:45 a.m., 11:15 a.m., 4:30 p.m., and 5:30 p.m. Check schedules at 685-5032.

By Car: The trip from Nicoya is approximately 40 kilometers and takes 45 minutes on paved roads. The road from Nosara is unpaved. We drove it in a four-wheel drive in the rainy season with no problem. Sámara is 4.5 hours from San José by car and 2 hours from Liberia.

By Air: Sámara is a 15-minute drive from Playa Carrillo. See "By Air" in Playa Carrillo below for more information.

PLAYA CARRILLO   Playa Carrillo, just a 15-minute drive east of Sámara, is a beautiful white-sand beach with waters kept calm by a reef outside a small semi-circular bay. Majestic palms at the beach's edge provide shade for campers and day-trippers. Unlike Sámara, where hotels and restaurants line the beach, Carrillo beach is business free. The town of Carrillo is uphill at the eastern end of the beach. The western end is best for swimming and snorkeling. Carrillo is an ecological Blue Flag beach. **Popo's Adventures** (656-0086; www.poposcostarica.com, e-mail: info@poposcostarica.com) offers rubber-duckie trips through the estuaries of the Río Ora and sea kayaking to Isla Chora. He'll tell you where the secret surfing spots are.

El Mirador (open daily, 10 a.m. to 10 p.m.) is a large open-air bar and restaurant at the entrance to the village of Carrillo. Up on a seacliff, it receives refreshing breezes and has a great view. Reasonably priced jumbo shrimp, lobster, and whole fried fish star on the menu; it's a bit greasy but there's no better place for watching the sunset.

Dining at **Pizzeria El Tucan** is like being in Italy. When we were there, it was crowded with Italians who all seemed to know each other. The food had that authentic Italian flavor. It's down a side street, across from El Rancho Bar.

Puerto Carrillo Sunset B & B (private bath, solar hot water, fans, air conditioning, pool; $110-$120 for up to four, including breakfast; 656-0011, fax: 656-0009; e-mail: puertocarrillosunset@yahoo.com), owned by a gringo/Tica couple, has a splendid view from the hills above the beach and very comfortable rooms. It's uphill to the left at the entrance to Puerto Carrillo. The German-owned **Club Carrillo** (private bath, hot water, pool, restaurant; $40-$50, including breakfast; 656-0316; www.carrilloclub.com, e-mail: info@carrilloclub.com), uphill at the same entrance, has rooms with an excellent view of the beach from their wide porches, and high-tech European showers with five sprayers.

Hotel la Esperanza (private bath, hot water; $40-$50, including breakfast; 656-0564; www.hotelesperanza.com, e-mail: esperanz@racsa.co.cr) is right on the main street, and yet the young French-Canadian owners have created a very peaceful atmosphere within their lush garden, which borders a wide, welcoming veranda in front of the rooms. Generous gourmet breakfasts are served in the garden and tastefully prepared dinners can be ordered in advance. Owners Marisa and Guy Orfali are helpful and informative. Local buses run several times a day, making it quick and easy to get to and from the beach. Recommended.

Cabinas Congo Real (private bath, hot water, ceiling fans; $30-$40; with kitchens, $50-$60; phone/fax: 656-0606) are cute cabinas that creatively use the possibilities of a narrow lot in town so that each has its own plant-filled patio. Cabins can easily be made into suites to accommodate families. Next door, **Apartamentos Colibrí** (private bath, heated water, ceiling fans; $40; with kitchens and room for four, $50; 656-0656) are clean and well-run.

In rows descending the hilly southern rim of the bay are the comfortable units of sportfishing hotel **Guanamar** (private bath, hot water, ceiling fans, air conditioning, satellite TV, phones, pool, bar, restaurant; $80-$90; with view, $100-110; suites that sleep five, $180-$190; breakfast included; children under 12 free; 656-0054, fax: 656-0001; www.hotelguanamar. com). Many rooms as well as the restaurant/bar complex have stunning ocean views.

Two kilometers inland from Puerto Carrillo, and one and a half kilometers from Camaronal, the next beach south of Carrillo, is **El Sueño Tropical** (private bath, heated water, ceiling fans, pools; $50-$60; two-bedroom apartments with kitchens, $90-$100; children under 12 free; 656-0151, fax: 656-0152; www.elsuenotropical.com, e-mail: suetrop@racsa.co.cr). This small Italian hotel, with a renowned Italian restaurant, is on a hilltop next to an appealing pool. They give guests free rides to the beach.

GETTING THERE: By Bus: The 12:30 p.m. and 6:15 p.m. San José–Sámara buses continue to Carrillo. Call 222-2666 to check schedules. Buy tickets a day in advance. The private, air-conditioned buses of Interbus (283-5573; www.interbus online.com) also take you to Carrillo.

By Car: From the Nicoya–Sámara road, turn left immediately before arriving in Sámara, at the Belvedere hotel. It's 15 minutes and about five kilometers from there to Carrillo, all on paved roads.

By Air: A SANSA flight (221-9414, fax: 255-2176; www.flysansa.com; $71) goes to Playa Carrillo. It leaves San José daily at 7:30 a.m., stopping in Punta Islita on the way. Nature Air flies to Playa Carrillo (220-3054, fax: 220-0413; $80 one way) daily at 1 p.m., returning at 2:05 p.m. Check flight schedules at www.natureair.com.

PUNTA ISLITA   Eight kilometers south of Carrillo, **Punta Islita** (private bath, hot water, fans, air conditioning, satellite TV; $200-$210; villas with private pools, $300-$700; 231-6122, fax: 231-0715; www.hotelpuntaislita. com, e-mail: info@hotelpuntaislita.com) is a remote luxury resort (gym and spa, conference room, pool, mountain bikes, kayaks, horseback riding, and sportfishing). They have a canopy tour and nature walks in their large tropical dry-forest reserve combed by trails. Punta Islita has a Blue Flag.

GETTING THERE: By Air: Punta Islita is most easily accessible by air. SANSA flies there daily on its way to Sámara and Nosara (www.flysansa.com). Nature Air's (www.natureair.com) daily flight to Tambor continues to Punta Islita. If you decide to drive to Punta Islita, take a four-wheel-drive vehicle and consult with the management about the best route.

By Car: Don't expect to make it to Punta Islita from Carrillo in the rainy season. In the dry season you can drive all the way from Carrillo to Playas Santa Teresita and Malpais, near Cabo Blanco, if you have four-wheel drive and go at low tide. (See Central Pacific Zone chapter.)

BARRA HONDA NATIONAL PARK

El Cerro Barra Honda is part of a flat-topped ridge that juts up out of the dry cattle-grazing land of the Nicoya Peninsula. People used to call the ridge a volcano because it's covered with large white limestone rocks piled around deep holes that look like craters. In the 1960s and '70s speleologists discovered that the holes were entrances to an intricate series of caves, some as deep as 240 meters. The caves are so spectacular that the area was made into a national park in 1974.

When the region was under the sea millions of years ago, marine animals deposited calcium carbonate that hardened and became limestone. Later, when the land was pushed up out of the ocean, rainfall combined with carbon dioxide and dissolved the limestone to hollow out the caves. In a process similar to how icicles form, dripping water carrying calcium carbonate formed stalactites and stalagmites that resemble curtains, pipe organs, fried eggs, and pearls.

In the **Nicoa cave**, speleologists discovered human skeletons that were quite old—a stalagmite was growing on one skull. It is assumed that indigenous people used this cave as a *cenote* (chamber for religious rituals), since some artifacts were found near the skeletons. Fortunately, the deep vertical drops at the entrances have discouraged all but the best-equipped spelunkers from entering, so the caves have suffered almost no vandalism.

The 62-meter deep **Terciopelo** cavern is the only one open to the general public. Three local guides must accompany you—whether you visit alone or with a group. In addition to the $6 park entrance fee, they charge $12 to $25 per descent. All equipment is included. To get there, first walk one hour to the cave entrance; then, assisted by your guides and the equipment (harness, ropes, helmets, ladder), enter by way of a ladder. Visitors who suffer from vertigo, claustrophobia, or hypertension are not allowed to go down and you had better like bats. You must wear pants and good shoes with closed toes, and bring your own drinking water and flashlight.

Arrange your descent in advance by visiting the park headquarters the day before or by calling the Conservation Area Office in Nicoya (686-6760). Many beach hotels arrange tours to Barra Honda. The caves are usually closed in the rainy season.

Even if you can't get down into the caves, a visit to Barra Honda is rewarding. You can explore the flat top of the ridge on trails where birds screech, iguanas stand motionless, and howler and white-faced monkeys fill the trees. The 1400-feet-above-sea-level lookout point, reached by following the seven-kilometer **Sendero Los Laureles** trail, affords wide views of the peninsula and the Gulf of Nicoya. You can take a six-kilometer hike (guide required) to a waterfall decorated with lacy calcium carbonate formations, and individual-sized bathing pools formed by the build-up of calcareous deposits in the waterfall's gently sloping path.

In the dry season it's very hot, so wear a wide-brimmed hat and bring a canteen. An unprepared European couple died several years ago from dehydration and heat exhaustion during their hike through the park.

LODGING   The park offers inexpensive and simple meals and lodging (private bath, cold water; $6/person) in dormitory-style rooms that accommodate up to eight. Meals cost about $7 per day; let them know in advance if you want them to cook for you.

GETTING THERE: By Bus: You can catch a bus at noon from Nicoya to the village of Santa Ana (an hour-and-a-half trip) and walk one kilometer to Barra Honda National Park. The bus returns the next morning at 7 a.m. A taxi from Nicoya to the park costs about $7.

By Car: Barra Honda is a half-hour from Nicoya by car. Take the main road east and make a left when you see signs for Barra Honda village. Follow signs to the park. You can also come from the east via the Tempisque bridge and turn right at the Barra Honda turnoff. The road to the village is full of potholes. Beyond that, the dirt road to the park gets narrower and bumpier, but national park signs clearly mark the way.

NORTH OF LIBERIA

GUANACASTE CONSERVATION AREA

The Guanacaste Conservation Area north of Liberia has been declared a UNESCO World Heritage site. It not only protects one of the last well-preserved stands of tropical dry forest in Central America, but also ensures migratory habitat from the Pacific coast to 6000 feet above sea level for an estimated 230,000 species of animals, birds, and insects: 65 percent of Costa Rica's biodiversity. It includes cloud forests at the top of Orosi and Cacao volcanoes, as well as the rainforests on their Atlantic slopes and 43,000 hectares of marine habitat.

Northern Guanacaste's parks benefited from the debt-for-nature swaps of the late 1980s and early 1990s and now form one of the best-endowed conservation areas in the country, and one of the most consolidated conservation areas in Latin America. Communities here have over a decade of experience in forming a model for non-destructive human use of biodiversity. Several of the ecotourism lodges mentioned in the following pages were, and still are, large haciendas involved in cattle ranching. But now these large holdings are incorporated into the conservation area as buffer zones for the national parks, and are actively preserving their forests, reforesting with native species, practicing organic agriculture, and welcoming visitors to their canopy tours, hot springs, and nature trails.

RINCÓN DE LA VIEJA NATIONAL PARK

Rincón de la Vieja is one of Costa Rica's richest and most varied parks. The centerpiece is a broad massif formed by the Rincón de la Vieja and Santa María volcanoes, with nine craters that melded about a million years ago. Its flanks are pocked by mudpots and fumaroles, which help the volcano vent its heat. The crater that is currently active cups a steaming lake, and periodically erupts, sending hot mud and volcanic ash into the sky and down the rivers to the north of the volcano. Its most active episode in recent history was between 1966 and 1970, but in 1995 and 1998 eruptions caused its campesino neighbors to flee their volcano-side homes. The damage has always occurred on the northern slopes of the volcano because the southern rim of the crater is higher than the northern rim. All lodging and park attractions are on the south and west sides. For current information, call the Guanacaste Conservation Area in Santa Rosa National Park (666-5051; www.acguanacaste.co.cr, e-mail acg@acguanacaste.ac.cr).

The park is a watershed for 32 rivers, many of which empty into the Tempisque. Three hundred species of birds have been identified there, as well as deer, collared peccaries, coatis, pacas, agoutis, raccoons, jaguars, two-toed sloths, and three species of monkeys. When we were there, we easily observed toucans, manakins, and crested jays.

There are two entrances to the national park: Rincón–Las Pailas, above the village of Curubandé, and Rincón–Santa María, five kilometers beyond the village of San Jorge, which is 25 kilometers northeast of Liberia on a dirt road. The Las Pailas entrance offers the more spectacular thermal sites, while Santa María has trails through a forest that is unusually moist for Guanacaste, due to its Atlantic exposure, and offers easier access to the hot springs.

It is actually easier to access both sections of the park from Rincón de la Vieja Lodge (see below), which is two and a half kilometers from Las Pailas. The hot springs in the Santa María Sector are a seven-kilometer hike from the Las Pailas Sector, but only four kilometers by way of trails on the lodge's property.

RINCÓN–LAS PAILAS Las Pailas (The Cauldrons) is a 124-acre wonderland of pits of boiling hot water; vapor geysers that stain the rocks around them red, green, and yellow because of the iron, copper, and sulfur in the steam; minivolcanoes that emerge spontaneously, last a few days or weeks, then dry out, leaving a conical pile of mud; fumaroles, which are deep holes that emit billows of sulfurous vapor; and seven bubbling pots of gray mud called the *Sala de Belleza* (Beauty Salon). Face masks made from this smooth glop are supposed to have rejuvenating and refreshing powers, but the Park Service no longer allows you to reach in and pull out a stick covered with the mud because too many beauty-seekers have been scalded. Albergue Rincón de La Vieja or Hacienda Guachipelín, on the way to Rincón and Hotel Borínquen, north of the park, have access to mud baths you *can* go to (see below).

Note: In Las Pailas, the dry, crusty earth around the mudpots is brittle and thin in some places; unsafe areas are clearly marked. Be sure to stay away from any area that has warning signs and fences. People have been burned when the ground under them gave way and they fell into boiling water or mud. Don't believe anyone who tells you about "shortcuts" off the marked trails. Sulfur fumes can cause bad headaches for some.

The Río Blanco forms a lovely **swimming hole** that's reachable by following a path to the left, about 100 meters beyond the ranger station. At the ranger station you can get a map that shows you how to get to **Catarata La Cangreja** (5.1 kilometers), a 75-foot waterfall with a gorgeous blue-green pool at its base, and **Cataratas Escondidas** (4.3 kilometers). You can see two of the waterfalls from the rim of a canyon, and can reach a third by walking along a creek.

Note: Signs along streams and pools in the park state that the water is drinkable (*agua potable*), but that refers to the concentration of minerals in the water and not to the absence of bacteria. We have heard of people getting severe intestinal upsets from these streams.

The park is great for hiking because it is largely untouched, and the trails are not too steep and are dry most of the year. Unlike the slippery, muddy cloud forests and rainforests, Rincón is a transitional area between dry forest and cloud forest. The trails get a bit muddy only at higher altitudes, right before the forest gives way to rocky, windblown volcanic terrain.

If you want to hike to the volcano's craters, and Von Seebach peak, 7.3 kilometers from the ranger station, start out by 10 a.m. in order to be back by nightfall. If you'd like to go at a more relaxed pace, it's best to camp overnight. March and April are the best months for this, but it is always wise to bring rainsuits, warm clothes, several changes of clothing wrapped in plastic, good hiking boots, a waterproof tent, and a compass. We saw a well-prepared group of campers in July who had made the trip with no problem.

Note: It's a good idea to hire a guide from a local hotel or tour company if you are going to the volcano because the paths are not clearly marked in the rocky terrain near the top, and thick mists come up frequently. If you go without a guide, the Park Service recommends that you turn back when you emerge from the forest to the barren crater area if you see that the crater is obscured by clouds. In the dry season the lava flows at the top can be extremely windy. It is tempting to walk closer to the edge

Collared peccary

than you should. But note that the crater's edge is made of gravel and ash, which can give way in a miniature landslide, taking you with it, toward the lake of boiling acid, 200 meters down. You can contact guides through the park administration, 666-5051; e-mail: acg@acguanacaste.ac.cr.

LODGING   The **camping spots** ($1.50/person) are in a shady river glen, a five-minute walk from the park administration center.

Rincón de la Vieja Lodge (private bath; $60-$80; meals about $27/ day; 661-8198; www.rincondelaviejalodge.com, e-mail: info@rincondela viejalodge.com) is a rustic and relaxed lodge located two kilometers from the Las Pailas entrance to the park. Rooms have porches with hammocks or rocking chairs. The main lodge has cozy areas for reading or meeting other travelers. Meals are served family-style. They offer half- to full-day hiking and horseback-riding expeditions, and rent bikes for exploring their 900-acre reserve or for riding to the park. Their **canopy tour** is a series of 21 platforms and 11 cables that glide you through the tree tops in a two- to four-hour tour. Try to go with as small a group as possible so you won't have to wait too long between glides. You have to be in good shape physically and emotionally to do 11 cables. Daredevils can do the tour at night and sleep on the last and biggest platform.

Several kilometers before you get to the park, **Hacienda Guachipelín** (private bath, water, fans; $50-$60; 442-2818, fax: 442-1910, cell phone: 384-2049; www.guachipelin.com, e-mail: info@guachipelin.com) is a classic Guanacaste cattle ranch. Rooms are arranged around a green area, playground, and pool near the century-old ranch house. There is a cool porch to sit on, a comfortable TV room, and a family-style dining area; a hot mud pool is located about half an hour from the lodge. You can cover yourself with mud, let it dry in the sun, wash it off in a tank of water, then take a final dip in a cold river nearby. They offer horseback tours and hikes to Las Pailas, a waterfall, and the mud baths with a Spanish-speaking guide. Their **Kazm Cañon Canopy Tour** takes you into a canyon where ten platforms, three wall climbs, and a "Tarzan swing" await the adventurous. You can spend the day and participate in as many activities as you can fit in with their Adventure Pass ($70 including lunch).

GETTING THERE: By Bus: No public buses run all the way to the Rincón–Las Pailas entrance, but a bus leaves Liberia for Curubandé daily at 2 p.m., returning the next morning at 6 a.m. You could walk or hitch the remaining eight kilometers from there, especially if you were planning to camp overnight. (If you're not planning to camp or stay in a nearby lodge, this alternative won't work.) Otherwise you must take a jeep taxi from Liberia ($25 one way).

, *By Car:* Go four and a half kilometers north of Liberia on the Interamerican Highway to the turnoff for Curubandé. You'll see signs directing you to the Las Pailas entrance of the park. It's 12 kilometers to Curubandé over a fairly good gravel road, interesting because it was cut through deposits of white and pinkish pumice. From Curubandé, it's about three kilometers farther up to Hacienda Guachipelín, another three to the turnoff to Albergue Rincón de la Vieja and two more to the park entrance. Just beyond Curubandé you have to pay $3 to enter the part of the road maintained by Hacienda Guachipelín. It takes about 45 minutes to drive from the Interamerican Highway to the park entrance.

RINCÓN–SANTA MARÍA   This entrance to the park has a park administration center and a small historical exhibit, with campsites nearby. Fifteen kilometers of trails are explorable on your own, but you should not walk to Las Pailas without a guide, since it's easy to get lost.

Three kilometers from the Santa María entrance are **Los Azufrales**, hot sulfur springs at a perfect bathtub temperature, right next to a cold stream to splash in (don't let the sulfurous water get in your eyes, and don't stay in longer than five minutes before alternating with the cold water). These springs can also be accessed by a four-kilometer trail from Rincón de la Vieja Lodge.

In San Jorge, three kilometers toward Liberia from the park entrance, there are a couple of inexpensive lodges (Rinconcito and Miravieja), but they are not worth the long bumpy trip.

GETTING THERE: No buses run to San Jorge or the Rincón–Santa María entrance (25 kilometers). The road is passable only with four-wheel drive. By car, take the Barrio La Victoria road.

BUENA VISTA LODGE   Thirteen kilometers north of Liberia on the Interamerican Highway, you come to the entrance to Cañas Dulces. Beyond that, **Buena Vista Lodge and Adventure Center** (private bath, hot water; $40-$60; 661-8158; www.buenavistacr.com, e-mail: info@buenavistacr. com) has a thrilling 1300 foot **waterslide** in the forest, ending in a swimming pool. Buena Vista offers two **canopy tours**: one has 10 cables and the other, for adrenaline freaks, features a 2400-foot cable where you can really pick up speed. This near-death experience ends at the **Buena Vista Spa**, two miles from the main lodge, where you can soak in five thermal pools, sweat in the stone steam room, and have a massage or a mud pack. If you choose not to take the zipline there, you can hike there through the forest, or go there on a tractor cart. They also have a series of 17 **hanging bridges** for bird and wildlife watchers in their 1000-acre forest reserve. They offer a guided night hike on the bridges to see nocturnal animals and insects. You can watch the sunset from their **Mirador Bar**, learn about snakes in their serpentarium, or see crocodiles in their lagoon. Buena Vista is a working organic farm and cattle ranch, so most of the food served in their restaurants is raised right there.

Hotel Borínquen (private bath, hot water, air conditioning, fans, refrigerator, satellite TV, pool; $240-$250, including breakfast and use of spa; 690-1900, fax: 666-2136; www.borinquenresort.com, e-mail: info@borinquen resort.com) has large, well-appointed individual and duplex bungalows, a fancy restaurant, and little golf carts to take you up and down its nicely paved roads. They offer a spa and mud treatments but seem somehow out of place, like a retirement community in the wilderness.

Buena Vista offers horseback tours to Rincón de la Vieja National Park, but the trip is long and difficult. If you want to hike to the craters, start from the park itself, using the Las Pailas entrance from the Interamerican Highway.

GETTING THERE: Drive north from Liberia about 15 minutes until you see signs for Cañas Dulces. Turn right and follow the road 18 kilometers to the entrances to the hotel. Borínquen is to the left before the Buena Vista gate. The road is bumpy in some places but you can make it in a regular car.

SANTA ROSA NATIONAL PARK

While most of Costa Rica's parks aim to preserve virgin forest, **Santa Rosa National Park** (666-5051 ext. 219, fax: 666-5020; www.acguana caste.ac.cr, e-mail: mfennell@acguanacaste.ac.cr) not only protects the little remaining tropical dry forest, but promotes its regeneration. This park encompasses almost every ecosystem that exists in Guanacaste. Part of the park was a large tract of pastureland, overgrazed and biologically bankrupt, where biologists have applied research findings about how forests propagate themselves. You will see, from the lush greenery as you drive in, that these methods have worked very well.

Seeds for forest regeneration are primarily carried by the wind and by mammals and birds who eat seeds and then defecate in treeless pastures. By encouraging this kind of seed dispersal and burning fire lanes to control the spread of wildfires, the scientists are allowing the dry forest to renew itself. The latest addition to the park, by the way, includes the location of the clandestine airstrip that figured in the Iran-Contra fiasco. The North American owner of this land won a legal dispute with the Costa Rican government over the expropriation that made it part of the park, and will be paid $22 million for the property. This part of the park is closed.

Frigates

The three times that Costa Rica has been attacked by military, the invaders were defeated at the **Hacienda Santa Rosa's Casona** (big house). The Casona was destroyed by arson in March 2001 and, thanks to a nation-wide fundraising campaign, an exact replica opened in March 2002. School children re-enacted the 280-kilometer march from the Central Valley taken by Costa Rica's troops in 1856 to defeat William Walker in the famous 15-minute Battle of Santa Rosa (see history section in Chapter One). Near the museum is a trail you can follow for a short natural-history jaunt.

There is **camping** (minimal fee) in a central area of Santa Rosa, with water, toilets, showers, and nice big shade trees. The ranger will tell you which parts of the park are especially rich in wildlife at the moment. Lodging and meals at the **Centro de Investigación** (research station) can be arranged by calling the above numbers. You can eat lunch with the park personnel if you give them three hours' notice.

A 12-kilometer trail will take you to **Playa Naranjo**, a long stretch of white sand that you can usually have all to yourself. Near the ranger station, right off the beach, there is a camping area, an outhouse, and a water well for washing, but not for drinking. Off Playa Naranjo is **Witch Rock**, famous with surfers the world over for creating the perfect wave. Surfers must pay the $6 park entrance fee to go to Witch Rock.

The six-kilometer **Carbonal** trail takes you through dry forest, rock formations, and mangroves. It starts 300 meters before the ranger station at Playa Naranjo.

If you don't want to go all the way down to the beach, the trail to **Mirador Valle Naranjo**, where you can get a panoramic view of the coast, starts from six kilometers down the road to Playa Naranjo. It takes about half an hour to hike the one and a half kilometers to the *mirador* from the entrance to the Mirador Trail.

The road to Playa Naranjo is probably a creek in the rainy season, and is only open to vehicles from December 15 to April 1. We have heard that this road has been greatly improved, but call the park before driving it because when it is in bad condition the typical four-wheel-drive Suzuki Sidekick rent-a-cars routinely get stuck near the beach. The rangers have to call a tow-truck from Liberia to get them out, which costs the tourists $150. **Bahía Junquillal Wildlife Refuge**, accessible by the Cuajiniquil entrance, about five minutes north of the main entrance to Santa Rosa on the Interamerican Highway, is a lovely place to camp and much easier to drive to, though it's not as wild (see below). The walk to Playa Naranjo takes three hours, and you must start early because of the heat.

Santa Rosa is home to a wide variety of easily observed animals, including three types of monkeys: loud howler monkeys, agile spider monkeys, and white-throated capuchin monkeys. You'll also see vultures, falcons, and the *urraca*, a blue-and-white jay, which has a feather on top of its head that looks like a curled ribbon on a birthday present. This bird's beauty is contradicted by its obnoxious squawk. Twenty-two species of bats inhabit the park, including two vampire varieties (they rarely attack humans—their victims are almost always livestock). Pelicans, gulls, herons, and sandpipers are the most common birds on the beach. Cicadas buzz from tree branches so loud you sometimes have to shout to be heard.

There are collared and white-lipped peccaries whose reputation for ferocity is misleading, according to a Santa Rosa biologist we talked to. Peccaries are actually afraid of humans and flee when they are near. White-tailed deer wander in the savannah, coatimundis prowl around the forests, and caimans live in the estuaries of Playa Naranjo. As in most areas of the Pacific coast, iguanas are everywhere.

Olive ridley turtles nest in the park from July to November at **Playa Nancite**, the next beach north from Playa Naranjo. Their *arribadas* (arrivals by sea) take place on moonless nights, with the largest (thousands at a time) arrival in October and November. After an approximately 45-day incubation period, the baby turtles hatch and crawl into the sea. About five percent survive all the hazards of turtle "childhood" to become adults.

Playa Nancite is covered with turtle eggshell fragments and a few shells and skeletons of unfortunate mother turtles who didn't make it. You can't stay at Nancite overnight without a permit from the ecotourism office at Santa Rosa (666-5051 ext. 219)—it serves mainly as a biological research station. Only 25 people are allowed on the beach at one time. To see olive ridley *arribadas* more easily, go to Ostional Wildlife Refuge (earlier in this chapter).

GETTING THERE: By Bus: Buses that go to La Cruz and Peñas Blancas on the Nicaragua border pass the entrance to Santa Rosa. Check www.monteverde

info.com for current schedules. You have to buy tickets in advance. Because of the tremendous heat, it's better to take a San José–Liberia bus, stay overnight, then take a La Cruz (not Santa Cruz) bus from Liberia at 5:30 a.m. (check the bus schedule the night before). Ask to be let off at the "entrada a Santa Rosa." You must walk or hitchhike about seven kilometers to the *casona* and camping area before you start the 12-kilometer hike to Playa Naranjo. It's easy to hitchhike this distance in the dry season because there are many people going to and from the park.

By Car: Santa Rosa is only 20 minutes north of Liberia on the Interamerican Highway, to the left. The entrance to the Murciélago Sector, through Cuajiniquil, is about five minutes (ten kilometers) beyond Santa Rosa, also to the left.

BAHÍA JUNQUILLAL WILDLIFE REFUGE AREA

North of Santa Rosa, the beautiful **Bahía Junquillal Wildlife Refuge** (679-9692; admission $4), near the picturesque inlet of **Cuajiniquil**, protects a calm bay that is good for swimming and snorkeling, a tropical dry forest, and a mangrove swamp. Three species of turtles lay eggs there, and whales visit in December. A lovely campground has showers and toilets ($2/person). This is one of our favorite camping and swimming spots, but beware of the jellyfish. Bring your own water and toilet paper. Camping is first-come, first-served. This beach has the Blue Flag.

Playa El Hachal is another lovely beach known for its multicolored stones. It's five kilometers beyond the Murciélago Ranger Station, south of Cuajiniquil, and only open in the dry season. You can get information through the Santa Rosa contact numbers.

West of Cuajiniquil on the Santa Elena peninsula are peaceful **Bahía Santa Elena** and **Bahía Playa Blanca**, accessible by car only in the dry season. There is a camping and picnic area with baths and potable water at the Murciélago ranger station, nine kilometers west of Cuajiniquil. Confirm that there is space at 666-5051, fax: 666-5020. From the campground you can hike 600 meters to a swimming hole, **Poza del General**. It's easy to spot monkeys, birds, and iguanas in this area.

GETTING THERE: By Bus: Buses to Cuajiniquil leave Liberia daily at 5:45 a.m. and 3:30 p.m., returning at 7 a.m. and 4:30 p.m. There is also a 12:30 p.m. bus from La Cruz (see below), which returns at 6 a.m. It takes about an hour to walk to the Bahía Junquillal campground from Cuajiniquil.

By Car: If you're going by car, keep on the Interamerican Highway for ten kilometers beyond the Santa Rosa turnoff, then turn left on the nicely paved road to Cuajiniquil (seven kilometers). Playa Junquillal campground is four kilometers to the north of Cuajiniquil on a good gravel road. The Murciélago campground is nine kilometers southwest of Cuajiniquil, Playa El Hachal is five kilometers to the southwest. Bahía Santa Elena is 12 more kilometers southwest on a difficult road, and Playa Blanca is another six kilometers beyond that. These last three trips are best done in the dry season with a four-wheel-drive vehicle.

GUANACASTE NATIONAL PARK

Guanacaste National Park was created in 1989 to protect the migratory paths of animals that live in Santa Rosa, so it extends from the Interamerican Highway east to the Orosi and Cacao volcanoes. Many species of moths procreate in the high mountains during the dry season, then fly down to spend the rainy season at a lower, warmer altitude. The *zahino,* a wild pig, retreats from the volcanoes to the dry forest in January to search for seeds of the *encino* (evergreen oak) tree. Scientists studying the wildlife in Santa Rosa have found that in order to protect these and other animals, the environments so necessary to their existence must also be protected. The whole Guanacaste Conservation Area now protects 220,000 hectares of land.

Although Costa Rica has about .001 percent of the world's landmass, it has 5 percent of the world's biodiversity. For instance, an estimated 3800 species of moths live in Santa Rosa alone. Studying all of them would take years. However, under the auspices of **InBio** (see Chapter Five) local park employees are being trained in biological inventory techniques by some of the best scientists in the world. By all reports, the program is a tremendous success due to the sharp powers of observation of the campesinos, their familiarity with the region and its wildlife, and their motivation to learn a new career that was not open to them until a few years ago (45 percent of the conservation area's employees are women). People from parks all over the country are being trained in the same techniques. All specimens will be turned over to InBio in Santo Domingo de Heredia, which hopes to identify every plant and animal species in Costa Rica.

LA CRUZ AND BAHÍA SALINAS

The region around La Cruz, near the Nicaraguan border, is still off the beaten track for tourists. There are spectacular views from the breezy west side of town.

Isla Bolaños, a small island in Bahía Salinas west of La Cruz, is part of Santa Rosa National Park. It is the only place in Costa Rica where frigate birds and American oyster catchers nest. Several hundred nesting pairs of frigate birds inhabit the cliffs on the southwestern side of the island; 500 to 600 pairs of brown pelicans nest on the northern side from December to July.

On Bahía Salinas, the **Kite Surfing Center** (shared bath; $20-$30; 826-5221; www.suntoursandfun.com, e-mail: bertoldi@racsa.co.cr) offers hotel style accommodations and teaches kite surfing. The lively **Restaurante Copal** serves good food nearby.

In the town of La Cruz, **Soda Santa María** (679-9347) is good for *comida típica.*

Cabinas Santa Rita (shared bath, small rooms; $7-$12; private bath, cold water, fans, $12-$20; with air conditioning, $20-$30; with kitchen, $50-$60; 679-9062, phone/fax: 679-9305) has well-kept, spacious rooms across from the Tribunales de Justicia. You can leave your car there if you want to take side trips by bus. Good value. Recommended for budget travelers.

Right on the edge of the cliff, with a stunning view of Bahía Salinas, is **Villa Amalia** (private bath, hot or heated water, satellite TV, pool; no children under 14; $30-$40; phone/fax: 679-9181), originally built as a gallery for the paintings of American artist Lester Bounds. His widow, Doña Amalia, is a charming hostess. The rooms are eclectic; all have their own sitting areas. There is also a restaurant to the left of the hotel.

GETTING THERE: By Bus: Check www.monteverdeinfo.com for current bus schedules to La Cruz. You can get a bus or taxi from La Cruz to the Nicaraguan border.

By Car: La Cruz is a straight shot up the Interamerican Highway from Liberia.

LOS INOCENTES   South of La Cruz is the turnoff for **Los Inocentes** (private or shared bath, solar-heated water, pool; $40-$50/person, including meals; phone/fax: 679-9190, fax: 265-4385; www.losinocenteslodge.com), the large estate of the Víquez family in the shadow of beautiful Volcán Orosi. This was one of the first *haciendas* to open its doors to tourists, and served as inspiration to many of the area's lodges. The food and service at Los Inocentes are excellent. The morning we were there we saw a toucan, a scarlet macaw, montezuma *oropéndolas,* and a fiery-billed aracari frequenting their bird feeders. The hotel's reserve is actually part of the Guanacaste Conservation area, so it is like a national park. Accommodations are in the main house with bathrooms downstairs, or in nice but simple cabins by the river. Both overnight guests and day visitors may take a two-hour horseback or tractor ride through the ranch to see birds, monkeys, and sloths. To get there, turn right at the security post about five minutes north of the turnoff to Cuajiniquil (the sign points to Upala and Santa Cecilia). After 15 kilometers, turn right at the "Los Inocentes" sign. Recommended.

ELEVEN

The Central Pacific Zone

Puntarenas Province extends along the Pacific Coast from Guanacaste to the Panamanian border. The Central Pacific Zone roughly corresponds to the northern part of the province, from the town of Puntarenas to the Nicoya Peninsula, to Quepos and Manuel Antonio National Park, about halfway down Costa Rica's Pacific Coast. Like Guanacaste, the Central Pacific is famous for its beaches—from the rocky coves of Montezuma on the Nicoya Peninsula to the half-moon jewels of Manuel Antonio.

The climate of the Central Pacific is not as dry as that of Guanacaste, however. You'll feel the heat and the heaviness of the moist, tropical air, so be prepared to slow down and let your body adjust to the change. Bring sunblock, insect repellent, and an umbrella to use in the sun or in case of sudden showers.

Note: Sanitary conditions are generally good on the Pacific Coast, but if you don't want to take chances, bottled water is readily available. Don't swim in estuaries or rivers; most of them are polluted. However, the heavy surf and currents of the Pacific keep the beaches free of contamination. (Be sure to read the section on how to handle rip currents in Chapter Five.)

PUNTARENAS

The town of Puntarenas was Costa Rica's main port for most of the 1800s. The treacherous terrain between San José and the Atlantic Coast made an eastern port impossible until the railway was completed in 1890. So ox-carts laden with coffee rumbled down to Puntarenas, from which the precious beans were shipped to Chile, to be re-exported to Europe. In 1843, English Captain William Le Lacheur landed in Puntarenas on the way back from a business failure in Seattle, Washington. Worried about the danger of sailing with an empty ship, he traveled five days by mule to San José, hoping to find some cargo for ballast. It turned out that coffee had been overproduced that year, and growers were desperate for new markets. Even though he was a stranger and had no money to give them, the growers entrusted him with a weighty shipment. He came back two years later with the payment, and a thriving trade with England was established.

Traditionally the vacation spot for Ticos from the Central Valley, Puntarenas underwent a facelift in late 1999 when it inaugurated new facilities to receive thousands of cruise ship passengers during their September to May season. A tourist information and communications center, a crafts market, a restaurant, and an amphitheater are housed in airy well-designed buildings across from the huge new dock on the ocean side of downtown. The **Puntarenas Marine Park** (open Tuesday through Sunday, 9 a.m to 5 p.m.; 661-5272; admission $7, students $4, seniors over 65 free) is an indoor aquarium showcasing the sea creatures of the Pacific Coast and the Gulf of Nicoya. The tanks are full of hermaphroditic fish, yellow seahorses, coral, and anemones. A whale jawbone and vertebrae, a resident pelican, and crocodiles in a pond are also featured. The snack bar, souvenir shop, ecology information stand, and playground are run by local women trained especially for the project. The marine park is 200 meters east of the cruise dock near the bus station.

The main reason foreign tourists go to Puntarenas is to catch a ferry boat to Playa Naranjo or to Paquera en route to the Nicoya Peninsula, or to make bus connections from Guanacaste and Monteverde to Manuel Antonio.

The town is only four blocks wide for most of its length because it is built on a narrow spit. Fishing boats and ferries dock on the estuary side; a beach runs along the Gulf of Nicoya side. The Ministry of Health warns against bathing in the estuary. The beaches in town have been cleaned up in the last few years and recent tests show they are now safe for bathing, but with so many other beautiful beaches to see, we would not make Puntarenas a final destination.

Calypso Tours takes you around the gulf in a luxurious Manta Raya, a speedy yacht with on-deck jacuzzi pools and trampolines and a spacious air-conditioned cabin with a bar ($99, including transportation to and from San José; wheelchairs can be accommodated; 256-8585; www.calypso tours.com, e-mail: info@calypsotours.com). The crew offers fresh tropical fruit snacks, and serves ceviche and a gourmet lunch on Tortuga Island, where you can swim and snorkel. Weekdays the beach is more tranquil

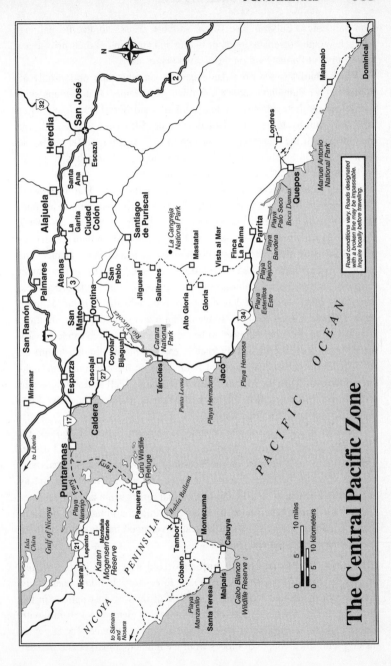

Road conditions vary. Roads designated with a broken line may be impassable. Inquire locally before traveling.

The Central Pacific Zone

than weekends. Calypso also offers sailboat cruises to Pacific national parks, bike and horseback tours, or hiking and kayaking at their private nature reserve at Punta Coral on the Nicoya Peninsula.

Finca Daniel (www.finca-daniel.com) is an adventure option only 35 minutes from Puntarenas above the town of Miramar. Cruise ships send many tourists there for canopy tours, hiking, and horseback riding. They offer two **canopy tours**: the 11-platform tour ($45) goes through the tree tops for part of the tour, then ziplines up to 2100 feet long offer incredible views of the Gulf of Nicoya; the 25-platform tour ($79), reached on horseback, crosses 11 waterfalls and can include plunges into waterfall pools, swimming in narrow canyon passageways, and rappelling. **Hotel Vista del Golfo** (private bath, hot water, cable TV, pool, exercise room, restaurant, internet access, conference center; $50-$60, including breakfast; 639-9900, fax: 639-8130; www.finca-daniel.com, e-mail: info@finca-daniel.com) has a beautiful view and offers clean, comfortable rooms at Finca Daniel. The German owners have planted over 350 fruit trees near the lodge that attract toucans, parrots, hummingbirds, monkeys, sloths, kinkajous, armadillos, and many other animals and birds. A drive up into the **Alberto Manuel Brenes Cloud Forest Reserve** above the farm can yield a quetzal sighting. If you want to stay cool but need to be close to Puntarenas to catch an early ferry, this is a good option. Day visitors can use the pool and a hammock for $10. To get there, head north of Puntarenas on the Interamerican highway. Soon you'll see the Miramar turnoff at a large Shell station. Turn right and climb six kilometers to the town of Miramar, then continue five kilometers farther uphill to Finca Daniel.

Back in Puntarenas, on the oceanfront between Calles 21 and 23, **La Caravelle** serves expensive food in an elegant setting. Nearby, **El Jorón** (open 10 a.m. to midnight; closed Tuesday) is popular among locals and visitors alike for beer and *bocas*. The restaurant at the **Hotel Las Brisas** has a clean kitchen, is well-lit and breezy, and serves some tasty Greek specialties. **La Yunta** (open noon to midnight), in a charming older building with a wide veranda overlooking the sea, serves good traditional Tico food, specializing in seafood and steak.

LODGING   The **Gran Hotel Chorotega** (cold water, ceiling fan, shared or private bath; $20-$40; 661-0998), a three-story building diagonally across from the Banco Nacional, is the best of the low-cost options in the crowded, funky downtown area of Puntarenas. It's clean and well-run, with secure parking, a refrigerator for guests, and laundry service. Try to get an inside room. It's a couple of blocks from the municipal market and passenger ferry dock—convenient for the early-morning passenger boat to the Montezuma area.

The beachfront hotels have more pleasant surroundings. **Hotel Tioga** (private bath, air conditioning, TV, phone, pool, hot water; $50-$100, including breakfast; 661-0271, fax: 661-0127; www.hoteltioga.com, e-mail: costa rica@hoteltioga.com) is comfortable and well-maintained, with a cafeteria.

The other places are at the western end of the Paseo de los Turistas, a few blocks from the dock for the car ferries. **Las Brisas** (private bath, heated water, TV, phones, air conditioning, pool; $70-$90, including breakfast; 661-4040, fax: 661-2120; e-mail: hbrisas@racsa.co.cr) is clean, with large, plain rooms and effective, no-nonsense management. **Apartotel Alamar** (private bath, hot water, kitchen, pool, jacuzzi; $70-$80; 661-4343, fax: 661-2726; www.alamarcr.com, e-mail: info@alamarcr.com) next door has rooms with fully equipped kitchens.

GETTING THERE: By Bus: San José–Puntarenas buses (Calle 16, Avenidas 10/12; 222-0064; $2.50) leave every 40 minutes between 6 a.m. and 7 p.m. Get there early on weekends and holidays. *Directo* buses take two and a half hours. In Puntarenas, the bus stop is at Calle 4, Avenidas 2/4 (661-2158). Return buses begin departing at 4:15 a.m. Buses leave the Monteverde Cheese Factory for Puntarenas daily at 5:30 a.m. (by way of Las Juntas de Abangares) and 6 a.m. (via Lagarto). Buses to Puntarenas from Liberia leave at 5 a.m., 8:30 a.m., 10 a.m., 11:15 a.m., and 3:15 p.m.

By Car: On the map, it looks like the Interamerican Highway is the most direct route to Puntarenas, but the last 31 kilometers between San Ramon and Esparza can take 45 minutes to an hour if there are a lot of trucks. The best route is the Atenas–Orotina road, accessed by the Atenas turnoff on the Interamerican Highway about 15 minutes west of the airport. Big freight trucks are not allowed on this road because it is so curvy. For this reason, the Atenas route can be a faster way to get to the Pacific (if you don't mind winding roads) because there is less traffic. When you get to the Jacó turnoff, ignore it and go straight to Caldera. The turnoff to Puntarenas is about 30 minutes from the Jacó turnoff, a few kilometers north of Caldera.

NICOYA PENINSULA

The southern edge of Guanacaste's Nicoya Peninsula is part of Puntarenas Province. This is because ferries have traditionally connected the eastern side of the Gulf of Nicoya with the mainland through the port of Puntarenas. Except for flying to the Tambor airstrip, the fastest way to get to the Nicoya Peninsula from San José is by boat, although it's still a time-consuming adventure. The area is a good three hours from Liberia in the dry season, and five hours in the rainy season. Tourism in the area has centered around Playa Naranjo, where one of the car ferries from Puntarenas docks; Bahía Ballena, located midway down the coast; the beaches of Montezuma to the south; the Cabo Blanco Absolute Biological Reserve at the very tip of the peninsula; and, most recently, the beaches of Malpaís and Santa Teresa. A terrific website for maps and information about this area is **www.nicoya peninsula.com**.

THE PENINSULAR BIOLOGICAL CORRIDOR AND THE KAREN MOGENSEN RESERVE

Apart from being one of Costa Rica's fastest growing tourism destination, the Nicoya Peninsula has one of the most developed biological corridors in

ADVENTURE REPORT: CERRO ESCONDIDO LODGE

The car ferry ride across the Gulf of Nicoya to Playa Naranjo was a "trip," with salsa blaring on the upper deck, seagulls screaming overhead, and pelicans skimming the water's surface as the ferry glided by the verdant islands of the Gulf. From Playa Naranjo, it was a short drive west to Lepanto, where we stopped at El Sol Naciente, ASEPALECO's tourism and culture office. After a warm greeting, they stored our luggage and took us to the village of Montaña Grande, where we saddled up on small, gentle horses for the ride up to the Karen Mogensen Reserve. Bushes with yellow flowers arched over the trail as we climbed. In about an hour we could see the islands of the Gulf, then we descended into the hidden valley at the top of the mountain and saw the red roofs of Valle Escondido Lodge below.

Luis Mena, biologist extraordinaire and one of the principal movers behind ASEPALECO, told us that when he was growing up, he had heard about the farm in this hidden valley, but that it seemed "as far off as Africa." In the early 1990s, he visited the elderly campesino couple that had homesteaded on the farm for 50 years. They were getting old and wanted to sell. Luis saw that several rivers that supply drinking water to the whole peninsula were born on the farm. Before she died, Doña Karen Mogensen heard about the farm and offered to bequeath money to ASEPALECO to buy it.

the country. ASEPALECO, the ecological association named after the peninsula's three main towns, Paquera, Lepanto, and Cóbano, has a model recycling and landfill program in Lepanto, on the peninsula's northern coast, has trained an active volunteer fire department, and has made great progress toward a biological corridor extending from Cabo Blanco Reserve to Barra Honda National Park, 55 miles to the north. Their enthusiastic work has put an end to the droughts, forest fires, and illegal logging that used to plague the area. They recently won the government's Improved Quality of Life Award.

Central to the Peninsular Biological Corridor is the **Karen Mogensen Reserve**, which offers opportunities for wilderness adventure that are rare in this area. Doña Karen and her husband, Nils Olof Wessberg, came to

---

The old farmhouse is still there. The wood stove is made of rocks and ashes, and the kitchen is just as it was in the old days. Now there are attractive wooden cabins near the farmhouse, each with two bunkbeds and a private bath. Doña Mary cooks when guests are there, and polishes the old stove with ashes each time she prepares a meal, adding to the stove's burnished glow. The meals were delicious, and we slept well in the quiet cabins.

In the morning, Don Arnaldo led us on a 90-minute hike down into the gorge. The steep trail had cement steps built into it all the way down. Someone had worked hard to make the trail safe and secure. When we reached the Río Blanco, we walked upstream over some slippery rocks until we could see the jewel of the Karen Mogensen Reserve: **Catarata Velo de Novia**, or **Bridal Veil Falls**, an incredible 60-foot waterfall that spreads out over a curved cliff like a lacy bridal veil. Below the falls, there is a pristine swimming hole with the most amazing pale-green crystalline water, a testament to ASEPALECO's work in assuring the water supply for the surrounding area.

On the hike out to the village of San Ramón, we met the two campesino brothers who had carefully laid cement blocks into the trail from the cabins. You could tell that this was a labor of love for them, and that they were totally involved in ASEPALECO's vision for the health of their community.

Nicoya in the 1950s. They were instrumental in the 1963 founding of Costa Rica's first biological reserve, Cabo Blanco, at the end of the Nicoya Peninsula. When Doña Karen passed away in 1993, she bequeathed money to ASEPALECO, which used it to buy the 1556-acre reserve that protects the headwaters of several important rivers. The reserve can only be reached by horse or on foot.

To visit ASEPALECO's attractive ✿ **Cerro Escondido Lodge** (private bath, solar heated water; $30-$40/person, including meals; 650-0607, fax: 650-0201; www.asepaleco.org, e-mail: asepalec@racsa.co.cr), you must arrange for transportation and guides in advance. See "Adventure Report" on page 366. Highly recommended.

ASEPALECO can arrange for you to visit other community-based initiatives in the region, like mangrove bird-watching bicycle tours with the women of ✿ **Isla Chira** (661-3261), a large island in the gulf, or to learn about solar ovens at the Casa del Sol (681-1015) near Guaitil. From February through April, they can take you to see the orchids at Monte Alto Forest Reserve (659-9347), near the pleasant mountain town of Hojancha.

PLAYA NARANJO

Travel notes: If you want to get from Guanacaste to the Nicoya Peninsula in the rainy season, you have to go through Playa Naranjo. The roads coming into Playa Naranjo from Guanacaste are paved, so even if it looks longer on the map, it's quicker to go from Sámara or Nosara to Montezuma by way of Playa Naranjo rather than dealing with the even rougher roads along the Guanacaste coast and, especially, the Río Ora and the Río Bongo between Malpaís and Playa Carrillo, which are impossible to cross in the rainy season. Staying in Playa Naranjo is convenient if you are coming from Guanacaste en route to Montezuma. The 27-kilometer stretch between Playa Naranjo and Paquera is unpaved. It takes three hours to get from Playa Naranjo to Montezuma or Malpaís in the rainy season. In the dry season you can take a short cut from Malpaís to Carmona on the way to the town of Nicoya. Ask at your hotel for exact directions.

A couple of hundred meters toward Lepanto from Playa Naranjo is the pleasant, clean **Hotel El Paso** (cold water, pool, private bath, ceiling fan or air conditioning, TV, restaurant; $40-$50, including breakfast; phone/fax: 661-2610). A good value. Use of their small pool costs $2, an option you might want to exercise to break up the trip. Also here is a compact complex including a gas station, convenience store, and bar/restaurant.

Toward Lepanto and Jicaral, the French-owned **Hotel Maquinay** (private bath, heated water, fans, air conditioning, pool; $20-$30; 641-8011) serves fish, fondue, and crepes suzette in its restaurant and offers ping-pong, tennis courts, and a pool table.

GETTING THERE: By Car and Boat: A ferry boat (661-1069, 661-3834; $1.40/adult, 75 cents/child, $10/car) leaves Puntarenas five times daily, with exact schedules varying according to the season. To reach the dock, drive right through downtown Puntarenas on the same street you came in on until you see a little sign directing you to turn right. The dock is near the northwestern end of town. Make sure you take the Naranjo ferry, not the Paquera/Tambor one. Snacks are sold on board.

Note: If you have a car, be sure to get in line at least an hour before the ferry leaves from either end because only a limited number of cars can fit. It is especially crowded on weekends and during the dry season. Allow two hours for the trip, including boarding and disembarking time. Only drivers are allowed to board the ferry in their cars. Passengers must walk on. A bus to Lepanto and Jicaral meets the ferry. There are numerous car-watchers at the ferry landing whom you can pay to watch your car while you buy tickets or have lunch.

By Bus: There are no buses south to Paquera.

PAQUERA AND CURÚ WILDLIFE REFUGE

Paquera is one hour from Playa Naranjo by car (on a gravel road), or an hour and 15 minutes from Puntarenas on either of two car ferries: the Naviera Tambor or Ferry Peninsular. You can also get there on the *lancha,* a smaller boat that carries people only. The ferry landing is a 15-minute drive east from Paquera itself, a small town that has gas stations, food and clothing stores, a bank, and pharmacies. The commercial center for the beach towns and farming communities on the lower Nicoya Peninsula, Paquera is not where you'd want to spend your vacation, but it's convenient for visiting Curú or if you need to spend a night near the ferry docks.

Twenty minutes north of Paquera, in a lush horseshoe valley downhill from the road, is **Hotel Bahía Luminosa** (private bath, hot water, pool, wall fans or air conditioning; $60-$70, including breakfast; 641-0386, in the U.S.: 530-842-3322; www.bahialuminosa.com, e-mail: tropics@racsa.co.cr), with both hilltop and poolside cabinas. Water-sports activities like sportfishing, diving, windsurfing, or canoeing through a local mangrove swamp can be coordinated through the hotel, as well as horseback rides to nearby waterfalls.

In Paquera, the **Cabinas Ginana** (private bath, cold water, ceiling fans, restaurant; $7-$12; with air conditioning, $20-$30; 641-0119, fax: 641-0419) are clean and inexpensive. **Cabinas El Paraíso** (private bath, cold water, table fans; $12-$20; 641-0240, fax: 641-0234), across from the

Guardia Rural after you turn right toward Cóbano, are very clean and have a nice *soda*. The owner will pick you up at the ferry.

Located on a private farm seven kilometers south of Paquera is the **Curú Wildlife Refuge** (open 7:30 a.m. to 3 p.m.; 641-0590; e-mail: refugio curu@yahoo.com; admission $6). Its beach is home to thousands of phantom crabs, one of which stole my watch while I was enjoying the warm, gentle waters of the picturesque, cup-shaped bay. Luckily, we spotted the watchband at the bottom of the nearest crab hole and we fished it out with a stick. Snorkeling is supposed to be good there, but we didn't stay long enough to find out because no-see-ums and other nasty biting bugs were making mincemeat of us.

A recent study rated Curú as the ecologically richest reserve on the Nicoya Peninsula due to its diversity of habitats, including mangroves, rainforest, and a lagoon, which is the only one left on the peninsula. The farm has banana plantations that are specifically for wildlife, so it's not difficult to see howler and white-faced monkeys, coatimundis, iguanas, and more than 150 species of birds from the 11 different hiking trails. Three kinds of turtles nest on the beach. Curú is better as a day trip, although there are very rustic accommodations ($25/person, including food) for groups of students and researchers. The bus from Paquera passes the entrance, which is easy to miss—if you're coming from the north it's on the left next to a green house on stilts, seven kilometers south of Paquera.

BAHÍA BALLENA

The waters of this deep, round bay on the southeastern end of the Nicoya Peninsula are gentle and warm, but are not very clear near the shore. This bay is the site of one of the largest beach hotel and condo projects in Central America, owned by the Spanish chain Barceló. You'll see the guarded entrance to the hotel and the brightly painted condos lined up in rows as you enter Tambor. You'll also notice that the road is in perfect condition between Barceló's ferry landing in Paquera and their hotel.

LODGING   We recommend that you continue on to Tango Mar, Montezuma, or Malpaís/Santa Teresa, but if you need a place to stay in this area, **Hotel Dos Lagartos** (cold water, ceiling fans, shared or private bath; $20-$30; phone/fax 683-0236; e-mail: aulwes@costarica.net) is clean, friendly, low-key, and quiet (and has good mattresses). From the beach in front of the hotel you can see two points in the distance that resemble crocodiles or lizards, hence the name.

Inland from the beach, **Pulpería Super Lapa** is a well-stocked and friendly grocery store. Meals are plentiful, inexpensive, and good at **Cris-**

tina's, next to Super Lapa. Cristina also rents rooms (cold water; with shared bath and wall fans, $12-$20; with private bath and ceiling fans, $20-$30; phone/fax: 683-0028) above the restaurant.

Tango Mar (683-0001, fax: 683-0003; www.tangomar.com, e-mail: tangomar@racsa.co.cr) is a unique resort on a beautiful stretch of beach south of Bahía Ballena. It has a variety of accommodations (all with hot water, ceiling fans, air conditioning, cable TV, phones; $190-$250; two- to five-bedroom villas, $500-$1200): some on the beach, some with views, some with private jacuzzis. All rates include a lavish breakfast. Tango Mar boasts a massage and yoga studio, a seaside golf course, and offers sport-fishing, sailing, surfing, scuba diving, tennis courts, two spring-fed swimming pools, horseback riding, mountain biking, and beach volleyball. They'll arrange to have you picked up six kilometers away in Paquera, or you can fly from San José to the airstrip at Bahía Tambor. By car, Tango Mar is about an hour south of Paquera; follow the signs south of Tambor. Reservations are required.

GETTING THERE: See "Getting There" in Montezuma section, below.

MONTEZUMA

Like other beautiful places in Costa Rica, Montezuma is having to adjust to its sudden fame as a tourist destination. Enchanted visitors have spread the word about its lovely rocky coves and waterfalls. Because of the rocky coastline, it is not ideal for swimming, but the many tidepools lend themselves to a refreshing dip. Of all the beach towns in Costa Rica, Montezuma is the one that has attracted the strongest "alternative" community, with a thriving population of hippie farmers, natural-foods producers and consumers, itinerant artisans, and the like.

Montezuma was for many years known as a campers' free haven, but now things are changing. The only public campground (often full) is at the northern end of the first beach ("Rincón de los Monos") and is only open during high season.

The first few rocky bays to the north of the village have very strong currents, especially during high tide. **Playa Grande**, about 30 minutes north by foot, is calm and shallow, the best and safest place for bathing, especially at low tide. At the far end of Playa Grande is a picturesque waterfall where you can sit and watch pelicans dive. Several locals offer horseback trips here. Read our cautions about riding horses in hot climates (see Chapter Five); there is a tragic history of horses in this area being mistreated and overused. Ask your hotel owner which guides they recommend.

Montezuma Expeditions (462-0919; www.montezumaexpeditions. com) arranges kayaking, mountain biking, and snorkeling trips, as well as tours to Tortuga Island and Malpaís. They will pick you up in San José and deliver you in an air-conditioned bus to Montezuma for $25, including breakfast. The **Waterfall Canopy Tour** (389-3139, 642-0307; www.monte zumatraveladventures.com) in the hills above Montezuma offers three tours a day. **Aventuras de Montezuma** (642-6050) and **Montezuma Travel Adventures** (823-6111) also provide a variety of trips. All have internet access and digital photo processing, and will arrange transfers. **Cabo Blanco Divers** (642-0482) offers diving trips.

There are **boatmen** in Montezuma who provide transportation across the gulf to Puntarenas and Jacó, or around Cabo Blanco to Carrillo, Sámara, and Nosara (see Guanacaste chapter). Contact them through the information kiosk across from Hotel Montezuma or the travel agencies in town. Come to the Saturday morning open-air market for fresh fruits and vegetables (some organic!).

There is a series of gorgeous waterfalls about 30 minutes out of town with pools that are nice for swimming. People like to cliff-dive here, but it's dangerous, so be very careful. Several people have slipped and fallen to their deaths in recent years. To get there, walk along the road to Cabo Blanco until you get to Restaurant La Cascada (about ten minutes). At the bridge, scramble upstream over the rocks for half an hour to an hour. You should be surefooted to attempt this hike. We used to recommend that people wear shoes that could get wet, but we've heard reports of many a twisted ankle on this slippery, rocky stream bed, so good hiking boots would be the best choice.

Cóbano, seven kilometers inland from Montezuma, has the only bank, post office, clinic, pharmacy, and car rental agency in the area. The Banco Nacional is almost always crowded, so try to get money changed before you get to the peninsula. They only accept American Express traveler's checks, and you must bring your passport. The supermarkets will sometimes change traveler's checks if you buy something. Bring *colones* in small denominations to pay for buses and restaurants. For medical problems, call the clinic at 642-0208. For emergencies, call 642-0630. There is also a dentist, as well as a chiropractor who comes once a week.

RESTAURANTS   Montezuma has some excellent dining choices. You might almost miss **Playa de los Artistas** (open 10 a.m. to 4:30 p.m., closed Sunday; 642-0920), on the beach across from Hotel Los Mangos, and if you enter the gate and see the rickety tables set in the sand, you might not think it's much, but taste the stuffed eggplant or the homemade breads and

organic salads and you'll know you are in a very special place. The tiny
Restaurante Rico Rico (open 5 p.m. to 10:30 p.m.) is toward town from
Playa de los Artistas, by a little stream. Its exuberant Italian owner makes
his own pasta. We have heard that the shrimp ravioli is incredible.

El Sano Banano (open 7 a.m. to 9:30 p.m.), in the center of town, has
excellent vegetarian and vegan food and a varied menu, which includes
Caribbean curry, pasta, Mexican dishes, and seafood specialties like tropical
shrimp with pineapple. It's open for breakfast, lunch and dinner. On the
north side of the village, the European-owned **Cocolores** (open 11 a.m. to
11 p.m.) specializes in seafood curry and pasta but also makes tasty sandwiches and salads. The nearby **Bakery Café** serves delicious breakfasts and
baked treats. Down in Cabuya, **El Celaje** offers authentic Belgian cuisine.

LODGING   In the dry season, Montezuma books up; call for reservations.
As in most beach towns, hotels here offer significant discounts, sometimes
up to 50 percent, in the "green season" (May through November). "Downtown" Montezuma can be very noisy at night due to the mighty sound systems at the two bars. A helpful service for booking any hotel, house, or
activity in this area is **Cabo Blanco Enterprises** (in the U.S.: 805-773-
9700; www.caboblancoent.com, e-mail: caboent@aol.com). Other useful
websites are **www.playamontezuma.net** and **www.nicoyapeninsula.com**.

You'll see a couple of places as you drive toward Montezuma from Cóbano. The turnoff for **The Nature Lodge Finca Los Caballos** (private
bath, hot water, fans, pool; $70-$80; phone/fax: 642-0124; www.nature
lodge.net, e-mail: naturelc@racsa.co.cr) is about halfway between Cóbano
and Montezuma. Rooms are tastefully designed and comfortable, and the
breezy open-air restaurant has an international menu with a Latin flair and
a lovely view of the ocean in the distance. Organic produce is used as
much as possible. Excellent horseback trips are offered, as well as a quieter
and more relaxing atmosphere than in downtown Montezuma.

In the hills 1.8 kilometers above the town, **Horizontes de Montezuma**
is a tranquil place to learn Spanish. It is also a lovely B&B (private bath,
hot water, pool; $50-$70; 642-0534; www.horizontes-montezuma.com, e-
mail: collina@racsa.co.cr). Rooms with balconies and hammocks offer
ocean and jungle views, and a central atrium with skylight keeps interior
spaces bright. The German owner gives a week-long Spanish survival
course as well as longer courses.

As you enter town, to the right is **El Jardín** (private bath, cold or
heated water, ceiling fans, some with air conditioning, refrigerator, pool;
$60-$80; 642-0548). These spacious rooms have wide, tiled balconies and

porches with hammocks. The houses up the hill sleep four and provide views ($70-$100). Across the street is **Hotel La Aurora** (shared or private bath, some hot water, some air conditioning, ceiling fans, screened windows, communal kitchen; $20-$50; rates include morning coffee, tea, purified water; phone/fax: 642-0051; e-mail: hotelaurora@racsa.co.cr), with a hammock-strewn balcony upstairs where it's easy to meet fellow travelers. The owners, a German-Tico couple, are passionate community activists. The hotel is in front of the shady, well-maintained town playground—a boon for families with kids.

Hotel El Tajalín (private bath, heated water, ceiling fans; $50-$60; with air conditioning, $60-$90; 642-0061, fax: 642-0527; www.tajalin.com, e-mail info@tajalin.com) overlooks the park and has ocean views from its third-floor café. The owner is very helpful to his guests.

Next door is **Hotel Montezuma Pacific** (private bath, heated water, shared refrigerator; with fans, $20-$30; with air conditioning, $30-$50; 642-0204, 222-7746), which has a nice upstairs porch.

The main street of Montezuma has become a brightly painted block of souvenir stands, trendy beach boutiques, travel agencies, an ice cream shop and a laundry. In the midst of all this is **El Sano Banano** (see page 373). This is the unofficial tourist meeting place in town. **El Sano Banano Beach Hotel**, in a gorgeous setting, consists of peaceful round bungalows and comfortable suites (private bath, hot water, fans; $110-$120; with kitchen, $110-$170; all rates include breakfast; 642-0638, fax: 642-0631; www.elbanano.com, e-mail: elbanano@racsa.co.cr) set in their forested preserve on the second beach to the north (a ten-minute walk from downtown). You cannot drive there, but the owners will transport your luggage. Because of the walk, these cabins are not the best for little children, but older kids are welcome. Be sure to get there by 4 p.m. so you can check in at the restaurant in town and do your first beach walk before dark. The bungalows are very near the beach, and the surf is strong. Some people find the sound of the waves too loud, but we found it an incredible lullaby. Also here is a lovely swimming pool with a waterfall that massages your shoulders and lush gardens full of flowers and monkeys. The owners rent comfortable rooms (private bath, hot water, air conditioning, cable TV; $70-$80) above and behind the El Sano Banano restaurant in town. If you stay there, you can still hang out at the pool and beach. Recommended.

Cabinas Mar y Cielo (private bath, cold water, fans; $20-$40; phone/fax: 642-0261) are on a rocky point behind Chico's Bar and the **Mamatea Delicatessen** (open daily, 7 a.m. to 9 p.m.), a well-stocked mini-market.

Up the road a bit and on the left is **Luz de Mono** (phone/fax: 642-0010; e-mail: luzdmono@racsa.co.cr), a large restaurant and bar with artistic bas-relief murals of monkeys doing all sorts of naughty things. They serve sushi and sashimi, and seafood delicacies like fish steamed in banana leaf with coconut and spices for dinner, accompanied by Italian wine made from local grapes by the owner's father. A full breakfast buffet costs $5, and lunch is also served. In back are rooms (private bath, heated water, fans, screened windows; $100-$110) with a moat around them and little stair-bridges over the moat. Cabins with kitchens run from $110-$190. The high-end cabins have panoramic views and jacuzzis on their sun decks.

At this end of town you'll also find **Librería Topsy**, where you can rent books, trade or sell used books, and buy souvenirs. They have a good selection of local and international newspapers.

South of downtown, along the coastal road (the one that leads all the way to Cabo Blanco), are several more good places to stay. The farthest are only a five- to ten-minute walk from downtown, and all are accessible by car:

Hotel Los Mangos (pool, restaurant; 642-0076, fax: 642-0259; www.hotellosmangos.com, e-mail: homangos@racsa.co.cr) has comfortable precious-wood bungalows (private bath, hot water, ceiling fans) dotting a hillside orchard, and other rooms with shared or private bath ($20-$80). Yoga classes are offered daily.

Down the street is **Hotel Lucy** (shared or private bath, cold water, table fans; $12-$20; 642-0273). In 1993, just as we were about to leave town, some friends informed us that the municipality had a bulldozer on its way to destroy Lucy's. Like many other establishments at Montezuma, Lucy's is built within 50 meters of the high-tide line, a zone the Costa Rican government has wisely established as an inviolable public area. But destroying Lucy's would be a case of selective enforcement. Since the owner of Lucy's is a feisty guy without connections to politicians, his hotel was targeted. We went to Lucy's that morning and saw half of the town staked out in front of the hotel in defiance of the approaching bulldozer. Along with the dozer came several rural guards and the mayor of Cóbano. The crowd successfully intimidated the officials; Lucy's still stands, and has been recently renovated.

The well-maintained, friendly **Hotel Amor de Mar** (cold or heated water, table fans; with shared bath, $40-$50; with private bath, $40-$90; phone/fax: 642-0262; www.amordemar.com, e-mail: shoebox@racsa.co.cr) features quiet rooms, some with verandas and ocean views, and has spacious grounds, its own private tidepool, and hammocks overlooking a stream that flows into the ocean. They also rent a house ($110-$150) for up to six people. The restaurant (open for breakfast and lunch) serves home-made bread. It's located a few hundred meters south of Lucy's, across the street from the waterfall trailhead. Recommended.

Three kilometers from Montezuma is **Playa Cedros**, a good beach for beginning surfers. Just before you get to Playa Cedros you'll see signs for **Las Rocas** (642-0393; www.cabloblancopark.com, e-mail: lasrocas@racsa. co.cr), owned by a Swiss family that offers rooms above their home (shared bath, cold water; $20-$30) and apartments in a two-story house (private bath, cold water, fans, kitchen; $50-$70; kids under 8 free). They have free snorkeling and fishing equipment for guests and provide bikes for riding into town. They can also tell you how to get to a nearby hidden waterfall. Las Rocas is a five-minute walk from the Río Cedros, a good place for kids to romp.

GETTING THERE: By Bus and Boat: From the dock behind the *mercado* in Puntarenas take the *lancha* (passenger ferry) to Paquera, which leaves Puntarenas at 6 a.m., 11 a.m., and 3 p.m. Several public buses wait for the *lancha* at Paquera. Be sure to take the one marked Montezuma ($3.50), which makes the trip down bumpy roads, through beautiful country, in about two hours. If you want to take the 6 a.m. boat, you'll have to spend the night in Puntarenas. Buses leave Monte-zuma for Paquera every two hours. Check schedules at www.playamontezuma. net. You can also take the more comfortable car ferry (see below). Buses don't al-ways meet the car ferry, but you can get a taxi into Montezuma for about $40 per carload. It's much faster than the bus.

By Private Bus and Boat: A great option for getting to Montezuma in a quick (five hours) and efficient way is Montezuma Expeditions (642-0919). They will pick you up at the airport, let you stay at Hotel Los Volcanes in Alajuela, and transport you to Montezuma for $45-$60. They will also take you from Mon-tezuma to Hotel Los Volcanes and deliver you to the airport in the morning. The same service without hotel and airport pick-up costs $25.

By Car and Boat: It is not really necessary to have a car to go to Montezuma, but if you do, car ferries leave Puntarenas nine times a day from the dock near the far end of town. To get to the ferry landing, drive through Puntarenas on the same street you come in on, until a sign directs you to turn right. If in doubt, ask. Find current schedules at www.playamontezuma.net.

You have to leave your car and go inside the terminal to buy your tickets. Be sure you are in the line for cars if you want a car ticket, for passengers if you want a passenger ticket. On Barceló's Naviera Tambor (661-2084) you can opt for a first-class seat in the air-conditioned (freezing) snack-bar and TV lounge. Otherwise, you ride on rather uncomfortable benches on top of the boat. The older, funkier Ferry Peninsular (641-0515) doesn't offer a first-class option.

Check schedules at www.playamontezuma.net. Cars start boarding about 50 minutes before departure time, so drivers should get there an hour early at either end. Only drivers can drive onto the ferries—all other passengers must walk on. The trip takes an hour and a quarter, with another 15 minutes to disembark. The landing is a 15-minute drive from Paquera. After that, the roads are perfectly paved until you get to Hotel Playa Tambor; from there it's a straight shot 45 minutes on good gravel road to Cóbano, where you make a left for the final seven kilometers (15 minutes) downhill to Montezuma. The trip from Paquera takes about two hours. The nearest gas station to Montezuma is in Cóbano.

By Air: The nearest airstrip to Montezuma is in Tambor, about an hour from Montezuma by car ($30-$40 in a taxi). Ask the airline or your hotel in Montezuma to help coordinate transportation in advance. SANSA flies to Tambor from San José (221-9414, fax: 255-2176; www.flysansa.com; $58 one way) twice daily. Nature Air also flies to Tambor twice daily (220-3054, fax: 220-0413; www.natureair.com; $66 one way, $132 roundtrip). See Chapter Four for information about making reservations on SANSA and Nature Air.

CABUYA AND CABO BLANCO WILDLIFE RESERVE

A road continues south from Montezuma through Cabuya and on to Cabo Blanco Wildlife Reserve. Cabo Blanco was the first national reserve in Costa Rica—its founding in 1963 was the initial step in the development of the country's extensive national park system. Preserved with the encouragement of Swedish biologist Nils Olof Wessberg and his wife Karen, who were concerned about the encroaching deforestation that was threatening the area's rich and varied wildlife, it is an "absolute reserve," which means most of the area is accessible only to scientific researchers.

Stop at the "Area Turistica" building to get an entrance permit (open 8 a.m. to 4 p.m.; closed Monday and Tuesday; 642-0093; $8). You can take a fairly strenuous two-hour hike up the Sendero Sueco and down to Playa Cabo Blanco (bring food and plenty of water). You'll see lots of howler monkeys. (Don't stand directly underneath them—they like to pee on sightseers.) There are pelican colonies on the point, which has beautiful pinkish coral sand. Another trail is the semicircular Sendero Danés, which takes about an hour to complete. Bring insect repellent and boots in the rainy season.

LODGING   For assistance in booking hotels or activities in this area, see www.caboblancoent.com.

Near the town of Cabuya, two kilometers before the reserve entrance, is an island that holds an indigenous cemetery. You can walk to the island at low tide (wear water walkers because of the rocky sea floor). Snorkeling is

Howler monkey

good there during the dry season, and reef-protected areas and tide pools make for safe swimming.

The nicest place to stay in Cabuya is **El Celaje** (private bath, heated water, ceiling fans, pool; $50-$60, including breakfast; 642-0374; www.celaje.com, e-mail: celaje@racsa.co.cr), two kilometers from the entrance to Cabo Blanco. It is right on the beach and features Belgian cuisine.

MALPAÍS AND SANTA TERESA

The long white beaches at Malpaís and Santa Teresa (both have Blue Flags) are renowned among surfers, and have been a well-kept secret among the area's aficionados. Swells are especially high at Santa Teresa, but nonsurfers will enjoy the tidepools and shell-strewn beach. Locals tell us that the area in front of Hotel Tropico Latino is the best for playing in the waves.

A lively community of Brazilians, Israelis, French Canadians, Czechs, Belgians, Swiss, Italians, gringos and Ticos makes for good food and lots of internet cafés. Both foreigners and locals participate in beach clean-ups, recycling, and environmental education.

Of course, the area has its own nine-platform **Canopy del Pacífico** (640-0071) canopy tour, located at the southern end of Malpaís, with a 1000-foot cable over a canyon, cables with ocean views combined with an ethnobotanical tour. **Pacific Divers** run scuba trips from their office at the Bar Tabú in Santa Teresa.

Santa Teresa and Malpaís are among Costa Rica's trendiest destinations and are developing at a rapid pace, but the roads are still bad, and 4WD is still needed.

First we'll talk about lodging to the south on Malpaís. Santa Teresa is to the north. See www.malpais.net or www.nicoyapeninsula.com for maps and information.

If you are interested in marine biology, a fascinating opportunity to study the marine ecosystems of this area, which have been off-limits to humans for 40 years, is now available. Milton and Diana Lieberman, researchers from the University of Georgia who founded the San Luis Ecolodge near Monteverde, have established the **San Miguel Marine Research Center** (shared bath, cold water, bunk beds; $30-$40/person, including meals; 645-5277, 645-5890, 640-0201; e-mail: liebermv@racsa.co.cr) within the reserve. You do not have to be a professional biologist—lay people with a sincere interest in this very special region are welcome, as long as they come in a group. To get there, you must hike two kilometers from Malpaís; reservations must be made in advance.

MALPAÍS   The road from Cóbano intersects with the coastal road at **Frank's Place** (restaurant, pool; phone/fax: 640-0096; e-mail frank5@racsa.co.cr), just 200 meters from a good surfing spot and the main area for beach camping. Over the years, Frank has studied what surfers need and provides good, clean, cheap rooms (shared bath, cold water; $12/person) and a wide range of other possibilities (private bath, some with kitchens; $30-$60). His corner kiosk also has internet, phone and fax access, and a Sansa reservation center. Recommended for budget travelers.

Two hundred meters to the left, **The Place** (private bath, heated water, mosquito nets; $70-$80; 640-0001; www.theplacemalpais.com, e-mail: theplace@caramail.com) wins our prize for the best-designed cabins in Malpaís. The charming Swiss owner has used a variety of colors and styles to create light, airy rooms with louvered wooden doors opening onto private patios, about 200 meters from the beach. Her restaurant, **La Cantina Mexicana**, is open daily in the high season, serving seafood and vegetarian specialties. Recommended.

Apartotel Oasis (private bath, hot water, ceiling fans, kitchen, pool, snack bar; $60-$70; 640-0259; www.oasis.malpais.net, e-mail: oasis@malpais.net) has comfortable two-room bungalows with kitchens and views of the ocean 200 meters away.

Next on the left, you'll see the North American–owned **Malpaís Surf Camp** (pool, gym, cable TV, billiards, horses, bikes, restaurant; 640-0031; www.malpaissurfcamp.com, e-mail: surfcamp@racsa.co.cr), which also offers a variety of options. If you've brought a tent, camping is $7 per person. Their breezy ocean-view *ranchos* (shared bath, cold water; $40-$50 for up to four) have gravel floors and are open on all sides, with bamboo curtains for privacy. There are swings and hammocks in the rooms and a big wooden trunk to store things in. There are also smaller rooms with shared bath ($20-$30) and spacious, elegant pool-side cabinas (private bath, hot water, ceiling fans, screened windows; $90-$100). Individual surfers can share a *rancho* with other surfers for $10. During the high season they do nightly pig roasts. They offer many services, from surfing instruction and board rental to laundry and babysitting. They welcome families—children under 12 stay for free. Their van will take you to or from Tamarindo or San José ($250 for up to eight people).

About one kilometer farther south down a side road to the beach, **Restaurante Piedra del Mar** (640-0069) serves freshly caught fish and lobster, Tico style. This inexpensive *soda* is popular with locals at sunset. Recommended.

Back on the main road, **Moana Lodge** (private bath, hot water, fan, some kitchens, pool; $50-$70; with air conditioning, $70-$80; phone/fax: 640-0230; www.moanalodge.com, e-mail: mail@moanalodge.com) is owned by a friendly Belgian surfer who has decorated his place with African sculpture. Cabins have two interconnecting rooms and open onto private decks. Guests can prepare meals in an open-air *rancho* near the pool.

About 400 meters south, on the right, **La Bella Napoli** (closed Monday; 640-0073) is worth a trip to Malpaís. We enjoyed delicious smoked fish made in Montezuma, lasagna prepared with homemade pasta and basil from the garden, and fantastic bruschetta, beautifully served and topped off with homemade lemon liqueur. Recommended. Across the road is the clean, quiet **Bosque Mar** (private bath, heated water, ceiling fans, kitchen; $30-$40; phone/fax: 640-0074; e-mail: bosquemar@malpais.net), with a nice swimming pool behind the rooms.

Less than a kilometer south, **Soda Restaurante Ambiente Marino** (640-0261) specializes in ceviche, fresh fish filets and *comida típica* at the Cabuya turnoff. (Cabuya is only accessible by this road between December and May).

If you'd like to combine your beach vacation with a rainforest experience, **Star Mountain Eco Resort** (private bath, hot water, ceiling fans, pool, waterfall jacuzzi; $80-$90, including breakfast; half price for children under 6; 640-0101, fax: 640-0102; www.starmountaineco.com, e-mail: star mountain@racsa.co.cr) is the place to do it. Managed by a very hospitable Belgian couple, Daniel and Dominique, Star Mountain is a quiet 216-acre nature retreat surrounded by forest, wildlife, and birds, bordering Cabo Blanco Reserve. The attractively decorated rooms open onto a tiled veranda where hammocks and rockers invite relaxation. There is also a *casita* that can sleep a whole family ($32/person). Meals are prepared with the freshest local ingredients and gourmet flair by Dominique and served family style. Daniel, who clearly knows and loves this place, leads guests on hikes through the reserve. Experienced riders can go on horseback. The lodge is closed from September through November. To get there, drive about two kilometers inland on the road to Cabuya. Recommended.

SANTA TERESA   If you turn north at the intersection of the Cóbano road and the coastal road (at Frank's Place), you head toward Santa Teresa. About 800 meters away, the **Trópico Latino** (private bath, hot water, ceiling fans, air conditioning, pool; $80-$100; phone/fax: 640-0062, fax: 640-0117; www.hoteltropicolatino.com, e-mail: tropilat@racsa.co.cr) is a beautiful retreat, with spacious, well-ventilated rooms. Only the front cabinas have an ocean view. They offer horseback riding, fishing trips, and surfboard rentals. Their **Playa Boa Restaurant** is a good place to go for freshly caught seafood and fusion cuisine on the beach.

Luz de Vida Resort (private bath, heated water, ceiling fans, some air conditioning, refrigerators, pool, communal kitchen; $60-$80; phone/fax: 640-0319; www.luzdevida-resort.com) is the dream of seven friends from Israel who moved here with their families and collaborated on every aspect of the project's design. The bungalows are scattered among tall trees near the beach. They sometimes host poolside dance parties, and their bar is open until the wee hours of the night. About 200 meters beyond is **Camping Sunset**, a shady campground right on the beach.

Restaurante Amapola (open daily, 7:15 a.m. to 9 p.m.; 640-0114), across from the soccer field in Santa Teresa, offers a complete Tico menu with fresh fruit smoothies and juices in a clean, friendly setting. It's one of the few places open early for breakfast. Recommended. Nearby is a place to rent bikes.

Jungle Juice Bar, 200 meters after the soccer field, serves organic juices, smoothies, veggie burgers, and burritos. Next door are a surf shop, internet café, and **Tuanis**, selling beach and adventure clothing. Uphill at that corner, the **Funky Monkey Lodge** (private bath, heated water, fans; $70-$100; dormitories, $8/person; 640-0317; www.funky-monkey-lodge.com) rents well-designed bungalows that sleep four to eight. They rent surfboards and have surfboard storage racks in the rooms. Their restaurant serves fresh fish sushi.

Two hundred meters farther, on the ocean side of the road, look for the friendly **Cabinas Zeneida's** (private and shared bath, cold water, table fans; $15-$30; 640-0118). The comfortable rooms are kept very clean. There is one family-size cabina and a camping area ($4/person). We have heard numerous recommendations for the inexpensive, delicious food at

Zeneida's. She obviously cares about her guests, and has a basketball court for days when the waves aren't good. Recommended for budget travelers.

About three kilometers from Frank's Place, **Cabinas Playa Santa Teresa** (private bath, cold water, ceiling fans, some kitchens; $20-$40; phone/fax: 640-0137) are clean quarters with a shady plant-filled front yard 150 meters from another of the area's prime surfing spots. The German owner is friendly.

One of our favorite places in this area is **Milarepa** (private bath, hot water, ceiling fans, pool; $110-$140; phone/fax 640-0023, fax: 640-0168; www.milarepahotel.com), which is worth the bumpy drive. Four bungalows, decorated with a relaxed grace, feature antique Indonesian canopy beds that are draped with filmy mosquito nets, giving them a medieval air. Folding wooden doors lead to beach-front stone terraces. Bamboo curtains roll down to block the sun and wind if needed. The outside is invited in, yet you are sheltered in a lovely way. Even the bathrooms are open to the sky, with lush tropical gardens inside. Tide pools in front are safe for kids at low tide. Milarepa's restaurant features cuisine from the south of France, with meals served at a leisurely pace and topped off by excellent coffee and homemade desserts. Recommended.

The masterpiece of Santa Teresa hotels is **Florblanca Resort** (private bath, hot water, ceiling fans, air conditioning, kitchenettes, phones, internet access in rooms, pool; $330-$570, including breakfast; 640-0232, fax: 640-0226; www.florblanca.com, e-mail: florblanca@expressmail.net) at the north end of the beach. We can't express it better than the *Condé Nast Traveler*, which called Florblanca "the perfect balance between nature and luxury." An artistic eye for space, form, and color shapes every aspect of Florblanca, from the open-air bathroom/gardens with driftwood towel racks, to the molded Santa Fe–style plasterwork and *vigas* in the rooms, to the yoga studio with statues of Balinese deities in each corner, inspiring reverence. The one- and two-bedroom villas are open to the air and gardens, but can be closed off in case of rain. Two swimming pools joined by a waterfall are off the Nectar Restaurant, where fusion cuisine includes vegetarian selections, and a pastry chef is in residence. Also in residence is a naturalist guide, who can take you to a nearby nature reserve. A music and TV room, a massage space, and a gym complete the amenities. For a truly special beach vacation or honeymoon, this would be one of our top choices. You can also rent all ten villas for a retreat, workshop, or wedding. Recommended.

GETTING THERE: *By Bus:* A minibus leaves Montezuma for Cabo Blanco daily at 8 a.m., 10 a.m., 2 p.m., and 6 p.m., returning to Montezuma at 8:15 a.m., 10:15 a.m., 2:15 p.m., and 6:15 p.m. Follow directions in the Montezuma section for arriving at Cóbano. Two buses leave Cóbano daily to Malpaís and Santa Teresa ($2; 10:30 a.m. and 2:30 p.m.) from the town's main intersection. Scheduling is unreliable in the rainy season.

By Car: Before driving your own car, check with the hotels about road conditions. It takes half an hour to drive the eight kilometers from Cóbano to Malpaís. You can drive from the southern end of Malpaís to Cabuya and Cabo Blanco in the dry season, but the road was closed when we were there in November. A taxi from Montezuma to Cabo Blanco costs about $6.50. Driving there takes about 45 minutes.

If you want to explore the road going west to Río Negro and Manzanillo from Cóbano on your way to Playa Sámara in Guanacaste, keep asking people if you're going the right way—there are no signs. We would have made it to Sámara in about four hours by jeep if we hadn't hit Río Ora at high tide. You can avoid this by heading inland at Pueblo Nuevo, crossing the river on a bridge at Santa Marta, and heading down the coast again after the bridge. In the rainy season this route is impassable. It's best to go back to Paquera and Playa Naranjo, then on paved roads to Nicoya and then to Sámara and Nosara.

CARARA NATIONAL PARK AND ENVIRONS

Located near Orotina, Carara National Park (open daily, 7 a.m. to 4 p.m.; admission $8; children 6 to 12 $1) is one of the closest wildlife observation spots to San José. The 5242-hectare park is in a transitional area between the dry climate of Guanacaste and the humid climate of the southern coast. It has wildlife common to both regions, including scarlet macaws, toucans, trogons, waterfowl, monkeys, crocodiles, armadillos, sloths, and peccaries. Jaguars, pumas, ocelots, margays, and jaguarundis are also present, but rarely seen. Birders stand on the bridge over the Río Tárcoles about 5 p.m. to witness the scarlet macaws' nightly migration from the Carara forest to the mangroves at the mouth of the river. You can see crocodiles measuring up to 12 feet long from this bridge as well. The name "Carara" is derived from the Huetar Indian word for crocodile. No camping is allowed in the reserve. Many tour companies in San José, Playa Jacó, and Manuel Antonio offer guided tours to Carara. Your hotel can set one up for you. Carara is a great place to stop on your way from Arenal to Manuel Antonio. The new visitors center at Carara has ample parking, an information desk, a cafeteria, and gift stores. It is the starting point of the well-maintained trail system, including one accessible for wheelchairs.

The riverside complex at **Villa Lapas** (private bath, hot water, ceiling fans and air conditioning, phones; $89/person, including meals, snacks, and drinks; 222-5191, fax: 222-3450; www.villalapas.com, e-mail: info@villa lapas.com) is composed of beautifully cared-for gardens, an open-air restaurant, a pool, and a 120-person conference center. The hotel protects a natural reserve that follows the Río Tarcolitos, bordering Carara National Park to the south. Their **Skyway** is a system of trails and hanging bridges similar to the famous Monteverde SkyWalk. The 2.5-kilometer trail has a downward slope and is safe for children. They also have a seven-platform **canopy tour**. Even though this is a fairly touristy hotel, friends have told us that the birding there is great. Over 225 species have been seen on the grounds and in the reserve. It's easy to find: the sign is on the left as you head toward Jacó from the north, and it's 600 meters from the highway turnoff.

If you continue up the Villa Lapas road, after about four kilometers you will come to the small community of **Bijagual**, where there is a 200-meter waterfall (open daily, 7 a.m. to 3 p.m.; 661-8263; admission $10). The trail is steep and can be slippery even in the dry season. You start at the top of the waterfall gorge and descend several hundred meters, then it's a scramble over slippery rocks to get a good view of the waterfall's base. Several side trails lead to swimming holes in the river—the waterfall pool is too dangerous to swim in. You will probably need to grab onto large tree roots for balance on the way down and leverage on the way up, so bring plenty of water and food in a backpack to keep your hands free, and watch out for snakes when you grab.

The **Pura Vida Botanical Garden** (open 9 a.m. to 5 p.m.; 200-5040; admission $15; children $10), on the same road, has a great view of the coast from manicured walkways through gardens of tropical flowers and orchids. There is a restaurant and gift shop. By bus, get off the Jacó bus at the Villa Lapas sign and hitchhike in. The local bus gets there too late for good hiking. Or you can take a taxi from Jacó.

The backcountry near Bijagual is beautiful and unspoiled. **Arbofilia**, a widely respected organization specializing in grassroots ecological regeneration, operates a field station in the town of El Sur de Turrubares, a tiny village bordering Carara National Park, and five kilometers northwest of Bijagual. For hardy, hard workers with at least two weeks to spare, there are volunteer opportunities here. Contact them at 294-6219, www.arbo filia.net, or e-mail: info@arbofilia.net.

GETTING THERE: By Bus: To reach Carara by bus, take a Jacó or Quepos bus from San José or Puntarenas. Get out at the entrance to Carara.

By Car: By car, you will pass the entrance to Carara on your left as you head south to Playa Jacó.

PURISCAL AREA   The mountains between the Central Valley and the Pacific are a new frontier for tourism. Because of their rugged terrain, they have been skirted by the roads leading to the Pacific. These mountains supplied hardwoods for Costa Rica's development throughout its history, and by the late 20th century they were largely deforested. During the late 1980s and early 1990s, the town of Puriscal was the site of daily earth tremors. You can still see cracks in the large church in the center of town, unusable since then.

The town of Turrubares, about a third of the way between Orotina (near the Jacó turnoff on the Atenas highway) and Puriscal, is becoming famous because of **Turu Ba Ri** (428-6070; www.turubari.com), a huge project started by the Saborío family, former owners of one of Costa Rica's major grocery chains. In an attempt to make Costa Rica into a Disneyland for foreigners, Turu Ba Ri starts out with a state-of-the-art electric funicular on which tourists make their grandiose entrance from a dizzying height of 265 feet into the Saborío *finca* on the floor of a river valley. The more adventurous can enter the park by horseback or two kinds of ziplines. The park boasts a huge butterfly garden and exhibits of bromeliads, orchids and bamboo. The forested area has paved trails and bridges over streams, completely eliminating the unsightly and troublesome mud found in less civilized rainforests. There is even a countryside farm and restaurant where gnome-like Ticos and Ticas clad in bright typical costumes serve a native buffet. All this for only $75! Turu Ba Ri is obviously geared to the hundreds of cruise passengers who disembark for a few hours in Puntarenas, hoping to get a glimpse of Costa Rica's wonders. The good thing is that it has brought over a hundred jobs to this formerly impoverished area.

If you would like to get off the beaten track but need your creature comforts too, treat yourself to a relaxing long weekend at **La Finca Que Ama** (private bath, hot water, bathtub with Jacuzzi, refrigerator, phone, internet access, cable TV, pool, restaurant, gym, $170-$180, including breakfast; 419-0110; www.costaricafinca.com, e-mail: information@costaricafinca.com), a quiet mountain retreat owned by a friendly, helpful Israeli couple. The junior suites are very well appointed, with comfy sitting rooms and a cable TV with a DVD player. You can choose your favorite movie from their extensive DVD collection. The restaurant menu is a combination of home cooking and gourmet world cuisine, served on their terrace overlooking hilly farms and forests. They are located about 35 minutes east of Orotina on the road to Puriscal, two minutes after San Pablo de Turrubares, on the left. Recommended.

LA CANGREJA NATIONAL PARK   Costa Rica's newest national park protects the last virgin rainforest of the remote mountainous area between Santiago de Puriscal and the coast. Sloths, monkeys, boa constrictors, poison-dart frogs, coyotes, anteaters, blue morpho butterflies, scarlet macaws, toucans, motmots, and many other species live in La Cangreja National Park (admission $4, children 6 to 12 $1), a largely undiscovered region.

The hospitable agricultural village of **Mastatal**, at the entrance to La Cangreja, is a great place to get a glimpse of campesino life.

Rancho Mastatal (770-8314, messages in Spanish only; www.rancho mastatal.com, e-mail: info@ranchomastatal.com) is a learning center and lodge that practices and promotes responsible living in the tropics. They will help you get to know the community, and you can hike their seven kilometers of trails to rivers and waterfalls. They sponsor a wide array of workshops such as building solar ovens, building with bamboo, and a wilderness first responder course. They also host many high school and college educational programs. You can choose to stay in rooms, tents, or hammocks (shared bath, solar hot water; $15-$50). Rates include wholesome and delicious vegetarian meals prepared with locally grown ingredients. A handcrafted house that sleeps six rents for $125/night, and home stays with local families can be arranged ($17-$20/person, including meals). Volunteers are needed.

GETTING THERE: By Bus: From downtown San José, take one of the frequent buses to Puriscal (Calle 16, Avenidas 1/3). One bus a day leaves from near the church in Puriscal around 3 p.m. and gets to Mastatal around 6 p.m.

By Car: Four kilometers northwest of Parrita on the Pacific Coast, you'll see signs for Puriscal and La Gloria. This mostly gravel road takes you up into the mountains for an hour and a half to a right turn with a bus stop and a La Cangreja sign. Mastatal and the national park are about five kilometers to the right. You can also get there following signs from Purisal to La Gloria and Parrita (about 90 minutes on unpaved winding roads).

CENTRAL PACIFIC BEACHES

PUNTA LEONA   This unique development is striving to combine environmental conservation with intense tourist development. Surrounded by 750 acres of primary rainforest, the hotel has allowed Universidad Nacional researchers to build artificial nests for scarlet macaws. Researcher Chris Vaughn estimates that about 300 macaws may live in the Carara–Punta Leona area, with 16 or 17 chicks hatching each year. The nests at Punta Leona are protected from poachers to help this endangered bird population expand. Free guided nature walks are offered daily. Its beautiful beaches have all been awarded the Blue Flag for cleanliness and safety.

You must drive through two gates and several kilometers of rainforest to reach **Selva Mar** (private bath, hot water, ceiling fans and air conditioning, phone, cable TV, refrigerator; $90-$100; 231-3131, fax: 232-0791; www.hotelpuntaleona.com, e-mail: info@hotelpuntaleona.com), Punta Leona's jungle hotel. The three-story condo complex **Leona Mar** (suites with kitchens; $190-$280) is on a cliff above Playa Blanca. There are also one- and two-bedroom apartments ($120-$210). Guests have access to the two white-sand beaches, by far the cleanest and most beautiful in this area. The resort offers several pools, playing fields, mini-golf, tennis, basketball and volleyball courts, aerobics and Latin dance classes, several restaurants, a discotheque, and vans and buses to ferry you around from one point to another. For families with children of various ages and interests, Punta Leona could make everyone happy. Watch for the turnoff to Punta Leona on the right, a few kilometers south of Tárcoles.

Built in a charming French Colonial style and perched on a hilltop 1000 feet above the Pacific with magnificent views, **Villa Caletas** (private bath, hot water, air conditioning, ceiling fans, cable TV, phone; in main building, $160-$180; in more private villas, $200-$210; suites with private jacuzzis or swimming pools, $270-$400; 637-0606, fax 637-0404; www. hotelvillacaletas.com) is real elegance. Its two restaurants specialize in excellent French and international cuisine. The 150-person Greek amphitheater has been the scene of many sunset weddings. Each luxury suite has its own crystal-clear swimming pool in a lush private garden (three-night honeymoon packages run $900-$1400, including breakfast, welcome cocktails, and a champagne dinner; their spa packages include mud wraps, aromatherapy, and massage). The entrance is between Punta Leona and Playa Herradura, then it's about three kilometers up on a paved but precipitous road.

PLAYA HERRADURA   Besides Puntarenas and Punta Leona, Playas Jacó and Herradura are the closest swimmable beaches to San José. Playa Herradura is right after the Río Caña Blanca, about seven kilometers north of Jacó, and three kilometers down a paved road from the main highway. It is smaller than Jacó, its waves are gentler, and it has more shade and good trees for hammocks. The north side of the bay is now dominated by **Los Sueños**, a giant golf and tourism complex with a 200-slip marina, built by the Marriott chain. We must say that Marriott in Costa Rica has proven to be a creative and dynamic force, and Los Sueños is no exception. Before they even began digging the foundations for the condos, they hired a biologist and planted trees that attract scarlet macaws. Half of their 1100-acre property will remain untouched. The golf course was built following recommendations from the Audubon Society. They work in conjunction with the public school in Jacó to teach English and provide training in tourism. We hope that the other complexes springing up all over Costa Rica's Pacific coast will follow their example.

Los Sueños Marriott Beach and Golf Resort (private bath, hot water, air conditioning, ceiling fans, pool, cable TV, voice mail, internet access; $340-$380; 630-9000, fax: 630-9090, in the U.S.: 800-228-9290; www.marriotthotels.com) is patterned after a Spanish colonial village and displays all the fine attention to detail that characterizes the San José Marriott.

GETTING THERE: By Bus: See below under Jacó for bus directions. Get off at the entrance to Herradura; taxis wait for the bus.

By Car: Watch for the turnoff about 13 kilometers south of the Tárcoles turnoff, after you descend from the high point where the Villa Caletas road branches off.

PLAYA JACÓ

Playa Jacó is not an ecotourism destination. It has a "fun and sun" reputation, and, as the closest readily accessible beach to San José, that is still true. But people are starting to plant trees and flowers that attract birds and butterflies, and there are many tours in the area that will connect you to nature.

School of the World (643-1064; www.schooloftheworld.org, e-mail: info@schooloftheworld.org) lets you combine one to four weeks of Spanish with surfing, art, or photography sessions. Hiking and kayaking are included in the cost ($1025 for two weeks). The school has a healthy café and an art gallery, and gives classes in Latin dance, tropical cooking, yoga, and guitar. Students live in attractive quarters at the school, which is within walking distance of the beach and downtown. See their website for amazing wildlife photos. Recommended.

Kayak Jacó ($45 for a half-day tour; phone/fax: 643-1233; www.kayakjaco.com, e-mail: info@kayakjaco.com) takes you whitewater kayaking on the Río Dulce, an hour from Jacó; no experience necessary. They also have stable, eight-person outrigger canoes that glide over the ocean almost effortlessly. Outriggers paddle much more easily than kayaks, and are almost impossible to flip. These tours are great for families, but bring sunhats and sunscreen. For those who want more, advanced instruction in sea and whitewater kayaking is available.

J.D.'s Watersports (257-3857, 800-477-8971; www.jdwatersports.com), based in Punta Leona, picks you up at your hotel and takes you on a

Jungle River Cruise, exploring the Tarcoles River and mangrove estuary. They can also teach you to scuba dive or take you sportfishing or on a cruise at sunset.

Surfers use Jacó as a base for trips to nearby beaches like **Boca Barranca** (a very long left), **Playas Tivives** and **Valor** (rights and lefts), **Escondida** (accessible by boat from Herradura), **Playa Hermosa** (the site of an annual surfing contest—very strong beach break, three kilometers south of Jacó), and **Playas Esterillos Este, Esterillos Oeste, Bejuco,** and **Boca Damas**, which are all on the way to Quepos. Many hotels give surfers discounts from May to December, and there are several surfing teachers in town.

Warning: It's not wise to swim in the estuary or near river mouths. The rip currents at Playa Jacó can be dangerous, as can sudden large waves. People drown there each year. The southern end of the beach is cleanest and safest. Drugs and prostitution are not uncommon at Jacó's nightspots.

CANOPY TOURS   Doing a canopy tour in Jacó might be a nice way to take a break as you head down the coast. The 12-platform, two-kilometer **Canopy Adventure** takes you up into the hills south of Jacó for incredible views of the beach and town as you zip. The 13-platform **Waterfalls Canopy Tour** (643-1103) starts out with a hike to a waterfall. About halfway through, you rest and have refreshments at a tree house, then continue onto a Tarzan swing before you rappel down 90 feet at the end. **Chiclet's Tree Tour** (643-1880) in nearby Playa Hermosa has 13 platforms and 1.2 kilometers of cable. Prices run around $55/person.

If you would like a more sedate adventure, there is now a branch of the **Rainforest Aerial Tram** (257-5961; www.rainforesttram.com; $55), two kilometers northeast of Jacó. Eight-person gondolas glide silently on an electric cable while a naturalist guide tells you about the flora and fauna of the 225-acre reserve.

Bobby Chappell of **Coast to Costa Rica** (www.coast2costarica.com) will take you across the Gulf of Nicoya to Curú Wildlife Refuge on the Nicoya Peninsula, then on a hike to Playa Quesada, a beautiful, deserted white-sand beach, for a picnic, then snorkeling around Isla Tortuga—sounds like a great way to see that part of the country. He operates out of **Jacó Café** (643-2601), an internet café and information center located at El Paso Mall in downtown Jacó. He will also download your digital photos, burn them onto CDs, or create high-quality prints.

RESTAURANTS   Jacó's main drag is a clutter of ever-changing restaurants and a crowded and hectic place to be. Nevertheless, you can find some good food there. **Hotel Poseidon** (open daily for appetizers, 2 p.m. to 5 p.m., and for dinner, 6 p.m. to 10 p.m.; 643-1642) has become the place to go for fine food in a tranquil atmosphere in Playa Jacó. Thai jumbo prawns, tuna in coconut curry sauce, and bananas Foster are among the tasteful menu offerings. **Gilligan's** (643-2874), in the center of town across from Pop's ice cream, is popular with locals for generous servings of well-prepared food at reasonable prices. The **Coffee Shop** (643-3240) next door has breakfasts with homemade bread and great sandwiches for lunch. **Tsunami**, across from Wishbone's downtown, features excellent sushi and other Asian dishes, and showcases local artists. Nearby, **Monica's Pasta Italiana** (643-1776) is good for salads and bruschetta.

Heading into the southern section of town, the simple typical **Estrella de David** near the bridge serves good, cheap meals.

CAR RENTALS   You can stay in lower-priced Jacó and make day trips to Manuel Antonio (90 minutes one way). There are plenty of car rental agencies in Jacó, and the driving is less nerve-wracking than in other areas because the roads are relatively straight, flat, and in good condition. **Zuma Rentacar** (phone/fax: 643-3207; e-mail: zumaway@racsa.co.cr) in central Jacó has good rates and is responsive to clients' needs. **Elegante Car Rental** (643-3224; e-mail: elegante@racsa.co.cr) is also a good bet.

SERVICES   The **Serenity Spa** (open 9 a.m. to 6 p.m.; closed Sunday; 643-1624), in El Paso Mall, offers massage, facials, salt-glows, and volcanic mud treatments.

For day trippers, **Camping Madrigal** rents showers and changing rooms at the southern end of the beach. **Puro Blanco Laundry** (643-1025) will pick up your clothes at your hotel and return them clean and nicely folded. In the center of town, the **Rayo Azul** supermarket is a good source for groceries; they also have an ice cream stand in front. Next door, **Ciclo Jacó** rents bikes ($1.50/hour).

LODGING   There are plenty of hotels, cabinas, and campsites in Jacó. Many have kitchenettes complete with utensils. Although Jacó does not have the dramatic views that you see from the hills near Manuel Antonio, it has many more lodgings that are right on the beach. So if you like the sound of the waves, you might prefer Jacó. Just make sure you're not within earshot of Disco La Central. Most hotels give substantial discounts during the off-season, and Jacó is often sunny when it's raining in San José. We'll mention some of the quietest places in order of their appearance, north to south.

The Austrian-owned **Villas Miramar** (private bath, hot water, ceiling fans, kitchen, pools; $60-$70, including breakfast; 643-3003, fax: 643-3617; www.hotels.co.cr/miramar.html, e-mail: miramar@hotels.co.cr), in a garden setting, is one of the loveliest and most tranquil places in Jacó. It is located down the next road to your right. **Apartotel Flamboyant** (private bath, hot water, ceiling fans, kitchen; $40-$50; 643-3146; fax: 643-1068; www.accommodations.co.cr/flamboyant.htm) is tastefully designed and right on the beach.

Cabinas Alice (private bath, heated water, ceiling fans; $30-$40; with kitchens, $40-$50; 643-4107) are toward the beach from the Red Cross. Doña Alice's husband, Don Antonio, cooks good food that's served by their son at shady outdoor tables.

Apartotel Sole d'Oro (private bath, hot water, ceiling fans, pool, kitchen, air conditioning; $70-$80; 643-3441, phone/fax: 643-3172) is a row of neat apartments parallel to the beach, but half a block away, with a pool and grassy area at the end. Half a block toward the beach, **Apartamentos El Mar** (private bath, hot water, ceiling fans, kitchen, pool; $20-$30; 643-3165, fax: 272-2280) are secure, clean, and spacious.

Aparthotel Girasol (private bath, hot water, ceiling fans, air conditioning, kitchens, pool; $90-$100; kids under 12 free; 643-1591, in the U.S.: 800-923-2779; www.girasol.com, e-mail: girasol@girasol.com) offers modern one-bedroom apartments that sleep four right on the beach.

Near the southern end of the beach, **Camping Madrigal** ($2.50/person; 643-3521) has shaded campsites with toilets, showers, makeshift tables, and barbecue pits.

Club del Mar is on a quiet cove at the southern end of the beach (phone/fax: 643-3194; www.clubdelmarcostarica.com, e-mail: hotelclubdelmar@racsa.co.cr). The one- and two-bedroom condominiums that sleep up to six ($150-$320) are tastefully decorated and have private balconies with lovely sea views. There is a good restaurant, a pool, and their own **Serenity Spa**. This is the most peaceful place to relax in Jacó, and swimming is safer here than at any other part of the beach. To get here, continue south on the Costanera highway a few kilometers past Jacó until you see the Club del Mar sign on the right. Recommended.

Another peaceful spot is **Docelunas Hotel and Spa** (private bath, heated water, fans, air conditioning, phone, cable TV, pool; $120-$150; 643-2211, fax: 643-3633; www.docelunas.com), at the base of a mountain away from the beach. Many mango trees and flowering plants grace the grounds, and a wood-floored studio is fully equipped for yoga and movement classes. Their **Eclipse Restaurant** serves wholesome meals with vegetarian selections, and massage is offered at their **New Horizons Spa**. Two rooms are wheelchair accessible.

GETTING THERE: By Bus: San José–Jacó buses (223-5567; $2) leave the Coca Cola at 7:30 a.m., 10:30 a.m., 1 p.m., and 3:30 p.m., returning at 5 a.m., 7:30 a.m., 11 a.m., 3 p.m., and 5 p.m. They add extra buses on holidays and weekends. The trip takes three hours. When the bus arrives in Jacó, it makes a big loop along the boulevard from south to north, so you can get off at your hotel/campground of choice. Buy your ticket back to San José a day or two before you want to leave because (especially on weekends) return tickets go fast. And get to the bus stop (across from the Best Western) early on weekends because you'll be waiting with a big crowd of *Joséfinos*. Buses leave Jacó for Quepos at 6:30 a.m., 12:30 p.m., and 4 p.m., returning from Quepos at 4:30 a.m., 10:30 a.m., and 3 p.m. Catch Puntarenas–Quepos buses to Jacó at 5 a.m., 11 a.m., or 2:30 p.m. They return to Puntarenas at 6:30 a.m., 12:30 p.m., and 5 p.m. Catch these buses across from the Mas por Menos. Check schedules with your hotel.

Gray Line (220-2126; www.graylinecostarica.com) runs a daily bus between San José and Jacó, with connections to Liberia and Tamarindo, for $25 per trip; They also have connecting buses from Jacó to Arenal, Liberia, Playa Flamingo, and Tamarindo. Interbus (283-5573; www.interbusonline.com) will also take you there.

By Taxi: A taxi from the airport to Playa Jacó costs $50 to $75. Taxi drivers will accept dollars or *colones*. Within Jacó, taxis charge about $1.25.

By Car: Herradura and Jacó are a two-hour drive from San José on a winding road through beautiful countryside. Take the Atenas turnoff on the Interamerican Highway to Puntarenas. The road is in fairly good repair most of the way through the mountains and offers some magnificent views. Near Orotina, you can buy watermelon, mangos, and sugarcane juice. After Orotina, the road becomes a four-lane highway for a few miles. Be careful when a median forms at underpasses because you can easily get in the wrong lane if you're not alert. After the turnoff for Jacó (again, pay attention—it's easy to miss it and find yourself en route to Caldera/Puntarenas), the road becomes a two-lane highway again, with sea views on one side and green rice fields on the other. You'll pass the entrance to Carara National Park (see above) about 20 minutes before Jacó. If you feel more comfortable with less-winding roads, skip the Atenas route and take the Interamerican Highway from San José west to Puntarenas, then drive south to Jacó. The trade-off is that there is a lot more truck traffic on the Puntarenas road. You can continue on to Quepos (70 kilometers farther), Dominical, and points farther south on the same road.

PLAYA HERMOSA   Surfers like Playa Hermosa for its consistent, strong break. There are southern swells between April and December, with the biggest waves in June and July. All the lodgings here are right on the beach. This is not a good beach for children because of the wild waves.

Jungle Surf Café (643-1495) has great atmosphere and service and outstanding food. The menu changes daily with the fresh seafood available. They rent basic rooms ($10/person).

Fuego del Sol (private bath, hot water, ceiling fans, air conditioning, satellite TV, pool; $70-$80; with kitchens, $120-150; breakfast included; kids 6 to 12 $5; 289-6060, 440-6768, fax: 440-6725; www.fuegodelsolhotel.com, e-mail: info@fuegodelsol.com) is our favorite at Playa Hermosa. The well-designed rooms have balconies and fanciful decorations on the walls, the gardens are lovely, and there is a world-class gym and a business center.

Las Olas (private bath, heated water, ceiling fans, kitchens, pool; $40-$50; 643-3687; e-mail: lasolas@racsa.co.cr) is a friendly, gringo-run surfers' hostel with some rooms in the main house, a row of thatched A-frames with kitchens, and a popular beachside restaurant. Waves are good right in front of the hotel. **Wavehunters** (888-899-8823; www.wave hunters.com) puts together five- to seven-day surfing trips based at Las Olas, including transport from San José for $550-$900. The **Backyard Hotel** (private bath, hot water, fans, air conditioning, cable TV, pool; $110-$120; suites for five, $160-$170; 643-3936; www.backyardhotel.com, e-mail: info@backyardhotel.com) has wide porches overlooking the surf. Their restaurant and bar features barbecued chicken and steak, burgers, pizza, and a very festive atmosphere.

GETTING THERE: Playa Hermosa is ten minutes by car from the south end of Jacó. Without a car, walk, hitch, or wait for a Quepos bus on the main road and get off in Hermosa.

ESTERILLOS ESTE   A rough beach 27 kilometers south of Jacó, Esterillos Este is home to some peaceful French Canadian–run retreats. Just 20 minutes south of Jacó and 45 minutes north of Manuel Antonio, this area would be a great base for trips to both with plenty of tranquility in between. **Auberge du Pélican** (hot water, ceiling fans, pool, private bath; $60-$70; phone/fax: 778-8105; www.aubergepelican.com, e-mail: auberge pelican@racsa.co.cr) is a well-designed place to go when you really need a break. They pay attention to detail in a way that many places don't: the main lodge is totally screened in; two cabins, the restaurant, and the grounds are wheelchair accessible; and rooms have built-in counters and benches. The restaurant serves Continental and Mediterranean dishes. **Flor de Esterillos** (private bath, hot water, ceiling fans, kitchenettes, pool, restaurant; $50-$70; 778-8045; pages.infinit.net/taus, e-mail: business@ racsa.co.cr) is a cluster of spacious cabins, some of which sleep up to six, surrounded by flowering bushes. Their **Restaurante Tulú** (open 8 a.m. to 8 p.m.) is a great place to have a relaxed lunch.

GETTING THERE: By Bus: The San José–Quepos or Puntarenas–Quepos buses will drop you off at the entrance to town. For schedules, see Quepos "Getting There" below.

By Car: The beach is one kilometer off the highway. The turnoff is clearly marked.

By Air: See Quepos for SANSA and Nature Air schedules.

PLAYA PALO SECO   Just south of the town of Parrita, five kilometers off the Costanera, **Palo Seco** is home to another French retreat, **El Beso del Viento** (private bath, heated water, fans, kitchens, pool, cable TV, some air conditioning; $60-$70; 779-9674, fax: 779-9575; www.besodelviento.com, e-mail: bviento@racsa.co.cr). The attractive apartments have spacious, tiled kitchens and good cross-ventilation. They sleep up to four people ($100). Horses are for rent, and there is a lovely pool. Children are welcome.

GETTING THERE: By Bus: Take the San José–Quepos or Puntarenas–Quepos bus (see below in the "Quepos" section), and get off at Parrita. Take a taxi from Parrita to Playa Palo Seco (about $4).

By Car: Follow signs five kilometers down a pretty good gravel road from Parrita. Palo Seco is about a half-hour drive from Esterillos Este.

QUEPOS AND MANUEL ANTONIO

Before you get to the inspiring vistas of Manuel Antonio, you pass through the bustling former United Fruit banana port of **Quepos**, where lodging is generally less expensive than the low-cost alternatives near the beach. It's about another three miles to the reason why you're here: Manuel Antonio National Park.

When you first glimpse the sea from the hills above Manuel Antonio, the word "paradise" might cross your mind. Then you'll go a little farther and see what happens when mortals fight to get the best view of paradise. These hills have become one of Costa Rica's most elegant destinations, but overdevelopment is encroaching on the elegance. Blessedly saved from development within its boundaries, **Manuel Antonio National Park**, one of the smallest in the country, is the area's crowning glory. The park is one of the few remaining habitats of the *mono tití* (squirrel monkey). Only 4000 *mono titís* remain in the area, according to a study by University of Florida researcher Sue Boinski, down from an estimated 200,000 in 1983. **ASCO-MOTI**, the local wildlife protection group, is collaborating with the Electricity Institute to convert the electric lines in the area to shock-free ones, thus eliminating one of the main causes of death of these tiny monkeys.

They are also planting fruit trees along the banks of the Río Naranjo to connect the Manuel Antonio area with Cerro Nara inland, creating a biological corridor that will restore the habitat of the *mono tití* and strengthen its gene pool. In order to do this, they have established nurseries of native species trees at five local schools.

They are also working to make sure that environmental laws are enforced. According to ASCOMOTI, "Destruction of the area's forests and subsequent new construction is occurring at an alarming rate. When one begins to look carefully at the status of permits and environmental impact evaluations for these changes, an even more alarming picture is drawn of irregularities, confusion, and mistakes. It appears that Quepos/Manuel Antonio is being permanently transformed—not on the basis of careful planning and responsible environmental management, but rather due to shoddy and irregular enforcement of the many good environmental laws which are on the books." ASCOMOTI has published a pamphlet that familiarizes potential developers with the government's development and environmental policies (www.ascomoti.org/investorinfo).

Volunteers with ASCOMOTI are currently tracking *mono tití* populations and monitoring habitat. Volunteers live with local families and pay about $350 a month for room and board. A one- to three-month commitment is required. Find out more at www.ascomoti.org, or 224-5703, e-mail: monotiti@racsa.co.cr. The website also has a current list of businesses that contribute to ASCOMOTI. Most of the businesses listed here are ASCOMOTI members.

MANUEL ANTONIO NATIONAL PARK   In addition to the *mono tití,* howler and white-face monkeys, two-toed sloths, coatimundis, and raccoons frequent the beaches, which are shaded by leafy trees. Manuel Antonio includes one of the best beaches on Costa Rica's Pacific coast for swimming and snorkeling, as well as trails where you can hike for at least a full day.

The wedge-shaped piece of land that is now Cathedral Point was once an island. A neck of land connects it to the beach. This rare phenomenon is known as a *tombolo*: a deposit of sand that builds up over thousands of years and finally connects an island to the mainland. North-flowing currents pushed water and sand through the opening between the island and the beach, and then flowed on to Punta Quepos, farther north, which forced the water back. The sand-bridge was formed after about 100,000 years of this action. Grass and shrubs gained a foothold on it, followed by the present-day trees that keep the formation from returning to the sea. The Manuel Antonio *tombolo* is one of the most perfect in the world.

The indigenous people who lived in Manuel Antonio 1000 years ago observed that while female green turtles were laying their eggs in the sand at high tide, the male turtles were waiting for them in the water. They fash-ioned balsawood models of female turtles to attract the males into an area surrounded by rocks. The males would stay with the decoy females and be trapped by the rocks when the tide went out. These pre-Columbian turtle traps are still visible on either end of Manuel Antonio Beach at low tide.

A trail takes you through the jungle to the top of Cathedral Point, where you can look down the vertical cliffs to the blue ocean 300 feet below. You start from Playa Espadilla Sur (the second beach) and take a circular route, about an hour from start to finish. At low tide, you can also begin or end on Playa Manuel Antonio, the third beach. The trail is very steep in some parts and muddy and slippery in the rainy season, so don't go alone. Sandals with good treads and straps that attach them firmly to your feet are proba-bly the most appropriate footwear. In the rainy season you will want to wear hiking boots or rubber boots with long socks.

Snorkeling is a rewarding adventure at Manuel Antonio. In the dry sea-son, when the water is clear, you'll see iridescent, peacock-colored fish, con-servative pin-striped fish, and outrageous yellow fish with diaphanous capes, all going in and out between the coral rocks—especially at Playa Escondida, a half-hour walk beyond Playa Manuel Antonio. Fins and a mask are all you need. If you burn easily, watch out—you'll lose track of time staring at the fish while the sun is reddening your back. It's best to wear a T-shirt in addi-tion to waterproof sunblock. Ask for the hour of low tide at your hotel or as you enter the park. Playa Escondida can only be accessed at low tide. At high tide snorkeling is good at the turtle traps at the third beach.

The entrance to the park is a 200-meter walk south of the end of the Quepos–Manuel Antonio road, and is clearly indicated (open 7 a.m. to 4 p.m.; closed Monday; $7, children 6 to 12 $1). A bridge is being built across the stream at the entrance so you don't have to wade across. Be sure to take food and water with you into the park because it is a hassle to go in and out. If you do wish to leave the park for lunch, the ranger will stamp your hand so you can re-enter without paying again.

Camping is not allowed within the park.

Note: Do not leave your belongings unattended on the beach. If anyone offers to guide you through remote areas of the park, they should have an official ID card, or be in a park service uniform. To contact AGUILA, the guides' association, call 777-0850. Perhaps more of a risk than *ladrones* are the white-faced monkeys on the beach. They have become very bold about stealing food and will grab your backpack and carry it up into a tree if you don't keep an eye on them. When they are through investigating your bags, they will unceremoniously drop them—not good for cameras or binoculars. Don't feed the monkeys anywhere in this area.

If you long to visit this still-beautiful area, try to go in the off-season (May through November). As we've stated elsewhere, you'll still have most of the day to play, you can relax with a book in your hammock if it rains, there are substantial discounts on lodging in most hotels, and you'll be able to enjoy Manuel Antonio in its more pristine, uncrowded state.

For good updated information on Quepos and Manuel Antonio, see www.quepolandia.com on the web.

ACTIVITIES **Iguana Tours** (777-1262; www.iguanatours.com, e-mail: iguana@racsa.co.cr) offers sea-kayaking ($65) and whitewater-rafting ($60-$90) tours down the Río Savegre as well as horseback, dolphin watching and natural history tours. The offices are across from the soccer field in Quepos. **Amigos del Rio** (www.amigosdelrio.com) also offers rafting and kayaking trips. Their office is on the left as you climb the hill to Manuel Antonio.

The five-hour **Canopy Safari** ($80, including breakfast, lunch, or dinner; 777-0100; e-mail: info@canopy-tour.com) swings you through the treetops and ends with a refreshing swim in a secluded water hole. It has been approved by the ACCT for safety. They have special equipment for children, and will take anyone over the age of five. **Dream Forest Canopy Tour** (777-3030, fax: 777-1924; e-mail: fattan@racsa.co.cr) offers some cables up to 2000 feet. They also offer a tour where you descend a waterfall on safety lines.

Manuel Antonio

The Nature Farm and Butterfly Botanical Gardens (open 9 a.m. to 3 p.m.; closed Saturday; 777-0973; www.avenatura.com, e-mail: fincasnatur ales@racsa.co.cr), across from Sí Como No hotel, is a 30-acre reserve bordering the national park. A short hike takes you to a beautifully designed 400-square meter atrium where you can see many butterfly species, including the heavenly blue morpho. It's best to go on a sunny day because the butterflies are more active. The tour is also a great botany lesson as you learn the relationship between plants and butterfly life cycle. At night, the atrium's amphitheater is the setting for an audio-visual presentation where animals' sounds are paired with their images so that you can recognize a toucan, for instance, before you see it. You can take the night tour in combination with a great dinner at Sí Como No.

Rainmaker is a private 1500-acre reserve protecting part of the Quepoa biological corridor used by migrating birds and animals. It also protects the streams that supply some of Manuel Antonio's water. In a well-run tour, visitors learn about rainforest botany on a guided hike ($15) along one of these streams to several magnificent waterfalls, ending at a swimming hole. A circular canopy walk along suspension bridges gives beautiful views of the forest, ocean, and waterfalls ($65; 777-3565; www.rainmaker costarica.com).

In **Londres**, 13 kilometers inland from Quepos, **Brisas del Nara** (779-1235, fax: 779-1049; www.horsebacktour.com, e-mail: brisasnara@racsa.co. cr) offers horseback tours to nearby waterfalls ($55, including transportation, breakfast, and lunch; $45 half day). They have special horses for kids.

Run by an agricultural cooperative that has been together since the early 1970s, ✿ **El Silencio** (private bath, heated water; $30/person, including meals; 771-1938, phone/fax: 779-9545, cell phone: 380-5581; www. turismoruralcr.com, e-mail: cooprena@racsa.co.cr) is an ecotourism project, about an hour inland from Manuel Antonio, that also protects the watershed. They are a rescue and release point for green and scarlet macaws and many other injured or confiscated animals. They have a good restaurant, clean cabins, nature trails, orchid propagation projects, and a butterfly garden, and will guide you to waterfall pools in the jungle. Volunteers are needed to help with the animals. To get there, turn left at kilometer 22 of the Quepos-Dominical road, and continue another six very bumpy kilometers to the village of El Silencio. A bus to El Silencio leaves Quepos at 4 p.m. every day but Sunday.

Beyond the entrance to El Silencio, **Rafiki** (private bath, hot water, pool with waterslide; $220-$230, including meals; children 6 to 12, $35;

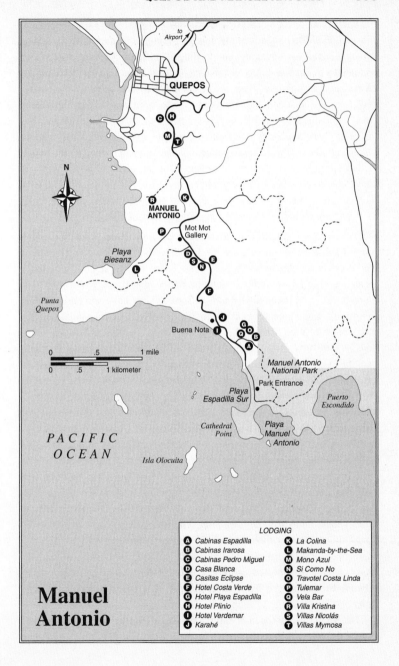

N

to
Airport

QUEPOS

Ⓒ Ⓗ
Ⓜ
Ⓣ

Ⓡ Ⓚ
**MANUEL
ANTONIO**

Ⓟ
Mot Mot
Gallery

*Playa
Biesanz*
Ⓛ Ⓓ Ⓔ
Ⓢ Ⓝ

*Punta
Quepos*
Ⓕ

Ⓙ
Buena Nota Ⓘ Ⓖ Ⓞ
Ⓠ Ⓑ
Ⓐ

0   .5   1 mile
0   .5   1 kilometer

*Manuel Antonio
National Park*

Park Entrance

*Playa
Espadilla Sur*

*Puerto
Escondido*

*Cathedral
Point*   *Playa
Manuel
Antonio*

**PACIFIC
OCEAN**

Isla Olocuita

**Manuel
Antonio**

LODGING

Ⓐ Cabinas Espadilla
Ⓑ Cabinas Irarosa
Ⓒ Cabinas Pedro Miguel
Ⓓ Casa Blanca
Ⓔ Casitas Eclipse
Ⓕ Hotel Costa Verde
Ⓖ Hotel Playa Espadilla
Ⓗ Hotel Plinio
Ⓘ Hotel Verdemar
Ⓙ Karahé

Ⓚ La Colina
Ⓛ Makanda-by-the-Sea
Ⓜ Mono Azul
Ⓝ Si Como No
Ⓞ Travotel Costa Linda
Ⓟ Tulemar
Ⓠ Vela Bar
Ⓡ Villa Kristina
Ⓢ Villas Nicolás
Ⓣ Villas Mymosa

777-2250, 777-5327; www.rafikisafari.com, e-mail: info@rafikisafari.com)
is a unique wilderness adventure site for hiking, horseback riding, fishing,
whitewater rafting, kayaking, and birding. The South African owners have
recreated a safari tent camp on wooden platforms that make as little impact
on the area as possible. Huge safari tents sleep four in very comfortable
beds, and the spacious bathrooms are made from rocks from the nearby
river. Rocking chairs and fresh flowers make these simple structures very
inviting. There is a honeymoon suite in the forest. The menu at the open-air
restaurant adds to the safari elegance: chicken souvlaki with tzatziki sauce,
grilled tarragon tuna, pork with tropical fruit salsa. Rafiki arranges horseback rides to Reserva Los Campesinos, over the hill on the other side of
the river (see above). They have two- to three-day packages for $340-
$525/person, including meals, rafting, and horseback riding.

SOUVENIRS   **L'Aventura**, across the street from Hotel Kamuk, displays
tasteful and creative clothes, pottery, wood, leather, and jewelry; **Regalame**
(pronounced ray-ga-la-may: a very Costa Rican way of saying "give me"),
located next to La Marquesa Restaurant on the oceanfront, features original
work from Costa Rican artists and craftsmen. They have another branch in
the small shopping center next to the Si Como No in Manuel Antonio. One
block north of the Catholic church in Quepos is **La Botánica** (open weekdays, 8 a.m. to 4 p.m.; phone/fax: 777-1223), an enticing shop that sells
packets of organically grown herbs and spices such as vanilla, cinnamon,
cardamon, and pepper. While you're looking around you can sip a cup of
their tea *du jour*. If you're under the weather, they might be able to mix up
an herbal remedy. If you're interested in the workings of a self-sustainable
farm, you can drive or take a taxi to their place near Londres, several kilometers inland. The U.S. expatriate who owns it will show you around. His
wife, a friendly, bilingual Tica, runs the shop; ask her for directions.

   Kids Saving the Rainforest (777-2592; www.kidssavingtherainforest.
org) was started by Janine Licare-Andrews and her friend when they were
nine and a half years old. At first they sold their artwork to raise money to
protect local land from deforestation. Their project has now grown to include reforestation with native species, building monkey bridges, an environmental summer camp, and links with children and youth around the
world. Their store, located online and in the Hotel Mono Azul, still features
artwork by Janine and her friends as well as donated works from local
artists. All proceeds go to support KSTR.

   La Buena Nota (open 8 a.m. to 5 p.m.; 777-1002) is a well-stocked
beachwear and gift shop that sells *The Tico Times* and *The New York Times*.

It's on the Manuel Antonio road, close to the beach between Karahé Hotel and Cabinas Piscis.

LANGUAGE SCHOOLS **Escuela de Idiomas D'Amore** (phone/fax: 777-1143; www.escueladamore.com, e-mail: damore@racsa.co.cr) offers a Spanish immersion course in a pleasant building overlooking the sea on the road to Manuel Antonio. Students are housed at the beach or with local families in not-so-elegant Quepos. If you have the discipline to study in such a heady tropical environment, this school might be a great learning vacation. At least one correspondent was very pleased with it. **Centro de Idiomas del Pacifico** (e-mail: cipacifico@racsa.co.cr) also offers language classes at Cabinas Pedro Miguel. **COSI** (777-0021; www.professionalspan ish.com) has its beach campus here.

DIVING **Costa Rica Adventure Divers** (777-0234; www.costaricadiv ing.com) offers diving tours and PADI certification as well as resort and open-water courses.

SPORTFISHING *Marlin Magazine* named Quepos the second-best location in the world for "all around action." There are over a dozen sportfishing companies that will take you out, and The Banco Bar, El Gran Escape, and the Dos Locos (see below) will cook your catch.

IMPORTANT NUMBERS *Hospital*: 777-0922; *Red Cross*: 777-0116; *Police*: 911 or 777-2117; *OIJ* (investigative police): 777-0511; *Taxi*: 777-1695, 777-1068, 777-0425, 777-1207, 777-0734.

BANKING There are three ATMs and four banks in Quepos and one in Manuel Antonio (Banco Promerica; open Monday through Saturday, 10 a.m. to 2 p.m.; 777-5101) in the shopping center next to Hotel Divisamar. You can usually exchange money at your hotel for a slightly lower rate.

CAR RENTALS You really do not need a car once you are in Manuel Antonio because buses are frequent and taxis are cheap ($4-$10 to go anywhere in the area). But if you want to fly here and rent a car to drive down the coast, Elegante (777-0115) and Alamo (777-3344; www.alamocosta rica.com) will meet you at the plane or at your hotel. Adobe (777-4242) and Excelente (777-3052) also have offices in Quepos. It costs about $30 extra to drop the car off in San José.

OTHER SERVICES There is a chiropractor, an acupuncturist, and quite a few massage and energy workers in Manuel Antonio, including **Sea Glass Spa** (777-2607; www.seaglassspa.com), 200 meters to the right after Villas El Parque.

ADVENTURE REPORT:
RESERVA LOS CAMPESINOS

After a four-hour trip to the coast, we arrived in Quepos, near famous Manuel Antonio National Park. Our destination was not the beautiful but over-visited beach, but an isolated community about an hour and a half inland. In Londres, about 30 minutes from Quepos, we changed from our 15-seater bus to a four-wheel-drive taxi to negotiate the 45-minute trip to the village of Quebrada Arroyo and ✿ **Reserva Los Campesinos** (private bath, cold water; $36/person, including meals and tours). After a delicious dinner in their open-air restaurant, we retired to our spacious cabins overlooking a forested gorge. The railings on the porch emphasized the natural shapes of the branches used in their construction.

In the morning, Don Miguel, president of the Vanilla Producers Association, talked about the history of the village. They had been successful in raising chocolate until monilia started ruining the cacao pods. Then they had a successful business raising vanilla and making extract, until another disease wiped out the vanilla crop. He showed us beautiful crafts that villagers had made out of the vanilla pods, still sweet smelling after eight years. Now they are starting to raise vanilla again, only organically, and are supplementing their farm earnings with income from their cabins and tours.

Miguel and his friend Misael led us up through the Los Campesinos reserve, stopping often to tell us the uses of different flowers, trees, and plants. Almost everything is used for food or medicine—and Miguel and Misael even showed us which plants they used to make into toys when they were kids. The wide, round leaves of one tree make terrific pinwheels. Miguel deftly shaved off part of the stiff hairs on "monkey's comb" pods with his machete, making monkey faces on the pods to give to the kids.

LODGING, RESTAURANTS, AND NIGHTLIFE

QUEPOS LODGING   You might like staying in Quepos if you like bars and nightlife. If we were going to Manuel Antonio, we would not stay in Quepos. If you want to save money, you might as well go to another area entirely. Although there are many hotels in Quepos, we list just a few of the cheap and good ones below. Some hotels are putting in security boxes for

Halfway up the trail, at the edge of a deep gorge, is an *andarivel*, a sturdy metal box suspended from a cable. Four people can fit inside the contraption, which zips maybe 75 feet across to the other side of the gorge, controlled by ropes and pulleys that Miguel and Misael handle. It was a quick and exciting ride, and saved us having to hike down into the gorge and up again.

Not long after that, we reached the covered lookout at the top of the ridge, from where you can see the coast south of Manuel Antonio. I asked Miguel if he had ever imagined that all the things he learned working beside his father in the countryside would someday be so fascinating to foreign tourists. "I never imagined it," he said. "Never." What an incredible way of preserving culture!

Misael told me that with farming as precarious economically as it is, his eight children would have had to move to the city to look for work, where they might have fallen in with the wrong people and developed bad habits. With the village ecotourism project, the family can stay together and make a living in the country.

Pineapple grown in the village awaited us when we came down, and then we were off across a narrow 380-foot suspended bridge that offers a view of the village's spectacular waterfall. At the other end of the bridge is a large waterfall-fed swimming hole, refreshingly cool after our long walk. We were in paradise! Our lunch featured heart of palm, which we had seen freshly harvested that morning. Reluctantly, we left Reserva Los Campesinos, and made our way back over the steep, muddy roads to our little bus.

To visit Reserva Los Campesinos, contact ACTUAR (228-5695; www.actuarcostarica.com, e-mail: actuar@racsa.co.cr).

valuables; be sure and use one if you can. *Note:* The beach at Quepos is polluted. Do not swim there.

On the northwest corner of the soccer field, near the post office, **Cabinas Doña Alicia** (private or shared bath, cold water, ceiling fans; $7-$20; 777-0419) are recommended for their cleanliness and the friendly owners. Some of the cabinas have three rooms, handy for families. They are on a quiet street with guarded parking.

Hotel Quepos (shared and private baths, cold water, ceiling fans; $12-$20; 777-0274) has small, second-story rooms with hardwood floors. Rooms are back from the street, and there is a night guard. It is across from the southwest corner of the soccer field. They give discounts for extended stays.

The German-owned **Hotel Villa Romántica** (private bath, hot water, ceiling fans; $60-$80, including breakfast; 777-0037, fax: 777-0604; www.villaromantica.com/us, e-mail: villarom@racsa.co.cr), tucked in on the right as you leave town, has a pool and shady sitting area.

QUEPOS RESTAURANTS AND NIGHTLIFE   Owned by a transplanted gringa, **El Gran Escape** whips up some of the best food in town. Mexican food is their specialty, but they also serve a hearty breakfast and desserts. Connoisseurs recommend the Dirty Banana. Around the corner is **Tropical Sushi** (open 5 p.m. to 10 p.m.; closed Tuesday; 777-0395).

Also around the corner, the Texan-owned **Banco Bar** (open daily, 3 p.m. until late, opens at noon on weekends; 777-0478), housed in a former bank, is known for authentic Tex-Mex cooking and great hamburgers and sandwiches. While on the oceanfront, check out **Café Milagro**, located one block north of El Gran Escapa, which roasts and distributes pure Tarrazú coffee, the best that Costa Rica has to offer. For an extra buzz, accompany your cup or glass with a rich, chewy brownie. You can't always find decaf in Costa Rica, but they have it. Their delicious breakfasts feature bagels, croissants, and Belgian waffles. They have a branch in Manuel Antonio across from the Barba Roja.

Our favorite seafood place is **Jiuberth's** (pronounced "Hubert's"; 777-1292), located in the Boca Vieja neighborhood 200 meters before the bridge at the northern entrance to Quepos. This is a real mom-and-pop place, with brightly colored oilcloth tablecloths, and decorations all over the walls and ceiling—full-size dried fish, wonderful wood carvings of saints, iguanas, and toucans, and beautiful paintings by Jiuberth's wife Isabel. Jiuberth runs a sportfishing operation and will prepare your catch for you. Recommended.

The market at the bus terminal is a good place to grab a quick bite to eat and to stock up on fruits and vegetables. Across the street from the market, **Restaurant Quepoa** (open daily, 8 a.m to 1 a.m.) serves good Tico food, and has karaoke on Wednesday and Friday nights. Half a block toward the ocean, **Dos Locos** features Mexican food and a lively open-air atmosphere with live music Wednesday and Friday. Try their Guaro Sour, a creative new use of the local firewater. **Escalofrio** (open daily from 2:30 p.m.; closed Monday; 777-0833), next door, serves brick-oven pizza and ice cream.

On a hillside near the Quepos school, **Restaurante Mar Luna** (777-5107) is popular with locals for fresh seafood at reasonable prices and attentive service.

Internet cafés: **Internet Tropical** (open daily, 8 a.m. to 8 p.m.; 777-2460), across the Banco Bar, serves delicious sandwiches and great tropical fruit drinks. They have Net2Phone for $10/hour so you can make high-speed connections and talk right from the computer headset. **Internet Quepos**, on the first street to the left as you enter town, has a number of high-speed computers. Other internet cafés come and go. Ask your hotel for the nearest one.

MANUEL ANTONIO LODGING AND RESTAURANTS   Near Manuel Antonio, the most beautiful places to stay are in the hills between Quepos and the park. There you'll find small, elegant hotels owned by tropics-lovers of many nationalities.

Make reservations six months in advance for Christmas or Easter, and several months in advance during the rest of the tourist season (December through April). Most of these places offer a 20-50 percent discount during the green season (May to November). Make sure that rooms you reserve are back from the road. If you're trying to save money, keep in mind that this area as a whole is not for budget travelers. Those who can afford $70-$150 per day will find some of the most beautiful accommodations in the country, but if you're looking for budget beachfront places, go south to Dominical or the Golfito area or east to the Caribbean coast.

House rentals: If you have more time to spend, you might want to rent a house by the week or month. For example: Fully equipped houses and apartments with breathtaking ocean views rent for about $200-$600 per week or $700-$2000 per month during the high season, and half that in the low season. Contact **La Buena Nota** (777-1002, 777-0292), **Geminis del Pacifico** (in the U.S. 773-472-7127; http://itsmycasa.com), **Condominios Biesanz** (228-1811; www.biesanz.com), or **Villa La Macha** (www.villala macha.com).

We will mention facilities in order of their appearance on the road between Quepos and Manuel Antonio.

The family-run **Cabinas Pedro Miguel** (private bath, cold water, ceiling fans; phone/fax: 777-0035; www.cabinaspedromiguel.com, e-mail: reservations@cabinaspedromiguel.com) have two types of lodging: a two-story construction ($20-$40), and large rooms with kitchens and a wall-sized screened window overlooking jungle with the sound of a rushing stream in the background. There's a small pool. This is the home of **Centro de Idiomas del Pacifico** (777-0805; www.cipacifico.com), a Spanish language school. The family that runs the cabins encourages guests to learn about Costa Rican cooking by participating in meal preparation.

Across the road, the European-owned **Hotel Plinio** (private bath, hot water, ceiling fans, pool; breakfast included; 777-0055, fax: 777-0558; www.hotelplinio.com, e-mail: plinio@racsa.co.cr) has single-story jungle-view rooms ($60-$70; with air conditioning, $80-$90), and suites of either two ($90-$100) or three levels ($120-$130), featuring raised king-size beds from which you can enjoy a coastal view. The hotel is surrounded by lush foliage, and has acquired a 70-acre forest reserve with a nature trail that leads up the mountain to a 15-meter observation tower. The hotel's **restaurant** (open daily for breakfast, lunch, and dinner), one of the most popular in Manuel Antonio, offers delicious pasta, lasagna, eggplant parmigiana, and Thai specialties. Its homemade bread is worth a trip in itself. Call for reservations.

Next on the right, the **Mono Azul** (private bath, heated water, ceiling fans, some with air conditioning, some cable TV, three pools; $60-$80; 777-1548, fax: 777-1954; www.monoazul.com, e-mail: monoazul@racsa. co.cr) is the home of Kids Saving the Rainforest. Their **restaurant** (open daily, 7 a.m. to 10 p.m.) delivers delicious pizza, burgers, fish, Mexican and Tico specialties, salad, and homemade cake anywhere in the area. The atmosphere is relaxed, the owners are very helpful, and internet access is provided. As one writer put it, the Mono Azul is "just like home, only you don't have to do the dishes." Some rooms have patios and jungle views.

A small road leads to the left to **Villas Mymosa** (private bath, hot water, ceiling fans, air conditioning, kitchens, pool; $70-$120, phone/fax: 777-1254; www.villasmymosa.com, e-mail: mymosa@racsa.co.cr), spacious, clean one- and two-bedroom condos with balconies that sleep up to six, around a large pool. There are no railings on the stairs, so these might not be good for toddlers. Their restaurant serves gourmet Spanish cuisine.

Back on the main road, go down a road to the right to get to **Villa Kristina** (private bath, hot water, air conditioning, kitchen, cable TV; $60-$100; $330-$495/week; phone/fax: 777-2134, http://members.aon.at/pwallner, e-mail: villa_kristina@hotmail.com), secluded, cozy apartments with ocean views, balconies with hammocks, and quiet gardens, 400 meters from Playa La Macha. You need four-wheel drive to get there

La Colina (private bath, hot water, ceiling fans, cable TV, air conditioning, pool, restaurant; breakfast included; children under 3 free; 777-0231, fax: 777-1553; www.lacolina.com, e-mail: lacolina@racsa.co.cr) offers garden rooms ($60-$70), apartments with kitchenettes ($80-$90), and suites with an ocean view ($90-$100) around their two-tiered pool with swim-up bar. They also have two-bedroom villas ($110-$120) for extended stays. This friendly hotel is a good value.

Next on the right is the gated entrance to **Tulemar** (private bath, hot water, ceiling fans, air conditioning, TV with VCR, hairdryer, kitchen, pool; $270-$280 for up to four, including breakfast; children under 12 free; 777-0580, 777-1325, fax: 777-1579; www.tulemar.com, e-mail: tulemar@ racsa.co.cr), luxurious octagonal houses with skylights, which accommodate four people; there are also one- and two-bedroom villas ($300-$450). Use of sea kayaks and snorkeling equipment is included. Far from the road, with stunning ocean views, a small private beach 800 meters from the bungalows, and kayaks for guests, Tulemar offers the quintessential Manuel Antonio experience. Their poolside restaurant, **Tulecafe**, features international and multiethnic cuisine. Their three-night honeymoon package ($700-$1400) includes champagne and flowers on arrival, massages, and dinner for two.

At the top of the hill is the **Barba Roja** (open 7:30 a.m. to midnight; closed Monday), a favorite with visitors because of its gringo-style lunches and dinners, such as burgers, nachos, and BLTs, and its sinful desserts—try the macadamia pie à la mode! Above the Barba Roja is the **Mot Mot Gallery** (open 4 p.m. to 9 p.m.; closed Monday), with tasteful exhibits by local artists. Behind them, at **Karola's** restaurant (open daily, 7 a.m. to 10 p.m.; 777-1557), you can drink margaritas or enjoy Mexican and seafood specialties in a garden setting.

Casa Blanca (private bath, hot water, ceiling fans, refrigerators, pool, wheelchair accessible; with air conditioning, $90-$100; with kitchen, $130-$140; two-bedroom suites, $200-$210; phone/fax: 777-0253; www.hotel casablanca.com, e-mail: cblanca@racsa.co.cr) is an intimate and private gay resort catering to gay men, lesbians, and their open-minded relatives and friends. Be sure to ask for the rooms or apartments with ocean views—they are spectacular.

Down a steep gravel road, one kilometer from the main road, is **Makanda-by-the-Sea** (private bath, hot water, ceiling fans, some air conditioning, kitchen, pool; $260-$410, including breakfast delivered to your room; 777-0442, fax: 777-1032; www.makanda.com, e-mail: makanda@ racsa.co.cr), secluded villas with wide balconies and a sunset ocean view set in a 12-acre nature reserve. It's much closer to Biesanz beach than hotels nearer the road. No children under 16 allowed. Honeymoon packages available. Makanda's **Sunspot Grill** (open 11 a.m. to 10 p.m.; 777-0442) is gaining a reputation as *the* place to go for lunch or dinner. Lobster with saffron-garlic dipping sauce, wasabi tuna, and pork tenderloin with chipotle marinade are among the dinner offerings. Recommended.

Returning to the main road, past a rather dense highrise hotel, are the comfortable and well-designed **Villas Nicolás** (private bath, hot water, ceiling fans, pool; $90-$110; with kitchen, $120-$232; 777-0481, phone/fax: 777-0451; www.villasnicolas.com, e-mail: sales@villasnicolas.com), with private terraces. The floor plans of the various-sized villas give an open, airy feel. The larger ones sleep four and two can be combined to sleep six. A trail from the hotel leads to the beach. Some have beautiful ocean views.

Si Como No (private bath, hot water, ceiling fans, air conditioning, kitchenette or wet bar, pool, jacuzzi, spa, restaurant/bar; $200-$280, including breakfast; children under 6 free; 777-0777, fax: 777-1093, 800-282-0488; www.sicomono.com, e-mail: sicomono@racsa.co.cr) is a wonderland of gardens, waterfalls, and cascading pools. Our kids loved the waterslide, and now there is an "adult" pool also. The **Rico Tico**, a swim-up bar and grill, serves California-style food and icy fruit smoothies. The air-conditioned restaurant, **Claro Que Sí**, features seafood. They even have a 46-seat movie theater under the lobby, free for guests of the hotel or restaurants. They welcome gay and straight people alike. Their two-night honeymoon package costs $900; wedding packages are also available. This luxury resort is a showcase of eco-friendly alternative technologies for saving energy and water (double-paned windows and insulated ceilings, low-voltage lighting, solar-heated jacuzzi, self-cleaning pool, graywater recycling system, etc.). Recommended.

Casitas Eclipse (private bath, hot water, ceiling fans, air conditioning, pools; $120-$130; with kitchen, $180-$200; houses for up to five people, $320-$330, including breakfast; 777-0408, phone/fax: 777-1738; www.casitas eclipse.com, e-mail eclipseh@racsa.co.cr) features whimsical Mediterranean-style houses, with three pools. Its romantic Italian restaurant, **El Gato Negro**, is known for its excellent homemade pasta and seafood dishes. Try their carpaccio, raw fish marinated in lemon juice and spices. Make reservations. Expensive.

Hotel Costa Verde (private bath, hot water, ceiling fans, air conditioning, some cable TV, kitchen, pool, restaurant; $100-$150; penthouse or bungalows, $180-$190; 777-0584, 777-0187, fax: 777-0560; www.hotelcosta verde.com, e-mail: reservations@costaverde.com) offers spacious rooms with kitchens and balconies. The Studio Plus rooms have ocean views. There is a separate building and pool for adults only, and others where children are welcome. Ask for rooms off the road. They have nature trails through 30 acres of rainforest, a restaurant, and an internet café.

BEACH AREA LODGING AND RESTAURANTS   The following hotels have easy access to **Playa Espadilla**, a long beach known for its dangerous rip currents. Access to the national park is from the south end of Espadilla. Some of Manuel Antonio's least expensive rooms are in this area, although several comfortable, luxurious hotels are here, too.

Karahé (777-0170, fax: 777-1075; www.karahe.com, e-mail: informa tion@karahe.com) offers three types of rooms: the villas (private bath, so-lar-heated water, ceiling fans, kitchenettes, air conditioning; $90-$100), which have magnificent views, but you must walk up more than a hundred steps to get to them; the newer "deluxe" rooms near the road (private bath, solar-heated water, air conditioning; $100-$110), which have terraces; and the junior suites (private bath, solar-heated water, air conditioning; $120-$130). The suites, which also have terraces, are across the road, near the pool and 200 meters from the beach. Breakfast is included in all rates. The solar showers are hottest in the afternoon.

Next on the right is **Buena Nota**, a well-stocked newsstand and beach shop. High-quality souvenirs and beachwear plus lots of tourism informa-tion make this a worthwhile stop.

Hotel Verdemar (private bath, hot water, ceiling fans, air conditioning; $70-$80; with kitchens, $90-$130; 777-1805, fax 777-1311; www.verde mar.com, e-mail: inq@verdemar.com) has pleasantly decorated rooms with a pool and a raised wooden walkway to the beach.

With shady tables on the beach, the **Restaurant Mar y Sombra** is the traditional place to eat on Playa Espadilla. It's about 500 meters north of the entrance to the national park; you'll see the entrance from the main road as well. Seafood, including delicious calamari and tropical *batidos*, are featured on their menu. They have a big disco dance on Saturday nights.

Across from the beach, the popular and affordable **Restaurant Marlin** (777-1543) serves Tex-Mex, seafood, soups, and salads, on an airy upstairs terrace.

Next comes a row of restaurants (not recommended) and souvenir shacks where you can rent surfboards, umbrella chairs, and snorkeling equipment. Many vendors in this area sell bottled water, and we highly rec-ommend that you bring some with you to the park. A road to the left in the middle of these establishments leads to the following hotels, some of the best at the beach: **Cabinas Espadilla** (private bath, heated water, fans, kitchen, some with air conditioning; $70-$80; 777-0416) has clean cabins in a tranquil garden atmosphere. Owned by the same family, the newer **Hotel Playa Espadilla** (hot water, air conditioning, cable TV, phones, pool; $120-$130; with kitchen, $140-$150; breakfast included; phone/fax: 777-0903; www.espadilla.com, e-mail: cabinas@espadilla.com), down the street on the left, has light, spacious rooms with tiled floors. There are tennis courts and a private nature reserve. Recommended.

Across the street from Cabinas Espadilla, the German-owned **Travotel Costa Linda** (cold water, table fans, shared bath; $8-$10/person; phone/fax: 777-0304) is basic, but rooms are clean and neat, the atmosphere is appealing. Their restaurant serves inexpensive breakfast and dinner.

The **Vela Bar** offers seafood and vegetarian specialties with a Spanish touch. Their rooms (private bath, ceiling fans, security boxes; with hot and heated water, some with air conditioning and kitchens; $40-$80; 777-0413, fax: 777-1071; www.velabar.com, e-mail: velabar@velabar.com) offer a lot of options and are reasonably priced.

Cabinas Irarosa (shared bath, cold water, $8/person; private bath, hot water, TV, $20-$30; 777-5084), near the park administration office, is good for budget travelers.

GETTING THERE: By Bus: A direct San José–Manuel Antonio bus (223-5567; $5) leaves the Coca Cola at 6 a.m., noon, 6 p.m., and 7:30 p.m., returning at 6 a.m., 9:30 a.m., noon and 5 p.m. Buy tickets in advance on weekends and holidays and purchase return tickets as soon as you arrive. The Quepos ticket office (777-0263) is open Monday through Saturday, 7 a.m. to 11 a.m., 1 p.m. to 5 p.m.; Sunday, 7 a.m. to noon. This bus will pick you up at your hotel on its way from Manuel Antonio to Quepos, but you must be out on the road to flag it down. (Do not let anyone but the bus driver load or unload your baggage. Try to keep it with you if possible. Things have been stolen from the luggage compartment.) One driver on this route makes the trip in three hours, a fact that defies conventional concepts of space and time. We have heard of several people who have become quite religious on this bus. The bus will let you off at the airport near San José if you ask. The trip should take three and a half to four hours and cost about $5. (Watch out for pickpockets at the Coca Cola.)

Quepos–Manuel Antonio: From the southeast corner of the market, take a 20-minute bus ride (30 cents) seven scenic kilometers to the entrance of the park. They leave on the hour and half hour between 7 a.m. and 7 p.m. Buses also leave Quepos for Manuel Antonio at 5:45 a.m., 6:45 a.m., and 10 p.m. (Check schedules at 777-0263) or visit www.quepolandia.com. Watch out for robberies in the tumult to get on this bus. A taxi to Manuel Antonio from Quepos costs about $4, or about half that if you hail it when it's coming back to Quepos.

Quepos–Puntarenas buses leave at 4:30 a.m., 7:30 a.m., 10:30 a.m., and 3 p.m., returning at 5 a.m., 11 a.m., 2:30 p.m, and 4:30 p.m. (two and a half hours; $3). (All of the above buses pass by Playa Jacó, an hour and a half north from Quepos.)

Buses leave San Isidro de El General (771-2550) for Quepos at 7 a.m. and 1:30 p.m., passing through Dominical. They return from Quepos at 5 a.m. and 1:30 p.m.

Interbus (283-5573; www.interbusonline.com) runs shuttles to Manuel Antonio from San José daily ($25). Lynch Travel (777-1170; www.lynchtravel.com, e-mail: lyntur@racsa.co.cr) is their representative in Quepos. Recommended if you feel too shaky in your Spanish to take the public bus.

By Boat: Manuel Antonio and Drake Bay are included in the itinerary of the Cruise West (888-851-8133; www.cruisewest.com), which has a week-long family cruise.

By Car: The trip from San José is about three and a half hours if you take the Atenas turnoff and drive the narrow, winding road through the Aguacate mountains. This route is scenic and gives you a glimpse of rural life. You can buy sugarcane juice and fruit along the way. You can also take the Interamerican Highway to Puntarenas and then turn south, but you might be traveling with a line of trailer trucks.

By Air: SANSA has six flights a day to Quepos during the high season (221-9414, fax: 255-2176; $45 one way). Buy tickets at least two weeks in advance during dry season. A private bus ($2.50) will deliver you to your hotel in Quepos or Manuel Antonio, and pick you up to get you to your return flight. SANSA also has Quepos–Tamarindo and Quepos–Puerto Jimenez flights. Check schedules at www.flysansa.com. Nature Air (220-3054, fax: 220-0413; $50 one way, $100 roundtrip) has four flights to Quepos daily. Check schedules at www.nature air.com. (Some of their flights continue on to Palmar Sur, the point of departure for Drake Bay, and to Puerto Jiménez, gateway to the Osa Peninsula.)

MATAPALO

An hour south of Manuel Antonio along the bumpy Costanera Sur road is Matapalo, a small, quiet beach town set in the middle of a seemingly unending stretch of beach. (One section of Matapalo is on the road, and its oceanside twin, with all the cabinas and restaurants, is a couple of kilometers away on the beach.) The surf here is not what you would call gentle, but it is much less rough than it is at Dominical, about 15 kilometers farther south (see Southern Zone chapter). The firm beach at low tide is great for horseback riding or bike riding, and sea kayaks are for rent to explore nearby mangroves. At night the starlight is brighter than in more developed areas.

In the pueblo, enjoy good Tico food at **Soda Mango** or **Soda Chasta**.

Just at the beach road, across the little bridge south of the football plaza, is a wonderful restaurant and equally fantastic *pulpería*. **La Pulpería Espiral** has lots of items that gringos and Europeans want but can rarely find— especially in remote areas like this one. Next door, **Express del Pacífico** serves up hand-tossed pizzas, rotisserie chicken, and a few Tico dishes.

The first place you come to on the beach is **El Oasis**, clean economical cabins with an adjacent bar/restaurant serving Tex-Mex and gringo food along with a few Tico dishes.

The Swiss-owned **El Coquito del Pacífico** (private bath, cold or hot water, ceiling fans, pool; $50-$70; phone/fax: 384-7220) has spacious, bright cabinas with good screens and reading lamps. Their restaurant has a Swiss chef.

Down the road on the right 150 meters is one of the nicest places to stay or eat in Matapalo: **Albergue Suizo** (private bath, heated water, ceiling fans; $30-$50; 382-7122). Rooms are spacious and clean. The Swiss owners serve tasty meals on their balcony.

A funky French restaurant, **La Terraza del Sol**, is a few hundred meters north. Reservations recommended (779-9255). Open for dinner only.

Almost a kilometer farther north, **La Piedra Buena** (private bath, cold water, ceiling fans, mosquito nets, some kitchens, restaurant; $30-$50; e-mail: lapiedra_buena@hotmail.com), owned by an industrious Swiss woman, is a wooden duplex set back from the beach in a groomed sand yard (with geese) and a house closer to the road. Beatrice, the owner, is an excellent chef.

Next door is the **Jungle House** (private bath, heated water, fans; $20-$50; phone/fax: 787-5005; www.junglehouse.com, e-mail: charlie@jungle house.com), with American-owned rooms and cabins, with kitchenettes. There's direct TV, pool table, and direct beach access.

El Castillo ($90-$100; phone/fax: 777-3634, cell phone: 392-3460; www.elcastillo.net, e-mail: dc@elcastillo.net) is a B&B in the hills with awesome views of Playa Matapalo and an in-house trained chef to cook meals aside from breakfast if you like.

GETTING THERE: By Bus: Take a San Isidro bus from Quepos at 5 a.m. or 1:30 p.m., a Quepos bus from San Isidro at 7 a.m. or 1:30 p.m., or a Quepos–Matapalo bus at 10 a.m.

By Car: Drive south along the gravel Costanera Highway from Manuel Antonio, or north from Dominical (see Southern Zone chapter). Travel time is one hour from Quepos, half an hour from Dominical; ask before you set out. Don't drive this road at night. It is in the process of being paved.

TWELVE

Southern Zone

Costa Rica's *Zona Sur*, or Southern Zone, encompasses the southern half of coastal Puntarenas Province (from Playa Dominical to the Osa Peninsula, to Punta Burica on the Panamanian border), as well as the mountainous southern half of San José Province and inland Limón and Puntarenas provinces, including Chirripó National Park and La Amistad International Park, which extends across the border into Panama. For hikers, naturalists, anglers, and those who want to get off the beaten track, this area has a tremendous amount to offer.

Despite its reputation nationally as a center of agroindustry (bananas, pineapples, palm oil, coffee), it has a larger percentage of national parks and forest reserves than any other region of Costa Rica. It also has the largest concentration of indigenous people, especially the Guaymis and Borucas, centering around the towns of Buenos Aires and San Vito. Because the area is not really on the tourist trail, budget accommodations are plentiful. The Southern Zone is also becoming known for small, aesthetically designed nature lodges that fund private reserves where you can get up close and personal with monkeys, macaws, and dolphins.

SANTA MARÍA DE DOTA AND COPEY

Los Santos is a mountainous region southeast of San José covered with well-groomed coffee farms. The higher reaches are cloud forest frequented by the beautiful resplendent quetzal, making this one of the closest quetzal-viewing areas to San José. Start by heading toward Cartago on the *autopista*, then up the Interamerican Highway toward San Isidro. The turnoff for Santa María de Dota is at El Empalme, 29 kilometers from Cartago. Stop to buy the tart apples and hard balls of sharp, white *palmito* cheese produced here. Or warm up with a cup of *agua dulce* and a hot *tortilla de queso*.

Continue down the road on the right to **Santa María de Dota** (11 kilometers). These mountains were the scene of the beginnings of the 1948 Civil War—the late Don Pepe Figueres' farm, La Lucha Sin Fin (The Endless Struggle), is located near Santa María. In the plaza is a monument to those who lost their lives in Costa Rica's battle to preserve the integrity of electoral process. **Santos Tours** (546-5446) helps you explore the forests, villages, and coffee *beneficios* of this lovely region.

For hikes through narrow mountain valleys and native oak forests, following rushing rivers and mesmerizing waterfalls, spend at least a day in **Copey**, seven kilometers uphill from Santa María. Its brisk climate at 7000 feet above sea level is refreshing, especially if you're feeling worn out from the lowland heat. Treat yourself to a trout lunch at **Pesca Río Blanco** (541-1816) or **La Catarata** and buy crisp, local apples for dessert. The old wooden **church** in Copey is a national monument.

Copey is part of the **Cerro Vueltas Biological Reserve**, which borders Tapantí/Maciso de la Muerte National Park to the northeast and Los Santos Forest reserve to the south. These protected areas are connected to Chirripó National Park and La Amistad International Park stretching down into Panama, making this the largest biological corridor in the country.

El Toucanet (private bath, hot water; children under 10 free; $50-$60, including breakfast; 541-1435; www.eltoucanet.com, e-mail: toucanet@racsa.co.cr) is the only lodge in Copey, with cabins and a good **restaurant** serving delicious trout overlooking a peaceful forest and a rushing mountain stream. It can get quite chilly in these hills, so the cabins have thick blankets and the restaurant has a cozy sunken sitting area around a fireplace. Owners Edna and Gary Roberts give a free guided tour every morning to search for the resplendent quetzal. Sightings are common from December to July just 15 minutes from the lodge. From August to November, Gary or his sons will take you to a higher altitude to find them. They also offer a horseback tour with breathtaking views for experienced riders, a tour of a local coffee factory, or hiking in the cloud forest and paramo. It is one kilometer east of the church in Copey.

A bit beyond El Toucanet, Urs and Isabel, a Swiss-French couple, offer horseback and hiking tours at **Finca Pelota de Roble** (541-1299). They will take you around the region, or even as far as Londres, near Quepos and Manuel Antonio—a two- or three-day camping trip. They also rent a rustic cabin that sleeps four (gas hot water, no electricity, woodstove; $12-$20,

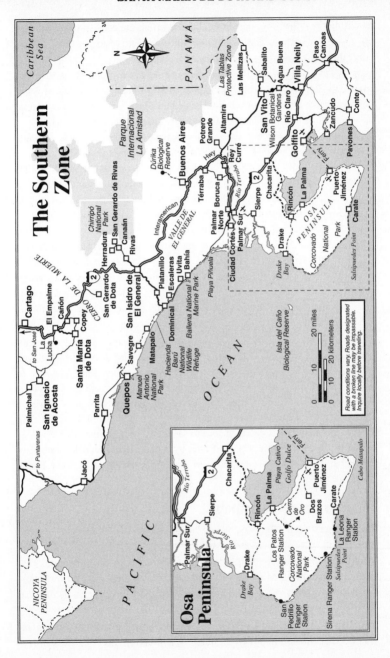

including breakfast; long-term rental possible) on the edge of the cloud forest. Great for birders. You must have four-wheel drive to get there. If you don't they will pick you up in Copey or Santa María.

GETTING THERE: By Bus: You can catch the bus to Santa María from San José (Calle 21, Avenida 16 bis; 223-1002; $1.80). Check the schedule at www.monteverdeinfo.com/costa-rica/bus-schedule.htm. Buses return to San José from the main square in Santa María six times a day. The trip takes about two hours.

Copey has its own bus service now, leaving from Santa María de Dota. Check schedules at 541-1449. A taxi from Santa Maria costs about $10.

To get to Copey without going through Santa María, take a San Isidro bus (Calle 16, Avenidas 1/3) to Cañón del Guarco, kilometer 58 on the Interamerican Highway. (You'll see the little yellow markers on the side of the road that tell you how many kilometers you are from San José.) From Cañón it's seven kilometers downhill on a dirt road to Copey. Santa María is another seven kilometers downhill. You can either walk or hitchhike. If you drive up from Santa María, make sure you have a four-wheel drive, or at least a powerful engine and a high clearance.

By Car: Head east of San José on the Interamerican Highway past Cartago and drive toward San Isidro. At Empalme turn right toward Santa María, or continue to kilometer 58 and turn right to go directly to Copey. It takes about one and a half hours.

To get to this area and avoid the hectic traffic of San José, go south of the international airport to Villa Colón and climb up to Palmichal de Acosta, where you can stay at Nacientes Palmichal (see p. 172). From there, find your way to Acosta, then San Gabriel, where you turn right and travel though the Los Santos area: San Pablo de León Cortés, San Marcos de Tarrazú, and Santa María de Dota. The roads are nicely paved, and the churches and plazas of these charming villages are picturesque. Take a detour to see the views from the hillside village of San Isidro de San Pablo de León Cortés by taking a right turn before you enter San Pablo. It takes about three hours to drive from the airport to Santa María. Recommended.

CERRO DE LA MUERTE

The Interamerican Highway, which becomes San José's Central Avenue, crossing the city from west to east, turns right at Cartago to connect the Central Valley with the Southern Zone. It winds into the mountains that surround fog-shrouded Cerro de la Muerte, the highest pass on the Interamerican Highway. This entire area is part of the Cerro Vueltas Biological Reserve, mentioned above.

As you wind around **Cerro de la Muerte**, you will see the lush vegetation become stunted and then diminish. When taking this trip, dress in layers and try to go early in the day, before fog and rain reduce the visibility to zero. This can happen even in the dry season. Landslides are also a very real danger during heavy rains. If you are cold in your car and intimidated by the driving conditions, imagine how Costa Ricans hiking or driving ox carts must have felt before the road was built. That's why this area is called "Mountain of Death." Several high-altitude mountain lodges are on or near Cerro de la Muerte.

Albergue Mirador de Quetzales (heated water; shared bath, $20-$30/ person; private bath, $30-$40/person; dinner, breakfast, and morning tour included; 771-4582, fax: 771-8841; www.exploringcostarica.com/mirador/ quetzales.html, e-mail: recajhi@racsa.co.cr) virtually guarantees that you will see quetzals in their reserve between November and May. The Serrano Obando family guides are intimate with the birds' hangouts and habits, but even if you're unlucky, the guided hike is lovely and punctuated with curiosities: huge *cipresillo* trees that naturally hollow out in their old age, and marine fossils in the rocks beside one of their creeks. Most visitors spend the night in the rustic-but-homey A-frame cabins because quetzal sightings are most likely in the early morning, but you can also stop in for a guided or a self-guided tour ($6) and a delicious campesino lunch. To get there, go one kilometer west after you turn off the Interamerican Highway at marker 70.

Several roadside cafeterias on the Cerro specialize in quick *comida típica* for bus passengers. The classic **La Georgina**, in Villa Mills, serves a wide variety of local treats. They have hummingbird feeders set up outside the window at the back of the restaurant so you can watch while you eat. Recommended. They also rent basic rooms with electric blankets (private bath, heated water, TV; $15-$20; 770-8043) above the restaurant. On a rare clear day you can see Volcán Irazú to the north and Chirripó to the south.

SAN GERARDO DE DOTA   San Gerardo de Dota, a narrow, pristine mountain valley at 6900 feet, has become a mecca for birders, hikers, and trout fishers. The first lodge you come to is the **Trogon Lodge** (private bath, hot water; $50-$60/person; meals, $25/day; 293-8181, fax: 222-5463; www.grupomawamba.com), with duplexes of dark-stained wood overlooking lovely flowering gardens next to a stream where you can catch your dinner. One and a half kilometers of trail lead through a primary-forest reserve in which quetzals and woodpeckers, among other birds, abound. The lodge offers horseback trips. One-day packages and two-day tours, including roundtrip transportation from San José, are available.

Cabinas El Quetzal (private bath, heated water; $30-$40/person, including meals; 740-1036), about a kilometer before the Albergue de Montaña Río Savegre, are good for families or groups that come to enjoy nature or fishing. Don Rodolfo Chacón can show you around the area and put you in contact with neighbors who rent horses. The cabins lack atmosphere, but the guests-only dining room has a beautiful river view.

Don Efraín Chacón and his family rent cabinas at **Hotel de Montaña Río Savegre** (private bath, heated water; $78/person, including three meals; 740-1029, fax: 740-1027; www.savegre.co.cr). Be prepared: it's cool, and gets downright chilly at night. The Chacón family has taken advantage of the crisp weather to grow apples, plums, Chilean papayas, and peaches, which you sample in meals. Trout abound in the nearby Río Savegre. Over 170 bird species have been observed from the 16 kilometers of hiking trails here. This is known as one of the best places in the country to observe quetzals, who live there year-round. The *albergue* hosts the Quetzal Education Research Complex, a cooperative venture between the Albergue and Southern Nazarene University in Oklahoma. Students who come to study quetzals share information with local residents and visitors through a series of public talks at the hotel. Be sure to make reservations: the lodge has grown quite popular lately.

GETTING THERE: By Bus: Take a San Isidro bus (see below) and ask to be left at the "*entrada a San Gerardo*" at the 80-kilometer mark on the Interamerican Highway. San Gerardo is nine kilometers downhill from there, a scenic two-and-a-half- to three-hour walk. The lodge will pick you up for $10.

By Car: If you are driving from San José, follow the directions in "Getting There" for San Isidro de El General, and turn right at the 80-kilometer mark. Make sure your vehicle has a powerful engine since the road is extremely steep and narrow. It is paved in the steepest parts.

SAN ISIDRO DE EL GENERAL

The **Valle de El General** is one of Costa Rica's natural jewels. When the fog clears after you pass Cerro de la Muerte, the surrounding small towns in the valley offer beautiful flowers and a lovely climate.

The bustling, fast-growing town of **San Isidro de El General** is the gateway to Chirripó National Park and Playa Dominical. The clean public market in San Isidro is a delight, offering an array of beautiful fruits and vegetables, and good, inexpensive places to eat. **Soda Popeye** (pronounced poh-pay-yay) is one of the best in the market. There is a farmer's market behind the Escuela del Valle Thursday afternoons and Friday mornings.

Twenty minutes (by car) before arriving in San Isidro, you can stop at the friendly **Vista del Valle** for a panoramic view and well-prepared, inexpensive *comida típica*. They serve fresh-squeezed orange juice. You can eat inside the homey restaurant or out on the balcony. They sell original crafts, including painted wooden platters, sun hats, and woven baskets, and have a cute little cabin with a great view and a balcony (private bath, hot water; $40-$50, including breakfast; 384-4685).

On the central plaza, the **Restaurant/Bar Chirripó**, at the hotel of the same name, is a favorite for local gringo residents. **El Tenedor** (closed Monday) is a good restaurant down from the central plaza, 75 meters toward the Hotel Iguazú on the second floor. Locals have recommended **Restaurante Mexico Lindo** for tasty Mexican food at reasonable prices, as well as for wonderful personal attention provided by the owners, Don Armando Tapia and his wife. You'll find Mexico Lindo inside the Centro Comercial Pedro Perez Zeledon on the south side of the Plaza.

Selva Mar (771-4582, fax: 771-8841; e-mail: selvamar@racsa.co.cr), around the corner from Hotel Chirripó, is a travel agency committed to ecotourism. You can change money, send documents by courier, buy airline tickets, and leave film to be developed there. They will also help you make reservations for any lodges listed below. They specialize in one- to five-day treks up Chirripó, and tours to Dominical, Uvita, Ballena National Marine Park, Drake Bay, Corcovado, the Osa Peninsula, and the Golfo Dulce. There are ATMs at the Banco de San José and Coopealianza.

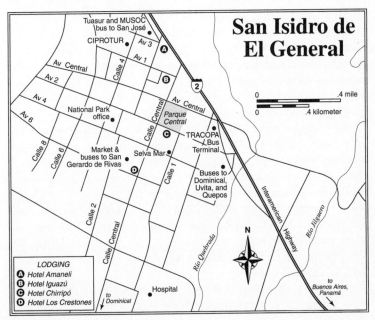

San Isidro de El General

LODGING
A Hotel Amaneli
B Hotel Iguazú
C Hotel Chirripó
D Hotel Los Crestones

SEPA (770-1457; www.sabalolodge.com/sepa.html, e-mail: spanish@ sabalolodge.com) offers one- to three-week Spanish instruction combined with tours or volunteer work.

Brunca.net Internet Cafe (open Monday through Saturday, 8 a.m. to 8 p.m.; Sunday, 9 a.m. to 5 p.m.; 771-3235) has offices on both the north and south side of the plaza for international calls, faxes, and e-mail. Open Monday through Saturday, 8 a.m. to 8 p.m.; Sunday, 9 a.m. to 5 p.m. You can also make telephone calls from the ICE, two blocks north of the Parque Central.

LODGING   There are several clean and inexpensive hotels in town. Near the bus stops and close to the Interamerican Highway you will find the relatively noisy **Hotel Amaneli** (private bath, heated water, wall fans, TV; $10/person; 771-0352) and the quieter **Hotel Iguazú** (wall fans, cable TV, private bath, heated water; $20-$30; 771-2571). **Hotel Chirripó** (hot water, fans, TV; with shared bath, $5/person; with private bath, $13/person; 771-0529) is the least expensive, and is much quieter.

Hotel Los Crestones (private bath, hot water, ceiling fans, air conditioning, cable TV, pool; $40-$50; 770-1200, fax: 771-6012; www.ecotourism. co.cr, e-mail: hcrestonespz@hotmail.com) is clean and airy. It's on the southwest side of the stadium in San Isidro, near the road to Dominical. Some rooms are wheelchair accessible.

Six kilometers south of San Isidro, on the left, is the large, comfortable **Hotel del Sur** (private bath, solar-heated water, fans or air conditioning, phones, TV, pools; $40-$70; 771-3033, fax: 771-0527; www.hoteldelsur.co. cr), with well-tended gardens, tennis courts, playground equipment, large conference rooms, a casino, and a good restaurant. Their *ceviche de camarón* is fresh and filling. Quiet cabins that sleep five are at the back of the property (refrigerators, heated water; $60-$70). A good value.

By far the most peaceful alternative is the friendly **Albergue de Montaña Talari** (private bath, solar, heated water, refrigerator, pool; $50-$60, including breakfast; children 6 to 12, $10; phone/fax: 771-0341; www.talari. co.cr, e-mail: talaripz@sol.racsa.co.cr; closed in September and October), a small, unpretentious farm on the banks of the Río El General, six kilometers (15 minutes) from San Isidro toward Chirripó National Park. The attentive Tica-Dutch hosts can arrange four-day treks up Chirripó. Their restaurant offers good food at reasonable prices, and even has a piano. Over 200 species of birds have been spotted on the property; birding tours are available. Recommended.

At ✿ **Montaña Verde**, near Rivas, you can learn about organic coffee farming and visit a *trapiche*, where brown sugar is made. The farmers of

Montaña Verde have a lodge (shared bath, cold water; $20/person, including meals) where you can stay and get to know the community. Contact them through ACTUAR (228-5695; www.actuarcostarica.com, e-mail: actuar@ra csa.co.cr).

GETTING THERE: By Bus: Comfortable buses leave San José for the three-hour trip to San Isidro from the spiffy new MUSOC station (on Calle Central, Avenida 22, across from Maternidad Carit) at 5:30 a.m., 7:30 a.m., 10:30 a.m., 11:30 a.m., 1:30 p.m., 2:30 p.m., 4:30 p.m., 5 p.m., and 5:30 p.m. (222-2422). Tuasur buses leave from Calle 16 outside the Coca Cola at 6:30 a.m., 8:30 a.m., 9:30 a.m., 12:30 p.m., and 3:30 p.m. (222-9763). Buy tickets in advance, especially on weekends and holidays. Buses back to San José leave hourly. (San Isidro: Tuasur, 771-0419; MUSOC, 771-0414.)

By Car: Follow San José's Avenida Central toward Cartago, then follow signs to San Isidro. There is a tricky spot just before Cartago where you should continue straight ahead on a smaller road toward San Isidro instead of following the freeway left into Cartago. The trip is a precipitous 125 kilometers, and takes three hours. Do not try to rush this trip because there is almost always some delay on this part of the Interamerican—road work or an accident. Once, some non-uniformed campesinos moved dayglo cones into the road. We could see some heavy machinery in the distance. They told us we would have to wait for an hour. Then they tried to sell us bags of potato chips. After a while we figured out that the machines were not blocking the road up ahead, and that the two men had stopped us so they could sell us chips. We continued on our way.

CHIRRIPÓ NATIONAL PARK AND ENVIRONS

San Gerardo de Rivas and **Herradura** are small mountain villages at the entrance to Chirripó National Park. Most people stop on their way to the famous Cerro Chirripó, but even if you are not up to climbing the mountain, the scenery in this area is beautiful and birds of all kinds are abundant. Not to be missed is the wood sculpture of Rafael (Macho) Elizondo of El Pelícano (see below). This prolific artist sees birds, people, and animals in wood and stone, and does what is necessary to bring out what he sees. He does not sell his *artesania*, but sometimes trades with other crafters. Highly recommended.

Narrow gravel roads follow the Chirripó Pacífico river and the neighboring Río Blanco through scenic valleys lined with vegetable, coffee, and dairy farms, perfect for invigorating day hikes. You can see quetzals halfway up the mountain; it's best to go with a guide who can show you where they nest. There is a **hot spring** (admission $2, children $1; pay at a small *soda* near the springs) in a lovely natural setting nearby: walk half a

Kingfisher

kilometer up the road to Herradura, then 20 minutes uphill through the pastures. It's clean, thanks to entrance fee revenue, and the bathtub-like temperature is maintained with a trickle of cold water from another stream above. Any of the hotels listed in this section can provide you with specific directions and guides for exploring this verdant area.

LODGING   The **El Pelícano** (shared baths, heated water; $20-$30; cell phone: 382-3000, 771-4582; e-mail: selvamar@racsa.co.cr) has wood-paneled rooms with comfortable beds and valley views above a restaurant high on a hill. The entrance to the lodge is up a steep hill paved with rocks; it would help to have a car with fairly high clearance.

Río Chirripo Lodge (private bath, heated water; $40-$50, including breakfast; in the U.S.: 707-937-3775; www.riochirripo.com, e-mail: riochirripo@yahoo.com) is a nice new place to stay. It overlooks the beautiful river that gave it its name and has a heated pool and vegetarian cuisine. Yoga, massage, and meditation retreats are held there.

Cabinas Marín (shared bath, heated water; $8-$15; 308-6753), next to the ranger station, have nine rooms behind their *soda/casa/pulpería*.

Francisco Elizondo offers simple, clean lodging at his **Posada del Descanso** (shared bath, heated water, laundry service; $7-$12; private bath, $20-$30; 375-3752; e-mail eldescanso@ecotourism.co.cr), 400 meters toward San Gerardo from the ranger station. He is a font of information and can take you on tours of the area, including his own *finca*. Don Francisco has won the *Carrera a Chirripó* several times, running up and down the mountain in three and a half hours!

Roca Dura (shared bath, $6; private bath, heated water, $15-$20; 771-1866; e-mail luisrocadura@hotmail.com) is a multistory cabina/*soda* built on top of a giant boulder overlooking the river. It's right in town, across from the soccer field.

Albergue Urán (shared bath, heated water, $7-$12; cabin with private bath, $30-$40; 388-2333, phone/fax 771-1669; www.hoteluran.com, e-mail rohelr@yahoo.com) is the closest lodge to the trailhead, located two and a half kilometers beyond the National Park ranger station. They have a store where you can buy what you will need on the mountain and a laundry service. Their restaurant serves tasty Tico food.

CLIMBING CHIRRIPÓ   Chirripó means "Land of Eternal Waters." It is regarded as sacred land by the local indigenous people, who do not venture up the mountain. The area is magnetically charged. Watches and compasses can be affected. Then there are the *nímbolos*, or dwarves, that play tricks on you up there. The old rangers have lots of stories. The trek up Chirripó can be painful, tiring, frustrating, and freezing, but it's so satisfying to reach the summit, which is really the top of this part of the world, being the highest peak in southern Central America at 12,503 feet. A climb up Chirripó, with only one day at the summit, will take a minimum of five days, including transportation to and from San José.

Making reservations for lodging within the park: The weeks before Easter and before New Year's are the Ticos' favorite time to climb Chirripó because they are on vacation and the weather is usually dry, so it is usually crowded at those times. The *Carrera a Chirripó* is in mid-February, so it might be hard to get reservations then, too. The park is closed during the month of May. No matter when you want to go, you must make reservations because they allow only a limited number of trekkers into the park at one time. Call or visit La Amistad Conservation Area office in San Isidro (150 meters west and 50 meters south of the Parque Central, in front of the Cámara de Cañeros; phone/fax: 771-3155, 771-5116) to make your reservations. Once they confirm that there's space, you must deposit the fee for your stay in their bank account and fax them the receipt. Charges per person include $15 for two days, plus $10 per night for lodging in the *albergue* near the top of the mountain. Each extra day costs $10 admission and $10 for lodging. The *albergue* has two bunkbeds with vinyl-covered mattresses and four security boxes in each room. There are shared baths. You can rent blankets ($1), sleeping bags ($2), and camping stoves and gas for camping stoves ($2) at the top. There is potable water, but you have to bring your own food.

To prevent fires, only stoves can be used, and only within the *albergue*. Smoking is not allowed in the park, only at the lodge in permitted areas.

Porters: There is an association of local men who will lug your backpack and equipment up the mountain by horse ($20-$25 for up to 15 kilos or 33 pounds) in the dry season or on their backs (a few dollars more) in the rainy season. This will probably make your hike a lot more enjoyable. To arrange for *porteros*, you must get to San Gerardo the day before you plan to hike and ask around to find who's available, or contact Selva Mar

(771-4582; e-mail: selvamar@racsa.co.cr) to arrange a porter for you. This service is not for hikers with inferiority complexes—just as you're struggling up another hill halfway up the mountain, you will meet the man who hauled up your stuff whistling gaily down the trail. Payment is made when you arrive in San Gerardo de Rivas.

Guides: Trails are well-marked, so there's no problem in going alone, but there are many advantages of going with a bilingual guide. You learn more about the history, legends, wildlife, and plants of the area. You don't have to make any arrangements yourself, and don't have to carry anything. While other tired hikers are struggling to boil water with their campstoves at the top, you'll be treated to gourmet meals prepared by someone experienced in high-altitude cooking. Selvamar (771-4582; e-mail: selvamar@rac sa.co.cr) offers guided tours up the mountain and has a lot of good information about Chirripó on its web page.

Check-in: To climb Chirripó, check in at the ranger station, near the final bus stop in San Gerardo de Rivas. It's open 5 a.m. to 5 p.m. If you want to leave before 5 a.m., as we did, check in the day before. Don't start any later than 8 a.m.—start earlier if it's raining or windy. You cannot enter the park after 10 a.m.

What to bring: The summit area is above timberline, so once you get there you can always see where you are as long as inclement weather and fog do not envelop you. Watch out for lightning and falling trees. Be sure to bring:

- A water bottle, at least one liter per person, to replenish all the liquid you'll lose sweating.

- Warm clothes and a warm sleeping bag. It gets very cold at night—between -5ºC (23ºF) in the windy dry season and 3ºC (37ºF) in the rainy season. Bring or rent extra blankets. I slept in a Polarguard sleeping bag with one blanket inside it, another on top, another underneath, all my clothes on, and a friend beside me. I was almost warm. You can rent blankets and sleeping bags at the top.

- Snacks for the hikes. Dried bananas and peanuts are good for energy when you're climbing. Carrots proved to be our lifesaver on the Cuesta de Agua. They quench your thirst and give you something to do slowly and steadily as you climb that never-ending hill.

- A kerosene or alcohol burner to cook your meals. Building fires in the park is not allowed. You can rent camping stoves at the top.

- A poncho to keep you dry during the daily multiple rainshowers. Veteran Chirripó climbers warn against getting wet during the hike. It might seem okay while you are heated up on the trail, but it can be dangerous when you get to the top.

• Binoculars and a camera (200 ISO film).

The hike: The first day is long and grueling. Hikers make the 14 straight uphill kilometers to the lodge in anywhere from seven hours to two days. It took us 11 hours; we left at 4:30 a.m. The average time is seven to nine hours. Follow the road through San Gerardo, across two bridges. Half a kilometer past the second bridge, follow the sign that directs you up through a coffee field. This is the *termómetro* shortcut, and connects with the main trail, which is well-marked. Signs every half kilometer give the altitude and distance to the summit. You will be slapping flies, sweating, and slipping on your long haul, but if you can take your mind off these annoyances, you'll enjoy your surroundings.

The trail climbs through a dense cloud forest, where *jilgueros* (black-faced solitaires) sing their amazing song—which sounds like it's blown through a glass flute. The song is simple, but very fine. The birds like to stay up in the highest treetops, so they're difficult to spot. The *jilguero's* natural habitat is the cloud forest. Sadly, as people destroy the cloud forests in Costa Rica, they are destroying the *jilguero* as well.

The first opportunity to get potable water is at "Llano Bonito" (Lovely Plain). This is four or five hours into the hike. There is a rustic hut here where you should stay only if you are sick or injured. The park service doesn't like to have hikers stay here because there is no ranger to supervise. After Llano Bonito comes **La Cuesta del Agua** (Water Hill), which is the longest haul of them all—it takes two to three hours to climb. It ends at **Monte Sin Fé** (Faithless Mountain), where you walk into a new kind of landscape. Almost 20,000 acres of Chirripó, including Monte Sin Fé, were ravaged in April 1992 by a fire started by careless hikers.

Next you have to climb **La Cuesta de los Arrepentidos** (Repentant's Hill), then the trail traces around the side of a mountain. Soon you'll see **Los Crestones** (The Outcrop) on the top of a ridge straight ahead. These are huge, sharp rocks that look like they were folded accordion-style. The lodge is in the valley just below them.

Herradura Route: You can travel a different route altogether that takes off from Herradura. It passes over Cerro Urán and then Chirripó. You have to camp two nights before arriving at the Los Crestones Base Camp. This is a new trail and you must hire a guide. Tell Parques Nacionales that you plan to take this route. Rodolfo Elizondo is a local guide who makes this trip. It is also offered by Selva Mar in San Isidro.

No matter which route you take, arriving at the lodge is a relief. If you're lucky, someone will have a pot of water boiling and will offer you a cup of hot tea.

Mornings are clear in the summer, then the valley fills with fog. Wisps of fog drift in until they crowd together and form dense clouds. Visibility decreases, and at 2 or 3 p.m. it rains for about 45 minutes, so be sure you're on the trail by dawn. Besides having a better chance to see both the Atlantic and Pacific oceans, you'll get to enjoy this time of day—the sun touches the frost-covered leaves and grasses, the ice melts, the plants stretch, and whole meadows squeak softly.

Day hikes from Los Crestones: There are many places to explore on day hikes. Of course you should go to the summit of Chirripó, two hours up the same trail. You pass through the **Valle de los Conejos** (Rabbit Valley). *Lagartijas* (spiny lizards, endemic to this area) now occupy the valley. Each lizard has a different sheen that perfectly matches the rock it suns itself on. On the top of Chirripó you can see both the Pacific Ocean and the Caribbean Sea if the clouds haven't rolled in by the time you get there. There's a register to sign in a metal container at the summit cairn. Below the summit is **Lago Chirripó**. You can swing by it on your way down.

The lake-filled **Valle de las Morrenas** (Valley of the Moraines, or glacier lakes) is on the other side of the peak. If you want to continue hiking in that direction, you can pass over Cerro Urán and continue along the **Camino de los Indios** (Indians' Path), a trail known and used almost solely by the locals. Talk to Parques Nacionales in San José for a special permit and hire a guide for this hike.

Other day-hike possibilities are **Cerro Ventisqueros**, the second-highest mountain in southern Central America, whose trail leads from the main trail a bit below the Valle de los Conejos. This is a very steep hike. You can also hike from the lodge to Los Crestones. The top of the ridge above the valley is reached by going up to the left of Los Crestones. Follow the ridge left to **Cerro Terbi**, a mild 15 minutes. There's a register there, too. To make this hike a roundtrip, continue on the ridge a few hundred meters and descend on a trail that goes through a steep chimney and ends up in Valle de los Conejos. You can also continue walking along Terbi's curving ridge, ascending and descending the peaks, and go down into Valle de los Conejos when you get tired.

Note: When you go on your day hikes, take a map, a compass, a flashlight, a sweater, a rain jacket, snacks, and water.

GETTING THERE: By Bus: The 6 a.m. San Gerardo bus leaves from the west side of San Isidro's Central Park; the 2 p.m. bus leaves from the south side of the market ($1). The trip takes about 90 minutes. When asking which of the many buses to take, specify San Gerardo de *Rivas*, because there's another San Gerardo. To be able to start your hike before dawn, arrive a day early and spend the night in San Gerardo de Rivas. The 10:30 a.m. bus from San José will get you to San Isidro in time to catch the 2 p.m. bus to San Gerardo. If you miss the bus, a taxi will take you to San Gerardo for about $20. Buses leave San Gerardo for San Isidro at 7 a.m. and 4 p.m. As mentioned above, Francisco Elizondo of Posada del Descanso can take you to San Isidro for about $20.

By Car: It's about 45 minutes from San Isidro to San Gerardo de Rivas. Take the paved road, which you'll see going uphill on your left just south of San Isidro, after the second bridge (there's a small sign for Parque Nacional Chirripó). It's nine kilometers to the town of Rivas. San Gerardo de Rivas is 11 kilometers on good gravel roads from there.

PASO DE LA DANTA BIOLOGICAL CORRIDOR

Danta is the Spanish word for Baird's tapir, the largest land mammal in Central America. The tapir's closest relative is the horse and rhino. The tapir's most unusual feature is its prehensile nose, which it uses to eat leaves, much like an elephant uses its longer trunk. The tapir has a stocky body and short legs. Though it weighs 200 to 400 kilos, it is very agile and elusive and is mostly nocturnal in areas where it is hunted. Tapirs make distinctive trails through the forests they inhabit. The Paso de la Danta Biological Corridor (787-0254; www.pasodeladanta.org) seeks to bring the endangered tapir back to the Fila Costeña, the mountain range that rises up from the coast between the Río Savegre, south of Quepos, and the Río Térraba near Palmar Norte. Tapirs now exist only in the Osa Peninsula and in the high mountains of La Amistad International Park. The Paso de la Danta hopes to connect these two habitats, increasing the tapir's chances of survival.

Headquarters for the biological corridor are at the office of ASANA, a grassroots conservation organization founded in the early 1990s. With funding from the UN Development Program, Nature Conservancy, and other NGOs, ASANA is fortifying local conservation groups, providing environmental education, and helping farmers submit the paperwork involved in getting environmental services payments for leaving their forests intact. The 130,000-hectare biological corridor encompasses 55 communities, with a total of 10,000 inhabitants.

During the July 15 to November 15 turtle nesting season, ASANA patrols Playa Matapalo, Playa Burú, Playa Dominical, and Playa Ballena to make sure that turtle eggs are not stolen. They gathered 15,000 eggs in

2003, put them in hatcheries, and helped the baby turtles reach the sea when they emerged from their nests. Tourists can participate in their "Adopt-a-Turtle" program and committed volunteers can help with these efforts by contacting ASANA (787-0254).

DOMINICAL

The scenery along the Costanera Sur Highway south of Playa Dominical is reminiscent of California's Big Sur coast—with lush tropical vegetation, of course. Soon the Costanera will become the major north–south route through Costa Rica, connecting Puntarenas with Ciudad Cortés in an easy couple of hours. The gravel road between Manuel Antonio (Quepos) and Dominical, although it can be driven throughout the year, is still bumpy, but the road between Dominical and Cortés is fully paved. For information on this area, see www.dominical.biz.

The area has numerous beaches, many with rough waves and strong currents. Swimming at the long beach at the village of Dominical can be dangerous, though surfers love it. On the other hand, the warm, reef-protected waters of Ballena National Marine Park, half an hour's drive to the south, are perfect for swimming and snorkeling. The small beaches near Costa Paraíso (below) are also safe for swimming, as is Playa Hermosa, just before Ballena Park.

Legendary Kayak Tours (361-4396) runs sea kayaking tours to Las Ventanas and Ballena National Marine Park. **Mystic Dive Center** (788-8636; www.mysticdivecenter.com) handles diving excursions of the region.

The area's numerous and spectacular waterfalls provide a refreshing break from the sea level's sweltering climate. **Don Lulo's Cataratas Nauyaca** (787-8013, fax: 787-0006; www.nauyaca.com; $40) takes you on horseback from Platanillo, a small town between San Isidro and Dominical, to two beautiful waterfalls with a large swimming hole. Breakfast, lunch, and a snooze in a hammock are offered at Don Lulo's ranch. The two private biological reserves in the area offer even more to do. (See descriptions below of Hacienda Barú and Rancho La Merced.)

On the way to Dominical in Platanillo, the **Restaurant El Barú** offers good roast chicken and grilled meats. **Paraíso Tropical** (private bath, heated water, refrigerators $40-$60; phone/fax: 787-8016; www.villas paraisotropical.com), also in Platanillo, is a nice place to stop for a meal. Restaurant customers can also take a swim in their pools; one has a waterslide. Their two-room cabinas are nicely decorated and quite peaceful.

As you approach Dominical from San Isidro, you follow the peaceful **Río Barú**. If you go right instead of left to cross the bridge into the village, you'll come, in about a kilometer, to the area's only gas station, where you can buy tide tables, fishing supplies, film, maps, and *The Tico Times*. They cash traveler's checks if they have enough money on hand. They also repair flat tires.

A bit farther north, **Hacienda Barú National Wildlife Refuge** offers many activities on their 830-acre private reserve. Their **Flight of the Toucan** canopy tour has eight cables with spans that range from 20 meters (65 feet) to 91 meters (296 feet), where you reach velocities of up to 35 kph (22 mph) between the 15 different takeoff and landing platforms, some on the ground and some in trees. The tour is set up to show how the primary forest forms layers of canopy so you can find out first-hand what the word biodiversity means. You will learn and observe more about nature on the Flight of the Toucan than on most other canopy tours. If you don't want to zip, you can ascend over 105 feet to a platform suspended in the canopy of a magnificent tree and just observe. Another tour involves camping in a tent on a platform in a jungle clearing. This gives you a good opportunity to look for nocturnal mammals.

The book, *Monkeys Are Made of Chocolate*, is a fascinating series of essays and stories by Jack Ewing, founder of Hacienda Barú, recounting his experiences and observations from his last 30 years of tropical living. He began farming rice and cacao and raising cattle on Hacienda Barú in the early 1970s, then started noticing how trees connecting forest patches allowed monkeys, birds, and finally sloths to repopulate the area. Now the monkeys harvest the cacao trees, and Hacienda Barú has become a center for learning about nature, both for tourists and the communities within the Paso de la Danta Biological Corridor. You can buy *Monkeys Are Made of Chocolate* and many other natural gifts at the shop in the reception building at Hacienda Barú.

Hacienda Barú also operates **Cabinas Hacienda Barú** (private bath, heated water, ceiling and table fans, kitchen, restaurant; $60-$70, including breakfast; 787-0003, fax: 787-0004; www.haciendabaru.com, e-mail: hacbaru@racsa.co.cr), simple three-room cottages on a grassy field close to the reserve and about 400 meters from Playa Barú.

SURFING   Dominical is an important surfing destination (see www.crsurf.com, a Dominical-based web page), and most of the cabinas on the beach in the town itself are designed to attract surfers, complete with blaring rap music. Even without a car, you can get to several places on the bus that offer more peace and quiet than the town.

Green Iguana Surf Camp (825-1381; www.greeniguanasurfcamp.com) offers surfing and Spanish lessons, taught by bilingual Costa Ricans for adults and teens. **Angels Surf Camp and Rainforest Experience** (825-1381; www.angelssurfcamp.com), affiliated with Green Iguana, offers surf instruction for girls only. Its hillside campus is near rainforest waterfalls and has great views of the coast.

SPANISH   **Adventure Education Center** (787-0023, in the U.S.: 800 237-2730; www.adventurespanishschool.com) combines surfing and Spanish, as well as offering classes in Medical Spanish and courses for families. Students can get to know the country by studying at their Turrialba and Arenal campuses as well.

LODGING AND RESTAURANTS   Dominical itself is not a particularly charming beachside village, but it is where most of the lodging and restaurants are concentrated. There are a couple of supermarkets in Dominical, but no banks. Water quality in the town is poor except in places that have their own wells; bottled water is available.

A few minutes upriver from the village of Dominical is the **Villas Río Mar Resort** (private bath, hot water, ceiling fans, refrigerator; $80-$90, $400/week; children under 12 free; 787-0052, fax: 787-0054; www.villasrio mar.com, e-mail: riomar@racsa.co.cr) with pool, jacuzzi, mini-gym, tennis court, etc. The thatched bungalows have spacious porches with mosquito-net curtains and a terrace sitting area with hammocks.

Zaidy Jimenez (787-0024) rents houses in the area, and is also a force behind local COVIRENAS and conservation efforts.

Another half-kilometer up the river road, you will come to a narrow hanging bridge over the Barú. We wouldn't recommend driving over it since it swings and groans under the weight of a car, but it is quite beautiful and makes a nice stroll from Dominical.

The **Plaza Pacífica** shopping center, just south of the entrance to town along the Costanera, includes **Banana Bay**, a souvenir shop with a selection of clothing and gifts from the world around, and **Dos Hermanos**, a well-stocked supermarket open 8 a.m. to 6 p.m. daily.

There are public phones in town at Cabinas DiuWak and by the soccer field in front of Restaurant San Clemente (see below). To use them, you must purchase a phone card at San Clemente.

Jazzy's River House (787-0310) has live music twice a week, a full-course vegetarian dinner on Wednesdays, yoga classes in the mornings, and basket-weaving lessons. It's on the river, through a white gate next to the market.

Restaurant San Clemente has inexpensive Tex-Mex specialties; pool tables, surfing videos, and a satellite TV define the ambience. There is also a public phone. Across the street is **Restaurante su Raza**, where a television and inexpensive food attract crowds of Ticos and gringo tourists every night.

Nearby is **Posada del Sol** (private bath, heated water, wall fans, screens; $20-$30; two-bedroom apartment with kitchen, $40-$50; phone/fax: 787-0085), clean and pleasant, and with its own well-water supply.

Veering right at the Y in the road will take you to a couple of cabinas in front of the best surf break on the beach. **Cabinas DiuWak** (private bath, heated water, ceiling fans, phones, jacuzzi; $60-$80; with kitchen, $80-$90; 787-0087, fax: 787-0089; www.diuwak.com, e-mail: diuwak@racsa.co.cr) is a surfers' information center and internet café. **Tortilla Flats** (private bath, heated water, ceiling fans or air conditioning; $30-$40 for up to three people; phone/fax: 787-0033) has good Tex-Mex specials. **Cabinas San Clemente** (private bath, heated water, ceiling fans; in the basement, $20-$30; with fans or air conditioning, $30-$40; phone/fax: 787-0026, 787-0055) are fairly nice rooms run by a transplanted California surfer, the owner of Restaurant San Clemente. They rent surfboards. The **Restaurant Atardecer** at the beach offers pitas, falafels, and smoothies.

Antorchas Camping (787-0307), a block inland from the corner of Cabinas San Clemente and Om Massage, has camping space with bathrooms, tent rentals ($5/person), safe parking, hammocks, and a basketball court. They also rent rooms ($8/person).

Two kilometers from Dominical, the **Costa Paraíso Lodge** (heated water, ceiling fans, some air conditioning; $60-$70; private bath, kitchen, $90-$110; 787-0025; www.costaparaisodominical.com, e-mail: costapar@racsa.co.cr) is quiet and secluded. Picturesque rock formations on the beach in front of the hotel form a lagoon; nearby beaches, protected by a reef, are safe for swimming. The tastefully decorated cabinas are designed with natural ventilation and there is a lovely *rancho* with hammocks near the water. You can also rent rooms by the week or the month. Their **Seaside Gallery of Fine Art** is open daily.

GETTING THERE: By Bus: Dominical is served by two bus lines from San Isidro. The San Isidro–Uvita line leaves the Empresa Blanco terminal near the Interamerican Highway in San Isidro for Dominical every day at 8 a.m. and 4 p.m., passing through Dominical an hour later. A slower Uvita bus leaves San José daily at 3 p.m., stopping in Dominical at 9 p.m., and returning through Dominical at 5 a.m. This bus is agonizingly slow, not recommended. On weekends there is also a 5:30 a.m. bus from San José to Dominical. The San Isidro–Quepos bus leaves Empresa Blanco at 7 a.m. and 1:30 p.m., arriving in Dominical an hour later. The San José–San Isidro–Dominical route is the most efficient. You can also take the three-hour San José–San Isidro bus (see San Isidro section earlier in this chapter) and get a taxi to Dominical for about $20. From Quepos, take the 5 a.m. or 1:30 p.m. San Isidro bus, which passes through Dominical two hours later. Check schedules at your hotel.

By Car: Dominical is about 45 minutes from San Isidro on a paved road. Follow the signs through San Isidro. If you are coming from Quepos ask about road and bridge conditions before leaving. The Quepos–Dominical trip takes about an hour and a half.

ESCALERAS AREA

About three kilometers south of Costa Paraíso, a road to the left climbs steeply up to the Escaleras area. Several lodges, cooled by mountain breezes and affording breathtaking views of the Pacific, can be found here. The road is an inverted U; the other end meets the Costanera a few kilometers down the road. Access is often only possible in a four-wheel-drive vehicle; most of the lodges will pick you up in their own vehicles, if you prefer. You can also hike, but it's quite steep. Before driving up, call your lodge to ask which side of the U is in better condition.

The beautifully designed **Necochea Inn** (shared bath, hot water, ceiling fans; $70-$80; private bath, $80-$130, including breakfast; children under 10 free; 395-2984; www.thenecocheainn.com) is the dream come true of a California couple. They have decorated their comfortable B&B with antiques and original art. The most expensive room has a jacuzzi, and all rooms have balconies with views of forest and ocean. Breakfast is served on the deck near their small pool, and other gourmet meals are available on request. The lodge has many nice touches, like handcrafted mosaic countertops and a game room for kids. Recommended.

Bella Vista Lodge (private bath, solar-heated water, ceiling fans; $50-$60; with kitchen, $70-$80; cell phone: 388-0155, 800-909-4469, access code 01; www.bellavistalodge.com, e-mail: reservations@bellavistalodge.com) has a beautiful view of the ocean from high atop the Escaleras road. Accommodations are simple but comfortable, and the lodge has a wide, breezy veranda. The two-bedroom house down the hill is probably quieter than the rooms in the main lodge.

Back on the Costanera, in the middle of the inverted U, there is a road heading up one kilometer to **Pacific Edge** (private bath, heated water; $50-$60; larger cabina with kitchen, $80-$90; cell phone: 381-4369; www.exploringcostarica.com/pacificedge/pacific_edge.html), which has individual rustic but comfortable cabins with broad, covered porches and a fantastic view. The cheery owners, a British-U.S. couple, can arrange catch-and-release fishing trips with local fishermen. They have two observation towers. With advance notice they will pick you up from the bus stop (the Uvita bus from San Isidro) on the Costanera, or in Dominical. Four-wheel drive is best. Recommended.

A few kilometers down the road, **Las Casitas de Puertocito** (private bath, hot water, ceiling fans, pool; $40-$50, including breakfast; with kitchens, $50-$60; 393-4327, 200-0139; www.lascasitashotel.com, e-mail las casitas@pocketmail.com) are thatch-roofed fourplexes (the sleeping lofts have ocean views) and some new wooden cabins at the edge of the forest. A candlelit restaurant only for guests serves pasta and seafood dishes with fine Italian wines. By foot, they are about ten minutes away from a beach and a waterfall. They also rent a house that sleeps four with a large balcony overlooking the sea ($1000/week).

A few kilometers south, turn left, go uphill, then turn left again and take the left fork to **Rancho Remo** (306-5171), a campesino-owned campground with beautiful ocean views. There is a small restaurant and cooking facilities. Take the right fork to go to ✿ **Proyecto Turistico Playa Hermosa** (shared bath, cold water, no fans; $7/person; 306-5171). There are simple rooms with a terrific view of the ocean and access to a 73-hectare primary forest reserve. Access to these two projects is quite steep and unpaved, so four-wheel drive is recommended. These projects are supported by APRE-FLOFAS (www.preserveplanet.org). They can help you stay there or volunteer there through their tour company, **Raccoon Tours**.

GETTING THERE: By Bus: The lodges on the main road are right on the San Isidro–Uvita bus line. A bus leaves the Empresa Blanco terminal in San Isidro (just off the Interamerican Highway) daily at 8 a.m. and 4 p.m., arriving in the Escaleras area at 10:30 a.m. and 5:30 p.m. You can also take the 1:30 p.m. San Isidro–Quepos bus and get off in Dominical. If you are staying at one of the lodges on the Escaleras horseshoe, ask the management to help coordinate transportation from the coastal road. Schedules change, so be sure you check.

By Car: The Costanera Sur road between Quepos and Dominical is still unpaved; it's in good condition, although the rough gravel is hard on tires. South of Dominical the road is paved. The San Isidro–Dominical road is paved, with a few potholes.

BALLENA NATIONAL MARINE PARK

Ballena National Marine Park (743-8236) is one of Costa Rica's newest national parks, and one of only two marine parks. The first 50 meters inland from the high tide line are part of the park; the rest is ocean.

The park protects the largest coral reef on the Pacific side of Costa Rica and the Ballena Islands, where humpback whales are seen with their young between December and April and in September and October. Local boatmen like Chume of **Ballena Tour** (818-4100) can take you out to the reef for snorkeling, skindiving, fishing, dolphin watching, or birdwatching. They can also take you an hour and a half south to the great snorkeling spots at Isla del Caño, which you can see in the distance. Frigate birds, brown boobies, and ibises all nest on Isla Ballena. If it's sunny and hasn't been raining lately, snorkeling and skindiving can be rewarding. At low tide you can walk to good snorkeling spots off **Punta Uvita**, the rocky point that spreads out like a whale's tail at the end of the sandy *tómbolo* near park headquarters. The water here is gentle and at bathtub temperature.

To the south, **Playa Colonia** is good for camping because you can drive right up to the campsites, and there are sinks, bathrooms, and showers. The road leading to Playa Colonia is about a kilometer past the second entrance to Bahía on the Costanera. There is a ranger station there and the beach is patrolled at night. Tips: Don't camp under a coconut tree—the coconuts can fall on your head. Bring your own toilet paper.

Eight kilometers south of Punta Uvita is **Playa Ballena**. The rocky half of the beach has a natural swimming pool at low tide and the other half is sandy. MINAE has its ranger station at this beach, and charges $6 admission. If you are not staying at La Cusinga Lodge (see below), this is the best way to access the amazing **Playa del Arco**, one kilometer north of Ballena. The hike to Playa del Arco can only be done at the beginning of low tide. Ask rangers to point you toward the path. Playa del Arco is divided in two by a small, forested point which has a beautiful natural tunnel that you can walk through at low tide.

South of Playa Ballena, is **Playa Piñuela**, a lovely little beach, where local fishermen moor their boats and sell their catch.

Kayakers and sightseers will be awed by the tunnels and caves of **Playa Ventanas**, just around the point south from Playa Piñuela. Over millennia, the sea has carved huge arches in the limestone cliffs that form the small bay. The other tunnels and caves offer plenty of chances for an adrenaline rush to jolt Class IV and V sea kayakers out of their tropical lethargy. **Caves n' Waves** (787-0226, 813-0249) kayak tours in Dominical will take you there. Wading is recommended over swimming, since the waves can be quite rough. During low tide you can walk halfway through the cave at the northern end of the beach; at high tide there is an awesome boom and a cloud of sea vapor as each wave hits the other opening of the cave and the water rushes through.

Ballena is unique on the west coast in that the local community runs the park in partnership with MINAE. The suggested donation at the Punta

Uvita, Playa Colonia, and Playa Piñuela ranger stations is $1 per person. Unlike the admission fees collected at most national parks, which go to Costa Rica's general fund, the much smaller donation you give here goes directly to the community for park maintenance and security, schools and other community needs. There are several *sodas* in Bahía near the park entrance where you can get sandwiches and *casados*.

UVITA   Eighteen kilometers south of Dominical, you will see signs for **Oro Verde Nature Reserve** (743-8072, 843-8833; www.costarica-birding-oroverde.com) 3.5 kilometers to the left. They offer three-hour birding hikes ($30) and two-hour nature hikes ($15). Birders will find this trip rewarding, as it covers a wide range of habitats and altitudes.

Staying at **Rancho La Merced** is a great way to enter into Costa Rican rural life. David Sequeira, who oversees the ranch, is a dedicated animal observer and protector. He takes guests to the beach on horseback, or hiking to waterfalls in the forested wildlife refuge in the hills above the ranch. Inéz, his wife, cooks wonderful country cuisine, served in their home. Lodging is in a simple campesino house in the hills, **El Kurukuzungo** (shared bath, solar-heated water, kitchen; $55/person, including meals and a daily tour; 771-4582; e-mail: selvamar@racsa.co.cr). These two reserves offer some of the best birding in the country. Recommended.

The village of Uvita, a couple of kilometers inland from Bahía and park headquarters, has two simple cabinas owned by friendly local families. Both families offer horseback rides and hikes through their own and surrounding farms and to a nearby waterfall, and they arrange boat rides at the national park. **Los Laureles** (private bath, cold water, table fans; $20-$30; 743-8008) consists of three small concrete houses in a grassy forest clearing—very quiet and peaceful—and some rooms nearer the road. A bit farther is **El Coco Tico** (private bath, cold water; $20-$30; 743-8016), with a large, clean *soda* on the premises. Some of the rooms are in a row set back from the road, others in a new two-story building next to the *soda*. **Toucan Hotel** (shared bath, $8/person; private bath and cooking area, $12-$20; with air conditioning, $30-$40; 743-8140; www.tucanhotel.com, e-mail: tucanhotel@yahoo.com) is a gringo-owned place for backpackers and surfers across from the church. There are hammocks and internet access.

The **Casitas y Restaurante Balcón de Uvita** (private bath, hot water, ceiling fans, pool; $50-$60 for up to three people; $330/week; 743-8034; www.balcondeuvita.com) is a quiet retreat for nature lovers. Three ample, individual bungalows overlook forest and sea, their porches strung with hammocks. The young Dutch owners serve authentic Indonesian (including vegetarian) dishes in their open-air **restaurant** (open Thursday through

Sunday, 11 a.m. to 9 p.m.), which has become one of the most popular in the area. They even prepare the famous Indonesian *rijstafel*. To get there, go left at the first road after the gas station in Uvita. It's best to have four-wheel drive to get up this road in the rainy season. Recommended.

Cascada Verde (shared and private rooms, $10-$20/person; dorms, no phone, $7/person; www.cascadaverde.org, e-mail: cascadaverde@hotmail.com) welcomes guests into its communal experiment in sustainable living. Permaculture, cleansing vegetarian foods, body/mind healing, arts and crafts, and Spanish classes are all offered there. There is a house for volunteers and a lodge with private rooms. The yoga and meditation platform has a distant view of the sea. When we were there, the delicious scent of fresh basil and greens from their garden permeated the atmosphere. They are two kilometers uphill from Coopeuvita. Get there before dark so you can find your way.

BAHÍA   This is the closest village to the park, a couple of kilometers west of the Costanera (when traveling south, make the first or second right after the bridge over the Uvita river). If you're looking for a quiet beach town where you can live as the Ticos do, this might be for you. There are several options: **Villa Hegalva** (private bath, cold water, table fans; $12-$20; 743-8016) has clean rooms and a covered patio strung with hammocks. They allow camping in their yard for $2.50 per person. Nearby, **Cabinas Dagmar** (private bath, heated water, some kitchens; $20-$30; 743-8181) are on the second floor of a well-tended older building. Camping is $2.50/person.

Cabinas Las Gemelas (private bath, cold water, ceiling fans, air conditioning, TV; $12-$20; 743-8009) are 150 meters north of the school.

Cabinas la Rana Roja (private bath, cold or heated water, fans, refrigerator, TV; $20-$30; 743-8047, 819-0697) are new, clean, have good mattresses, and have plenty of room for families. They are on a corner 100 meters west of the soccer field. ✿ **El Canto de la Ballena** (private bath, cold water, fan, screened windows, restaurant; $50-$60, including breakfast; 743-8085; www.turismoruralcr.com, e-mail: cooprena@racsa.co.cr) is owned by a local cooperative. It is very nicely designed with comfortable rooms and mattresses, but has an uninteresting location 500 meters from the first entrance to Bahía and a kilometer from the beach.

A few kilometers south, **La Cusinga Lodge** (private bath, solar hot water, natural ventilation; $90-$100/person, including meals; children under 12, 50 percent discount; 770-2549; www.lacusingalodge.com, e-mail: info@lacusingalodge.com) is a beautiful rainforest reserve overlooking the ocean. The breezy cabins all have great ocean views. Personalized rainforest tours, surfing lessons, snorkeling, fishing, and other activities are included in the rates, and meals are organic. All materials used in construction are natural and display their innate beauty. There are not many coastal areas (besides Corcovado) where virgin forest comes right down to the beach as it does here, and visitors will be rewarded with many bird and wildlife sightings. There is a waterfall-fed swimming hole near the lodge for those who do not want to hike 20 minutes through the forest to beautiful Playa del Arco. It is definitely a place for people who are self-sufficient and in good physical condition, and prefer a quiet environment. For an engrossing recounting of cross-cultural experiences and conservation on this amazing piece of land, read Jon Marañón's *The Gringo's Hawk,* available at online bookstores or at La Cusinga's gift shop. Recommended.

GETTING THERE: By Bus: Buses leave daily at 9 a.m. and 4 p.m. from San Isidro's Empresa Blanco terminal (just off the Interamerican Highway, one block south of the main bus station), arriving in Bahia two hours later. From Quepos, follow the directions in the "Getting There" section for Dominical. Travelers from Quepos can intercept the San Isidro–Uvita bus in Dominical around 11 a.m. When leaving the area, there are buses (6 a.m. and 2 p.m.) to San Isidro; the very slow Uvita–San José bus leaves at 5 a.m. and 1 p.m., passing through Quepos.

By Car: The Costanera Sur between Dominical and Uvita is paved and in good condition. The drive takes about 20 minutes. To reach Dominical from San Isidro or Quepos follow the directions in the "Getting There" section under Dominical. The recent "completion" of the Costanera has opened up the coast between Uvita and Puerto Cortés. This makes roundtrip circuits through the Southern Zone more reasonable: you can drive one way from San José to Jacó or Manuel Antonio, south along the coast to Cortés and Palmar, and then north, inland along the Térraba River, through San Isidro, and over Cerro de la Muerte.

By Air: You can cut many hours from your trip by flying as far as Palmar Sur (about ten kilometers from Cortés) and taking a bus or taxi the rest of the way to Uvita. SANSA (221-9414, fax: 255-2176; www.flysansa.com) and Nature Air (232-7883, 220-3054, fax: 220-0413; www.natureair.com) fly there daily.

OSA PENINSULA

The Osa Peninsula reaches out of southwestern Costa Rica into the Pacific Ocean. Historically it has been one of the most remote areas of the country, unknown to most Costa Ricans. Now, nature-loving Ticos and foreign tourists are arriving in large numbers to explore the incredible richness of the peninsula. Its large virgin rainforests receive 150 to 230 inches of precipitation a year, and it hosts an incredible variety of tropical flora and fauna. In the Osa alone, 375 species of birds have been identified. This is about half the number of species in the whole United States. Of the eleven endemic freshwater fish species in Costa Rica, nine are found only in the Osa. Over 124 species of mammals live there, 58 of them bats. Within the Osa Conservation Area, which extends from Dominical to the Panama border, 34.5 percent of the land is protected. These protected areas are home to 28 endangered bird species and 13 endangered mammal species, like tapirs, scarlet macaws, spider monkeys, jaguars and pumas.

The biological richness of the Osa is due to the fact that three million years ago, part of the peninsula was an island. Later, during the last Ice Age, approximately 20,000 years ago, the high mountains north of the Los Santos region were frozen. The slow freezing process gave some plants and animals time to move to lower altitudes, where they remained after the ice had melted. So today's Osa has plants that originated at both low and high altitudes. The Osa contains the most extensive rainforests on the Pacific coast of Mesoamerica (between México and Panamá). The 600-foot-deep Golfo Dulce, between the eastern coast of the peninsula and the mainland, holds biological riches that are just beginning to be known. Humpback whales and dolphins can be observed there, as well as on the Pacific side. The extensive mangrove swamps that line the coast are important nurseries for marine wildlife.

The Osa Conservation Area, Corcovado Foundation, and the Nature Conservancy are working with local community groups to form a biological corridor that would link Corcovado, Piedras Blancas National Park northwest of Golfito, and the Sierpe-Térraba wetlands north of Drake Bay in order to insure a viable future for both the people and wildlife of the region.

The peninsula has been the site of much ecological destruction by lumbermen, campesino settlers, and gold miners. The creation of Corcovado National Park in 1975 and the cooperative work of both international and grassroots organizations has served to protect much of the region's natural wealth, but illegal logging and poaching are still serious threats. In March 2004, the Minister of the Environment said that the chronically underfunded park system was in a state of emergency, unable to control a fierce wave of hunting that was threatening to wipe out the population of collared peccaries and jaguars within Corcovado National Park. He threatened to close the park if the government and local ecotourism businesses did not chip in to help pay for the environmental services that the park provides for them: scenic beauty, water, and the attraction of biodiversity, which makes big bucks for local hotels and tour companies.

The Corcovado Foundation, made up of local hotel and tourism operators, donates money for park administration. See who their members are at www.corcovadofoundation.org.

Most visitors in the 1980s had to go on a hardcore mission to backpack through Corcovado National Park. In the last few years, options have sprung up for softer-core tourists who want to see the rainforest but want their strawberry macadamia nut pancakes for breakfast, too. Most of the prime land for tourism, with the magnificent views, is owned by foreigners, mainly North Americans.

PALMAR NORTE AND SUR

Palmar Norte and **Palmar Sur**, while not tourist destinations in themselves, are the gateways to Drake Bay, the Osa Peninsula, and Golfito to the south. Also, if you have traveled down the Costanera to Ciudad Cortéz, you can turn north in Palmar to visit Boruca and the Dúrika Reserve, or cross the Río Térraba at Paso Real to continue south to the Altamira entrance of Parque Internacional La Amistad and San Vito (see below). You can also fly into the airport in Palmar Sur and continue to the above destinations or head up the Costanera to Uvita and Dominical. If you must stay in Palmar en route to somewhere else, the best place is the **Casa Amarilla** (cold water, table or ceiling fans; with shared bath, $7-$12; with private bath, $20-$30; 786-6251), next to the Plaza de Deportes in Palmar Norte. The upstairs rooms have balconies. It is often full, so make reservations.

The airport is in Palmar Sur, across the Río Térraba. Taxis are usually around when flights come in.

GETTING THERE: See "Drake Bay" section below for air, bus, and car directions to Sierpe and Palmar.

SIERPE

Sierpe used to be a steamy riverside village that you'd just pass through to get to well-known Drake Bay, but recently it has developed a tourism industry of its own. The **Oleaje Sereno** (private bath, hot water, ceiling fans, air conditioning; $30-$40; 786-7580; e-mail: elfenix@racsa.co.cr), located right at the dock, is very clean. They have a fenced parking lot and will watch your car for you for a nominal fee while you go to Drake Bay. **Hotel Margarita** (shared bath, cold water; $7-$12; with private bath, $12-$20; 786-7574) is "el cheapo" in Sierpe. It has clean, small rooms with screened windows and is run by friendly local people. It's across the plaza from the discotheque, so you might not want to stay there on weekends. They arrange trips to Poor Man's Paradise, south of Drake Bay.

Restaurante Las Vegas, on the river side of the plaza, serves good fish and chicken, and **Rosita's** is popular for *comida típica*. **Sonia's** *pulpería* is the communications center for Sierpe, with telephones, faxes, radios, etc., for public use, plus an incredibly wide variety of items for sale.

DRAKE BAY

Drake Bay, purported to be where Sir Francis Drake anchored the *Golden Hinde* and set foot in Costa Rica in 1579, is on the northern coast of the Osa Peninsula, accessible by boat from Sierpe or by plane from San José or Quepos. Scarlet macaws and monkeys are easy to spot there as you hike along the trail above the rocky coves south of the Río Agujitas. The bay is rich in marine life. Four types of whales visit the bay. **Elderhostel** sponsors a whale research expedition based at Drake Bay Wilderness Resort (see below). All the hotels in the area will take you to see the dolphins, which seem to love to gather around boats, arcing out of the water and leaping high into the air. You can also spend a fascinating evening with biologist **Tracie the Bug Lady** (382-1619; www.thenighttour.com), who will lead you into the jungle with hand-held night-vision optics devices that cast an eerie green color on everything but allow you to see clearly in the dark without disturbing the animals. She and her partner teach you how to see the eye-glow from frogs and spiders, and explain the weird mating rituals of leaf-cutter ants and stick insects. You might even see a boa. It's well worth the $35 fee. She supplies you with boots and walking sticks. She also rents a beautiful house in the forest ($200/night; e-mail: eyeshine@racsa.co.cr).

The **Original Canopy Tour** has a nine-platform, six-cable zipline ($45) in Drake. Your hotel can book it for you.

All the lodges on Drake Bay offer fishing trips and guided tours to Corcovado National Park and **Isla del Caño**, a small, round, forest-covered island about 20 kilometers off the coast that is thought to be the site of a pre-Columbian cemetery. Stones carved into perfect spheres can be found on the island; their significance is still unknown. Snorkeling and scuba diving are especially good at Isla del Caño because the water is often crystal-clear in the dry season and five coral platforms surround the island. The lodges all lend out snorkeling equipment in the dry season, and many offer PADI-certified diving programs. Kayaks are also available.

Even though tourism in this area largely depends on dolphins, whales, coral reefs, and marine biodiversity, the offshore area between Corcovado and Ballena Marine Park is completely unprotected, except for the area surrounding Isla de Caño. These waters are unscrupulously exploited by shrimp boats, which operate at night, notoriously hauling up everything in their nets just to get the shrimp, and letting the by-catch die. Ask your hotel how you can help support the formation of a marine wildlife refuge in this area, and boycott shrimp whenever you see it on the menu.

GETTING ORIENTED AND GETTING AROUND: The most common way of getting to Drake Bay involves a 75-minute boat trip down the Sierpe

River and across the river mouth to the open sea before you get to the lodges. The San Pedrillo entrance to Corcovado is about half an hour's boat ride beyond Drake Bay, or a four-hour hike. It's a 40-minute boat ride from Drake Bay to Isla del Caño.

The lodges listed first are south of the village of Drake Bay. Drake Bay Wilderness Camp, Aguila de Osa, and La Paloma are clustered around the Río Agujitas where the main docks are. The next seven are scattered along isolated beaches between Drake and the border of Corcovado National Park. While these more-remote lodges offer boat transportation, reaching them on foot from the Agujitas area is also possible at low tide. For instance, Delfia Amor, Marenco, and Punte Marenco are 40 to 50 minutes by foot south of the Agujitas River. Poor Man's Paradise is a three-hour hike south of the Agujitas, and Campanario is one hour beyond that. Just south of Drake Bay are Las Caletas, a series of small coves bordered by rocky outcroppings. The trail goes up above the coves. It's a lovely hike, with plenty of chances to swim and snorkel if you want to. South of Marenco the landscape flattens out and the trail is sometimes on the beach itself.

Note: It really is smart to bring well-fitting rubber boots to this area. They give much-needed traction on the muddy trails, and can keep you dry through most stream crossings at low tide. Otherwise, sand gets in your wet sandals and rubs your feet—the same happens with wet sneakers. If you bring boots, be sure to bring several pairs of thick socks that extend above the rim of the boots. If you don't, the boots rub against your calves. Also, don't expect to find an ATM or bank in this area. Bring cash for small purchases and find out in advance whether your hotel accepts credit cards. Most rates are all-inclusive so you don't need a lot of money here.

LODGING   Most lodges require a two-night minimum and offer packages including meals and transfers from San José. Prices are for double occupancy. On the north side of the Río Agujitas is **Aguila de Osa** (private bath, hot water, ceiling fans; $560/person for two nights, including meals and transfers; discount for children; 296-2190, fax: 232-7722, in the U.S.: 866-924-8452; www.aguiladeosa.com, e-mail: info@aguiladeosa.com), with stunning views, excellent tropical cuisine, and good service.

Across the Río Agujitas is **Drake Bay Wilderness Resort** (solar- and gas-heated water, ceiling fans; $606/person for two nights, including meals, transfers, and two tours; discount for children; 256-7394, phone/fax: 770-8012, in the U.S.: 561-371-3437; www.drakebay.com, e-mail: emichaud@drakebay.com), right at the mouth of the Río Agujitas with good American- and Tico-style food served in a breezy bar and lunch room overlooking the water, and plenty to do near the lodge. Snorkeling is good both right at the resort and ten minutes away by boat at Punta San Joseçito. They will lend you masks, fins, and canoes and kayaks for exploring the Río Agujitas, known for its needlefish. You can canoe up the river in search of monkeys, then relax in the giant tidepools at the far end of the property or in their saltwater swimming pool. There's a butterfly farm you can ride to on horseback or mountain bike, an hour and a half from the lodge. Sea-kayaking instruction is also offered, as well as an excellent dolphin tour. A three-day package, including transportation to the Drake airstrip from San José or Quepos, costs $780/person. A weekend getaway costs $530. Boat transfers can be arranged from Dominical for groups. Laundry service is free for guests. You might not grasp what an important service this is unless you have tried to dry your clothes in the tropics. It can take several days. The gas-run dryers seem heaven-sent.

Staying in the *ranchos* at **La Paloma Lodge** (private bath, solar-heated water, ceiling fans, pool; three-night package: $1000 to $1210/person, including meals, transportation from San José, and tours to Corcovado and Isla del Caño; 293-7502, 293-5400, fax 239-0954; www.lapalomalodge.com, e-mail: info@lapalomalodge.com) is like waking up in the jungle. Perched high on a hill, the private, two-story *ranchos* are surrounded by greenery and birds, with views of Drake Bay and Caño Island beyond. A winding staircase connects the two floors, and louvered wooden shutters open to let in air and light. Their tiled swimming pool offers spectacular ocean views. Free guided nature walks with staff naturalists were included when we were there; a guide took our 13-year-old son kayaking while the rest of us relaxed on our balcony hammocks. The staff does everything it can to please its guests. The airy dining room serves delicious food. Kayaks, canoes, boogie boards, and snorkeling equipment are free for guests, and there is PADI-certified scuba instruction. Three- to five-night scuba packages are also offered. Getting to La Paloma from the landing dock on the river involves a fairly steep 15-minute uphill climb, so it is not recommended for those with heart problems or trouble walking. Recommended.

A half-hour's hike along the lovely trail above Las Caletas brings you to **Delfin Amor Eco-Lodge** (shared bath, cold water, no fans; three-night package: $600/person, including meals, transportation, and two tours; in the U.S.: 831-345-8484; www.divinedolphin.com, e-mail reservations@divinedolphin.com), whose mission is "enriching the deep connection that humans have with dolphins and whales" and helping protect the sea mammals as well. Delfin Amor's Wild Dolphin Encounters ($95) epitomize respect—the animals are never chased or fed, and the choice to interact is always their choice. Dolphins are not as easy to see when the seas are rough—the trip will be cancelled if conditions are not right. Guests at the lodge dine family-style, and gather on the stone veranda of the dining room overlooking the sea to watch the sunset. Jerry, the Pirate Chef, dishes out some awesome fare, and will cook up the fish you catch on your way back from communing with the dolphins (dolphins' sonar keeps them away from hooks). Lodging consists of five simple screened rooms with two double beds in each, and a shared bath area. Volunteering is a possibility if your skills match their needs. Because they do not have a landing dock, Delfin Amor is not recommended for children under 10 or people who are not agile enough to jump out of the boat between waves.

A 15-minute walk south of Delfin Amor brings you to **Marenco Beach and Rainforest Lodge** (private bath, cold water, fans; $50-$80; 258-1919, fax: 255-1346, in the U.S.: 800-278-6223; www.marencolodge.com, e-mail: info@marencolodge.com), one of the original ecotourism projects in Costa Rica. Cabins, high on a hill with private porches, look out at gardens that attract birds and butterflies, and at Isla del Caño beyond. Researchers are always in residence at Marenco, and double as naturalist guides. Their rates are per room, not per person—a bargain in this area. Marenco Beach Lodge shares the view and a 500-hectare forest reserve with its neighbor, **Punta Marenco Lodge** (private bath, cold water, no fans, mosquito nets; $399/ person for a three-night package, including meals, tours, and roundtrip transportation from Palmar Sur; 222-3305, 268-9441; www.puntamarenco. com, e-mail: info@puntamarenco.com), individual *ranchos* with one side totally open to the view, owned and operated by Guillermo Miranda, the founder of the reserve, and his family. Rates do not include meals or transportation. A half-hour hike from either lodge through a series of lovely rocky coves ends at the Río Claro, where a deep natural pool lends itself to a refreshing swim.

Poor Man's Paradise (three-night package: $376-$421/person, including meals, tours, and transfers from Palmar Sur; 786-6150, 771-4582, fax: 771-8841; www.mypoormansparadise.com, e-mail: poormans@cheqnet.net) is a family-run project on isolated Playa Rincón, a three-hour hike (go at low tide only) or a 20-minute boat ride south of Drake. A little grass-roofed *rancho* on the beach, which serves as an evangelical church for the community, is the only sign you see from the water. In back of it are simple, clean cabins with good mattresses (private bath, cold water, table fans), a common hanging-out area, and a platform with tents (shared bath, cold water). Farther back is the restaurant where Doña Carmen takes care of her guests as if they were family. Her husband, Don Concho, learned herbal medicine when he lived with the Guaymi Indians. Their son Pincho specializes in low-cost sportfishing trips. They offer horseback riding and have a sheltered reef ideal for snorkeling at low tide.

Proyecto Campanario (shared baths, cold water, no fans; $50-$60/person, including meals; 258-5778, fax: 256-0374, 282-8750; www.campana rio.org, e-mail: campanario@racsa.co.cr) is a biological reserve and field station on a beautiful cove about an hour's walk or a short boat ride south of Poor Man's Paradise. It's the brainchild of Nancy Aitken, a high school teacher with a dream to help people understand the rainforest. She has set up tables and benches in the most beautiful parts of the reserve so you can spend time being quiet and listening to the forest. The no-frills field station provides bunkbed accommodations with shared baths downstairs. Large tents on platforms up the hill from the field station are more private. Their three-night package ($397) includes meals and transportation from Sierpe plus guided trips to the reserve and Corcovado. They also offer a six-day Rainforest Conservation camp ($635), a ten-day course in Tropical Biology for students ($1022), and a two-week Tropical Biology course for teachers. The last three include transport from San José. This is a great volunteer opportunity for people willing to do trail maintenance work and help in the kitchen. Visiting Campanario is a friendly, educational, and inexpensive way to see this beautiful area.

Casa Corcovado (private baths, hot water, ceiling fans; $140/person, including meals and tours; 256-3181, fax: 256-7409, in the U.S.: 888-896-6097; www.casacorcovado.com, e-mail: corcovdo@racsa.co.cr; closed September 1 through November 15) is on the border of Corcovado National Park, a half-hour boat ride from Drake Bay. After a beach landing that has to be done at exactly the right gap in the waves, guests are transported straight uphill for a welcome cocktail at a simple but elegant screened bar with a great view of Isla del Caño. The bungalows are set back at the edge of the forest and do not have views. They are private and well-designed, with good mattresses and spacious, tiled bathrooms. Another attractive open-air bar is cantilevered over the jungle where chances for birdwatching abound. There is a spacious recreation room with videos and a library, and a fresh-water pool surrounded by jungle. Casa Corcovado is known for excellent service. Their three-night package costs $925 including meals and air transport from San José and trips to Corcovado and Caño Island.

DRAKE VILLAGE   North of Río Agujitas, toward the town of Drake (pronounced "Drah-kay" in Spanish), are several places. There is also an administered public telephone at the *pulpería* about two-thirds of the way down the beach. There is a steep but not-too-slippery trail leading from the entrance to La Paloma Lodge down to a hanging bridge across the Agujitas river. It leads uphill on the other side, goes by Aguila de Osa, and takes you into the village. It takes about half an hour to walk to the *pulpería* that way. If you don't want to make the hike, you or your hotel can usually find someone to ferry you the short distance across the river.

Albergue Jinetes de Osa (solar-heated water, ceiling fans, shared or private bath; $70-$90/person, meals included, transfers extra; 236-5637, 800-317-0333; www.costaricadiving.com, e-mail: oamonge@racsa.co.cr) specializes in scuba diving, rents snorkel equipment, and can arrange inexpensive small-craft fishing trips in the bay.

Halfway down the beach, an uphill road next to the *pulpería* leads you to **Cabinas Jade Mar** (private bath, cold water, table fans, mosquito nets; $45/person, including meals; cell phone: 384-6681, 786-7591), simple but very clean cabins run by a local woman who is a certified nature guide. You will really get a sense of life in this small beach town by staying with Doña Marta, and though we didn't get to eat there, the tempting aroma of fried fish emanating from her breezy, open-air dining room indicated that she's a very good cook. She can take you to her family's farm, where you can swim in a waterfall-fed lagoon, and she offers group rates to Corcovado and Isla de Caño. Recommended.

At the end of the beach you'll see a road coming from the north and following a river inland. This is the Rincón–Rancho Quemado road, which could change the face of Drake forever if it becomes viable year-round. If you wade across the river and scramble up the embankment and over the road, you'll see a steep trail that will bring you to **Mirador Lodge** (private bath, cold water, natural ventilation; no electricity; $40/person, including meals; cell phone: 831-1488; www.mirador.co.cr, e-mail: info@mriador.co.cr), rustic accommodations with a beautiful view of Drake Bay and nearby rivers and waterfalls. A steep hike uphill from the cabins is a covered camping area ($15/person, including meals) with an even more amazing view. Owner Don Toño and his family are ardent vegetarians and organic gardeners. They cook soymeat specialties on their woodstove. Recommended for budget travelers who like to hike.

LOS PLANES   Four kilometers uphill from Agujitas, in the village of Los Planes, a conservation organization started by two local women has converted a former park ranger station into ✿ **Tesoro Verde** (shared bath, cold water; $25-$35, including meals; 849-9848, 827-9807; www.ecolodge-costa-rica.com, e-mail: tesoroverdedrake2003@yahoo.com), a charming inn with sunny rooms and access to their 12-hectare rainforest reserve. Staying at Tesoro Verde puts you in the center of village life, with plenty of opportunities for intercultural exchanges. The dedication of the people to preserving the land and stopping illegal hunting and logging is impressive. You can hike to an isolated *finca* in the forest where Oldemar and his family will guide you to secluded waterfall pools ($25), or take an hour's horseback ride ($50) to the Río Claro. Tesoro Verde lodge is only four kilometers by foot from Corcovado. To get there, take the fork to the right at Cabinas Jade Mar in Drake and walk four kilometers, passing over a hanging bridge, to the village of Los Planes, or arrange a $5 taxi from Drake.

ON THE RÍO SERPE   Back down the Río Sierpe again, you'll come to **Río Sierpe Lodge** (private bath, solar-heated water, fans, screens; three-night package: $255-$475, including meals, tours, and transportation from Palmar; 253-2412, phone/fax: 225-8553; www.riosierpelodge.com, e-mail: info@riosierpelodge.com), a good place for serious birders, naturalists, and anglers. Owner Mike Stiles is a bird expert with years of experience in the region, and particular knowledge of the birds that frequent the estuarine and primary forest systems near the lodge. Try to get one of the cabins that has a screened upstairs bedroom and views of the jungle or the river. Mike has a great library of nature books.

GETTING THERE: You should definitely make reservations and travel arrangements before you go to Drake Bay because crossing the river mouth is best done with the tides. Also, many lodges do not have their own docks, and landings need to be coordinated by captains and assistants experienced with each place. For these reasons it is best to let your lodge arrange transportation for you from San José, Palmar, or Sierpe. You can get to Palmar by bus or plane, or drive to Sierpe if you have a car (the Hotel Oleaje Sereno, next to the main dock in Sierpe, will watch your car while you are in Drake). Many travelers leave Drake Bay for the end of their trip, turn in their rental cars in Quepos and fly to Drake, or drive to Palmar and taxi and boat to the coast, then fly back to San José. You are met at each step by people from your hotel. If you have a package deal, transportation costs are included.

By Bus to Sierpe: If you want to get there on your own, take the 5 a.m. TRACOPA bus to Palmar (Calle 14, Avenida 5; 221-4214; $5). The trip takes six hours. After you get to Palmar, follow directions for boat travel from Sierpe, below.

By Car to Sierpe: At Palmar Sur on the Interamerican Highway, drive south through a maze of banana plantations to the town of Sierpe. Ask the banana workers for directions at every intersection (there are no signs and it's easy to get lost). From Sierpe, follow boat directions below.

By Car to Drake: A new road connects Drake with the Rincón on the Golfo Dulce. If you take the Interamerican Highway all the way to Chacarita and head towards Puerto Jiménez, you will come to the town of Rincón. This is the road that has been facilitating logging operations north of Corcovado. It runs from Rincón to Rancho Quemado and on to Drake Village. It doesn't cross the Agujitas River, so you'd have to leave your car on the village side if you wanted to visit lodges to the south in Drake Bay. Jade Mar will watch your car for you. This road can only be driven by a high-clearance vehicle, and only in the dry season. Check with your hotel regarding road conditions and driving times.

By Bus and Taxi: A bus will take you from San José to Rincón, north of Puerto Jimenez (Transportes Blanco, Calle 14, Avenidas 9/11; 257-4121; 6 a.m.; $6.50, 7 hours). From there you can hire a taxi-truck to Drake Bay on the Rincón road, a bumpy 32 kilometers.

By Air to Palmar: You can take a plane to Palmar. SANSA (221-9414, fax: 255-2176; $66 one way; www.flysansa.com) leaves at 9:30 a.m., returning at 10:30 a.m. Nature Air (220-3054, 232-7883, fax: 220-0413; www.natureair.com; $66) leaves every morning at 8:30 a.m. You can pick up the flight in Quepos if coming from Manuel Antonio. It returns at 10 a.m. with a stop in Quepos.

By Air to Drake: Nature Air (www.natureair.com) flies to Drake Bay at 8:30 a.m., 8:45 a.m., and 2 p.m. for $85 one way. The flight is in a single-engine plane. SANSA (www.flysansa.com) flies twice a day to Drake, at 9:30 a.m. and 2:05 p.m. ($73 one way).

PUERTO JIMÉNEZ

Puerto Jiménez is the largest town on the Osa Peninsula. People say its first inhabitants were prisoners sent away from the mainland with machetes and a warning never to come back.

Despite, or perhaps as a result of, its tawdry history, Puerto Jiménez is now the gateway to some of the most beautiful and inspiring tourism projects in the country. Because the Osa was considered such a no-man's land, it opened to tourism much later than the rest of Costa Rica. The people who started tourism projects here did not do so to jump on the bandwagon, but because they had a vision that the beauty of the land could be the key to its preservation. The ecotourism projects in this area are principled, and are already seeing the effects of their efforts: scarlet macaws and monkeys are coming back. You can probably see as much wildlife in the private reserves of these lodges, or from their terraces, as you can by going to Corcovado itself. And it has its positive effects on the local community: Don Alfredo Mesén, an employee of one of the lodges, heard that a neighboring campesino was about to cut the trees on his land—virgin forest. Don Alfredo suggested that in one year, his neighbor could make more money by guiding tourists through his forest than he could by cutting it down. The campesino took him up on it, and Señor Mesén sent him a steady supply of tourists from his beach hotel. At the end of one year the farmer was better off economically, and will be for years to come. Now other campesinos are calling the hotel, asking to be supplied with tourists.

We should not paint too rosy a picture, however: deforestation and poaching are still serious problems.

Puerto Jimenez has two internet cafés. **Osa Natural**, located across the street from the soccer field, is run by a local tourism cooperative. Its competition is **Café Internet Sol** in the center of town. They have links to local hotels on their website: www.soldeosa.com. As you come into "downtown" Puerto Jimenez, they are at the end of the first block, on the left. Either internet café can make hotel and tour reservations for you or watch your luggage while you run errands.

Isabel Esquivel, the well-organized bilingual radio operator at **Osa Tropical** (735-5062, fax: 735-5043; e-mail: osatropi@racsa.co.cr; 50 meters south of the Catholic Church), offers a variety of naturalist expeditions; she can also make reservations for the lodges on the Osa Peninsula. If you have trouble contacting any business in this region, she will help you. **El Tigre**, just south of La Carolina on the main street, is a general store where you can cash traveler's checks, change money, and stock up on food or camping supplies. They run a collective taxi service to Cabo Matapalo ($2.50) and Carate ($7) that leaves at 6 a.m. and 1:30 p.m. and returns at 8:30 a.m. and 4 p.m. every day but Sunday ($60 per carload at other times). There is a gas station at the southern end of Puerto Jiménez, where you turn right to go to Matapalo and Carate.

There is a full-service **Banco Nacional** in Puerto Jimenez.

You can observe **turtle nesting** at Playa Piro or Playa Platanares between June and December. Starting in August, you can see baby turtles scrambling to the sea if you go early in the morning.

Luis Quintero gives great wildlife tours of the area. He also does an unforgettable half-day horseback tour of the beach. Ask your hotel to get in touch with him for you. You can arrange sea kayak trips or sunset dolphin watches at the downtown **Escondido Trex** (phone/fax: 735-5210; e-mail: osatrex@racsa.co.cr) office in Restaurant Carolina. Joel Stewart (735-5569) of **El Remanso** (see Cabo Matapalo below) helps you climb 180-foot forest giants or rappel down waterfalls. **Bosque del Cabo** (381-4847) has an observation platform high in the forest canopy that you can slide to on a cable. **Osaventures** (735-3541) specializes in bird and wildlife observation. **Aventuras Tropicales** (735-5195, 735-5692; e-mail: kayak@racsa.co.cr) is located on the street leading to the kayak launch in the "gringolandia" district south of town. Alberto Robleto, owner and chief guide, is a Costa

Rican biologist who now delights in offering tours of the Golfo Dulce and its mangroves.

LODGING   Right off the pier, with a back wall on the mangrove swamp (big bathroom windows provide almost an aquarium effect at high tide), are the **Cabinas Agua Luna** (private bath, cold water, air conditioning, cable TV, phone, refrigerator; $45/person; 735-5393).

On the way into town from the dock, **Cabinas Brisas del Mar** (private bath, some with heated water, ceiling fans; $10-$20; 735-5012) have windows facing the gulf. **Cabinas Puerto Jiménez** (private bath, table fans, cold water; $10-$20; 735-5090, 735-5152) are simple, clean, and right on the water.

Away from the waterfront there are several inexpensive hotels and cabinas, all locally owned, with rooms in the $7-$15 range. **Cabinas Carolina** is behind Restaurant Carolina on the main street. Walk to the next corner, turn left, and you will pass the **Hotel Oro Verde** (private bath, cold water, fans; $7/person; 735-5241). Turn the next corner where the street dead-ends at the mangrove and you will find the **Hotel Bosque Mar** (private bath, heated water, fans, air conditioning, cable TV; $15-$30; 735-5681). Return to Café Internet Sol and continue one block farther and you will come to the bus station, the hub for budget travelers.

Cabinas Marcelina (private bath, heated water, fans, some air conditioning; $20-$40; 735-5007) are nicely tiled and decorated and have a pleasant yard. A few blocks down the main street across from the gas station you will find **Cabinas Maricel** with the **Cabinas Eylin** farther down the road to Carate. All of these budget lodgings provide respectable but very basic accommodations.

A five-minute walk toward the airport are **Cabinas Manglares** (private bath, cold water, table fans, some air conditioned; $20-$30; 735-5605, fax: 735-5002). To find Manglares, make a left off the main street at Cabinas Marcelina, and continue two blocks. Make a right, cross a little bridge over the mangrove swamp; Manglares is around the bend. Hospitable owners Augustine and Catalina Quintero provide meals and tour arrangements for their guests. The large natural garden behind the inn shelters birds and wildlife. Don Augustine usually puts out a banana or two in the birdfeeder in the morning, and a retinue of tanagers, woodpeckers, monkeys, and raccoons, often appears for breakfast. Recommended.

Parrot's Bay Village (private bath, hot water, ceiling fans, air conditioning; $70-$110; 735-5180, 735-5748, fax: 735-5568; www.parrotbayvillage.com, e-mail: mail@parrotbayvillage.com) is a group of attractive, comfortable cabins on the far side of the airport. A shady dirt road through a campground called the Puerto Jiménez Yacht Club takes you to their entrance. While the lodge has its own sportfishing program, it also welcomes families and eco-travelers, rents kayaks, and arranges sea and land tours. Their restaurant and bar are very popular with locals and tourists. Across the road from the cabins is a nature trail into the mangroves, where you can see cayman, monkeys, egrets, and ibis.

RESTAURANTS   **Agua Luna** is a restaurant formed by a series of *ranchitos* (round, indigenous-style buildings with pointy, thatched roofs) on the spit between the gulf and the mangrove, right near the dock. Food is good here. The owner runs the cabinas of the same name (see above).

The open-air restaurant at **Parrot's Bay Village** is one of the more pleasant eating places in Puerto Jiménez. They offer an excellent bistro-style menu for lunch and dinner. Dona Catalina at **Los Manglares** will prepare delicious meals for both guests and outside customers. **Restaurant Carolina** is a popular meeting place for expats in the center of town, and the **Soda Oro Verde** offers sidewalk meal service and really good ice cream. Sanjuana Cranford from Monterrey, Mexico, has opened **Juanita's Mexican Bar and Grille** (378-3013), next to the Café Internet Sol, serving authentic Mexican cuisine including fajitas, chimichangas, tequila chicken, and seafood.

You should also try some of the local *sodas* like **El Ranchito**, across from the soccer field, **Soda Morales**, near the waterfront, and the surprisingly good *soda* located in the town bus station. If it's Italian you crave, you will find a popular pizzeria called **Pizza Rock** as you walk from downtown to the public pier. Caution in Puerto Jiménez restaurants: Too rapid growth in the town center has created problems with drinking water quality, so it's a good idea to stick to bottled drinks and ditch the ice.

GETTING THERE: By Bus: Take the Empresa Blanco bus from San José at 6 a.m. or noon ($7; Calle 12, Avenidas 7/9; 257-4121, 771-2550). The trip lasts eight hours. The bus passes through San Isidro at 9 a.m. and 3 p.m.—catch it one block south of the main bus station. Buses also leave San Isidro for Puerto Jiménez at 6 a.m. and noon. The bus returns from Puerto Jiménez at 5 a.m. and 11 a.m. If you are coming from some other point, intercept the Villa Neily–Puerto Jiménez bus at 6:30 a.m. or 3 p.m. at Chacarita (Piedras Blancas), at the entrance to the Osa Peninsula on the Interamerican Highway.

By Car: Follow the Interamerican Highway to Piedras Blancas (Chacarita) and turn right. It can take as much as three hours to drive the 75 kilometers between Chacarita and Puerto Jiménez. The road gets totally destroyed by the huge lumber trucks that constantly traverse it, and by flooding during the rainy season.

Rumor has it that the road will be fixed soon, but don't plan to drive here unless you check with your hotel on road conditions and driving times. Be really alert for bicycle riders along the Interamerican Highway. There are a lot of them, especially at dawn and dusk, and they don't have lights.

By Boat: An old launch leaves the municipal *muelle* in Golfito for Puerto Jiménez every day at 11:30 a.m., returning the next morning from Jiménez at 6 a.m. The enjoyable ride across the gulf takes an hour and a half. Dolphins often swim and dive alongside the boat. Zancudo Boat Tours (776-0012) will take you from Zancudo to Puerto Jiménez for $30 for two.

By Air: SANSA offers a daily flight for Puerto Jiménez (221-9414, fax: 255-2176; www.flysansa.com). Nature Air (220-3054, fax: 220-0413; www.natureair.com) also flies to Puerto Jiménez daily.

SOUTH OF PUERTO JIMÉNEZ

The following projects are located south of Puerto Jiménez, an area that is not serviced by public electricity. All of them rely on private generators or solar and candle power, so be sure to bring a flashlight. The phone numbers we give are where the lodges pick up their messages, so call for reservations as far ahead of your arrival as possible. Lodges in the area north of Puerto Jiménez are listed after those to the south.

PLAYA PLATANARES **Playa Platanares** is a long, peaceful beach on the Golfo Dulce six kilometers south of Puerto Jiménez. Whales can be spotted there in October and November and it's a turtle beach. A local couple, Don Efraín Mesén and his wife, have a homegrown turtle protection project there. Don Efraín patrols the beach nightly from May to November and moves the nests to a protected area. They date the reburied nests, and then help the baby turtles with their trip to the water when they hatch 60 days later. Don Efraín has also built some whimsical driftwood sculptures on the beach. They will gladly show you their project. Donations are gratefully accepted.

The waves at Playa Platanares are gentle and safe for children, and all three of the following lodges welcome families.

Black Turtle Lodge (shared bath, hot water, fans; $80-$100/person, including meals; children $20-$40; 735-5005; www.blackturtlelodge.com, e-mail: info@blackturtlelodge.com), to the left at the beach, has individual raised bungalows with balconies at canopy level, and *cabinettas* that are closer to the ground. There is a shaded platform on the beach for hammocks and a large, beautiful screened yoga platform under the trees.

Iguana Lodge (private bath, solar hot water, ceiling fans; $70-$90/person, including meals; 735-5205; www.iguanalodge.com, e-mail: lauren@

iguanalodge.com), next door, has spacious cabins on stilts so that each has an ocean view; the screened walls are louvered so you can catch the breeze. There are two beds upstairs and two below, so it's a great place for families. Meals, featuring freshly caught seafood and lots of veggies, are really special and served in a huge two-story *rancho*. There is a lovely Japanese hot tub. Tasteful sofas and rockers make for a congenial sitting area. The owners are very active in the community and can direct you to the most interesting things to do. Recommended.

They also own the nearby **Pearl of the Osa** (private bath, cold water, ceiling fans; $50-$60, including breakfast; 735-5205, fax: 735-5043; www.thepearloftheosa.com, e-mail: info@thepearloftheosa.com). Eight simple but spacious and airy rooms are located on the second floor, above a restaurant/bar that closes at 9 p.m. so you won't be kept awake by the noise.

CABO MATAPALO   As you head south of Puerto Jiménez, the road is bumpy and unpaved. If you are not a four-wheel-drive wizard, it's better to fly into Jiménez and let your hotel transport you out here.

Buena Esperanza is a restaurant and bar just after the Río Carbonera on the left, where an enthusiastic California chef turns out "low fat, high flavor" food to go. It's the only restaurant between there and Carate. They also rent colorful open-air cabins (shared bath, cold water; $25/person). **Playa Matapalo** is *the* surfing beach in the Osa, reachable by an unmarked but obviously well-used road on the left as you climb toward Lapa Ríos.

Tierra de Milagros (shared and private baths, cold water; $60-80, including meals; www.tierrademilagros.com, e-mail: info@tierrademilagros.com) hosts yoga retreats from December through April. Their shady open-air yoga deck overlooks a river. Bonfires, drumming circles, and organic gardening happen there. Accommodations are in candlelit open-air cabins (with beds on platforms for increased air flow) and in tents. Volunteer work exchanges are possible.

The locally owned **Vida de Osa** (shared bath, cold water; $20-$30; 735-5062; www.osatropical.com, e-mail: osatropi@racsa.co.cr), 200 meters from the surfer's haven, Playa Matapalo, has simple, palm-roofed, screened rooms with fans and reading lamps

Lapa Ríos (private bath, solar hot water, natural ventilation, screens and mosquito nets, pool, wheelchair accessible; $210/person, including meals; children under 10, $110; 735-5130, fax: 735-5179; www.laparios.com, e-mail: info@laparios.com) is a luxury resort on a 1000-acre reserve containing primary and secondary rainforest, and reforested pastureland. Thatch-roofed bungalows dot the side of a hill, at the top of which is a spacious restaurant. Up a tall spiral staircase is an observation deck with a beautiful view of the Golfo Dulce. The rooms are tastefully designed with wide private balconies. Each balcony has a shower surrounded by lush foliage so you can bathe outside while enjoying the view. Guests can learn about medicinal plants from a local shaman, visit waterfalls in the reserve, take a night hike, learn to surf, or visit the calm beach at the bottom of the hill. They are given the opportunity to plant a tree in the reforested sector. Monkeys, toucans, and macaws are often visible from the elegant restaurant terrace, which hangs over the jungle high above the sea. The resort came in second on Condé Nast's list of the top 15 small hotels in the Caribbean and Latin America.

The land owned by the next two hotels is also a wildlife refuge.

Bosque del Cabo (private bath, some hot water, fans, spring-fed pool; $120-$140/person, including meals; children 3 to 12 $50, under 3 free; cell phone: 381-4847, phone/fax: 735-5206; www.bosquedelcabo.com, e-mail: phil@bosquedelcabo.com), a few kilometers farther down the road and left down a mile-long driveway through the forest, has a spectacular view of the ocean from above Playa Matapalo at the very southern tip of the Osa Peninsula. You can take a horseback ride down to the beach where there is a beautiful waterfall with macaws nesting above the pool, or slide Tarzan-like on a cable to a wildlife observation platform 110 feet up in a *manú* tree in the middle of the forest. Yoga classes and massage are also offered. The chic, tropical-style individual bungalows are perched at the edge of a semi-circular cliff overlooking the sea. They are spacious, with porches and unique outdoor showers decorated with creative mosaic work. Screened and louvered windows allow you to adjust the natural air conditioning. The restaurant serves good international food and is receptive to vegetarians. Three houses are available for a weekly rental of $1400-$2000/week, meals not included. With advance notice, they can arrange a taxi from Puerto Jiménez for $25 each way. Recommended.

Just after the entrance to Bosque del Cabo is the long driveway down to **El Remanso** (private bath, hot water, natural ventilation, spring-fed pool; $105/person, including meals; 735-5569; www.elremanso.com, e-mail: elremanso@racsa.co.cr), owned by Belén Momeñe of Spain and Joel Stewart, a North American who runs tree-climbing and waterfall-rappelling adventure tours from their property. They met while working on Greenpeace's boats. The four spacious bungalows are designed for those who like quiet and privacy, and are decorated with delightful murals of angels. One has water views. There is a house that sleeps seven. Meals feature fresh seafood and exotic fruits. The beach is a ten-minute walk downhill. You can take a zip-line to a platform in the forest with a picnic breakfast at 5 a.m. for bird observation. Closed October and November. Recommended.

GETTING THERE: It takes about an hour to get from Puerto Jiménez to Cabo Matapalo. Your hotel can arrange taxi transport for about $25 per car. Note that you shouldn't try to drive down Bosque del Cabo's driveway if it starts to look mucky; leave your car by the side of the road and walk the rest of the way.

CARATE   The road gets better after Lapa Ríos, continuing an hour through pleasant cattle country to the Río Aguas Buenas, which sometimes becomes too deep to cross in the rainy season. You can ask the local taxi driver to arrange for horses to meet you at the river if it looks like crossing on foot is impossible. Carate is another eight kilometers after the river.

The **National Save the Sea Turtle Foundation** (in the U.S.: 954-351-9333; www.savetheseaturtle.org, e-mail: nststf@bellsouth.net) in Fort Lauderdale, Florida, runs a volunteer program here to protect olive ridley turtle nests. Their hatchery has a 60 percent success rate.

Just before you get to Carate, you'll see **The Lookout** (private bath, pool, hot water; $100-$110/person, including meals; discounts for children; 735-5431; www.lookout-inn.com, e-mail: info@lookout-inn.com). It offers bungalows in a hillside garden about an hour by foot from the La Leona station. Their popular bar has great ocean views, as do the rooms in the lodge itself.

Luna Lodge (private bath, hot water; $125/person, including meals and waterfall tour; in secluded one-room tent, $75/person, including meals; 380-5036, in the U.S.: 888-409-8448; www.lunalodge.com, e-mail: information@lunalodge.com), on a mesa high above the Carate River, is a wonderland of waterfalls and wildlife, with individual bungalows, rockers on the porches, and its own version of the open-air shower. Its Wellness Center hosts yoga, massage, and creative visualization, with classes at their spacious, elegant yoga studio overlooking the jungle and sea. Meals are made from fresh fruits and vegetables grown at the lodge's organic gardens. Luna Lodge borders Corcovado, but its lofty elevation makes for cool, comfortable nights. It is located two and a half kilometers north of the Carate airstrip up a long, muddy, and bumpy road.

Costa Rica Expeditions' **Corcovado Lodge and Tent Camp** (shared bath, cold water, natural ventilation; $60-$70/person, including meals; 257-0766, 222-0033, fax: 257-1665; www.corcovadolodge.com, e-mail: corcovado@expeditions.co.cr) has an enviable setting: off a pristine beach near La Leona entrance to Corcovado National Park. Guests arrive via plane or vehicle from Puerto Jiménez, and stay in ten-by-ten-foot tents on wooden platforms. There is a large *rancho* up the hill that has hammocks for reading and relaxing, and a family camp–style restaurant. A three-night package is $350/person, including meals and airfare to Puerto Jiménez (tours extra).

La Leona Lodge (shared bath, cold water; $60/person, including meals; 735-5704; www.laleonalodge.com, e-mail: info@laleonalodge.com), just down the beach, also has a tent camp and six kilometers of trails going to two lookout points. Their restaurant is the last place to eat before you enter the park.

GETTING THERE: There is no public bus service south of Jiménez. Your lodge can arrange transportation from Puerto Jiménez, for about $60. Taxi-trucks leave from Supermercado El Tigre in Puerto Jiménez daily at 6 a.m. and 1:30 p.m. ($7/person to Carate). If you wish to go later in the day, it costs $60 per taxi to Carate. If the Río Aguas Buenas is too high, the truck only goes to the river, and you have to hike the remaining eight kilometers to Carate. The truck/taxi driver can arrange for horses to meet you at the river. There is no problem crossing the river in the dry season.

By Car: The gravel road south of Puerto Jiménez was passable only for four-wheel-drive vehicles in the rainy season. It takes about two hours to get to Carate. Check with your hotel about current road conditions and driving times.

By Air: It costs about $600 to charter a five-passenger plane from San José to Carate, $100 from Puerto Jiménez to Carate (a seven-minute flight), $200 from Jiménez to Sirena. Alfa Romeo Aero Taxi (735-5178) is the company most familiar with the zone. They have offices near the airport in Puerto Jiménez. To get from Puerto Jimenez to Drake Bay, take SANSA or Nature Air.

NORTH OF PUERTO JIMÉNEZ

The locally owned **Río Nuevo Lodge** (shared bath, cold water; $50/person, including meals and transportation from Puerto Jiménez; 735-5095; www.rionuevolodge.com, e-mail: reserve@rionuevolodge.com) is a lovely tent camp at the juncture of three rivers. The home-cooked food is very good and the gardens are tended with *cariño*. This is a little oasis, truly off the beaten track. It is accessible by a turnoff about ten minutes north of Puerto Jiménez, but let them take you there—you have to ford several rivers and cross a hanging bridge in the process. Horseback riding, hiking, and relaxing are the main activities. Recommended.

A few kilometers north of town and eight bumpy kilometers inland is the village of **Dos Brazos**. **Bosque del Río Tigre Sanctuary and Lodge** (private or shared bath, cold water, natural ventilation, mosquito nets; $88/person, including meals; 383-3905, 735-5725, in the U.S.: 888-875-9453;

www.osaadventures.com, e-mail: info@osaadventures.com) is a 31-acre private reserve just beyond Dos Brazos. Owned by Abraham Gallo and Liz Jones, a hospitable Tico-gringa couple who are ardent rainforest and birding enthusiasts, the lodge has an open design that makes electric fans unnecessary. Mosquito netting protects sleeping guests from wayward insects. The second floor of the lodge contains four corner rooms (shared bath), separated from each other by an attractive reading area, well-stocked with natural history books and identification guides. There is also a secluded riverside cabin (private bath) surrounded by lush foliage. Meals, personally supervised by Abraham, are a point of pride—delicious, wholesome, and gourmet. Quality birding binoculars are available to guests to help them get the most from their fascinating hiking and birdwatching expeditions. To get there by car, take a clearly marked turnoff four kilometers north of Puerto Jiménez, and follow the road eight kilometers to Dos Brazos. Make a left at the concrete bridge at the entrance to town. Follow signs to the lodge. In the dry season you may be able to drive across the river to the lodge. In the rainy season leave your car at a nearby *soda*. They will show you the best place to wade across the Río Tigre (it's about two feet deep). Liz and Abraham can arrange for a taxi to meet you at the airport or bus stop. It is best to make reservations at this small lodge before you come. Recommended for birders.

Antonio Garbanzo runs a collective taxi service to Dos Brazos. He leaves Super 96 in Puerto Jiménez at 5 a.m., 11 a.m., and 4 p.m. daily.

Birding is great at the Swiss/Tico-owned **Suital Lodge** (private or shared bath, hot water, fans, mosquito nets; $30-$50; 382-1314; homepage.mac.com/suital, e-mail: suitalcr@hotmail.com), 17 kilometers east of the town of Rincón. The rustic cabins have verandas for hummingbird watching. This 70-acre reserve's well-marked trails take you to the shore; the sea here is gentle for kayaking. Horseback riding is also offered.

GOLFO DULCE

On the Golfo Dulce, between the Osa Peninsula and the mainland, the *costa* is *rica* indeed: lush vegetation; breezy, rocky beaches; deep, green waters. There are several ecotourism projects set on the eastern rim of the gulf, which really make the area worth visiting. Because all the lodges are isolated and accessible only by boat, prices are per person, including meals and sometimes transportation from Puerto Jiménez. For the same reason, credit cards and personal checks are not accepted. Bring traveler's checks or cash. The best way to contact any of these lodges is through **Osa Tropi-**

cal (735-5062; e-mail: osatropi@sol.racsa.co.cr), a Puerto Jiménez travel agency that has radio contact with all the hotels in the area.

Dolphin Quest (rustic *ranchos*, shared baths, natural ventilation; with double occupancy: $50-$60/person in private *ranchos*; camping, $20-$30; prices include meals but not transportation; fax: 775-0373; www.dolphin questcostarica.com, e-mail: dolphinquest@email.com), located down the beach from Golfo Dulce Lodge, is a laidback farm where you can explore the jungle, help with gardening, ride horses, kayak, snorkel, or swim with dolphins. It's definitely for people who are comfortable with alternative lifestyles. They are interested in hosting retreats and workshops in their large, open-sided, cement-floored, thatched *rancho*.

Casa Orquídeas is a beautifully landscaped private botanical garden overlooking the sea. Longtime residents Ron and Trudy McAllister take you on an hour's tour of the garden, where you can see what the spices and fruits in your kitchen look like on the vine—and taste them if they're in season. You'll see ginger, vanilla, black pepper, cinnamon, cacao, cashew, mango, avocado, and papaya, as well as tons of beautiful orchids and famil- iar houseplants in their native habitat. Tours begin around 8:15 a.m. Sunday through Thursday, $5 per person, minimum four visitors or $20. They also rent a simple but very pleasant screened cabin (private bath, kitchen; $150/ week; $500/month) at the back of the garden. All the nearby lodges plus Zancudo Boat Tours (see below) will take you there, or you can rent a boat in Golfito.

Playa Nicuesa Lodge (private bath, hot water, mosquito nets; $130- $150/person, including meals, transportation from Puerto Jiménez or Golfito, and an introductory tour; 735-5237, in the U.S.: 866-348-7610; www.nicu esalodge.com) is a unique ecotourism opportunity on the Golfo Dulce. The 2800-foot main lodge, with its massive beams, is reminiscent of a woodsy lodge in Maine, but it's open to nature on all sides. I spent a tranquil after- noon in that welcoming space just relaxing in a hammock and watching the changing reflections in the fascinating glass and shell mobile at the center

of the upper floor. The rooms are very well done, with molded plaster open-air bathrooms that add such a charming, creative touch to the hotels of the Osa. Some of the cabins have two bedrooms, ideal for families; others are more secluded for honeymooners. The water on this part of the gulf is protected and lake-like, good for kids. Their dock is the perfect place to see bioluminescence at night. The fish glow as they swim by. Trails into the rainforest behind the lodge are flat and comfortable for walking. Snorkeling is good at nearby shallow reefs, and the use of kayaks is free for guests. The very creative chef and the friendly local guides make this a good place to get to know the Costa Rican staff as well as the North American owners. A three-night package ($850-$895) includes transportation from San José and several tours. Readers that have stayed a week say there is plenty to do. The lodge is closed from October 1 to November 15. Recommended.

Caña Blanca Beach and Rainforest Lodge (private bath, cold water, natural ventilation; $150/person, including gourmet meals, tours, and transportation from Puerto Jiménez; three-night minimum stay; voice mail: 383-5707, fax: 735-5043; www.canablanca.com, e-mail: canablan@racsa.co.cr), the dream of a couple of gourmet cooks and bird lovers, is a rescue center for injured or confiscated birds. The three private cabins are totally open to the jungle and to the resident macaw, toucan, and parrot, the owners' pets. Located on an isolated cove about nine miles from Puerto Jiménez, the cabins all overlook the gentle waters of the Golfo Dulce. A 750-acre reserve backs the property, with six miles of trails. Closed in May and October.

CORCOVADO NATIONAL PARK

In the 1970s, scientists realized that the Osa Peninsula was one of the richest, most diverse tropical areas on earth. The tremendous rainfall, remote location, and variety of unique habitats (eight in all, ranging from mountain forest to swamp), made protection from development imperative. Fortunately scientists won the battle against lumbermen and other proponents of rainforest destruction, and the 108,022-acre national park was founded in 1975.

Since then, the park has been the site of much scientific research, and biologists have identified at least 500 species of trees, 285 birds, 139 mammals, 116 amphibians and reptiles, and 16 freshwater fishes. The rainforest canopy reaches higher than anywhere else in the country, due to the abundant rainfall and low altitude.

Besides its ecological wealth, the area has an interesting human history as well. Some of the best-known and most notorious inhabitants of the national park have been the *oreros* (gold panners). The *oreros* are independent, solitary types who know the peninsula like the backs of their hands. During their heyday, they sifted for their fortunes in the streams and rivers of Corcovado National Park, camping in crude lean-tos and hunting wild animals for food. They would only venture out to Puerto Jiménez once in a while to sell their gold nuggets to the Banco Central's special gold-buying office there. But in the mid-1980s, due to massive unemployment in the region, the gold panners' numbers grew so large that their activity started causing real destruction. The silt from their panning was filling up the rivers and the lake in the park's basin. In 1986, the park service and the Costa Rican Civil Guard physically removed all of the gold panners, promising them an indemnity for their lost jobs. After a year without payment, the *oreros* camped out in protest in the city parks of San José until the government came through with the checks they had promised. Many *oreros* are back in Osa, panning in the forest reserve that borders Corcovado. Even though their activity is destructive, the park service has decided to let it continue rather than risk the panners retreating into Corcovado.

Many migrant farmers came to the peninsula after the all-weather road connected the peninsula with the mainland in the mid-1980s. Most new arrivals settled in the traditional way, by burning off all the forest covering their little plot of land and then cultivating or grazing cattle on it. This approach is productive for a very short period of time. Rainforest soil is quite poor when there's no forest covering it: once the trees are gone, the rainforest's self-fertilization by dead leaves, plants, and animals stops, and the soil becomes infertile. When it rains, the soil erodes and silt fills the rivers. Because there is little biomass left to absorb excess moisture, floods become a problem.

Visiting the Osa Peninsula is a good way to learn firsthand about the conflict between the conservation of natural resources that humans need in the long-term, and the short-term options that many people consider their only means of survival.

VISITING CORCOVADO   To visit Corcovado National Park, call the Osa Conservation Area office in Puerto Jiménez (open weekdays, 8 a.m. to 4 p.m.; 735-5036 or 735-5580; e-mail corcovado@minae.go.cr) as far ahead as possible for a reservation. Give them the desired dates of your trip, where you will want to stay each night. Campsites are available only at La Leona, Los Patos, and San Pedrillo ($4/night; bring your own food). Bunk-bed, dorm-style lodging costs $8 per person per night and is only available at Sirena; camping at Sirena is $4 per person per night. Meals are approxi-

mately $21 per day, and are served at certain times only, often correspon-
ding to the tides so that people can leave or arrive safely. An entrance fee
of $17 entitles you to five days in the park, including Isla del Caño.

The park needs volunteers. Call PROVCA at 222-7549 to see how you
can help.

During the dry season you can camp fairly comfortably, but the
beaches are infested with *purrujas*, invisible biting insects that leave itchy
welts that seem to never go away. Do not plan to just sack out on the
beach—bring a tent and always camp at the ranger stations. Do not plan to
hike or camp here alone—it's a jungle out there.

Additional things you will need to bring for a comfortable stay include:

- a tent with good screens if you are camping
- a lightweight sleeping bag or a sheet or two—bedding is not provided
- a mosquito net
- at least two types of insect repellent, in case one doesn't work
- sunscreen
- several changes of cotton clothing, with long pants and long sleeves
  to protect you from sun and bugs
- a wide-brimmed hat and a bandanna
- a rain poncho or umbrella
- a towel
- a flashlight
- candles and matches
- a Swiss Army knife
- plan to carry all the water you will need (at least four liters of water
  or more); water in the park is not potable and the river water is salty
- snacks—a generous supply in case you're delayed on your way
  to one of the park's stations
- binoculars
- one pair of good hiking boots that will stand up to getting wet, and
  a pair of tennis shoes. Sandals are not recommended because of the
  danger of snakes. River crossings should be done in hiking boots,
  and the tennies can be worn when you're between treks
- rubber boots, if you are comfortable in them
- several pairs of long socks
- a clothesline

Following are the main entrances and routes through the park:

CARATE–LA LEONA–SIRENA   This route traces the coast. Trucks leave Puerto Jiménez every morning but Sunday at 6 a.m. and 1:30 p.m., returning at 8:30 a.m. and 4 p.m. ($7/person). If you want to go at another hour, you must hire a taxi (at El Tigre in Puerto Jiménez), which costs about $60 per trip. If you'd rather walk, it's about an eight-hour trip, with no stores along the way.

At Carate, stop at the *pulpería* for a meal or a *refresco*. They have a radio and can call for airplanes, taxis, or emergency help.

To get to La Leona park entrance from Carate, turn right and walk along the soft sand beach 3.5 kilometers (about 45 minutes) to **La Leona** ranger station. There is no food or lodging at the station. (Don't swim— there are sharks and the current is strong.)

The walk from La Leona to Sirena spans 16 kilometers and takes five to seven hours. It is almost entirely along the soft sand beach. You must do it at low tide, because you walk around a couple of rocky points covered at high tide. There is a rusty shipwreck at Punta Chancha, with huge engines scattered around the rocks.

A bit later you reach **Salsipuedes** (Get-out-if-you-can) **Point**, which has a pretty cave hollowed out of the coast. At some of the rock points there are trails that cut inland for a few hundred meters. The best way to find them is to start looking as soon as the coast seems impassable. The Salsipuedes trail gives you a break from the soft sand for a kilometer or two, but coat yourself up with repellent before starting into the jungle.

There are many monkeys along this trail. You will probably see scarlet macaws singing raucously and winging awkwardly through the sky. *Pizotes* (coatimundis) also come to the coast frequently. After you cross the Río Claro, cut in either on the Sirena trail or at the airstrip a bit farther down.

Sirena is a 15-bed research station populated by ecotourists and biological researchers who are mostly from the United States or Europe. We have heard that cleanliness at the station is inconsistent, and that the food is not that good. Do not bathe in the ocean because there are sharks; there are crocodiles in the nearby Río Claro and Río Sirena. You can rent canoes at the station for $3/hour.

SIRENA–SAN PEDRILLO   If you want to reward yourself after your wet, buggy time in Corcovado, consider spending a night or two in one of the resorts at Drake Bay (see above), half an hour by boat from San Pedrillo, the northwestern entrance station. The resorts will pick you up there, or you can hike to Drake in five or six hours.

The walk from Sirena to San Pedrillo is 25 kilometers: 20 along wide, flat, hard beach, and 5 through rainforest. The entire walk can take seven to nine hours. Make sure you walk the beaches at low tide. The park service does not allow people to do this hike in the rainy season.

One kilometer from the Sirena research station is the Río Sirena, the deepest river (three to four feet) with the strongest current that you'll have to cross on this hike. There is a boat you can use to get across, holding onto a rope; ask the rangers to unlock it for you. If you start out at high tide and use this boat to cross the river, you will arrive at the next rivers at low tide. It is very important to plan your hike to correspond with the tides. After Río Sirena, it's about two hours to the **Río Corcovado**, which has a sandy bottom and is two feet deep at low tide. Two hours later is the **Río Llorona**, comparable to the Corcovado. A couple of hundred meters later is the **Piedra Arco**, a huge rock arch covered with greenery. Twenty meters after Piedra Arco is the trail to **La Llorona**, a 100-foot waterfall that cascades onto the beach. Don't be fooled by the tiny waterfall that you see immediately after leaving the sandy beach; continue on another 15 minutes to get to La Llorona. Do not attempt this except at low tide.

The trail through the rainforest climbs steeply at first, then rises and descends to creeks along the way. Much of the trail is level, winding through the jungle. For the most part it is a good, wide path, but watch the ascents and descents, because there the trail is eroded and slippery. Toward the end of the hike, you descend back to a beach. It's another hour to the Río San Pedrillo. With long legs you can jump it near the mouth; otherwise, test the waters and wade. If you want to keep walking, take the trail that follows the coast to Drake Bay, ten kilometers (four to five hours) away. It's not hard to get a ride back to Drake Bay with the tour boats that drop people off at San Pedrillo. The ride costs about $30.

GETTING THERE: By Air: Five-passenger charter planes will fly you directly to the Sirena airstrip. Taxi Alfa Romeo (735-5178) flies for $200 one way from Puerto Jiménez.

LA PALMA–LOS PATOS–SIRENA   La Palma is a small town about 25 kilometers north of Puerto Jiménez. A bus leaves Puerto Jiménez at 5 and 5:30 a.m. for La Palma. It's an hour-long trip.

There are a couple of inexpensive cabinas in La Palma, and a restaurant or two as well. **Cabinas El Tucán** (private bath, cold water; under $7) on the main street has clean rooms.

From La Palma it's a 12-kilometer, three-hour walk to the park's northeastern entrance at **Los Patos**, crossing the Río Rincón 26 times in an ever-narrowing valley. There's a taxi-jeep in town that will take you there for $25; everyone in La Palma knows the driver.

The trail in this stretch is a narrow gravel road. The worst stretches of the whole trip are immediately before and after Los Patos, where the trail can be swampy and slippery, especially in the rainy season.

When you enter the park at Los Patos, there are five kilometers of steep trails through high mountain forests, then fifteen kilometers of flat walking in low, dense rainforest to the research station at Sirena. The trail is clearly marked, but at some river crossings you have to check up- or downstream for where the trail takes off again. Some of the rivers can be thigh-deep in the rainy season. Don't do this walk at night. Most snakes are nocturnal, and they like water. Don't cross the rivers in sandals.

Be careful not to walk into biting spiders, whose webs span the trail; bring repellent and plenty of patience for the horseflies. On the way you might see frogs, morpho butterflies, and monkeys, and perhaps the tracks of tapirs and ocelots.

GOLFITO

The port town of Golfito has a gorgeous setting—lush, forested hills surrounding a deep bay on the Golfo Dulce with the misty outline of the Península de Osa in the distance.

The town is stretched along one main road squeezed between the gulf and the mountains. Virgin forest blankets the mountains, which have been made into a wildlife and watershed reserve. Behind the airstrip a botanical garden and experimental bamboo plots are managed by the University of Costa Rica.

The northern part of town is the Zona Americana. United Fruit administrators once lived in this neighborhood in big wooden houses on stilts, surrounded by large lawns and gardens. The southern part of town is called the Pueblo Civil and is a noisy collection of bars, restaurants, and hotels. Buses run along the road the length of the town, passing about every 15 minutes during the day. At the northern end of town, they stop at the airport and the *depósito*. Taxis are plentiful (it's about 75 cents to travel anywhere in town).

Many Central Valley shoppers visit the **Depósito Libre**, a huge outdoor mall with air-conditioned shops filled with *electrodomésticos* (household appliances) and luxury items.

The government established the town as a duty-free port in 1990. Ticos and foreigners alike are allowed to buy $500 worth of merchandise every six months. The imported items are still sold with a hefty tax, which will not make them of much interest to tourists, but does make them cheaper than in San José. Shoppers come mainly on weekends, so during the week Golfito is relatively empty, except before Christmas.

For a good orientation to the Zona Sur, pick up a copy of Alexander del Sol's *The Southern Costa Rica Guide*, a very informative booklet that gives complete details about some of the author's favorite places in the area. It's distributed widely in San José and the Zona Sur.

Land Sea Services (phone/fax: 775-1614, VHF marine radio ch. 16; www.marinaservices-yachtdelivery.com, e-mail: landsea@racsa.co.cr) is a tourist information center next to the Banana Bay Marina on the left as you enter Golfito. They book national and international flights, have a trading library, and rent four-wheel-drive vehicles. They send faxes and radio messages, and can help arrange transport for medical emergencies. On top of that, they run a laundry service! Open Monday through Saturday, 8 a.m. to 5 p.m. **Banana Bay Marina** (775-0838; www.bananabaymarina.com, e-mail: info@bananabaymarina.com), next door, is a full-fledged marina with a popular restaurant serving gringo food.

We've heard that the best place to change money is with Doña Rosa at the *bomba*—the large gas station to the left of the municipal dock. She also has telephone and fax services. Nearby, at the **Soda Muellecita** or the **Coconut Café** across the street (great cappuccino, homemade treats, and internet access; 775-0518), you can ask about transport to Zancudo and Pavones. Traveler's checks must be cashed at the Depósito Libre (closed Monday) or at the Banco Nacional on the far side of the soccer field.

LODGING AND RESTAURANTS   The following hotels and restaurants are presented in order of appearance south to north—the order you'll come across them if you drive or take the bus to Golfito. The order is the opposite if you fly there; the airstrip is at the extreme north point of town.

Seven kilometers before the entrance to town, in a grassy orchard with cabins and camping spots, is **La Purruja Lodge** (private bath, cold water, ceiling fans; $20-$30; camping, $2/tent; phone/fax: 775-1054; www.purruja.com, e-mail: purruja@purruja.com). The rooms are very clean, with separate bathing and laundry facilities for campers, all in a beautiful setting. Breakfast and dinner are served at the lodge, and the owners provide tours to see crocodiles and caves nearby. It's a great place to stay with kids, because it's away from the road with lots of room to run around. Buses to Golfito pass in front every half hour. Recommended.

Two hundred meters more will bring you to **Bar Río de Janeiro** (also known as **Mike's Place**), famous in Golfito for spare ribs. Stuffed peppers and goulash are also on the menu—the owner is a Hungarian-American wed to a Tica. In 800 meters more, you'll come to **Margarita's Rancho Grande** (775-1951), known for *comida típica* cooked over a wood fire, as well as filet mignon and *sopa de mariscos*.

At the entrance to town, **El Gran Ceibo** (private bath, hot water, cable TV, pool; with ceiling fans, $20-$30; with air conditioning, $30-$40; 775-0403, fax: 775-2303; www.soldeosa.com/granceibo, e-mail: elgranceibo@ soldeosa.com) is clean and friendly. Every room has local original paintings.

In the heart of the Pueblo Civil are several open-air restaurants overlooking the coastal road: **La Eurekita**, the most popular, has an ice cream parlor. **La Cubana** is also a good choice.

Continuing north along the coastal road, **Samoa del Sur** (private bath, hot water, ceiling fans, phone, cable TV, pool; $40-$50; 775-0264, 775-0237, fax: 775-0573; e-mail samoadelsur@racsa.co.cr) has spacious rooms, the nicest in Golfito. The thatched open-air restaurant **Le Coquillage** offers a varied international menu at moderate prices and has dart boards, Foosball, and billiards, all contributing to its lively atmosphere.

Dozens of homes in the Zona Americana, near the Depósito Libre, have been converted into guesthouses, mostly catering to shoppers. As many beds as possible are crowded into each room. One of the nicest is **Cabinas Casa Blanca** (private bath, cold water, ceiling fans; $12-$20; 775-0124), which has rooms on the first floor of the owner's house and a row of cabinas in the yard. It is located about 350 meters south of the Depósito.

Nearby, **Hotel Golfo Azul** (private bath, heated water, ceiling fans, air conditioning; $20-$30; 775-0871, fax: 775-1849) is clean and well-run.

Hotel Sierra (private bath, hot water, ceiling fans, air conditioning, phone, TV, pools; $50-$60; 775-0666; www.hotelsierra.com), next to the airstrip, is a large, rather faceless hotel near the Deposito Libre.

GETTING THERE: By Bus: Golfito buses leave the Alfaro–Tracopa station (Calle 14, Avenida 5; 222-2160, 222-2666, 223-7685) at 7 a.m. and 3 p.m., and cost $6.50. They return at 4 a.m., 7:30 a.m., 9 a.m., and 3 p.m. It's a seven-hour trip. Or you can take any Zona Sur bus to Río Claro—that's the turnoff to Golfito. Villa Neily–Golfito buses pass through Río Claro hourly. It's a half-hour trip. Buy your return tickets as soon as you get to Golfito.

By Car: Follow the Interamerican Highway from San José to Río Claro and turn right. The trip takes about seven hours. If you want to do the trip in two days, San Isidro de El General or Playa Dominical are good places to stay overnight.

By Air: You can avoid the long, winding (though scenic) bus ride by flying SANSA to Golfito (221-9414, fax: 255-2176; $71 one way). Check schedules at www.flysansa.com. Nature Air (220-3054, fax: 220-0413; $84 one way) also flies to Golfito. Check schedules at www.natureair.com.

PIEDRAS BLANCAS NATIONAL PARK   In 1991, the President of Costa Rica declared 14,000 hectares in the Esquinas Rainforest, on the eastern side of the Golfo Dulce, a national park. The land is blanketed by lush virgin forest. There are many endemic species of plants and animals, especially birds. It is also a refuge for migratory birds.

Esquinas Rainforest Lodge (private bath, heated water, ceiling fans; $95/person, including meals; 775-0901; www.esquinaslodge.com) is a cluster of well-appointed duplexes, kept cool because three of the four walls have large, screened windows and there is a layer of insulation between the roof and ceiling. There's a chlorine-free, stream-fed pool whose outflow feeds a pond with tilapia and caimans. The reception area, library, and restaurant are in a large building topped with a locally woven palm roof; the advantage of this type of roof is clear as soon as you walk inside and feel the cool temperature. All profits from the lodge are used for improvement projects proposed by the people of La Gamba, a village near the park entrance.

GETTING THERE: By Car: Drive toward Golfito as far as Villa Briceño, at kilometer marker 37 on the Interamerican Highway. Make a right, and follow signs for five kilometers on a gravel road that has several small wooden bridges without guardrails. If you take the Golfito bus or fly to Golfito, the lodge can pick you up for $10. There is a mountainous back road that will take you from Golfito to Esquinas in about 15 minutes in the dry season.

ZANCUDO

Playa Zancudo, on a strip between the ocean and the Coto River, is one of the Zona Sur's most popular beaches during the dry season. The fine black-sand beach stretches for miles, and the surf is mostly gentle. This safe beach is ideal for families with children. The southern section of Zancudo (in front of Zancudo Beach Club) offers good surfing, with beach breaks in both directions. Because it is relatively unknown, there is no line-up. Zancudo has earned the prestigious Bandera Azul from the government, indicating that residents work together to keep the beach and water clean.

The mangroves along the Río Coto and the Atrocha canal connecting Zancudo with Golfito serve as a safe nursery for the area's rich fishing grounds. **Zancudo Boat Tours** (776-0012) offers scenic kayak trips along the Río Coto to view birds, crocodiles, monkeys, and otters. Trips to Casa Orquídeas botanical garden (see above), and the Osa Peninsula are available as well. It's only $30 for two people to go by boat from Zancudo to Puerto Jiménez—a pleasant way to arrive at the gateway to Cocovado. Andrew Robertson, a transplant from the U.K., is ZBT's witty and entertaining captain.

LODGING   Hotels and cabinas are plentiful, and a better value than those at many other Costa Rican beaches. We'll describe them in order from north to south. If you drive (not recommended—it's a long, bumpy trip, possible only with four-wheel drive during rainy season), reverse the order. If your boat lets you off at the public dock, turn left on the main road for the cabinas listed below.

In "downtown" Zancudo, left from the dock, is **Soda Katherin** (open every day, all day), a great place to eat. We had baby shrimp there that were perfectly cooked and seasoned. And it's very inexpensive. **Cabinas Tío Froilan** (private bath, cold water, ceiling fans; $12-$20; 776-0103) offers two parallel rows of simple cabinas; the first row blocks the breeze and view for the second. Down the street on the left is the locally acclaimed **Macondo** (open noon to 3 p.m. and 5:30 p.m. to 9:30 p.m.; 776-0157), a second-floor Italian restaurant that overlooks the mangrove estuary. They also rent cabins (shared bath, heated water, ceiling fans; $20-$40) and have a small pool.

Abastecdor El Buen Precio is a good place to stock up on groceries or make telephone calls. Next door, the **Shangri-La** has a nicely displayed selection of local arts and crafts. Across the street, **La Puerta Negra** is a small Italian restaurant with lots of character, owned by excellent chef Alberto. Open for dinner only.

The owners of Zancudo Boat Tours also operate **Cabinas Los Cocos** (private bath, heated water, table fans, kitchens; $50-$60; weekly and monthly rates available; 776-0012; www.loscocos.com, e-mail: loscocos@los cocos.com), about two kilometers or a 20-minute walk south of the municipal dock. Los Cocos consists of three individual houses, two of which are reconditioned banana company cabins, with big decks overlooking the ocean, and several thatch-roofed *ranchos*, one with a loft that sleeps four. They are quiet, private, and shipshape. Bikes, kayaks, and boogieboards are available for guests. Recommended.

Next door, **Cabinas Sol y Mar** (private bath, heated water, ceiling fans; $20-$50; 776-0014; www.zancudo.com/sol_main.htm, e-mail: solymar@zan cudo.com), with cabinas and a restaurant, offers horseshoe and volleyball tournaments, and surfboards for rent. The cabins have good air circulation. There's also a house for rent ($700/month).

The last hotel south is the friendly, U.S.-owned **Zancudo Beach Club** (private bath, solar hot water with back-up, fans, refrigerator; $50-$60 for up to three people; villas, $70-$80; 776-0087, fax: 776-0052; www.zancudo beachclub.com, e-mail: zbc@costarica.net), right on the beach, with individual elevated cabins and a breezy restaurant/bar (open 7 a.m. to 9 p.m.), which is becoming a meeting-place for the gringo community. We happened to arrive on Thanksgiving and had an excellent turkey dinner with all the trimmings. Quite a feat in Zancudo. The cabins are well-appointed and very comfortable and come complete with refrigerators, microwaves, and coffee makers. Surfing is good here. Recommended. **Los Tres Amigos** (775-0123) down the street sells clothes, sandwiches, and familiar U.S. groceries.

Cabinas y Restaurante El Coloso del Mar (private bath, heated water, fans; $30-$40; 776-0050; www.coloso-del-mar.com, e-mail: info@coloso-del-mar.com), 300 meters north of Zancudo Beach Club, has quiet cabinas on the beach and a restaurant (open in high season only) specializing in Caribbean treats like conch fritters, jerk chicken, and tropical cocktails. They have the only **internet café** in Zancudo.

GETTING THERE: By Car: If you have a four-wheel-drive vehicle, driving is usually possible, and the trip from Golfito takes between one and two hours. Locals say that the trip can be done in a regular car in the dry season, but it's always best to have a high clearance. Look for the Rodeo bar at kilometer 14 of the Río Claro–Golfito road, and turn south. Fifteen minutes later on paved road you come to an old-fashioned barge that takes about five minutes to ferry you across the Coto River. The ferry shuts down at 6 p.m., so be sure to get there before dark. In another half hour you'll get to the place where the road goes south to Pavones and north to Zancudo. There are signs in most crucial places. It's good to ask directions as often as possible. When in doubt, turn right.

By Boat: The *Macarela,* a public ferry ($2), leaves the municipal *muelle* in Golfito at 5 a.m. and noon, Monday through Friday only. Since the schedule depends on the tide, the ferry will take either the Atrocha (mangrove canal shortcut, only possible in high tide) or the ocean route (beach landing; you have to walk ashore). The trip takes an hour and a half. Not for people with a lot of luggage. The easiest way to get there is with Zancudo Boat Tours (776-0012; $25 minimum; more than two passengers, $12.50/person extra); they take you to your hotel so that you don't have to walk 30 or 40 minutes in the hot sun—and it is hot!

By Taxi: A land taxi costs $30 to $40 from Golfito.

PAVONES

Pavones is highly publicized in surfer magazines for having the longest wave in the world but we have heard that this legendary wave only occurs about ten times a year. When it does happen, expect rides more than a minute long, and between 50 and 80 surfers in the water. This wave is for experts only.

It is a beautiful area, much more lush and green than Zancudo, and there are some delightful places to stay. The area is now attracting nature lovers, bird watchers and lovers of tropical flowers and fruits. Dr. Bob Bacher, a tai chi teacher with 35 years of experience, organizes trainings and retreats through **Tai Chi Tropical Tours** (www.chentaijiinternational.com) centered in Pavones, where you can learn this ancient "inner" martial art for health, long life, and inner peace.

The **Manta Club** is owned by an Israeli couple who are surfing aficionados. They film the surfing every day at Pavones and show the videos at night, often as a prelude to DVD movies, while admiring surfers eat their shish kebab and falafel. The Israeli-owned **Café Vegetariano** in the center of town is also popular.

Mira Olas (private bath, cold water, fans, mosquito nets, hammocks, kitchens; $20-$40, $120-$180/week; 393-7742; www.miraolas.com, e-mail: miraolas@hotmail.com) are two private cabins on a hill full of fruit trees. One is rustic, the other is "Jungle Deluxe." Monkeys and birds are frequently seen there. The *finca*, owned by a U.S.-German couple, is accessed by a dirt road heading a quarter mile inland from the fishermen's co-op at the entrance to town. It's great for couples or families who like peace and quiet, and is an easy walk to the river or the beach. Recommended.

South of town are several places to stay, described in order of appearance. To get there, go back a quarter mile to the fish co-op and turn inland. Turn right at the supermarket and cross the bridge over the Río Claro.

An attractive, spacious bed and breakfast built on a hill overlooking the sea, **Casa Siempre Domingo** (private bath, heated water; $50-$60; 820-4709; www.casa-domingo.com, e-mail: heidi@casa-domingo.com) is owned by a couple from Cape Cod, and has a fantastic view. You should have a car to stay here.

One and a half kilometers south of town are **Cabinas La Ponderosa** (private bath, hot water, some with air conditioning, ceiling fans; $50-$60/person, including meals; $30-$40 without meals; 824-4145; www.cabinas laponderosa.com), which are well-designed, completely screened-in cabins owned by two friendly Florida brothers who have put a tremendous amount of love and care into their project. There is a volleyball court and a large, screened game room with satellite TV, ping pong, and hammocks. It's just 50 meters from the ocean. They have a two-bedroom house for rent that sleeps up to six ($160 for two, including meals). Recommended.

Four and a half kilometers south, high on a jungle-covered hillside, is **Tiskita Lodge** (private bath, cold water, pool; $120/person, double occupancy, including meals; phone/fax: 296-8125, fax: 296-8133; www.tiskita-lo dge.co.cr, e-mail: info@tiskita-lodge.co.cr). The rustic but comfortable cabins all have superb ocean views and are cooled by sea breezes. Agronomist Peter Aspinall has planted more than 100 varieties of tropical fruits from around the world here, which attract many birds and monkeys. Peter has been working on re-establishing the scarlet macaw population. Today you can see and hear dozens of pairs of these large, colorful birds throughout the region. Guided nature walks are available and trails wind up and down the mountain backdrop in this 400-acre reserve. A 65-foot waterfall and swimmable ponds are close to the cabins. Three-night packages ($475) include charter flights to their private airstrip from Puerto Jiménez or Golfito. Package options also include trips to Corcovado.

GETTING THERE: By Bus: A bus for Pavones leaves at 10 a.m. and 3 p.m. every day from the *bomba* in Golfito, returning at 5:30 a.m. and 12:30 p.m. daily. A taxi to Pavones costs $40 to $50, depending on how far south you're going.

By Car: It takes a little over an hour to get from Zancudo to Pavones, with gorgeous views on the way. It takes about an hour and a half to get to Pavones from Golfito. As with Zancudo, look for the Rodeo Bar at kilometer 14 of the Río Claro–Golfito road, and turn south. The section up to the Río Coto is paved. Cars cross the river on a ferry contraption ($1.25 for car and driver, 15 cents for each passenger). The ferry shuts down at dark, so don't get stuck there. Roads south of the river to Pavones are gravel or dirt, very bumpy, but almost always passable without four-wheel drive (although it's good to have a high-clearance vehicle). You will probably want to ask directions frequently.

SAN VITO

Founded in the early 1950s by immigrants from postwar Italy, **San Vito** is in a high, mountainous valley with an invigorating climate. The town of 40,000 has a strong sense of its roots, with good Italian restaurants and the Dante Aligheri cultural center, which offers Italian films, exhibits, and language classes. **Pizzeria y Restaurante Lilliana** (773-3080), 50 meters west of the park, is a popular place run by an Italian family.

Two spurs off the Interamerican Highway lead to San Vito. From the north, cross the Térraba River on the Paso Real bridge, and drive 38 kilometers up the fertile backbone of the Coto Brus. This is the route the bus takes from San José. From the south, take the Villa Neily–San Vito road, built by the United States in 1945 during World War II as a strategic protection point, because the area is due west of the Panama Canal. The road rises so sharply that, in 20 minutes, Villa Neily's sweltering heat is forgotten in the cool misty mountains above San Vito. Views are spectacular, but the road is so winding that you should really pull over to enjoy the vista.

Halfway between San Vito and Wilson Botanical Gardens is the unique **Finca Cántaros** (open 9 a.m. to 5 p.m.; closed Monday; 773-3760; admis-

sion $1). The *finca* consists of grassy picnic grounds with a pond and pano-
ramic views, a renovated historic farmhouse with a children's reading
room, and a gift shop with high-quality, hand-painted ceramics, Boruca and
Guaymi woven goods, and delicious orange-guava jam, all at reasonable
prices. Proceeds from sales of the handicrafts, both locally produced and
brought from other areas of the country, go toward staffing the reading
room. Recommended.

LODGING   **Hotel El Ceibo** (private bath, hot water, some with TV; $30-
$50; phone/fax: 773-3025) is very clean and by far the most comfortable. It
is behind the Municipalidad, right in the center of town. The rooms in the
back have views.

   Albergue Firenze (private bath, heated water; $7-$12; 773-3741) is a
small, basic place, down a road to the left after the gas station at the entrance to town on the Paso Real (Río Térraba) route.

WILSON BOTANICAL GARDENS   San Vito's main attraction is un-
doubtedly **Las Cruces Biological Station** and **Wilson Botanical Gardens**,
5.4 kilometers uphill from town on the Villa Neily road. This floral wonderland is fascinating for lay visitors and the botanically inclined alike. Its
astonishingly diverse collection was gathered from around the world and
designed by the original owners, Robert and Catherine Wilson, with help
from the great Brazilian horticulturist Roberto Burle-Marx. The garden is
now owned by the Organization of Tropical Studies, a consortium of U.S.,
Latin American, and Australian universities. Much important botanical and
agro-ecological research takes place on the grounds and in the laboratories.

   One could spend days on the self-guided tours through the garden's 25
acres of cultivated sectors—trails are dedicated to heliconias, bamboos, orchids, lilies, gingers, palms, and ferns, to name a few. Nine kilometers of
trails in the 632-acre forest reserve offer mountain vistas, overlooks of the
rainforest canopy, and hikes to the lovely, rocky pools of the Río Java. The
gardens' bird list of 330 species includes some aquatic species of the
nearby San Joaquín marsh.

   Day visits cost $30 for a full day, $15 for a half day; children $20 and
$10; student and researcher rates are available. Lodging is in comfortable
cabins with balconies (private bath, heated water; $70-$80/person, including
meals and a guided walk). Some units are wheelchair accessible. There is
library and video room for rainy afternoons. Regular guided tours leave at
8 a.m. and 1:30 p.m.; special birding tours start at 6 a.m. You must make
reservations before you visit: contact the San José office of the Organization
for Tropical Studies (240-6696, fax: 240-6783; www.ots.ac.cr/en/lascruces,
e-mail: reservas@ots.ac.cr). Recommended.

GETTING THERE: By Air: You can charter a five-passenger plane to San Vito, or fly to Coto 47 with SANSA (221-9414, fax: 255-2176; www.flysansa. com; $71 one way) and take a taxi ($40) to the botanical gardens.

By Bus: A direct bus to San Vito leaves San José at 5:45 a.m., 8:15 a.m., 11:30 a.m., and 2:45 p.m. from Empresa Alfaro (Calle 14, Avenida 5; 222-2666; $6.65). It's a five-hour trip. Buy tickets in advance. Most of these buses pass the botanical gardens after a stop in San Vito. Check with the driver. The bus that returns to San José at 4:30 a.m. passes by Wilson Gardens on its way to San Vito at 4:10 a.m. The Alfaro office in San Vito is around the curve from the Municipalidad (city hall). San Isidro–San Vito buses leave at 5:30 a.m. and 2 p.m., returning at 6:30 a.m. and 1:30 p.m.

A taxi from San Vito to Wilson Gardens is about $2.50.

By Car: The San José–San Vito trip takes five hours: two and a half hours to San Isidro, after which the road straightens out a bit, then one and a half hours to the Rio Térraba bridge, then another hour on the paved but pot-holed road to San Vito. Be sure not to miss the turnoff to the bridge at Paso Real, 15 kilometers after Buenos Aires. You'll see the river on your left, then you'll pass the bridge down below before you see a small sign indicating the road to San Vito. Once in San Vito, turn right onto the main street and follow it 15 minutes more to the botanical gardens.

PARQUE INTERNACIONAL LA AMISTAD

Parque Internacional La Amistad extends over the Talamanca mountains from the southern border of Chirripó National Park down into Panama. It is the largest park in the country (599,000 hectares), and its Panamanian counterpart is more than three times larger. Comprising eight life zones, La Amistad is one of the richest ecological zones in Central America. The United Nations has declared the park and its neighboring reserves and protected zones a World Heritage site and has given it the status of Biosphere.

Preliminary surveys indicate that two-thirds of the country's vertebrate species are found in this park. It is an extremely important refuge for animals that require large areas in order to hunt, forage, and reproduce, like the jaguar, margay, and puma.

The official gateway to La Amistad is the **Altamira** entrance (admission $5 for two days; camping $2/day). You'll see signs for it about halfway down the Paso Real–San Vito road. The signs are confusing, but it's a 20 kilometer (one hour) drive up a gravel road from the turnoff. On the way you'll pass through the village of **El Carmen**, where you can rent rooms, buy food supplies, or eat at the **Soda y Hospedaje La Amistad** (shared bath, cold water; $7-$12; 773-8153). Once you get to Altamira there are beautiful views, a campground with tiled bathrooms, and a covered cooking area with picnic tables. The park guards will lend you a gas stove. **Sendero los Gigantes del Bosque** is a circular four-kilometer hike. You can also hike to the 8000-foot **Valle del Silencio** from here in about eight hours. There is a shelter to stay in after about two hours of hiking.

No matter how adventurous you feel, don't undertake the trip without a guide. It's very easy to get lost, and hikers have died from hypothermia and falls in the slippery, precipitous terrain. Camping in this area is most enjoyable in the dry season (January through April).

To plan your trip, call or visit the office of La Amistad Conservation Area in San Isidro de El General (150 meters west and 50 meters south of Central Park; phone/fax: 771-3155, fax: 771-3297; e-mail: gdemarco@minae.go.cr) at least two weeks in advance, so that guides and porters can be contracted. Dúrika, below, will guide you into La Amistad as well.

GETTING THERE: See description above.

DÚRIKA BIOLOGICAL RESERVE   High in the Talamanca mountains above Buenos Aires is **Dúrika Biological Reserve** (730-0657; www.durika.org, e-mail: peregrino@racsa.co.cr), operated by a self-sufficient agricultural community. The 7500-hectare private reserve is a buffer zone for this section of La Amistad International Biosphere Reserve. The community's resident naturalist can lead hikes of one to five days through Reserva Biológica Dúrika and La Amistad, including a trek up Cerro Dúrika, a peak of over 11,000 feet, and a six-day trek visiting various indigenous communities. You can also hike to a *trapiche* where *tapa dulce*, the traditional hard brown sugar, is made.

With the money it earns from tourism, the community hopes to buy adjoining farms to make a biological corridor for local wildlife, which needs to migrate altitudinally according to the season. The community itself offers classes in vegetarian cooking, bread-baking, gardening, yoga, kung fu, and meditation techniques. Dúrika now has a naturopathic health center offering medical care as well as massage, hydrotherapy, and clay treatments; their laboratory makes soap, shampoo, and herbal teas.

Even if you can't visit the *finca*, it's worth stopping by their office in Buenos Aires to buy some of their healthy cookies and pastries (730-0657).

Accommodations (private or shared bath, solar-heated water; $30-$40/person, students $25/person) in the guest cabins are rustic but cozy. Prices include three delicious vegetarian meals per day. If you'd like to get to know the community, a stay of a week to ten days is recommended.

GETTING THERE: Call the reserve as far ahead as possible so they can prepare for your visit. Take a Tracopa–Alfaro bus to Buenos Aires (at 5 a.m., 6 a.m., 8:30 a.m., and 2:30 p.m.; Calle 14, Avenida 5; 4.5 hours); there are also buses from

San Isidro every two hours. Once you are in Buenos Aires, they will arrange for a taxi to pick you up and take you to the community ($30 for up to seven people). Their office is near the entrance to town. As you enter Buenos Aires you will see a sign on the right that says "Clinica." Turn right one street before that, go one block, and then a quarter block to the right.

By Car: It takes about 90 minutes to get to Dúrika from Buenos Aires. The last three and a half kilometers are on very bad road. Try to get to Buenos Aires no later than 4 p.m. so you can reach the reserve in daylight. Four-wheel drive is necessary. You can make it in a regular car to Buenos Aires and take a taxi ($30) 17 kilometers to the reserve.

BORUCA

Boruca is a small town cradled in a green valley in the southwestern part of Costa Rica. The surrounding countryside is beautiful—you can walk up the red dirt trails for views across mountains, valleys, and rivers.

The Borucas offer a glimpse into the traditions of Costa Rica's indigenous peoples. For instance, they traditionally celebrate the New Year with the Fiesta de los Diablitos, a dramatic re-enactment of the war between the Spanish conquistadores and the local native people, in which the locals win. (Native peoples throughout the Americas share the Diablitos tradition, though usually their drama represents a war between the Spanish and the Moors.) The Diablitos are boys disguised as devils. One boy is the bull. The Diablitos taunt the bull and the bull chases them. Costumes are fashioned from burlap sacks and balsa-wood masks carved by Boruca artisans.

The whole village meets on a hill the night of December 30. At midnight, a conch shell sounds, and they run down the hill into town. They spend the whole night going from house to house, giving a short performance at each, then relaxing to enjoy the *chicha* (homebrew) and tamales they are offered. The group visits most houses in town that night and during the next three days. On the third day of the fiesta, the Diablitos symbolically kill the bull. A huge bonfire reduces the bull to ashes.

The Borucas are known for their fine handicrafts. Men carve expressive balsa-wood masks. Both women and men etch elaborate scenes onto large, hollow *jícaras* (gourds). Boruca women are especially known for their weavings, done with yarn spun from species of cotton that grows only in Boruca. The cotton is dyed with natural tints, including a purple extracted from a terrestrial mollusk that lives on cliffs near the Terraba River delta. The men make periodic trips to gather this dye. To obtain it, they scale the cliffs, locate the now-scarce shells, remove them from the rock wall, blow on the animals so they will spray their dye, and then replace them on the cliff for their next visit. That's true sustainability.

You can buy the Borucas' handicrafts from families all over Boruca. Local ladies Marina Lazaro and Igenia Gonzalez (771-2533) do a demonstration of Borucan weaving and dying techniques at the **Museo Comunitario**, or you can call the Women Artisans Association (730-1673). Call them in advance if you would like them to set up a demonstration for you. If you don't have time to visit Boruca, you can buy the handicrafts at the cooperative stands in Rey Curré, an indigenous village along the Interamerican Highway between the Paso Real turnoff for San Vito and Palmar Norte. They are also sold at many hotels throughout the Zona Sur.

This community is being threatened by the construction of what could be Costa Rica's largest hydroelectric dam project.

We know of no formal hotels here, but you can probably arrange to stay with a local family or camp if you ask around. Be aware that loud music plays all night during the Diablitos. There are no restaurants and no banks, so bring enough *colones* to buy food at the store.

Note: You might want to combine a stop in Boruca with a visit to the Dúrika Biological Reserve, which borders La Amistad Biosphere Reserve above Buenos Aires.

GETTING THERE: By Bus: A bus leaves Buenos Aires at 11:30 a.m. and arrives in Boruca (18 kilometers up and down a mountainous dirt road) at 1 p.m. Get there early to get a seat. Or you can get off the Zona Sur bus at the Entrada de Boruca, about 30 minutes past the entrance to Buenos Aires, and walk eight kilometers up the path that takes off to the right of the highway. The hike takes about two hours.

By Car: Look for the Térraba turnoff from the Interamerican Highway about 12 kilometers south of the entrance to Buenos Aires and just after the Brujo gas station. Boruca is about 18 kilometers from there. Your car should have high clearance and a powerful engine.

ISLA DEL COCO

Isla del Coco (Coco Island), 500 kilometers off the Pacific Coast, boasts 200 dramatic waterfalls, many of which fall directly into the sea. It was made into a National Park in 1978, and declared a UNESCO World Heritage Site in 1997 because of the richness of its flora and fauna. Because the island is uninhabited, animals there are not afraid of humans. The fairy terns find humans so interesting that they hover about them curiously.

Although its geological origin remains a mystery, scientists believe Isla del Coco is a volcanic hot spot at the center of the Cocos tectonic plates. The Coco Island finch is a subspecies of the finch endemic to the Galápagos Islands that prompted Darwin's questions about evolution. Several species of birds, lizards, and freshwater fish found on the island have not been seen anywhere else on earth. Whereas on mainland Costa Rica there are so many species that the behavior of each is highly specialized, on Isla del Coco individual birds of the same species will have different feeding habits—very interesting from an evolutionary standpoint. Some 77 nonendemic species, mainly seabirds, can also be observed.

European sailors probably first discovered the island in the 1500s. Many early visitors were pirates who rested and restocked fresh water there during expeditions. They named the island after its many coconut palms, but apparently enjoyed the coconuts so much that there are almost none left today. Passing boats installed pigs, deer, and goats on the island to provide meat for return voyages. With no predators, these animals now constitute the majority of the wildlife there.

There are tales of buried treasure on the island. The Portuguese Benito Bonito, "The One of the Bloody Sword," is said to have buried his fabulous treasure there. Also during the early 19th century, at the time of Peru's wars of independence from Spain, the aristocracy and clergy entrusted their gold and jewels to Captain James Thompson, who promised to transport their riches to a safe port. Thompson disappeared with the loot and is supposed to have hidden it on Isla del Coco. Although many treasure hunters have searched the island, no one has found anything yet.

Hunting for gold doubloons might not be rewarding at Isla del Coco, but scuba divers find it rich in natural treasures. The ship **Sea Hunter** (228-6613, 800-203-2120; www.underseahunter.com, e-mail: info@underseahunter.com) takes divers to the island for ten days of heavy-duty diving. Several sailboat companies in Guanacaste offer trips to Coco.

To get direct information on Coco National Park, contact the Area de Conservación Marina Isla del Coco in San José (258-7295, fax: 258-7350; e-mail: ferqui@minae.go.cr).

Appendix

LIVING IN COSTA RICA

RESIDENCY

Tourists may own vehicles, property, and businesses in Costa Rica, and may generate income from their own companies, but the Immigration Department does not look kindly on this arrangement long-term. After a few renewals of your visa obtained by leaving the country and coming back in, you should apply for residency. Securing permanent residency in Costa Rica is a complicated and increasingly difficult process but still easy in comparison to other countries, and required if you plan to live here for more than a few months.

Do not plan to make your residency application yourself unless you have plenty of patience to deal with lines, national holidays, lunch breaks, misunderstandings, offices that have moved from where they were a month ago, impossible-to-find phone numbers, and so on. If you have comfortable shoes and love to meditate or read novels while waiting in line, you'll find *trámites* (bureaucratic machinations) just your cup of tea. If you are nervous and impatient or have fallen arches, you will suffer. Of course, you can have a professional handle this for you.

Potential residents will want to visit the **Asociación de Residentes de Costa Rica** (Avenida 4, Calle 40, San José; 233-8068, 221-2053, fax: 233-1152; www.arcr.net). Their website is a great resource for learning about current immigration policies. The association's contracted specialists will see potential residents through the lengthy approval process for *pensionado* or *rentista* status.

Christopher Howard of **Relocational and Retirement Consultants** (www.liveincostarica.com) offers similar services, but provides more personalized help.

WAYS TO WORK

The Costa Rican government doesn't want foreigners taking jobs from Costa Ricans. Therefore, most foreigners are not allowed to work unless they are performing a task that Ticos cannot do. But with some thought, you might be able to discover a skill you have that will help you establish temporary residency (*residencia temporal*). Qualified teachers are needed at the English-, French-, Japanese-, and German-speaking schools in San José. English teachers are often needed by the various language institutes. The National Symphony needs musicians; *The Tico Times* needs reporters. You would be surprised at how many gorgeous, isolated ecotourism projects need bilingual people with managerial experience—many educated Ticos are not willing to live so far from "civilization."

Doctors, lawyers, architects, and engineers are plentiful here and are protected by powerful professional associations that make entry difficult for foreigners.

LEGAL ADVICE

If you live here and have a business or buy land, sooner or later you will need to hire a lawyer. Legal fees vary greatly. Some very good lawyers charge more because they know that what they do is far superior to the run of the mill. If you have the money, it is worth every penny to have a good lawyer here.

The Legal Guide to Costa Rica (www.costaricalaw.com), currently in its third edition, offers information on real estate transactions, corporations, residency and immigration, commercial transactions, banking and finance, powers of attorney, environmental laws, copyrights, trademarks, worker's compensation, automobile regulations, taxation, social security, labor legislation, and much more. A fourth edition will come out as soon as Costa Rica's tax reform law is passed.

REAL ESTATE AND INVESTMENTS

According to an article in *The Tico Times*, ". . . the potential investor in Costa Rica should beware of *all* glib, 'fact-filled,' English-speaking promoters flogging *anything*, whether it's gold mines, beach property, condominiums, agribusiness, or mutual funds. Costa Rica has long been a haven for con artists whose favorite targets are trusting newcomers. This doesn't mean, however, that legitimate investment opportunities don't exist. Investors here, like everywhere else, are advised simply to move cautiously, ask lots of questions, and check with well-established, reputable companies before parting with any money. That way, investors can be confident of making a good choice."

Know that any land within 200 meters of the high tide line on the beach is public and cannot be legally owned. You can "buy" it and build on it only after meeting a series of prerequisites and dealing with the local municipality, often a hotbed of corruption and greed. Many environmental laws also must be complied with.

Owning land and houses anywhere in Costa Rica can transform it from paradise into living hell unless you follow a few rules of thumb: Hire a lawyer you trust before undertaking any transaction. Always place deposit money in an escrow account; never give it to the seller or the seller's attorney. Beware of being an absentee landlord or business-owner. It doesn't work.

The **American Chamber of Commerce of Costa Rica** (open 8 a.m. to 5 p.m.; Sabana Norte, 300 meters to the northeast of ICE; 220-2200, fax: 220-2300; www.amcham.co.cr, e-mail: chamber@amcham.co.cr) publishes a monthly magazine, *Business Costa Rica*, with information on economics, finance, legislation, and other related topics. Also, be sure to read *Potholes to Paradise* by Tessa Borner.

HEALTH CARE

The Social Security system makes low-cost medical care available to those who need it, but its clients must deal with long lines, short appointments, and delays lasting months between referral and delivery for X-rays, ultrasounds, operations, and other diagnostic treatment services. Doctors also have their private practices in the afternoons. A gynecological exam including Pap test costs around $30; a sonogram costs about $30; a complete cardiac stress exam runs about $70. Dental care is also considerably less expensive here. All of the above services are available to foreigners. Facelifts and other plastic surgeries cost a fraction of what they do elsewhere, and postoperative care is also a lot cheaper.

Well-qualified alternative medicine practitioners such as acupuncturists, homeopaths, chiropractors, and massage therapists are also available in Costa Rica and charge less than their northern counterparts. Check *The Tico Times*. Homeopaths are listed in the phone directory.

There are several English-speaking chapters of AA, CODA, and NA in Costa Rica. They list meetings in "Weekend" section of *The Tico Times*.

Long-term nursing home care is much less expensive here than in North America. We have heard wonderful things about Villa Alegria Nursing Home (www.costaricanursinghomes.com) in Alajuela.

One thing that few retirees take into consideration is that in Costa Rica it is illegal to refuse life-supporting devices such as respirators.

RESOURCES

See our guide to Costa Rica on the internet at the beginning of Chapter Three. Also, check out *Potholes to Paradise* by Tessa Borner.

RECOMMENDED READING

BIOLOGICAL CORRIDORS

Ewing, Jack. *Monkeys Are Made of Chocolate*. Dominical, CR: 2003. Available at www.haciendabaru.com. A fascinating collection of essays by a North American naturalist about wildlife and forest regeneration at Hacienda Barú, where he has lived, farmed, and philosophized for several decades. Lots of good information about biological corridors.

Miller, Kenton, Chang, Elsa, and Johnson, Nels. *Defining the Common Ground for The Mesoamerican Biological Corridor*. Washington, D.C.: World Resources Institute, 2001. An excellent history and summary of the challenges facing the Mesoamerican Biological Corridor. Also available online at www.wri.org.

ECOTOURISM

Honey, Martha. *Ecotourism and Sustainable Development: Who Owns Paradise?* Washington, D.C.: Island Press, 1998. Definitive analysis of the issues surrounding ecotourism and sustainable tourism certification by an expert.

HISTORY AND CULTURE

Bell, John. *Crisis in Costa Rica: The 1948 Revolution*. Austin: University of Texas Press, 1971. History of the 1948 civil war.

Biesanz, Mavis, Richard, and Karen. *The Costa Ricans*. Prospect Heights, IL: Waveland Press, Inc., 1988. A sympathetic portrayal of traditional Costa Rican culture.

Biesanz, Mavis and Richard. *The Ticos: Culture and Social Change in Costa Rica.* London: Lynne Rienner, 1998. A fun-to-read look at Costa Rican culture from Doña Mavis, who has been observing Ticos since the 1940s.

Borner, Tessa. *Potholes to Paradise: Living in Costa Rica: What You Need to Know.* Port Perry, Ontario: Silvio Mattacchione, 2001. A frank, very readable account of the experiences of several families and their ups and downs as immigrants. Full of practical advice.

Marañón, Jon. *The Gringo's Hawk.* Eugene, OR: Kenneth Group Publishing, 2001. An engrossing and beautifully written autobiography of a North American who has lived in Costa Rica since 1972, with great portraits of local people and nuanced recounting of his struggles as an environmentalist.

Palmer, Paula. *What Happen: A Folk-History of Costa Rica's Talamanca Coast.* San José: Publications in English, 1993. A revised edition of the classic oral history of the Afro-Caribbean Talamancans.

Palmer, Sanchez, Mayorga. *Taking Care of Sibö's Gifts, an Environmental Treatise.* San José: Editorama, 1993. The Kéködi tribe writes about its stewardship of nature.

Palmer, Steven Paul and Molina Jimenez, Ivan. *The Costa Rica Reader: History, Culture, Politics.* Durham, NC: Duke University Press, 2004. This brings together newspaper accounts, histories, petitions, memoirs, poems, and essays written by Costa Ricans, designed to reveal the complexity of the country's past and present, and showing how Costa Rican history challenges the idea that current dilemmas facing Latin America are inevitable or insoluble.

Ras, Barbara. *Costa Rica: A Traveler's Literary Companion.* San Francisco: Whereabouts Press, 1994. An excellent English translation of short stories by Costa Rica's best writers.

NATURAL HISTORY

Botanica Editors. *Botanica's Orchids: Over 1200 Species.* San Diego, CA: Laurel Glen Publishing, 2002.

Carr, Archie. *The Windward Road: Adventures of a Naturalist on Remote Caribbean Shores.* Gainesville: University Press of Florida, 1979. The book that inspired the worldwide turtle conservation movement.

Colesberry, Adrian. *Costa Rica: The Last Country the Gods Made.* Guilford, CT: Globe Pequot Press, 1993. Coffee table classic of travel writing with photographs.

DeVries, Philip. *The Butterflies of Costa Rica and Their Natural History*. Princeton: Princeton University Press, 1997. A color-filled volume about butterflies.

Forsyth, Adrian and Miyata, Ken. *Tropical Nature: Life and Death in the Rain Forests of Central and South America*. New York: Touchstone, 1995.

Franke, Joseph. *Costa Rica's National Parks and Preserves: A Visitor's Guide, Second Edition*. Seattle, WA: Mountaineers Books, 1999.

Haber, Zuchowski and Bello. *An Introduction to Cloud Forest Trees*, second edition. Puntarenas, CR: Mountain Gem Publications, 2000.

Henderson, Carrol L. *Field Guide to the Wildlife of Costa Rica*. Austin: University of Texas Press, 2002. Excellent guide.

Inbio. The Institute of Biodiversity has many bilingual guides on everything from bromeliads to cacti, beetles to whales. Order at www.inbio.ac.cr under Editorial.

Janzen, Daniel, ed. *Costa Rican Natural History*. Chicago: University of Chicago Press, 1983. The undisputed bible of Costa Rican ecology, with 174 biologist contributors covering almost everything there is to know about the subject. Entertaining and well-written. Also published in Spanish.

Leenders, Twan. *A Guide to Amphibians and Reptiles of Costa Rica*. San José: Distribuidores Zona Tropical, S.A., 2001.

Nadkarni and Wainright. *Monteverde: Ecology and Conservation of a Tropical Rain Forest*. New York: Oxford University Press, 2000.

Reid, Fiona. *A Field Guide to Mammals of Central America and Southeast Mexico*. New York: Oxford University Press, 1997.

Skutch, Alexander. *Trogons, Laughing Flacons, and Other Neotropical Birds*. Texas A&M University Press, 1999. Costa Rica's master birder, who passed away in 2004 at age 99 and was the author of 25 other books, describes the behavior of the trogon family, which includes the resplendent quetzal.

Stiles, Gary F., and Alexander Skutch. *A Guide to the Birds of Costa Rica*. Ithaca, NY: Cornell University Press, 1990. *The* birder's guide to Costa Rica. Illustrated by Dana Gardner. See companion audiotape, below.

Wainwright, Mark. *The Natural History of Costa Rican Mammals*. San José: Distribuidores Zona Tropical, S.A., 2003. A beautifully illustrated guide.

PERIODICALS

AMCOSTARICA.COM. A daily English-language online periodical. www. amcostarica.com.

The Tico Times. The best way to keep up with what is happening in Costa Rica. Apdo. 4632, San José. 258-1558, fax: 233-6378; www.tico times.net.

AUDIO FIELD GUIDES FOR BIRDERS AND NATURALISTS

The Cornell Laboratory of Ornithology's Library of Natural Sounds has several audiotapes that can help you identify birds and animals in the wild:

Costa Rican Bird Song Sampler has the songs of 180 bird species arranged by habitat. A booklet provides the page and plate numbers for the species as they are found in *A Guide to the Birds of Costa Rica* by Stiles, Skutch and Gardner (see "Books," above).

Sounds of Neotropical Rainforest Mammals is an audio companion to the book *Neotropical Rainforest Mammals* by Louise H. Emmons. Disc One features primates, Disc Two has all other mammals.

Voices of Costa Rican Birds: Caribbean Slope, a two-CD set containing 225 species, the largest compilation available.

Voices of the Cloud Forest, a CD of sounds from a day in the Monteverde Cloud Forest Biological Reserve. Sounds of cloud-forest denizens are identified at the end.

Index

Lodging Index

Dining Index

Notes from the Publisher

An alert, adventurous reader is as important as a travel writer in keeping a guidebook up-to-date and accurate. So if you happen upon a great restaurant, discover a hidden locale, or (heaven forbid) find an error in the text, we'd appreciate hearing from you. Just write to:

Ulysses Press
P.O. Box 3440
Berkeley, CA 94703
www.ulyssespress.com
e-mail: readermail@ulyssespress.com

It is our desire as publishers to create guidebooks that are responsible as well as informative. We hope that our guidebooks treat the people, country, and land we visit with respect. We ask that our readers do the same. The hiker's motto, "Walk softly on the Earth," applies to travelers everywhere . . . in the desert, on the beach, and in town.

We Need Your Help!

We have done the best we could to evaluate "ecotourism" projects that agreed to participate in our sustainable ecotourism survey. But we need your help to monitor those on our list, add new lodgings, and check on those that have made improvements since our last visit. As you travel through Costa Rica, keep your eyes open for positive and negative environmental, cultural, and economic impacts of the ecotourism-oriented hotels you visit. Hotel owners may be more open with you. You might catch things that we couldn't in our brief interview.

Please fill out this form or write to us. We promise to follow up on your tips, and if you request, we will be happy to write back to you and let you know what we have done with your suggestions. Your comments will help us determine the lodging facilities that are truly making extra-special efforts to have a positive effect on the environment and culture of Costa Rica, and thus deserve to be recognized in The New Key.

POSSIBLE ADDITION TO THE SUSTAINABLE TOURISM LIST:

Name of hotel: _____

Location: _____

Phone/fax (if there is one): _____

What environmental, sociocultural, and/or economic practices made you feel the lodging facility should be recognized?

POSSIBLE DELETION FROM THE SUSTAINABLE TOURISM LIST:

Name of hotel: _____

Location: _____

Phone/fax (if there is one): _____

What environmental, sociocultural, and/or economic practices made you feel this lodging facility should not be on our list?

Mail to: Key to Costa Rica, P.O. Box 73, East Blue Hill, ME 04629,
or e-mail your comments to info@keytocostarica.com

You're already helping!

Simply by purchasing *The New Key to Costa Rica*,
you have helped preserve Costa Rica's environment

Would you like to do more?

At Ulysses Press, we believe that ecotourism can have a positive impact on
a region's environment and can actually help preserve its natural state. In
line with this philosophy, we donate a percentage of the sales from all New
Key guides to conservation organizations working in the destination country—in Costa Rica, our environmental partner is the Resource Foundation.

The Resource Foundation, a nonprofit membership organization founded
in 1987, is working through its Costa Rican affiliate, Arbofilia (Asociación
Protectora de Árboles), to improve agricultural productivity and assist low-
income rural families, while at the same time protecting natural resources
and promoting conservation.

The target area is near Carara Biological Reserve, in the central part of
Costa Rica, on the west coast near the Pacific Ocean. From an ecological
standpoint, the area lies between the northern limits of the South American
tropical rainforests and the beginnings of the dry forests of Mesoamerica. It
has a number of major rivers that supply water for many important communities in the Central Pacific region.

Ulysses Press encourages you to further support this organization. For
more information, or to make a donation, contact:

The Resource Foundation
P.O. Box 3006
Larchmont, NY 10538
phone/fax: 914-834-5810
e-mail: resourcefnd@msn.com

HIDDEN GUIDES

Adventure travel or a relaxing vacation?—"Hidden" guidebooks are the only travel books in the business to provide detailed information on both. Aimed at environmentally aware travelers, our motto is "Where Vacations Meet Adventures." These books combine details on unique hotels, restaurants and sightseeing with information on camping, sports and hiking for the outdoor enthusiast.

PARADISE FAMILY GUIDES

Ideal for families traveling with kids of any age—toddlers to teenagers—Paradise Family Guides offer a blend of travel information unlike any other guides to the Hawaiian islands. With vacation ideas and tropical adventures that are sure to satisfy both action-hungry youngsters and relaxation-seeking parents, these guides meet the specific needs of each and every family member.

Ulysses Press books are available at bookstores everywhere. If any of the following titles are unavailable at your local bookstore, ask the bookseller to order them.

You can also order books directly from Ulysses Press
P.O. Box 3440, Berkeley, CA 94703
800-377-2542 or 510-601-8301
fax: 510-601-8307
www.ulyssespress.com
e-mail: ulysses@ulyssespress.com

HIDDEN GUIDEBOOKS

____ Hidden Arizona, $16.95
____ Hidden Bahamas, $14.95
____ Hidden Baja, $14.95
____ Hidden Belize, $15.95
____ Hidden Big Island of Hawaii, $13.95
____ Hidden Boston & Cape Cod, $14.95
____ Hidden British Columbia, $18.95
____ Hidden Cancún & the Yucatán, $16.95
____ Hidden Carolinas, $17.95
____ Hidden Coast of California, $18.95
____ Hidden Colorado, $15.95
____ Hidden Disneyland, $13.95
____ Hidden Florida, $18.95
____ Hidden Florida Keys & Everglades, $13.95
____ Hidden Georgia, $16.95
____ Hidden Guatemala, $16.95
____ Hidden Hawaii, $18.95
____ Hidden Idaho, $14.95
____ Hidden Kauai, $13.95
____ Hidden Los Angeles, $14.95
____ Hidden Maui, $13.95

____ Hidden Miami, $14.95
____ Hidden Montana, $15.95
____ Hidden New England, $18.95
____ Hidden New Mexico, $15.95
____ Hidden New Orleans, $14.95
____ Hidden Oahu, $13.95
____ Hidden Oregon, $15.95
____ Hidden Pacific Northwest, $18.95
____ Hidden San Diego, $14.95
____ Hidden Salt Lake City, $14.95
____ Hidden San Francisco & Northern California, $18.95
____ Hidden Seattle, $13.95
____ Hidden Southern California, $18.95
____ Hidden Southwest, $19.95
____ Hidden Tahiti, $17.95
____ Hidden Tennessee, $16.95
____ Hidden Utah, $16.95
____ Hidden Walt Disney World, $13.95
____ Hidden Washington, $15.95
____ Hidden Wine Country, $13.95
____ Hidden Wyoming, $15.95

PARADISE FAMILY GUIDES

____ Paradise Family Guides: Kaua'i, $16.95
____ Paradise Family Guides: Maui, $16.95

____ Paradise Family Guides: Big Island of Hawai'i, $16.95

Mark the book(s) you're ordering and enter the total cost here ⬅ ☐

California residents add 8.25% sales tax here ⬅ ☐

Shipping, check box for your preferred method and enter cost here ⬅ ☐

☐ BOOK RATE   **FREE! FREE! FREE!**

☐ PRIORITY MAIL/UPS GROUND   cost of postage

☐ UPS OVERNIGHT OR 2-DAY AIR   cost of postage

Billing, enter total amount due here and check method of payment ⬅ ☐

☐ CHECK   ☐ MONEY ORDER

☐ VISA/MASTERCARD _____ EXP. DATE _____

NAME _____PHONE _____

ADDRESS _____

CITY _____ STATE _____ ZIP _____

MONEY-BACK GUARANTEE ON DIRECT ORDERS PLACED THROUGH ULYSSES PRESS.

ABOUT THE AUTHORS

Beatrice Blake has been living or traveling in Costa Rica for more than 30 years. In 1985, she rewrote *The Key to Costa Rica*, which her mother, the late Jean Wallace, had originally published in 1978, and has been updating it every other year since then. Beatrice enjoys helping people plan their vacations (www.keytocostarica.com/costaricaconsults.htm) and is an expert in community-based ecotourism. She lives with her family in East Blue Hill, Maine.

Anne Becher is a freelance journalist and translator (M.A., Hispanic Linguistics). In addition to co-authoring *The New Key to Costa Rica*, she co-edits a bilingual literary magazine, *Selvática*, and writes reference books for publisher ABC-Clio. She has traveled the full length of the Americas by land; she now lives in Boulder, Colorado with her husband and their two children.

ABOUT THE PHOTOGRAPHER

David Gilbert, the photographer of the color insert, began his relationship with photography at an early age when his grandfather gave him an ancient Nikon. Almost 15 years later, his interest has grown into a way of life: he has chronicled California, Costa Rica, the Southwest, Ecuador, Mexico, Nicaragua, and Peru with his camera. A graduate of Brooks Institute of Photography, David regularly shoots for travel and nature publications. He currently resides in Berkeley, California.

ABOUT THE ILLUSTRATOR

Deidre Hyde is an illustrator working out of Costa Rica. A graduate of the University of Reading, England, with a degree in Fine Arts, her work has taken her throughout Central and South America, West Africa, and Italy. Her main focus is on conservation themes and she works closely with conservation groups such as the World Conservation Union. Hyde is painting for conservation.